WEB SERVICES:
A TECHNICAL INTRODUCTION
DEITEL™ DEVELOPER SERIES

Deitel™ Books, Cyber Classrooms, Complete Tra
published by

DEITEL™ *Developer* Series

C#: A Programmer's Introduction

C# for Experienced Programmers

Java™ Web Services for Experienced Programmers

Visual Basic® .NET for Experienced Programmers

*Visual C++® .NET: A Managed Code Approach
For Experienced Programmers*

Web Services: A Technical Introduction

Java 2 Micro Edition for Experienced Programmers (Spring 2003)

Java 2 Enterprise Edition for Experienced Programmers (Spring 2003)

*ASP .NET and Web Services with Visual Basic® .NET for Experienced
Programmers (Fall 2002)*

*ASP .NET and Web Services with C# for Experienced Programmers
(Spring 2003)*

How to Program Series

*Advanced Java™ 2 Platform How to
Program*

C How to Program, 3/E

C++ How to Program, 3/E

C# How to Program

*e-Business and e-Commerce How to
Program*

*Internet and World Wide Web How to
Program, 2/E*

Java™ How to Program, 4/E

Perl How to Program

Python How to Program

Visual Basic® 6 How to Program

*Visual Basic® .NET How to
Program, 2/E*

*Wireless Internet & Mobile Business
How to Program*

XML How to Program

.NET How to Program Series

C# How to Program

Visual Basic® .NET How to Program, 2/E

Visual Studio® Series

C# How to Program

Visual Basic® .NET How to Program, 2/E

*Getting Started with Microsoft® Visual
C++™ 6 with an Introduction to
MFC*

Visual Basic® 6 How to Program

For Managers Series

*e-Business and e-Commerce for
Managers*

Coming Soon

e-books and e-whitepapers

*Premium CourseCompass, WebCT and
Blackboard Multimedia Cyber
Classroom versions*

ining Courses and Web-Based Training Courses
Prentice Hall

Multimedia Cyber Classroom and Web-Based Training Series

(For information regarding Deitel™ Web-based training visit **www.ptgtraining.com**)

C++ Multimedia Cyber Classroom, 3/E

C# Multimedia Cyber Classroom

e-Business and e-Commerce Multimedia Cyber Classroom

Internet and World Wide Web Multimedia Cyber Classroom, 2/E

Java™ 2 Multimedia Cyber Classroom, 4/E

Perl Multimedia Cyber Classroom

Python Multimedia Cyber Classroom

Visual Basic® 6 Multimedia Cyber Classroom

Visual Basic® .NET Multimedia Cyber Classroom, 2/E

Wireless Internet & Mobile Business Programming Multimedia Cyber Classroom

XML Multimedia Cyber Classroom

The Complete Training Course Series

The Complete C++ Training Course, 3/E

The Complete C# Training Course

The Complete e-Business and e-Commerce Programming Training Course

The Complete Internet and World Wide Web Programming Training Course, 2/E

The Complete Java™ 2 Training Course, 4/E

The Complete Perl Training Course

The Complete Python Training Course

The Complete Visual Basic® 6 Training Course

The Complete Visual Basic® .NET Training Course, 2/E

The Complete Wireless Internet & Mobile Business Programming Training Course

The Complete XML Programming Training Course

To follow the Deitel publishing program, please register at

www.deitel.com/newsletter/subscribe.html

for the DEITEL™ BUZZ ONLINE e-mail newsletter.

To communicate with the authors, send e-mail to:

deitel@deitel.com

For information on corporate on-site seminars offered by Deitel & Associates, Inc. worldwide, visit:

www.deitel.com

For continuing updates on Prentice Hall and Deitel publications visit:

www.deitel.com,
www.prenhall.com/deitel or
www.InformIT.com/deitel

Library of Congress Cataloging-in-Publication Data

On file

Acquisitions Editor: *Karen McLean*
Project Manager: *Mike Ruel*
Executive Managing Editor: *Vince O'Brien*
Formatters: *Chirag Thakkar, John Lovell*
Director of Creative Services: *Paul Belfanti*
Art Editor: *Xiaohong Zhu*
Creative Director: *Carole Anson*
Design Technical Support: *John Christiana*
Chapter Opener and Cover Designers: *Laura Treibick, Dr. Harvey M. Deitel and Tamara L. Newnam*
Manufacturing Manager: *Trudy Pisciotti*
Manufacturing Buyer: *Lisa McDowell*
Marketing Manager: *Kate Hargett*
Marketing Assistant: *Corrine Mitchell*

 © 2003 Pearson Education, Inc.
Upper Saddle River, New Jersey 07458

Cover photo: *James Lamass/Index Stock Imagery, Inc.*

10 9 8 7 6 5 4 3 2 1

ISBN 0-13-046135-0

Pearson Education Ltd., *London*
Pearson Education Australia Pty. Ltd., *Sydney*
Pearson Education Singapore, Pte. Ltd.
Pearson Education North Asia Ltd., *Hong Kong*
Pearson Education Canada, Inc., *Toronto*
Pearson Educacion de Mexico, S.A. de C.V.
Pearson Education–Japan, *Tokyo*
Pearson Education Malaysia, Pte. Ltd.
Pearson Education, Inc., *Upper Saddle River, New Jersey*

WEB SERVICES
A TECHNICAL INTRODUCTION
DEITEL™ DEVELOPER SERIES

H. M. Deitel
Deitel & Associates, Inc.

P. J. Deitel
Deitel & Associates, Inc.

B. DuWaldt
Deitel & Associates, Inc.

L. K. Trees
Deitel & Associates, Inc.

Prentice Hall

PRENTICE HALL, Upper Saddle River, New Jersey 07458

Trademarks

Microsoft® and Visual Studio® .NET are either registered trademarks or trademarks of Microsoft Corporation in the United States and/or other countries.

Java and all Java-based marks are trademarks or registered trademarks of Sun Microsystems, Inc. in the United States and other countries. Prentice Hall is independent of Sun Microsystems, Inc.

CapeClear, CapeConnect, CapeStudio and CapeScience are trademarks of Cape Clear Software Limited in the United States and other countries.

IONA E2A™ is a trademark of IONA.

Systinet and Systinet WASP are trademarks of Systinet Corporation.

In loving memory of Julius and Miriam Zigman.

Harvey and Paul Deitel

To my mother:

For your patience, kindness and faith.

Betsy

To my parents, Douglas and Carolyn Trees:

Thank you for teaching me how to write, inspiring me to persevere and never letting me take the easy way out.

Lauren

Contents

11   Computer and Internet Security   249

12   Web Services Security   287

Illustrations

10   Java Web Services: A Conceptual Overview   224

11   Computer and Internet Security   249

12   Web Services Security   287

A   Introduction to XML Markup   318

B   Implementing Web Services in Visual Basic .NET   335

C   Implementing Web Services in Java   383

Preface

Live in fragments no longer. Only connect.
Edward Morgan Forster

We wove a web in childhood,
A web of sunny air.
Charlotte Brontë

Welcome to the world of Web services! This book is one of the first in the new *Deitel*™ *Developer Series*, which presents leading-edge computing technologies to software developers, technical managers and IT professionals.

Anyone familiar with the software industry is aware that Web services are one of 2002's hottest new technologies. Microsoft coined the term "Web services" in June 2000, when the company introduced Web services as a key component of its .NET initiative, a broad new vision for embracing the Internet in the development, engineering and use of software. As others began to investigate Web services, it became clear that the technology could revolutionize distributed computing. Software vendors quickly established Web services strategies and began to enhance their products with support for Web services standards. Now, nearly every major vendor—including Sun Microsystems, IBM, Hewlett-Packard, Oracle and BEA Systems—is marketing Web services tools and applications.

Web services encompass a set of related standards that can enable any two computer applications to communicate and exchange data via a network, such as the Internet. The primary standard used in Web services is the Extensible Markup Language (XML), developed by the World Wide Web Consortium (W3C). XML is a meta-language for describing data and creating markup languages; developers use XML tags to describe individual pieces of data, forming XML documents. Since XML documents are text-based, they can be processed on any platform. XML's portability and its rapid adoption throughout the industry made it an obvious choice for enabling cross-platform data communication in Web services.

XML provides the foundation for many core Web services standards, including the Simple Object Access Protocol (SOAP), the Web Services Description Language (WSDL) and the Universal Description, Discovery and Integration (UDDI) specification. SOAP is an XML vocabulary (i.e., an XML-based markup language developed for a specific industry or purpose) that enables programs on separate computers to interact across a network, such as the Internet or a company intranet. WSDL, another XML vocabulary created for Web services, allows developers to describe Web services and their capabilities in a standardized format. UDDI is a framework that defines XML-based registries in which businesses can publish information about themselves and the services they offer.

Almost every type of business—from small organizations to large, global enterprises—can benefit from Web services. Companies are already implementing Web services to facilitate a wide variety of business processes, such as expediting the development of corporate software, integrating applications and databases and automating transactions with suppliers, partners and clients. This book explains how developers and businesses can harness the potential of Web services technology to facilitate application-to-application communication and improve efficiency and profitability. For programmers, the book includes appendices on XML, implementing Web services in Java™ and implementing Web services in Visual Basic® .NET.

Who Should Read This Book

Deitel & Associates, Inc., offers several publications that discuss Web services, intended for various audiences. We provide information on **www.deitel.com**, here and inside this book's back cover to help you determine which publication is best for you.

Web Services A Technical Introduction is the first book in our *A Technical Introduction* series, which offers broad overviews of new technologies. We designed this publication to be a "literacy" book that explains Web services, explores the benefits they provide to businesses and discusses key concepts related to the technology. This is not a programming book, but it contains in-depth treatments of technical concepts. It also includes significant programming appendices that present Visual Basic .NET and Java Web services implementations. We believe that the information we present will be useful both to programmers, who must learn to incorporate Web services in their applications and networks, and to IT managers, who must decide when and how to adopt this important new technology.

This book is divided into several sections. Chapters 1–4 present the business case for Web services. We introduce the basics of Web services, describe Web services' strengths and limitations and examine the development of Web services standards. We also explore how companies can use Web services to improve productivity and enhance their business models. These chapters present numerous case studies that describe how specific companies are employing Web services to integrate systems and improve communication among departments, supply chains and partners.

Chapters 5–7 delve into more technical topics, including explanations of core Web services technologies and standards. We begin by introducing XML, its history and role in Web services. This leads to an analysis of various XML-derived technologies that incorporate Web services, including e-business XML (ebXML), Business Transaction Protocol (BTP), Business Process Modeling Language (BPML) and Web Services Flow Language (WSFL). We then examine the fundamentals of SOAP, including the SOAP messaging specification, the architecture of SOAP messages and Remote Procedure Calls (RPCs). We also discuss WSDL and present a sample WSDL document. We conclude by exploring various technologies for locating Web services on a network, including public and private UDDI registries, ebXML registries and WS-Inspection documents.

In Chapter 8, we describe a variety of software vendors and the Web services development tools they offer. We also discuss vendors that market Web services management and workflow products. This information is designed to help programmers and IT managers identify tools and products that best fit their Web services requirements. Following this broad overview of Web services development platforms, we examine two of the most popular platforms—.NET and Java—in detail. Chapter 9 examines Web services in the context of Microsoft's .NET platform, including the basics of creating and consuming Web services in .NET. Chapter 10 explores Sun Microsystems' *Java Web Services Developer Pack* and its capabilities for developing and deploying Web services that run on Java platforms.

The book's final chapters provide a detailed analysis of Web services security issues. In a memo to all Microsoft employees, Bill Gates stated that the company's highest priority is trustworthy computing—i.e., ensuring that Microsoft applications are reliable, available and secure. Gates's security emphasis has been echoed across the computing industry as organizations work to improve Internet and network security. Security is particularly crucial to Web services, and we therefore have included a two-chapter treatment of security issues. Chapter 11 presents general computer security concepts, such as cryptography, digital signatures and steganography. In Chapter 12, we examine the set of emerging XML-based security standards designed specifically for Web services.

The book concludes with programming appendices that introduce XML markup and .NET and Java Web services implementations. Appendices B and C contain complete, working examples of Web services and Web service clients built using the standards and tools we discuss throughout the book. We include this material as appendices, because readers must have substantial knowledge of Visual Basic .NET and Java to understand and run the programs. Readers interested in learning these languages should refer to our publications *Visual Basic .NET How to Program, Second Edition, Visual Basic .NET for Experienced Programmers* and *Java How to Program, Fourth Edition*; the inside back cover of this book contains additional information on choosing the right book. For a detailed listing of Deitel™ products and services, please see the "advertorial" pages at the back of this book or visit **www.deitel.com**. Readers also can register for our new *Deitel™ Buzz Online* e-mail newsletter (**www.deitel.net/newsletter/subscribe.html**), which provides information about our publications, company announcements, links to informative technical articles, programming tips, teaching tips, challenges, anecdotes and more.

As you proceed, if you would like to communicate with us, please send an e-mail to **deitel@deitel.com**—we always respond promptly. Please check our Web sites, **www.deitel.com**, **www.prenhall.com/deitel** and **www.InformIT.com/deitel** for frequent updates, errata, FAQs, etc. When sending an e-mail, please include the book's title and edition number. We sincerely hope that you enjoy learning about Web services with our publications.

Features of *Web Services A Technical Introduction*

This book contains many features, including:

- *XML (Extensible Markup Language)*. XML is gaining widespread popularity in the software-development and e-business communities. As a platform-independent standard for describing data and creating markup languages, XML is ideal for Web services. Many core Web services standards—including SOAP, WSDL and UDDI—are based on XML. Chapter 5, XML and Derivative Technologies, examines the basic structure of XML and overviews key concepts related to the technology. Appendix A, Introduction to XML Markup, describes the fundamentals of XML markup, including elements, attributes and character data.

- *Simple Object Access Protocol (SOAP)*. The Simple Object Access Protocol is the *lingua franca* of Web services, enabling interoperability among disparate applications. SOAP is a simple markup language for describing messages between applications. Built using XML, SOAP provides the platform and programming-language independence that developers require to integrate applications and business processes across the Web. Chapter 6, Understanding SOAP and WSDL, discusses the SOAP specification and SOAP messaging.

- *Web Services Description Language (WSDL)*. The Web Services Description Language provides developers with an XML-based language for describing Web services and exposing those Web services for public access. Chapter 6, Understanding SOAP and WSDL, examines the WSDL standard and provides an explanation of a sample WSDL document.

- *XML Registries and Universal Description, Discovery and Integration (UDDI)*. Before employing a Web service, an organization must locate the service and learn about its capabilities. XML registries, including those based on the Universal Description, Discovery and Integration (UDDI) specification, provide common repositories through which businesses can advertise themselves and their Web services. Chapter 7, UDDI, Discovery and Web Services Registries, introduces the fundamentals of UDDI and XML registries.

- *.NET Web Services*. The .NET platform is one of the most complete environments for building, deploying and accessing Web services. There are many benefits to implementing Web services in .NET, including .NET's support for multiple programming languages and its tools for code reuse. Chapter 9, .NET Web Services: A Conceptual Overview, introduces Microsoft's .NET strategy and describes .NET's support for Web services. Appendix B, Implementing Web Services in .NET, introduces Web services programming with Active Server Pages (ASP) .NET and Visual Basic .NET.

- *Java Web Services*. The Java 2 Platform provides rich support for Web services technologies. Java's portability, along with its support for XML and standard networking technologies, makes Java ideal for building Internet applications, including those based on Web services. Chapter 10, Java Web Services: A Conceptual Overview, introduces the Java Web Services Developer Pack, which includes APIs for building Java-based Web services and clients. Appendix C, Implementing Web Services in Java, introduces Web services programming with the Java API for XML Messaging (JAXM) and the Java API for XML-based RPC (JAX-RPC).

- **Web Services Security Standards**. By enabling organizations to move transactions beyond corporate firewalls, Web services create significant security challenges. The software industry has developed numerous XML-based standards to address Web services security, including the Security Assertion Markup Language (SAML), the XML Key Management Specification (XKMS), XML Signature and XML Encryption. Chapter 11, Computer and Internet Security, describes fundamental computer security concepts; Chapter 12, Web Services Security, examines Web services security standards and how organizations can ensure the security of Web services transactions.

Pedagogic Approach

Web Services A Technical Introduction contains a rich collection of illustrations, tables, and features that highlight significant topics discussed in the text. In addition, each chapter includes objectives, an outline and a summary to help readers identify the chapter's key goals. This organization, in combination with our extensive Index and glossary, enable the book to be used as a reference. For readers who want additional information on particular topics, all chapters conclude with Internet and Web resources sections; many chapters also include recommended reading lists.

Objectives
Each chapter begins with objectives that inform readers of what to expect and give them an opportunity, after reading the chapter, to determine whether they have met the intended goals.

Quotations
The chapter objectives are followed by sets of quotations. Some are humorous, some are philosophical, and some offer interesting insights. We have found that readers enjoy relating the quotations to the chapter material. Many of the quotations are worth a "second look" *after* you read each chapter.

Outline
The chapter outline enables readers to approach the material in top-down fashion. Along with the chapter objectives, the outline helps readers anticipate topics and quickly locate information that is of particular interest to them.

171 Illustrations/Figures
An abundance of charts, line drawings and Web screenshots is included. The illustrations and figures provide visual examples of business and technical topics. Charts and tables offer lists of additional resources and break information into an organized, easy-to-read format.

Features and Case Studies
Most chapters contain features, which highlight and build on concepts introduced in the body text. Many features provide case studies on businesses that are implementing Web services, whereas others highlight key Web services-related technologies.

Summary
Each chapter ends with a summary that helps readers review and reinforce key concepts. Readers also can use the summaries to discover what topics are discussed in each chapter.

Internet and Web Resources

Each chapter ends with an Internet and Web resources section, which lists Web sites that readers can visit for additional information on the chapter topics.

512 Works Cited

Almost every chapter includes a works cited section, which contains books, articles, Web sites and other resources from which we derived information for the chapter.

Recommended Reading

Most chapters include recommended reading lists, which refer to books, articles and other resources relevant to the chapter. In most cases, these reading suggestions represent the sources we found most informative while writing the book.

Glossary

The book's extensive glossary summarizes the key terms in each chapter. We include the glossary as a helpful reference.

Approximately 2268 Index Entries (with approximately 3,402 Page References)

We have included an extensive Index. This resource enables readers to search for any term or concept by keyword. The Index is especially useful to readers using the book as a reference.

Approximately 3,433 Lines of Code in 18 Example Programs (with Program Outputs)

For readers who are Java and/or Visual Basic .NET programmers, the appendices include complete, working programming examples. All examples are available as downloads from our Web site, **www.deitel.com**.

Appendices: Pedagogic Approach

Although *Web Services A Technical Introduction* is not a programming book, we have included several programming appendices that build on topics covered in the main text. These appendices contain a rich collection of programming examples designed to introduce the basics of XML markup and .NET and Java Web services. When presenting programming examples and concepts, we concentrate on the principles of good software engineering and stress program clarity.

Live-Code™ Teaching Approach

Several *Web Services A Technical Introduction* appendices contain LIVE-CODE™ examples. This style exemplifies the way we teach and write about programming and is the focus of our multimedia Cyber Classrooms and Web-based training courses, as well. Each programming concept is presented in the context of a complete, working example that is followed by one or more windows showing the program's input/output dialog. We call this method of teaching and writing the *LIVE-CODE™ Approach*. Readers have the option of downloading all of the code examples from **www.deitel.com**, under the **Downloads/Resources** link. Other links provide errata and answers to frequently asked questions. Features of our LIVE-CODE™ examples include:

- *Syntax Highlighting.* This book's implementation appendices use five-way syntax highlighting to emphasize various programming elements. Our syntax-highlighting conventions are as follows:

```
comments
keywords
literal values
errors and ASP .NET directives
text, class, method and variable names
```

- *"Code Washing."* This is our term for the process we use to format programs so that they have a carefully commented, open layout. The code is grouped into small, well-documented pieces. This greatly improves code readability.

World Wide Web Access

All the source code for the program examples in the appendices (and our other publications) is available on the Internet as downloads from:

```
www.deitel.com
www.prenhall.com/deitel
```

Registration is quick and easy and the downloads are free. If you read the programming appendices, we suggest downloading all the examples, then running each program as you read the corresponding discussion. Make changes to the examples and immediately see the effects of those changes—this is a great way to improve your programming skills. [*Note:* This is copyrighted material. Feel free to use it as you study, but you may not republish any portion of it in any form without explicit permission in writing from Prentice Hall and the authors.]

Programming Tips

In the appendices, we have included programming tips to help readers focus on important aspects of program development. We highlight these tips in the form of *Good Programming Practices*, *Common Programming Errors*, *Portability Tips* and *Software Engineering Observations*.

6 Good Programming Practices

Good Programming Practices *are tips that call attention to techniques that will help developers produce programs that are clearer, more understandable and more maintainable.*

16 Common Programming Errors

Developers learning a language tend to make certain kinds of errors frequently. Pointing out these Common Programming Errors *reduces the likelihood that readers will make the same mistakes.*

2 Portability Tips

We include Portability Tips *to help developers write portable code and to provide insights on how programming languages achieve a high degree of portability.*

1 Software Engineering Observation

Software Engineering Observations *highlight techniques, structural issues and design issues that affect the architecture and construction of software systems, especially large-scale systems.*

Deitel e-Learning Initiatives

e-Books and Support for Wireless Devices

Wireless devices will play an enormous role in the future of the Internet. Given recent band-width enhancements and the emergence of 3G wireless technologies, it is projected that, within two years, more people will access the Internet through wireless devices than through desktop computers. Deitel & Associates is committed to wireless accessibility and has published *Wireless Internet & Mobile Business How to Program*. To fulfill the needs of a wide range of customers, we are developing our content in traditional print formats and in new electronic formats, such as e-books, so that readers can access content virtually any-time, anywhere. Visit **www.deitel.com** and subscribe to the *Deitel™ Buzz Online* e-mail newsletter for periodic updates on all Deitel technology initiatives.

e-Matter

Deitel & Associates is partnering with Prentice Hall's parent company, Pearson PLC, and its information technology Web site, **InformIT.com**, to launch the Deitel e-Matter series at **www.InformIT.com/deitel** in Fall 2002. The Deitel e-Matter series will provide professionals with an additional source of information on specific programming topics at modest prices. e-Matter consists of stand-alone sections taken from published texts, forth-coming texts or pieces written during the Deitel research-and-development process. Devel-oping e-Matter based on pre-publication manuscripts allows us to offer significant amounts of the material well before our books are published.

Course Management Systems: WebCT, Blackboard, CourseCompass and Premium CourseCompass

We are working with Prentice Hall to integrate our *How to Program Series* courseware into four course management systems: WebCT, Blackboard™, CourseCompass and Premium CourseC-ompass. These enable instructors to create, manage and use sophisticated Web-based educational programs. Course management systems are used primarily in academic institutions and feature course customization (such as posting contact information, policies, syllabi, announcements, assignments, grades, performance evaluations and progress tracking), class and student manage-ment tools, a grade book, reporting tools, communication tools (such as chat rooms), a whiteboard, document sharing, bulletin boards and more. Instructors can use these products to communicate with their students, create online quizzes and exams from questions directly linked to the text and efficiently grade and track test results. For more information about these products, visit **www.prenhall.com/cms**. For demonstrations of existing WebCT, Blackboard and Course-Compass materials, visit **cms.prenhall.com/webct**, **cms.prenhall.com/blackboard** and **cms.prenhall.com/coursecompass**, respectively.

Deitel and InformIT Newsletters

Deitel Column in the InformIT Newsletters

Deitel & Associates, Inc., contributes articles to the free *InformIT* weekly e-mail newslet-ter, subscribed to by more than 750,000 IT professionals worldwide. For registration infor-mation, visit **www.InformIT.com** and click the **MyInformIT** tab.

Deitel™ Buzz Online Newsletter

Our own free newsletter, the *Deitel™ Buzz Online*, includes commentary on industry trends and developments, links to articles and resources from our published books and upcoming publications, product-release schedules, challenges, anecdotes and more. To subscribe, visit **www.deitel.com/newsletter/subscribe.html**.

The Deitel™ Developer Series

Deitel & Associates, Inc., is making a major commitment to covering Web services and other leading-edge technologies through the launch of our *Deitel™ Developer Series*. *Web Services A Technical Introduction* and *Java Web Services for Experienced Programmers* are the first Web services books in the series. These will be followed by several others, including *ASP .NET with Visual Basic .NET for Experienced Programmers* and *ASP .NET with C# for Experienced Programmers*. Additional *Deitel™ Developer Series* books include *C# A Programmer's Introduction*, *C# for Experienced Programmers*, *Visual Basic .NET for Experienced Programmers* and *Visual C++ .NET for Experienced Programmers*, which cover .NET topics.

The *Deitel™ Developer Series* is divided into three subseries. The *A Technical Introduction* subseries provides IT managers and developers with detailed overviews of emerging technologies. The *A Programmer's Introduction* subseries is designed to teach the fundamentals of new languages and software technologies to programmers and novices from the ground up. These books discuss programming fundamentals, followed by brief introductions to more sophisticated topics. The *For Experienced Programmers* subseries is designed for seasoned developers seeking to learn new programming languages and technologies without the encumbrance of introductory material. The books in this subseries move quickly to in-depth coverage of the features of the programming languages and software technologies being covered.

Acknowledgments

One of the great pleasures of writing a book is acknowledging the efforts of many people whose names may not appear on the cover, but whose hard work, cooperation, friendship and understanding were crucial to the production of the book. Many other people at Deitel & Associates devoted long hours to this project. Below is a list of our full-time employees who contributed to this publication:

- Tem R. Nieto, a graduate of the Massachusetts Institute of Technology, is Director of Product Development at Deitel & Associates, Inc. He is co-author of *C# A Programmer's Introduction*, *C# for Experienced Programmers*, *Visual Basic .NET for Experienced Programmers* and numerous texts in the *How to Program* series. Tem co-authored Chapter 5, XML and Derivative Technologies, and Appendix A, Introduction to XML Markup, and certified all of the book's technical chapters.

- Sean E. Santry, a graduate of Boston College with degrees in Computer Science and Philosophy, is Director of Software Development at Deitel & Associates, Inc., and co-author of *Java Web Services*. Sean co-authored Chapter 10, Java Web Services: A Conceptual Overview and Appendix C, Implementing Web Services in Java.

- Rashmi Jayaprakash, a graduate of Boston University with a degree in Computer Science, co-authored Chapter 7, UDDI, Discovery and Web Services Registries, and contributed to Chapter 8, Web Services Platforms, Vendors and Strategies.

- Su Zhang, a graduate of McGill University with a Master's in Computer Science, co-authored Chapter 10 and Appendix C and contributed to Chapter 5. Su also is a co-author of *Java Web Services*.

- Kyle Lomelí, a graduate of Oberlin College with a degree in Computer Science and a minor in East Asian Studies, co-authored Chapter 10 and Appendix C, contributed to Chapter 6, Understanding SOAP and WSDL, and reviewed many of the book's technical chapters. Kyle also is a co-author of *Java Web Services*.

- Jonathan Gadzik, a graduate of the Columbia University School of Engineering and Applied Science with a major in Computer Science, co-authored Chapter 10 and Appendix C, contributed to Chapter 6, Understanding SOAP and WSDL, and reviewed many of the book's technical chapters. Jonathan also is a co-author of *Java Web Services*.

- Cheryl Yaeger, a graduate of Boston University with a degree in Computer Science, is the Director of Microsoft® Software Publications at Deitel & Associates, Inc., and is the co-author of *C# A Programmer's Introduction, C# for Experienced Programmers* and *Visual Basic®.NET for Experienced Programmers*. She co-authored Chapter 9, .NET Web Services: A Conceptual Overview, and Appendix B, Implementing Web Services in Visual Basic .NET.

- Christina J. Courtemarche, a graduate at Boston University with a degree in Computer Science, contributed to Chapter 5.

- Laura Treibick, a graduate of the University of Colorado at Boulder with a degree in Photography and Multimedia, is Director of Multimedia at Deitel & Associates, Inc. She enhanced many of the graphics throughout the text, designed the cover and created the graphics in the inside front and back covers.

- Christi Kelsey, a graduate of Purdue University with a major in Management and a minor in Information Systems, co-authored several case studies in Chapter 4, Web Services and Enterprise Computing.

- Barbara Deitel applied copy edits to the manuscript and compiled the quotations for all the chapters.

- Abbey Deitel, a graduate of Carnegie Mellon University's Industrial Management Program and President of Deitel & Associates, Inc., co-authored Chapter 11, Computer and Internet Security, and Chapter 12, Web Services Security.

- Matthew R. Kowalewski, a graduate of Bentley College with a degree in Accounting Information Systems, contributed to Chapter 9.

We would also like to thank the participants in the Deitel & Associates, Inc., College Internship Program who contributed to this publication.[1]

- A. James O'Leary, a senior in Computer Science and Psychology at Rensselaer Polytechnic Institute, co-authored Chapter 11 and Chapter 12.

- Lucas Ballard, a senior at Brandeis University in Computer Science and Mathematics, contributed to Chapter 1 and Appendix D, Best Web Services Web Sites, created case studies for Chapter 4 and edited the entire manuscript.

- Jon Goldstein, a senior at Cornell in Computer Science and Economics, contributed to Chapter 1 and Appendix D, Best Web Services Web Sites, created case studies for Chapter 4 and edited the entire manuscript.

- Brian Foster, a sophomore at Northeastern University in Computer Science, contributed to Chapter 8.

- Ngale Truong, a sophomore at Northeastern University in Computer Science, contributed to Chapters 5 and 6.

- Matthew Rubino, a sophomore at Northeastern University in Computer Science, contributed to Chapter 5, Chapter 8 and Appendix D.

- Christina Carney, a senior in Psychology and Business at Framingham State College, researched and co-authored the Internet and Web Resources URLs and helped with the Preface and the glossary.

- Marc Marinaccio, a senior at Brown University in History, edited the entire manuscript and contributed to the glossary.

- Mike Dos'Santos, a senior at Northeastern University in Computer Science, contributed to Appendix C.

We are fortunate to have been able to work with the talented and dedicated team of publishing professionals at Prentice Hall. We especially appreciate the extraordinary efforts of our editor, Karen McLean of Prentice Hall/PTR, and Michael Ruel, who managed the extraordinary review processes for our *Deitel™ Developer Series* Web services publications. We would also like to thank Mark L. Taub, Editor-in-Chief for computer publications at PH/PTR, for conceptualizing the *Deitel™ Developer Series* and providing the necessary environment and resources to help us generate the many books in this series. A special note of appreciation goes to Marcia Horton, Editor-in-Chief of Engineering and Computer Science at Prentice Hall. Marcia has been our mentor and our friend for 18 years at Prentice Hall. She is responsible for all aspects of Deitel publications at all Pearson divisions, including Prentice Hall, PH/PTR and Pearson International.

---

1. The *Deitel & Associates, Inc. College Internship Program* offers a limited number of salaried positions to Boston-area college students majoring in Computer Science, Information Technology, Marketing, Management and English. Students work at our corporate headquarters in Maynard, Massachusetts full time in the summers and (for those attending college in the Boston area) part time during the academic year. We also offer full-time internship positions for students interested in taking a semester off from school to gain industry experience. Regular full-time positions are available to college graduates. For more information about this competitive program, please contact Abbey Deitel at `deitel@deitel.com` and visit `www.deitel.com`.

Laura Treibick, the Director of Multimedia at Deitel & Associates, Inc., designed the cover. Tamara Newnam (**smart_art@earthlink.net**) carried the cover through to completion and produced the artwork for our programming-tip icons.

We wish to acknowledge the efforts of our reviewers. Adhering to a tight time schedule, these reviewers scrutinized the text, providing countless suggestions for improving the accuracy and completeness of the presentation. We sincerely appreciate the time these people took from their busy professional schedules to help us ensure the quality, accuracy and timeliness of this book.

Christopher Fry (Clear Methods)
Kyle Gabhart (Independent Consultant)
Ari Goldberg (Alphawolf)
Corinne A. Gregory (Speaker, Author, Consultant)
Mason Ham (Zambit Technologies, Inc.)
Michael Hudson (Blueprint Technologies, Inc.)
Anne Thomas Manes (Systinet)
Paul Monday (J. D. Edwards & Co.)
JP Morganthal (iKimbo)
John Mueller (Consultant)
Neal Patel (Microsoft Corporation)
Mike Plusch (Clear Methods)
Teri Radichel (Radical Software)
Sazi Temel (BEA)
Priscilla Walmsley (Consultant)
David Weller (Valtech Technologies, Inc.)
Justin Whitney (Author and Web Services Game Designer)

We would sincerely appreciate your comments, criticisms, corrections and suggestions for improving the book. Please address all correspondence to:

deitel@deitel.com

We will respond promptly.

Well, that's it for now. Welcome to the exciting world of Web services. We hope you enjoy this presentation of business, technical and programming topics as much as we enjoyed writing it.

Dr. Harvey M. Deitel
Paul J. Deitel
Lauren K. Trees
Betsy DuWaldt

About the Authors

Dr. Harvey M. Deitel, Chairman and Chief Strategy Officer of Deitel & Associates, Inc., has 41 years experience in the computing field, including extensive industry and academic experience. Dr. Deitel earned B.S. and M.S. degrees from the Massachusetts Institute of Technology and a Ph.D. from Boston University. He worked on the pioneering virtual-memory operating-systems projects at IBM and MIT that developed techniques now widely implemented in systems such as Unix, Linux™ and Windows® XP. He has 20 years of college teaching experience, including earning tenure and serving as the Chairman of the Computer Science Department at Boston College before founding Deitel & Associates, Inc., with his son, Paul J. Deitel. He is the author or co-author of several dozen books and multimedia packages and is writing many more. With translations published in Japanese, Russian, Spanish, Traditional Chinese, Simplified Chinese, Korean, French, Polish, Italian, Portuguese and Greek, Dr. Deitel's texts have earned international recognition. Dr. Deitel has delivered professional seminars to major corporations, government organizations and various branches of the military.

Paul J. Deitel, CEO and Chief Technical Officer of Deitel & Associates, Inc., is a graduate of the Massachusetts Institute of Technology's Sloan School of Management, where he studied Information Technology. Through Deitel & Associates, Inc., he has delivered Java, C, C++ and Internet and World Wide Web programming courses to industry clients including Compaq, Hewlett-Packard, Sun Microsystems, White Sands Missile Range, Rogue Wave Software, Boeing, Dell, Stratus, Fidelity, Cambridge Technology Partners, Open Environment Corporation, One Wave, Hyperion Software, Lucent Technologies, Adra Systems, Entergy, CableData Systems, NASA at the Kennedy Space Center, the National Severe Storms Laboratory, IBM and many other organizations. He has lectured on C++ and Java for the Boston Chapter of the Association for Computing Machinery and has taught satellite-based Java courses through a cooperative venture of Deitel & Associates, Inc., Prentice Hall and the Technology Education Network. He and his father, Dr. Harvey M. Deitel, are the world's best-selling programming language textbook authors.

Lauren Trees is a graduate of Brown University with a concentration in Literatures in English. Lauren participated in the conceptualization of this book, performed much of the necessary research and acted as the primary author of Chapters 1–4. She also served as project manager and edited the entire manuscript for accuracy, clarity and effectiveness of presentation. Over the past two years, Lauren has contributed to numerous Deitel and Associates, Inc., publications, including *e-Business & e-Commerce for Managers*, *Wireless Internet & Mobile Business How to Program* and *Visual Basic® .NET How to Program*.

Betsy DuWaldt, Editorial Director of Deitel & Associates, Inc., is a graduate of Metropolitan State College of Denver with a major in Technical Communications (Technical Writing and Editing Emphasis). She acted as primary author of Chapters 5, 6, 8 and Appendix D. Betsy has contributed to numerous Deitel & Associates, Inc., publications, including *Wireless Internet & Mobile Business How to Program*, *C# How to Program* and *Python How to Program*.

About Deitel & Associates, Inc.

Deitel & Associates, Inc., is an internationally recognized corporate instructor-led training and content-creation organization specializing in Internet/World Wide Web software technology, e-business/e-commerce software technology, object technology and computer programming languages education. The company offers courses in Internet and World Wide Web programming, wireless Internet programming, Web services (in both Java and .NET languages), object technology, and major programming languages and platforms, such as Visual Basic .NET, C#, Visual C++ .NET, Java, Advanced Java, C, C++, XML, Perl, Python, ASP .NET, ADO .NET and more. Deitel & Associates, Inc., was founded by Dr. Harvey M. Deitel and Paul J. Deitel, the world's leading programming-language textbook authors. The company's clients include many of the world's largest companies and government agencies, branches of the military and business organizations. Through its 25-year publishing partnership with Prentice Hall, Deitel & Associates has published leading-edge programming textbooks, professional books, interactive CD-ROM-based multimedia *Cyber Classrooms*, *Complete Training Courses*, e-books, e-matter, Web-based training courses and course-management-systems e-content. Deitel & Associates, Inc., and the authors can be reached via e-mail at:

deitel@deitel.com

To learn more about Deitel & Associates, Inc., its publications and its worldwide corporate on-site curriculum, see the last few pages of this book or visit:

www.deitel.com

Individuals wishing to purchase Deitel products can do so through bookstores, online booksellers and:

www.deitel.com
www.prenhall.com/deitel
www.InformIT.com/deitel
www.InformIT.com/cyberclassrooms

Bulk orders by corporations and academic institutions should be placed directly with Prentice Hall. See the last few pages of this book for worldwide ordering details. To follow the Deitel publishing program through the *Deitel™ Buzz Online* e-mail newsletter, please register at

www.deitel.com/newsletter/subscribe.html.

The World Wide Web Consortium (W3C)

 Deitel & Associates, Inc., is a member of the *World Wide Web Consortium (W3C)*. The W3C was founded in 1994 "to develop common protocols for the evolution of the World Wide Web." As a W3C member, Deitel & Associates, Inc., holds a seat on the W3C Advisory Committee (the company's representative is our CEO and Chief Technology Officer, Paul Deitel). Advisory Committee members help provide "strategic direction" to the W3C through meetings held around the world. Member organizations also help develop standards recommendations for Web technologies (such as XHTML, XML and many others) through participation in W3C activities and groups. Membership in the W3C is intended for companies and large organizations. To obtain information on becoming a member of the W3C, visit **www.w3.org/Consortium/Prospectus/Joining**.

1

Introduction to Web Services

Objectives

- To review the history of the Internet, distributed computing and object technology.
- To explain enterprise communications requirements that have led to computing innovations.
- To understand the evolution of Web services.
- To discuss the potential of Web services and challenges to Web services adoption.
- To provide examples of companies benefiting from Web services.
- To tour the book.

Before beginning, plan carefully.
Marcus Tullius Cicero

Look with favor upon a bold beginning.
Virgil

I think I'm beginning to learn something about it.
Auguste Renoir

Outline

1.1 Introduction

Welcome to the world of Web services! Over the past several decades, computing has evolved at an unprecedented pace. This progress impacts organizations in significant ways, forcing information-technology (IT) managers and developers to accept new computing paradigms. Innovations in programming and hardware have led to more powerful and useful technologies, including object-oriented programming, distributed computing, Internet protocols and XML (Extensible Markup Language). At the same time, organizations have learned to leverage the power of their networks and the Internet to gain competitive advantages.

Web services technology—which represents the next stage in distributed computing—will profoundly affect organizations in 2002 and beyond. Web services encompass a set of related standards that can enable any two computer applications to communicate and exchange data via the Internet. Although the true impact of Web services is not yet known, many factors—including software vendors' widespread support for underlying standards—indicate that Web services will radically change IT architectures and partner relationships. Companies are already implementing Web services to facilitate a wide variety of business processes, such as application integration and business-to-business transactions.

When the topic of Web services began to appear in magazines and trade papers, we noticed that few people could concisely define what Web services are. At that point, we realized the need for a "literacy" book that explains Web services, explores the benefits they provide to businesses and discusses key concepts related to the technology. This book, one of the first in our new *Deitel Developer Series*, reflects our extensive research on Web services. We believe that the information we present will be useful both to programmers, who must learn to incorporate Web services in their applications and networks, and to IT managers, who must decide when and how to adopt this important new technology. As you proceed, if you would like to communicate with us, please send an e-mail to

deitel@deitel.com or browse our Web sites at **www.deitel.com**, **www.pren-hall.com/deitel** and **www.InformIT.com/deitel**. To learn about the latest developments in Web services and other leading-edge software technologies, please register at **www.deitel.com/newsletter/subscribe.html** for the new *Deitel™ Buzz Online* e-mail newsletter. We hope that you find *Web Services: A Technical Introduction* both informative and enjoyable.[1]

1.2 Computing Advancements and Web Services

Computer technology is constantly evolving to better serve the needs of programmers and users. Advances in programming and networking have improved software-development and communications capabilities, paving the way for Web services. This section overviews key developments in computing technology that have led to the creation of Web services.

1.2.1 Structured Programming to Object Technology

One of this book's authors, HMD, remembers the great frustration felt in the 1960s by software-development organizations, especially those creating large-scale projects. During the summers of his undergraduate years, HMD had the privilege of working at a leading computer vendor on the teams developing time-sharing, virtual-memory operating systems. It was a great experience for a college student, but, in the summer of 1967, reality set in. The company "decommitted" from commercially producing the particular system that hundreds of people had been working on for several years. Software development is a complicated process, and it was difficult to get this software right.

During the 1960s, many large software-development projects encountered severe difficulties. Development efforts typically ran behind schedule, costs often greatly exceeded budgets, and the finished products were unreliable. People began to realize that software development was a far more complex activity than they had imagined. Research activity, intended to address these issues, led to *structured programming*—a disciplined approach to creating programs that are clear, demonstrably correct and easy to modify.

As the benefits of structured programming (and the related disciplines of structured systems analysis and design) were realized in the 1970s, improved software technology did begin to appear. However, it was not until *object-oriented programming* became widely used in the 1980s and 1990s that software developers finally felt they had the necessary tools to improve the software-development process dramatically.

What are objects, and why are they special? Object technology is a packaging scheme that enables programmers to create meaningful software units. These units can be large and are focused on particular applications areas. There are date objects, time objects, paycheck objects, invoice objects, audio objects, video objects, file objects, record objects and so on. In fact, almost any noun can be reasonably represented as a software object. Objects have *properties* (i.e., *attributes*, such as color, size and weight) and perform *actions* (i.e., *behaviors*, such as moving, sleeping or drawing). *Classes* represent groups of related objects. A class is to an object as a blueprint is to a house. A class specifies the general format of its objects; the properties and actions available to an object depend on its class.

---

1. The *Deitel Developer Series* book *Java Web Services* provides more detailed information on creating and deploying Web services on Java platforms.

We live in a world of objects. Just look around you—there are cars, planes, people, animals, buildings, traffic lights, elevators and so on. Before object-oriented languages appeared, procedural programming languages (such as Fortran, Pascal, Basic and C) focused on actions (verbs) rather than objects (nouns). This paradigm shift made program writing a bit awkward. However, with the advent of popular object-oriented languages, such as C++, Java, C# and Visual Basic .NET, programmers can write code in an object-oriented manner that reflects the way in which they perceive the world. This process has resulted in significant productivity gains.

One of the key problems with procedural programming is that the software units created do not mirror real-world entities effectively and therefore are not particularly reusable. Programmers often write and rewrite similar software for various projects. This wastes time and money as developers repeatedly "reinvent the wheel." By contrast, object-oriented programming allows for code to be organized and encapsulated as classes, which facilitates the reuse of software components. Developers can group classes into *class libraries*, then make the libraries available to developers working on other projects.

Web services take advantage of object-oriented programming techniques in that Web services enable developers to build applications from existing software components. In this manner, the technology encourages a modular approach to programming, transforming a network such as the Internet into an enormous library of programmatic components available to developers. This can greatly reduce the effort required to implement certain kinds of systems—especially when compared to the effort involved in reinventing these capabilities for every new project.

1.2.2 Distributed Computing

When developers create substantial applications, often it is more efficient, or even necessary, for different tasks to be performed on different computers. The emergence of more powerful computers and networks led to the *distributed computing* phenomenon, in which an organization's computing is distributed over networks, instead of being performed only at a central computer installation. *N-tier applications* often split up applications over numerous computers. For example, a *three-tier application* might have a user interface on one computer, business-logic processing on a second and a database on a third—all interacting as the application runs.

For a distributed system to function correctly, application components (often encapsulated as programming objects) executing on different computers throughout a network must be able to communicate. In the early 1990s, many companies and organizations—including the *Object Management Group* (*OMG*), Microsoft, Sun Microsystems and IBM—realized the need for such functionality and began developing their own technologies to enable communication among distributed components. Each of the main technologies—OMG's *Common Object Request Broker Architecture* (*CORBA*), Microsoft's *Distributed Component Object Model* (*DCOM*), Sun Microsystem's *Remote Method Invocation* (*RMI*) and IBM's *Distributed System Object Model* (*DSOM*)—allow programs running in different locations to communicate as if they were on the same computer. This was a significant development, because businesses could use these technologies to integrate applications with business partners' computing systems.

Unfortunately, *interoperability* (the ability to communicate and share data with software from different vendors and platforms) is limited among these technologies. For example, the two most popular technologies, DCOM and CORBA, cannot communicate easily. DCOM and CORBA components often communicate via a *COM/CORBA bridge*. If DCOM's and CORBA's underlying protocols change, programmers must modify the bridge to reflect the changes. Such problems have impeded distributed computing's ability to facilitate business-process integration and automation.

Web services improve distributed-computing capabilities by addressing the issue of limited interoperability. Unlike DCOM and CORBA, Web services operate using *open* (i.e., non-proprietary) *standards*. This means that Web services can, theoretically, enable any two software components to communicate—regardless of the technologies used to create each component or the platform on which the component resides. Also, Web services-based applications are often easier to *debug* (i.e., for a programmer to locate and remove errors), because Web services use text-based communications protocols, rather than the *binary* (i.e, consisting of ones and zeros) communications protocols employed by DCOM and CORBA. Organizations are implementing Web services to improve communication between DCOM and CORBA components and to create standards-based distributed-computing systems. Thus, Web services might enable organizations to finally achieve the goals of distributed computing.

1.2.3 World Wide Web

Although the Internet was created more than three decades ago, the *World Wide Web* (*WWW*) is a relatively recent development. The Web allows computer users to locate and view multimedia-based documents (i.e., documents with text, graphics, animations, audios and/or videos) on almost any subject. In 1989, Tim Berners-Lee of CERN (the European Organization for Nuclear Research) began to develop a technology for sharing information via hyperlinked text documents. Basing the new language on the well-established *Standard Generalized Markup Language* (*SGML*)—a standard for data interchange—Berners-Lee called his invention the *HyperText Markup Language* (*HTML*). He also wrote communication protocols such as *Hypertext Transfer Protocol* (*HTTP*) to form the backbone of his new hypertext information system, which he referred to as the World Wide Web.

The Internet and Web will surely be listed among the most important and profound creations of the twentieth century. In the past, most applications ran on standalone computers. Today's applications can be written to communicate among the world's hundreds of millions of computers. The Internet and Web expedite and simplify our work, changing the way we do business and conduct our personal lives. Web services—which can operate over Internet and Web protocols, such as HTTP—extend the Web's capabilities to include direct communication between computer programs. However, Web services are just one of the many advancements made possible by the Web and its ubiquitous, platform-independent technologies.

1.2.4 Electronic Data Interchange (EDI)

As computers became integral to business, organizations wanted to use electronic capabilities to reach their markets faster and more efficiently. By shortening *lead time*, the time it takes to receive a product from a supplier after an order has been placed, businesses can lower their inventory costs and gain competitive advantage.[1] Many organizations have invested in *Electronic Data Interchange* (*EDI*) technology to link business partners and help manage supply chains.

Conventional EDI systems combine computers and communications equipment to enable businesses to conduct secure, reliable electronic transactions. Every supplier, manufacturer and distributor in a supply chain is linked to the EDI system through a *value-added network* (*VAN*)—a closed network that includes all members of a production process. EDI systems track and document a business's daily accounting and inventory data, including purchase orders, invoices and other transaction information. For example, operations personnel at a manufacturing plant might use an EDI system to buy supplies, track shipments and maintain accurate inventories. The EDI system transfers electronic documentation that verifies each party in a transaction, records the terms and conditions of the transaction and processes the order.[2]

Although EDI systems improve efficiency and promote better accounting practices, they can be expensive to operate. Many suppliers and distributors are small machine shops and shipping companies that do not have the technology to link into a traditional EDI system. The systems that send and receive EDI messages are not standardized, so a supplier or distributor that conducts business with multiple customers or partners might require separate EDI connections for each relationship. Also, EDI systems can be difficult to maintain, because they are *tightly coupled*. If a developer changes one component of a tightly coupled system, the developer must re-program all components in the system that rely on the altered component.[3] EDI traffic can now be carried over the Internet, which reduces costs and makes EDI accessible to more organizations. Nevertheless, EDI remains prohibitively expensive for many companies.[4]

Web services provide capabilities similar to those offered by EDI, but are simpler and less expensive to implement. Since Web services are built on open standards, fewer incompatibility problems arise. Also, Web services are more conducive to constructing *loosely coupled* systems—i.e., systems in which a developer can alter a programming component without modifying other components to reflect the original change.[5] Web services can be configured to work with EDI systems, which allows organizations to use the two technologies together or to phase out EDI while adopting Web services. Some companies are using Web services and EDI to implement more affordable business-process management systems.[6] We discuss business-process management in Chapter 5, XML and Derivative Technologies.

1.3 Emergence of Web Services

Although organizations are just beginning to implement Web services, the basic standards and ideas have existed for several years. In 1999, Hewlett-Packard became the first software vendor to introduce the concept of Web services. HP's product, *e-Speak*, was a platform that enabled developers to build and implement "e-services," program units similar to Web services. However, the proprietary nature of e-Speak's underlying technologies prevented the platform from gaining widespread industry support.

Microsoft coined the actual term "Web services" in June 2000, when the company introduced Web services as a key component of its *.NET initiative*, a broad new vision for embracing the Internet in the development, engineering and use of software. Microsoft announced that it was "betting the company" on Web services and, almost immediately, Web services became "the next big thing."[7] Now, nearly every major software vendor is marketing Web services tools and applications.

When Microsoft announced Web services, it was clear that the technology could revolutionize distributed computing. Previously, both CORBA and DCOM had been submitted to standards organizations with the expectation that companies would choose one as a universal distributed-computing standard. However, this did not occur, because organizations had already made significant investments in platforms that support specific distributed-computing technologies. Migration to a different platform costs businesses time, money and employee productivity.[8]

Microsoft's experience with interoperability problems caused the company to base Web services on open, standard technologies that could communicate with any platform or device. The main standard used in Web services is XML, a language for marking up data so that information can be exchanged between applications and platforms. Microsoft and DevelopMentor built the *Simple Object Access Protocol* (*SOAP*) as a messaging protocol for transporting information and instructions between Web services, using XML as a foundation for the protocol. Two other Web services specifications—*Web Services Description Language* (*WSDL*) and *Universal Description, Discovery and Integration* (*UDDI*)—are also based on XML. WSDL provides a standard method of describing Web services and their specific capabilities; UDDI defines XML-based rules for building directories in which companies advertise themselves and their Web services. We discuss these standards in Chapter 5, XML and Derivative Technologies; Chapter 6, Understanding SOAP and WSDL; and Chapter 7, UDDI, Discovery and Web Services Registries.

Most major software vendors have recognized that Web services technology represents a significant step forward for computing. Ariba, Apache, IBM, Sun, Oracle, Hewlett-Packard and others have contributed to the development of Web services standards and toolkits that enable programmers to create and deploy Web services.[9] Chapter 8, Web Services Vendors, Platforms and Strategies, discusses the roles of these and other companies in Web services.

1.4 Web Services Advantages

After the dot-com crash, businesses are more hesitant to invest significantly in new technologies. Readers might be wondering, "why is the computing industry so excited about Web services, given that many other promising technologies have failed?" To understand the answer to this question, let us consider some advantages associated with Web services.

- Web services operate using open, text-based standards, which enable components written in different languages and for different platforms to communicate.

- Web services promote a modular approach to programming, so multiple organizations can communicate with the same Web service.

- Web services are comparatively easy and inexpensive to implement, because they employ an existing infrastructure (a network, such as the Web) to exchange information. Moreover, most applications can be repackaged as Web services, so companies do not have to adopt entirely new software.

- Web services can significantly reduce the costs of enterprise application integration (EAI) and business-to-business (B2B) communications, thus offering companies tangible returns on their investments.[10] (We discuss these issues in Chapter 4, Web Services and Enterprise Computing.)

- Web services can be implemented incrementally, rather than all at once. This lessens the cost of adopting Web services and can reduce organizational disruption resulting from an abrupt switch in technologies.

The most important advantage of Web services over previous distributed-computing technologies is that they employ open standards. Because Web services facilitate communication among disparate applications and platforms, standardization and interoperability are crucial. The *World Wide Web Consortium* (*W3C*)—an organization that defines Web technologies—and other standards bodies are committed to ensuring that Web services protocols and specifications remain open and interoperable across vendor implementations. For example, the W3C established a *Web Services Activity*[2] to oversee the continued development of Web services technologies and to guarantee their compatibility with other W3C standards.[11]

Major software vendors, such as Microsoft and IBM, are also promoting interoperability among Web services implementations. The two companies are founding members of the *Web Services Interoperability Organization* (*WS-I*), a vendor consortium encompassing over a hundred companies from various industries (**www.ws-i.org**). The WS-I's goals include 1) developing guidelines and testing procedures for creating interoperable Web services, 2) establishing best practices for implementing Web services using SOAP, XML and UDDI, and 3) providing developers with example Web services that conform to WS-I guidelines. Although not a standards organization, the WS-I plans to help the W3C refine and improve Web services specifications.[12] Critics argue that Sun Microsystems's nonparticipation in the WS-I might limit the organization's effectiveness; nonetheless, the WS-I represents a major step towards vendor cooperation to promote interoperability.[13] Figure 1.1 lists current WS-I community members. We discuss the WS-I and W3C in greater detail in Chapter 2, Web Services: A New Computing Paradigm.

Web Services Interoperability Organization (WS-I) community members		
101communications	Accenture	Actional
Agentis Software	Akamai Technologies	Altova
Approva	Ascential Software	AT&T
Attachmate	Autodesk	Avinon
Bang Networks	BEA Systems	Blue Titan
Borland	Bowstreet	Business Objects
Cape Clear	Commerce One	CommerceQuest
ContentGuard	Corechange	Corel
Corillian	Cotagesoft	Cyclone Commerce
Daimler Chrysler	Dassault Systemes	DealEasy
Discrete Objects	E2Open	EDS
Epicentric	Epicor	ESRI

Fig. 1.1   Web Services Interoperability Organization (WS-I) community members.[14] (Part 1 of 2.)

2. A W3C Working Group is a unit of technical experts developing and improving a particular technology. Activity is the term that the W3C uses to represent an area of development around which one or more working groups are formed.

Web Services Interoperability Organization (WS-I) community members		
FileNET	Flamenco Networks	Ford Motor Company
Fox Island Partners	FrontRANGE Solutions	Fujitsu
FullTilt	Geac Computer Corporation	Grand Central
Groove Networks	Hewlett-Packard	HighJump Software
Hitachi	Hummingbird Limited	I/O Software
IBM Corporation	Intel	IONA
iWay Software	JamCracker	JD Edwards and Company
KANA	Kinzan	Loudcloud
Macromedia	McAfee	Mediapps
Mercator	Metapa	Micro Focus
Microsoft	Mogul Technology	move3d
NEON Systems	Netegrity	NetIQ Corporation
Onyx	Oracle Corporation	Parasoft
Peregrine Systems	Pivotal	Plumtree
Portera	POSC	Procter & Gamble
Promon IP	Quovadx	Qwest
Rational Software	Reactivity	RealNames
Reed Elsevier	Reuters	Sabre
SAP AG	SAS	SeguriDATA
SilverStream Software	Softronic	Software AG
Sonic Software	Suntail	Sybase
Systinet	Talking Blocks	Tata Consultancy Services
TIBCO	Toshiba	Tryllian
Unisys	United Airlines	UK Office of e-Envoy
Verisign	Versata	Vinsurance
Vitria	webMethods	WRQ

Fig. 1.1   Web Services Interoperability Organization (WS-I) community members.[14] (Part 2 of 2.)

1.5 Real Web Services

Web services technology is already reshaping business communications. Companies are recognizing the benefits of Web services, and many have deployed Web services to address specific business needs. This section describes Web services implementations in industries such as education, manufacturing, financial services and travel.

Organizations are employing Web services to integrate and improve communications systems. For example, the University of California, Berkeley, is using Web services to unify the school's e-mail, voice mail and facsimile service into individual in-boxes that are accessible from cell phones, PDAs, telephones or e-mail clients. With this new architecture, a single number can provide access to a cell phone, phone, fax and pager, and users can customize their personal settings. The set of Web services (called the *Unified Communications Technical Project*) will connect existing communications channels, allowing the school to integrate the channels while preserving legacy systems. The communications project also offers the flexibility to add new technologies or change vendors if necessary. At the time of this writing, the project was under development. If successful, the system will serve 50,000 students, faculty and staff by 2003.[15]

Manufacturing companies are implementing Web services to improve supply chains, inventory and customer-management systems. For instance, Eastman Chemical allows customers to access information about the company's numerous products via Web services. Eastman's distributors used to retrieve product information via the company's Web site or e-mail and, in turn, pass the information to customers. Since Eastman updates its product information frequently, this system caused distributors to supply customers with dated information. In response, Eastman implemented a Web services solution that allows distributors to query Eastman's product catalog directly, then push the information to customers in real time. Without Web services, this would have required each Eastman distributor to install a complex proprietary application. However, Web services enable Eastman to provide distributors with a standard application (i.e., a Web services client) that facilitates communication with Eastman's servers.[16]

Financial-services companies require the most current market statistics to make effective decisions. The consulting firm Accenture has developed Web services products, called *Live Information Models*, that enable stock traders to access real-time quotes and market information. Prior to Web services, brokerages had to install new terminals to access market information from subscription services. This situation often forced brokers to look at multiple screens to gather information. Accenture's Web services product allows brokers to receive real-time updates and to access different information sources from a single terminal.[17]

The travel industry also is benefitting from the Web services' integration capabilities. Airlines, travel agencies, rental-car companies and hotels all provide travel-related services. However, most of these organizations cannot integrate their computing systems because they do not use the same software or platforms. With Web services, companies in the travel business can streamline the reservation process. For example, consider the Web service implemented by business partners Dollar Rent a Car and Southwest Airlines. When Southwest approached Dollar about enabling customers to make rental-car reservations from the airline's site, it was obvious that connecting the reservation system and the Web site would benefit both businesses. However, integration would be difficult due to the companies' different operating systems—Southwest uses UNIX systems and Dollar uses Microsoft Windows. Dollar knew it could create a one-time solution to connect its electronic reservation system to Southwest's site, but it would not be able to reuse a customized system with other partners. Instead, Dollar turned its reservation system into a Web service. Since Web services communicate via the Internet using open standards, Dollar can connect additional businesses to its reservation system without creating customized functionality for each relationship.[18]

These examples illustrate ways that Web services can facilitate communication within an organization or between trusted business partners. Other organizations are developing public Web services, which are accessible to any interested party. Many public Web services are listed by Web services broker sites, such as **www.xmethods.net** and **www.salcentral.com**. At this time, XMethods lists approximately 175 Web services, and Salcentral lists approximately 400 Web services—the majority of these services are free, but some are fee-based. Figure 1.2 contains examples of public Web services and their capabilities. We discuss Web service brokers in Chapter 3, Web Services Business Models.

Web Services Can...

Offer updates on local traffic conditions or the status of an eBay auction.
(**alerts.microsoft.com/alerts/UserHome.asp**)

Provide computer and network security.
(**www.McAfee.com**)

Query Web documents directly from other computer applications.
(**www.google.com/apis**)

Return the distance in miles between two locations.
(**www.codebump.com**)

Locate entertainment, restaurants and lodging in a given area.
(**www.zagat.com**)

Return the name and postal address associated with a phone number.
(**www.serviceobject.com/products/dots_geophone.asp**)

Find information about ski resorts in a given city or zip code.
(**www.skiwhere.com**)

Locate trademark-status information from the U.S. Patent and Trademark Office's Web site.
(**www.serviceobjects.com/products/dots_tradetrack.asp**)

Conjugate verbs in over a hundred languages.
(**www.verbix.com**)

Find ATM locations in a given zip code.
(**www.serviceobjects.com/products/dots_atm_demo.asp**)

Return the position of the sun, moon and planets at a specific time.
(**www.orbitarium.com**)

Find the current price of any book at **barnesandnoble.com**.
(**www.esynaps.com/eSynaps_home.aspx**)

Communicate with e-mail servers to validate e-mail addresses.
(**www.cdyne.com/service.aspx**)

Find the current conversion rate between two currencies.
(**www.esynaps.com/eSynaps_home.aspx**)

Translate text between two languages.
(**babelfish.altavista.com**)

Process electronic payments—including credit cards, debit cards and e-checks.
(**www.richsolutions.com**).

Check and correct postal addresses.
(**www.cdynecom/services.aspx**)

Track the current location and status of a FedEx package.
(**fedex.com/us/tracking**)

Fig. 1.2   Examples of existing Web services and their capabilities. (Part 1 of 2.)

Web Services Can...

Perform financial calculations—including APR, tax and mortgage rates.
(**www.xmlbus.com/docs/5.2/demos**)

Report current weather conditions at airports and airfields.
(**capescience.capeclear.com/webservices/airportweather**)

Return stock quotes.
(**www.cdynecom/services.aspx**)

Send SMS messages and ring-tones to Internet-enabled wireless devices.
(**www.webservicebuy.com/x/smsreg.asp**)

Fig. 1.2   Examples of existing Web services and their capabilities. (Part 2 of 2.)

1.6 Web Services Challenges

Web services offer many benefits, but also create significant challenges for application developers and IT staffs. A key problem is that SOAP, WSDL and UDDI—the standards that drive Web services—are still in draft form. SOAP and WSDL are under development by the W3C, and UDDI has not yet been submitted to a standards organization. This means that the protocols and specifications are likely to change in the near term.[19] Many businesses want to wait until the underlying technologies are stable before adopting Web services. Others are nervous that the current cooperation among software vendors such as Microsoft, IBM and Sun to create interoperable implementations might fail, resulting in splinter standards and incompatible Web services implementations.[20] Also, Microsoft and IBM are refusing to release their intellectual property rights to certain Web services standards, suggesting that vendors might attempt to charge royalties on Web services technologies.[21] Throughout the book, we explain how standards immaturity affects Web services adoption and describe ways in which standards bodies and vendor consortia—including the W3C, OASIS and WS-I—are working to overcome these difficulties.

Another impediment to Web services adoption is the lack of standard security procedures. Web services typically allow direct access to a company's applications, which can expose corporate networks to security threats such as hackers and viruses. The core standards used in Web services, such as SOAP, are not designed to provide security. New Web services-specific security technologies are under development, but many companies are hesitant to deploy Web services outside corporate firewalls until security mechanisms are standardized.[22] This book provides an in-depth treatment of security issues in Chapter 11, Computer and Internet Security, and Chapter 12, Web Services Security.

Other Web services challenges involve defining and guaranteeing Quality of Service (QoS). Before invoking a Web service, customers often want to verify that the service will meet their expectations. Possible QoS problems with Web services include slow response times, infrequent updates and an inability to handle large numbers of requests. Some businesses have developed service-level agreements (SLAs), contracts between service providers and consumers that guarantee certain amounts of uptime, performance, security and so on. Also, independent companies have begun to provide third-party evaluations of Web services. In Chapter 3, Web Services Business Models, we describe the factors that comprise QoS and examine how organizations can address QoS concerns.

In the next section, we take a detailed tour of *Web Services: A Technical Introduction*. This book is divided into several sections. Chapters 1–4 explore the business case for Web services. We discuss the benefits and limitations of Web services, the development of Web services standards, Web services business models and the impact of Web services on enterprise computing. Chapters 5–7 describe the core technologies and standards associated with Web services. We discuss the history and role of XML, then cover the XML-derived technologies of e-Business XML (ebMXL), Business Transaction Protocol (BTP), Business Process Modeling Language (BPML), Business Process Query Language (BPQL) and Web Services Flow Language (WSFL). We also describe the architecture of SOAP messages, the role of WSDL in Web services and various discovery technologies, including UDDI and WS-Inspection. Chapters 9 and 10 overview two main Web services development platforms—.NET and Java—and Chapters 11 and 12 examine Web services security issues. The book concludes with programming appendices that introduce XML markup and .NET and Java Web services implementations.

1.7 Tour of the Book

In this section, we overview each chapter and outline the many topics discussed in *Web Services: A Technical Introduction*. Some of the terms mentioned here might be unfamiliar to you—they will be defined throughout the book. Every chapter ends with an Internet and Web Resources section, which lists Web sites that you can visit to learn more about the topics discussed in that chapter. Please visit our Web sites, **www.deitel.com** and **www.prenhall.com/deitel**, for updated information and additional learning resources. To follow the Deitel publishing program, including existing and forthcoming Web services publications, please register at **www.deitel.com/newsletter/subscribe.html** for the new *Deitel™ Buzz Online* e-mail newsletter.

Chapter 1—Introduction to Web Services
This chapter introduced Web services. We began by chronicling computing developments that make Web services possible, including object-oriented technology, distributed computing and Internet protocols. We described the emergence of Web services and explored their benefits, then introduced challenges to Web services adoption. We also discussed software vendors—including Microsoft, IBM, Sun and Hewlett Packard—that are cooperating to create open Web services standards and to ensure Web service interoperability. The chapter listed examples of existing Web services to illustrate the range of possible Web services capabilities. We also highlighted how certain industries—such as travel, financial services and manufacturing—are using Web services to integrate applications and improve B2B interactions. We concluded by touring the book.

Chapter 2—Web Services: A New Computing Paradigm
This chapter overviews technical and business topics relevant to Web services. We begin by defining Web services and discussing some of their distinguishing features, including modularity and platform independence. We introduce the Extensible Markup Language (XML), the underlying technology used in Web services, and explain how XML forms the basis for Web services standards such as SOAP, WSDL and UDDI. The chapter describes how organizations can use Web services and examines one Web service in a detailed case study. We discuss standards organizations and vendor consortia, such as the W3C and OASIS, and ex-

plore their roles in defining Web services specifications. We then overview key limitations of Web services, including performance, security and quality-of-service (QoS) concerns.

Chapter 3—Web Services Business Models

Web services offer opportunities for new businesses and lines of business. In this chapter, we divide Web services business models into two categories—businesses that offer services enabled by Web services standards and businesses that support the Web services industry. The first group is subdivided into service providers offering service-to-consumer (S2C), service-to-business (S2B) and service-to-employee (S2E) services. The second group—which facilitates Web services discovery and management—includes organizations that operate Web services registries, brokerages and networks. In discussing the stages of Web service development and deployment, we explain how service providers, brokers and requesters interact to complete Web services transactions. We also describe service-level agreements (SLAs) and explore possible payment methods.

Chapter 4—Web Services and Enterprise Computing

Companies can improve productivity and enhance various business processes through Web services. This chapter discusses how application developers and IT staffs can increase efficiency by incorporating Web services in enterprise systems. We explain the benefits of packaging business applications as services over the Internet, then describe how Web services can be used in specific enterprise software, such as portal, inventory, supply-chain-management and customer-relationship-management (CRM) applications. The chapter also contains case studies of how specific companies—including Microsoft, British Telecom, Alliance Airlines and Nordstrom—are using Web services to integrate systems and improve communication among departments, supply chains and partners.

Chapter 5—XML and Derivative Technologies

Understanding XML is essential to understanding Web services. This chapter begins by tracing the history of XML. We introduce the concept of markup languages, explaining how their standardization has increased interoperability among language platforms. We then overview a technology stack that illustrates the standards supporting Web services. We also discuss key XML-based technologies for describing and defining business processes. We explain the core components of ebXML, a technology that attempts to automate business processes. Other XML-derived technologies include Business Transaction Protocol (BTP), Business Process Modeling Language (BPML), Business Process Query Language (BPQL), Web Services Flow Language (WSFL) and Universal Business Language (UBL). The chapter concludes by introducing the basic structure of XML and defining key concepts such as tags, elements and namespaces.

Chapter 6—Understanding SOAP and WSDL

Simple Object Access Protocol (SOAP) and Web Services Description Language (WSDL) play crucial roles in Web services interactions. This chapter begins by chronicling the evolution of the SOAP and WSDL standards. We discuss the role of the SOAP messaging protocol in Web services architectures; topics include SOAP envelopes, Remote Procedure Calls (RPCs) and transport protocols. After providing an example of a SOAP message, we discuss interactions between SOAP senders and receivers. We also describe enhanced features of SOAP 1.2 and examine SOAP security issues. The chapter then introduces the

WSDL standard, an XML vocabulary used to provide specific information about Web services, and provides an explanation of a sample WSDL document. We conclude by examining SOAP implementations by Apache, Microsoft and IBM.

Chapter 7—UDDI, Discovery and Web Services Registries

For Web services to achieve widespread adoption, a unified system must enable developers and applications to locate specific Web services. Several organizations have developed Web services registry systems, but the leading registry is based on the Universal Description, Discovery and Integration (UDDI) specification. This chapter details aspects of UDDI, including dynamic discovery, the public UDDI Business Registry (UBR) and private registries. We describe the UDDI information model, which is composed of business information, business service information, bind information, service specification information and publisher assertion information. We then discuss the UDDI publishing and querying APIs. We also explain key limitations of UDDI and introduce alternative discovery methods provided by ebXML and WS-Inspection.

Chapter 8—Web Services Platforms, Vendors and Strategies

Many companies are creating tools and applications for the Web services market. This chapter overviews various vendors and their Web services offerings. We begin by describing major vendors' products and platforms that offer integrated support for Web services standards. These include BEA Systems' various Web services products, the Hewlett-Packard *HP Web Services Platform*, the IBM *WebSphere* product line and *Web Services Toolkit*, Microsoft's *.NET Platform*, the Oracle *9i Technology Suite* and Sun Microsystems's *Sun ONE* platform. We then consider mid-sized vendors' Web services platforms, such as the IONA *Orbix E2A™ Platform*, SilverStream Software's *eXtend™* product line, The Mind Electric's *GLUE* platform and Cape Clear's *CapeConnect* and *CapeStudio* tools. We also highlight Web services products created by smaller vendors and start-ups.

Chapter 9—.NET Web Services: A Conceptual Overview

Microsoft's .NET strategy embraces the Internet and Web as integral to the software-development and deployment processes. This chapter describes the .NET platform and its features for creating, publishing and consuming Web services. We highlight the benefits of implementing Web services in .NET, including .NET's support of multiple programming languages and its tools for code reuse. We illustrate "drag-and-drop" programming using Visual Studio .NET and explain how ASP .NET can improve Web service performance, testing and security. The chapter then presents the basic structure of both .NET Web services and .NET Web service clients. We introduce ASMX files, code-behind files and proxy classes. We also overview the Global XML Web Services Architecture (GXA), a set of specifications that extend Web services standards. We explain how Web services are invoked from wireless devices, and we conclude by investigating the use of Web services with Microsoft BizTalk and Microsoft's .NET Enterprise Servers.

Chapter 10—Java Web Services: A Conceptual Overview

The Java 2 Platform provides rich support for Web services technologies. Companies, organizations and individuals in the Java software community have developed various Web services platforms that enable programmers to build, deploy and publish Web services. Virtually every major application-server vendor provides Web services support for Java 2 Enterprise

Edition (J2EE) applications. This chapter discusses the extensive set of programming tools that Sun Microsystems provides to enable Java developers to build, access and integrate Web services. We overview Java technologies for Web services, including Java API for Remote Procedure Calls (JAX-RPC), Java API for XML Messaging (JAXM), SOAP with Attachments API for Java (SAAJ), Java API for XML Registries (JAXR) and various Java-based Web services deployment platforms. After reading this chapter, the reader will be familiar with the array of options for building Java-based Web services.

Chapter 11—Computer and Internet Security

Security breaches and network attacks can cause immense damage, costing organizations billions of dollars and affecting their productivity and even their credibility. To minimize these problems, it is essential that companies protect their data and ensure secure transactions. Effective security involves authenticating the identities of senders and receivers, verifying data integrity, ensuring that sensitive information remains private and proving that information was sent and properly received. This chapter begins by defining basic security terminology and exploring the history of cryptography. We examine and illustrate several cryptographic techniques used to encode information, including secret-key cryptography and public-key cryptography. We explore user authentication methods, such as digital signatures, digital certificates, digital watermarks and Kerberos. We also analyze the strengths and weaknesses of today's security standards—including Secure Sockets Layer (SSL), Internet Protocol Security (IPSec) and Virtual Private Networks (VPNs). Finally, we consider network security options, such as firewalls and intrusion-detection systems.

Chapter 12—Web Services Security

Web services can move transactions beyond corporate firewalls and enable outside entities to access corporate applications. This offers many benefits to organizations, but also increases the potential for security attacks and data corruption. This chapter addresses security—one of the main obstacles to widespread Web services adoption. We begin by describing why existing security technologies—such as HTTP and SSL—are insufficient to protect Web services transmissions. We then present several evolving Web services security specifications, including XML Signature and XML Encryption. These techniques authenticate messages and protect data during transmission, respectively. The XML Key Management Specification (XKMS), a specification for registering and distributing encryption keys, can be used with these techniques to authenticate each party in a transaction and to set up PKI (Public Key Infrastructure) for Web services. We also examine authorization and policy standards, such as the Security Assertion Markup Language (SAML) and the Extensible Access Control Markup Language (XACML). The chapter concludes by discussing Web services security with regard to firewalls and networks.

Appendix A—Introduction to XML Markup

Many Web services standards, such as SOAP, WSDL and UDDI, are XML-derived technologies. This appendix introduces the fundamentals of XML markup, including elements, attributes and character data. We explain the requirements for a well-formed document (i.e., a document that is syntactically correct) and provide a brief overview of parsers—programs that process XML documents and their data. We also introduce namespaces, which differentiate XML elements to avoid naming collisions. The appendix presents several complete XML documents, as well as an example of an XML Schema.

Appendix B—Implementing Web Services in Visual Basic .NET
This appendix introduces Web services programming with ASP .NET and Visual Basic .NET, building on concepts introduced in Chapter 9, .NET Web Services: A Conceptual Overview. The appendix shows complete working Visual Basic .NET LIVE-CODE™ examples; understanding these examples requires some familiarity with Visual Basic .NET and ASP .NET programming. The examples include Web services that manipulate integers up to 100 digits, simulate the Blackjack card game and implement a simple airline-reservation system. One particularly interesting example is our temperature server, a Web service that aggregates weather information for dozens of cities in the United States.

Appendix C—Implementing Web Services in Java
This appendix introduces how to build applications using the Java technologies discussed in Chapter 10, Java Web Services: A Conceptual Overview. We show complete working Java LIVE-CODE™ examples, so understanding these examples requires some familiarity with Java programming. Specifically, we show how to use the Java API for XML Remote Procedure Call (JAX-RPC) and the Java API for XML Messaging (JAXM)—technologies that Sun Microsystems provides for building Web services and the clients that invoke them. We show these technologies "at work," as we use these APIs and the Java programming language to develop two example programs. The first example is a JAX-RPC-based Web service that tallies votes for favorite programming languages. The second example is a JAXM-based business-to-business (B2B) architecture for purchasing and selling books. As we build these systems, we compare and contrast JAX-RPC and JAXM. We also include a Java-based client capable of invoking a Web service that provides stock information.

Appendix D—Best Web Services Web Sites
This appendix tours key Web services Web sites. First, we overview online resources provided by standards organizations and vendor consortia—such as the W3C, OASIS and the UDDI project. We direct readers to the most important information on these organizations' sites, including technical specifications and downloads. We then tour software vendors' Web sites that offer Web services articles and resources, including the IBM, Microsoft and Sun Microsystems sites. We also describe Web sites exclusively devoted to providing Web services articles and information, such as **www.webservices.org** and **www.webservicesarchitect.com**.

1.8 Summary

Web services technology—which represents the next stage in distributed computing—will profoundly affect organizations in 2002 and beyond. Web services encompass a set of related standards that can enable any two computer applications to communicate and exchange data via the Internet. Although the true impact of Web services is not yet known, many factors—including software vendors' widespread support for the technology—indicate that Web services will radically change IT architectures and partner relationships.

Web services take advantage of object-oriented programming techniques in that Web services enable developers to build applications from existing software components. This can greatly reduce the effort required to implement certain kinds of systems. Web services improve distributed-computing capabilities by addressing the issue of limited interoperability. Unlike DCOM and CORBA, Web services operate using open standards. This means that Web services can, theoretically, enable any two software components to communicate—regardless of differences in programming languages or platforms.

In 1999, Hewlett-Packard became the first software vendor to introduce the concept of Web services. Microsoft coined the term "Web services" in June 2000, when the company introduced Web services as a key component of its .NET initiative, a broad vision for embracing the Internet in the development, engineering and use of software. Now, nearly every major software vendor is marketing Web services tools and applications.

The main standard used to enable Web services is XML, a language for marking up data so that information can be exchanged between disparate applications and platforms. XML forms the foundation for the Simple Object Access Protocol (SOAP), a messaging protocol for transporting information and instructions between Web services. Two other Web services specifications—Web Services Description Language (WSDL) and Universal Description, Discovery and Integration (UDDI)—are also based on XML. WSDL provides a standard method of describing Web services and their specific capabilities; UDDI defines standard, XML-based rules for building Web services directories.

Web services promote a modular approach to programming, so multiple organizations can communicate with the same Web service. Web services are comparatively easy and inexpensive to implement, because they employ an already existing infrastructure (a network, such as the Web) to exchange information. Also, Web services significantly reduce the costs of enterprise application integration (EAI) and business-to-business (B2B) communications.

A challenge to Web services adoption is that SOAP, WSDL and UDDI are still in draft form. Many businesses want to wait until the underlying technologies are stable before adopting Web services. Others are nervous that the current cooperation among software vendors to create interoperable implementations might fail, resulting in splinter standards and incompatible Web services implementations. Web services also lack standard security procedures. Core standards used in Web services, such as SOAP, are designed to provide only the functions necessary to exchange information, which do not include security. Other Web services challenges involve defining and guaranteeing Quality of Service (QoS). Before invoking a Web service, customers often want to verify that the service will meet their expectations. Some businesses have developed service-level agreements (SLAs)—contracts between service providers and users that guarantee certain amounts of uptime, performance, security and so on. Independent companies have begun to provide third-party evaluations of Web services.

1.9 Internet and Web Resources

www.deitel.com
This site offers updates, corrections and additional resources for Deitel & Associates, Inc., publications.

www.prenhall.com/deitel
This is the Deitel & Associates, Inc., subsite on the Prentice Hall Web site, which contains information about Deitel products, publications, downloads and author information.

www.w3.org
The World Wide Web Consortium (W3C) develops technologies for the Internet and World Wide Web. This site includes links to W3C recommendations, news, mission statements and frequently asked questions (FAQs).

www.softlord.com/comp
This site outlines the history of computers, from the early days of computing through the evolution of modern machines.

www.elsop.com/wrc/h_comput.htm
The history of computing is summarized on this site, which features content on famous innovators, the evolution of programming languages and the development of operating systems.

www.w3.org/History.html
This site overviews the history of the Internet. After briefly covering developments from 1945 to 1988, the site details technological advances on a year-by-year basis from 1989 to the present day.

www.netvalley.com/intval.html
This site provides a short history of the Internet and the World Wide Web.

www.webservices.org
This portal aggregates information regarding nearly every aspect of Web services. Visitors can find updates on the latest Web services news, as well as information from standards organizations and articles discussing vendors, platforms, products, applications, case studies, security mechanisms and more. A search feature is included on the site.

www.webservicesarchitect.com
Web Services Architect is an online journal designed for Web services developers and the Web services community. The site provides in-depth articles on Web services development, tools, vendors and business models. The site also directs visitors to additional resources, including Web sites, books and white papers.

www.ws-i.org/
This is the home page of the Web Services Interoperability Organization (WS-I), an industry consortium designed to promote interoperability among Web services created in different programming languages on different platforms. The site provides white papers, news, FAQs and information regarding the organization and its members.

www.xml.com/lpt/a/2002/02/06/webservices.html
This article, entitled "Web Services Pitfalls," explains limitations of current Web services technologies and models. After introducing Web services, the author discusses the lack of standards for contracts and billing, unresolved security issues and problems surrounding Web service version control.

www.webservices.org/print.php?sid=201
In this article, "Web Services—A Reality Check," the author overviews technical concerns regarding Web services. The article focuses on three primary issues: transactions, security and quality of service (QoS). None of these issues are resolved by current Web services standards.

WORKS CITED

1.   R. F. Bruner, et al., *The Portable MBA* (New York: John Wiley & Sons, Inc., 1998) 146.

2.   K. Kaplan, "New Competitors for Dot-com," *LA Times* 10 July 2000 <**www.latimes.com**>.

3.   T. Clements, "Overview of SOAP," 17 August 2001 <**dcb.sun.com/practices/ webservices/overviews/overview_soap.jsp**>.

4.   M. McGarr, "Transforming Business Processes with EDI," *Electronic Commerce World* May 2002: 23.

5.   T. Clements, "Overview of SOAP," 17 August 2001 <**dcb.sun.com/practices/ webservices/overviews/overview_soap.jsp**>.

6.   M. McGarr, "Transforming Business Processes with EDI," *Electronic Commerce World* May 2002: 25.

7.   F. Harvey, "The Internet Reaches the Age of the Living Page," *Financial Times* 15 May 2002: 9.

8.   D. Gisolfi, "Web Services Architect, Part 3—Is Web Services the Reincarnation of CORBA?" July 2001 `<www-106.ibm.com/developerworks/webservices/library/ws-arc3/>`.

9.   F. Curbera, "Web Services Overview," 25 July 2001 `<www.llnl.gov/CASC/workshops/components_2001/viewgraphs/FranciscoCurbera.pdf>`.

10.   J. Borck, "*InfoWorld* Technology of the Year: Web Services," *InfoWorld* 4 February 2002: 48.

11.   J. Rapoza, "Web Services Standards Can't Be Rigged," *eWeek* 11 February 2002: 54.

12.   C. Purpi, "Web Services Organization Gets Down to Business," *Software Development Times* 15 May 2002: 1, 10.

13.   S. Vaughan-Nichols, "WS-I: Another Standards Battle Begins," *Software Development Times* 15 May 2002: 27.

14.   "WS-I Community," `<www.ws-i.org/Community.aspx?Alpha=All>`.

15.   J. Fontana, "XML the Glue for Unified Messaging," *Network World* 22 April 2002: 14–16.

16.   J. Fontana, "New Formula for Apps Access," *Network World* 15 April 2002: 18, 74.

17.   M. Vernon, "Transparency is the Key to Early Appearance on Trading Floors," *Financial Times* 1 May 2002: FT-IT 5.

18.   "Dollar Rent A Car E-Commerce Case Study on Microsoft Business," Microsoft Case Study 1 July 2001 `<www.microsoft.com/BUSINESS/casestudies/b2c/dollarrentacar.asp>`.

19.   S. Vaughan-Nichols, "WS-I: Another Standards Battle Begins," *Software Development Times* 15 May 2002: 27.

20.   J. McCarthy, "The Standards Body Politic," *InfoWorld* 20 May 2002: 44.

21.   D. Berlind, "IBM, Microsoft Plot Net Takeover," 11 April 2002 `<www.zdnet.com/filters/printerfriendly/0,6061,2861123-92,00.html>`.

22.   M. Vernon, "Why IT Managers Remain Cautious," *Financial Times* 1 May 2002: FT-IT 3.

Web Services: A New Computing Paradigm

Objectives

- To introduce the definition of, and concepts behind, Web services.
- To compare Web services to other distributed computing models and software services.
- To overview the major technologies that enable Web services: XML, SOAP, WSDL and UDDI.
- To explain the role of standards organizations and discuss the status of Web services standards.
- To explore the limitations of current Web services models.

Our technology, wiser than we, has given us the unforeseen and unforeseeable means of worldwide understanding at the moment when worldwide understanding is the only possible means to lasting peace.
Archibald MacLeish

Once a human being has arrived on this earth, communication is the largest single factor determining what kinds of relationships he makes with others and what happens to him in the world about him.
Virginia Satir

The open society, the unrestricted access to knowledge, the unplanned and uninhibited association of men for its furtherance—these are what may make a vast, complex, ever growing, ever changing, ever more specialized and expert technological world, nevertheless a world of human community.
J. Robert Oppenheimer

Outline

2.1 Introduction

Anyone familiar with the information-technology industry is aware of the current buzz surrounding Web services. Major software vendors—including Microsoft, Sun Microsystems, IBM and BEA Systems—have made significant commitments to Web services, and businesses are beginning to incorporate the services in their software systems. Over 66 percent of respondents to a 2001 *InfoWorld* magazine poll at least somewhat agreed that "Web services are likely to emerge as the next business model of the Internet."[1]   In the previous chapter, we introduced Web services and examined some of their benefits. But what are Web services, and how will they change the nature of business conducted over the Internet?

This chapter provides a general overview of Web services, focusing on what Web services mean to businesses and organizations. We begin by defining the term "Web services," around which some confusion has centered. We describe what Web services are and how they differ from previous computing and e-business models. We also discuss the technologies that enable Web services and the role of standards organizations in developing some of these technologies into official standards. The chapter explores a real Web service, including the functions that the service provides and how the service can be accessed over the Internet. Although many of this chapter's topics are covered in greater detail later in the book, the information here is intended to familiarize readers with key concepts relating to Web services. Additional information on many topics discussed in this chapter can be found at **www.webservices.org** and **www.webservicesarchitect.com**.

2.2 What Are Web Services?

To facilitate business tasks, enterprise applications must communicate with one another and share data. Historically, this was accomplished through proprietary specifications and data formats. However, the emergence of the World Wide Web and XML—an open standard for data exchange—has increased the possibility for interoperable system-to-system communications. Web services are software programs that use XML to exchange information with other software via common Internet protocols. Basically, a Web service communicates over a network to supply a specific set of *operations* (specific tasks performed by computers, often called *methods* or *functions*) that other applications can invoke (i.e., access and use). This means that an application residing on one computer can send requests to, and possibly receive responses from, applications on other computers. Web services can exchange information via many Internet protocols, but most employ *Hypertext Transfer Protocol* (*HTTP*)—the key communication protocol of the World Wide Web.

A Web service can perform almost any kind of task. For example, a Web portal might obtain top news headlines from an Associated Press Web service, whereas a financial application might employ a Web service that checks a stock quote and returns its current value. A Web service's functionality can be as trivial as multiplying two numbers together—or as complex as the functions carried out by an entire customer-relationship-management (CRM) software system.

Web services possess certain characteristics that, when considered collectively, distinguish Web services from other computing models. Paul Flessner, senior vice president of Microsoft's .NET Enterprise Server Division, identifies several of these traits in an article about Web services.[2] First, Web services are programmable. A Web service encapsulates a task; when an application passes data or instructions to it, the service processes that information and, if required, returns something to the application.[1] Second, Web services are based on XML. As an open, text-based standard, XML enables Web services to communicate with other applications, even if those applications are written in different programming languages and run on different platforms. Web services also are self-describing, meaning that they are accompanied by information explaining what they do and how other applications can access and use them. These descriptions typically are written in WSDL (Web Services Description Language), an XML-based standard explored later in this chapter. In addition, Web services are discoverable. This refers to the ability of applications and developers to search for and locate desired Web services through registries, such as those based on UDDI (Universal Description, Discovery and Integration), another emerging Web services standard.

---

1. In some cases, an application sends a message to a Web service, then suspends program execution while waiting for a response. In other cases, an application that invokes a Web service does not require or expect an immediate response. These differences are discussed in Chapter 6, Understanding SOAP and WSDL.

2.3 Web Services: Additional Web Tool—or New Distributed Computing Environment?

The concepts behind Web services are complex, so it is not surprising that people disagree about what Web services are and what they mean to the computing industry. Various developers, businesses and organizations think about Web services differently because they use them differently. Annrai O'Toole is the executive chairman of Cape Clear, a software company that is pioneering a range of software products for Web services. He summarizes the dichotomy in thinking that surrounds Web services today:

> Web services have a wide variety of uses. One group of users sees Web services as a simple Internet technology that can be used to replace some of the existing Internet screen-scraping techniques.[2] Rather than trawling a site and pulling data from pages based on an implicit understanding of how that data is formatted, [Web services] can provide an explicit, well-formed interface to the data.... [These users] do not perceive Web services as a new programming environment, but rather as a useful adjunct to their existing collection of Web tools.... At the other end of the spectrum is a group of users who sees Web services as a new distributed computing environment.[3]

To explain the idea of Web services as a new kind of Web tool, we must overview the basic structure of Web-based applications. Typical Web-based applications are programs that create Web content— including HTML, images and other material—for Web browser clients. Like many distributed applications, Web application are built on a multi-tier, or *n-tier*, architecture; this means that the application's functionality is divided into separate, logical groupings (Fig. 2.1). The *information tier* (also called the *data tier* or *bottom tier*) stores information. This tier can be comprised of one or more databases, which together contain the data relevant to the application. The *middle tier* (also called the *business tier* or *business-logic tier*) acts as an intermediary between data in the information tier and the application's clients, managing interactions between application clients and application data. The middle tier controls and processes *business logic* (i.e., rules to execute tasks performed by businesses), including how clients access data, how the application processes data and how content is presented to clients. The *client tier* (also called the *presentation tier* or *top tier*) provides the application's user interface, which typically runs in a Web browser. Users communicate with the application through the user interface. The client tier interacts with the middle tier to make requests and to retrieve data from the information tier. The client tier then displays to the user the data retrieved from the middle tier.

Often, different applications need to use the same data. However, it has been difficult to find an effective method of integrating Web-based applications, or enabling them to communicate with one another. Prior to the advent of Web services, most efforts to share information among Web-based applications involved one application interacting with another's client tier. Using this kind of integration, applications access information from other applications via their HTML markup, then attempt to distinguish the needed data from the other information that the markup contains. For example, an application that aggregates financial information might retrieve data from the markup of banking applications, stock applications and other sources. Screen scraping, which we mention earlier, is one method of performing client-tier integration. Although applications can share basic

---

2. In this context, screen scraping refers to processing HTML Web pages with applications designed to locate certain data or patterns of content. Applications that use screen-scraping techniques often are unstable, because the applications must be adapted every time a Web site's layout changes.

Client Tier   Middle Tier   Information Tier

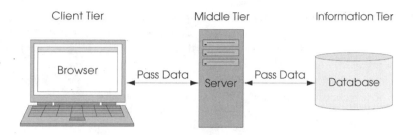

Fig. 2.1   Three-tier Web-based application.

information in this manner, communication via client-tier integration is limited in scope and prone to errors.

In situations where a specific set of applications need to share large quantities of data, it is possible to enable direct communication between applications' middle tiers without employing Web services. For example, an organization can integrate an inventory application and a sales-analysis application so that the two applications share the same product data. However, this often requires that IT departments or consultants develop customized connections between applications, which are costly to deploy and maintain. Applications running on different platforms are even more difficult to integrate. Furthermore, companies rarely integrate applications located across firewalls (such as partners' applications) because of security and performance problems. (We discuss application integration in Chapter 4, Web Services and Enterprise Computing; security is covered in Chapter 11, Computer and Internet Security, and Chapter 12, Web Services Security.)

By contrast, Web services provide a standard method for enabling communication between applications' middle tiers over a network. When packaged as a Web service or set of Web services, an application provides a reusable interface that can communicate with other properly configured applications. This means that applications can share processes (i.e., computing tasks), rather than only content, without the need for customized, one-to-one solutions. Since Web services' XML-based standards are not tied to a particular software vendor or platform, Web services theoretically can be deployed between any two systems, regardless of the underlying platforms.

The widespread adoption of Web services could result in a much higher level of data integration both within and between businesses, helping companies improve relationships with partners and customers. Within organizations, different departments can use Web services to share customer and inventory data and to work collaboratively in applications. When different corporate applications can access the same data, it becomes easier to manage such aspects of business as supply chains and inventory systems. Web services also fuel business-to-business relationships, in that companies can offer partners access to pieces of their applications. The ability of partner organizations to communicate effectively and exchange data increases both the quantity and the quality of partner interactions.

The opportunities that Web services offer to e-businesses are even more extensive. Instead of building all its own Web-site functionality, an e-business can locate Web services that perform specific tasks, then incorporate those services on its own site. For example, a grocery chain developing a national Web site might want to provide driving directions to local stores through the company's site. Instead of building the necessary functionality from scratch, which would be costly, the chain could incorporate a Web service that provides directions between a location input by a user and the chain's closest store.

The second description of Web services—as a new distributed computing environment—is much broader, and many would argue that it better reflects the scope of Web services technologies. By enabling applications to communicate effectively in a distributed environment, Web services can help developers change the way in which they design software. In the next section, we compare Web services to previous distributed computing technologies and demonstrate why Web services represent a major step forward for distributed computing.

2.4 Benefits of Web Services over Other Distributed Computing Technologies

Steve Benfield is chief technology officer of SilverStream Software, a company that is creating tools for developing and deploying Web services. When asked about Web services, he responds with this paradox: "1. There is nothing special about Web services. 2. Web services will change the world."[4] Benfield's two statements—which might at first appear contradictory—actually reveal a lot about the nature of Web services. Although the standards that enable Web services are not revolutionary in themselves, the situation surrounding their adoption is unique. Therefore, many believe that Web services will deliver on the promises of seamless integration made by various previous distributed-computing technologies.

From a purely technical perspective, there is "nothing special" about Web services. As we established in Chapter 1, Introduction to Web Services, protocols enabling applications to communicate and share processes in a distributed environment have existed for years. However, most of these technologies have a downside. Either they are overly complex, prone to errors, do not work well across firewalls or are not scalable enough to support use over a large distributed network like the Internet. Furthermore, most are in some manner specific to the vendor or platform for which they were designed, and none offers true interoperability.[5]

The infrastructure of Web services solves many problems inherent in previous distributed-computing technologies, and this is the reason why Benfield believes they "will change the world." First, the Internet is ubiquitous today, and Web services function over HTTP, so companies can expose and access Web services using technology that they already have in place. Because companies do not have to invest in significant new infrastructure before using and deploying Web services, the technology has a better chance of being adopted quickly. Another advantage of Web services is that they are more interoperable, because they employ an open, text-based standard—XML—to communicate among systems. Furthermore, nearly all major software vendors have agreed to use the same core standards to enable Web services: SOAP, WSDL and UDDI. (To learn more about these standards, read the sections describing them later in this chapter.) When previous distributed computing technologies emerged, different vendors or groups of vendors supported their own solutions, resulting in a fragmented marketplace.

All these factors indicate that Web services have the capability to provide direct application-to-application communication, opening the door for a wide range of potential communications uses. In Chapter 1, Introduction to Web Services, we outlined situations in which companies could employ Web services to facilitate business processes. However, Web services also have the potential to change the entire process of designing, developing and deploying software. In this context, they represent a new paradigm for distributed computing.

First, Web services could vastly improve collaborative software development. This is because Web services allow developers to create applications by combining code written in any language on any platform. Using Web services, developers can write code in the programming languages with which they are most comfortable, then merge their work with that of other developers writing in other languages for different platforms. This lessens the need for developers to learn multiple programming languages.

Furthermore, the widespread adoption of Web services could result in the emergence of more modular applications. Each business function in an application can be exposed as a separate Web service and offered over the Internet. Modular programs are less prone to errors and enable programmers to reuse components. When such components are available over the Internet, customers (individuals or businesses) can create their own unique applications by mixing and matching pieces, choosing only the Web services that provide functionality they need. Such software would be deployed as services accessible over networks, rather than as standalone applications residing on desktop computers. This concept is explored in greater detail in the next section.

2.5 Benefits of Web Services over Software Hosted by Application Service Providers (ASPs)

The idea of offering software as a service over the Internet is not unique to Web services. Since 1998, *Application Service Providers (ASPs)* have provided customized business software applications over the Web. ASPs typically develop a set of commonly used applications, then customize the applications to suit individual clients. By using an ASP to access business applications, companies eliminate the costs associated with developing and maintaining applications themselves. Instead, each company pays a fee, and its employees can access the necessary applications over the Internet. ASPs also assume responsibility for maintaining the applications and updating them as necessary.

However, ASPs have struggled financially and never gained widespread acceptance. The expense of maintaining and updating hosted software has resulted in high overhead costs, diminishing the viability of the ASP as a business model. For example, ASPs that maintain commerce applications for customers must update product, pricing and inventory information constantly so that applications reflect relevant data. Other types of hosted business applications require the complicated, manual integration of multiple data sources. Most ASPs charge according to the number of application users in a given time period (usually a month); often, billing does not sufficiently account for all these costs.[6]

Web services offer a new model for deploying software as an Internet-based service, and the many advantages that Web services provide likely will improve the success of software-as-service initiatives.[3] First, Web services sometimes are developed and maintained by the same entity, whereas most ASPs host software created and owned by others. The possible elimination of this intermediary makes software hosting more economically viable. ASPs usually offer large, complete applications with limited customization for individual clients; by contrast, Web services can be smaller components that perform specific

---

3. Readers should note that hosted applications and Web services differ in that hosted applications typically provide a user interface, whereas Web services provide a programming interface.

functions. This makes software upgrades easier to deploy and means that Web services customers have increased flexibility to assemble their own, unique applications from multiple vendors' offerings. Web services also can simplify the process of supplying data to business applications. Using Web services technology, a company can enable hosted software to access database applications directly and query them for needed information. This reduces the need for costly data updates.[7]

Perceiving the relative benefits of Web services, some ASPs are modifying their technical infrastructures and business models to be more like those of Web service providers. Most such ASPs will continue to manage their hosted applications while building a set of Web services and a customer base for the services. ASPs also can use Web services technology to facilitate communication between their hosted applications and databases that maintain a specific company's data. The role of Web service providers is discussed in detail in Chapter 3, Web Services Business Models.

2.6 ZipCode Resolver: A Simple Web Service

To understand better what a Web service is, let us explore a real service that readers can locate and access via the Internet. The Web site **www.xmethods.net** is one of the best sources for locating deployable Web services, and our example is taken from this site. If readers visit the XMethods home page, they will see a **Service List**, which contains Web services that perform a range of simple tasks (Fig. 2.2). Available services include credit-card validation services, currency converters, daily horoscopes by astrological sign, NFL headlines and a service that returns the current bid price of an eBay auction.

XMethods' **Service List** provides certain basic information for each service. The list's left-hand column identifies a service's publisher (i.e., the organization that owns or manages the Web service); although XMethods lists its own Web services, the site also catalogues services developed and hosted by third parties. After supplying publisher information, the site indicates the Web service's name and a brief description of the service. In the right-hand column (not shown in Fig. 2.2), XMethods specifies the service *implementation* (i.e., the specific application or toolkit used to develop the service). Possible implementations include *Microsoft .NET*, *Apache SOAP* or Cape Clear's *CapeConnect*. Additional information about vendors and their Web services implementations is provided in Chapter 8, Web Services Platforms, Vendors and Strategies.

Among the many services listed at **www.xmethods.net** is a service called the *ZipCode Resolver*, which is published by **eraserver.net** and uses data maintained by the United States Postal Service. The Web service accepts as input an address or partial address, then returns the zip code associated with that address.

To access the ZipCode Resolver, a user must scroll down the list of XMethods services and click the link labeled **ZipCode Resolver**. This link directs the user to another XMethods page that contains details about the service; information includes the owner of the service, the URL for the service, the SOAP implementation that the service employs, a description of the service and notes regarding usage. Clicking the link labeled **Service Home Page** directs the user to the main Web page for the service. This page offers a more in-depth description of the service, including a list of the methods (computing tasks) that the service provides (Fig. 2.3). The ZipCode Resolver offers several methods, each accepting some form of incomplete address and returning a complete address or zip code.

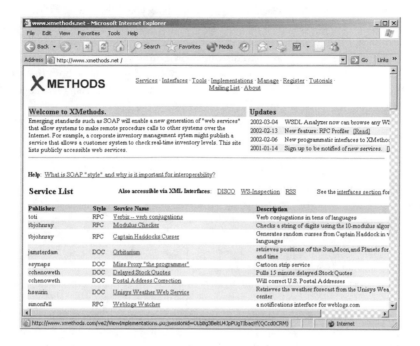

Fig. 2.2   XMethods Web site, which lists available Web services. (Courtesy of XMethods.)

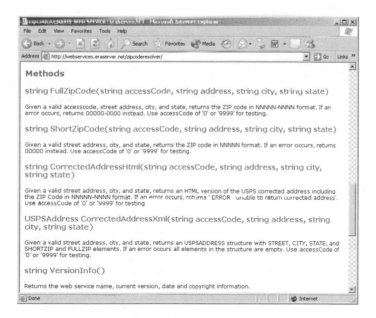

Fig. 2.3   Services available as part of the ZipCode Resolver. (Courtesy of **eraserver.net**.)

The service's home page also contains a version history and links to view the service's WSDL document and to access a test page. If a developer wants to incorporate the ZipCode Resolver into an application, the developer can use the service's WSDL document. This document describes the service and explains how programs can invoke the service's various methods. The developer then downloads certain software components that enable a program to communicate with the service. These concepts are beyond the scope of this chapter, but are covered in detail later in the book.

For the purposes of this example, we focus on the capabilities of the Web service, which are illustrated by the ZipCode Resolver test page (Fig. 2.4). The test page demonstrates the functionality the Web service, simulating via a Web page the tasks that the service can perform. On the test page, we input the address of the White House (1600 Pennsylvania Avenue, Washington, DC) to determine whether the service could locate a correct zip code.

After inputting the street address, we clicked the **ShortZipCode** button on the test page, which invokes a method that accepts a street address, then produces the associated five-digit zip code. When we performed our test, the service returned **20500**, the correct zip code for the White House (Fig. 2.5).

This Web service performs a simple task. After looking at the example, readers might be saying, "Web sites already exist where a user can enter an address and receive an appropriate zip code—why is this so special?" Of course, many Web sites enable users to perform functions similar to those performed by current-generation Web services. The capabilities that the ZipCode Resolver provides are not unique; it is the technologies behind these capabilities that are innovative. The most important factor is that, unlike Web sites, Web services are designed to be accessed and employed by other applications.

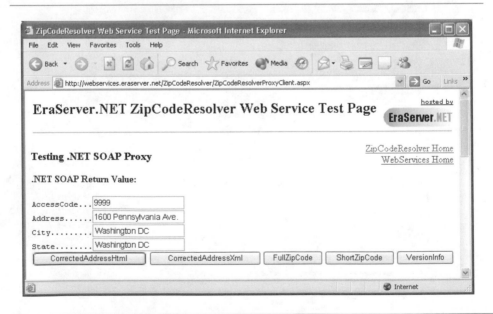

Fig. 2.4   ZipCode Resolver test site, where we input the address of the White House. (Courtesy of **eraserver.net**.)

Fig. 2.5   ZipCode Resolver test page displaying the zip code for the White House. (Courtesy of **eraserver.net**.)

Although the ZipCode Resolver is intended only for personal use, a similar service could be created and marketed to businesses. Imagine that a programmer is designing a database application for storing a business's customer information. However, the company's files contain only partial addresses for many customers. Instead of looking up every complete address and zip code, the developer could incorporate a service similar to the Zip-Code Resolver in the application. If appropriately configured, the database application conceivably could access the Web service, send it each incomplete address, then enter each response (i.e., complete address) into the database. In this manner, the application could update address data automatically, requiring only minimal human intervention.

2.7 Key Web Services Technologies

As we explained earlier, part of what distinguishes Web services from similar computing models is the use of XML and XML-based standards—most commonly SOAP, WSDL and UDDI. These technologies enable communication among applications in a manner that is independent of specific programming languages, operating systems and hardware platforms. SOAP provides a communication mechanism between services and applications, WSDL offers a uniform method of describing services to other programs and UDDI enables the creation of searchable Web services registries. When deployed together, these technologies allow developers to package applications as services and publish those services on a network.

Figure 2.6 depicts the role of various standards in common Web services architectures.[4] Although readers might be unfamiliar with the technologies and relationships portrayed in the diagram, the next sections provide clarification by describing each core Web

---

4. For simplicity, Fig. 2.6 depicts a Web service that returns a response to a client. However, readers should note that some Web services do not return immediate responses.

services standard. We discuss these standards in greater detail in Chapter 5, XML and Derivative Technologies; Chapter 6, Understanding SOAP and WSDL; and Chapter 7, UDDI, Discovery and Web Services Registries.

2.7.1 XML (Extensible Markup Language)

Developed from the *Standard Generalized Markup Language* (*SGML*), XML is a widely accepted standard for describing data and creating markup languages. Unlike many technologies, which begin as proprietary solutions and become standards, XML was defined by the W3C as an open, standard technology. In 1998, the XML version 1.0 specification was accepted as a W3C Recommendation, which means that the technology is stable for deployment in industry.

Data independence, or the separation of content from its presentation, is the essential characteristic of XML. Because XML documents describe only data, any application that understands XML—regardless of the application's programming language or platform—has the ability to format XML in a variety of different ways. Recognizing this, software developers are integrating XML into their applications to improve Web functionality and interoperability. XML documents contain data, but no formatting instructions, so applications that process XML documents must decide how to display the documents' data. For example, a PDA (personal digital assistant) might render an XML document differently than a wireless phone or desktop computer would render that document.

An *XML parser* is a software program that checks an XML document's syntax and makes the XML document's data available to applications. If the syntax is correct, then the document conforms to the XML 1.0 specification and therefore is considered *well formed*. If the syntax is not correct, the parser generates one or more errors, and applications cannot use the document. An XML document optionally can reference another document that defines the XML document's structure. This other document is either a *Document Type Def-*

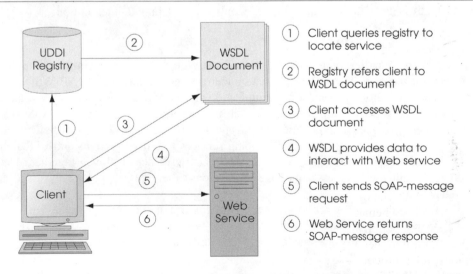

Fig. 2.6   SOAP, UDDI and WSDL in a Web service interaction.

inition (DTD) or a *Schema*. When an XML document references a DTD or Schema, some parsers (called *validating parsers*) can read the DTD/Schema and check that the XML document adheres to the structure that the DTD/Schema defines. If the XML document adheres to the structure defined in the DTD/Schema, then the XML document is *valid*.

As applications become more Web enabled, it seems likely that XML will become the universal technology for representing data passed between Web applications. All applications employing XML will be able to communicate, provided that they can understand each others' XML markup, or vocabulary. This high level of interoperability makes XML an ideal technology to enable Web services, which communicate among systems without regard to operating systems and hardware platforms. The core standards enabling Web services, which are described in the next three sections, are based on XML.

2.7.2 SOAP (Simple Object Access Protocol)

SOAP is one of the most common standards used to deliver Web services. Initially developed by representatives from DevelopMentor, Userland Software and Microsoft, SOAP was conceptualized in 1998 and published as SOAP 0.9 in 1999.[8] The companies released several subsequent versions of SOAP before submitting the protocol to the W3C. The newest version of SOAP, SOAP 1.2, is currently being defined by the W3C. When finalized, SOAP 1.2 will represent a major progression of the standard, which in part explains the current industry excitement regarding SOAP and Web services deployments.

The purpose of SOAP is to enable data transfer between systems distributed over a network. When an application communicates with a Web service, SOAP messages are the most common means through which the two systems exchange data. A SOAP message sent to a Web service invokes a method provided by the service, meaning that the message requests that the service execute a particular task. The service then uses information contained in the SOAP message to perform its function; if necessary, the Web service returns the result via another SOAP message.

As an XML-based communication protocol, SOAP basically consists of a set of standardized XML Schemas. The Schemas define a format for transmitting XML messages over a network, including the types of data that the message can include and the way in which the message must be structured so that the server on the other end can interpret it correctly.[9] SOAP is layered over an Internet protocol, such as HTTP, and can be used to transfer data across the Web and other networks. The use of HTTP allows Web services to communicate across firewalls, because most firewalls are designed to accept HTTP service requests.[10]

A SOAP message consists of three main parts: an *envelope*, a *header* and a *body*. The envelope wraps the entire message and contains the header and body elements; the header is an optional element that provides information regarding such topics as security and routing. The body of the SOAP message contains the application-specific data that is being communicated. The data is marked up as XML and adheres to a specific format, which is defined by the Schemas we mentioned earlier. This formatting enables the recipient to process the data correctly. SOAP messages are received and interpreted by SOAP servers, which, in turn, trigger Web services to perform their tasks.

Several protocols could be used instead of SOAP to enable Web services. For example, *XML-RPC* is an older technology that provides similar functionality. However, most major software vendors have chosen to support SOAP over other possible technologies. There are several technical reasons for industry support of SOAP, many of which refer to aspects of the protocol beyond the scope of this text. However, it is important to note the main advantages of SOAP—simplicity, extensibility and interoperability.[11] Basic SOAP messages do not involve extensive amounts of code, and there is little "special software" needed either to send or to receive SOAP messages. SOAP also provides mechanisms that enable developers to extend the standard to meet specific needs. Furthermore, because SOAP employs XML to communicate over HTTP, SOAP theoretically can be used to transfer data between any two systems that are connected to the Internet, regardless of programming languages, operating systems and hardware platforms. A more detailed description of SOAP and several common SOAP implementations is provided in Chapter 6, Understanding SOAP and WSDL.

2.7.3 WSDL (Web Services Description Language)

Another standard that plays a crucial role in enabling Web services is WSDL. We mentioned earlier that a defining feature of Web services is that they are self-describing, meaning that every Web service is accompanied by information that enables developers to employ the service. These descriptions typically are written in WSDL, an XML-based language through which a Web service can convey to other applications the methods that the service provides and how those methods can be accessed.

When SOAP and other Web services technologies were first developed, software vendors realized that applications calling services across a network would need information about a specific service before interacting with it. However, each vendor began building its own method of description, resulting in service descriptions that were incompatible with one another. The WSDL specification emerged when vendors Microsoft and IBM decided to combine their description technologies into a universal standard. In March 2001, Microsoft, IBM and Ariba submitted WSDL 1.1 to the W3C; the W3C is working to standardize the language further. Although the technology is still under development, nearly all Web services products now provide support for WSDL 1.1.

Nearly every Web service published on the Internet is accompanied by an associated WSDL document, which lists the service's capabilities, states its location on the Web and provides instructions regarding its use. A WSDL document defines the kinds of messages a Web service can send and receive, as well as specifying the data that a calling application must provide for the Web service to perform its task. WSDL documents also provide specific technical information that informs applications about how to connect to and communicate with Web services over HTTP or another communications protocol.

It is important to realize that WSDL is a language meant to be read by applications, rather than by humans. Although the structure of WSDL documents might appear complex, computers that understand WSDL can process the documents and extract the information they need. Furthermore, most Web services development tools generate WSDL documents automatically. This means that, if a programmer develops a Web service, the software used to build the service creates an appropriate WSDL document for that service. Therefore, it is not necessary for developers to understand the syntax of WSDL fully when building and deploying Web services. WSDL and its role in Web services are discussed in Chapter 6, Understanding SOAP and WSDL.

2.7.4 UDDI (Universal Description, Discovery and Integration)

The third major Web services standard, UDDI, enables developers and businesses to publish and locate Web services on a network. Originally designed by Microsoft, IBM and Ariba, UDDI began as a way for users of B2B exchanges to share information about their businesses and business processes with potential partners and affiliates.[12] As its name implies, the specification allows companies to describe their own services and electronic processes, discover those of other companies and integrate others' services into their systems. Although UDDI is a relatively new standard (the first version was published in September 2000), it has acquired significant industry backing. The most recent version of UDDI, UDDI 2.0, was released in June 2001; UDDI 3.0 is under development.[13]

UDDI defines an XML-based format in which companies can describe their electronic capabilities and business processes; the specification also provides a standardized method of registering and locating the descriptions on a network, such as the Internet. Part of the information that companies can supply is data regarding available Web services. Companies can store their information either in private UDDI registries, which are accessible only to approved business partners, or in public UDDI registries, which any interested party can use. The largest, most comprehensive public UDDI registry is the UDDI Business Registry (UBR), which was developed to facilitate the formation of new business relationships. Microsoft and IBM host implementations of the UBR that adhere to UDDI 1.0, and Microsoft, IBM, Hewlett-Packard and SAP host UBR implementations that adhere to UDDI 2.0. The UBR implementations that adhere to UDDI 1.0 are synchronized, so information entered in one is replicated in the other. The UBR implementations that adhere to UDDI 2.0 are expected to support replication by fall 2002.

A UDDI registry's structure is conceptually similar to that of a phone book. Registries contain "white pages," where companies list contact information and textual description of themselves; "yellow pages," which provide classification information about companies and details on companies' electronic capabilities; and "green pages," which list technical data relating to services and business processes.[14] Information regarding businesses and services is highly categorized, enabling companies to search for desired partners or services. IT staffs then can use the technical information in the registries to link electronically to other businesses. In this manner, UDDI simplifies the process of creating B2B relationships and connecting electronic systems to exchange data and services.

Vendor interest in UDDI registries is already strong—most Web services players support UDDI and have incorporated the standard into their products. NTT Communications of Tokyo and other companies are in the process of building additional implementations of the UDDI Business Registry. However, businesses have been slow to enter information in the public registries. This has not surprised industry experts, who believe that companies will begin by building private registries to share services with partners. Large organizations also can create private registries to organize their own Web services and make the services available to other departments. Some experts believe that, once the technology has matured and users are comfortable with it, public exchanges will become more popular.

It is difficult for large organizations to change the way in which they communicate, form partnerships, locate clients and transact business. Some companies are hesitant to abandon older B2B communications mechanisms, whereas others are concerned about the security issues raised by exposing corporate data or applications on the Web. However, organizations are slowly realizing that technologies such as UDDI can improve business processes and provide competitive advantages. Chapter 7, UDDI, Discovery and Web Services Registries, contains additional information about registries and the UDDI specification.

2.8 Development of Web Services Standards

A major goal of technologies such as XML and Web services is to facilitate interoperability among computers and networks using different software, platforms or operating systems. However, true interoperability requires that software vendors and developers agree to employ the same or compatible underlying technologies. If every software vendor created its own proprietary specifications to enable Web services, it is unlikely that systems would be able to communicate effectively. Vendors and other relevant players need a structure through which to discuss emerging technologies and make unilateral decisions regarding their development.

Many standards organizations promote the adoption of open and interoperable specifications. According to the *ISO (International Organization for Standardization)*, "standards are documented agreements containing technical specifications or other precise criteria to be used consistently as rules, guidelines, or definitions of characteristics, to ensure that materials, products, processes and services are fit for their purpose."[15] In the area of information technology, standardization refers to the creation of a set of rules that form and guide implementations of a technology so that everyone employing that technology is using the same or compatible versions. Several key standards organizations are overseeing the development of the protocols involved in Web services.

2.8.1 Standards Bodies[5]

With approximately 500 member organizations, the W3C is the largest and most influential standards body involved in the advancement of Web services technologies. Tim Berners-Lee, one of the inventors of the World Wide Web, founded the W3C in 1994. At that time, many industry leaders were afraid that a lack of standards governing World Wide Web technologies would result in technological chaos. In an attempt to minimize such problems, the W3C provides an established forum through which qualified individuals and companies can cooperate to define and standardize Web technologies.

A W3C *Working Group* is a unit of technical experts who work to develop and improve a particular Web technology. *Activity* is the term used by the W3C to represent an area of development around which one or more working groups are formed. Individuals, companies and groups who create new technologies can submit them to the W3C; the W3C then evaluates such submissions and, if appropriate, establishes activities and working groups to hone the technologies. Eventually, these working groups present specifications called *Recommendations*, which define the technologies. This process improves technologies through collaboration and limits the control that any individual or company has over the development of important specifications.

Recommendations are not actual software products, but documents that specify the role, syntax and rules of a technology. Before becoming a W3C Recommendation, a document

---

5. The W3C and OASIS technically are vendor consortia, rather than official standards bodies. However, we refer to them as standards organizations, because they define and build consensus for technologies.

passes through three major phases: *Working Draft*—which, as its name implies, specifies an evolving draft; *Candidate Recommendation*—a stable version of the document that industry can begin to implement; and *Proposed Recommendation*—a Candidate Recommendation that is considered mature (i.e., has been implemented and tested over a period of time) and is ready to be considered for W3C Recommendation status. Since its inception, the W3C has released Recommendations for many key Internet technologies, including HTML, XHTML and XML (the root technology of Web services).[16] Additional information about the W3C, its structure and various projects is available at **www.w3.org**.

The *Organization of the Advancement of Structured Information Standards (OASIS)* is another key standards body working to develop Web services specifications. Founded in 1993 as SGML Open, OASIS began as a group of software vendors and large companies that wanted to improve interoperability among various SGML products. When XML evolved from SGML as a simpler and more Web-friendly technology, XML quickly overtook SGML in popularity. In response to this industry shift, OASIS adopted its current name and now focuses on the development and standardization of XML-based technologies.

The organization, which consists of over 400 individual and corporate members, aims to create consensus regarding XML technologies and to improve those technologies so that they fit the requirements of the widest possible range of users.[17] Among its other activities, OASIS operates **XML.org**, a clearinghouse for XML documentation and a registry of XML vocabularies, and *XML Cover Pages*, a collection of online reference materials regarding markup language standards. To learn more about OASIS and its initiatives, visit **www.oasis-open.org**.

A host of other standards organizations also are involved in the development of Internet protocols. For example, the *Internet Engineering Task Force (IETF)* is an international consortium of network and Internet experts who work to further Internet architecture and technologies (**www.ietf.org**). This body governs the evolution of several standard Internet operating protocols, such as TCP/IP.[18] The International Organization for Standardization (ISO) is a standards body whose mission is much broader in scope (**www.iso.org**). Comprised of representatives from standards organizations in approximately 140 member countries, ISO facilitates international commerce by developing protocols in many diverse areas, from standardized ATM cards to universal systems of measurement. Its work in the information technology arena has included the standardization of SGML, XML's parent language.[19]

2.8.2 W3C and Web Services

The W3C develops nonproprietary technologies for the World Wide Web. One of the W3C's primary goals is to make the Web universally accessible, regardless of users' "hardware, software [and] network infrastructure," among many other factors. Another, equally emphasized W3C goal is to ensure interoperability among Web technologies.[20] The concepts and technologies that underlie Web services adhere to and further these W3C goals. The W3C has recognized this and has, in turn, made significant contributions to Web services initiatives.

The W3C became significantly involved with Web services standards in May 2000. At that time, Microsoft, the creator of the initial SOAP specification, joined with Ariba, Commerce One, Hewlett-Packard, IBM, IONA and Lotus Development to submit SOAP 1.1 to the W3C for standardization. All these companies saw a need to establish a common method of XML application-to-application messaging, and they decided to support the SOAP specification to fill that need. The W3C was chosen to develop SOAP further because XML itself is a W3C standard.[21]

The W3C acknowledged the submission and, in September 2000, established the *XML Protocol Activity* to address the standardization of SOAP and related protocols. The corresponding *XML Protocol Working Group* then began to develop a standard protocol for XML messaging, basing its work on the SOAP submission. In July 2001, the W3C published an initial Working Draft of SOAP Version 1.2; a second Working Draft was published in December 2001.[22] Although still under development, SOAP 1.2 is a more stable protocol that resolves many of SOAP's previous problems and ambiguities. (For a detailed analysis of SOAP and SOAP Version 1.2, see Chapter 6, Understanding SOAP and WSDL.)

In January 2002, the W3C increased its commitment to Web services by forming a Web Services Activity to oversee the further development of Web services technologies. The new Activity encompasses a *Coordination Group* (which facilitates communication among related groups) and three Working Groups, including the XML Protocol Working Group that is developing SOAP Version 1.2.

One of the new working groups is a *Web Services Architecture* Working Group, which must identify the technologies necessary for Web services and define how those technologies relate to each other. The primary goals of this working group are to ensure that Web services architecture is modular, based on XML, platform-independent, integrated into the overall architecture of the Web and supports the extensibility that exists on the Web.[23] The other new working group, called the *Web Services Description* Working Group, was established to design an XML-based language for describing Web services and ways in which other applications can interact with those services. This group plans to base its work on WSDL 1.1, which was submitted to the W3C for standardization in March 2001.[24]

2.8.3 OASIS and Web Services

Rather than competing with the W3C to develop basic standards such as SOAP and WSDL, OASIS is working on projects to ensure that specific industries acquire e-business tools that meet their unique needs.[25] However, OASIS's efforts have made significant contributions to various Web services-related initiatives. Most relevant to the advancement of Web services is OASIS's joint project with the *United Nations Centre for Trade Facilitation and Electronic Business (UN/CEFACT)*, which resulted in the creation of *electronic business XML (ebXML)*.

In late 1999, OASIS and UN/CEFACT initiated a project to consolidate and standardize the many competing XML specifications for facilitating electronic business. The two organizations established the *Electronic Business XML Working Group* to oversee an 18-month project. The working group aimed to create a technical framework through which companies of any size in any industry could communicate and exchange data via the Internet.[26] In May 2001, OASIS members approved a set of XML specifications known collectively as ebXML.

Patrick Gannon, president and CEO of OASIS, states that OASIS's role with regard to Web services is to "combine tools together and construct new business processes."[27] In many ways, ebXML is a realization of that statement, in that it encompasses aspects of core

Web services technologies into a framework that enables e-business. ebXML is a modular set of XML-based specifications and protocols that are designed for exchanging XML messages and conducting business transactions over the Internet. Whereas the core Web services technologies are versatile and designed for a wide range of uses, ebXML addresses a more focused list of e-business requirements. The ebXML framework incorporates SOAP into its Messaging Service, but goes beyond other Web services standards to enable the modeling of business processes. For example, ebXML has specific mechanisms that facilitate B2B transactions and complex supply-chain systems. Although ebXML employs its own registry technology, rather than using UDDI, applications can be designed to access both ebXML and UDDI registries.[28] Many vendors and businesses see ebXML as a key to Web services adoption, because it provides the tools that real businesses need to realize the potential of Web services. For additional information on ebXML and its capabilities, see Chapter 5, XML and Derivative Technologies.

In 2002, OASIS is continuing its work on Web services standards by forming two new technical committees. One committee, called the *OASIS Web Services for Remote Portals (WSRP)* technical committee, is developing a standard that would enable content to be plugged into corporate portals via Web services. A *portlet* refers to dynamic content, a service or an application designed to be added to portals. When portal developers want to incorporate a portlet, they must integrate the portlet manually into the portal. WSRP aims to provide a standard by which portlets could be packaged as Web services and published in UDDI registries. Then, any developer using the portlet simply would call the appropriate Web service, eliminating the need for additional coding.[29]

OASIS established the second new technical committee as the *Web Services Component Model (WSCM)* committee. However, once organized, members voted to change this name to the *Web Services for Interactive Applications (WSIA)* committee. The group is working to develop an XML-based protocol that functions with other, established standards and governs the display components of Web services. Using such a standard, businesses easily could distribute interactive Web applications through multiple channels, such as Web browsers, mobile devices and portal applications. The standard possibly will incorporate aspects of both the *Web Services User Interface (WSUI)* specification and IBM's *Web Services Experience Language (WSEL)*.[30]

2.8.4 Vendors and Standardization

Although standards organizations have played a key role in the development of Web services technologies, major software vendors also are contributing to standardization. After previous distributed computing technologies failed to reach their potential due to a lack of universal standards, vendors are working together to achieve interoperability among competing technologies. For example, multiple vendors collaborated to develop both SOAP and WSDL and to submit them to the W3C.

To facilitate collaboration among industry players, vendors have established several forums through which they can communicate and reach consensus regarding Web services technologies. One of these efforts is the *UDDI project*, which began as a joint initiative for developing a Web services discovery standard. Microsoft, IBM and Ariba established the UDDI project so that technology providers and customers could agree on a system for publishing and locating Web services. Now, the UDDI project community consists of over 300 member companies that work collaboratively to improve the UDDI specification and to encourage the use of UDDI registries. The industry-led group plans to submit UDDI to a standards organization at a future date.[31]

In February 2002, major software vendors announced the launch of the *Web Services Interoperability Organization* (*WS-I*), an industry consortium that we discuss in Chapter 1, Introduction to Web Services. According to two founding members, Microsoft and IBM, the group's objectives are "to provide implementation guidance to support customers deploying Web services, promote consistent and reliable interoperability among Web services, and articulate a common industry vision for Web services."[32] The WS-I plans to create a set of tools for testing the compatibility of various Web services implementations and ensuring that Web services products adhere to standards such as SOAP, WSDL and UDDI. In addition, the group will identify necessary future specifications and work to develop such standards. Through this organization, the software community hopes to develop standards collaboratively and to maintain interoperability among present and future Web services implementations.

2.9 Web Services Limitations

Although Web services are a promising new technology with a great deal of potential, many problems regarding development and deployment have yet to be addressed. One important concern is that the standards on which most Web services are based—SOAP, WSDL and UDDI—are new and will require further development before they are finalized. For example, W3C working groups are enhancing SOAP and WSDL, and UDDI has not yet been submitted to a standards organization. Developers are worried that Web services created with current software tools will not be compliant with future versions of standards. In addition, the lack of set standards could cause vendors to add proprietary features to technologies such as SOAP, thus limiting interoperability among Web services developed using different platforms.

Another issue plaguing adoption of Web services standards is the controversy over royalty fees. Major software vendors—most notably Microsoft and IBM—hold intellectual property (IP) rights to SOAP, WSDL, UDDI and other key Web services technologies. Although the industry hopes that IP owners will make the standards available on a royalty-free basis, some technologies might be licensed under *reasonable and non-discriminatory* (*RAND*) agreements—that is, contracts in which every licensee (in this case, companies that create tools and applications for Web services development) must pay the same small fee to the licensor. If vendors charge RAND fees to users of Web services technologies, the companies might be able to impose taxes on all Internet transactions that rely on Web services. Microsoft and IBM have stated that they are unwilling to release their intellectual property rights, enabling them to implement RAND licensing schemes in the future.[33]

In reaction to Microsoft and IBM's intellectual-property claims, the W3C has taken steps to ensure the open status of standards under the organization's control. For example, the XML Protocol Working Group charter states that technologies it develops will be royalty free, and a W3C policy that enforces a royalty-free framework is in draft form.[34] Microsoft and IBM have tentatively agreed to offer SOAP 1.2 and WSDL on a royalty-free basis, but fees might be charged to software vendors whose products incorporate other technologies, such as security specifications, certain SOAP extensions and UDDI. Such charges would significantly diminish the advantages of using Web services technologies.

Even if Web services technologies remain free and open, some developers fear that Web services will be too slow for use in high-performance situations and will put unprecedented strain on network resources. Because SOAP is an XML-based technology, SOAP messages must be parsed so that they can be processed. Parsing XML takes time, which means that applications using SOAP to transmit data will not perform as quickly as comparable applications that do not communicate with XML-based remote services. Furthermore, the fact that SOAP uses a verbose syntax and is reliant on Internet communications might increase traffic on networks. Some IT experts wonder whether current network and Internet infrastructures can handle the quantity of SOAP-message transmissions that Web service interactions might generate.

 The lack of security standards for Web services is another important factor holding back adoption. Although there are many options for Web services security, the industry has not agreed on specific methods of authenticating Web services users and securing data. For example, one Web service might simply require that a user supply a username and password to access the service, whereas another might be secured via digital signatures. (Digital signatures and other methods of securing Web services are discussed in Chapter 11, Computer and Internet Security, and Chapter 12, Web Services Security.) Without uniformity in the area of Web services security, many companies are hesitant to employ Web services in applications containing sensitive data, such as financial, sales or customer information.

Network strain, performance problems and security breaches could cause applications that rely on Web services to fail or function inefficiently. In addition, if service providers' computing systems break down or must be taken offline, applications that use the providers' services might crash. As the number of systems involved in a single application or transaction increases, so does the possibility that an error will occur. Most companies cannot tolerate these kinds of problems. Even small periods of downtime in enterprise systems can cause chaos within companies, missing data, incomplete transactions, lost revenue and decreased consumer confidence.

When applications are contained on stand-alone machines or corporate networks, IT staffs can find and address the source of an error. However, if the broken or malfunctioning part of an application resides beyond the company firewall, the process of identifying and fixing the problem becomes more complex. For these reasons, companies must have a high degree of confidence in the Web services they use. Before agreeing to employ a particular Web service, organizations likely would want to review statistics regarding the service's capabilities, speed, reliability and security provisions. If the Web service is involved in critical applications, the organization would require that the service provide a "back-up plan" in case of system or network failure. In addition, service providers and users must agree to policies that specify who is responsible for maintaining applications and services, as well as how problems are remedied when they occur.

The computing industry has not yet established standard procedures for describing the quality (i.e., levels of performance, reliability, security etc.) of particular Web services. Current standards such as SOAP, WSDL and UDDI do not contain mechanisms for monitoring Web services or collecting data on service performance. Although Web services management products exist, they are not standardized. Because many service providers offer minimal information regarding service quality, it is difficult for organizations to evaluate whether Web services meet the requirements of specific processes or applications. Although some service providers maintain contracts that guarantee certain levels of uptime and reliability, customers are unsure whether such contracts will be honored. In addition, service providers are still experimenting with payment plans for Web services, and standard billing schemes have not emerged. Many organizations are waiting for resolution of these issues before they begin to use Web services—especially Web services that reside outside their firewalls.

Although Web services technologies offer important new computing capabilities, software vendors and service providers still need to work out many details regarding Web services interactions. Payment plans, standards for service quality and contracts that guarantee levels of quality are important factors that will affect the adoption of Web services. We discuss these topics, as well as many others relating the business of buying and selling Web services, in the next chapter, Web Services Business Models.

2.10 Summary

The emergence of the Web and XML has increased the possibility for interoperable system-to-system communications. Web services are software programs that use XML to exchange information via common Internet protocols. A Web service communicates over a network to supply a specific set of operations (specific tasks performed by computers, often called methods or functions) that other applications can invoke (i.e., access and use). Web services can exchange information via many Internet protocols, but most employ Hypertext Transfer Protocol (HTTP).

Prior to the advent of Web services, most efforts to share information among Web-based applications involved one application interacting with another's client tier. Using this kind of integration, applications access information from other applications via their HTML markup, then attempt to distinguish the needed data from the other information that the markup contains. In situations where a specific applications need to share large quantities of data, it is possible to enable direct communication between applications' middle tiers without employing Web services. However, this often requires that IT departments or consultants develop customized connections, which are costly to deploy and maintain. By contrast, Web services provide a standard method for enabling communication between applications' middle tiers over a network. This means that applications can share processes, rather than only content, without the need for customized, one-to-one solutions.

The idea of offering software as a service over the Internet is not unique to Web services. Since 1998, Application Service Providers (ASPs) have provided customized business software applications over the Web. However, ASPs have struggled financially and never gained widespread acceptance. Web services offer a new model for deploying software as an Internet-based service, and the many advantages that Web services provide likely will improve the success of software-as-service initiatives. ASPs usually offer large, complete applications with limited customization for individual clients; by contrast, Web services can be smaller components that perform specific functions. This makes software upgrades easier to deploy and means that Web services customers have increased flexibility to assemble their own, unique applications from multiple vendors' offerings.

Part of what distinguishes Web services from similar computing models is the use of XML-based standards—most commonly SOAP, WSDL and UDDI. These technologies enable communication among applications in a manner that is independent of specific programming languages, operating systems and hardware platforms. SOAP provides a communication mechanism between services and applications, WSDL offers a uniform method of describing services to other programs and UDDI enables the creation of searchable Web services registries. When deployed together, these technologies allow developers to package applications as services and publish those services on a network.

Several key standards organizations are overseeing the development of Web services standards. The W3C, which defines nonproprietary technologies for the World Wide Web, is overseeing the development of SOAP and WSDL. OASIS is not directly involved in core Web services standards, but is working on related standards such as ebXML. Major software vendors also are contributing to standardization. For example, the UDDI project is a joint initiative for developing a Web services discovery standard, and the Web Services Interoperability Organization (WS-I) is an industry consortium that promotes interoperability among Web services implementations.

Although Web services have great deal of potential, many problems regarding development and deployment exist. One important concern is that SOAP, WSDL and UDDI are new standards and will require further development before they are finalized. Another issue plaguing adoption of Web services is the controversy over royalty fees. Even if Web services technologies remain free and open, some developers fear that Web services will be too slow for use in high-performance situations and will put unprecedented strain on network resources. The lack of security standards for Web services is also holding back adoption. These problems must be addressed before Web services gain widespread adoption.

2.11 Internet and Web Resources

www.webservices.org
This portal aggregates information regarding nearly every aspect of Web services. Visitors can find updates on the latest Web services news, as well as information from standards organizations and articles discussing vendors, platforms, products, applications, case studies, security mechanisms and more. A search feature is included on the site.

www.webservicesarchitect.com
Web Services Architect is an online journal designed for Web services developers and the Web services community. The site provides in-depth articles on Web services development, tools, vendors and business models. The site also directs visitors to additional resources, including Web sites, books and white papers.

www.the400resource.com/CONTENT/MONTHLY/200111/webservices11.html
This article introduces the concepts behind Web services in a simple, comprehensible style. The author—Rick Stevens, a senior software engineer at IBM—provides a detailed definition of Web services, examples of services, discussions of core standards and an explanation of Web services' evolution from other distributed computing technologies.

www.sdtimes.com/opinions/guestview2_036.htm
In this article, Paul Flessner—senior vice president of Microsoft's .NET Enterprise Server Division—explains what Web services are by listing their defining characteristics. The article overviews the advantages of Web services-enabled interoperability and discusses how Web services can help IT staffs reach their goals.

www.cfoinfo.com/overview/asp_wsp.htm
This site contains a chart listing differences between Web service providers (WSPs) and application service providers (ASPs). The table compares the two types of service provider with regard to business models, license models, payment plans, accessibility and capabilities to customize and support applications.

www.xmethods.net
XMethods is a Web services broker, which aggregates information regarding publicly available Web services. Visitors can browse through services listings, then view more detailed data on particular services. The Web service we employ in our case study, the ZipCode Resolver, is listed at this site.

www.eraserver.net
Eraserver.net is a hosting company and Web service provider. The organization develops and hosts Microsoft .NET Web services, as well as other .NET Web applications. The ZipCode Resolver Web service is owned by this company.

www.w3.org/2002/ws
Part of the W3C Web site, this page contains content relating to the W3C Web Services Activity. The site defines Web services and the Activity's mission, then provides links to the Activity Statement and the home pages of the Activity's various Working Groups. The page also lists W3C events relevant to Web services and links to Web services-related Working Drafts and publications.

www.w3.org/2002/ws/Activity
This section of the W3C Web site contains the W3C Web Services Activity Statement. The Activity Statement introduces Web services, defines the role of the W3C with regard to Web services technologies, outlines the current status of technologies being developed by the Activity's Working Groups and discusses the Activity's future plans.

www.w3.org/TR/2001/WD-soap12-20010709/
This section of the W3C Web site contains the latest m of the SOAP specification—SOAP 1.2. The page provides an abstract, a summary of the document's status and a full copy of the document.

www.w3.org/TR/wsdl
This section of the W3C Web site contains the latest version of the WSDL document—WSDL 1.1. The page lists the authors of the document, then provides an abstract, a summary of the document's status and a full copy of the document.

www.uddi.org
This is the home page for the UDDI project, an industry initiative for developing UDDI. The site explains the UDDI project and the potential business benefits of UDDI. Visitors also can view a list of UDDI community members, search the UDDI Business Registry, read about UDDI news and events, join UDDI-related discussion groups and locate UDDI specifications, FAQs and white papers.

www.eweek.com/article/0,3658,s=722&a=22053,00.asp
This article offers an introduction to UDDI and UDDI registries. In the article, the author explains the origins of UDDI, the goals of the UDDI Project and ways in which UDDI can improve B2B communication. The article also covers the role of private UDDI registries and the evolution of public UDDI Business Registries.

www.oasis-open.org
This site is the home page for OASIS, an organization that develops XML and Web services technologies. The site provides links to OASIS's technical work and standards. Visitors also can read OASIS-related news and find information on the organization and its members.

www.ebxml.org
This site provides information regarding OASIS's ebXML standard, including an introduction to the technology and its business benefits. Visitors to the site can read FAQs, news and articles relating to ebXML; locate additional resources; view specifications; and learn about technical work on ebXML.

www.oasis-open.org/committees/wsia/
This OASIS site provides information about the Web Services for Interactive Applications standard, which currently is under development by an OASIS technical committee. The site also contains links to related documents and press releases.

www.oasis-open.org/committees/wsrp/
This OASIS site provides information about the Web Services for Remote Portals standard. The site provides an overview of WSRP and contains links to relevant documents and press releases.

www.ws-i.org/
This is the home page of the Web Services Interoperability Organization (WS-I), an industry consortium designed to promote interoperability among Web services created in different programming languages on different platforms. The site provides white papers, news, FAQs and information regarding the organization and its members.

www.xml.com/lpt/a/2002/02/06/webservices.html
This article, entitled "Web Services Pitfalls," explains limitations of current Web services technologies and models. After introducing Web services, the author discusses the lack of standards for contracts and billing, unresolved security issues and problems surrounding Web service version control.

www.webservices.org/print.php?sid=201
In this article, "Web Services—A Reality Check," the author overviews technical concerns regarding Web services. The article focuses on three primary issues: transactions, security and quality of service (QoS). None of these issues are resolved by current Web services standards.

WORKS CITED

1. J. Borck, "Leaders of the Web Services Pack," *InfoWorld* 17 September 2001: 52.

2. P. Flessner, "XML Web Services: More Than Protocols and Acronyms," *Software Development Times* 15 August 2001: 31.

3. A. O'Toole, "It's a Web Services World," 3 December 2001 **<e-serv.ebizq.net/wbs/otoole_1.html>**.

4. S. Benfield, "Web Services: The Power to Change the World?" *Web Services Journal* June 2001: 22.

5. B. Howerton, "Keeping Promises," *Intelligent Enterprise* 1 January 2002: 46-47.

6. J. Fonstad, "From Hosted Applications to Web Services," *Red Herring* 1 September 2001: 36.

7. J. Fonstad, "From Hosted Applications to Web Services," *Red Herring* 1 September 2001: 36.

8. W. Oellermann, Jr., *Architecting Web Services* (Berkeley, CA: Apress, 2001) 602.

9. B. Howerton, "Keeping Promises," *Intelligent Enterprise* 1 January 2002: 46.

10. S. Hildreth, "Web Services: The Next Generation of Distributed Computing," 9 April 2001 **<e-serv.ebizq.net/wbs/hildreth_1.html>**.

11. P. Cauldwell, et al., *Professional XML Web Services* (Birmingham, UK: Wrox Press 200) 21.

12. P. Korzeniowski, "A Little Slice of the UDDI Pie," *eWeek* 4 February 2002: 50.

13. P. Korzeniowski, "A Little Slice of the UDDI Pie," *eWeek* 4 February 2002: 51.

14. T. Wilson, "UDDI Promises Link to Web Services," *Internet Week* 26 November 2001: 26.

15. "What are Standards?" **<www.iso.org/iso/en/aboutiso/introduction/index.html>**.

16. "About the World Wide Web Consortium (W3C)," **<www.w3.org/Consortium>**.

17. "About Oasis," <www.oasis-open.org/who/organization.shtml>.

18. "Overview of the IETF," **<www.ietf.org/overview.html>**.

19. "What is ISO?" **<www.iso.org/iso/en/aboutiso/introduction/whatisISO.html>**.

20. "W3C in 7 Points," 18 December 2001 `<www.w3.org/Consortium/Points>`.

21. "Microsoft Submits SOAP Specification to W3C," *Microsoft press release* 5 May 2000 `<www.microsoft.com/presspass/press/2000/May00/SoapW3CPR.asp>`.

22. "Web Services Activity Statement," 25 January 2002 `<www.w3.org/2002/ws/Activity>`.

23. "Web Services Architecture Working Group Charter," 26 January 2002 `<www.w3.or/2002/01/ws-arch-charter>`.

24. "Web Services Activity Statement," 25 January 2002 `<www.w3.org/2002/ws/Activity>`.

25. B. McLaughlin, "ebXML: Not just another acronym," `<www.javaworld.com/javaone00/j1-00-ebxml_p.html>`.

26. "United Nations and OASIS Join Forces to Produce Global XML Framework for Electronic Business," 15 September 1999 `<www.ebxml.org/news/pr_19990915.htm>`.

27. K. Ohlson, "Q&A: Oasis exec discusses role in Web services," *Network World Fusion* 1 October 2001 `<www.nwfusion.com/news/2001/1001oasis.html>`.

28. J. Borck, "Building a Better B-to-B Marketplace," *InfoWorld* 17 September 2001: 50.

29. "Oracle Spurs Innovation of Portal Standards," 29 January 2002 `<biz.yahoo.com/prnews/020129/sftu062_1.html>`.

30. J. Perez, "OASIS Unveils New Technical Committee for Standardizing Interactive Web Services," *Intelligent Enterprise* 1 February 2002: 15.

31. "About UDDI," `<www.uddi.org/about.html>`.

32. "Industry Leaders Align Around Web Services Interoperability," Microsoft/ IBM press release 6 February 2002 `<www-916.ibm.com/press/prnews.nsf/jan/3320A50B103498C185256B590066D319>`.

33. D. Berlind, "IBM, Microsoft Plot Net Takeover," *ZDNet* 11 April 2002 `<www.zdnet.com/filters/printerfriendly/0,6061,2861123-92,00.html>`.

34. D. Berlind, "HP Withdraws Support," *ZDNet* 11 April 2002 `<techupdate.zdnet.com/techupdate/stories/main/0,14179,2861123-2,00.html>`.

RECOMMENDED READING

Andrews, W. "As Good As It Gets," *Internet World* 1 September 2001: 23.

Benfield, S. "Web Services: The Power to Change the World?" *Web Services Journal* January 2002: 22.

Fisher, M. "Introduction to Web Services," `<java.sun.com/webservices/docs/ea1/tutorial/doc/IntroWS.html>`.

Flessner, P. "XML Web Services: More Than Protocols and Acronyms," *Software Development Times* 15 August 2001: 31.

Fonstad, J. "From Hosted Applications to Web Services," *Red Herring* 1 September 2001: 36.

Gilmor, S. "Keeping It Simple," *InfoWorld* 28 January 2002: 70.

Ham, M. and T. Olson. "Web Service—Tiptoeing Through the Snarl," *Web Services Journal* January 2002: 58–62.

Hildreth, S. "Web Services: The Next Generation of Distributed Computing," 9 March 2001 `<e-serv.ebizq.net/wbs/hildreth_1,html>`.

Howerton, B. "Keeping Promises," *Intelligent Enterprise* 1 January 2002: 46–47.

Jenz, D. E. "Web Services—A Reality Check," 26 July 2001 **<www.webservices.org/ print.php?sid=201>**.

King, N. "Have Web Services, Will Travel," *Intelligence Enterprise* 29 June 2001: 60–62.

Kulchenko, P. "Web Services Acronyms, Demystified," 9 January 2002 **<www.xml.com/pub/a/ 2002/01/09/soap.html>**.

Leibs, S. "Web Services: The Great Buildup," *CFO* May 2001: 27–28.

Morgenthal, J. P. "Where Are Web Services Going?" *Web Services Journal* January 2002: 6–7.

Phipps, S. "It's About More Than Just the Plumbing," *Web Services Journal* January 2002: 42.

Powers, T. "Web Services—Long Overdue," 19 November 2001 **<www.webreview.com/ 2001/11_19/strategists/index01.shtml>**.

Sullivan, T. "Web Services," 9 March 2001 **<iwsun4.infoworld.com/articles/hn/xml/ 01/03/12/010312hnweserv.xml>**.

Swartz, S. "Web Services Are Coming: Panacea Or Pandora?" 1 November 2001 **<news.com.com/2010-1072-281593.htm?legacy=cnet>**.

Trombly, M. "Web Services," *Computer World* 24 September 2001: 56.

3

Web Services Business Models

Objectives

- To explore the infrastructure though which Web service providers deliver their services.
- To discuss service-level agreements (SLAs) and how they help ensure the quality of Web services.
- To introduce payment mechanisms for Web services, and to discuss available billing solutions.
- To examine service-to-consumer (S2C), service-to-business (S2B) and service-to-employee (S2E) Web services, and to provide examples of each.
- To examine Web services registries, brokerages and networks, and to provide examples of each.

It is an immutable law in business that words are words, explanations are explanations, promises are promises—but only performance is reality.
Harold S. Green

To be of true service I must know two things: his need, my capacity.
Nikita Nikolayevich Panin

Sometimes give your services for nothing...
Hippocrates

Outline

3.1 Introduction

As we discussed in the previous chapter, new development tools and technical standards allow programmers to create interoperable Web services. However, for Web services to reach their potential in the business world, companies must establish plans encompassing all aspects of Web services transactions, including how services are marketed, distributed, paid for and managed. In this chapter, we explore the business models of companies that develop Web services, as well as those of companies that support Web services.

First, we introduce frameworks for providing business-grade Web services, including who the key players are and how they interact to facilitate Web services transactions. Two important aspects of these models are service-level agreements and payment mechanisms, which we cover in detail. We discuss the process of publishing Web services and the types of available services, including services designed for individual consumers, businesses and employees. We then explore the business models of organizations that host and support Web services, such as Web services networks, registries and brokerages. We also provide case studies outlining the business models of companies involved in Web services.

Many companies are adopting Web services to simplify internal business processes. Although Web services deployed only within an organization can provide substantial benefits—such as simplifying the integration of corporate applications—these services do not require the kinds of business models that we discuss here. We explore these Web services in detail in the next chapter, Web Services and Enterprise Computing.

3.2 Frameworks for Delivering Web Services

Web services technologies can create new business opportunities. For software vendors, Web services represent a new method of distributing their products—i.e., as subscription-based services offered over the Internet. Other companies develop software applications in house to fill corporate needs, such as supply-chain management, human-resources administration or inventory control. These companies can enhance their business models and increase revenue by packaging their business processes as Web services, then marketing the services to other companies that require similar functionality. In addition, new businesses are required to serve the Web services industry and to act as intermediaries between Web services and their customers. In this section, we outline possible frameworks though which businesses can create, distribute, sell and use Web services.

3.2.1 Service-Oriented Architecture

IBM, a vendor of Web services development tools and software, has created a model to depict Web services interactions. Referred to as a *service-oriented architecture*, IBM's representation (Fig. 3.1) comprises relationships among three entities: a Web service provider, a Web service requester and a Web service broker.[1]

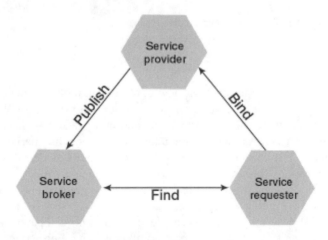

Fig. 3.1   Service-oriented architecture representation. (Courtesy of IBM Corporation.)

---

1. IBM's service-oriented architecture is a generic model describing service collaboration. However, this chapter presents service-oriented architectures in the context of Web services. For a general introduction to service-oriented architectures, visit **www-106.ibm.com/developer-works/library/ws-tao/index.html**.

In the IBM diagram, the *service provider* is a server or system that makes a Web service available over a network, such as the Internet. The provider achieves this through a *service interface*, a software component that enables other applications to access the service. After creating a service interface, a service provider publishes the service to a *service broker*, a networked server or system that maintains a directory or clearinghouse for Web services. Although service brokers can take many forms, all act as liaisons between service providers and service requesters. A *service requester*—a networked server or system that accesses and employs a Web service—interacts with a service broker to find a Web service that fills a specific computing need. For example, the requester might be looking for a currency converter or a service that performs computations of large numbers. Often, service brokers allow requesters to search for services on the basis of categories or keywords. After locating an appropriate service via the broker, the requester then *binds* to, or initiates contact with, the service provider's service interface. Thus, communication is established between two applications or computing systems.

Although the provider, requester and broker technically are computing systems, we can use the terms more generally to refer to the individuals or businesses that manage those systems.[2] For instance, a financial institution employing a Web service to supply its computers with updated stock quotes would be a service requester. Companies that aggregate either content or services can benefit most directly from becoming service requesters. Companies that aggregate content communicate with a variety of data sources to amass information and present it to customers. For example, portals, such as **yahoo.com** or **msn.com**, rely heavily on combining information from multiple sources. *Service aggregation* is a newer concept referring to businesses that combine electronic services to provide a single, more comprehensive service to customers. One example is OnStar (**www.onstar.com**), a company that offers a composite service for automobile owners by combining features such as on-demand directions, roadside assistance, online concierge and stolen vehicle tracking.[2] These companies can employ Web services to simplify the accumulation of data or processes that the companies supply to end users.

Businesses that assume the role of service provider must communicate with and perform computing tasks for others. Application service providers (ASPs) are prime candidates to become Web service providers, because ASPs already possess infrastructure for providing and maintaining hosted software. *Independent software vendors* (ISVs)—companies that specialize in the development and sale of software not directly associated with a specific platform—also might become Web service providers. However, a service provider can be any organization that creates or hosts software and wants to make that software available over a network. Many companies are becoming service providers by creating Web services available only within their organizations or to trusted business partners. It is hoped that, once standards mature and confidence in Web services technologies increases, some of these companies will make their Web services more widely accessible.

The service provider for a particular service is not necessarily the creator of the service. Sometimes, the service developer employs a third party to host and maintain the service. In such cases, the hosting entity is the Web service provider, because it manages the computing system on which the service resides. The creator of the service is called the *asset owner*—if a company both develops and hosts a Web service, that company is both the ser-

---

2. When Web services are deployed to simplify internal business processes, a single business might represent the service provider, service requester and service broker.

vice provider and the asset owner. Asset owners usually maintain legal control over their Web services and any related intellectual property, including the code for the services and any data that the services use.[3]

Service brokers communicate with service requesters and direct them to appropriate service providers. For example, the operators of the public UDDI Business Registry (UBR) act as service brokers, offering information about service providers and their available Web services. Other types of service brokers include Web services brokerages and portals that aggregate Web services targeted to a specific industry. Different brokers might specialize in breadth of listings, depth of listings for a particular category or accuracy of listings.[4] In Section 3.9, we explore different types of service brokers and their respective functions.

3.2.2 Stages of Web Service Development and Deployment

Service requesters, providers and brokers represent the three most integral players in Web services transactions. Most Web services interactions, however, are more complex and involve a larger number of participants. In this section, we discuss the tasks that comprise the Web service development process, from generating an idea for a service to actually deploying and selling that service.[3] The business lifecycle of a Web service can be broken into four stages: creation, publication, promotion and sale (Fig. 3.2).[5]

The *creation* stage includes not only the initial construction of the Web service, but also the steps required to prove that the service operates correctly. The first participant in creation is the Web service designer, an individual or team that initiates the idea for a Web service and presents an overall model for the service's implementation. The designer passes the idea to the developer, an individual or team that builds the actual service according to the designer's specifications. The next step is to assemble documentation that describes the Web service, including how it is accessed and used. Although we separate design, development and documentation in this explanation, these tasks can be performed by the same individual or team.

Stage	Activities
Creation	Design, development, documentation, testing and distribution.
Publication	Web service hosting and maintenance.
Promotion	Directory services, value-added services and accreditation.
Sale	Auditing and accounts management.

Fig. 3.2   Web service lifecycle stages.

---

3. Information in this section is based partially on articles by Mike Clark, a senior analyst at Lucin and the principal designer of the Web services brokerage Salcentral. Readers can view Clark's articles at **www.webservicesarchitect.com**

Once a Web service and its accompanying documentation have been constructed, the service must be tested to establish that it performs a particular task, can handle certain traffic volumes and is interoperable with applications running on different platforms. Organizations that develop Web services can test them in house. Ideally, however, an independent third party that specializes in the assessment of Web services functionality and interoperability should administer the tests and provide a form of certification. Testing and certification enable Web services consumers to evaluate the quality of a particular service before agreeing to use it; these processes also help customers differentiate among similar Web services. Universally accepted testing and certification procedures have not yet arisen, but, once these processes are standardized, they will be crucial to Web services development. The WS-I, a vendor consortium that we discuss in Chapter 1, Introduction to Web Services, is developing guidelines and testing procedures for creating high-quality, interoperable Web services.

The final step in the creation process is handled by a distributor. Distributors—who can be either the same as or separate from the service's owners—package all the code and documentation relating to the Web service in a format that can be understood and used by other applications. Distributors also make decisions regarding the publication of the Web service (the next stage in our lifecycle), such as what entity hosts the service.

The *publication* stage involves exposing all necessary pieces of a Web service on a network. Although the organization that develops a Web service can host the service on its own servers and maintain the service's data, the organization alternatively can outsource these tasks. Large software vendors might manage all aspects of the Web services they develop, but businesses that provide only a small number of services likely will outsource service hosting and maintenance. ASPs, Internet service providers (ISPs) and Web-hosting companies are the most obvious choices to host Web services, because such organizations already possess Web-hosting infrastructure. These types of organizations also might develop and market their own Web services.

After a Web service is developed and published on the Internet, third parties must enable service requesters to locate the service. *Promotion* of a Web service is carried out by brokers. (We introduced the concept of service broker in the previous section.) The most common examples of brokers are UDDI registries—both public UDDI registries, such as the UDDI Business Registry (UBR), and private registries, which promote Web services available within an organization or among partners. Web sites such as **www.xmethods.net** and **www.salcentral.com** have created their own Web services directories. These sites list available Web services; some also offer *value-added services* (*VAS*), which support Web services transactions and provide information about services' performance, reliability, etc. Another aspect of promotion likely will be accreditation of service providers, but standardized accreditation procedures have not yet been developed.

The final stage in Web services development, the *sale* of services, involves two main participants. The first is a company or organization that manages Web services accounts—this can be the entity that hosts the service or a separate organization that specializes in billing. The *accounts manager* collects money from the subscribers to a particular Web service, then distributes the money to the asset owner, hosting company and any other involved parties. Section 3.4 explores payment mechanisms for Web services in detail.

The other participant is a Web service *auditor,* an individual or organization responsible for reviewing the functionality of Web services. Service providers typically employ third parties to audit their Web services during the creation stage as part of testing and certification. Once a Web service is operational, the service provider might ask an auditor to reevaluate the service on a regular basis; this helps the service provider verify that the service continues to perform its tasks efficiently and reliably.

A service requester also can employ an auditor to ensure that a Web service is functioning correctly. It is less efficient for service requesters to hire auditors, because multiple requesters might pay to audit the same Web service. However, because standard testing and certification processes have not yet developed, some service requesters prefer to employ auditors, rather than trusting service providers to do so. If an auditor employed by a service requester finds that a Web service is not performing to the level that it guarantees in its contract, the auditor informs the service requester. The requester then can take whatever action it sees fit, including replacing the service with another, similar one. Most interactions among asset owners, service providers and service requesters are controlled by contracts called service-level agreements (SLAs). We discuss the contents and parameters of SLAs in the next section.

3.3 Service-Level Agreements (SLAs)

Most business customers who buy software products do so by purchasing licenses. Software licenses outline terms of use for a piece of software, and customers typically pay a one-time fee to use a specific version of the software in accordance with the licensing agreement. By contrast, many *fee-based Web services*, or Web services accessible only to paying customers, are purchased on a subscription basis. The parameters of Web services subscriptions are determined by *service-level agreements (SLAs)*—legal contracts in which a service provider outlines the level of service it guarantees for a specific Web service. Unlike software licenses, SLAs cover a specific time period, after which the agreements must be renegotiated. When customers purchase Web service subscriptions, their subscriptions guarantee service according the contents of the SLA.

Most SLAs define relationships between Web service providers and requesters. However, if the developer or owner of a Web service is separate from the provider, the provider and owner also might maintain an SLA. SLAs between requesters and providers delineate the requester's needs and goals with regard to the service, as well as the capabilities of the provider to meet those requirements. In SLAs between developers and providers, the developer specifies the capabilities of the service, and the provider outlines the level of service it will provide to the service's requesters.[6]

Since the participants determine the exact contents of Web service SLAs, no specific formula guides the creation of these contracts. However, an important function of SLAs is to address *quality of service (QoS)*, which refers to the level of service that a particular Web service provides.[4] QoS is defined by factors such as the probability that a service can respond to a request at a given time, how well a service executes its tasks, how quickly a service works and how reliable and secure it is. Many SLAs stipulate QoS requirements,

---

4. The QoS definitions in this section are based partially on an article by Anbazhagan Mani and Arun Nagarajan, but we have modified some explanations. To read the original descriptions, visit **www-106.ibm.com/developerworks/webservices/library/ws-quality.html?dwzone=webservices**.

including specific levels of availability, accessibility, integrity, performance, reliability, security and conformance to standards.[7]

- *Availability* describes the probability that a Web service is ready for use (i.e., available). A higher availability rating means that the service is more likely to be able to process a request at a given time. Availability often is measured as a percentage—for example, a Web service might be available to service requesters 99.99 percent of the time.

- *Accessibility* describes the group of users that can access a service, as well as how difficult it is to access the service. A higher level of accessibility means that a service is available to a larger number of users and that users can access the service more easily. For example, a Web service that supports multiple languages (such as Spanish, Japanese, etc.) would more accessible than a Web service that supports only English.

- *Integrity* describes the probability with which a service performs its tasks in the exact manner described in the service's WSDL document or service-level agreement (SLA). A higher integrity rating indicates that the service's functionality resembles more closely the service description in the WSDL document or SLA.

- *Performance* is comprised of two main factors: *throughput* and *latency*. Throughput represents the number of requests that a Web service processes in a given time period, and latency represents the length of time that the service takes to respond to each request. Better performance is indicated by a higher throughput value and a lower latency value.

- *Reliability* describes the ability of a Web service to function correctly and provide consistent service, even in the event of a system or network failure. The reliability of a Web service usually is represented by the number of transaction failures per month or year. Reliability also encompasses procedures for data backup and redundancy.

- *Conformance to standards* describes whether a Web service employs the specific standards and implementations—for example, SOAP Version 1.2—that it claims to use. Service providers must adhere to standards agreed upon in SLAs, because, otherwise, requesters might not be able to access the services.

- *Security* involves technologies and processes such as authentication, message encryption and digital signatures. An SLA defines the amount of security that a particular Web service requires, and the service provider then must maintain that level of security. We discuss security in greater detail in Chapter 11, Computer and Internet Security, and Chapter 12, Web Services Security.

SLAs are crucial to the success of the Web services industry, because Web service customers must be able to trust that services will adhere to certain quality-of-service requirements. SLAs help ensure the reliability of a Web service, because, if a service provider fails to fulfill the requirements of the SLA, the requester can terminate the contract. Some SLA agreements also include information regarding liability—this means that if a deficiency in service impacts the requester's business, the provider is legally responsible to compensate the requester. However, even with SLAs in place, quality of service is not guaranteed. Service providers still might not honor their contracts, because providers know that the cost of litigation often is far greater than the cost of switching to another provider.[8]

Most Web services SLAs represent agreements between partner companies or members of a supply chain. Although these agreements involve some legal risk, liability concerns are lessened, because the involved parties have already established a level of trust with one another. However, as the Web services industry grows, providers and requesters might not know each other prior to establishing Web service agreements. How can businesses develop trust with new partners and, at the same time, protect themselves from Web services that do not live up to their contracts?

First, companies that request Web services must be precise about the level of service they need. Requestors should assess the transaction volumes that the Web service must process, as well as the necessary latency (response time). In addition, requesters should ensure that their SLAs require service providers to perform periodic QoS testing. The most basic testing should evaluate response times for normal and peak traffic loads, response times in various locations where the service is consumed and whether the service still operates if the system or network fails.[9]

Although service providers can administer their own tests, it often is preferable to employ an independent organization to perform testing. Several companies offer technologies and services that perform tests to verify SLA compliance. For example, Santra Technology (**www.santra.com**) provides the *iON* service, which monitors and tests the performance of Web services. iON continually examines Web service functionality, then notifies customers of any changes. The Web service brokerage Salcentral (**www.salcentral.com**) also offers testing services. For service providers that want to perform their own tests, Empirix (**www.empirix.com**) offers *FirstACT,* a set of tools for testing the performance and functionality of Web services. WestGlobal's *mScape™* is a Web services management tool that monitors Web services performance, as well as performing other management tasks (**www.westglobal.com**). Other testing tools include PushToTest's Load (**www.pushtotest.com**), which is a Java-based open-source utility for Web service testing, and Red Gate Software's *Advanced .NET Testing System* (**www.redgate.com**), which facilitates load and scalability testing of .NET Web services. Some Web services development environments also provide features that enable Web services testing and monitoring.

Another way that customers can alleviate concerns regarding QoS and liability is to purchase services through a Web services brokerage. The primary business of a brokerage is to facilitate Web services interactions, so it is in the brokerage's best interest to maintain the trust of its customers and avoid acquiring a bad reputation. It also is likely that brokerages would test Web services extensively before agreeing to list them, so customers could expect a higher base level of QoS.[10]

3.4 Web Services Payment Models

To become profitable enterprises, organizations that wish to sell Web services must develop effective billing methods. The market for fee-based Web services is still in its early stages, and few Web services payment models have been sufficiently tested in real-world environments. However, industry players have outlined possible payment scenarios, and several companies are working to create billing solutions. In this section, we overview options for Web services payments, as well as the implementation of charging mechanisms. We also describe several companies and organizations that are developing tools and services in this area.

3.4.1 Payment Mechanisms

Industry players have defined various methods that service providers can use to charge for Web services. Figure 3.3 summarizes several payment mechanisms.

Paradoxically, the first payment mechanism that we list is to offer Web services free of charge. This is a popular model—most publicly available Web services are free. It is important that service providers supply free services to publicize Web services and to encourage users to experiment with the technology. Often, free services are designed to provide an immediate benefit while requiring little commitment on the part of the requester. For example, service providers supply news-headline services and calendar services for free. Some service providers offer free services in exchange for displaying the provider's brand or logo. Other free services are limited versions of more comprehensive, fee-based services. Many people are concerned that customers will have difficulty with the transition from free to fee-based Web services. However, service providers hope that, after successfully using free services, requesters will return and subscribe to more complex, fee-based services.[11]

Although free services can be appealing, fee-based services usually are more reliable—many free services are not governed by SLAs or other QoS assurances. Of the fee-based models, the *pay-per-use* model involves the smallest commitment from customers. Most pay-per-use services require that requesters purchase a set number of service invocations. Requestors prepay for a certain volume of service, then can decide whether to renew once they exhaust their prepaid limits. [12]

Every pay-per-use service must include a mechanism that counts and records the number of times each requester uses the service. Many such services charge on a sliding scale, which means that requesters who buy more service invocations incur a smaller cost per unit. Some service providers create pay-per-use models in which requesters use the service before paying, then are billed according to the number of times they invoke the service. However, such models are riskier for providers, because they cannot be sure that customers will pay. Furthermore, if there is no minimum to the amount of service that customers can buy, the small usage fees might not justify the cost of billing.

Payment Mechanism	Description
Free	Web service is available to customers without charge. The service (or a limited version of the service) can be free indefinitely, or the service can be free for a specified trial period, after which customers must pay for the service.
Pay per use	Customers prepay to use a Web service a specified number of times. When the customer invokes the service, a mechanism records the interaction. When the customer exhausts the prepaid quantity of service, the provider informs the customer that it is time to renew.
Flat-fee subscription	Customers pay to use a Web service for a specific period of time. During the subscription period, the customer has unlimited use of the service. When a subscription expires, the provider either can notify the customer or can automatically charge for the next billing period.

Fig. 3.3   Payment mechanisms for fee-based Web services.[13] (Part 1 of 2.)

Payment Mechanism	Description
One charge	Customers make a single payment for the right to use a Web service for the entire duration of that service.

Fig. 3.3   Payment mechanisms for fee-based Web services.[13] (Part 2 of 2.)

Most experts believe that, eventually, *flat-fee subscription* will become the most common way to charge for Web services. Under this model, service requesters pay a fee for unlimited use of a Web service during a specific time period. Most subscriptions are renewed monthly, but some providers offer subscriptions that span several months, a year or even longer. Customers either authorize each subscription renewal or agree to automatic renewal, which means that providers can bill customers for the next period without notifying them. Service providers benefit from flat-fee subscriptions, in that the providers can better predict their incomes. Similarly, requesters know up front what the per-month cost of the service will be, regardless of how frequently they use it. However, flat-fee subscriptions can place service providers at a disadvantage if providers underestimate the amount of service that requesters will use.[14]

Another payment mechanism is the *one-time charge* model—requesters pay a single fee in exchange for unlimited access to the service for the entire lifetime of the service. For most services, this billing model is impractical. A one-time charge usually equates to a high cost of entry, and customers often are unsure whether the longevity or quality of the service will justify the cost. However, one-time payment is an ideal charging mechanism for *perishable services*, or services that exist for a finite period of time. For example, a Web service that provides special-events news coverage—such as information on a specific Olympic games, World Series or presidential campaign—might charge a one-time fee for unlimited use.[15]

Payment mechanisms can be combined. For instance, a service provider might offer a Web service for free initially, then begin to charge for the service after a trial period expires. Similarly, a Web service can be designed so that customers subscribe for a flat monthly fee, but incur additional pay-per-use charges if they exceed a set volume of service during the month. Although combination payment mechanisms can attract new customers and improve pricing flexibility, service providers must be clear about their exact methods of charging.[16] Customers might be upset if they incorporate a Web service into their systems on the understanding that the service is free, then learn that they must pay for the service after a two-week trial period. Service providers that lure new customers using misleading information could quickly develop bad reputations.

The list of payment mechanisms we provide is not exhaustive. For example, when business partners or members of a supply chain access each other's Web services, payment mechanisms might not be limited to monetary exchanges. Companies might offer Web services to their partners for free as a way to build trust and improve communication between the organizations. Unlike publicly available free Web services, free services among partners likely would remain free. Partners also can barter Web services for other goods, services or Web services. In cases where one partner controls highly valuable Web services, the partner might offer access to the services in exchange for equity in the other partner company or a percentage of that company's gross revenue.[17]

3.4.2 Payment Tools and Solutions

Payment tools allow service providers to identify service requesters, record the quantity of service that requesters use and bill requesters accordingly. All fee-based Web services should include authentication capabilities, which allow the service to confirm the identity and access rights of the customer requesting the service. Without proper authentication, service providers cannot bar nonpaying users from invoking services. Methods for identifying service requesters include passwords, the exchange of public keys, digital certificates and digital signatures. We discuss these technologies in detail in Chapter 11, Computer and Internet Security, and Chapter 12, Web Services Security.

Although it is too soon to determine exactly how fee-based Web service implementations will develop, most services will connect to an application or another Web service that handles *metering and accounting*. In this context, metering and accounting refer to recording a Web service requester's usage information—i.e., the times when a requester begins using a service, the times when the requester disconnects from the service and the total quantity of service resources that the requester uses. It is mandatory for Web services that charge on a pay-per-use basis to collect detailed usage information.

When a service requester subscribes to a metered Web service, the provider *enrolls* the requester in the service—i.e., the provider supplies the requester's identification information to the meter service or application. Then, every time the requester uses the Web service, the service provider transmits the requester's identification data to the metering mechanism. The metering service or application records the requester's usage information, which an appropriate billing application or service later uses to charge the requester.[18]

IBM has introduced some of the most advanced development tools for implementing functional, fee-based Web services. Version 3.0 of IBM's *Web Services Toolkit* (*WSTK*), a set of development tools for Web services, includes a new tool called *Web Services Hosting Technology* (*WSHT*). WSHT 1.0 enables service providers to implement metering and billing mechanisms more easily, without altering the actual code that comprises a Web service.[19]

WSHT provides tools to package Web services or groups of related Web services so that they can be sold via an online catalog. The technology also supplies an enrollment system that manages requesters' identification information and generates SLAs for new subscribers. Other WSHT tools record requesters' usage information, pass that information to a billing system and create customer invoices based on the usage information. A WSHT portal provides a user interface through which service providers can access the technology's various functions.[20] IBM provides WSHT as part of the WSTK 3.0 or as a stand-alone package; both are available as free, renewable 90-day downloads from IBM's alphaWorks Web site (**www.alphaworks.ibm.com**).[5] For additional information regarding the IBM Web Services Toolkit, see Chapter 6, Understanding SOAP and WSDL.

Another billing option for Web service providers is to use XML-based payment software. In 2001, a company called MetraTech® (**www.metratech.com**) introduced a billing platform designed especially for Web services (though it can be used for other purposes, such as charging for hosted applications). MetraTech's product, *MetraNet*™, allows Web service providers to bill customers and to share revenue among various parties, such as service providers, partners, asset owners and brokerages.[21] The fact that the software is XML based adds flexibility, enabling businesses to configure and customize the system

---

5. Free downloads of the WSHT and WSTK 3.0 are for testing and evaluation purposes only.

without coding. MetraNet encompasses six components: MetraBill, MetraView, Metra-Partner, MetraPay, MetraCare and MetraSDK (Fig. 3.4).

MetraBill is a billing engine that tracks service usage and supports paper and online invoicing, complex pricing schemes and customized rates for subscribers (i.e., a provider can charge different customers at different rates). A complementary component, MetraPay, provides payment-processing capabilities. MetraPartner facilitates multiple revenue-sharing relationships, so companies can properly distribute the money they collect from service subscriptions. MetraView presents itemized, online bills to customers, and Metra-Care provides additional customer-service features. The last component, MetraSDK, facil-itates integration between MetraNet and a company's existing billing system. Companies that wish to use MetraNet can either purchase the software or employ MetraTech Managed Services, which offers MetraNet as an outsourced solution.

Other companies also offer payment solutions that incorporate XML, although none was created specifically for Web services billing. For example, software from Erogo (**www.erogo.com**) and Ican SP (**www.icansp.com**) enable companies to bill for Web services on the basis of customers' usage information. Alternatively, service providers can employ third parties to administer authentication, metering and billing. MetraTech's Man-aged Services is one outsourced billing solution, but other organizations offer similar ser-vices. For example, several Web services brokerages and networks, including Salcentral (**www.salcentral.com**) and Grand Central™ Communications (**www.grandcen-tral.com**), provide Web services billing support. We discuss these companies in greater detail in Sections 3.9 and 3.10, respectively.

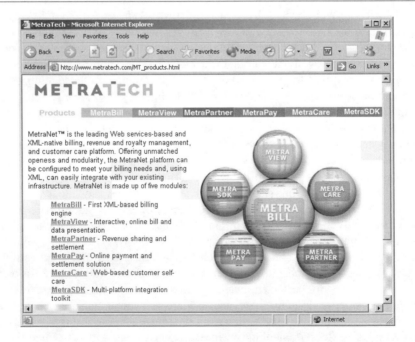

Fig. 3.4   Metratech provides an XML-based billing solution for Web services. (Courtesy of MetraTech Corporation.)

3.5 Business of Publishing Web Services

Now that we have outlined the major requirements for providing business-grade Web services, we discuss specific Web services business models in more detail. The first models that we explore are those of companies that publish Web services—i.e., provide software components or applications as network-enabled services. We break these business models into three main categories: models that support *service-to-consumer* (*S2C*) Web services, models that support *service-to-business* (*S2B*) Web services and models that support *service-to-employee* (*S2E*) Web services. Service providers offer S2C services directly to individuals for personal use, whereas S2B services are marketed to and used by businesses. Businesses purchase S2E services to improve communication within organizations and to provide employees with relevant content or applications.

Although Web services technologies facilitate these business models, it is important to recognize that the actual items for sale are specific services, rather than Web services in general. A Web service must be supported by appropriate technologies and infrastructure, or the service likely will not survive in the marketplace. However, the quality and marketability of each individual service determines the ultimate success or failure of its provider's business model.[22]

3.6 Service-to-Consumer (S2C) Web Services

Due to the benefits that Web services can provide to businesses, corporate Web services have developed more quickly than consumer services have. However, many companies are creating Web services intended for consumption by individuals, rather than businesses. In this section, we explore the range of possible S2C Web services, as well as the methods that service providers use to develop, distribute and sell these services.

Individuals can find S2C services though Web services brokerages, such as XMethods (**www.xmethods.net**) and Salcentral (**www.salcentral.com**). In Chapter 2, Web Services: A New Computing Paradigm, we discussed one such service in detail—the ZipCode Resolver. Brokerages list many S2C services that provide general information, such as news headlines, sports scores or stock quotes. More involved services accept input from requesters, then return customized content. These services might supply the definition of a requested word, information regarding traffic on a particular highway, a map to a specific location or the current temperature for a given zip code. XMethods developed and maintains one notable service that takes a customer's FedEx package tracking number, then returns FedEx's most current status information on that package. Other available services convert between currencies or languages, verify phone numbers or e-mail addresses and enable users to communicate with interactive, online games.

As we mentioned in the preceding chapter, Web sites and other resources can supply the same functionality that the current generation of S2C services provide. However, Web services represent a new distribution channel, one that offers advantages in certain situations. Web services can simplify the process of communicating content or requested data to users—especially if the information changes regularly and must be updated. Some S2C services allow users to store information, then access the information from any Internet-enabled device. Since Web services can communicate directly with applications, they can automatically enter information, such as a user's shipping address or password, at Web sites.

Because S2C services are such a new concept, many are free and offer only trivial functionality. This means that most service creators do not have defined business models or immediate plans for profitability. Some developers create services "just for fun" or to advertise the technology, whereas others hope to charge for their services once the services develop into more valuable entities. However, the transition to fee-based services already has begun. Organizations are starting to market services that include more extensive capabilities while making the services available only to paying customers. For example, Salcentral lists several services that charge nominal fees for usage, including a U.K. Web service that charges users several cents to send text messages to cell phones.

In addition, some companies are including Web services as part of larger offerings, such as travel services or customer-relationship management. For example, Expedia, Inc., maintains an online travel agency (**www.expedia.com**) where users can book air travel, car rentals and hotel accommodations. Using Expedia's Web services, customers can access updated travel information, such as flight status, from any computer or Web-enabled device. Expedia's Web services also enable travelers to integrate the latest travel information into their personal calendar applications. Expedia does not charge its customers additional fees to use these Web services. However, the company believes that, by providing these capabilities, it can differentiate itself from competitors in the online travel industry.[23]

Large software vendors are creating many of the newer, more comprehensive S2C Web services. The most prominent example of this trend is Microsoft's *.NET My Services*, a set of S2C Web services that stores users' personal information—such as username and password pairs, appointment schedules, travel information and credit-card data.[24] Microsoft currently operates two components of .NET My Services: Microsoft *.NET Passport* (see the feature, Case Study: Microsoft .NET Passport) and *.NET Alerts*, a notification system. We provide further information on .NET My Services in Chapter 9, .NET Web Services: A Conceptual Overview.

Case Study: Microsoft .NET Passport

In 1999, Microsoft began running .NET Passport (**www.passport.com**), a *single sign-on (SSO)* service that stores users' authentication information and enables automatic sign-on (i.e., users do not have to enter usernames and passwords) at participating Web sites. Each Passport account encompasses four components: a Passport Unique Identifier (PUID), a user profile, credential information and an optional wallet feature called Express Purchase. When individuals set up Passport accounts, the system assigns a PUID to each, enabling Passport to distinguish among users. A user profile is associated with each Passport account. Although the profile must contain either a phone number or a Hotmail or MSN e-mail address, users also can include additional information, such as their address, gender, birthday and occupation. Figure 3.5 depicts the Microsoft Web site from which users can establish Passport accounts.

Case Study: Microsoft .NET Passport (Cont.)

Fig. 3.5   Microsoft Passport home page. (Courtesy of Microsoft Corporation.)

Credential information consists of an e-mail address or phone number, then a password containing a minimum of six characters. Each Passport user also selects a four-digit security key, which Web sites can use to provide an additional layer of authentication. Express Purchase holds users' credit-card information and shipping addresses. If a user employs Express Purchase, Passport can enter shipping and billing information automatically when the user shops at participating Passport sites.[25]

Single sign-on services are a popular early application of Web services technologies. A large number of businesses—including eBay, **McAfee.com**, **Monster.com** and Office Depot—allow visitors to log into their Web sites via the Passport authentication system. (A full list of participating sites can be found at **www.passport.com**.) Microsoft claims that over 200 million users have established Passport accounts. However, this number does not reflect the number of individuals who actually employ Passport, because Microsoft creates a Passport account for anyone who uses **MSN.com** or the Hotmail e-mail service. It is unclear how many Internet users have signed up specifically to use Passport.[26]

Case Study: Microsoft .NET Passport (Cont.)

Although Passport offers many benefits to customers, critics have raised significant concerns regarding security and privacy. For example, security experts have identified ways in which hackers can impersonate Passport users. Furthermore, many customers are hesitant to let any company manage their personal and financial data. According to a 2001 Gartner survey, approximately one-third of Internet users are "very concerned" that Microsoft either will not secure their information properly or will share the information with third parties without consent. Although these consumer concerns likely are not a direct reflection on Microsoft—users would worry about any company handling their personal information—such hesitation might limit Passport's success.[27]

Microsoft is working to improve Passport security and claims that it will not sell or use inappropriately the information it collects via Passport. It is nevertheless difficult to alter customer opinion. Several companies are developing alternative single sign-on services—AOL's Magic Carpet service and the Liberty Alliance Project, which is backed by Sun Microsystems, also offer single sign-on capabilities. Many experts believe that, for S2C Web services to become popular, major industry players must agree on a universal single sign-on system, or at least enable their sign-in services to interoperate. We examine single sign-on alternatives in greater detail in Chapter 8, Web Services Platforms, Vendors and Strategies, and Chapter 12, Web Services Security.

3.7 Service-to-Business (S2B) Web Services

One of the most powerful benefits that Web services offer is the ability for businesses to communicate with one another and share data, regardless of platform. Recognizing the advantages of interacting via Web services, many companies are developing S2B Web services, which are designed to be accessed by other companies. These Web services can simplify existing transaction processes, as well as enable the formation of new, more streamlined relationships among organizations. Partners can link their databases and applications, and companies can share updated data regarding orders and inventory with the members of their supply chains. Furthermore, none of the participants is required to maintain complex, expensive Electronic Data Interchange (EDI) systems.

Currently, most businesses allow only trusted partners to access their S2B Web services. Such services can address a wide range of business-communications needs. For instance, by using Web services to connect to a partner's commerce application, an e-business can sell that partner's products or services through its own Web site. Dollar Rent A Car Systems (**www.dollar.com**) pioneered this type of implementation when it developed a Web service linking its reservation system directly to Southwest Airlines Company's Web site (**www.southwest.com**). Now, when Internet users visit Southwest's site to purchase plane tickets, they can make rental-car reservations from the same Web page. Furthermore, Dollar can reuse the Web service to connect its reservation system to other partners' Web sites.[28] Dollar's Web service is free to partners, and therefore does not create a new line of business for either company. However, the service does improve Dollar's business model by enabling the company to market and sell its car-rental service through new channels—i.e., partners' Web sites.

Companies also can use Web services to communicate with their client businesses. An example of this is Zagat Survey, a company that produces restaurant, hotel and travel guides to various cities and regions around the world. Zagat derives one of its main revenue streams from licensing its content to other organizations. E-businesses such as Ticket-master's Citysearch pay to include Zagat restaurant reviews and other writings on their Web sites.[29] Prior to implementing Web services, Zagat provided copies of its database to clients every month, which required converting data into multiple formats to accommodate the various client Web sites. After receiving the data, clients then updated the information on their sites manually.

Zagat has built a Web services-enabled system that directly connects its content to partners' Web sites over the Internet. Providing data to clients via Web services has improved Zagat's B2B business model. Zagat does not have to convert its data into multiple formats, which saves the company time and money. The Web services also free Zagat's clients from the task of updating content on a monthly basis. Instead, client Web sites configure their systems to receive regularly updated content from Zagat, and the new content is incorporated automatically. The system allows Zagat to add new clients easily and to offer more flexible content-licensing options. Rather than paying flat licensing fees, Zagat clients now can purchase varying amounts of content to fit their individual needs.[30] Although Zagat does not charge directly for its Web services, the services enable the company to attract new clients and increase licensing revenue.

Most businesses restrict use of their Web services to a limited number of companies with whom they have established relationships. This hesitation stems in part from the security and quality of service (QoS) concerns that we outlined earlier in this chapter. However, a handful of companies are beginning to develop fee-based Web services available to any business. Such companies center their business models around the provision of Web services, rather than incorporating Web services into some other part of their business models. Most of these companies offer extremely general services, such as news content for Web sites, financial information or payment processing. For example, EarthConnect is developing Web services that provide stock quotes, charting and stock and equities histories. Although this information is available from Web sites, EarthConnect's Web services offer more current data, which is crucial in the financial industry. EarthConnect plans to market the Web services to financial institutions, which will pay to include the services in personal financial applications.[31] A similar fee-based Web service from Concord EFS Inc. provides credit-card processing capabilities (see the feature, Case Study: Concord EFS Inc.).

Case Study: Concord EFS Inc.

Concord EFS Inc. (www.concordefs.com) is a major provider of electronic-payment services. Among its capabilities, Concord offers credit-card authorization services to businesses, including e-commerce Web sites and stores that operate point-of-sale terminals. In July 2001, Concord became the first known payment processor to offer credit-card authorization over the Internet as a Web service. Initially, Concord offered the system, called *Web Payment Services*, only to e-businesses; however, the company now communicates via Web services with point-of-sale terminals, as well.[32]

Case Study: Concord EFS Inc. (Cont.)

Typical services that offer credit-card authorization over the Internet require client businesses either to employ third-party middleware (i.e., software that links two separate applications) or to build custom connections to the payment-processing application. Concord wanted to create a situation in which companies could connect directly to the authorization service. To do this, Concord used Microsoft .NET technology to build *ESFnet*[sm], a gateway (i.e., an entrance point into Concord's network) that translates between clients' computing systems and Concord's proprietary protocol. Clients' commerce applications use Web services standards to send data to Concord. This means that any application able to interpret EFSnet's XML markup can use the system, regardless of the application's programming language or platform. ESFnet translates the information so that it can be processed by Concord's payment platform. A response message then is translated back to XML and sent to the client application. The Concord system is designed to handle high transaction volumes quickly, and the company claims that clients can integrate to ESFnet in one day. Concord charges setup and annual subscription fees in exchange for unlimited use of its authorization service.[33]

According to the head of Concord's emerging technologies group, the company has benefited significantly from the introduction of Web Payment Services. During the first six months that Concord operated the authorization system, the number of participating merchants grew approximately 30 percent per month, and transaction volume grew over 78 percent per month.[34] In the near future, the company hopes to extend the system's capabilities to include typical B2B Internet payment forms.[35]

3.8 Service-to-Employee (S2E) Web Services

S2E Web services are Web services specifically designed for use by employees. The services can take many forms; some S2E Web services help companies deliver information to employees, whereas others simplify interactions among employees. For instance, a business might use Web services to link applications and data to customized employee portals accessible over any Internet connection. The portals would enable employees with appropriate access rights to use corporate applications and modify files over the Web.[36] Another S2E Web service might enable companies to update applications on employees' cell phones or PDAs. For example, if a company sends an employee a notification regarding a meeting time, a Web service might access an electronic schedule on the employee's PDA and make appropriate changes.

Several companies are developing business models that rely on the provision of S2E Web services. Most of these services are tied to more comprehensive industries, such as outsourced human-resources administration or customer-relationship management (CRM). For example, Hewitt Associates LLC is building Web services that companies can incorporate in corporate portals, enabling employees to access benefits information directly from the portals (see the feature, Case Study: Hewitt Associates LLC).

Case Study: Hewitt Associates LLC

Hewitt Associates LLC is a consulting and outsourcing firm that provides human-resources and employee-benefits services to businesses. With more than 250 client companies, Hewitt manages retirement plans, healthcare benefits and other services for over 15 million employees worldwide.[37] One of Hewitt's goals is to offer employees convenient access to their personal retirement and benefits information; employees can retrieve data or change options through customer-service representatives, an automated telephone service or Hewitt's Web site (**www.hewitt.com**).[38]

However, Hewitt's client companies requested that the firm provide more direct access to benefit data. Employees wanted the ability to retrieve information regarding 401k accounts and health-care policies from their companies' corporate portals, without going through Hewitt's site. Hewitt realized it could achieve this by creating custom connections between its computing system and those of its clients, but the costs and development time involved seemed unreasonable. Instead, Hewitt is using Web services technologies to build a platform-independent system that all its corporate clients can integrate into corporate portals or other applications. Hewitt decided to build its Web services using IBM's development tools, in part because the Hewitt's mainframes run IBM software.

Hewitt's Web services enable Web applications, such as corporate portals, to access and retrieve information directly from Hewitt's databases. When an employee wants certain information from Hewitt, such as a 401K balance, the employee provides appropriate authorization information, then registers the request through a corporate portal. The portal translates the request to XML and sends it in a SOAP envelope over the Internet. On the other end, this message is received by Hewitt's IBM WebSphere *application server* (a server that maintains Web applications). The application server unwraps the SOAP envelope and passes the request to Hewitt's mainframe, which translates the request from XML and processes it. The mainframe returns an XML response to the application server, which places the data in a SOAP envelope and transmits it back to the client application. For more information on SOAP and SOAP envelopes, see Chapter 6, Understanding SOAP and WSDL.[39]

Hewitt's initial Web services infrastructure allows employees to check the balances of their 401K accounts, change the contribution rates and allocations of their 401Ks, determine their eligibility for healthcare benefits and check the coverage of their specific health plans.[40] Tim Hilgenberg, Hewitt's CTO of applications, claims that the company is extremely happy to be using Web services—the system, he says, is cost effective and improves the experiences of Hewitt's customers.[41] The company is considering several additional Web services development projects.

3.9 Web Services Registries and Brokerages

Throughout the previous sections of this chapter, we concentrated our discussion on the business models of companies that develop and provide Web services. From this point on, we focus on businesses that serve the emerging Web services industry. We refer to these organizations as third parties, because the organizations are separate from both service providers and service requesters and therefore represent third participants in Web services transactions. Earlier in this chapter, we discussed Web services brokers, which are third-party organizations that enable companies to locate Web services. Other third-party Web services business models offer value-added services and provide support for Web services interactions.

Discovery involves locating Web services to fill specific needs. For example, if a company decides to perform credit-card authorization via a Web service, the company would need to discover an appropriate service (such as the one developed by Concord EFS). Web services registries and brokerages are third parties that facilitate connections between service requesters and service providers. Although few of these organizations charge for their services, many expect that, eventually, they will be able to collect referral revenues by enabling businesses to discover each other's Web services.

3.9.1 UDDI Registries

UDDI registries are the most commonly known method of discovering Web services. The UDDI Business Registry (UBR) provides information about and access to publicly available Web services (services that anyone can invoke). The ebXML specification defines a similar registry structure, which we discuss in Chapter 7, UDDI, Discovery and Web Services Registries.

A UDDI registry's structure is conceptually similar to a that of a phone book. Registries contain "white pages," where companies list contact information and textual description of themselves; "yellow pages," which provide classification information about companies and details on companies' electronic capabilities; and "green pages," which list technical data regarding services and business processes.[42] Information about businesses and services is highly organized, so companies can search registries by business entity, business service and other categories. IT staffs then can use the technical information in the registries to link electronically to other businesses.

Several companies maintain UDDI *operator nodes*, or locations on the Web where interested parties can access the UDDI Business Registry. In September 2000, IBM and Microsoft launched the first registry nodes, which adhere to version 1.0 of the UDDI specification; these can be found at **www.ibm.com/services/uddi** and **uddi.microsoft.com**, respectively. At the time of this writing, four operator nodes—Hewlett-Packard, IBM, Microsoft and SAP—host beta implementations of the UBR that adhere to the UDDI Version 2.0, and two operator nodes—IBM and Microsoft—host implementations of the UBR that adhere to the UDDI Version 1.0. In January 2002, NTT Communications Corp. of Japan announced its plan to become Asia's first UDDI Business Registry node.[43]

Companies are still experimenting with UDDI technology's capabilities. Although the registries boast over 7000 registrants, only a handful of the registered companies are actually providing services through the nodes.[44] Most companies do not want to expose their Web services so publicly until standard Web services security mechanisms are developed. However, once the technology matures and security issues are addressed, public UDDI registries might enable companies to form new B2B relationships. We discuss the details of UDDI and UDDI registries in Chapter 7, UDDI, Discovery and Web Services Registries.

3.9.2 Web Services Brokerages

Organizations also can discover Web services through *Web services brokerages*—Web sites that list available Web services. Like UDDI registries, brokerages allow service providers to input the Web addresses of, and information about, available Web services. Users search this information to locate services that provide specific functionality. However, most brokerages also supply value-added services, which can include advanced search capabilities, service monitoring and service support.

We have already mentioned two of the largest Web services brokerages, XMethods and Salcentral. XMethods maintains a list of free Web services, along with links to additional information about those services. XMethods listings are available through a browser interface, enabling developers to search for services, and a series of programmatic interfaces, which allow applications to search for services. The site also offers Web services-related resources, such as a tool that validates WSDL documents, descriptions of specific Web services implementations and user-contributed tutorials that explain how to install and use the implementations. However, XMethods does not provide advanced value-added services, such as monitoring or technical support. This is because XMethods presents itself primarily as a free resource for developers, rather than as a comprehensive brokerage.

By contrast, Salcentral maintains a wide range of value-added services. Before service providers register their Web services with Salcentral, Salcentral will test the services and provide an analysis of the results. Once a service is registered, Salcentral can include the service in its e-mail newsletter or create a tailored marketing campaign for the service. In addition, Salcentral's monitoring capabilities can supply providers with information regarding the reliability, popularity and profitability of their Web services.

Salcentral also offers value-added services that benefit service requesters. When browsing Salcentral service listings, potential requesters can search by category, organization name or schema type. Once a user becomes interested in a particular service, the user can opt to "watch" that service. This means that Salcentral e-mails the user if the service fails to respond to any request, if the service's XML Schema changes or if a review of the service is completed. A user can watch a Web service before employing it to find out how reliable it is, or, after a user incorporates a service into an application, the user can watch the service to learn about any changes that might affect the calling application.[45]

Another function of Salcentral is to provide payment mechanisms for fee-based Web services. Service requesters can purchase subscriptions directly from Salcentral; most requesters see this as an advantage because they do not have to reveal financial information (such as credit-card numbers) to multiple service providers. Payment support also benefits service providers, who do not have to implement their own payment mechanisms. Figure 3.6 depicts a fictional Salcentral user account. The page contains a chart listing a username, the Web service to which the user subscribes and the number of calls that remain in the user's subscription. Since the page is only a demonstration, it includes descriptions of the fields in the chart. All registered users can access this type of customized page, from which they can change passkeys and buy additional calls.

Other Web services brokerages include Allesta Web Service Agency (**www.allesta.com**) and serviceFORGE (**www.serviceforge.com**). Allesta lists available Web services, as well as providing service testing, monitoring and other support. ServiceFORGE offers security, metering and billing capabilities to service providers.

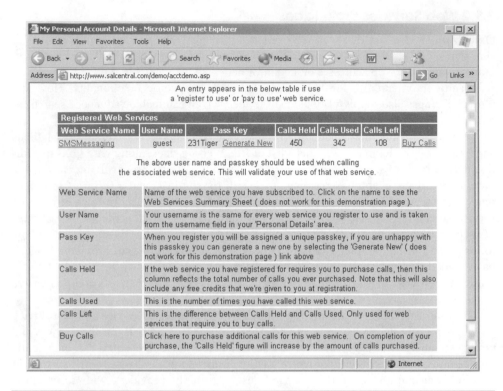

Fig. 3.6   User account for fee-based Web services at **www.salcentral.com**. (Courtesy of Lucin.)

At this point, most brokerages are independent start-up companies. Although these brokerages have developed the necessary technology to host Web services and provide value-added features, the organizations do not have hosting experience, and it is unclear whether they will be able to attract sufficient customer bases. Industry analysts expect that many Internet Service Providers (ISPs) and Application Service Providers (ASPs) eventually will develop their own brokerage capabilities or will partner with existing brokerages. ISPs and ASPs already have customer bases and hosting infrastructures; therefore, these entities might be able to build larger, more comprehensive brokerages.[46]

3.10 Web Services Networks

Although some brokerages provide services such as security, metering and billing, most enterprises that use Web services require more comprehensive, end-to-end support for Web services transactions. Furthermore, many companies offer Web services only to partners or affiliates, so the services are not maintained by brokerages. In these situations, *Web services networks*—companies that oversee Web services communications by offering authentication, security, routing, etc.—can provide additional service support.

Web services networks offer comprehensive delivery services that are similar to the package delivery services provided by UPS and FedEx.[47] In the physical world, when two businesses need to exchange products, they employ a package delivery service to route the package; the delivery service guarantees that the package reaches the appropriate recipient, that it arrives by a certain time and that it remains undamaged. The deliverer also adheres to customized protocols that address contextual situations, such as where the package can be left if the recipient's office is closed.

Web services interactions between companies require these kinds of guarantees, as well. Organizations will not be comfortable conducting important business via Web services unless the participants can ensure that messages arrive securely, on time and intact. Web services networks act as intermediaries between enterprises that exchange Web services; as such, the networks provide a variety of services that address QoS, network reliability, security, metering and billing (Fig. 3.7).[48]

For example, a Web services network can authenticate the participants in Web services transactions and encrypt messages to ensure the security of transmitted information. Networks also guarantee the reliability of Web services and provide *nonrepudiation* of messages (legal proof that a message was received). If a Web service message must pass through multiple parties, the network can ensure that the message is routed correctly. Another function of networks is to monitor Web services usage, which facilitates billing and error management. Some networks also maintain private UDDI registries for customers; only authorized parties can access these registries.[49]

The two most comprehensive Web services networks are operated by Grand Central Communications and Flamenco Networks. Although both companies' networks offer similar capabilities, the networks have different architectures. Grand Central uses a centralized hub infrastructure, which means that all Web services transactions are routed through Grand Central's internal network, then forwarded to their intended recipients. By contrast, Flamenco Networks employs a decentralized, *peer-to-peer* infrastructure (i.e., a network in which each computing system has the same capabilities and responsibilities). In this setup, transactions flow directly from sender to recipient, without passing through Flamenco's systems. (To learn more about peer-to-peer networking and its connection to Web services, see Chapter 4, Web Services and Enterprise Computing.) Grand Central's centralized system is ideal for enterprises with limited computing resources that cannot handle high traffic volumes. However, Flamenco's peer-to-peer architecture simplifies the process of

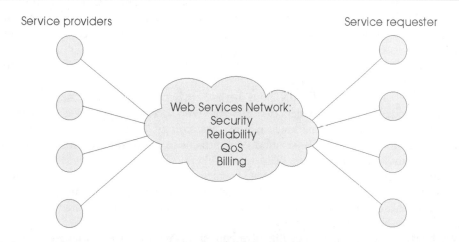

Service providers   Service requester

Web Services Network:
Security
Reliability
QoS
Billing

Fig. 3.7   Web services networks act as intermediaries in Web services interactions.

transmitting a message, which results in fewer delayed deliveries. Flamenco's approach also increases security, because messages that are transmitted directly from senders to authenticated recipients must be encrypted and decrypted only once. (We discuss encryption in Chapter 11, Computer and Internet Security, and Chapter 12, Web Services Security.)[50] Other companies that operate Web services networks are Kenamea (**www.kanemea.com**) and Bang Networks (**www.bangnetworks.com**).

Web services networks supply many of the features—such as security and reliability—that enterprises require to embrace Web services technologies. If a company can subscribe to a network that guarantees the quality of the Web services the company uses, that company will be more likely to employ Web services to transmit critical data. In the next chapter, Web Services and Enterprise Computing, we discuss in detail how companies can use Web services to improve the way in which they interact and communicate.

3.11 Summary

A service provider is a server or system that makes a Web service available over a network. The provider achieves this through a service interface, a software component that enables other applications to access the service. After creating a service interface, a service provider publishes the service to a service broker, a networked server or system that maintains a directory or clearinghouse for Web services. A service requester—a networked server or system that accesses and employs a Web service—interacts with a service broker to find a Web service that fills a specific computing need.

The business lifecycle of a Web service can be broken into four stages: creation, publication, promotion and sale. The creation stage includes not only the initial construction of the Web service, but also the steps required to prove that the service operates correctly. The publication stage involves exposing all necessary pieces of a Web service on a network. The promotion stage is carried out by brokers that help service requesters locate the service. The sale of services involves auditing and billing.

The parameters of Web services subscriptions are determined by service-level agreements (SLAs)—legal contracts in which a service provider outlines the level of service it guarantees for a specific Web service. An important function of SLAs is to address quality of service (QoS), which refers to the level of service that a particular Web service provides. QoS is defined by factors such as the probability that a service can respond to a request at a given time, how well a service executes its tasks, how quickly a service works and how reliable and secure it is. SLAs are crucial to the success of the Web services industry, because Web service customers must be able to trust that services will adhere to certain quality-of-service requirements.

Industry players have defined various methods by which service providers can charge for Web services. Service providers can offer free Web services to publicize Web services and to encourage users to experiment with the technology. Of the fee-based models, the pay-per-use model involves the smallest commitment from customers. Most pay-per-use services require that requesters purchase a set number of service invocations. Providers also can employ a flat-fee subscription model, in which service requesters pay a fee for unlimited use of a Web service during a specific time period. Another payment mechanism is the one-time charge model—requesters pay a single fee in exchange for unlimited access to the service for the entire lifetime of the service.

We break business models that involve publishing Web services into three main categories: models that support service-to-consumer (S2C) Web services, models that support service-to-business (S2B) Web services and models that support service-to-employee (S2E) Web services. Service providers offer S2C services directly to individuals for personal use, whereas S2B services are marketed to and used by businesses. Businesses purchase S2E services to improve communication within organizations and to provide employees with relevant content or applications.

Other Web services business models relate to third-party organizations that serve the Web services industry. These third-party organizations include Web services registries, brokerages and networks. The UDDI Business Registry (UBR) provides information about and access to publicly available Web services. Organizations also can discover Web services through Web services brokerages—Web sites that list available Web services and supply value-added services, which can include advanced search capabilities, service monitoring and service support. Companies that require more comprehensive, end-to-end support for Web services transactions can employ Web services networks—companies that oversee Web services communications by offering authentication, security, routing and other services.

3.12 Internet and Web Resources

www-106.ibm.com/developerworks/webservices/?loc=dwmain
This site, which is part of IBM's DeveloperWorks, offers resources to programmers and others interested in the Web services industry. The site contains links to Web services news, articles, tutorials and information regarding Web services tools and products

www.webservices.org/print.php?sid=361
In this article, the founder and editor of **webservices.org** explains various business models that companies can build using Web services technologies.

www-106.ibm.com/developerworks/library/ws-arc2.html
This article explains the roles of various participants in a service-oriented architecture, then lists reasons why businesses should adopt Web services technologies.

www-106.ibm.com/developerworks/webservices/library/ws-quality.html?dwzone=webservices
This article overviews the various factors that affect the quality of service (QoS) for Web services; it also explains how developers can improve the performance of their Web services.

www-106.ibm.com/developerworks/webservices/library/ws-arc4/
This article discusses how the Web services industry might develop over the next five years; it also defines terminology related to fee-based Web services.

www.metratech.com
Metratech provides solutions for Web services billing. At this site, visitors can learn about Metratech's XML billing platform and its various components.

www.microsoft.com/myservices
This site contains introductory information regarding .NET My Services, as well as links to FAQs and articles. Article topics include Microsoft's .NET strategy, .NET Passport, .NET Alerts and security in .NET. Visitors also can register to use .NET Passport from this site.

www.uddi.org
This site provides a wide variety of resources relating to UDDI. At the site, visitors can find UDDI specifications, white papers, FAQs, discussions and news. The site also contains information about the UDDI Project and companies that support UDDI.

`www.xmethods.net`
XMethods is a Web services brokerage. At this site, visitors can browse Web services listings, access specific services and learn about various Web services implementations.

`www.salcentral.com`
Salcentral is a Web services brokerage that offers many value-added services. At this site, visitors can search Web services by category, subscribe to services and request to receive e-mails regarding a particular service.

`www.grandcentral.com`
Grand Central Communications is a Web services network. At this site, visitors can learn about Web services networks, as well as the specific services that Grand Central provides.

`www.flamenconetworks.com`
Flamenco Networks is a Web services network. At this site, visitors can find a wide variety of information regarding Web services and Web services networks.

`www-106.ibm.com/developerworks/webservices/library/ws-netwrk.html`
This article describes the various functions that a Web services network must provide to businesses.

WORKS CITED

1. D. Gisolfi, "Web Services Architect, Part 1: An Introduction to Dynamic E-business," April 2001 <`www-106.ibm.com/developerworks/webservices/library/ws-arc1/`>.

2. D. Gisolfi, "Web Services Architect, Part 2: Models for Dynamic E-business," April 2001 <`www-106.ibm.com/developerworks/library/ws-arc2.html`>.

3. D. Gisolfi, "Fee-Based Web Services: Terminology," October 2001 <`www-106.ibm.com/developerworks/webservices/library/ws-arc4/`>.

4. S. Burbeck, "The Tao of E-business Services," October 2000 <`www-106.ibm.com/developerworks/webservices/library/ws-tao/index.html?dwzone=webservices`>.

5. M. Clark, "Business Architecture of a Web Services Brokerage: Understanding the Business Context of Web Services," 1 August 2001 <`www.webservicesarchitect.com/content/articles/clark01print.asp`>.

6. "The Importance of an SLA," <`thewhir.com/find/resellers/articles/sla.cfm`>.

7. A. Main and A. Nagarajan, "Understanding Quality of Service for Web Services," January 2002 <`www-106.ibm.com/developerworks/webservices/library/ws-quality.html?dwzone=webservices`>.

8. C. James, "Can You Trust Web Services SLAs?" *Software Development Times* 1 September 2001: 31.

9. C. James, "Can You Trust Web Services SLAs?" *Software Development Times* 1 September 2001: 31.

10. M. Clark, "Business Architecture of a Web Services Brokerage: Understanding the Business Context of Web Services," 1 August 2001 <`www.webservicesarchitect.com/content/articles/clark01print.asp`>.

11. M. Clark, "Making Money out of Selling Web Services—Part I," 22 August 2001 <`www.webservicesarchitect.com/content/articles/clark02print.asp`>.

12. D. Gisolfi, "Web Services Architect, Part 2: Models for Dynamic E-business," April 2001 <`www-106.ibm.com/developerworks/library/ws-arc2.html`>.

13. M. Clark, "Making Money out of Selling Web Services—Part II," 29 August 2001 `<www.webservicesarchitect.com/content/articles/clark03print.asp>`.

14. M. Clark, "Making Money out of Selling Web Services—Part I," 22 August 2001 `<www.webservicesarchitect.com/content/articles/clark02print.asp>`.

15. D. Gisolfi, "Web Services Architect, Part 2: Models for Dynamic E-business," April 2001 `<www-106.ibm.com/developerworks/library/ws-arc2.html>`.

16. M. Clark, "Making Money out of Selling Web Services—Part I," 22 August 2001 `<www.webservicesarchitect.com/content/articles/clark02print.asp>`.

17. D. Gisolfi, "Web Services Architect, Part 2: Models for Dynamic E-business," April 2001 `<www-106.ibm.com/developerworks/library/ws-arc2.html>`.

18. W. Eibach and D. Kuebler, "Metering and Accounting for Web Services," July 2001 `<www-106.ibm.com/developerworks/webservices/library/ws-maws/?dwzone=webservices>`.

19. D. Taft, "Raising the Services Stakes," *eWeek* 14 January 2002 `<www.eweek.com/article/0,3658,s%3D701%26a%3D21059,00.asp>`.

20. M. Polan, "Web Services Provisioning: Understanding and Using Web Services Hosting Technology," January 2002 `<www-106.ibm.com/developerworks/webservices/library/ws-wsht/>`.

21. M. Vizard, "CEO Discusses MetraTech's Place in the Web Services Space," *Infoworld* 17 December 2001 `<www.infoworld.com/articles/hn/xml/01/12/17/011217hnmetratech.xml>`.

22. C. Adam, "Web Services Business Models," 7 November 2001 `<www.webservices.org/print.php?sid=361>`.

23. "Expedia, Inc.: XML Web Services Provide Travelers with Unprecedented Advantages," Microsoft Case Study 13 July 2001 `<www.microsoft.com/servers/evaluation/casestudies/Expedia.asp>`.

24. T. Olavsrud, "Microsoft Launches .NET Alerts Preview," 8 October 2001 `<www.internetnews.com/asp-news/print/0,,3411_898911,00.html>`.

25. A. Conry–Murray, "Emerging Technology: Microsoft's Passport to Controversy," *Network Magazine* 4 March 2002 `<www.networkmagazine.com/article/printableArticle?doc_id=NMG20020304S0003>`.

26. C. Adam, "Two Single Sign-Ons, Passport and Liberty," 19 November 2001 `<www.webservices.org/article.php?sid=370&mode=thread&order=0>`.

27. M. Rosoff, "A Closer Look at Passport," 10 September 2001 `<www.directionsonmicrosoft.com/sample/DOMIS/update/2001/10oct/1001aclap.htm>`.

28. W. Wong, "Pitch: Why Web Services Make Business Sense," *CNET News* 8 November 2001 `<news.com.com/2102-1017-275442.html>`.

29. T. Sullivan, "Expanding the Menu," *Infoworld* 29 October 2001: S22.

30. "Zagat Survey: .NET Framework Helps Restaurant-Review Leader Cut Development Time in Half," Microsoft Case Study 12 July 2001 `<www.microsoft.com/servers/evaluation/casestudies/zagat.asp>`.

31. M. Wagner, "Web Services Show Promise," *InternetWeek* 29 October 2001: 11.

32. P. Krill, "Brick-and-Mortars Get Credit Card Authorization via Internet," *Infoworld* 17 January 2002 `<www.infoworld.com/articles/hn/xml/02/01/17/020117hnconcordefs.xml>`.

33. "Web Payment Services: A Ground-Breaking Solution," <**www.concordefs.com/ web_payments/index.htm**>.

34. "Payment Solution Built Using New Internet Standards Unveiled at XML World Trade Show," 7 December 2001 <**www.webservices.org/ article.php?sid=406&mode=thread&order=0**>.

35. P. Krill, "Brick-and-Mortars Get Credit Card Authorization via Internet," *Infoworld* 17 January 2002   <**www.infoworld.com/articles/hn/xml/02/01/17/ 020117hnconcordefs.xml**>.

36. C. Moore, "Take It All With You," *Infoworld* 29 October 2001: 39.

37. P. McDougall, "Decoding Web Services," *Information Week* 1 October 2001: <**www,informationweek.com/story/IWK20010928S0008**>.

38. M. Hicks, "E-Biz Building Blocks," *eWeek* 13 August 2001 <**www.eweek.com/ print_article/0,3668,a=12366,00.asp**>.

39. J. Fontana, "Web Services Making Headway in Large Firms," *Network World* 14 January 2002 <**www.nwfusion.com/cgi-bin/mailto/x.cgi**>.

40. M. Hicks, "E-Biz Building Blocks," *eWeek* 13 August 2001 <**www.eweek.com/ print_article/0,3668,a=12366,00.asp**>.

41. T. Sullivan, "At Your Web Service," *InfoWorld* 1 June 2001 <**www.infoworld.com/ articles/fe/xml/01/06/04/010604fetrend.xml**>.

42. T. Wilson, "UDDI Promises Link to Web Services," *Internet Week* 26 November 2001: 26.

43. "NTT Communications to Become Asia's First UDDI Business Registry Node Operator," NTT press release 15 January 2002 <**www.ntt.com/NEWS_RELEASE_E/news02/0001/ 0115.html**>.

44. M. Meehan, "Updated B2B Registry Debuts," *ComputerWorld* 19 November 2001 <**www.computerworld.com/itresources/rcstory/ 0,4167,STO65907_KEY52,00.html**>.

45. "Web Service Watch," <**www.salcentral.com/watchx/run.asp**>.

46. "How Can We Build Trust Between a Consumer of a Web Service and Developer?" Value Added Web Service Suppliers white paper <**www.vawss.org/ca/v001.aspx**>.

47. K. Truelove, "Web Services Networks: Intermediaries that Simplify Inter-Enterprise Projects," October 2001 <**www-106.ibm.com/developerworks/webservices/library/ ws-netwrk.html**>.

48. J. Harney, "Web Services Networks," *Intelligent EAI* 1 February 2002 <**www.intelligenteai.com/020201/503feat1_1.shtml**>.

49. K. Truelove, "Web Services Networks: Intermediaries that Simplify Inter-Enterprise Projects," October 2001 <**www-106.ibm.com/developerworks/webservices/library/ ws-netwrk.html**>.

50. J. Borck, "Shoring Up Web Services," *InfoWorld* 3 December 2001: 36.

RECOMMENDED READING

Adam, C. "Web Services Business Models," 7 November 2001 <**www.webservices.org/ print.php?sid=361**>.

Borck, J. "Shoring Up Web Services," *InfoWorld* 3 December 2001: 36.

Clark, M. "Business Architecture of a Web Services Brokerage: Understanding the Business Context of Web Services," 1 August 2001 <`www.webservicesarchitect.com/content/articles/clark01print.asp`>.

Clark, M. "Making Money out of Selling Web Services—Part I," 22 August 2001 <`www.webservicesarchitect.com/content/articles/clark02print.asp`>.

Clark, M. "Making Money out of Selling Web Services—Part II," 29 August 2001 <`www.webservicesarchitect.com/content/articles/clark03print.asp`>.

Eibach, W., and D. Kuebler, "Metering and Accounting for Web Services," July 2001 <`www-106.ibm.com/developerworks/webservices/library/ws-maws/?dwzone=webservices`>.

Gisolfi, D. "Web Services Architect, Part 1: An Introduction to Dynamic E-business," April 2001 <`www-106.ibm.com/developerworks/webservices/library/ws-arc1/`>.

Gisolfi, D. "Web Services Architect, Part 2: Models for Dynamic E-business," April 2001 <`www-106.ibm.com/developerworks/library/ws-arc2.html`>.

Harvey, J. "From Web Services Report: Issues and Insights," <`www.esj.com/webservices/insights/print.asp?EditorialsID=27`>.

James, C. "Can You Trust Web Services SLAs?" *Software Development Times* 1 September 2001: 31.

Main, A., and A. Nagarajan, "Understanding Quality of Service for Web Services," January 2002 <`www-106.ibm.com/developerworks/webservices/library/ws-quality.html?dwzone=webservices`>.

Rubinstein, D. "Market for Web Services Networks Grows," *Software Development Times* 1 October 2001 <`www.sdtimes.com/news/039/story3.htm`>.

Truelove, K. "Web Services Networks: Intermediaries that Simplify Inter-Enterprise Projects," October 2001 <`www-106.ibm.com/developerworks/webservices/library/ws-netwrk.html`>.

"Web Services and the Need for Web Services Networks," 28 November 2001 <`www.webservices.org/article.php?sid=377`>.

Wong, W. "Pitch: Why Web Services Make Business Sense," 8 November 2001 <`news.com.com/2009-1017-275442.html?legacy=cnet`>.

Web Services and Enterprise Computing

Objectives

- To discuss how Web services can increase the efficiency of software development projects.
- To examine the benefits of using Web services to integrate applications.
- To explain how organizations can use Web services to create Web-enabled applications and corporate portals.
- To discuss the potential role of Web services in supply-chain management and customer-relationship management (CRM).
- To explain how Web services can enable B2B transactions and improve partner relationships.

Take the tone of the company that you are in.
Philip Dormer Stanhope, Earl of Chesterfield

Making mental connections is our most crucial learning tool, the essence of human intelligence: to forge links; to go beyond the given; to see patterns, relationship, context.
Marilyn Ferguson

I have entered on an enterprise which is without precedent, and will have no imitator.
Jean-Jacques Rousseau

When you stop talking, you've lost your customer.
Estée Lauder

Outline

4.1 Introduction

In the preceding chapter, we examined ways in which companies can expand their businesses and increase revenue by creating, selling or managing enterprise Web services. However, many companies are waiting until standards mature and security and Quality of Service (QoS) concerns are resolved before deploying publicly accessible Web services. Instead, organizations are beginning with internal Web services implementations, such as using Web services to connect applications across departments. Other companies are making a limited number of Web services available to trusted business partners.[1]

This chapter investigates how organizations can create and consume Web services to improve communications and productivity. We begin by discussing how application developers and IT staffs can enhance the software-development process by incorporating Web services in corporate applications. We examine enterprise application integration (EAI) and ways in which Web services can improve integration projects. We then consider the use of Web services in specific enterprise software, such as corporate-portal, customer-relationship-management (CRM), supply-chain-management (SCM) and inventory applications. The chapter also contains case studies on companies—including Microsoft, British Telecom, Alliance Airlines and Nordstrom—that are using Web services to integrate systems and improve communication among departments, supply chains and partners.

4.2 Web Services and Corporate Software Development

Web services can improve corporate software development by reducing the time and expense involved in developing a software application. As companies adopt Web services, they are beginning to develop private UDDI or ebXML registries, which catalog the Web services maintained by a company or a group of partner companies. Instead of designing software "from scratch," programmers can use registries to locate existing Web services, then incorporate those services into applications. Programmers can find additional Web services by searching public registries, such as the UDDI Business Registry (discussed in

Chapter 7, UDDI, Discovery and Web Services Registries). A programmer might compile an e-commerce application from numerous publicly and privately held Web services, such as a Web service that processes credit-card payments and a Web service that provides driving directions to the company's closest store. Since the developer does not have to create new software to perform these tasks, the application can be completed faster and at less cost. According to Gartner, Web services could increase the efficiency of software-development projects by up to 30 percent.[2]

Web services also can decrease the complexity and cost of *integrating* applications, or connecting them to enable direct communication and information exchange. Forrester research estimates that, without using Web services, the average company spends up to one million dollars to research, test, implement and maintain software that can link two separate applications over the Internet.[3] By contrast, Web services facilitate less expensive and more flexible integration solutions—especially when connecting applications written in different languages for different platforms. Companies can employ Web services to integrate their own applications or to integrate with suppliers, distributors, partners and corporate clients. We discuss various forms of Web services-enabled application integration throughout this chapter.

Realizing these advantages, many organizations are beginning to adopt Web services. Figure 4.1 summarizes the results of a 2002 Jupiter Media Metrix survey, in which companies were polled regarding their plans to deploy Web services over the next year. The survey indicated that only 23 percent of companies had no plans to adopt Web services.

Web services are not an ideal solution for every software-development project. As we mention throughout this book, Web services security and QoS protocols are not fully developed. Therefore, some experts believe that Web services should not yet be used to transmit highly confidential or business-critical data across organizational boundaries.[1] Also, Web services are not recommended for systems that handle a large number of transactions, because processing SOAP messages can impede performance.[4] (We discussed Web service performance in Chapter 2, Web Services: A New Computing Paradigm.) Companies should implement Web services slowly, beginning with internal integration projects or services that are shared among trusted partners. Once Web services and security standards mature, companies might deploy Web services that are more widely accessible.[5]

Percentage of companies	Projected Web services implementation(s) within the next year
16 percent	Businesses planning to employ Web services to locate and communicate with new business suppliers, distributors or partners.
53 percent	Businesses planning to employ Web services to integrate and transact business with existing suppliers, distributors or partners.

Fig. 4.1   Percentages of companies that plan to implement Web services within the next year.[6] (Part 1 of 2.)

1. Web services networks can significantly increase the security and reliability of Web services. We discuss Web services networks in Chapter 3, Web Services Business Models.

Percentage of companies	Projected Web services implementation(s) within the next year
60 percent	Businesses planning to employ Web services to integrate applications and data sources within their organizations.
23 percent	Businesses that do not plan to employ Web services.

Fig. 4.1   Percentages of companies that plan to implement Web services within the next year.[6] (Part 2 of 2.)

4.3 Web Services and Enterprise Application Integration (EAI)

Large corporations often have many departments, each using applications and platforms that are best suited to the department's particular needs. Since most enterprise applications are designed to function independently, interdepartmental communication can be difficult. Before a company can automate B2B transactions and conduct e-business with suppliers, partners and clients, the company's internal applications and business processes should be integrated.[7] Companies traditionally integrated applications via point-to-point connections (direct connections between two systems). More recently, organizations have invested in *Enterprise Application Integration* (*EAI*)—infrastructures that link multiple applications and databases so that they can share information and business processes.

EAI typically uses *middleware* (software that links separate applications) to connect a company's many applications. A custom interface is built to link each separate application to the EAI system. Several types of EAI exist, including data integration, business-process integration and method integration.[8] *Data integration*, the most common form of EAI, involves linking databases to applications or other databases. *Business-process integration* and *method integration* involve connecting applications so that they can communicate and access each other's functionality. [*Note*: We discuss business processes and business-process management in Chapter 5, XML and Derivative Technologies.]

Figure 4.2 depicts an EAI infrastructure that integrates various applications and data sources—including a Web-application server, databases and *legacy applications* (older applications in which companies have invested significant resources).[2] Most EAI systems connect applications using *adaptors*, or software components that enable applications to communicate with other applications. This type of integration offers many benefits. For instance, imagine that a company provides a Web application that enables customers to check whether certain products are in stock. However, the Web application resides on the company's Web-application server, and the needed inventory data is maintained in a legacy application. EAI would allow the Web application to access and use the legacy application's data.

---

2. Figure 4.2 address some aspects of EAI that are beyond the scope of this discussion. For additional information on EAI, readers can visit `eai.ittoolbox.com`.

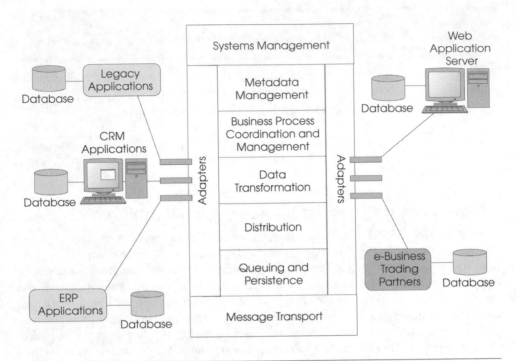

Fig. 4.2   EAI infrastructure. (Courtesy of Computer Sciences Corporation.)

There are several drawbacks to traditional EAI. Most EAI solutions aim to integrate an entire enterprise, including all relevant applications and data sources. Although this type of comprehensive integration improves overall communication, it makes EAI complex and expensive. Middleware products are usually costly, and most companies must hire specialized integration consultants to implement EAI solutions.[9] Furthermore, companies usually cannot reuse EAI interfaces for other purposes, such as integrating with partners.

As a result, some businesses are adopting Web services to integrate applications. Web services' open standards enable organizations to create reusable interfaces to applications. When packaged as a Web service or set of Web services, any application theoretically can communicate with any other application via SOAP messages. Thus, Web services provide a standard for linking all software, whereas traditional EAI links only specific applications. Many companies see internal integration as an appropriate first Web service implementation, because security and QoS concerns are lessened when Web services communicate only within an organization. According to a February 2002 Hurwitz Group survey, over 50 percent of IT managers reported that their first Web services projects involve or would involve integrating internal applications.[10] Many EAI software vendors are responding to this trend by enhancing their products to support Web services standards, such as SOAP, WSDL, UDDI and ebXML.[11]

Web services are less complex to develop and maintain than are most EAI systems, which means that integration projects require less time and money. Toolkits for designing and deploying Web services are significantly less expensive than most EAI solutions are.[12] Web services provide flexibility in that companies can start by connecting two or three applications, then integrate additional applications into the system as necessary. Also, Web services allow companies to break applications into separate units, which makes integration more efficient. For example, a company can divide its human-resources software into units that deal with employee-contact information, employee salaries, employee reviews and so on. Each unit then is packaged as a separate Web service. If another application needs to access employee contact information, the application can communicate directly with the employee-contact-information Web service, rather than with the entire human-resources application.[13]

Although Web services technology can enable EAI, it does not constitute an entire EAI solution. Not all integration issues can be solved using Web services—for example, Web services might not provide the levels of security, reliability, performance and uptime required by some organizations.[14] For companies that have already developed integration solutions, it is usually less expensive to enhance current EAI systems than to adopt new technology.[15] Organizations that are implementing new EAI solutions should weigh the benefits and costs associated with Web services before forming an integration strategy.

The following sections describe companies that are adopting Web services to integrate internal applications. For information regarding EAI software vendors—including Vitria, SeeBeyond, Tibco, and webMethods—and their support for Web services standards, see Chapter 8, Web services Platforms, Vendors and Strategies.

4.3.1 Case Study: British Telecom

British Telecom (BT, **www.bt.com**) is a U.K.-based telecommunications company that provides local and long-distance phone service, mobile-communications service and Internet service. With more than 28 million exchange lines and 7 million mobile customers on three continents, BT relies heavily on the ability to communicate across different media and technologies.[16] In December 2001, BT adopted Web services to improve the company's technological infrastructure. The company chose Cape Clear Software (discussed in Chapter 8, Web Services Platforms, Vendors and Strategies) to design and implement a Web services solution.[17]

BT's computing infrastructure incorporates a diverse collection of technologies and platforms, including mainframes, CORBA, J2EE and *MQSeries*[3] technology. The incompatibility of various technologies limited interoperability between departments, and translation between platforms slowed BT's network. BT wanted its systems to be flexible and interoperable, but did not want to upgrade to an entirely new platform. Jon Calladine, BT's application-integration consultant, addressed these concerns: "We require a standard means for protecting our investment in existing systems while also enabling the development of new applications. While most IT platforms offer the means of interoperating, they are not inherently designed to do so. As a result they use proprietary protocols and increase the complexity of the development process."[18]

Using Cape Clear's *CapeConnect* Web services platform, BT created a solution that uses XML and SOAP messages to communicate across platforms. The standardization that Web services provide allowed the company to integrate previously incompatible objects, but did not force BT's developers to adopt new platforms or programming languages. Since Web services can be incorporated into existing software, the company did not have to

---

3. MQSeries (now called WebSphere MQ) is IBM's middleware product line for application and business-process integration.

replace its infrastructure. BT's Web services implementation is not tied to a particular vendor's product line, and it provides the flexibility to add and integrate new applications as necessary.[19] Although BT has not completed its Web services project, the company is confident that Web services will facilitate effective communication among its existing heterogeneous systems.

4.3.2 Case Study: `Nordstrom.com`

Nordstrom is one of the most popular department stores in the United States. The company is also an e-commerce leader, offering a wide variety of products through its Web site, **nordstrom.com**. In December 2001, Nordstrom hired IONA Technologies (discussed in Chapter 8, Web Services Platforms, Vendors and Strategies) to improve communication between Nordstrom's e-commerce site and its other applications.[20]

Before adopting Web services, communication among Nordstrom's applications was limited due to the company's many disparate computing platforms. **Nordstrom.com** uses Microsoft software, but the company's *enterprise resource planning* (*ERP*) applications—which it employs to check inventory, place orders and organize company resources—run on Hewlett-Packard UNIX servers, and inventory data resides on IBM mainframes. The company considered connecting these systems using traditional middleware products, but decided that the available solutions were too expensive and time-consuming. Instead, Nordstrom is using Web services technology to ensure interoperable transactions among systems. Nordstrom's CTO, Paul Onnen, observed that Web services are more cost-effective because one Web service can be accessed by multiple applications: "The key with Web services is that you only have to build [them] a single time."[21] Web services also can be implemented quickly—**nordstrom.com** installed its first Web services in only a few hours.[22]

Nordstrom is using Web services to connect its e-commerce site to its gift-card-management and cosmetics-replenishment applications, which reside on legacy systems. The Web services that link **nordstrom.com** to the gift-card-management system allow customers to redeem Nordstrom gift cards through the Web site. The other Web services implementation is designed to improve Nordstrom's cosmetics-inventory system—when a customer purchases a cosmetics product from **nordstrom.com**, a Web service automatically updates the cosmetics-replenishment application to reflect the changed inventory. Although security concerns have caused Nordstrom to deploy Web services only on the company's private network, Nordstrom is happy with its Web services implementations. The company plans to use Web services to create a universal inventory system that connects each store's separate inventory applications. Onnen highlights why Web services will allow them to accomplish this goal: "I don't have to reinvent the wheel. We can define interfaces one at a time and use them over again multiple times."[23]

4.4 Corporate Portals and Knowledge Management

Corporate portals are browser-based applications that offer single-access points to information or applications aggregated from disparate sources. Companies usually implement corporate portals to improve communication with customers, partners and employees. For example, a company's customers and partners might query a portal to access information such as product availability and pricing. Employees typically use portals to perform various tasks, from retrieving corporate policies or human-resource information to booking work-related trips and accessing scheduling applications.[24]

As organizations grow more complex, they are developing portals that offer enhanced functionality, such as the ability to supply confidential information to users. When attempting to access sensitive data via a portal, users enter authorization information, such as usernames and passwords. After authenticating a user's identity, the corporate portal displays information appropriate for that user. For instance, a corporate portal might allow an authorized sales associate to view information on company products and services, but restrict the sales associate's access to fellow employees' personnel data. Likewise, a corporate portal might allow trusted business partners to view information about new or existing services while restricting access to information about the company's financial assets.

To facilitate business processes and ensure maximum security, corporate portals should be customized on the basis of users' identities, positions or job titles. As the technology evolves, portals will employ Web services to supply users with personalized information.[25] Web services also can link portals with disparate applications and data sources. For example, imagine that a company wants to connect its portal to a business partner's application, but the business partner uses a different programming platform that does not interoperate with the portal. In this scenario, the company could use Web services to enable communication between its portal and the partner's application. To address these kinds of interoperability issues, organizations that develop portal software are incorporating Web services standards into new versions of their products.

Portal users often want to access only content that pertains to a particular topic. In these cases, portals employ *portlets*, which are application modules that encapsulate specific, real-time information from a portal and present that information to a user.[26] Portlets often are proprietary programming components and therefore pose potential interoperability problems. As Web services standards develop, it is likely that many companies will incorporate Web services technologies to perform portlet functions.

A crucial aspect of creating effective portals is managing portal information. Without *content management*—rules for creating, storing and presenting content so that information is accessible and useful—portals can become "information dumps" that are difficult to navigate. However, when content is managed effectively, portals become significant *knowledge-management* tools. This means that businesses gain value from portals that present company information assets in a logical, useful manner.[27] Many software vendors that market portal solutions also offer content-management software, and other portal vendors are partnering with content-management vendors. For example, portal vendor Plumtree has partnerships with content-management vendors Interwoven and Documentum.[28]

Several major software vendors are including portal applications in their overall Web services strategies. These include BEA Systems, which has developed the *WebLogic Portal 7.0* for its *WebLogic Platform 7.0*; Microsoft, which has introduced the *SharePoint Portal Server* to be used with its .NET platform; and Sun Microsystems, which has created the *Sun™ ONE Portal Server* for its *Sun ONE* Web services initiative.[29] In addition, numerous portal and content-management vendors are enhancing their products by integrating support for Web services standards (Fig. 4.3).

Vendor	Application
Portal	
BEA, www.bea.com	WebLogic Portal
BroadVision, www.broadvision.com	One-To-One Portal
Epicentric, www.epicentric.com	Foundation Server
IBM, www.ibm.com	WebSphere Portal Server
Microsoft, www.microsoft.com	SharePoint Portal Server
Oracle, www.oracle.com	Oracle9iAS Portal Studio
Plumtree, www.plumtree.com	Corporate Portal
Sun, www.sun.com	Sun ONE Portal Server
Tibco, www.tibco.com	Active Portal
Content Management	
divine, www.divine.com	divine Content Server
Documentum, www.documentum.com	eContent Services for Portals
OnePage Inc., www.onepage.com	Content Connect Studio
Vignette, www.vignette.com	Vignette V6

Fig. 4.3   Portal and content-management vendors and their products that support Web services standards.

To promote standardization among corporate portals, several organizations—including Epicentric, Documentum and Instraspect—formed the *Web Services User Interface (WSUI)* initiative, which describes how organizations can leverage XML technologies to create portals that interact with Web services.[30] In October 2001, the WSUI specification was contributed to OASIS's *Web Services Component Model (WSCM)* Technical Committee, now called the *Web Services for Interactive Applications (WSIA)* Technical Committee. The WSIA TC is incorporating the WSUI specification in a Web services framework for interactive Web applications.[31] We discuss the role of XML in Web services in Chapter 5, XML and Derivative Technologies.

Another OASIS initiative is the *Web Services for Remote Portals (WSRP)* Technical Committee, which is defining a standard that will allow Web services to be "plugged into" platforms that aggregate content, such as corporate portals or other Web applications. The committee will work to define self-describing services that can be published and discovered in standard way.[32]

Many companies that supply content to other organizations are incorporating Web services in their content-delivery systems. By exposing content as Web services, a content provider can allow clients to access updated data directly and incorporate that data in Web sites and portals. For more information on this type of Web services implementation, see the feature, Case Study: Standard and Poor's.

Case Study: Standard and Poor's

Standard and Poor's (S&P, **www.standardandpoors.com**), a division of the McGraw-Hill Companies, provides financial information, industry analysis and data on fiscal performance and trends for the financial-services industry. The company's main goal is to offer outside, objective resources that help individuals and corporations make well-informed investment decisions.[33] To assess the performance of companies and investments, managers and business executives require the most up-to-date financial reporting possible. Thus, S&P constantly seeks out new ways to keep its clients informed. In 1998, S&P began offering some of its printed material online—the company soon realized that the Web could vastly improve its ability to deliver financial information to clients.

As the Web evolved, S&P has experimented with new ways of delivering its information and services—including the use of Web services technology. The company is developing more than 60 Web services. Initially, S&P's Web services were available only as a complete package, so interested customers had to purchase access to all 60 services at once. However, the company now is packaging each Web service separately. This enables customers to pick and choose the specific applications to which they subscribe. S&P maintains over 40 Oracle databases to contain the services' information, and each database is updated regularly to include current and accurate financial data.[34]

Using the Sun ONE platform (discussed in Chapter 8, Web Services Platforms, Vendors and Strategies), S&P created each application as a modular J2EE component. The component is packaged in a SOAP envelope and described using WSDL. The SOAP envelope then is passed to an internal directory, from which other business units within the company can access the information. These components also can be published externally, which allows client businesses to incorporate the services on their own Web sites or portals.[35] Examples of available S&P Web services include a quote engine, rules-based screening tools, equity-quote services and financial calculators.

Through Web services, S&P can provide more current data and value-added services to customers. Web services also allow S&P to attract new customers and expand into new markets without significantly increasing the company's infrastructure. Since S&P's Web services are available worldwide via the Internet, international customers can access up-to-date financial reports and industry data, regardless of location.[36]

4.5 Web Services and Customer-Relationship Management

One way that companies can differentiate themselves from competitors is by providing superior customer service. *Customer-Relationship Management* (*CRM*) encompasses every aspect of interaction between an organization and its customers—including sales, service and support. An effective CRM strategy combines technology and marketing to help companies better understand their customers, identify profitable customers, resolve customers' concerns, target customers with appropriate promotions and automate customer-service tasks. [37]

Data and application integration are crucial to successful CRM. Many companies store customer data in decentralized databases, and it is common for different departments to maintain duplicate information. One of CRM's main goals is to enable a company's employees to access a complete customer profile from a single application or location.[38] To accomplish this, the company's CRM system must facilitate communication among various corporate applications and databases. Also, as B2B partnerships become more common, many partner organizations want to integrate their CRM data.[39] This requires CRM systems to communicate remotely with applications that run on different platforms.

As we discussed in Section 4.3, traditional methods of linking applications and databases require expensive, customized connections. In a typical CRM implementation, integration represents 30 to 50 percent of the project's total cost.[40] Web services can provide a less expensive method of integrating customer data. Moreover, since Web services employ open standards, companies can more easily integrate their own customer data with that of partners. This allows organizations to develop more complete customer profiles, which helps marketing departments target customers with appropriate advertisements and promotions. As a company's CRM strategy evolves, it is relatively simple to integrate new applications and data sources into a Web services-enabled CRM system.[41]

Companies also can use Web services to communicate directly with customers. If Web services are used to link a company's internal databases to a Web application, customers can access data such as billing and order-status information over the Internet. A customer can directly query a company's database through its Web site and receive personalized, up-to-date information. In addition, Web services can be used to automate customer-service tasks, such as sending information regarding sales and promotions to customers on the basis of their preferences and purchasing histories.

As the software industry has embraced Web services, many CRM application vendors have modified their products to support Web services standards. In summer 2002, Siebel Systems (the CRM-application market leader, **www.siebel.com**) is due to release *Siebel 7.5*, which will provide support for SOAP and WSDL. Support for UDDI will be available in future versions of Siebel software. Other CRM software vendors are also adding support for Web services. For example, Oracle supports SOAP, UDDI, and XML; E.piphany (**www.epiphany.com**) supports SOAP and XML; and PeopleSoft (**www.people-soft.com**) exposes CRM-application functions to XML.[42] Other vendors, such as Onyx (**www.onyx.com**) and SAP (**www.sap.com**), are rebuilding their applications using XML and Web services, instead of merely offering support for standards.[43]

At this stage, most Web services capabilities provided by off-the-shelf CRM applications are too basic to facilitate meaningful communication. However, analysts expect that Web services will eventually provide a standard for integrating packaged CRM applications.[44] The following sections explore the experiences of two companies—Putnam Lovell Securities and Microsoft—that are integrating their customer data and CRM applications via Web services technology.

4.5.1 Case Study: Putnam Lovell Securities

Putnam Lovell Securities (**www.putnamlovell.com**) is an investment bank that targets financial institutions, private investment firms, brokerages, mutual-fund companies and insurance companies.[45] One of Putnam's functions is to provide research reports on particular investments, but the company lacked an effective method of supplying clients with current information.

Putnam's problems were caused in part by its many disparate, unintegrated applications—**salesforce.com**, an ASP that specializes in CRM solutions, stores and manages Putnam's customer data, whereas Blue Matrix distributes financial research to Putnam clients. The inability of these applications to share data made it difficult for the company to analyze customer information and provide appropriate services. Putnam bankers had to request reports that might interest specific clients, then ship the reports via courier mail or e-mail. This process was expensive and inefficient, and reports were often out-of-date when they arrived.[46] Furthermore, the system made it impractical for Putnam employees to taylor reports to specific clients. Instead, Putnam sent composite reports, which were more costly to transmit and less valuable to customers.[47]

Putnam has adopted Web services technology to improve the company's integration and customer-service capabilities. Putnam hired Grand Central Communications (a Web services network discussed in Chapter 3, Web Services Business Models) to serve as an intermediary between **salesforce.com** and Blue Matrix, effectively integrating the two online applications. Through Grand Central's Web services network, Blue Matrix can query **salesforce.com** to determine which Putnam customers might be interested in a particular research report. **salesforce.com** analyzes Putnam's customer data and transmits a list of appropriate clients to Grand Central, which passes the information to Blue Matrix. Blue Matrix then sends the research report to appropriate clients via e-mail.[48]

This automated system reduces mailing costs, improves efficiency and enables Putnam to distribute personalized research reports to clients. Putnam has realized many benefits from its Web services implementation, including cost savings, increased trading and higher customer-retention rates. The company is planning several additional Web services projects, which will automate tasks such as creating expense reports and updating employee contact information.[49]

4.5.2 Case Study: Microsoft Sales & Support IT Team (SSIT)

The Microsoft Sales & Support IT team (SSIT) is responsible for managing and controlling all of Microsoft's data-storage systems that contain information on account contacts, business opportunities, sales reports, customer support, sponsored events and marketing functions. Sales teams and representatives use each system to gather data on clients and sales performance. This enables the sales teams to analyze trends and forecast future results, as well as track individual client preferences and purchasing behaviors. Originally, each system had its own unique functionality and interface with which the sales teams interacted. This meant that employees had to know how to use five or more different systems before they could obtain a compete picture of a customer's account.[50] This type of infrastructure made tasks complex and time-consuming. Furthermore, the information in the systems was not always up-to-date, which impeded the staff's ability to provide effective customer-relationship management (CRM).

Working with .NET technology, SSIT set out to build an integrated data-retrieval infrastructure that would allow sales representatives to access data from a set of XML Web services. A Web-based tool called Account Explorer enables sales representatives to review a complete set of data on any one client from a central location.[51] Account Explorer calls various XML Web services to retrieve necessary information from the core data systems and present it in a unified, easy-to-read manner. By employing the system, managers can quickly analyze accounts and make appropriate, well-informed decisions about customers and sales trends.[52]

To further improve CRM, the SSIT group used Microsoft's Mobile Internet Toolkit to create a wireless version of the *Account Explorer* Web services. Using the wireless system, sales representatives can access customer information in the field using Pocket PC devices running on the Windows CE or Windows CE .NET platform. The ability to access information remotely from wireless devices further enhances sales performance and sales teams' decision-making capabilities, which improves overall CRM. We introduce Microsoft's Mobile Internet Toolkit in Chapter 9, .NET Web Services: A Conceptual Overview.

4.6 Web Services and B2B Collaboration

The preceding sections of this chapter focused on how Web services can facilitate integration and automation within an organization. However, as we discussed throughout this book's first three chapters, businesses also can employ Web services to communicate with other businesses. B2B Web services implementations extend data and application integration beyond corporate firewalls, enabling companies to share data and business processes with partners, suppliers, distributors and corporate clients. Using Web services, partners can gain access to each other's applications and data, which improves collaboration and strengthens relationships between businesses. Readers should note that deploying inter-organizational Web services can raise significant concerns regarding security and Quality of Service (QoS). We discuss QoS in Chapter 3, Web Services Business Models; security is examined in Chapter 11, Computer and Internet Security, and Chapter 12, Web Services Security.

A particularly significant B2B integration scenario involves using Web services to connect every member of a *supply chain*—i.e., a network of organizations involved in creating a particular product or service. A typical supply chain might include businesses that procure raw materials, businesses that process those materials into intermediate and finished products, businesses that transport and distribute the product during various production stages and businesses that market and sell the final product to customers (Fig. 4.4). *Supply-chain management (SCM)* organizes all these supply-chain members to better coordinate daily business interactions—including procurement, transactions, production and distribution.[53]

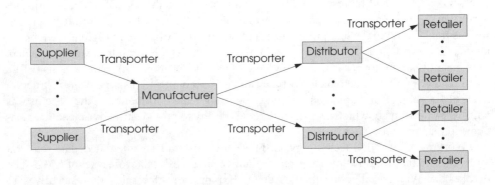

Fig. 4.4   Manufacturing supply-chain example.

Historically, integrating an entire supply chain's computing systems required every participant to adopt the same computing platform or integration solution. Since many supply-chain members interact with numerous different supply chains, true integration was expensive and, in most cases, impractical. Web services enhance the possibility for supply-chain integration by providing a relatively inexpensive, standardized method of platform-independent communication among applications.[54]

Integration improves a supply chain's ability to perform basic transactions—such as placing orders and confirming delivery times—over the Web or a shared network, instead of by fax or phone. This increases efficiency while reducing communications costs.[55] Moreover, businesses can package components of their applications as Web services, then allow suppliers and distributors to access those components directly. For example, imagine that a manufacturer exposes its inventory applications as a set of Web services and places the Web services in a private ebXML or UDDI registry (discussed in Chapter 7, UDDI, Discovery and Web Services Registries). Suppliers would use the registry to access the manufacturer's inventory system, then analyze the inventory data to determine when the manufacturer will need a new shipment of raw materials. This type of collaboration decreases uncertainty in the supply chain—if suppliers can determine when the manufacturer will need additional materials, the suppliers can deliver those materials at the exact time they are needed.[56] This enables the manufacturer to maintain less inventory of extra materials. Since storing inventory can cost up to 40 percent of the inventory's value, lowering inventories can result in significant savings.[57]

Web services can improve an organization's relationships with partners in similar ways. Through Web services, partners can create more flexible pricing contracts for complementary products or services. For example, most travel agencies maintain affiliations with hotels, airlines, car-rental agencies and tour groups. If a travel agency's computing system can communicate with partners' applications via Web services, the travel agency 's system can incorporate the most up-to-date prices for various travel and accommodation services. This enables the travel agency to adjust vacation-package costs to reflect fluctuations in air-travel, hotel and tour prices.[58]

As we discussed in Section 4.5, partners can link their CRM applications to exchange and share information about customers and purchasing patterns. This enables both partners to create more complete customer profiles, which improves customer service and facilitates the creation of personalized marketing campaigns. Partners also can employ Web services to notify each other automatically about new products or services, press releases and other business-critical information. In addition, Web services can be used to integrate partners' e-commerce applications. For instance, by using Web services to connect to a partner's purchasing application, an e-business can sell the partner's products or services through its own Web site. An example of this is the Web services implementation developed by Dollar Rent A Car and SouthWest Airlines, which we discussed in Chapter 3, Web Services Business Models.

In some cases, Web services can even enable partners and supply chains to automate B2B transactions. Automation involves one company's application or Web service accessing another company's Web service to request a particular business function, such as ordering materials or billing for services rendered. To enable automation, an application is programmed to perform certain actions on the basis of pre-established criteria—for example, if a sweater manufacturer's inventory of wool falls below a certain quantity, the application would contact the wool supplier and order additional materials. This type of automation theoretically can reduce costs by limiting the human intervention necessary to perform business tasks. For more information on supply-chain Web services implementations and B2B automation, see the feature, Case Study: Alliance Airlines.[59]

Business culture must evolve significantly before automation of B2B transactions becomes commonplace. Many companies are not comfortable allowing computers to make business-critical decisions.[60] Managers worry that Web services do not yet provide sufficient security or QoS assurances. For example, what if an automated ordering system malfunctions and purchases the same supplies twice? To address these concerns, software vendors and standards organizations are developing XML-based business-process-management technologies, which help organizations define rules for secure, reliable, automated B2B transactions. We discuss many of these standards—including ebXML, Business Transaction Protocol (BTP) and Web Services Flow Language (WSFL)—in Chapter 5, Web Services and Derivative Technologies.

Case Study: Alliance Airlines

Alliance Airlines (**www.allianceairlines.com**) provides airline cargo-handling and scheduled interline road feeder services to over 110 international airline carriers.[61] In 2001, Alliance handled approximately 20,000 aircraft movements and 700 million pounds of cargo. However, before adopting Web services, Alliance's computing infrastructure was impeding the company's growth. Various Alliance departments used applications that ran on different platforms; these applications could not communicate with each other or with members of the company's supply chain. Company employees were forced to input data manually, which reduced efficiency and caused errors.[62]

Alliance hired SilverStream Software (discussed in Chapter 8, Web Services Platforms, Vendors and Strategies) to improve interdepartmental and supply-chain communication. Using Web services technology, SilverStream connected Alliance's various computing systems, allowing data to flow among applications. The *SilverStream eXtend™* product suite enabled Alliance to develop 3A Track, a system through which Alliance's employees and supply-chain members can learn the status of cargo shipments. 3A Track traces the location of all cargo and communicates directly with airlines' and trucking companies' computing systems, providing real-time updates when shipments depart and arrive.

As a result of this upgrade, Alliance's clients have direct access to status information, which improves Alliance's relationships with its customers. Web services have improved the company's billing and accounting systems, enabling Alliance to eliminate many billing errors and shorten its billing cycle from 70 to 30 days.[63] Alliance's Web service implementation has also created a new revenue stream for the company. Prior to implementing Web services, Alliance was unable to charge fees for holding cargo at storage locations, because the company could not accurately track how long freight was stored. However, with 3A Track, detailed status information is available on all cargo. This enables Alliance to enforce service and storage fees.[64]

4.7 Summary

Web services can improve corporate-software development by reducing the time and expense involved in developing a software application. Instead of designing software "from scratch," programmers use registries to locate existing Web services, then incorporate those services into applications. However, Web services are not ideal for every software-development project. Web services security and QoS protocols are not fully developed, and Web services are not recommended for systems that handle a large number of transactions. Companies should implement Web services slowly, beginning with internal integration projects or services shared among a limited number of trusted partners.

Companies traditionally integrated applications via point-to-point connections (direct connections between two systems). More recently, organizations have invested in Enterprise Application Integration (EAI)—infrastructures that link multiple applications and databases so that they can share information and business processes. EAI is complicated and expensive, and EAI's custom interfaces are not reusable. Web services are less complex to develop and maintain than are most EAI systems, which means that integration projects require less time and money. Web services also allow companies to break applications into separate units, which makes integration more efficient.

Corporate portals are browser-based applications that offer single-access points to information or applications aggregated from disparate sources. Companies usually implement corporate portals to improve communication with customers, partners and employees. As the technology evolves, portals will use Web services to supply users with personalized information. Web services also can be used to link portals with disparate applications and data sources.

Customer-relationship management (CRM) encompasses every aspect of interaction between an organization and its customers—including sales, service and support. An effective CRM strategy combines technology and marketing to help companies better understand their customers, identify profitable customers, resolve customers' concerns, target customers with appropriate promotions and automate customer-service tasks. Web services can provide a less expensive method of integrating customer data. Since Web services employ open standards, companies can more easily integrate their own customer data with that of partners. This allows organizations to develop more complete customer profiles, which helps marketing departments target customers with appropriate advertisements and promotions.

B2B Web services implementations extend data and application integration beyond corporate firewalls, enabling companies to share data and business processes with partners, suppliers, distributors and corporate clients. Using Web services, partners can gain access to each other's applications and data, which improves collaboration and strengthens relationships between businesses. A particularly significant B2B integration scenario involves using Web services to connect every member of a supply chain. Web services enhance the possibility for supply-chain integration by providing a relatively inexpensive, standardized method of platform-independent communication among applications.

Web services also can improve an organization's relationships with partners. Through Web services, partners can create more flexible pricing contracts for complementary products or services. Web services can be used to integrate partners' e-commerce applications. In addition, partners can employ Web services to notify each other automatically about new products or services, press releases and other business-critical information. In some cases, Web services can even enable partners and supply chains to automate B2B transactions.

4.8 Internet and Web Resources

www.webservices.org/index.php/article/articleview/102/1/20
This article summarizes the results of a Jupiter Media Metrix survey in which businesses revealed their plans to deploy Web services over the next year.

www.webservicesarchitect.com/content/articles/samtani01.asp
The authors of this *Web Services Architect* article introduce basic EAI concepts and discuss how Web services can improve integration projects.

www.adtmag.com/article.asp?id=6403
In this article, the author relates various companies' experiences with Web services-enabled integration projects. The article is designed to help companies determine whether to adopt Web services for integration.

www.informationweek.com/731/31erall.htm
This *InformationWeek* article examines the benefits of corporate portals.

www.oasis-open.org/cover/wsui.html
This *XML Cover Pages* article discusses the WSUI initiative to standardize implementation of corporate portals.

www.oasis-open.org/committees/wsia/
This OASIS site provides information about the Web Services for Interactive Applications initiative, which currently is under development by an OASIS technical committee. The site also contains links to related documents and press releases.

www.oasis-open.org/committees/wsrp/
This OASIS site provides information about the Web Services for Remote Portals initiative. The site provides an overview of WSRP and contains links to relevant documents and press releases.

wwww.eaijournal.com/Article.asp?ArticleID=422&DepartmentID=1
This article from *eAI Journal* overviews how to integrate CRM technologies into existing corporate software.

www.ittoolbox.com/help/crmoverview.asp
A brief overview of CRM is provided in this IT Toolbox article. The article overviews the history of CRM, explains CRM's importance and provides statistics on the expected growth rate of CRM-enabled technologies.

silmaril.smeal.psu.edu/misc/supply_chain_intro.html
Written by professors at Penn State University, this article overviews supply-chain management and how businesses can make intelligent supply-chain decisions.

www.webservicesarchitect.com/content/articles/samtani02print.asp
This article defines business-to-business integration (B2Bi) and the role that Web services can play in integrating with partners, suppliers and customers.

www.zdnet.com/filters/printerfriendly/0,6061,2852816-92,00.html
The author of this article examines how companies can use Web services technology to improve relationships with partners.

www.microsoft.com/net/use/casestudies.asp
This site provides links Microsoft Web services case studies. Each case study describes how a particular company or organization is using Microsoft technology to build and maintain Web services.

www-4.ibm.com/software/solutions/webservices/casestudies/
This site provides links to IBM Web services case studies. Each case study describes how a particular company or organization is using IBM technology to build and maintain Web services.

WORKS CITED

1. J. McCarthy, "A Platform for Developers," *InfoWorld* 27 May 2002: 52.

2. P. Fingar, "Web Services Among Peers," *Internet World* January 2002: 21.

3. J. Webster, "Will Web Services Do The Trick?" *InternetWeek* 10 April 2001 <www.internetweek.com/indepth01/indepth041001.htm>.

4. J. Ambrosio, "Web Services: Report from the Field," *Application Development Trends* June 2002: 28.

5. J. Hagel, J. Brown and D. Layton-Rodin, "Go Slowly with Web Services," *CIO* 15 February 2002: 40.

6. Report Suggests Only 23% of Companies Plan Not to Use Web Services," 5 March 2002 <www.webservices.org/index.php/article/articleview/102/1/20>.

7. G. Samtani and D. Sadhwani, "EAI and Web Services: Easier Enterprise Application Integration?" 17 October 2001 <www.webservicesarchitect.com/content/articles/samtani01.asp>.

8. G. Samtani and D. Sadhwani, "EAI and Web Services: Easier Enterprise Application Integration?" 17 October 2001 <www.webservicesarchitect.com/content/articles/samtani01.asp>.

9. T. Yager, "The Windows Way to Web Services," *InfoWorld* 10 January 2002 <www.infoworld.com/articles/tc/xml/02/01/14/020114tcmicrosoft.xml>.

10. J. Ambrosio, "Web Services: Report from the Field," *Application Development Trends* June 2002: 25.

11. H. Harreld, "EAI Seeks to Remold," *InfoWorld* 1 April 2002: 33.

12. J. Ambrosio, "Web Services: Report from the Field," *Application Development Trends* June 2002: 26.

13. G. Samtani and D. Sadhwani, "EAI and Web Services: Easier Enterprise Application Integration?" 17 October 2001 <www.webservicesarchitect.com/content/articles/samtani01.asp>.

14. D. Rubinstein, "Web Services: EAI's Newest Battleground," *Software Development Times* 15 June 2002: 23.

15. H. Harreld, "EAI Seeks to Remold," *InfoWorld* 1 April 2002: 34.

16. "British Telecom and Web Services," *Cape Clear Software Case Study* <www.capeclear.com/customers/BT_and_CC.pdf>.

17. M. Migliore, "British Telecom Testing on Web Services Platform," 28 December 2001 <esj.com/webservices/news/print.asp?EditorialsID=93>.

18. "British Telecom and Web Services," *Cape Clear Software Case Study* <www.capeclear.com/customers/BT_and_CC.pdf>.

19. J. Zipperer, "Calling For Web Services: British Telecom Looks to XML to Meet Integration Challenge," *Internet World* December 2001: 54.

20. S. Patton, "Web Services in the Real World," *CIO Magazine* 1 April 2002 <www.cio.com/archive/040102/real_content.html>.

21. S. Patton, "Web Services in the Real World," *CIO Magazine* 1 April 2002 <www.cio.com/archive/040102/real_content.html>.

22. S. Johnston, "State of Web Services," *InfoWorld* 1 February 2002 <www.infoworld.com/articles/pl/xml/02/02/04/020204plwebstate.xml>.

23. R. Karpinksi, "Web Services Crack App Integration Nut," *Internet Week* 12 November 2001: 44.

24. M. Santosus, "Portal Power," *CIO* 19 February 2002 `<www.cio.com/knowledge/edit/k021902_portal.html>`.

25. C. Moore, "Take it All with You," *InfoWorld* October 2001 `<www.infoworld.com/articles/fe/xml/01/10/29/011029feportal.xml>`.

26. "What is a Portlet?" `<www.3-ibm.com/softwarewebservers/portal/portlet.html>`.

27. M. Santosus and J. Surmacz, "The ABCs of Knowledge Management," *CIO* `<www.cio.com/research/knowledge/edit/kmasbs.html>`.

28. J. Mears, "Vendors Bolster Portal Intelligence," *Network World* 15 April 2002 `<www.nwfusion.com/news/2002/131646_04-15-2002.html>`.

29. C. Moore, "Take it All with You," *InfoWorld* October 2001 `<www.infoworld.com/articles/fe/xml/01/10/29/011029feportal.xml>`.

30. R. Cover, "The XML Cover Pages: Web Services User Interface (WSUI) Initiative," November 2001 `<www.oasis-open.org/cover/wsui.html>`.

31. "OASIS Web Services for Interactive Applications TC," `<www.oasis-open.org/committees/wsia>`.

32. "OASIS Web Services for Remote Portals (WSRP) Technical Committee Purpose," `<www.oasis-open.org/committees/wsrp/charter.shtml>`.

33. "About Us," `<www.standardandpoors.com/AboutUs/index.html>`.

34. K. Cassie, "S&P Turns Java Beans into Web Services," 22 March 2002 `<techupdate.zdnet.com/techupdate/stories/main/014179,2855469,00.html>`.

35. R. Karpinski, "S&P's Web Services Play," *InternetWeek* 11 November 2001 `<www.internetweek.com/transtoday/ttoday110101.htm>`.

36. L. Liebermann, "Know Your Web Sites Inside & Out," *InternetWeek* 1 January 2002 `<www.internetweek.com/indepth02/indepth010202.htm>`.

37. "ITToolbox CRM Overview," `<www.ittoolbox.com/help/crmoverview.asp>`.

38. C. Saunders, "No Integration, No CRM," *eAI Journal* 24 September 2001 `<www.eaijournal.com/Article.asp?ArticleID=422&DepartmentID=1>`.

39. P. Krill, "CRM Seeks Web Exposure," *InfoWorld* 11 March 2002: 35.

40. A. Mello, "When CRM and Web Services Collide," 3 April 2002 `<techupdate.zdnet.com/techupdate/stories/main/0,14179,2859862,00.html>`.

41. R. Whiting, "Web Services Take Integration to a New Level," *InformationWeek*, 15 April 2002 `<www.informationweek.com/story/IWK20020411S0009>`.

42. A. Mello, "When CRM and Web Services Collide," 3 April 2002 `<techupdate.zdnet.com/techupdate/stories/main/0,14179,2859862,00.html>` .

43. R.Whiting "Web Services Take Integration to a New Level," *InformationWeek* 15 April 2002 `<www.informationweek.com/story/IWK20020411S0009>`.

44. E. Kinikin, "CRM and Web Services," *Line56* 9 April 2002 `<www.line56.com/print/default.asp?ArticleID=3541>`.

45. "Putnam Lovell Securities, Inc.," *Grand Central Communications Case Study* `<www.grand-central.com/services/cs_putnam_lovell.html>`.

46. "**Salesforce.com**'s XML Interface Enables Putnam Lovell Securities's Web Services Strategy," *salesforce.com Case Study* <**www.salesforce.com/us/customers/ casestudy.jsp?name=putnamlovell**>.

47. E. Corcoran, "Web Repair," *Forbes* 29 October 2001: 83.

48. E. Corcoran, "Web Repair" *Forbes* 29 October 2001: 84.

49. P. Buxbaum, "XML Stars in First Act of Investment Bank's Web Services Strategy," 12 November 2001 <**searchebusiness.techtarget.com/ originalContent/0,289142,sid19_gci780837,00.html**>.

50. "Microsoft Uses .NET to Unlock Customer Data for Sales Teams," April 2002 <**www.microsoft.com/business/casestudies/net/microsoft_ssit.asp**>.

51. "Microsoft Uses .NET to Unlock Customer Data for Sales Teams," April 2002 <**www.microsoft.com/business/casestudies/net/microsoft_ssit.asp**>.

52. "Microsoft Uses .NET to Unlock Customer Data for Sales Teams," April 2002 <**www.microsoft.com/business/casestudies/net/microsoft_ssit.asp**>.

53. R. Ganeshan and T. Harrison, "An Introduction to Supply-Chain Management," <**silmaril.smeal.psu.edu/misc/supply_chain_intro.html**>.

54. G. Samtani and D. Sadhawani, "B2Bi and Web Services: An Intimidating Task?" 2 January 2002 <**www.webservicesarchitect.com/content/ articles/samtani02print.asp**>.

55. S. Durchslag, "Beyond the Hype... The Reality of Early Web Services Adoption," *Web Services Journal* March 2002: 30.

56. J. Lewis, "Web Services Should Unlock Potential of B2B Connectivity," *InternetWeek* 30 July 2001: 23.

57. R. Ganeshan and T. Harrison, "An Introduction to Supply-Chain Management," <**silmaril.smeal.psu.edu/misc/supply_chain_intro.html**>.

58. A. Mello, "Getting Down to Business with Web Services," 6 March 2002 <**www.zdnet.com/filters/printerfriendly/0,6061,2852816-92,00.html**>.

59. J. Borck, "Web Services Integration to Automate Supply-Chain Management," *InfoWorld* 20 April 2001 <**www.itworld.com/AppDev/4162/IWD010423opborck/**>.

60. A. Mello, "Getting down to business with Web services," March 2002 <**www.zdnet.com/ filters/printerfriendly/0,6061,2852816-92,00.html**>.

61. "The Evolution of Alliance Airlines," <**www.allianceairlines.com/backgrnd/ backgrnd_1.html**>.

62. L. Ellingson, "Transforming Alliance Airlines' Business Operations," *Web Services Journal* January 2002: 57.

63. "Alliance Airlines Transforms Business Operations Using SilverStream eXtend Software," *Business Wire* 15 October 2001 <**industry.java.sun.com/javanews/stories/ print/0,1797,39487,00.html**>.

64. L. Ellingson, "Transforming Alliance Airlines' Business Operations," *Web Services Journal* January 2002: 56.

RECOMMENDED READING

Ambrosio, J. "Web Services: Report from the Field," *Application Development Trends* June 2002: 28.

Borck, J.R. "Web Services Integration To Automate Supply Chain Management," *InfoWorld* 20 April 2001 <**www.itworld.com/AppDev/4162/IWD010423opborck**>.

Donato, C., S. Durchslag and J. Hagel. "Web Services: Enabling the Collaborative Enterprise," 29 October 2001 <**e-serv.ebizq.net/wbs/donato_1a.html**>.

Falla, J. "Much Ado About Web Services," *e-Business Advisor* July/August 2001: 9.

Karinski, R. "Web Services Crack App Integration Nut," *Internet Week* 12 November 2001: 1, 44, 47.

Lewis, J. "Web Services Should Unlock Potential of B2B Connectivity," *Internet Week* 30 July 2001: 23.

McDougall, P. "Decoding Web Services," *Information Week* 1 October 2001: 28, 84–86.

Mello, A. "Getting down to business with Web services," March 2002 <**www.zdnet.com/ filters/printerfriendly/0,6061,2852816-92,00.html**>.

Saunders, C. "No Integration, No CRM," 24 September 2001 <**www.waijournal.com/ Article.asp?ArticleID=422&DepartmentID=1**>.

Samtani, G., and D. Sadhwani. "EAI and Web Services: Easier Enterprise Application Integration?" 17 October 2001 <**www.webservicesarchitect.com/content/articles/ samtani01.asp**>.

Trott, B. "Web Services to Enhance CRM," 4 May 2001 <**www.itworld.com/AppDev/4162/ IWD010507hnwebcrm/pfindex.html**>.

Wreden, N. "From Chaos to Cooperation," *Enterprise Systems* October 2001: 53–58.

XML and Derivative Technologies

- To become familiar with XML.
- To understand how XML forms the basis of key Web services standards.
- To explore XML-based business-process technologies—including ebXML, BPML and BTP.
- To overview XML markup.
- To introduce XML concepts—including DTDs, schemas and namespaces.

Proper words in proper places make the true definition of a style.
Jonathan Swift

Let us make distinctions, call things by the right names.
Henry David Thoreau

What signifies knowing the Names, if you know not the Nature of Things.
Benjamin Franklin

If names be not correct, language is not in accordance with the truth of things. If language be not in accordance with the truth of things, affairs cannot be carried on to success.
Confucius

Outline

5.1 Introduction

The terms Web services and *XML Web services* often are used interchangeably, illustrating Web services' dependence on the *Extensible Markup Language (XML)*. In fact, Web services in its current form would not exist without XML. XML provides Web services with a markup technology that is platform-independent, flexible and extensible. All of the core Web services standards—SOAP, WSDL and UDDI—are based on XML.

The treatment of XML in this book is divided into two parts—this chapter, and Appendix A, Introduction to XML Markup, which provides markup examples and explanations of the markup. This chapter examines XML and XML-derivative technologies relevant to Web services. We detail the history of XML and discuss the W3C—the organization that oversees XML's development. We present a conceptual technology stack that illustrates how technologies use underlying standards—in this chapter, how XML supports the Web services architecture. We introduce key technical aspects of XML, including elements, attributes, namespaces, DTDs and schemas.[1] The chapter concludes by overviewing XML-based business-process technologies that incorporate Web services.

---

1. Although this chapter overviews certain technical concepts, we present XML in depth in Appendix A, Introduction to XML Markup.

5.2 History of Extensible Markup Language (XML)

In the late 1960s, communications between computer systems at IBM were hindered by a profusion of different file formats. IBM researchers Charles Goldfarb, Edward Mosher and Raymond Lorie addressed the problem by building a powerful, yet portable, system for exchanging and manipulating documents. The researchers realized that a system-independent, common way of describing data would best facilitate communication. They decided to use a *markup language* as the basis of their system. A markup language is not a programming language; rather, it is a way of tagging data to identify the structure and/or describe the data of a document.[1] The IBM team's prototype language described data, rather than how that data should be formatted. The formatting information was located in separate files called *style sheets*, which computers use to format the data and render a finished document. This method of structuring data made it possible to repurpose information for a wide variety of client applications.

Documents could be processed reliably, the IBM team realized, only if the documents were structured correctly—i.e., if they conformed to a *syntax* (a specific format that conforms to the rules defined by a grammar). However, it would be time consuming and error-prone for a programmer to look at a document containing markup and determine that the document was correct and complete. The researchers needed a system that could recognize *valid* documents (i.e., documents that were structured correctly) and reject invalid documents (such as documents with missing or extraneous data). To automate document processing, a technology called *Document Type Definition (DTD)* was developed to specify the correct rules to which a document must adhere for that document to be correct. A system then processes and verifies the document against these rules. A document that conforms to a DTD is a *valid document*. Documents that do not conform to DTDs, but are syntactically correct, are called *well-formed documents*. DTDs are used to verify that documents are correct and allow machines to process the documents quickly and reliably. We discuss DTDs and the technology that is replacing DTDs, *XML Schema*, in Section 5.10.1

By 1969, the IBM research team had developed a language with all of these capabilities, called the *Generalized Markup Language (GML)*. In 1974, Goldfarb proved that a *parser* (i.e., software capable of analyzing the structure and syntax of a document) was easy to create and could validate a GML document. The use of parsers to validate documents furthered the development of GML, eventually leading to the 1986 adoption of the *Standard Generalized Markup Language (SGML)* as an International Organization for Standardization (ISO) standard. (We discussed ISO in Chapter 2, Web Services: A New Computing Paradigm.) SGML quickly became the worldwide business standard for data storage and interchange. The *Document Style Semantics and Specification Language (DSSSL)*, another ISO standard, standardized the creation of style sheets used for SGML documents.[2]

In 1989, Tim Berners-Lee of CERN (the European Organization for Nuclear Physics) began to develop a technology for sharing information via hyperlinked text documents. Berners-Lee based his new language on SGML and called it the *HyperText Markup Language (HTML)*. He also wrote communication protocols, such as HTTP, to form the backbone of his new hypertext information system, which he termed the *World Wide Web*.[3]

As the popularity of the Web exploded in the 1990s, HTML's limitations became apparent. Although HTML was created as a common format for the Web, HTML's lack of *extensibility* (the ability to change or add features) frustrated developers, and the lack of correctly structured documents allowed erroneous HTML to proliferate. Browser vendors attempting to gain market share created platform-specific *tags,* which are names enclosed in angle brackets, as HTML extensions. This forced Web developers to support multiple browsers, which significantly complicated Web development. To address these and other problems, the W3C developed XML.[4]

XML combines the power and extensibility of its parent language, SGML, with simplicity.[5] XML is a *meta-language*—a language used as a basis for other languages—that offers a high level of extensibility. Using XML, the W3C created the *Extensible HyperText Markup Language (XHTML)*, an XML *vocabulary* (i.e., an XML-based markup language that is developed for a specific industry or purpose) that provides a common, extensible format for the Web. XHTML is expected to replace HTML. The W3C also developed the *Extensible Stylesheet Language (XSL)*, which is composed of several technologies, to manipulate data in XML documents for presentation purposes. XSL provides developers the flexibility to transform data from an XML document into other types of documents— for example, Web pages or reports. In addition to serving as the basis for other markup languages, developers use XML for data interchange and e-commerce systems.[6] At the time of this writing, there were more than 450 XML standards.[7]

Unlike many technologies, which begin as proprietary solutions and become standards, XML was defined as an open, standard technology. XML's development has been supervised by the W3C's *XML Working Group*, which prepared the XML specification and approved it for publication. In 1998, the XML version 1.0 specification (**www.w3.org/ TR/REC-xml**) was accepted as a *W3C Recommendation*. This means that the technology is stable for wide deployment in industry.

The W3C continues to oversee the development of XML, as well as SOAP and WSDL. Other standardization organizations and vendor consortia also are developing XML-derived languages and Web services technologies—for example, the *Internet Engineering Task Force (IETF,* **www.ietf.org***)* is working with the W3C on the development of SOAP and the *Organization for the Advancement of Structured Information Standards (OASIS,* **www.oasis-open.org***)*, is developing Electronic Business XML (ebXML), Business Transaction Protocol (BTP) and Universal Business Language (UBL), which we discuss in Sections 5.6, 5.7 and 5.10, respectively.

5.3 Web Services Technology Stack

Bill Smith, the director of Sun Microsystems' *XML Technology Center*, introduced the concept of a *Web services technology stack* at a *2001 XML One/Web Services One conference* keynote speech. Technology stacks illustrate how technologies build on other technologies. Typically, the bottom layers in a technology stack support lower-level computer processing and transport details—for example, the Internet transport protocol, TCP/IP, is part of the lowest layer in the Web services stack. Technologies higher in the stack use the lower-level technologies, but "hide" the more technical details from the programmer. Developers creating applications using technologies higher in a stack usually can develop programs quickly and without having to understand all the lower-layers' underlying details. Although the computer industry does not formally recognize the Web services technology stack, the illustration demonstrates the underlying technologies that support Web services and other XML technologies.[8]

The organizations that developed Web services based the new paradigm on well-understood, widely implemented technologies. Internet and Web protocols (e.g., TCP/IP and HTTP, respectively) form the foundational layer for Web services (Fig. 5.1). The next layer contains the core XML-processing technologies, which include XML and associated technologies, such as XSL, DTDs and XML Schema.

The next layer introduces *horizontal XML vocabularies*. Horizontal vocabularies provide functionality that can be used across industries. An example of a horizontal vocabulary is *Electronic Business XML (ebXML)*, which is a framework for enabling global e-business. EbXML uses XML to define, and subsequently automate, business processes. Developers and industry consortia are building consensus for such technologies. It is expected that Web services will be deployed in business processes described by horizontal vocabularies.

The technologies that enable Web services compose the layer above the XML horizontal vocabularies. XML markup provides platform independence and interoperability for the Web services' messaging standard—the Simple Object Access Protocol (SOAP). Web Services Description Language (WSDL), the technology that describes Web services, is an XML vocabulary. UDDI registries use XML to mark up data about businesses and their Web services.

The top layer contains *vertical languages*, which are XML-based technologies that define specific processes for a single industry or group of industries. Although many industries share common processes, which can be described in horizontal vocabularies, each industry also supports unique processes and products. For example, all industries send invoices, but the products and product specifications contained in the invoices are different. The RosettaNet consortium defines a vertical language for information-technology industries (see RosettaNet feature).[9]

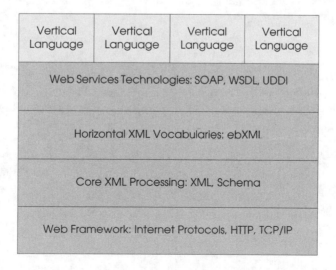

RosettaNet

RosettaNet (**www.rosettanet.org**) is a non-profit consortium that is developing an e-business framework to define business processes for the information-technology, electronics and semiconductor industries. More than 400 companies are members of the organization, including American Express, Intel, Cisco Systems, Hewlett-Packard, IBM, Microsoft, National Semiconductor and Nokia. RosettaNet is creating open standards so that members of a supply chain can coordinate and align their processes to conduct e-business more efficiently.[10]

To accomplish the goal of enhanced e-business, RosettaNet has developed dictionaries and frameworks that help companies implement business-process standards. RosettaNet plans to define approximately 10,000 terms used in the information-technology, electronics and semiconductor industries, such as price, end user and confirmation number. This set of definitions provides the core properties for the RosettaNet *Partner Interface Processes (PIPs)*. PIPs are XML specifications that describe processes and business documents that are shared between business partners. Using PIPs, developers implement RosettaNet-compliant applications. RosettaNet categorizes hundreds of PIPs for processes into eight clusters:

- Administration

- Partner, Product and Services Review

- Product Information

- Order Management

- Inventory Management

- Marketing and Information Management

- Service and Support

- Manufacturing

The *RosettaNet Implementation Framework (RNIF)* is a specification that describes how RosettaNet partners exchange information. The RNIF provides information on packaging, routing and transmitting *PIP messages*—the electronic messages that RosettaNet business processes use to communicate. The consortium has adopted the ebXML framework for the RNIF. We discuss ebXML in Section 5.5.[11]

Intel and several other RosettaNet members are implementing RosettaNet standards to communicate with business partners. For example, National Semiconductor, a computer chip manufacturer with $2.1 billion in sales, implemented a RosettaNet framework to simplify customer searches of the National Semiconductor extensive product database.[12] To encourage additional member companies to implement RosettaNet systems, RosettaNet has launched a *Basics Program* that simplifies the process of applying RosettaNet technologies to business systems.[13] Vendors, such as NEC Systems, also are developing products that integrate RosettaNet standards and technologies.[14]

Horizontal vocabularies are some of the most talked-about emerging technologies. Smith remarked in his keynote that XML developers need to learn about and become involved in XML business-process technologies.[15] The next section discusses various business-process technologies and how each incorporates Web services and/or Web services technologies.

5.4 XML Technologies that Enable Business-Processing Systems

Organizations and industries are developing various XML-based technologies that define business processes to help solve real-world business issues. For example, many people have experienced the frustration of contacting companies to correct personal data, such as a shipping address. When erroneous information exists between business partners, shipments are not received, and invoices are not paid promptly. When using XML-based business-process systems, all data must be validated by either a DTD or a schema. This means that, if information is missing, the document will not be processed, and, therefore, incorrect information will not enter a system. Of course, certain types of data can be mis-entered and accepted by an XML-based system, but DTDs and schemas will reduce the amount of erroneous information that enters an organization.[16]

However, simply marking up documents in XML does not guarantee that the files are available for transactions; business partners must establish sets of business rules that every partner implements. Participating organizations must collaborate on standardizing the markup and processes. The following sections discuss the technologies that define and automate business processes among organizations and across industries. One popular XML-based business-process technology we do not include is Microsoft's BizTalk™, which we examine in Chapter 9, .NET Web Services: A Conceptual Overview. Many of the technologies explicitly describe incorporating Web services and its related technologies, such as SOAP, WSDL and UDDI, into the processes.

It is crucial to understand that the technologies we describe in this section are specifications, rather than applications. Although many of the technologies define specific XML vocabularies, the technologies neither include explicit programming instructions nor restrict developers to a specific programming language, such as Visual Basic® .NET, Java or C#. The technologies also do not specify the types of platforms (such as UNIX®, Windows® or Linux) that should implement the systems.

5.5 ebXML

Electronic Business XML (ebXML) is an open, XML-based infrastructure that enables global companies to conduct reliable, interoperable e-business.[17] As we described in Chapter 2, Web Services: A New Computing Paradigm, ebXML was created by a joint initiative of OASIS and UN/CEFACT. Industry support for the ebXML technology includes companies, industry consortia (such as RosettaNet and the Korean Institute for Electronic Commerce) and individuals from more than 30 countries.[18]

EbXML offers a set of specifications that defines an alternative to Electronic Data Interchange (EDI) systems. EbXML allows businesses of various sizes to partner and conduct global business-to-business transactions using XML and the Internet. Although EDI offers many of these capabilities, EDI generally is restricted to larger companies, because of its costs. EDI, however, forms a basis for ebXML—EDI systems have been implemented since the 1960s and have defined and automated many business processes and ebXML uses these processes. A business process details the roles and responsibilities that a business partner must fulfill in a business collaboration.[19]

Corporations that have large investments in EDI systems do not want to abandon their EDI infrastructures. EbXML addresses this issue by providing a framework in which organizations can maintain existing EDI systems while incorporating ebXML so that they begin trading with other ebXML adopters. With ebXML, organizations exchange business messages, maintain trading relationships, define and register business processes and transfer data using a set of specifications that describe the implementation of such systems.[20]

This section examines the key components of the ebXML framework—business-partner information, business-process and information modeling, *core components* (i.e., reusable business processes), ebXML *registries* (also called the *registries/repositories*) and the *ebXML Messaging Service*. EbXML registries support discovery mechanisms, which allow users to locate specific documents. We discuss this capability in detail in Chapter 7, UDDI, Discovery and Web Services Registries. For additional information about ebXML, visit **www.ebxml.org**.

5.5.1 Trading Partners

Organizations involved in ebXML transactions are called *trading partners*. EbXML defines two document types that contain trading partner-information—*Collaboration Protocol Profiles (CPPs)* and *Collaboration Protocol Agreements (CPAs)*. CPPs and CPAs are XML documents that provide a standard, portable way of describing companies' services. CPPs contain information about a trading partner's capabilities—including business collaboration and business-information exchange. XML elements in a CPP describe information about the types of agreements that the trading partner is willing to accept, information for exchanging and transporting documents and the characteristics of messages, such as security and reliability. CPAs contain information about business collaborations, including the seller's business processes and message-exchange capabilities, as well as the buying processes of the buyer. A business process also can provide constraints for using ebXML core components and can include a framework for creating CPAs.[21]

When two or more trading partners want to conduct business, the partners negotiate a CPA. The CPA is a combination of the participating businesses' CPPs and is an agreement to transact business. The CPA describes the specific messaging service and business-process requirements to which the trading partners agree. A CPA must be updated if aspects of an agreement change after the CPA has been formed and accepted. Together, CPPs and CPAs are similar to the *trading-partner agreements* of EDI systems. Trading partners can register their CPAs in a searchable ebXML registry, but it is not mandatory. EbXML registries are discussed in further detail in this section.[22]

Figure 5.2 overviews the ebXML architecture. An ebXML registry, accessible via the Internet, stores CPPs, CPAs and other documents that contain information about businesses that support ebXML transactions. Trading Partner A, which stores its business information in the repository, searches the registry for a suitable trading partner. The search returns Trading Partner B's CPP, which documents Trading Partner B's ebXML capabilities and restrictions. Trading Partner A sends a request to Trading Partner B to engage in a business process using ebXML Message Service. Before the process begins, Trading Partner A submits a *business arrangement* proposal (i.e., CPA) to Trading Partner B's ebXML-compliant software. This proposal includes the intended business interaction(s) and agreements, as well as messaging requirements and security information. Trading Partner A and B negotiate the agreement. When trading partners agree on the CPA, the companies can begin the electronic business transaction using ebXML.[23]

5.5.2 Business Process and Information Modeling

To help an organization describe its business processes and scenarios in a CPP, ebXML offers a specification called the *Business Process and Information Meta Model.* Developers can use the Business Process and Information Meta Model to compose processes defined in CPPs. For example, some of the scenarios included in the Model describe how to define a business process, how to define a transaction and how to execute the process.[24]

A subset of the Business Process and Information Model is the *Business Process Specification Schema (BPSS).* The BPSS is a set of XML vocabularies and guidelines for creating applications that enable business systems to implement ebXML.[25] This schema declares the XML elements and attributes used to describe the business processes of ebXML.[26]

5.5.3 Core Components

The ebXML framework distills the aspects of business processes that are universal across most industries into reusable core components. Core components, which are stored in ebXML registries, are "building blocks" for common, reusable processes that developers use as a basis for CPPs. Developers can extend core components to create custom components specific to an organization's CPP. A core component can be a single piece of business information or can consist of a set of business information components.[27]

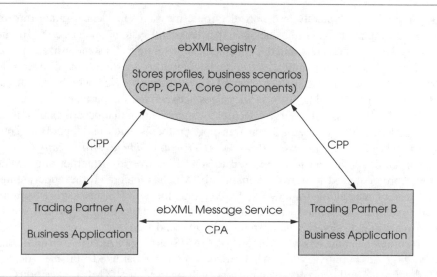

Fig. 5.2 ebXML architecture.

5.5.4 Registries

Much like UDDI registries, *ebXML registries* allow trading partners to store and share information. In fact, companies can define and register ebXML registries in UDDI registries. It is then possible to search for ebXML registries via UDDI registries.[28]

EbXML registries enable trading partners to learn about other trading partners and to share information. The registries store CPPs, CPAs, schemas, DTDs, business-process models and more. Also, registries include services that help companies form business agreements and perform business transactions. A business submits *Business Profile* information, which describes a company's ebXML capabilities and constraints, as well as the *business scenarios*—i.e., XML files that define how business activities are accomplished—that the company supports. The registry also stores reusable business collaboration definitions and business documents.

The ebXML registry can reside on a Web server or can be hosted by an application service provider (ASP) that distributes and manages services over a distributed-computing network from a central data source. Each item within the registry needs to be uniquely identified. To accomplish this, every item in a registry is assigned a *Unique Identifier (UID)*. UIDs can be assigned through several different methods. For example, a UID can be a reference, such as a *uniform resource identifier (URI)*, which represents the name or address of an object or a resource on a network—for example, a URL (such as **http://www.deitel.com**) is a type of URI. Using URIs as UIDs can ensure that each item has a unique reference. There are also identifiers called *Universally Unique Identifiers (UUIDs)*, which are used for global uniqueness within a registry. UUIDs are created by using a combination of the host's network address, a timestamp and a random, generated component. This combination guarantees that the UUID is unique.[29] When a user queries the registry via a UUID, only one result should be returned. This unique identification simplifies the process of querying registries.

5.5.5 Messaging Service

Messaging systems typically transport electronic messages that encapsulate information between trading partners. For businesses to participate in systems such as ebXML, the process of exchanging messages and documents must be reliable and standardized. To accomplish interoperable communication among computing systems in a decentralized, distributed network, ebXML offers the *ebXML Messaging Service*, which provides a standard method for exchanging business messages between trading partners.

The ebXML Messaging Service includes a specification that describes how to encapsulate ebXML messages for different transport protocols, such as HyperText Transport Protocol (HTTP), *File Transfer Protocol (FTP)* and *Simple Mail Transfer Protocol (SMTP)*. (Both HTTP and FTP are used to send files over the Internet and SMTP is a common protocol used to transfer e-mail.) EbXML has integrated the widely employed Web services messaging framework, SOAP, into the ebXML messaging system.[30] A SOAP envelope encapsulates ebXML information to send to a trading partner. We discuss SOAP in detail in Chapter 6, Understanding SOAP and WSDL.[31]

To complement the ebXML framework, OASIS has organized the *Universal Business Language (UBL)* initiative, which will produce a set of standardized e-business documents. UBL documents will be freely available and will be used in ebXML transactions, as well as in other business-to-business transactions. We discuss UBL in Section 5.9.

5.6 Business Transaction Protocol (BTP)

The OASIS *Business Transactions Technical Committee (BTTC,* **www.oasis-open.org***)* developed the XML-based *Business Transaction Protocol (BTP)* to work with existing business-messaging standards, including ebXML and RosettaNet, to coordinate and manage complex transactions between businesses using Web services or other B2B technology. Initial members of the BTTC were BEA Systems, Bowstreet, Interwoven and Sun Microsystems; newer members include Choreology (a transaction-processing vendor), Entrust (an Internet security solutions vendor), Hewlett-Packard, IONA (a Web services vendor), Oracle, SeeBeyond (an Enterprise Application Integration vendor) and Talking Blocks (a Web services vendor).[32] The complexity of the processes BTP defines has resulted in slow adoption of the technology; only a few companies—BEA, Hewlett-Packard, Choreology and Talking Blocks—have implemented the protocol in products and systems. For example, Hewlett-Packard has based their Web Services Transaction Server 1.0 on the BTP specification.[33] Updates to the specification can be found at **www.oasis-open.org/committees/business-transactions**.[34]

The protocol's goal is to define how organizations can coordinate their systems to achieve automated business transactions.[35] The BTP specification defines a transaction as the point at which the two business' processes, which are private, intersect to accomplish a goal (such as a transaction). The intersection becomes a *public* process.[36]

BTP describes a transaction as either an *atom* or a *cohesion*.[37] An atom takes part in a *two-phase commit transaction*—i.e., a process either fully commits to a transaction or *rolls back* (i.e., cancels) the transaction. A single Web services operation and the internal processes that support the operation is an example of an atom. However, many transactions are not this simple. Cohesion is a group of atoms that work as a unit to complete a transaction. Cohesion allows certain portions of transactions that involve multiple participants to fail without cancelling the transaction. This is applicable to many types of transactions. For example, when a customer purchases an item from a Web site, the order has to go to a warehouse, the customer's credit-card needs to be authorized and a shipping company needs to be notified of the pending shipment. The credit-card authorization might fail, but the order still can be sent to the warehouse to prepare the inventory to ship, and the authorization can be re-tried, rather than forcing the customer to begin the process again.[38]

5.7 Business Process Modeling Language (BPML) and Business Process Query Language (BPQL)

The *Business Process Management Initiative (BPMI,* **www.bpmi.org***)* is an organization with more than 130 members. BPMI was formed to promote the standardization of processes across applications, platforms and partners.[39] To manage processes, BPMI developed the *Business Process Modeling Language (BPML)*, which is a meta-language for modeling business processes, and the *Business Process Query Language (BPQL)*, which deploys processes.[40]

BPMI created BPML and BPQL using open standards, which facilitates integration with other technologies and systems, including SOAP, WSDL, ebXML and RosettaNet. BPML provides a method for describing business processes and to share business-process details using XML. Companies can use BPML to model, deploy and manage order, customer-care, demand-planning and product-development processes. Ultimately, BPMI will release a *Business Process Management System (BPMS)*—i.e., a framework for managing a system of integrated processes, from the strategic planning phase to implementation.[41]

BPML offers a model for businesses to communicate by exchanging messages. Certain messages support specific processes that are sent between participants. Message definitions use XML schemas to describe the structure and type of message content so that messages encapsulate the correct processing instructions.[42]

BPMI considers an e-business transaction to consist of at least three components. The first component is a *public interface*, which is the interaction shared by partners involved in a business process and is supported by RosettaNet and ebXML protocols. The remaining components are two *private implementations*—i.e., the proprietary processes that are specific to the partners that participate in the business interaction. Private implementations are defined by each company and can be described by any language, including BPML.[43]

Once the private implementation for a business process is developed, the private implementation must be deployed on a platform that can execute the process. BPMI developed BPQL to interact with a business-process-management infrastructure that includes a *process server*, which executes processes and a *process repository*, on which processes are deployed. BPQL allows business managers to send queries to a process server and to control the execution of processes, using a messaging technology that will be based on SOAP. BPQL also manages process models (created using BPML) that reside in the process repository.[44] BPQL employs UDDI, the Web services mechanism for service discovery, to register and discover business processes deployed on a process repository.[45]

5.8 Web Services Flow Language (WSFL)

The *Web Services Flow Language (WSFL)* is an XML-based language created by IBM to incorporate Web services as part of a business's *workflow*—i.e., the operations required to accomplish a process or transaction. The specification is available at **www-3.ibm.com/software/solutions/webservices/pdf/WSFL.pdf**. WSFL offers a framework in which Web services providers and Web services consumers can define the work to perform and the flow the work needs to follow to implement business processes.[46]

IBM developed WSFL to function as a layer on top of WSDL. WSFL uses WSDL for describing Web services characteristics, but WSFL also describes characteristics of services not covered by WSDL, such as Quality of Service (QoS).

WSFL describes Web services *compositions*—i.e., collections of Web services that work together. The two types of WSFL composition models are the *flow model* and the *global model*. The WSFL flow model describes the sequence of steps required by a collection of Web Services to accomplish a business process, such as a transaction.[47] The global model describes an *interaction pattern composition*, which specifies how the Web services in a composed Web service relate to each other, rather than the sequence of interactions. WSFL supports both hierarchical (often found in more stable, long-term relationships) and peer-to-peer (established dynamically and on individual bases) interactions. "Global" refers to the decentralized and distributed aspect of these interactions.[48]

Recursive compositions also are an essential part of WSFL; every composition can become a part of another composition to create a new Web service. This capability ensures that the language is scalable. Recursive compositions have become an important aspect of WSFL.[49]

5.9 Universal Business Language (UBL)

An OASIS committee oversees the *Universal Business Language (UBL)* initiative. The UBL uses ebXML parameters and systems to develop a set of XML business documents. The committee's goal is the creation of a set of international, freely available, unlicensed e-commerce standard documents.[50]

To accomplish this objective, the committee has based the language on an existing XML technology, the *XML Common Business Language (xCBL) 3.0*—a freely available, widely implemented standard that defines numerous sets of document formats. Using xCBL, the UBL committee is developing standard, yet customizable, documents that are compatible with ebXML specifications. In addition to ensuring compatibility with ebXML, the UBL committee is creating the documents to integrate with the standards and specifications from a variety of organizations, including UN/CEFACT, W3C, IETF and others.[51]

The UBL Technical Committee has committed to three deliverables—a *component library*, standard XML documents and an *extension methodology*. The component library consists of reusable parts, which, when combined, create e-business schemas, from which the UBL standard XML documents are created. The UBL Technical Committee has created seven document categories: *Core Library* (e.g., parts from the component library that form the basis for all the other categories); *Trade/Procurement* (e.g., purchase order, purchase order response), *Materials Management* (e.g., shipping schedule, goods receipt), *Trade/ Payment* (e.g., remittance advice, commercial invoice), *Transport/Logistics* (e.g., transport contract, consignment status report), *Catalog* (e.g., price catalog, product catalog) and *Statistical Reports* (e.g., accounting report). Finally, an extension methodology would allow businesses to customize the documents for a particular transaction or industry. For more information on UBL, visit **www.oasis-open.org/committees/ubl**.[52]

5.10 Introduction to XML Markup

In this section, we present key technical concepts of XML to provide a foundation for the next chapter, Understanding SOAP and WSDL. We discuss XML technology in more detail in Appendix A, Introduction to XML Markup.

The following markup is an example of XML:

```
<memo id = "643070">
    <message>Welcome to XML!</message>
</memo>
```

In XML, data is marked up using tags, which are names enclosed in *angle brackets* (**< >**). Tags are used in pairs to delimit the beginning and end of markup. A tag that begins markup is called a *start tag*; a tag that terminates markup is called an *end tag*. An example of a start tag is **<message>**. End tags differ from start tags in that they contain a *forward slash* (**/**) character. An example of an end tag is **</message>**.

Individual units of markup (i.e., everything from a start tag to an end tag, inclusive) are called *elements*. Elements are the most fundamental building blocks of an XML document. XML documents contain one element—called a *root element* (e.g., **memo**) that contains all other elements in the document. Elements can be *nested* (or *embedded*) within other elements to form hierarchies—the root element is at the top of the hierarchy. For example, **message** is the nested element. Organizing elements in this manner allows document authors to create explicit, hierarchical relationships between data. XML documents can contain any number of elements.

In addition to being placed between tags, data can be placed in *attributes*, which are located in start tags and provide additional information about the elements. Elements can have any number of attributes. In the start tag,

```
<memo id = "643070">
```

for example, attribute **id** is assigned the value **"643070"**. XML element and attribute names can be of any length and can contain letters, digits, underscores, hyphens and periods; however, they must begin with a letter or an underscore.

5.10.1 Document Type Definitions and Schemas

The XML Recommendation includes Document Type Definitions (DTDs), for describing an XML document's structure. However, in most cases, DTDs are not flexible enough to meet today's programming needs. For example, DTDs cannot be manipulated (e.g., searched, transformed into different representations such as XML, etc.) in the same manner as XML documents can, because DTDs do not use XML syntax. In 1999, the W3C began developing an XML vocabulary to be an alternative to DTDs, called XML Schema. In 2001, the W3C accepted XML Schema as a Recommendation. Although documents can be validated against DTDs or schemas, schemas are expected to replace DTDs as the primary means of describing XML document structure.

5.10.2 XML Namespaces

Object-oriented programming languages, such as Java and standard C++, group language features into packages and namespaces, respectively. These packages and namespaces prevent *naming collisions* between programmer-defined identifiers, third-party identifiers and class-library identifiers. For example, a class named **Transaction** might represent a monetary transaction between two large companies; however, a bank might use class **Transaction** to represent a monetary transaction with a Federal Reserve Bank. A naming collision would occur if these two classes were used in the same Java application without their fully qualified package names.

Like standard C++, XML supports *namespaces*[2], which provide a means of uniquely identifying XML elements. Because document authors create their own markup languages, or vocabularies, namespaces are needed to group a vocabulary's elements.

Element names can be qualified with *namespace prefixes*, which identify the namespaces to which elements belong. For example,

```
<deitel:book>Web Services: A Technical Introduction
</deitel:book>
```

qualifies element **book** with the namespace prefix **deitel**. This indicates that element **book** is part of namespace **deitel**.

Document authors create their own namespace prefixes and *uniform resource identifiers (URIs)*, which represents the location or address of an object or a resource on a net-

---

2. XML Namespaces is a W3C Recommendation (**www.w3.org/TR/REC-xml-names**).

work for their vocabularies. For example, a URL (such as **www.deitel.com**) is a type of URI. Using URLs ensures that the namespaces are unique. For example

```
<text:directory xmlns:text =
    "http://www.deitel.com/text_data_info"
    xmlns:image = "http://www.deitel.com/image_data_info">
```

uses URLs **http://www.deitel.com/text_data_info** and **http://www.deitel.com/image_data_info** as URIs. The URLs in this example relate to the Deitel & Associates, Inc., domain name. During the processing of this document, the parser never visits the URLs—the URLs simply represent a series of characters used to differentiate names.

In this chapter, we examined the circumstances that led to the development of XML and introduced XML markup. We discussed XML's impact on Web services. We also overviewed various XML technologies that define business processes. In the next chapter, we detail two crucial Web services technologies—SOAP and WSDL. We explain the technical aspects of both technologies and provide code examples to illustrate the elements in each.

5.11 Summary

The terms Web services and XML Web services often are used interchangeably, which illustrates the dependence of Web services on the Extensible Markup Language (XML). In fact, Web services in its current form would not exist without XML. XML provides Web services with a markup technology that is platform-independent, flexible and extensible. The W3C developed XML to combine the power and extensibility of its parent language, SGML, with the simplicity that the Web community demands. The development of XML has been supervised by the W3C's XML Working Group, which prepared the XML specification and approved it for publication. The XML version 1.0 specification was accepted as a W3C Recommendation in 1998.

XML is the foundation for key Web services technologies. XML markup provides platform independence and interoperability for the Simple Object Access Protocol (SOAP)—the Web services messaging technology. Web Services Description Language, (WSDL), the technology that describes Web services, also is an XML-derived technology; a WSDL document is a type of XML document. UDDI registries use XML to store data about businesses and their Web services.

Organizations and industries have developed various XML-based technologies that define business processes. Industries are pursuing these technologies to define and automate processes, which could result in savings for businesses. To define and automate processes successfully, business partners must agree to standards and coordinate their systems.

OASIS has developed Electronic Business XML (ebXML), an open, XML-based infrastructure that enables global companies to conduct reliable, interoperable e-business internationally. EbXML offers a set of specifications that defines an alternative to Electronic Data Interchange (EDI) systems. EbXML allows businesses of various sizes to partner and conduct global business-to-business transactions using XML and the Internet. Business processes can include such information as the exact steps involved in ebXML transactions and any necessary contact information. The key components that comprise the ebXML framework include trading-partner information, business-process and information modeling, the ebXML registry and the ebXML messaging service.

Several other business-process technologies include Business Process Management Initiative's (BPMI's) Business Process Modeling Language (BPML), which models business processes, and the Business Process Query Language (BPQL), which provides a tool to deploy processes. The Web Services Flow Language (WSFL) is an XML-based language that incorporates Web services as part of a business's workflow—i.e., the operations required to accomplish a process or transaction. The Universal Business Language (UBL) initiative is guided by an OASIS committee that builds on ebXML by developing a set of XML business documents. The committee's goal is the creation of a set of international, freely available, unlicensed e-commerce standard documents.

In XML, data is marked up using tags, which are names enclosed in angle brackets. Tags are used in pairs to delimit the beginning and end of markup. A tag that begins the markup is called a start tag; a tag that terminates markup is called an end tag. Individual units of markup (i.e., everything from a start tag to an end tag, inclusive) are called elements, which are the most fundamental building blocks of an XML document. XML documents contain a root element that contains all the other elements in the document. Elements are embedded or nested (i.e., placed inside) other elements to form hierarchies— with the root element at the top of the hierarchy. Organizing elements using nesting allows document authors to create explicit, hierarchical relationships between data. XML documents can contain any number of elements.

5.12 Internet and Web Resources

www.xml.com
XML information, resources, tutorials and links are available at this site, including articles, news, seminar information, tools and Frequently Asked Questions (FAQs).

www.xml.org
"The XML Industry Portal" includes links to various XML resources, such as news, FAQs and descriptions of XML-derived markup languages.

www.w3.org/XML
The W3C's XML home page contains links to related XML technologies, recommended books, a time-line for pending publications, developer discussions, translations and software downloads.

www.oasis-open.org/cover
The Oasis XML Cover Pages is a comprehensive XML reference. The site includes links to news, articles, software and events.

www.ebxml.org
This site provides specifications, resources, news and articles on ebXML.

www.bpmi.org
The BPMI organization site was designed to offer information about business-process management. It contains specifications for BPML and information about BPQL.

www.ebpml.org/bpml.htm
This site provides information and diagrams to explain BPML.

www.oasis-open.org/committees/business-transactions
The OASIS site contains the latest information about BTP, including links to draft specifications and relevant articles.

www.oasis-open.org/committees/ubl
This site provides information about UBL's development, including current meetings and documentation.

www-4.ibm.com/software/solutions/webservices/pdf/WSFL.pdf
IBM published the WSFL specification to familiar readers with the various aspects of the technology.

www.w3schools.com/xml
This site offers a tutorial with examples that introduce XML.

html.about.com/compute/html/cs/xmlandjava/index.htm
This site contains articles about using XML with Java technologies.

WORKS CITED

1. "SGML Users' Group History," <**www.oasis-open.org/cover/sgmlhist0.html**>.

2. C. Goldfarb and P. Prescod, *The XML Handbook, Third Edition*. (Upper Saddle River, New Jersey: Prentice Hall, 2001) 19.

3. C. Goldfarb and P. Prescod, *The XML Handbook, Third Edition*. (Upper Saddle River, New Jersey: Prentice Hall, 2001) 20.

4. C. Goldfarb and P. Prescod, *The XML Handbook, Third Edition*. (Upper Saddle River, New Jersey: Prentice Hall, 2001) 21.

5. J. Norton, "XML Fundamentals," *DB2 Magazine* Quarter 2, 2001: 52.

6. R. Boeri, "XML Across the Publishing Lifecycle," *eContent* October 2001: 21.

7. "Key XML Standards and Specifications," *Electronic Commerce World* insert May 2002.

8. K. Kayl, "Evolution or Revolution? Standardizing XML Technology," 4 October 2001 <**java.sun.com/features/2001/10/xmlone.p.html**>.

9. K. Kayl, "Evolution or Revolution? Standardizing XML Technology," 4 October 2001 <**java.sun.com/features/2001/10/xmlone.p.html**>.

10. R. Covers, "XML Cover Pages: RosettaNet," 26 February 2002 <**www.oasis-open.org/cover/rosettanet.html**>.

11. <**www.rosettanet.org**>.

12. M. McGarr, "Transforming Processes with EDI," *Electronic Commerce World* May 2002: 25.

13. G. Roos, "RosettaNet for the Masses," 1 October 2001 <**www.ebnews.com/story/OEG20010928S0071**>.

14. "RosettaNet," <**www.necsystems.com/ibs/pdf/rosettanet.pdf**>.

15. K. Kayl, "Evolution or Revolution? Standardizing XML Technology," 4 October 2001 <**java.sun.com/features/2001/10/xmlone.p.html**>.

16. M. Gibbs, "Covering Web Services," *NetworkWorld* 29 April 2002: 102.

17. <**www.ebxml.org**>.

18. M. Siddalingaiah, "Best Practices: Overview of ebXML," 17 August 2001 <**dcb.sun.com/practices/webservices/overviews/overview_ebxml.jsp**>.

19. "ebXML Technical Architecture Specification v1.0.4," 16 February 2001 <**www.ebxml.org/spec/ebTA.pdf**>.

20. K. Kayl, "EbXML: The Key Components," 5 September 2001 <**java.sun.com/features/2001/09/ebxmlkey.html**>.

21. "ebXML Technical Architecture Specification v1.0.4," 16 February 2001 <**www.ebxml.org/specs/ebTA.pdf**>.

22. "Collaboration-Protocol Profile and Agreement Specification," 10 May 2001 <**www.ebxml.org/specs/ebCPP.pdf**>.

23. "ebXML Technical Architecture Specification v1.04," 16 February 2001 `<www.ebxml.org/spec/ebTA.pdf>`.

24. "ebXML Technical Architecture Specification v1.0.4," 16 February 2001 `<www.ebxml.org/spec/ebTA.pdf>`.

25. "ebXML Business Process Specification Schema Version 1.01," 11 May 2001 `<www.ebxml.org/specs/ebBPSS.pdf>`.

26. "ebXML Technical Architecture Specification v1.0.4," 16 February 2001 `<www.ebxml.org/spec/ebTA.pdf>`.

27. "Core Component Overview Version 1.05," 10 May 2001 `<www.ebxml.org/specs/ccOVER.pdf>`.

28. "Using UDDI to Find ebXML Reg/Reps," 8 May 2001 `<www.ebxml.org/specs/rrUDDI.pdf>`.

29. "UUID," `<searchwebservices.techtarget.com/sDefinition/0,,sid26_gci805876,00.html>`.

30. R. Cover, "The XML Cover Pages," 22 February 2001 `<xml.coverpages.org/ni2001-02-22-b.html>`.

31. M. Siddalingaiah, "Best Practices: Overview of ebXML," 17 August 2001 `<dcb.sun.com/practices/webservices/overviews/overview_ebxml.jsp>`.

32. `<www.oasis-open.org>`.

33. R. Karpinski, "HP Adds Transaction Support to Web Services: Java One," 25 May 2002 `<www.internetwk.com/story/INW20020325S0005>`.

34. "Business Transaction Protocol Version 1.0 [0.9.6.1]," 14 May 2002 `<www.oasis-open.org/committees/business-transactions/documents/2002-05-14.BTP_draft_0.9.6.1.pdf>`.

35. R. Covers, "The XML Cover Pages," 29 October 2001 `<xml.coverpage.org/ni2001-10-29-a.html>`.

36. A. Green, "The OASIS Business Transaction Protocol," High Performance Transaction Systems Workshop presentation 14–17 October 2001.

37. R. Covers, "The XML Cover Pages," 29 October 2001 `<xml.coverpages.org/ni2001-10-29-a.html>`.

38. T. Jewell, "The Business Transaction Protocol: A Critical Infrastructure Component," `<www.sys-con.com/webservices/>`.

39. `<www.bpmi.org>`.

40. "Industry Leaders Publish Standard for Business Process Management: Release of BPML Specification Paves Way for Implementations," 8 March 2001 `<xml.coverpages.org/bpml20010308Ann.html>`.

41. M. Lenhardt, "BPMS–Business Process-Management System," `<www.boc-eu.com/english/bpms.shtml>`.

42. A. Arkin, "Business Process Modeling Language (BPML) Working Draft 0.4 8 March 2001 `<www.bpmi.org/bpmi-downloads/WD-BPML-20010308.pdf>`.

43. A. Arkin, "Business Process Modeling Language (BPML) Working Draft 0.4 8 March 2001 `<www.bpmi.org/bpmi-downloads/WD-BPML-20010308.pdf>`.

44. G. Heidel, "Web Services Standards," `<www.momentumsoftware.com/pdf/web_services.pdf>`.

45. <`www.bpmi.org/bpql.esp`>.

46. J. Snell, "The Web Services Insider, Part 6: Assuming Responsibility, Implementing Roles in WSFL," July 2001 <`www-106.ibm.com/developerworks/webservices/library/ws-ref6/?dwzone=webservices`>.

47. F. Leymann, "Web Services Flow Language (WSFL 1.0)," May 2001 <`www-3.ibm.com/software/solutions/webservices/pdf/WSFL.pdf`>.

48. F. Leymann, "Web Services Flow Language (WSFL 1.0)," May 2001 <`www-3.ibm.com/software/solutions/webservices/pdf/WSFL.pdf`>.

49. F. Leymann, "Web Services Flow Language (WSFL 1.0)," May 2001 <`www-3.ibm.com/software/solutions/webservices/pdf/WSFL.pdf`>.

50. <`www.oasis-open.org`>.

51. <`www.oasis-open.org`>.

52. "UBL: The Next Step for Global E-Commerce," UBL Marketing Subcommittee Marketing Document 2 April 2002 <`www.oasis-open.org`>.

6

Understanding SOAP and WSDL

Objectives

- To discuss the Simple Object Access Protocol (SOAP).
- To understand the structure of a SOAP message.
- To review alternatives to SOAP.
- To discuss the Web Services Description Language (WSDL).
- To understand the role of WSDL documents in a Web services architecture.

It is very hard to be simple enough to be good.
Ralph Waldo Emerson

You know more of a road by having traveled it than by all the conjectures and descriptions in the world.
William Hazlitt

...it is always the simple that produces the marvelous.
Amelia Barr

It is a capital mistake to theorize before one has data.
Sir Arthur Conan Doyle

Outline

6.1 Introduction

In the previous chapter, XML and Derivative Technologies, we learned that XML is the underlying technology used in Web services transactions. XML's data portability allows Web services to communicate with applications that run on disparate computing platforms. However, to achieve XML-based interaction, developers need to establish a standard transport and data-exchange framework. The nature of Web services dictates that this framework enable interoperability. Many applications employ proprietary data specifications, which complicates communication among applications; Web services require a protocol that uses a standard, open data format. In addition, Web services need a way to work with the basic security mechanisms of remote networks. Most enterprise applications reside behind *firewalls*—security barriers that restrict communication between networks. For Web services to succeed, they must operate through firewalls. Although several technologies meet these requirements, the Web services industry supports one—the *Simple Object Access Protocol* (*SOAP*).[1]

SOAP facilitates interoperable communication among computing systems in a decentralized, distributed network. The protocol specifies a *messaging framework*—i.e., a software system that enables applications to communicate with one another by exchanging messages—to send XML documents, called SOAP *messages*, over the Internet. In the SOAP messaging framework, messages encapsulate information transmitted to and from a Web service. SOAP messages do not provide programming instructions; rather, they specify to a Web services server which operation to invoke. Designed to be extensible, SOAP supports such features as attachments, security, routing information and transactions. SOAP's extensibility is expected to become more critical as organizations begin to deploy highly secure and reliable Web services, such as those performing billing and payment transactions.[1]

This chapter explains how SOAP facilitates communication between applications over the Internet. We introduce the SOAP messaging specification, as well as the various components that comprise the SOAP architecture. The chapter also discusses the XML vocabulary, *Web Services Description Language (WSDL),* which enables applications to determine the capabilities of Web services. Web services often are accompanied by WSDL documents, which contain information that applications use to "learn" about the functionality that Web services provide. The chapter explains the role of WSDL in Web services interactions and includes an example of a WSDL document. The chapter concludes with an overview of three applications that developers use to create and deploy Web services. [*Note*: This chapter examines the lower-level protocols of Web services communication. For information on programming-level technologies, we discuss the .NET platform and its support for Web services development in Chapter 9, .NET Web Services: A Conceptual Overview, and the Java Web Services Developer Pack in Chapter 10, Java Web Services: A Conceptual Overview.]

6.2 History of Simple Object Access Protocol (SOAP)

Rather than being developed specifically for Web services, SOAP was created before the advent of Web services, as a communications protocol that could be used over the Internet. When the W3C released XML 1.0 as a recommendation in 1998, a group of developers realized that, in addition to describing data, XML also could describe programmatic actions, or *behaviors*. Consequently, IBM, Lotus Development Corporation, Microsoft, DevelopMentor and Userland Software began collaborating to develop an XML-messaging protocol to define a non-platform specific (interoperable) way to invoke remote operations. The work resulted in the development of SOAP.[2]

The organizations that developed SOAP published the first SOAP specification, SOAP 0.9, in 1999. The founding organizations released several subsequent versions of SOAP before submitting the protocol to the W3C. In July 2001, the W3C released SOAP 1.2 as a *Working Draft*. This means that the W3C published the SOAP specification document, but continued to accept comments and suggestions for changes to the document. Working

---

1. Many in the industry believe that the terms that spell SOAP are misleading; SOAP is neither simple nor is it designed explicitly for objects. Many in the computer industry, including the W3C, no longer treat the word as an acronym.

drafts are unstable and subject to change and, therefore, are not suitable for industry-wide implementation. The Working Draft of the specification is available in three parts: *Primer*, *Messaging Framework* and *Adjuncts*, at **www.w3.org/TR/soap12-part0**, **www.w3.org/TR/soap12-part1** and **www.w3.org/TR/soap12-part2**, respectively. Most existing SOAP implementations adhere to SOAP 1.1, because, as a Working Draft, SOAP 1.2 might change significantly—the final version might include new features or exclude existing ones.[3]

The *W3C XML Protocol Working Group* is the primary organization developing the SOAP specification. The Working Group is comprised of more than 60 participants from 34 organizations, including IBM, Microsoft, MITRE, Software AG, DevelopMentor, Sun, SAP, Cisco Systems, Oracle, Intel, Unisys, Hewlett-Packard and Netscape.[4] Several Working Group members, such as Apache, IBM and Microsoft, have released applications that help developers implement SOAP in enterprise systems. These implementations include Apache's *Axis*, Microsoft's *SOAP Toolkit* and IBM's *Web Services Toolkit*. We discuss these applications in more detail later in this chapter.

6.3 SOAP Architecture

Although SOAP can be used for other types of computer communications, the protocol is best known for its use in Web services. This section first overviews the structure of the software systems that use Web services. Then we examine the basic messaging framework in which SOAP operates and discuss the individual components of SOAP's messaging system.

Web services often are part of larger, object-based architectures. Good systems architectures promote *loosely coupled* systems—i.e., systems in which each software component's implementation is independent of those surrounding it. When an application resides in a loosely coupled system, changes to one component or application do not affect other applications in the system. For example, if the Web service implementation is modified to enhance performance, the developer does not have to modify other applications in the system. The advantage of loosely coupled systems is that a developer can change a particular component without going through the error-prone process of modifying other system components. By contrast, if a developer changes a component in a *tightly coupled* system, the other system components must be altered.

The SOAP specification offers a protocol by which XML messages can communicate programmatic instructions between applications. This specification encompasses four main parts:

1. The first is the SOAP envelope, which describes the format of a SOAP message. We discuss SOAP envelopes and envelope components in Section 6.3.2.

2. The second part defines a set of rules that *encode data types*—i.e., the structures or representations of information (data) that are sent in a message. Most programming languages require developers to specify the types of data that an application uses; this allows programs that receive the data to interpret the information correctly. Section 6.3.3 discusses data types and encoding.

3. The third part defines how a SOAP message can execute *remote procedure calls* (i.e., requests to execute a program component on a remote computer). This is detailed in Section 6.3.4.

4. The last part of the SOAP specification involves the SOAP *binding framework*, which defines the protocol through which SOAP messages are transmitted to applications. We discuss this in Section 6.3.5.[5]

It is crucial to understand that SOAP is not an executable application. The SOAP specification neither includes explicit programming instructions, nor restricts developers to a specific programming language, such as Visual Basic® .NET, Java or C#. The SOAP specification was designed to include only the functions and capabilities necessary to achieve platform- and language-independent communications. Developers who apply the protocols can create SOAP applications that achieve interoperable messaging across platforms. Processing basic SOAP messages does not involve extensive amounts of code, and there is little "special software" needed either to send or to receive SOAP messages. Any programming language that can understand SOAP messages and XML can implement the protocol—third-party software enables developers to use SOAP messaging in more than 60 programming languages.[6]

The SOAP Version 1.2 specification defines the protocol's key components and presents a model for exchanging messages in a distributed-computing environment. The following section overviews this conceptual model, the *SOAP Message Exchange Model*, which provides a framework in which components send and receive SOAP messages.

6.3.1 SOAP Message Exchange Model

The SOAP Version 1.2 Working Draft describes a model of the most basic SOAP-message transmission. The *SOAP Message Exchange Model* defines how components exchange messages, as well as the basic requirements for processing one-way transmissions from a SOAP *sender* to a SOAP *receiver*.

In this model, SOAP *nodes* (i.e., applications or programming components that understand SOAP) process SOAP messages. A node that sends a SOAP message is called a SOAP *sender*, whereas a node that receives a message is called a SOAP *receiver*. When a SOAP node processes a SOAP message, that node is called a SOAP *actor*. SOAP actors are identified by an *actor name*, which is a Uniform Resource Identifier (URI). A SOAP message uses the SOAP actor name to identify intermediaries and SOAP receivers. Figure 6.1 illustrates the *one-way message model*.

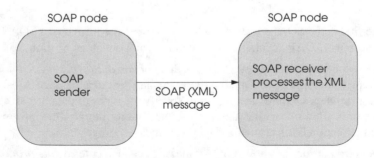

Fig. 6.1   SOAP message one-way transmission model.

This model represents the simplest type of SOAP transmission. Using the model as a base, developers can create more complex communication architectures. For example, developers can incorporate intermediate nodes, called *intermediaries*, or can create a *request/response* model (Fig. 6.2). An example of a request/response model is one in which a client sends a message to a Web service and the Web service returns information to the client.

6.3.2 SOAP Messages

The main section of the SOAP specification defines the structure of a SOAP message, a specific type of XML document. SOAP encapsulates data in messages that are transferred to and from Web services. Each SOAP message contains an initial envelope element, ***Envelope***, which is composed of an optional ***Header*** element and a required ***Body*** element (Fig. 6.3). The SOAP ***Envelope*** element requires information that specifies the namespace and schema information for the message. The envelope does not define the actual contents of the header and body; this information is provided by the application sending the message.[7]

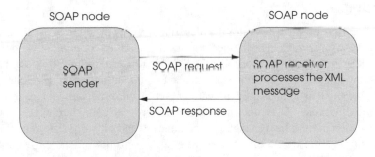

Fig. 6.2   SOAP message request/response transmission model.

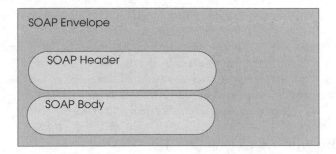

Fig. 6.3   SOAP message structure.

The SOAP header can contain information about the message, parsing instructions for nodes that receive the message and security information. A SOAP message does not always travel directly from its sender to the intended recipient. For example, imagine that a client sends a SOAP message to a Web service that performs payment processing; the header of the message might include *routing* information that instructs an intermediary to verify the identity of source of the message before it is processed at the final node. An intermediary processes the information specific to that node, then sends the message to its next destination. If a node receives a SOAP message and the header contains no instructions for the node, the node passes the message to the next node. As we mentioned, the SOAP header is optional. However, if a SOAP message includes a header, it must precede the **Body** element.

The body of a SOAP message describes the purpose of the SOAP message and contains the SOAP *payload*—i.e., the data or instructions intended for the receiving application. For example, the body can include instructions for tasks that the receiver must perform, such as calling a method, or can include information that must be processed by an application.

If the final recipient of the message cannot process the information in the header or the body, the recipient returns a SOAP message containing error information. For example, if the header format is incorrect, the node is unable to read the instructions contained in the header. In such cases, a SOAP *Fault* element containing the error information is returned to the sending node.

6.3.3 Encoding

The SOAP specification provides rules that describe how specific kinds of data can be represented in a SOAP message. These rules, known as *SOAP encoding,* enable applications that receive SOAP messages to recognize the format of, and therefore process, data in the messages. Although the specification defines a set of encoding rules, developers can use any encoding method, as long as they indicate the set of rules they are using. This is particularly important, because SOAP does not specify the programming languages in which developers can program, and many languages can understand only specific sets of encoding rules. Flexibility to choose a set of encoding rules allows programmers to use the encoding with which they are most familiar, rather than being forced to learn and apply new rules.[8]

The SOAP *encoding style* specifies the rules for defining the data types of individual data elements within the SOAP message. For example, when a SOAP message contains an integer to send to a Web service, the particular value can be encoded to convey to the receiving node that the value (e.g., the number **2002**) is an integer, as opposed to a string. When the node can determine that it is receiving an integer, the node can process the data correctly.

The SOAP **Header** or **Body** element can have the SOAP **encodingStyle** attribute, which is the attribute that contains a URI that maps to the encoding rules. SOAP encoding supports *simple* data types, such as strings and integers, as well as complex types. The specification provides numerous encoding rules that are beyond the scope of this text; definitions are available at **www.w3.org/TR/soap12-part2**.

6.3.4 Remote Procedure Call (RPC)

A *procedure* is a set of instructions that tells an application how to carry out a particular task. Procedures (also called methods, in the context of object-oriented programming) are used in almost every aspect of computing. A *procedure call* is the command that *invokes* a procedure—i.e., directs an application to execute a procedure to perform a specific operation. A procedure call contains the name of the operation and the operation's *parameters* (data that the procedure requires to complete its task).

Remote Procedure Call (*RPC*) is a technology by which one application invokes (executes) a procedure residing on another computer. RPC is a common mechanism by which applications interact with Web services, and the concept is crucial to understanding the role of SOAP in Web services interactions. Because one purpose of a SOAP message is to execute a procedure from across a network, a SOAP message sent to a Web service represents an RPC. When using the RPC convention, the SOAP specification requires that the SOAP-message body contains the Web service method to be invoked, any parameters the method takes and the target procedure's URI. After an RPC is executed, the Web service can communicate information to the calling application; thus, the service sends the application another SOAP message containing the results of the procedure call.

SOAP also supports *document-style* communication in which no method is invoked; this type typically is used for notification or status information. For example, a Web service that tracks shipping could receive a document-style message notifying it that a certain package had been sent. This situation does not require a response.

Remote procedure calls can be transmitted either synchronously or asynchronously.[2] Using *synchronous* communications, an application sends a SOAP message to a Web service, then suspends program execution while waiting for a response. Synchronous communications are employed when an application expects a quick response or cannot continue without the data provided by the Web service. For example, synchronous communications would be used by a program that sends stock symbols to a Web service to receive real-time stock quotes. However, synchronous communications are not ideal for all situations. If every program that accesses a Web service must wait for a response—which could take minutes, hours or even days—performance could be severely hindered. Document-style messages typically employ *asynchronous* communications, which do not require a program to wait for a response from the remote procedure. The application invokes a remote operation and continues program execution; no immediate response is expected. Asynchronous communications would be appropriate for notifying a Web service of an inventory status, for example. It is an advantage that applications can transmit SOAP messages either synchronously or asynchronously, because each option is preferable in different situations.

We have described the structure of SOAP messages, the encoding styles used in SOAP messages and the methods by which SOAP messages invoke procedures from across a network. The remaining concept covered in the SOAP specification is how SOAP messages can be transmitted. The next section discusses this technology, the transport protocol.

6.3.5 Transport Protocols

The fourth part of the SOAP specification involves SOAP's bindings to transport protocols. Any transport protocol can be used to exchange SOAP messages, as long as the applications sending and receiving the messages understand the protocol.[9] HTTP is the most common protocol used to transmit data over the Internet, and as a result, the vast

---

2. Although an RPC can be transmitted asynchronously, it typically uses synchronous communication.

majority of computer systems can accept and process HTTP transmissions. HTTP is ubiquitous; therefore, the protocol also has become the primary transport mechanism for SOAP messages. The SOAP specification recognizes the popularity of HTTP by devoting a section to HTTP as an example of a transfer protocol. We focus on SOAP's binding to HTTP.

HTTP defines several *request types*—i.e., methods by which clients can communicate with an HTTP server. The **post** and **get** request types are most commonly used to send form data and retrieve Web pages, respectively. The SOAP specification details the transfer of SOAP messages via the HTTP **post** request type. If a Web service returns information in a SOAP message, the information is sent as part of an HTTP response.[10]

In addition to HTTP, there are SOAP bindings for other transport protocols, such as *Hypertext Transfer Protocol Secure (HTTPS)* and *Simple Mail Transfer Protocol (SMTP)*. HTTPS is a secure form of HTTP that uses *Secure Sockets Layer (SSL)*. SSL is a protocol that encrypts data sent across the Web to ensure that third parties do not compromise the information. When organizations must exchange confidential data, such as credit-card numbers, over the Web, applications transport the information via HTTPS. SMTP is a common protocol used to transfer e-mail.[11]

6.4 Example of a Simple SOAP Message

At this point, it might be helpful to clarify the concepts explained thus far by presenting an actual SOAP message, including the message format that performs an RPC. Figure 6.4 depicts a sample SOAP message sent to a Web service that receives an ISBN and returns a corresponding book title. The code is taken from the *Deitel™ Developer Series* book, *Java Web Services for Experienced Programmers*. This example illustrates a message in which a Java object of class **BookTitleClient**, invokes the Book Title Web service's **getBookTitle** method.

As we have explained, a SOAP message is an XML document—line 1 provides the XML version information, as well as the character encoding. Lines 5–21 define the SOAP XML element **Envelope**. Lines 5–9 specify the message's encoding style and bind three namespaces to their corresponding prefixes. This particular SOAP message does not include a header, because this SOAP request does not need special routing information or transaction processing. Lines 11–19 define the **Body**, which contains the elements that specify the Web service method to invoke. Line 15 defines the parameter that **getBookTitle** requires. Notice that the XML element is named according to the parameter name. The **ISBN** parameter element defines the parameter type—type **xsd:string** indicates that the parameter, **ISBN**, is a string. (The ISBN corresponds to *Advanced Java 2 Platform How to Program*, which can be confirmed by visiting **www.amazon.com/exec/obidos/ASIN/0130895601**.)

```
1    <?xml version="1.0" encoding="UTF-8"?>
2    <!-- Fig. 6.4: SOAPmessage        -->
3    <!-- Example of a SOAP message. -->
4
```

Fig. 6.4   SOAP message example. (Part 1 of 2.)

```
 5   <SOAP-ENV:Envelope
 6       SOAP-ENV:encodingStyle= "http://schemas.xmlsoap.org/soap/
encoding/"
 7           xmlns:SOAP-ENV="http://schemas.xmlsoap.org/soap/envelope/"
 8           xmlns:xsd="http://www.w3.org/2001/XMLSchema"
 9           xmlns:xsi="http://www.w3.org/2001/XMLSchema-instance">
10
11       <SOAP-ENV:Body>
12
13           <ns1:getBookTitle xmlns:ns1="urn:deitel:BookTitle">
14
15               <ISBN xsi:type="xsd:string">0130895601</ISBN>
16
17           </ns1:getBookTitle>
18
19       </SOAP-ENV:Body>
20
21   </SOAP-ENV:Envelope>
```

Fig. 6.4   SOAP message example. (Part 2 of 2.)

6.5 SOAP Clients and Servers

The previous sections detailed the integral parts of the SOAP messaging specification. Next, we discuss two important entities that interact with SOAP messages in a distributed computing network. This section explains the roles of SOAP *clients* (i.e., software that creates SOAP messages to interact with Web services) and SOAP *servers*[3] (i.e., software that processes SOAP messages for Web services).

A client application that wants to query a Web service uses a SOAP client to create and send a SOAP message. The SOAP specification does not indicate the types of applications that can function as SOAP clients; the applications could be simple programs or parts of more complex systems.[12] Before creating a SOAP message, a SOAP client can use a *Universal Description, Discovery and Integration (UDDI)* registry or other discovery mechanism to locate a Web service. UDDI registries store descriptions of service providers and their Web services, as well as links to the services' WSDL documents. We discuss WSDL later in this chapter and UDDI is introduced in Chapter 7, UDDI, Discovery and Web Services Registries. After a client searches the UDDI registry and locates a desired Web service, the client creates a SOAP message in accordance with the information found in the chosen Web service's WSDL file. WSDL information includes the location of the Web service (which is needed to address the SOAP message) and the parameters that the Web service requires from the requesting program.

A SOAP *server* is a program or part of a program that receives and processes a SOAP client's request.[13] The server listens for SOAP messages; when it encounters a SOAP message, the server accepts it and processes the information (e.g., a remote procedure call) into code that the receiving object, the Web service, understands. The SOAP server accom-

---

3. Although we use the terms client and server, the SOAP specification uses the terms sender and
    receiver.

plishes this by *parsing*—i.e., the server processes the message, then translates the encoding instructions to a data type that the receiving application can process.

Once the SOAP server sends the relevant data contained in the SOAP message to the intended Web service, the Web service performs the tasks defined in the SOAP message and sends the response data back to the SOAP server. The server translates the data to XML and creates a SOAP envelope that includes the Web service's response. The server then places the envelope in a SOAP message and sends the message back to the SOAP client.[14] The SOAP client that initially sent the request converts the response information to an appropriate format, then uses the data or directs it to an appropriate application.[4] Figure 6.5 illustrates a Web services transaction that depicts the SOAP client and the SOAP server functionality.

6.6 SOAP Enhancements

SOAP is still a relatively new specification, and it does not address all aspects of Web services interactions. As the W3C and other organizations develop the technology, new versions will enhance SOAP's functionality. This section overviews improvements made in Version 1.2 of SOAP, and discusses attachments to SOAP messages.[5]

The latest version of the SOAP specification defines everything in terms of the *XML Infoset*, a W3C Recommendation that defines a standard set of terminology for referencing the information presented in an XML document. Version 1.2 also has improved error handling. This version clarifies error messaging by enhancing and further defining the **fault** element. SOAP's encoding style also has been enhanced and clarified and some changes have been made to HTTP binding.[15]

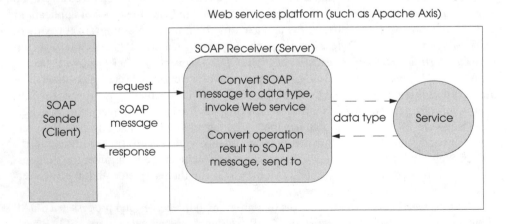

Fig. 6.5   Synchronous Web service typical invocation process.

---

4. Please note that the response in this example is returned synchronously.
5. The reader should note that some enhancements might change in the SOAP 1.2 specification, because the specification is not yet a recommendation.

The ability to attach files to SOAP messages greatly increases SOAP's versatility. Attachments enable Web services to exchange data that is difficult to represent in XML—such as images and audio files. The specification created to describe this technology is called *SOAP Messages with Attachments*.

In December 2000, Hewlett-Packard Labs and Microsoft submitted the SOAP Messages with Attachments document to the W3C as a *Note*. When the W3C publishes a Note, the W3C is neither endorsing the content nor is it controlling the document's contents. Instead, the W3C posts a Note to encourage discussion about the content of the document.

When applications transmit files across the Internet, the data is sent in some type of *binary* format (i.e., data represented as 1s and 0s). For example, most images on the Internet are transmitted using either *Graphics Interchange Format (GIF)* or *Joint Photographic Experts Group (JPEG)* data formats, which are binary. However, the SOAP Messages with Attachments document uses *Multipurpose Internet Mail Extensions (MIME)* to describe various media types, such as audio and video, so that the attachments can be processed by the receiving applications. MIME most often is used to send e-mail attachments. The SOAP Messages with Attachments document explains how MIME encapsulates the SOAP message and the accompanying attachment. The attachment information is included in the HTTP header (when HTTP is used as the transport protocol).[16]

Instead of using the SOAP with Attachments specification, Microsoft has created the *Direct Internet Message Encapsulation (DIME)* specification to use for SOAP message attachments. DIME is similar to MIME, but DIME is designed for simplicity, whereas MIME is designed for flexibility. DIME also offers enhanced performance. Visit **www.ietf.org/internet-drafts/draft-nielsen-dime-01.txt** to read the specification.[17]

6.7 Security

The SOAP 1.2 Working Draft of December 2001 provides no specific provisions for security. In fact, the specification states that "such issues will be addressed more fully in a future version(s) of this document."[18] This section provides only a brief introduction to Web services-related security issues, because we examine security in detail in Chapter 11, Internet Security, and Chapter 12, Web Services Security.

Most computer networks use firewalls to prevent unwanted or harmful transmissions from entering the network. *Ports* are numbers that identify network services a computer provides, such as e-mail and file transfer; network transmissions are routed to a specific port. Firewalls secure networks by blocking ports that might receive malicious files or programs. HTTP, the transport protocol used most often to exchange SOAP messages, communicates on a *trusted* port (one that is not blocked). Firewalls do not interfere with HTTP communications, because computer users on the network employ HTTP to receive Web pages, e-mail and other Internet transmissions. To increase network security, message senders can declare in the HTTP header whether a transmission contains a SOAP message. This enables network administrators to program firewalls so that they filter out all SOAP messages. Although this solution might prevent harmful messages from entering the network, it also prohibits the network's computers from using Web services. Thus, organizations that want to employ Web services must adopt other SOAP security mechanisms.

One option for such organizations is to use a Web services development application, such as IBM's Web Services Toolkit Version 3.0 or Systinet's *Web Applications and Ser-*

vices Platform (WASP). Both toolkits offer several SOAP *security extensions* that provide authorization and element-level encryption. One such SOAP security extension is the *SOAP Security Extensions: Digital Signature (SOAP-SEC)*, which provides a set of rules for digitally signing SOAP messages and validating message signatures. The W3C accepted SOAP-SEC as a Note; however, SOAP-SEC has been superseded by WS-Security. We discuss WS-Security in detail in Chapter 9, .NET Web Services: A Conceptual Overview and Systinet's WASP in Chapter 8, Web Services Platforms, Vendors and Strategies and Chapter 10, Java Web Services: A Conceptual Overview.

6.8 SOAP Alternatives

Although the computer industry and most major software vendors support SOAP as the standard method of Web services communication, other protocols offer similar functionality. Companies have used one such technology, *XML-RPC*, instead of SOAP for certain implementations.

For simple RPC, XML-RPC is easier to implement than SOAP. If a developer wants to link applications in a smaller, less complex distributed computing network—such as a local-area network (LAN)—within an organization, XML-RPC would be an appropriate technology to use. However, using XML-RPC is less appropriate than using SOAP when communicating in a wider, more diverse community, such as the Internet. This is because SOAP supplies extensible capabilities to support attachments, routing, transactions and other such features required by complex distributed computing applications. Such extensions will become even more important when people start using Web services to conduct business transactions that involve billing and that require high levels of reliability.[19]

Instead of using SOAP or XML-RPC, a developer alternatively can create a proprietary XML messaging framework for communicating messages on a distributed computing network. This is not feasible for many developers due to the time and expertise required. Also, vendors are developing SOAP products and services that will offer more features and better functionality than could most proprietary XML solutions.[20]

There are several technical reasons for the intense industry support that SOAP has garnered; most are beyond the scope of this text. However, it is important to note that the main advantages of SOAP include extensibility and interoperability. As more developers begin to use SOAP, vendors and organizations will create an increasing number of development tools designed to speed the incorporation of SOAP in distributed computing networks. The next section explains another crucial Web services standard, the Web Services Description Language (WSDL).

6.9 Web Service Description Language (WSDL)

In the previous sections, we described SOAP and the role that SOAP plays in the Web services paradigm. However, before an application can access a Web service, the application must learn about the available services and their capabilities. In such cases, a client can consult a lookup service, called a *registry*—i.e., a repository that stores the URLs of Web Services Description Language (WSDL) documents. Registries store files that provide specific technical information; using this data, applications can query and communicate with Web services. The client application uses WSDL, an XML-based language, to obtain such information. This section overviews the history of WSDL, explains the elements in WSDL documents and provides an illustration of a WSDL document.

6.10 History of WSDL

Before organizations adopted WSDL as a universal method of Web services description, each Web services development environment used a proprietary method to describe available Web services. There was no standard way to access the files containing the descriptions, and service descriptions were inconsistent and incompatible. To remedy this situation, Microsoft and IBM collaborated to create a language that describes Web services in a standard, structured way. The technologies of Microsoft's *SOAP Contract Language (SCL)* and IBM's *Network Accessible Service Specification Language (NASSL)* were combined to form the basis of WSDL.[21] SCL employs XML to describe the messages exchanged between applications, and NASSL describes the interface and the implementation details of a Web service. Microsoft and IBM, with contributions from Ariba, submitted WSDL Version 1.1 to the W3C in March 2001. Although the technology still is under development, nearly all Web services provide support for WSDL, and most development tools auto-generate WSDL files.[22]

6.11 Role of WSDL in Web Services

Many Web services published on the Internet have associated WSDL documents, which contain sets of definitions (marked up as XML) that describe the Web service. The WSDL document specifies the service's capabilities, its location on the Web and instructions regarding how to access it. A WSDL document defines the structure of the messages (i.e., indicate the data that a calling application must provide for the Web service) that a Web service sends and receives. Using this information, applications searching for a Web service to fill a specific need can analyze the WSDL files of several comparable services and choose between the services. In addition, WSDL files provide specific technical information that enables applications to connect to and communicate with Web services over HTTP or another communications protocol.[23] This section explains the role of WSDL in Web services discovery, then discusses several XML elements that are contained in WSDL documents.

Figure 6.6 illustrates the role of a WSDL file in a Web services interaction. When a Web service is published, a Web service administrator posts a link to the Web service's WSDL document in an XML registry or other WSDL repository (Step 1). The WSDL file then is available when an application, such as a SOAP client, searches a registry to locate a Web service.[6] A client accesses the WSDL document contained in the XML registry to acquire information about the Web service and to create a SOAP message with the appropriate structure to communicate with the service (Step 2). Then, using the information in the WSDL document, the client invokes the Web service (Step 3).

---

6. Registries are not the only mechanism for accessing WSDL files. An organization can send a WSDL file via e-mail or might provide a URL to access the file. Other options include using WS-Inspection—we discuss WS-Inspection in detail in Chapter 7, UDDI, Discovery and Web Services Registries and Chapter 9, .NET Web Services: A Conceptual Overview. WSDL files also can reside in file systems not associated with an XML registry or WSDL repository.

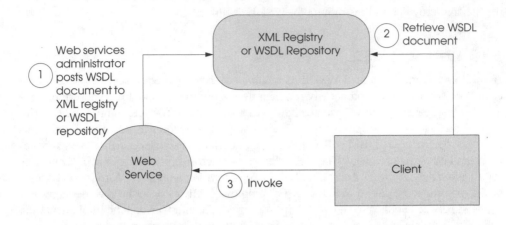

Fig. 6.6   WSDL role in Web services interactions.

WSDL specifies how to structure documents so that Web services communications can be automated. Each WSDL document contains XML elements that define the characteristics and capabilities of a Web service. The main elements belong to one of two categories: *abstract* definitions, which define general concepts that can apply to more than one instance, and *concrete* definitions, which define specific examples that apply to real interactions. Figure 6.7 overviews the main elements.[24]

WSDL element	Element description
Abstract Definitions	
message	Provides a definition of the message that is communicated.
portType	Defines the service interface of the operations that the Web service supports.
operation	Describes an action provided by the Web service. Is a child of **portType**.
type	Provides definitions for the data types that SOAP messages contain.
Concrete Definitions	
binding	Specifies the protocols by which nodes transport messages and for data encoding.
port	Specifies the address for a particular **binding**. Is a sub-element of **service**.
service	Specifies the actual location (URL) of the Web service on the server.

Fig. 6.7   Key WSDL elements and descriptions.

Developers do not need to understand WSDL to be able to build and deploy Web services, but developers who comprehend the underlying markup can customize WSDL documents when necessary. Figure 6.8 depicts a WSDL document for the Book Title Web service. To illustrate and explain WSDL elements, we include this sample document from the *Deitel*™ *Developer Series* book, *Java Web Services for Experienced Programmers.*

```
1   <?xml version="1.0"?>
2   <!-- Fig. 6.8: BookTitle.wsdl     -->
3   <!-- Example of a WSDL document. -->
4
5   <wsdl:definitions
6      name="com.deitel.jws1.soap.services.BookTitleImpl"
7      targetNamespace="urn:com.deitel.jws1.soap.services.BookTitle"
8      xmlns:wsdl="http://schemas.xmlsoap.org/wsdl/"
9      xmlns:xsd="http://www.w3.org/2001/XMLSchema"
10     xmlns:tns="urn:com.deitel.jws1.soap.services.BookTitle"
11     xmlns:soap="http://schemas.xmlsoap.org/wsdl/soap/"
12
13     <message name="BookTitleImpl_getBookTitle_Response">
14        <wsdl:part name="response" type="xsd:string" />
15     </wsdl:message>
16
17     <wsdl:message name="BookTitleImpl_getBookTitle_Request">
18        <wsdl:part name="ISBN" type="xsd:string" />
19     </wsdl:message>
20
21     <wsdl:portType name="BookTitleImpl">
22
23        <wsdl:operation name="getBookTitle" parameterOrder="p0">
24           <wsdl:input name="getBookTitle"
25              message="tns:BookTitleImpl_getBookTitle_Request" />
26
27           <wsdl:output name="getBookTitle"
28              message="tns:BookTitleImpl_getBookTitle_Response" />
29        </wsdl:operation>
30
31     </wsdl:portType>
32
33     <wsdl:binding name="BookTitleImplSOAPBinding0"
34        type="tns:BookTitleImpl">
35
36        <soap:binding
37           transport="http://schemas.xmlsoap.org/soap/http"
38           style="rpc" />
39
40        <wsdl:operation name="getBookTitle">
41
42           <soap:operation soapAction="" style="rpc" />
43
44           <wsdl:input name="getBookTitle">
45              <soap:body use="encoded"
46              encodingStyle="http://schemas.xmlsoap.org/soap/encoding/"
```

Fig. 6.8   WSDL document associated with **BookTitle** Web service. (Part 1 of 2.)

```
47                  namespace="urn:com.deitel.jws1.soap.services.BookTitle" />
48              </wsdl:input>
49
50              <wsdl:output name="getBookTitle">
51                  <soap:body use="encoded"
52                   encodingStyle="http://schemas.xmlsoap.org/soap/encoding/"
53                   namespace="urn:com.deitel.jws1.soap.services.BookTitle" />
54              </wsdl:output>
55
56          </wsdl:operation>
57
58      </wsdl:binding>
59
60      <wsdl:service name="BookTitle">
61
62          <wsdl:port name="BookTitle"
63             binding="tns:BookTitleImplSOAPBinding0">
64             <soap:address
65                 location="http://www.deitel.com:6060/BookTitle/" />
66          </wsdl:port>
67
68      </wsdl:service>
69
70  </wsdl:definitions>
```

Fig. 6.8   WSDL document associated with **BookTitle** Web service. (Part 2 of 2.)

Figure 6.8 contains all the information that a client application needs to determine which operations of the Web service are available to the client and how to communicate with those Web services. Line 1 specifies the XML declaration, because WSDL is an XML vocabulary. Line 5 contains the **definitions** element, which is the root element of a WSDL document. This element contains all the other elements that store information on the Web service. The **definitions** element also defines several namespaces (lines 8–11) that the WSDL document can use.

Lines 13–15 and 17–19 contain two **message** elements, which represent the variables that clients and Web services transfer between each other. These variables are either the argument types or the return types for the Web service's remote methods. A **message** element contains a **part** element (lines 14 and 18), which specifies the name and data type of the message exchanged. Lines 13–15 define a **message** element named **BookTitle-Impl_getBookTitle_Response**, which represents a **string**. Similarly, lines 17–19 define a **message** element named **BookTitleImpl_getBookTitle_Request**,[7] which also represents a **string**.

It seems logical that the **message** elements defined in lines 13–19 should represent the messages that the client receives from, and sends to, the Web service. However, the WSDL **message** element declares only the messages that will be used, but does not specify exactly how the client and Web service should send the messages. WSDL provides the **portType** element to accomplish this task. The **portType** element (lines 21–31) contains **opera-**

---

7. **BookTitleImpl_getBookTitle_Response**
   and **BookTitleImpl_getBookTitle_Request** are auto-generated names.

tion elements (lines 23–29), which translate the messages defined in the WSDL **message** elements to those passed to and from the actual services. Each **operation** element contains an **input** and **output** element, each of which associates a **message** element to a method parameter or method return type, respectively. Lines 23–29 contain an **operation** element that corresponds to the two **message** elements in lines 13–19. Lines 24–28 declare the *input* element that specifies that the **BookTitle** Web service receives as a parameter the **BookTitleImpl_getBookTitle_Request** message. Similarly, lines 27–28 declare the **output** element that specifies that the **BookTitle** Web service returns to the client the **BookTitleImpl_getBookTitle_Response** message. Note that the **message** element in lines 13–19 specified these messages as strings. Therefore, when the client sends a string as a parameter to the **BookTitle** Web service, the client will receive another string as a return value.

The *binding* elements (lines 33–58) specify how the client and Web service should send messages to one another. The client uses this information to access the Web service. Each **binding** element contains another **binding** element that specifies the protocol by which clients access the Web service. The second **binding** element is prefixed by the URI associated with that protocol. For this example, we use SOAP as the protocol that the client uses to invoke a service, as evidenced by the namespace **"http://schemas.xmlsoap.org/wsdl/soap"** prefix used on the **binding** element (line 36). A WSDL document allows us to use other protocols as well, such as MIME and HTTP (without using SOAP). If either of these protocols had been used, we would have declared the second **binding** element using the namespace prefixes associated with HTTP and MIME, respectively.

Line 37 sets the **transport** attribute of the **binding** element to **http://schemas.xmlsoap.org/soap/http**, which is an unique identifier for specifying SOAP over HTTP. Line 38 sets the **style** attribute of the **binding** element to **rpc**, which specifies that the client will make XML-based remote procedure calls to access the Web service. By using this value, the Web service platform—i.e., the environment on which a Web service resides, which includes the Web server, the SOAP server, etc.—can expect to receive a message that has a specific structure containing parameters (input) or return values (output). The other value that the **style** attribute can assume is **document**, which is the default value if the **style** attribute is omitted. This value specifies that the message contains an XML document that does not have this structure (i.e., one that is not "formatted" appropriately for remote procedure calls).

Lines 40–58 define an **operation** element that contains instructions on how to access the Book Title Web service. The **operation** element provides the actual method definition for accessing the Web service—i.e., this element defines the interface for the Web service. Lines 43–48 contain an **input** element, which in turn provides a **body** element that specifies how the Web service platform encodes SOAP requests to the Web service. This element has attributes **use**, **encodingStyle** and **namespace**. Attribute **use** determines whether the **part** elements of the **message** elements are encoded. Attributes **encodingStyle** and **namespace** specify the encoding and namespace used for the messages, respectively. Lines 50–54 define an **output** element, which specifies how the Web service platform encodes SOAP responses from the Web service. The attributes that an **output** element contains are identical to those of an **input** element.

The **service** element (lines 60–68) specifies the URL that clients use to invoke the Web service. The **service** element can contain several **port** elements—each **port** element contains a URL for a unique binding. Our example only contains one Web service—**BookTitle**—so we need to use only one **port** element to reveal the Web service location (lines 62–66). Lines 64–65 contain an **address** element that specifies that **http://www.deitel.com:6060/BookTitle/** is the URL that clients can access to invoke the Book Title Web service.

6.12 SOAP Implementations

Several companies have produced toolkits to facilitate the rapid development of Web services. These toolkits allow developers to create and publish Web services without having to learn the technical details of SOAP or WSDL. Toolkits often provide programming environments that hide the lower-level technical details. This allows programmers to develop applications quickly and to focus on the application's functionality, rather than on the details of implementing the Web service. Several development tools are available—this section focuses on Apache Axis, Microsoft's SOAP Toolkit and IBM's Web Services Toolkit. The IBM toolkit uses Axis as its SOAP implementation.

6.12.1 Apache Axis

In 2000, the Apache Software Foundation (**www.apache.org**) created a SOAP toolkit, called Apache SOAP, which was based on IBM's early SOAP toolkit, *SOAP4J*. Apache SOAP implements most of the features included in the SOAP Version 1.1 specification. After releasing several versions of Apache SOAP, Apache created the Java development tool called Axis. At the time of this writing, Axis has not been released in its final version, so many organizations still use Apache SOAP. We discuss Apache Axis in this section.

At the time of this writing, Apache Axis 1.0 was in the beta-testing phase. The toolkit fully supports SOAP 1.1, as well as many features of SOAP 1.2, and offers greater flexibility and more features than does Apache SOAP. To ensure interoperability, Apache and Microsoft have collaborated to resolve communications issues between Axis and Microsoft's SOAP implementations.[25]

To use Axis, a developer needs to install an application server, such as Apache's *Tomcat* (**jakarta.apache.org**), and an XML parser, such as *Xerces* (**xml.apache.org**). These components needs to be installed in addition to the Axis application.[26]

To deploy a Web service using one of the Apache toolkits, developers first create a Web service application in Java. Axis gives developers the option of using *Enterprise JavaBeans* (**java.sun.com/products/ejb**), a technology that creates reusable *server-side* (i.e., located on servers) *business logic* (i.e., programming code that processes data according to the application's business rules).

After a developer creates a Web service, Axis provides two options to deploy that service. Using the first option, called the *Instant Deployment*, system administrators can publish a Web service quickly and easily, but with limited customization options. Using instant deployment, Axis exposes all *public methods* (i.e., methods that are available to external entities) of the Java class as Web services. However, developers who desire greater control can use Axis' Custom Deployment features, which allow developers to specify which methods to expose. Often, a developer wants to expose only one method as a Web service and leave other methods private. To customize the deployment of a Web service, developers produce a specialized XML file, called a *Web Service Deployment Descriptor (WSDD)* file. Axis uses the WSDD file, which is an XML document, to detail exactly which methods to expose.

Axis also offers support for generating WSDL documents that can be published to a registry.[27] Axis provides two options for generating a WSDL document. In the first, and simplest, Axis auto-generates the file after a Web service has been deployed. The second option allows developers to generate WSDL documents using *command line* (e.g., DOS prompt) instructions; this enables greater customization of WSDL files. Apache's Axis is available free for download at **xml.apache.org/dist/axis**.[8]

6.12.2 Microsoft SOAP Toolkit

The *Microsoft SOAP Toolkit 2* enables programmers to deploy Web services on Windows platforms that do not include the .NET Framework.[9] Like Axis and the IBM Web Services Toolkit, the Microsoft SOAP Toolkit 2 fully supports the SOAP 1.1 specification, the WSDL 1.1 specification and Universal Description, Discovery and Integration (UDDI). This toolkit also offers proprietary technologies that Microsoft developed to tie Web services deployment explicitly to Microsoft programming components. Developers can download the Microsoft SOAP Toolkit for Visual Studio® 6 at **msdn.microsoft.com/xml**.

This toolkit includes both client-side and server-side components. The client-side components invoke Web services, and the server-side components map the invoked services to *Component Object Model (COM)* objects. COM is a Microsoft software architecture in which developers use binary program components to build applications that can communicate with other COM-based applications. Using the SOAP Toolkit, interaction with COM objects is described in WSDL and *Web Services Meta Language (WSML)*[10] files. To simplify the creation of WSDL and WSML files, the SOAP Toolkit provides the Web Services Description Language/Web Services Meta Language (WSDL/WSML) tool, which auto-generates WSDL and WSML files for the developer. Although WSML is not a standard, Microsoft employs this WSML in conjunction with WSDL to map the operations of a service to the methods that reside in a COM object. The Microsoft toolkit also employs the *Remote Object Proxy Engine (ROPE),* an infrastructure that provides a set of COM components to handle aspects of messaging. ROPE formats the remote procedure call, binds the message to HTTP and processes the returned information so that developers do not have to understand or implement the details of these processes.[28]

Another technology in the SOAP Toolkit that simplifies Web services application development is Microsoft's *SOAP Messaging Object (SMO)* framework. SMO simplifies the creation and processing of XML documents that reside in SOAP messages.[29]

---

8. At the time of this writing, Axis was in the Beta 2 testing phase.
9. When developers move to .NET, creating and transmitting SOAP messages to Web services will not require a separate toolkit—the functionality is built into .NET. We discuss .NET in Chapter 9 and Appendix B.
10. WSML is equivalent to Axis WSDD.

6.12.3 IBM Web Services ToolKit 3.0

IBM's *Web Services Toolkit (WSTK) 3.0* offers applications and resources, including documentation, tutorials and specifications, for a Web services developer to deploy Web services in Linux, Windows® 2000 or XP environments. The IBM toolkit provides a Web service environment, prototypes and previews of developing technologies for Web services. The toolkit is free for download at the IBM *alphaWorks* Web site, **www.al-phaworks.ibm.com/tech/webservicestoolkit**.[11]

The toolkit application contains an embedded, limited version of the IBM WebSphere Application Server, which provides an environment in which to run Web services. However, developers can opt to configure the toolkit to employ a standard version of the WebSphere Application Server or Apache's Tomcat.

When a developer downloads and installs the IBM toolkit, a wizard (an application that guides a user through the program setup) installs sample Web services, a private UDDI registry and plug-in components that enable the Web browser to search the UDDI registry. An *Aggregation Demo* illustrates the potential modularity of Web services by demonstrating how Web services can be combined to evolve new Web services. Another demonstration included in the toolkit is *Gourmet2Go*, which illustrates how Web services function in a B2B and B2C environment. Gourmet2Go is a fictional Web services application that demonstrates how a grocery delivery provider can employ Web services technology, such as online grocery ordering and delivery. The *Private UDDI Registry* is an example of a lookup service that might be used within an organization; private registries provide an alternative to publishing information to a public UDDI registry. IBM's Web Services Toolkit also installs *Web services base code*, which includes the WebSphere server, the Apache Axis engine and support for UDDI and WSDL.

Like Axis, the IBM WSTK provides developers with two options to create WSDL files that describe Web services. A developer either can code the description manually or can use the IBM Toolkit's *Web Service Generator Tool* to generate the necessary files.[30] The IBM WSTK also provides demonstrations that utilize SOAP-related technologies, such as SOAP encryption and SOAP messages with attachments.

This chapter overviewed two essential technologies involved in Web services—SOAP is the protocol by which applications communicate with Web services, and WSDL documents provide information that applications use to locate and invoke Web services. Developers often store WSDL documents in registries, such as those that operate using UDDI. The next chapter, UDDI, Discovery and Web Services Registries, explains the registries and the technologies that facilitate the discovery of Web services.

6.13 Summary

IBM, Lotus Development Corporation, Microsoft, DevelopMentor and Userland Software developed an XML-messaging protocol to define an interoperable way to invoke remote operations, called the Simple Object Access Protocol (SOAP). The most recent version of the SOAP specification is Version 1.2, released as a W3C Working Draft in December 2001. Although SOAP can be employed for other types of computer communications, the protocol is best known for its adoption by the industry as the standard messaging protocol used in Web services.

---

11. The toolkit is updated periodically. Check the Web site for latest download.

SOAP facilitates interoperable communication among computing systems in a decentralized, distributed network. The protocol specifies a messaging framework to send XML documents, called SOAP messages, over the Internet. SOAP messages encapsulate information transmitted to and from a Web service but SOAP messages do not provide programming instructions; rather, they specify to a Web services server which operation to invoke. Designed to be extensible, SOAP supports such features as attachments, security, routing information and transactions.

SOAP is not an executable application; it neither includes explicit programming instructions, nor restricts developers to a specific programming language, such as Visual Basic .NET, Java or C#. The SOAP specification was designed to include only the functions and capabilities necessary to achieve platform- and language-independent communications. Developers who apply the protocol can create SOAP applications that achieve interoperable messaging across platforms.

The SOAP specification describes four main parts of the protocol. The first part is the SOAP envelope, which describes the format of a SOAP message. The second part is a set of rules that encode data types that are sent in a SOAP message. Most programming languages require developers to specify the types of data that an application uses; this allows programs that receive the data to interpret the information correctly. The third part defines how a SOAP message can execute remote procedure calls (i.e., requests to execute a program component on a remote computer). The fourth part of the specification involves the SOAP binding framework, which defines the protocol through which SOAP messages are transmitted to applications.

A client application that wants to query a Web service uses a SOAP client to create and send a SOAP message. SOAP client applications can be simple programs or parts of more complex systems. A SOAP server is a program or part of a program that receives and processes a SOAP client's request

The ability to attach files to SOAP messages greatly increases SOAP's versatility. Attachments enable Web services to exchange data that is difficult to represent in XML—such as documents and multimedia files. One specification, called SOAP Messages with Attachments, describes how send attached files with SOAP messages. Microsoft created an alternative to the SOAP Messages with Attachments specification, called the Direct Internet Message Encapsulation (DIME) specification.

Although the computer industry and most major software vendors support SOAP as the standard method of Web services communication, other protocols offer similar functionality. Companies have used one such technology, XML-RPC, for certain implementations. Another alternative is for developers to create proprietary messaging solutions.

Before an application can access a Web service, the application must learn about the available services and their capabilities. In such cases, a client can consult a registry for URLs of Web Services Description Language (WSDL) documents. Registries store files that provide specific technical information; using this data, applications can query and communicate with Web services. The client application uses WSDL, an XML-based language, to obtain such information. Microsoft and IBM, with contributions from Ariba, submitted WSDL Version 1.1 to the W3C in March 2001. Although the technology still is under development, nearly all Web services provide support for WSDL, and most development tools auto-generate WSDL files.

Many Web services published on the Internet have associated WSDL documents, which contain sets of definitions (marked up as XML) that describe the Web services. The

WSDL document specifies the service's capabilities, its location on the Web and instructions regarding how to access it. A WSDL document defines the structure of the messages that a Web service sends and receives. Using this information, applications searching for a Web service to fill a specific need can analyze the WSDL files of several comparable services and choose between the services. In addition, WSDL files provide specific technical information that enables applications to connect to and communicate with Web services over HTTP or another communications protocol.

Several companies have produced toolkit applications to facilitate the rapid development of Web services. These applications allow developers to create and publish Web services without having to learn the technical details of SOAP or WSDL. Toolkits often provide programming environments that hide the lower-level technical details. This allows programmers to develop applications quickly and to focus on the application's functionality, rather than on the details of implementing the Web service. Several development tools are available, including Apache Axis, Microsoft's SOAP Toolkit and IBM's Web Services Toolkit.

6.14 Internet and Web Resources

SOAP

www.w3.org/TR/soap12-part2/#soapenc
This site defines and provides links to additional information on SOAP encoding and the SOAP data model.

xml.apache.org/axis
The Apache organization provides information about Apache's SOAP implementation, as well as documentation and downloads.

www.xml.com/pub/a/2002/02/20/endpoints.html
This article overviews WSDL and explains how SOAP accesses WSDL documents.

msdn.microsoft.com/msdnmag/issues/01/04/Toolkit20/Toolkit20.asp
Microsoft's Developer Network provides articles that discuss why Microsoft created WSML for its SOAP 2 Toolkit.

www.aspalliance.com/Yusuf/Article11.asp
An overview of Web services, including an explanation of SOAP and WSDL, is available at this site.

www.develop.com/soap
This site offers articles, resources and answers to frequently asked questions relating to SOAP.

xml.coverpages.org/soap.html
The SOAP Cover Pages provides synopses of books and articles, as well as links to numerous SOAP sites.

www.microsoft.com/mind/0100/soap/soap.asp
This article defines SOAP and discusses its uses.

www.wdvl.com/Authoring/Languages/XML/Schema.html
This section of the Web Developers Virtual Library provides information on XML Schema and SOAP. Links to presentations, articles, specifications and Schema software tools are provided.

WSDL

www.w3.org/TR/wsdl
This site introduces WSDL, provides examples and discusses how WSDL and SOAP are related.

`xml.coverpages.org/wsdl.html`
This site aggregates descriptions of, and links to, articles and books on the topic of WSDL.

`www-106.ibm.com/developerworks/webservices/library/ws-wsdl`
In a series of articles, IBM's DeveloperWorks details the various ways of using WSDL in a UDDI registry.

`www-106.ibm.com/developerworks/webservices/library/ws-peer4`
A definition and explanation of WSDL is available in this article.

`www.eweek.com/article/0,3658,s%253D701%2526a%253D22273,00.asp`
This *eWeek* article discusses the use of WSDL by vendors, as well as the W3C working group established to develop WSDL further.

`www.learnxmlws.com/tutors/wsdl/wsdl.aspx`
This article introduces WSDL and its use with SOAP and provides diagrams to clarify the explanations.

`www.webreference.com/js/column96/9.html`
This site discusses WSDL and provides an example of a WSDL document.

`www.itworld.com/nl/xml_prac/06212001`
This *IT World* article helps readers obtain a better understanding of WSDL and its purpose.

`www.gotdotnet.com/services/wsdl/wsdlverify.asmx?op=ValidateWSDL`
Visitors can validate the functionality of published WSDL files at this site.

WORKS CITED

1. "RE: Asynchronous Calls and More," `<aspn.activestate.com/ASPN/Mail/Message/Apache-Soap-Users/950352>`.

2. D. Box, "A Brief History of SOAP," `<www.xml.com/lpt/a/2001/04/04/soap.html>`.

3. D. Box, "A Brief History of SOAP," `<www.xml.com/lpt/a/2001/04/04/soap.html>`.

4. `<www.w3.org>`.

5. "SOAP Version 1.2 Working Draft," 9 July 2001 `<www.w3.org/TR/2001/WD-soap12-20010709>`.

6. T. Clements, "Overview of SOAP," 17 August 2001 `<dcb.sun.com/practices/webservices/overviews/overview_soap.jsp>`.

7. "SOAP Version 1.2 Part 0: Primer," W3C Working Draft 17 December 2001 `<www.w3.org/TR/2001/WD-soap12-part0-20011217>`.

8. M. Gudgin and T. Ewald, "Data Encoding or Data 'n Coding?" `<www.xml.com/lpt/a/2001/11/21/data-encoding.html>`.

9. "SOAP Version 1.2 Working Draft," 9 July 2001 `<www.w3.org/TR/2001/WD-soap12-20010709>`.

10. P. Cauldwell, et al., *Professional XML Web Services* (Birmingham, UK: Wrox, 2000) 21.

11. P. Cauldwell, et al., *Professional XML Web Services* (Birmingham, UK: Wrox, 2000) 21.

12. T. Clements, "Overview of SOAP," 17 August 2001 `<dcb.sun.com/practices/webservices/overviews/overview_soap.jsp>`.

13. T. Clements, "Overview of SOAP," 17 August 2001 `<dcb.sun.com/practices/webservices/overviews/overview_soap.jsp>`.

14. B. Decorum, "A Simple SOAP Client," `<www-106.ibm.com/developerworks/xml/library/x-soapcl/?dwzone=xml>`.

15. "SOAP Version 1.2 Part 0: Primer," W3C Working Draft 17 December 2001 `<www.w3.org/TR/2001/WD-soap12-part0-20011217>`.

16. I. Moraes, "SOAP Messages with Attachments," *XML Journal* Volume 3, Issue 1: 46–48.

17. M. Powell, "DIME: Sending Binary Data with Your SOAP Messages," 22 January 2002 `<msdn.microsoft.com/library/en-us/dn_voices_webservice/html/service01152002.asp?frame=true>`.

18. `<www.w3.org/TR/2001/WD-soap12-part0-20011217>`.

19. "RE: Asynchronous Calls and More," `<aspn.activestate.com/ASPN/Mail/Message/Apache-Soap-Users/950352>`.

20. "SOAP Frequently Asked Questions," `<www.develop.com/soap/soapfaq.htm>`.

21. "UDDI Advances with Web Services Description Language," 29 September 2000 `<www.advisor.com/Articles.nsf/aid/SMITT31>`.

22. P. Cauldwell, et al., *Professional XML Web Services* (Birmingham, UK: Wrox, 2001) 110.

23. B. Siddiqui, "Deploying Web Services with WSDL: Part 1, Introduction to Web Services and WSDL," November 2001 `<www-106.ibm.com/developerworks/library/ws-intwsdl>`.

24. `<www.w3.org/TR/wsdl>`.

25. T. Modi, "Axis: The Next Generation of Apache SOAP," *Java World* 25 January 2002 `<www-javaworld.com/javaworld/jw-01-2002/jw-0125-axis_p.html>`.

26. `<www.apache.org/dist/axis>`.

27. T. Modi, "Axis: The Next Generation of Apache SOAP," *Java World* 25 January 2002 `<www-javaworld.com/javaworld/jw-01-2002/jw-0125-axis_p.html>`.

28. A. Cartwright, "SOAP Soup," `<xml101.com/articles/adam/soapsoup/default.asp>`.

29. C. Weyer, "Implementing a Web Service with Microsoft SOAP Toolkit Version 2.0," `<www.vbxml.com/soap/articles/tk2>`.

30. "Implementing the Web Services ToolKit," `<www.ibm.com/developerworks>`.

7

UDDI, Discovery and Web Services Registries

Objectives

- To discuss Web services discovery.
- To explain how UDDI enables client applications to locate Web services.
- To overview the relationship among SOAP, UDDI and WSDL.
- To introduce the UDDI Business Registry, how it is organized and how users can search its contents.
- To discuss how organizations or partner businesses can create private UDDI registries.
- To introduce alternative discovery technologies, such as ebXML and WS-Inspection.

Knowledge is of two kinds. We know a subject ourselves, or we know where we can find information upon it.
Samuel Johnson

The secret of all those who make discoveries is that they regard nothing as impossible.
Justus Liebig

The people who get on in this world are the people who get up and look for the circumstances they want, and, if they can't find them, make them.
George Bernard Shaw

Outline

7.1 Introduction

As the popularity of the World Wide Web surged in the 1990s, many organizations began to conduct business on the Internet. To facilitate e-commerce, companies needed a way to locate one another and exchange information electronically. Organizations responded by creating their own methods of publishing business-related data on the Web and offering third parties access to the data. However, adding new business customers and suppliers to these proprietary systems often was inefficient, difficult and time-consuming.[1] To address this problem, IBM, Microsoft and Ariba developed *Universal Description, Discovery and Integration (UDDI)*, a specification that defines registries in which businesses can publish information about themselves and the services they provide. Service consumers can use UDDI registries to locate general and technical information about various service providers. With this information, consumers can initiate business transactions, form partnerships and purchase services.

In this chapter, we overview UDDI and UDDI registries. We explain how registries operate, the kinds of data they store and how users can search their contents. We also introduce alternative registry and discovery technologies, including *electronic business XML (ebXML)* and *Web Services Inspection (WS-Inspection)*. The widespread adoption of UDDI and other discovery mechanisms will enable service requestors to find and learn about specific Web services—which is key to the ultimate success of Web service initiatives.

7.2 Discovery

Discovery is the process of locating Web services through registries. Web services registries are repositories containing documents that describe business data. Web services registries also provide features such as search capabilities and programmatic access to remote applications. By using a registry, an organization that wishes to employ a Web service to process credit-card payments, for example, can locate all publicly available services that provide the necessary functionality. The organization can compare the services, then make an educated decision as to which service best fits the organization's needs.

Discovery can be categorized into *direct discovery* and *indirect discovery*. Direct discovery is the process of obtaining data from a registry maintained by the service provider. Obtaining data through direct discovery improves the likelihood that data is accurate, because the organization providing the information also operates the Web service. With indirect discovery, an organization obtains data through a third-party registry. Such data might not be as accurate, because service providers might not update information in third-party registries as frequently. When performing indirect discovery, organizations must pose the question: How often do third-party registries interact with service providers to ensure that the data is still accurate? Although indirect discovery has its drawbacks, it allows companies to evaluate Web services from various providers before committing to use a particular service.[2]

7.3 SOAP, UDDI and WSDL

As we described in previous chapters, SOAP, WSDL and UDDI are the core technologies used in Web services interactions. These technologies enable communication among applications in a manner that is independent of specific programming languages, operating systems and hardware platforms. SOAP provides a communication mechanism between Web services and other applications, WSDL offers a uniform method of describing Web services to other programs and UDDI enables the creation of searchable Web services registries. When deployed together, these technologies allow developers to package applications as services, publish the services on the Web and advertise the services to developers and applications.

Applications typically communicate with Web services via a SOAP messaging framework. SOAP messages encapsulate programmatic instructions that are transported to a SOAP server, which processes the messages and invokes the targeted Web services. The WSDL document associated with a particular Web service informs client applications how to format a SOAP message to send to that service. For more information on SOAP and WSDL, review Chapter 6, Understanding SOAP and WSDL.

Figure 7.1 depicts the general architecture in which Web services operate. The UDDI registry stores the locations of WSDL documents. To publish a Web service, a service provider registers the service's WSDL document with the UDDI registry. A service consumer discovers the service from the UDDI registry. Once the service consumer knows how to access the Web service, the consumer can communicate with the Web service directly via SOAP messages.

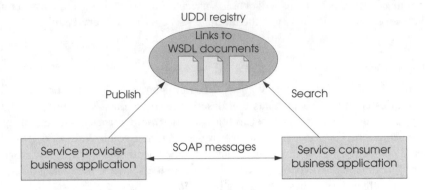

Fig. 7.1   Web services architecture.

7.4 Universal Description, Discovery and Integration (UDDI)

In September 2000, the UDDI project—led by IBM, Microsoft and Ariba—released Version 1.0 of the UDDI specification. This specification defines a framework for centralized registries that facilitate the storage, discovery and exchange of information about businesses and their Web services.[3] UDDI is used in the publicly accessible *UDDI Business Registry (UBR)* maintained by Microsoft, IBM, Hewlett-Packard and SAP. Companies also can implement UDDI in private registries, which are accessible only to authorized parties, such as a company's employees, business partners and suppliers.

In June 2001, the UDDI project released a beta specification of UDDI Version 2.0, which improves on several features of the original specification. One enhancement offers advanced searching capabilities, such as the ability to search using the wildcard character (%). UDDI Version 2.0 also increases the global scope of UDDI registries in that businesses can provide company and product descriptions in various languages, such as Chinese and French. Another new feature enables an organization to provide data regarding its infrastructure, such as details about departments (sales, marketing, research and development, etc.), partners and affiliates. In addition, UDDI Version 2.0 offers support for industry-specific identifiers, such as those of the *Standard Industrial Classification (SIC)* system, which assigns unique numerical identifiers to industries.[4] For example, 2621 represents Paper Mills, and 7371 represents Computer Programming Services.[5]

UDDI Version 2.0 is a beta implementation, so not all applications support it. This is because beta implementations are likely to contain bugs, which could affect the performance of some applications.[6] Furthermore, data stored using the beta implementation of a registry might be lost when the data is migrated to the final version.[7] [*Note*: The UDDI project is developing UDDI Version 3.0. After releasing Version 3.0, the UDDI project plans to submit the UDDI specification to a standards organization.][8]

At the time of this writing, more than 300 companies belong to the UDDI community.[9] These companies, known as community members, are committed to the enhancement, evolution and world-wide acceptance of the UDDI registry. Community members include many large and influential organizations, such as American Express, Boeing, Fujitsu, Hitachi and Sun Microsystems. A complete list of community members can be found at **www.uddi.org**.[10]

7.4.1 Operator Nodes and Registrars

An *operator node* is an organization that hosts an implementation of the *UDDI Business Registry (UBR)*. Four operator nodes—Hewlett-Packard, IBM, Microsoft and SAP—host beta implementations of the UBR that adhere to the UDDI Version 2.0, and two operator nodes—IBM and Microsoft—host implementations of the UBR that adhere to the UDDI Version 1.0. A company needs to register with only one operator node to be listed in the UBR. This is because the UBR is based on the "register once, publish everywhere" principle, which states that information contained in one registry is replicated in the other registries. *Replication* is the process of updating records so that all instances of those records are identical. Thus, when a company registers with one operator node (known as a *custodian*), the company's data appears in the other three registries, as well.[11] Although data is not replicated instantaneously, the operator nodes synchronize their data at least every 12 hours.[12]

At the time of this writing, only the UBR implementations that adhere to UDDI Version 1.0 support replication. However, the UBR implementations that adhere to UDDI Version 2.0 are expected to support replication by fall 2002. We list the URLs of the four operator nodes in the Internet and Web Resources section at the end of this chapter. [*Note*: The UDDI project announced that NTT Communications of Tokyo, Japan, will become an operator node in 2002.][13]

Although replication ensures that all four UBRs contain identical information, a company can update its information only through its custodian. This is because the *UDDI Version 2.0 API Specification* does not provide a protocol for reconciling disparate or duplicate data. Limiting companies to interaction with only one operator node prevents users from entering multiple versions of data in different operator nodes.[14]

Alternatively, companies can publish information in the UBR through a *registrar*—an organization that assists companies in creating data, such as business and service descriptions, to be stored in UDDI registries.[15] Note that registrars are not operator nodes, because registrars do not host implementations of the UDDI registry. A complete list of the registrars can be found at **www.uddi.org**.

7.4.2 Advantages of Registering

Registering in the UBR offers advantages to both service providers and service consumers. For service providers, the UBR is an effective method of advertising Web services. Because the UBR can be accessed from anywhere, service providers gain global visibility, enabling them to communicate and form alliances with organizations located throughout the world. This kind of worldwide exposure helps service providers expand their markets.[16]

For service consumers, the UBR saves time and simplifies the process of using Web services. The UBR stores technical details about Web services, so service consumers do not have to spend time locating service-related information, such as how to communicate with a particular Web service. By using the UBR, service consumers can integrate their applications with remote services more quickly and efficiently.[17]

The UBR also can reduce costs for service providers and service consumers. Service providers can advertise their businesses and services for free, and service consumers can locate compatible Web services for free. Without the UBR, organizations might have to pay fees to advertise and find Web services. [*Note*: Some service providers listed in the UBR charge consumers that access their Web services.][18]

7.5 Role of UDDI in Web Services

As stated previously, UDDI registries contain general and technical information about businesses and their Web services. Vendors often compare the UBR's structure to that of a phone book. In this section, we discuss the components of the UBR's phone-book structure—*white pages*, *yellow pages* and *green pages*.[19] We overview the schema for the UDDI information model, which specifies the XML elements and attributes used to describe a Web service. We also explain the UDDI publishing and inquiry APIs, which define rules for posting and searching registry content, respectively.

The UBR mainly supports indirect discovery, because it is hosted by four intermediaries. However, UDDI also can support direct discovery in private registries. This is because private registries usually are implemented by specific organizations and describe only services offered by those organizations.

7.5.1 Levels of UDDI

The UBR can be categorized into white pages, yellow pages and green pages. The white pages contain general information about a company, such as its name, address, contact information and identifiers. Identifiers are values (alphabetic or numeric) that uniquely distinguish companies. Examples of identifiers are Dun & Bradstreet's *D-U-N-S® (Data Universal Numbering System)* classifications, which are nine-digit numbers assigned to businesses.[20]

The yellow pages divide companies into various categories on the basis of their products or services. For example, a software company might be categorized under computer software or software engineering. The yellow pages allow registry users to search for companies or services that fit a particular category (such as sales, travel or books).[21]

The green pages contain technical information about a company's products, services and Web services. This data allows a service client to *bind* (i.e., establish a communication channel) to a Web service, because the information defines how to invoke the service.[22] The green pages usually include references to services' WSDL documents, which contain information on how to interact with Web services.[23]

7.5.2 Information Models in UDDI[1]

The *UDDI Version 2.0 Data Structure Reference* (available at **www.uddi.org**) stipulates that to transact business, a client company needs access to certain information about a provider's Web service. This information, known collectively as the *UDDI information model*, includes the following five components: business information, business-service information, binding information, service-specification information and publisher-assertion information. In this section, we discuss the five components of the UDDI information model.

Each component of the UDDI information model resides within a *data structure* that consists of XML elements and attributes. These XML elements and attributes describe the components of the information model. The XML representation of the UDDI information model is used when interfacing with a UDDI registry. Because there are five components, there exist five interrelated data structures. Figure 7.2 illustrates the relationships among the UDDI information model's five data-structure types.

---

1. Technical information in this section is based primarily on "UDDI Version 2.0 Data Structure Reference," 8 June 2001 **<www.uddi.org/pubs/DataStructure-V2.00-Open-20010608.pdf>**.

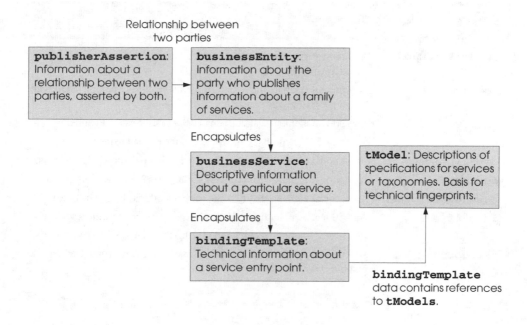

Fig. 7.2 UDDI information model. (Courtesy of UDDI.)

The *businessEntity* *structure* encapsulates a business's general information, such as its name, address and contact information. This structure references the *busi-nessService structure*, which describes different types of services offered by the company. Technical information about these services resides in the *bindingTemplate structure*, which contains references to *tModel structures*. A **tModel** structure contains information on how to interact with the Web services. The *publisherAssertions structure* describes the relationships (e.g., partnerships) between two business entities.

The *business information* component corresponds to the UDDI white and yellow pages in that it contains general data about a business and the products and services offered by that business. The business information resides in the **businessEntity** *top-level structure*, which categorizes businesses by their unique identifiers. In this context, a top-level structure encapsulates elements, attributes and other structures that describe a business and its Web services. Figure 7.3 summarizes the elements and attributes of the **businessEntity** structure.

Entity	Description
businessKey	A required attribute that contains a unique hexadecimal identifier for the business. The identifier is assigned by the custodian upon registration.

Fig. 7.3 **businessEntity** attributes and child elements. (Part 1 of 2.)

Entity	Description
authorizedName	An optional attribute that contains the name of the person who published the information.
operator	An optional attribute that contains the name of the operator node with which the business registered.
discoveryURLs	An optional element that contains URLs to discovery documents.
name	A required element that contains the name of the business.
description	An optional element that contains a brief description of the business.
contacts	An optional element that contains the business's contact information.
businessServices	An optional element that lists the services offered by the business.
identifierBag	An optional element that contains a list of unique identifiers (D-U-N-S® number, stock symbol, etc.) associated with the business.
categoryBag	An optional element that contains a list of industry, product or geographic classifications.

Fig. 7.3   **businessEntity** attributes and child elements. (Part 2 of 2.)

In this structure, **businessKey** is a required attribute that uniquely identifies a business. The custodian assigns a unique identifier to each **businessEntity** structure upon registration. Unique identifiers are referred to as *Universally Unique Identifiers (UUIDs)* and usually consist of hexadecimal values. The **businessServices** element contains zero or more references to the descriptions of services offered by an organization. This element references the **businessService** structure.

The *business service information* component corresponds to the UDDI green pages in that it contains technical data about the products and services offered by a particular business. The business service information resides in the ***businessService*** structure. Figure 7.4 summarizes the elements of **businessService**. Each **businessService** structure is identified uniquely by two UUIDs—**serviceKey** and **businessKey**. The required **bindingTemplates** structure contains the technical information about a Web service. The **bindingTemplates** structure includes zero or more references to the **bindingTemplate** structure, which contains the binding information.

Entity	Description
serviceKey	A required attribute that contains a unique, hexadecimal identifier for a service.
businessKey	An attribute that references the **businessKey** of the **businessEntity** structure.
name	A required element that contains the name(s) of a service.
description	An optional element that contains a brief description of a service.

Fig. 7.4   **businessService** attributes child elements. (Part 1 of 2.)

Entity	Description
bindingTemplates	A required structure that contains technical information about a service.
categoryBag	An optional element that contains a list of industry, product or geographic classifications.

Fig. 7.4 **businessService** attributes child elements. (Part 2 of 2.)

The *binding information* component also corresponds to the green pages in that it contains technical information pertaining to a Web service. This information specifies how clients can connect to a particular Web service. Figure 7.5 summarizes the elements and attributes of the **bindingTemplate** structure.

Attribute **bindingKey** is a UUID assigned to each **bindingTemplate** structure by the custodian. The **tModelInstanceDetails** structure contains references to one or more **tModelInstanceInfo** structures, which contain the elements and attributes that describe the service-specification information, or "blueprints," of a Web service. Structure **tModelInstanceInfo** references the **tModel** structure.

Entity	Description
bindingKey	A required attribute that contains a unique hexadecimal identifier. The identifier is assigned by the operator node upon registration.
serviceKey	An attribute that references the **serviceKey** of the **businessService** element. This attribute is required if the **bindingTemplate** structure is not contained in a fully qualified parent that contains another **serviceKey**.
description	An optional element that contains brief description(s) of Web service(s).
accessPoint	An element that states where to access a Web service. Valid **accessPoint** types include **mailto**, **http**, **https**, **ftp**, **fax**, **phone** and **other**. This element is required if **hostingRedirector** is not specified.
hostingRedirector	An element that contains a link to another **bindingTemplate** structure, which contains the description for a particular service. This element is required if **accessPoint** is not specified.
tModelInstanceDetails	A required structure that contains **tModelInstanceInfo** elements, which are "blueprints" of Web services. This structure specifies how to access a Web service.

Fig. 7.5 **bindingTemplate** attributes and child elements.

Whereas the binding information specifies where to access a Web service, the *service-specification information* component describes how to interact with the Web service. The service-specification information resides in the **tModel** structure, summarized in Fig. 7.6. The **tModel**, or *Service Type Registrations*, structure contains information that allows service consumers to use a service provider's Web service.[24]

In the **tModel** structure, the **tModelKey** is a UUID assigned to the structure. The custodian assigns the value to the **tModelKey**. Structure **overviewDoc** references documentation that provides information or instructions about the Web service. Usually, **overviewDoc** references WSDL documents, which contain technical ("blueprint") information about Web services. This "blueprint" information includes the parameters that a Web service receives, the data formats it accepts (**.dat**, **.txt**, etc.) and other application-specific information. This information allows programmers to determine whether a Web service is compatible with their programs.

The *publisher-assertion information* component indicates a relationship between two companies. To instantiate the relationship, both parties must agree to the relationship by declaring identical assertions (i.e., identical statements that specify a mutual relationship). A relationship is valid only when both parties reciprocate the assertions. The publisher assertion information resides in the **publisherAssertion** structure. Figure 7.7 summarizes the elements of the **publisherAssertion** structure.

Publisher-assertion information, a new feature of Version 2.0, allows organizations to acknowledge *parent-child*, *peer-peer* and *identity* relationships. A parent-child relationship indicates that one organization owns another, smaller organization (i.e., the organization identified in the **fromKey** owns the organization identified in the **toKey**). A peer-peer relationship states that the organizations identified in the **fromKey** and the **toKey** are partners or affiliates. An identity relationship states that the organization identified in the **fromKey** is the same as the organization identified in the **toKey**. Identity relationships typically are used to assert an organization's various divisions, units and departments.[25]

Entity	Descriptions
tModelKey	A required attribute that uniquely identifies the **tModel**. The identifier is assigned by the custodian upon registration.
authorizedName	An optional attribute that contains the name of the individual who published the information.
operator	An optional attribute that contains the name of the custodian.
name	A required element that contains a descriptive identifier for the **tModel**. Service consumers can use **name** to perform a search for a given **tModel**.
description	An optional element that describes the **tModel**.
overviewDoc	An optional element that redirects users to additional references, usually WSDL documents.

Fig. 7.6   **tModel** attributes and child elements. (Part 1 of 2.)

Entity	Descriptions
identifierBag	An optional element that contains a list of unique identifiers (e.g., D-U-N-S® number, stock symbol) associated with the business.
categoryBag	An optional element that contains a list of industry, product or geographic classifications.

Fig. 7.6   **tModel** attributes and child elements. (Part 2 of 2.)

Entity	Description
fromKey	A required element that uniquely identifies the business that instantiates the relationship.
toKey	A required element that uniquely identifies the business that accepts the relationship.
keyedReference	A required element that identifies the type of relationship.

Fig. 7.7   **publisherAssertion** child elements.

By providing publisher-assertion capabilities, UDDI allows large corporations to describe aspects of their businesses—such as divisions, departments, partners, affiliates and subsidiaries—to users of the UBR. This information is beneficial to service consumers who want to know how business A relates to business B before accessing the services of either business.

7.5.3 UDDI Publishing and Inquiry APIs

The UDDI Version 2.0 API Specification overviews the publishing and inquiry APIs for creating and searching registry content. The *publishing API* supports the *publish* operation, which enables companies to post and update information in the UDDI registry. Access to the publishing API is restricted, and the UDDI project requires that operator nodes implement an authentication protocol that verifies the identity of the individual or organization creating or updating the information. The publishing API consists of commands that service providers can use to create and update information. Access to the publishing API commands is available only via *HTTPS* (i.e., a variant of HTTP that uses Secure Sockets Layer to establish security).[26] For more information regarding HTTPS and Secure Sockets Layer, see Chapter 11, Computer and Internet Security, and Chapter 12, Web Services Security.

The *inquiry API* supports the *find* operation, which enables service consumers to browse the registry for service providers that offer a certain service or type of service. Anyone can use the inquiry API to perform queries on the UBR. The inquiry API supports three query patterns—browse, drill-down and invocation. The *browse pattern*, which supports the five information-model structures discussed in the previous section, allows service consumers to perform broad searches for businesses, services, templates or **tModel**s.

This query pattern returns the general, overview information (identification key, name and description) pertaining to the business, service, template or **tModel**.[27]

To obtain a more detailed description of a business, service, template or **tModel**, the inquiry API provides the *drill-down pattern*. This pattern typically is used in conjunction with the browse pattern, because it requires an identification key (obtained during the browse pattern) to retrieve the necessary information. The identification key is passed as an argument in a drill-down pattern. With the drill-down pattern, users can obtain technical information, such as integration capabilities and scalability.[28]

The *invocation pattern* queries the **bindingTemplate** structure, which contains information that programmers need to access a particular Web service. Because the location of a Web service might change, the invocation pattern searches the **bindingTemplate** structure for the service's current location. The access information always resides in the **bindingTemplate** structure; therefore, service consumers typically use automated tools that query the structure for the access information.[29]

After service consumers discover compatible Web services, the consumers must connect to, and communicate with, the computing systems of other businesses. The process of connecting to, and communicating with, a Web service is referred to as binding.[30]

7.6 UDDI Registries

As we stated previously, UDDI can be supported on both public and private registries. The UDDI Business Registry (UBR) is a free, public registry that can be accessed by individuals or businesses. Organizations that want to restrict access to their services can implement private registries, which impose additional security measures to safeguard against unauthorized access. In this section, we discuss the UBR and private registries in detail.

7.6.1 UDDI Business Registry

The UBR, which contains information about companies and their technical capabilities, allows service providers to organize and describe Web services in a central location. Service consumers can browse this registry to find information about businesses and Web services.[31] To post information in the UBR, businesses need to register with the UDDI project. However, any individual or business can perform searches on the UBR without registering.[32]

The UBR usually is referred to as a *Public Cloud*, because the "UDDI Business Registry" consists of several registries owned and maintained by public operator nodes. Although multiple organizations host implementations of the UBR, data entered in one registry is replicated in the other registries. The replication of data is guaranteed, because the operator nodes are governed by the *Operator's Council*, a committee that consists of the current operator nodes. The Operator's Council governs the UDDI specifications and quality-of-service (QoS) issues.[33] The list of companies that host public registries is provided at **www.uddi.org**.

Figure 7.8 depicts the home page for the UDDI project (**www.uddi.org**). From this Web site, users can register for, and search, the UBR. To register and publish information in the UBR, select the **Register** tab. Clicking this tab redirects the user to a page that lists the operator nodes for both Version 1.0 and Version 2.0 UDDI implementations. To register in the UBR, select an operator node and click **Go**. Then, complete the required information.

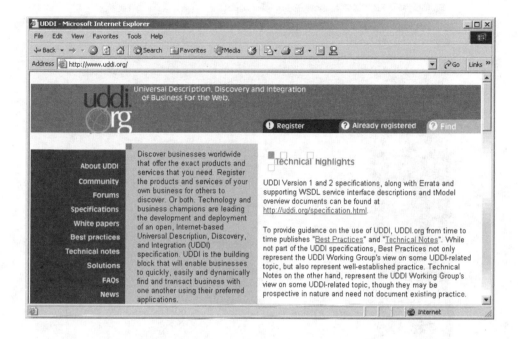

Fig. 7.8   UDDI home page. (Courtesy of UDDI.)

To search the UDDI registry for a specific Web service, select the **Find** tab. Clicking this tab redirects the user to a page that lists the operator nodes for both Version 1.0 and Version 2.0 (Fig. 7.9). To perform a search, the user selects an operator node and clicks **Go**. For demonstration purposes, we perform a search using IBM's implementation of the UBR Version 1.0 registry.

Figure 7.10 depicts the IBM **UDDI Business Registry** Web site. This site allows the user to perform searches on the basis of a **Business**, a **Service** or a **Service Type**. A search performed on a **Business** returns businesses whose names start with a particular word. Figure 7.11 demonstrates performing a **Business** search for companies whose names begin with **Books**.

Figure 7.12 illustrates the results of the search. From the results page, users can view a service provider's general information—the **businessEntity** information—by selecting a link listed under the **Business Name** column. Potential service consumers can use this information to learn about and compare service providers.

Performing a search using **Service** returns products or services that start with a specific word. In our example, we perform a search on products/services that start with the word **Books** (Fig. 7.13). From the results page, users can view the **businessService** and **bindingTemplate** information by selecting a link listed under the **Service Name** column. Potential service consumers can use this information to review descriptions of Web services.

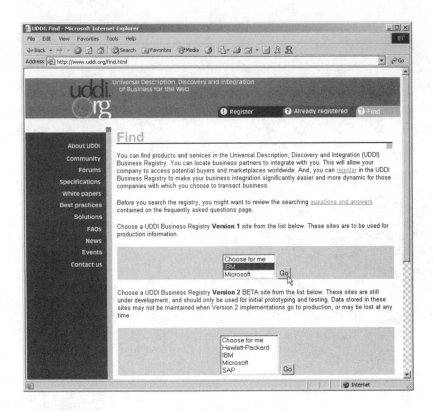

Fig. 7.9   Operator node selected. (Courtesy of UDDI.)

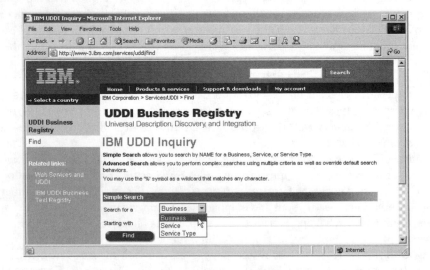

Fig. 7.10 UDDI Business Registry site hosted by IBM. (Courtesy of IBM Corporation.)

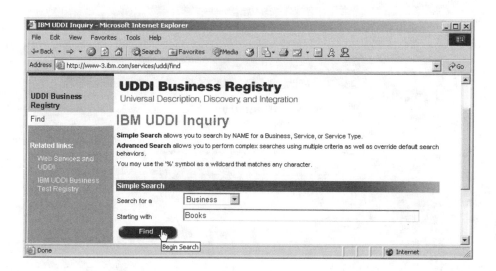

Fig. 7.11   UDDI registry used to perform a **Business** search. (Courtesy of IBM Corporation.)

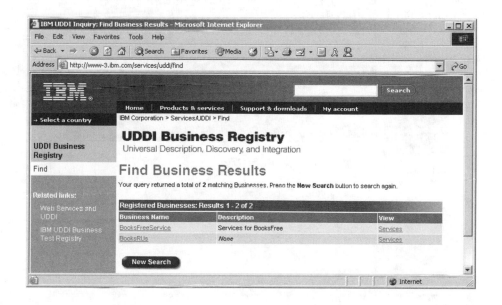

Fig. 7.12   **Business** results for search word **Books**. (Courtesy of IBM Corporation.)

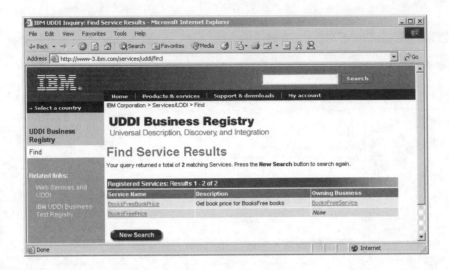

Fig. 7.13   **Service** results for search word **Books**. (Courtesy of IBM Corporation.)

Performing a search using **Service Type** returns the names of businesses that offer a service that contains a specific word. In our example, we perform a search on products/services that contain the word **Books** (Fig. 7.14). From the results page, users can view the **tModel** information by selecting a link listed under the **Service Type Name** column. This information allows users to review technical descriptions of Web services. With the information provided by the UBR, service consumers can discover, connect to and communicate with hundreds of Web services.

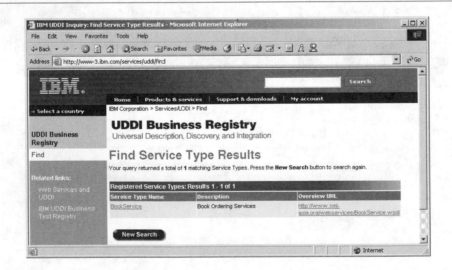

Fig. 7.14   **Service Type** results for search word **Books**. (Courtesy of IBM Corporation.)

7.6.2 Private Registries

The UBR is accessible to the general public, which means that anyone can search the UBR to discover a Web service. However, many organizations might want to limit access to their Web services. Restricting access to services can reduce concerns regarding service-level agreements (discussed in Chapter 3, Web Services Business Models) and security (discussed in Chapter 11, Computer and Internet Security, and Chapter 12, Web Services Security).

Organizations that are uncomfortable exposing services in a public forum can implement *private registries*, access to which is restricted to certain parties (often the employees, partners and affiliates of a particular company). Usually, private registries contain additional security features to ensure data integrity and to safeguard against unauthorized access. Many companies develop private registries to provide personalized services for clients. To support the cost and maintenance of personalized services, most companies charge fees to use private registries.[34]

Companies are adopting private registries more quickly than public registries. This is partly because most organizations want to experiment with Web services by deploying them internally before offering publicly accessible Web services.[35] Another reason for the popularity of private registries is that organizations can use private registries to locate services offered by their own departments or by their partners. As we discuss in Chapter 4, Web Services and Enterprise Computing, Web services accessible only within an organization or group of trusted partners can be used to expedite software-development projects and to integrate applications among departments or partners. According to Gartner, over 75 percent of Web services will reside in private registries by 2005.[36]

There are four varieties of private registries: *e-marketplace UDDI*, *portal UDDI*, *partner catalog UDDI* and *internal enterprise application integration UDDI*. An e-marketplace UDDI is a registry that is hosted by an industry and lists businesses that belong to an industry consortium. For example, an e-marketplace UDDI hosted by car manufacturers might consist of services offered by Ford, Honda and Volkswagen. The e-marketplace UDDI allows only those businesses that belong to a particular industry to publish and find information.[37]

A portal UDDI is a registry that resides on a company's firewall and contains information about a single company's Web services. The company publishes information about its services in the registry so that other companies can view the information. Usually, a portal UDDI operator enables the *find* function for external users, but disables the *publish* function. This means that only internal users (i.e., authorized employees of the company) can update and post information.[38]

The partner catalog UDDI is a registry that resides behind a company's firewall and lists Web services offered by an organization and its partners. A partner catalog UDDI is accessible only to internal users—*publish* and *find* functions are restricted to select employees of an organization and its partners.[39]

The internal enterprise application integration UDDI is a registry that resides behind a company's firewall and lists Web services offered by an organization. This type of registry is accessible only to internal users—*publish* and *find* operations are restricted to select employees of the organization.[40]

7.7 Limitations of UDDI

Although UDDI facilitates the discovery of Web services, there are certain limitations to UDDI and UDDI registries. The most significant limitation of UDDI is the immaturity of the UDDI specification. UDDI has not been submitted to a standards body, so no "official" organization is controlling its development. Also, the specification may change significantly in future versions or when it is finally submitted to a standards body.

Some UDDI registries also raise the question of data reliability. For companies to feel comfortable relying on registry data, the companies need to trust the data. However, the UBR, for instance, does not indicate when data was last updated or checked for accuracy. Because registry users do not know how often data is updated, users must question whether data, service descriptions and hyperlinks contained in registries reflect the most current information about businesses and Web services.[41]

Another limitation of UDDI is that UDDI registries describe Web services, but do not evaluate them. Before using a particular Web service, service consumers usually require information about the Web service's quality of service (QoS). For example, service consumers might want to know the following: How often can I access a certain Web service? Will the Web service "crash" if numerous companies use it simultaneously? Does the service provider offer technical support? If so, what is the turnaround time for resolving issues?[42] The answers to these types of questions would help service consumers distinguish among similar Web services. Quality-of-service information currently does not reside in UDDI registries; therefore, service consumers must perform extensive research to locate the necessary data. Although UDDI was not designed to provide quality-of-service information, registries containing such data would offer more value to service consumers. [*Note*: Quality of Service (QoS) is discussed in greater detail in Chapter 3, Web Services Business Models.]

7.8 Other Discovery Technologies

Although UDDI is the most common Web services discovery standard, other technologies also facilitate Web services discovery. It might seem redundant for the industry to support multiple discovery technologies, but different technologies are appropriate for different situations. For example, some technologies support direct discovery, whereas others support indirect discovery. In this section, we discuss two additional technologies that enable discovery—ebXML and WS-Inspection.

7.8.1 ebXML

Electronic business XML (ebXML) is a joint initiative led by the *United Nations Centre for Trade Facilitation and Electronic Business* (*UN/CEFACT*) and the *Organization for the Advancement of Structured Information Standards* (*OASIS*). UN/CEFACT, OASIS and other organizations designed the ebXML specification to standardize XML-based communication among organizations and to facilitate electronic business.[43] Currently, the ebXML initiative consists of over 1,400 organizations, including RosettaNet, Automotive Industry Action Group, Sun Microsystems and Open Travel Alliance.[44]

EbXML provides a technical framework through which companies of any size in any industry can communicate and exchange data via the Internet. Rather than supporting UDDI, ebXML defines its own registry structure through which service consumers can access XML documents that contain information about service providers. The registry includes capabilities that allow companies to initiate business agreements and perform business transactions. The ebXML registry is accessed through interfaces that expose registry services.[45]

The ebXML registry allows trading partners to share information, such as *Collaboration-Protocol Profiles* (*CPPs*), *Collaboration-Protocol Agreements* (*CPAs*), DTDs and business-process models. CPPs are XML documents that contain information about specific organizations and the services they offer.[46] A CPP includes information about a service interface and specifies the requirements to exchange documents with a particular trading partner. A CPP also contains industry classifications, contact information and a list of services offered by an organization.[47]

A CPA is a contract formed between trading partners; it defines the guidelines to which trading partners must adhere when transacting business.[48] For instance, a CPA can contain the parameters that trading partners must use to ensure that their applications are compatible. Trading partners must have identical copies of the CPA to ensure complete compatibility. It is not mandatory for trading partners to publish their CPAs in the ebXML registry.

Although UDDI and ebXML are separate technologies, organizations can combine them. For instance, organizations can use UDDI registries to advertise Web services and ebXML registries to store trading contracts/agreements. It is preferable to store contracts and agreements in ebXML registries, because ebXML provides a security model and UDDI currently does not. Thus, UDDI and ebXML can be used as complementary services.[49] EbXML registries mainly support indirect discovery, because they are supported by intermediaries. However, ebXML also can support direct discovery within private registries. This is because private registries usually are implemented by specific organizations and contain the services offered by those organizations. For more information on the ebXML specification, see Chapter 5, XML and Derivative Technologies.

7.8.2 WS-Inspection

Web Services Inspection (*WS Inspection*) is an XML-based discovery technology developed by IBM and Microsoft. WS-Inspection defines how a client application server can locate Web services descriptions, such as WSDL documents, that reside on a particular Web server. A WS-Inspection document is maintained by a service provider and contains references to all Web service description documents on the service provider's Web server. If a developer wants to use a particular Web service and knows the Web server on which the service resides, the developer can use WS-Inspection to find WSDL documents and other data about the Web service. In such cases, using WS-Inspection is faster and more efficient than searching the entire UDDI registry for the needed information. However, if the developer does not know the Web server that contains the desired Web service, the developer would use UDDI to locate the service. Thus, WS-Inspection is designed to complement, rather than to replace, UDDI.[50] Because WS-Inspection is hosted by an individual service provider, it supports only direct discovery.

Although WS-Inspection has not been submitted to a standards organization, interested companies can obtain a copy of the WS-Inspection specification from IBM (**www.alphaworks.ibm.com**) or from Microsoft (**msdn.microsoft.com**). The IBM Web Services Toolkit contains an implementation of the WS-Inspection specification; the most current version of Visual Studio® .NET also supports WS-Inspection.[51] WS-Inspection supersedes the Microsoft-specific *Discovery of Web Services* (*DISCO*) technology, which facilitates discovery of Web services in a particular directory on a server. For more information on WS-Inspection and DISCO, see Chapter 9, .NET Web Services: A Conceptual Overview.

In the last three chapters, we examined the core technologies used in Web services—including XML, SOAP, WSDL and UDDI. For organizations to adopt Web services on a large scale, software vendors must incorporate support for these technologies into enterprise software and must provide Web services application-development tools that hide low-level programming details. Chapter 8, Web Services Platforms, Vendors and Strategies, examines numerous software vendors, their products and the support they provide for Web services standards.

7.9 Summary

IBM, Microsoft and Ariba developed Universal Description, Discovery and Integration (UDDI), a specification that defines registries in which businesses can publish information about themselves and the services they provide. Service consumers can use the UDDI registry to locate general and technical information about various service providers. With this information, consumers can initiate business deals, form partnerships and purchase services.

Discovery is the process of locating Web services through registries. By using a registry, an organization that wishes to employ a Web service to process credit-card payments, for example, can locate all publicly available services that provide the necessary functionality. Discovery can be categorized into direct discovery and indirect discovery. Direct discovery is the process of obtaining data from registries maintained by the service provider. With indirect discovery, an organization obtains data through a third-party registry.

In September 2000, the UDDI project—led by IBM, Microsoft and Ariba—released Version 1.0 of the UDDI specification. This specification defines a framework for centralized registries that facilitate the storage, discovery and exchange of information about businesses and their Web services. In June 2001, the UDDI project released a beta specification of UDDI Version 2.0, which improves on several features of the original specification.

UDDI is used in the publicly accessible UDDI Business Registry (UBR) maintained by Microsoft, IBM, Hewlett-Packard and SAP. A company can enroll in the UBR through an operator node, an organization that hosts an implementation of the UBR. When a company registers with one operator node, the information is replicated in the other three registries. UDDI also can be implemented in private registries, which are accessible only to authorized parties. Usually, private registries enforce additional security features to ensure data integrity and to safeguard against unauthorized access.

The UDDI publishing API supports the publish operation, which enables companies to post and update information on a UDDI-based registry. Access to the publishing API is restricted. The inquiry API supports the find operation, which enables service consumers to browse the registry for service providers that offer a certain service. After service consumers discover compatible applications, they must connect to, and communicate with, the computing systems of other businesses. This process is referred to as a binding.

The UBR can be categorized into white pages, yellow pages and green pages. The UDDI white pages contain contact and general information about a company, the yellow pages divide companies into various categories, and the green pages contain technical information about a products, services and Web services.

A client company needs to know certain information about a provider's Web service. This information, known collectively as the UDDI information model, includes the following five components: business information, business service information, binding information, service-specification information and publisher assertion.

Other technologies (such as ebXML and WS-Inspection) also allow applications and developers to discover Web services. EbXML provides a technical framework through which companies can communicate and exchange data via the Internet. EbXML defines its own registry structure through which service consumers can access XML documents that contain information about service providers. Web Services Inspection (WS-Inspection) is an XML-based discovery technology that defines how a client application can locate Web services descriptions, such as WSDL documents, that reside on a particular Web server.

7.10 Internet and Web Resources

www.uddi.org
The UDDI project's site provides UDDI specifications and allows companies to register for the UDDI Business Registry. Anyone can query the UBR from this site.

www-3.ibm.com/services/uddi/find
IBM's implementation of the UDDI Version 1.0 registry can be accessed from this site. The site allows users to publish and find information. Users can perform searches on the basis of business names, service names and service types.

uddi.microsoft.com/search.aspx
This site contains Microsoft's implementation of the UDDI Version 1.0 registry. The site allows users to publish and find information. Users can perform searches on the basis of business names, business categories, business locations, **tModel** names, various taxonomic categories, URLs, etc.

uddi.hp.com/uddi/index.jsp
Hewlett-Packard's implementation of the UDDI Version 2.0 registry can be accessed from this site. The site allows users to publish and find information. It also contains links to the Hewlett-Packard home page, HP's products and services page, and a page detailing HP news and events.

www-3.ibm.com/services/uddi/v2beta/protect/registry.html
This site contains IBM's implementation of the UDDI Version 2.0 registry. The site allows users to publish and find information. Users can perform searches on the basis of business names, service names and **tModel** names. The site also contains links to Web services resources, UDDI features and UDDI specification issues.

uddi.rte.microsoft.com/search/frames.aspx
This site contains Microsoft's implementation of the UDDI Version 2.0 registry. The site allows users to publish and find information. Users can perform on the basis of service names, provider names or **tModel** names. The site also contains information about UDDI, a FAQ section and links to the Microsoft home page.

udditest.sap.com
SAP's implementation of the UDDI Version 2.0 registry can be accessed from this site. The site allows users to publish and find information; it also provides links to the SAP home page, services offered by the company, a listing of SAP partners and other resources.

www.oasis-open.org/cover/uddi.html
The XML Cover Pages provides an overview of UDDI and a brief history of the UDDI specification. The site also contains links to resources such as the UDDI technical white paper and XML Schema.

www.sun.com/software/xml/developers/uddi/
The Sun Microsystems Developer Connection site provides overviews of the UDDI Business Registry, the UDDI information model and the UDDI Programmer's API.

general.rau.ac.za/infosci/raujournal/default.asp?to=newsvol2nr4
The *South African Journal of Information Management* site discusses UDDI and the business benefits of using UDDI.

www.w3.org/2001/03/WSWS-popa/paper12
This W3C site contains information on Web services topics, such as transport and messaging protocols, security, transactions and registries. The site also contains links to references on SOAP, WSDL, UDDI and ebXML.

www-106.ibm.com/developerworks/webservices/library/ws-wsilspec.html
This IBM site contains the Web Services Inspection Language specification. The specification defines the document structure and services provided by WS-Inspection. The specification also explains how WS-Inspection interacts with WSDL and UDDI.

www.perfectxml.com/WebSvc3.asp
The Perfect XML site contains numerous links to references on WSDL, UDDI and DISCO.

WORKS CITED

1.   P. Korzeniowski, "Internet Insight: A Little Slice of the UDDI Pie," *eWeek* 4 February 2002 **<www.eweek.com/print_article/0,3668,a=22053,00.asp>**.

2.   W. Nagy and K. Ballinger, "The WS-Inspection and UDDI Relationship," November 2001 **<www-106.ibm.com/developerworks/webservices/library/ws-wsiluddi.html?dwzone=webservices>**.

3.   "About UDDI," **<www.uddi.org/about.html>**.

4.   P. Korzeniowski, "UDDI: Two Versions Down, One to Go," *eWeek* 4 February 2002 **<www.eweek.com/article/0,3658,s%253D722%2526a%253D22050,00.asp>**.

5.   "SIC Division Structure," **<155.103.6.10/cgi-bin/sic/sicser5>**.

6.   P. Cauldwell, et al., *Professional XML Web Services* (Birmingham: WROX 2001) 181.

7.   "**UDDI.org** Find," **<www.uddi.org/find.html>**.

8.   "UDDI   Specification   Index   Page,"   **<msdn.microsoft.com/library/default.asp?url=/library/en-us/dnuddispec/html/uddispecindex.asp>**.

9.   P. Korzeniowski, "Internet Insight: A Little Slice of the UDDI Pie," *eWeek* 4 February 2002 **<www.eweek.com/print_article/0,3668,a=22053,00.asp>**.

10. "**UDDI.org** Community," **<www.uddi.org/community.html>**.

11. "**UDDI.org** FAQs," **<www.uddi.org/faqs.html>**.

12. "UDDI Version 2.0 Operator's Specification," 8 June 2001 **<www.uddi.org/pubs/Operators-V2.00-Open-20010608.pdf>**.

13. W. Wong, "NTT Joins Web Services Directory Effort," 17 January 2002 **<news.com.com/2100-1001-817566.html?legacy=cnet&tag=dd.ne.dht.nl-sty.0>**.

14. "UDDI Version 2.0 API Specification," 8 June 2001 **<www.uddi.org/pubs/ProgrammersAPI-V2.00-Open-20010608.pdf>**.

15. "**UDDI.org** FAQs," **<www.uddi.org/faqs.html>**.

16. "**UDDI.org** FAQs," **<www.uddi.org/faqs.html>**.

17. "**UDDI.org** FAQs," **<www.uddi.org/faqs.html>**.

18. "**UDDI.org** FAQs," **<www.uddi.org/faqs.html>**.

19. A. Rajaram, "Overview of UDDI," 17 August 2001 **<dcb.sun.com/practices/webservices/overviews/overview_uddi.jsp>**.

20. A. Rajaram, "Overview of UDDI," 17 August 2001 **<dcb.sun.com/practices/webservices/overviews/overview_uddi.jsp>**.

21. A. Rajaram, "Overview of UDDI," 17 August 2001 <**dcb.sun.com/practices/webservices/overviews/overview_uddi.jsp**>.

22. A. Rajaram, "Overview of UDDI," 17 August 2001 <**dcb.sun.com/practices/webservices/overviews/overview_uddi.jsp**>.

23. P. Cauldwell, et al., *Professional XML Web Services* (Birmingham: WROX 2001) 191.

24. P. Cauldwell, et al., *Professional XML Web Services* (Birmingham: WROX 2001) 187.

25. D. Ehnebuske, C. Kurt and B. McKee, "UDDI tModels: Classification Schemes, Taxonomies, Identifier Systems, and Relationships," 15 November 2001 <**www.uddi.org/taxonomies/UDDI_Taxonomy_tModels.htm**>.

26. "UDDI Version 2.0 API Specification," 8 June 2001 <**www.uddi.org/pubs/ProgrammersAPI-V2.00-Open-20010608.pdf**>.

27. "UDDI Version 2.0 API Specification," 8 June 2001 <**www.uddi.org/pubs/ProgrammersAPI-V2.00-Open-20010608.pdf**>.

28. "UDDI Version 2.0 API Specification," 8 June 2001 <**www.uddi.org/pubs/ProgrammersAPI-V2.00-Open-20010608.pdf**>.

29. "UDDI Version 2.0 API Specification," 8 June 2001 <**www.uddi.org/pubs/ProgrammersAPI-V2.00-Open-20010608.pdf**>.

30. P. Cauldwell, et al., *Professional XML Web Services* (Birmingham: WROX 2001) 181.

31. R. Cover, "The XML Cover Pages: Universal Description, Discovery and Integration," 21 December 2001 <**www.oasis-open.org/cover/uddi.html**>.

32. "**UDDI.org** FAQs," <**www.uddi.org/faqs.html**>.

33. "**UDDI.org** FAQs," <**www.uddi.org/faqs.html**>.

34. P. Cauldwell, et al., *Professional XML Web Services* (Birmingham: WROX 2001) 186.

35. P. Krill, "UDDI Seeks Its Place," *InfoWorld* 3 June 2002: 41.

36. A. Chen, "Web Directories Dial In," *eWeek* 22 April 2002: 51.

37. S. Graham, "The Role of Private UDDI Nodes in Web Services, Part 1: Six Species of UDDI," May 2001 <**www-106.ibm.com/developerworks/webservices/library/ws-rup1.html**>.

38. S. Graham, "The Role of Private UDDI Nodes in Web Services, Part 1: Six Species of UDDI," May 2001 <**www-106.ibm.com/developerworks/webservices/library/ws-rup1.html**>.

39. S. Graham, "The Role of Private UDDI Nodes in Web Services, Part 1: Six Species of UDDI," May 2001 <**www-106.ibm.com/developerworks/webservices/library/ws-rup1.html**>.

40. S. Graham, "The Role of Private UDDI Nodes in Web Services, Part 1: Six Species of UDDI," May 2001 <**www-106.ibm.com/developerworks/webservices/library/ws-rup1.html**>.

41. A. Meyer, "UDDI Registries and Reuse," 28 January 2002 <**e-serv.ebizq.net/wbs/meyer_1.html**>.

42. A. Meyer, "UDDI Registries and Reuse," 28 January 2002 <**e-serv.ebizq.net/wbs/meyer_1.html**>.

43. "**ebXML.org** About," <**www.ebxml.org/geninfo.htm**>.

44. "**ebXML.org** Industry Support," <**www.ebxml.org/endorsements.htm**>.

45. "**ebXML.org** FAQ," <**www.ebxml.org/faq.htm**>.

46. "Oasis ebXML CPPA," 7 May 2002 <**www.oasis-open.org/committees/ebxml-cppa**>.

47. K. Kayl, "EbXML: The Key Components," 5 September 2001 <**java.sun.com/features/2001/09/ebxmlkey.html**>.

48. "Oasis ebXML CPPA," 7 May 2002 <**www.oasis-open.org/committees/ebxml-cppa**>.

49. S. Fordin, "ebXML Registry/Repository Implementation: Introducing the First J2EE™-Based ebXML Registry/Repository Implementation," August 2001 <**wwws.sun.com/software/xml/developers/regrep/article**>.

50. R. Cover, "IBM and Microsoft Issue Specification and Software for Web Services Inspection Language," 2 November 2001 <**xml.coverpages.org/ni2001-11-02-a.html**>.

51. J. Borck, "Expressway to Discovery," *InfoWorld* 19 November 2001 <**www.infoworld.com/articles/op/xml/01/11/19/011119opborck.xml**>.

RECOMMENDED READING

Ballinger, K. and W. Nagy, "The WS-Inspection and UDDI Relationship," November 2001 <**www-106.ibm.com/developerworks/webservices/library/ws-wsiluddi.html?dwzone=webservices**>.

Cover, R. "The XML Cover Pages: Universal Description, Discovery and Integration," 21 December 2001 <**www.oasis-open.org/cover/uddi.html**>.

Graham, S. "The Role of Private UDDI Nodes in Web Services, Part 1: Six Species of UDDI," May 2001 <**www-106.ibm.com/developerworks/webservices/library/ws-rup1.html**>.

Kayl, K. "EbXML: The Key Components," 5 September 2001 <**java.sun.com/features/2001/09/ebxmlkey.html**>.

Korzeniowski, P. "A Little Slice of the UDDI Pie," *eWeek* 4 February 2002 <**www.eweek.com/print_article/0,3668,a=22053,00.asp**>.

Korzeniowski, P. "UDDI: Two Versions Down, One to Go," *eWeek* 4 February 2002 <**www.eweek.com/article/0,3658,s%253D722%2526a%253D22050,00.asp**>.

Rajaram, A. "Overview of UDDI," 17 August 2001 <**dcb.sun.com/practices/webservices/overviews/overview_uddi.jsp**>.

"UDDI Version 2.0 API Specification," 8 June 2001 <**www.uddi.org/pubs/ProgrammersAPI-V2.00-Open-20010608.pdf**>.

"UDDI Version 2.0 Operator's Specification," 8 June 2001 <**www.uddi.org/pubs/Operators-V2.00-Open-20010608.pdf**>.

Web Services Platforms, Vendors and Strategies

- To understand vendor strategies for marketing Web services solutions.
- To overview Web services deployment platforms and development tools.
- To discuss companies that offer Web services workflow solutions.
- To learn about Web services management applications.
- To understand vendor strategies for incorporating Web services in enterprise application integration (EAI) products.

The engine which drives enterprise is not thrift, but profit.
John Maynard Keynes

In real life, of course, it is the hare who wins. Every time. Look around you. And in any case it is my contention that Aesop was writing for the tortoise market...Hares have not time to read. They are too busy winning the game.
Anita Brookner

The best strategy is always to be very strong, first generally, then at the decisive point.
Karl von Clausewitz

8.1 Introduction

As Web services standards develop, organizations are realizing the importance of implementing Web services as soon as possible. Companies worldwide are formulating strategies to adopt Web services technologies in their earliest stages. Gartner forecasts that 75 percent of corporations with annual earnings exceeding $100 million dollars will have incorporated Web services by mid-2002.[1]

Many software vendors have created Web services platforms, which consist of programming tools with which developers construct and deploy Web services and server software. Web services platforms "hide" many of the programmatic details and enable programmers to create and deploy Web services easily. When a developer creates a Web service using a Web services platform, the Web service must be deployed using the server software associated with the programming tool. Many software vendors are marketing Web services deployment platforms and other products that help companies implement Web services.

In the future, organizations will purchase Web services on a per-use basis or integrate pre-packaged Web services into enterprise systems. However, few organizations offer such products; this chapter's main focus is on companies that offer Web services deployment platforms and other products that support Web services.

How does an IT manager decide on a Web services solution provider? First, a manager must match Web services products to the company's requirements. Second, the manager must determine the level of vendor support offered to clients. For example, some companies might feel more comfortable trusting a smaller vendor that offers more personalized service and support. Other organizations might prefer the support and product variety provided by a large, established vendor like IBM or Sun. This chapter examines numerous vendors, their products and their market strategies.[1] We discuss major corporations that are offering Web services products and support, including BEA, Hewlett-Packard, IBM, Microsoft, Oracle and Sun Microsystems. We describe other vendors—including Borland, IONA and SilverStream—that either incorporate Web services in their own platforms or offer Web services development and deployment tools. We introduce start-up companies such as Cape Clear Software, Systinet and The Mind Electric. We discuss the need for Web services management and workflow products, and we list the key vendors that offer such products. We also examine Enterprise Application Integration (EAI) and highlight EAI vendors that are incorporating Web services into their products. We conclude with examples of smaller organizations that offer niche products.

8.2 Major Vendors and Their Web Services Strategies

Enterprise-software vendors participate in the Web services industry in several ways. Major organizations often join Web services standards consortia to be involved in the early development of the technologies. Large companies also incorporate support for Web services standards into new versions of already-established products. This way, clients purchasing the new versions have the option to develop and publish Web services if they choose. Typically, larger vendors also offer development toolkits that enable clients to create and deploy Web services. These strategies can result in enterprise-software vendors supplying and supporting clients' Web services. This section discusses BEA, Hewlett-Packard, IBM, Microsoft, Oracle and Sun and the support each offers for Web services development.

8.2.1 BEA Systems and WebLogic

BEA Systems (**www.bea.com**) is a well-known enterprise-application server vendor that has entered the Web services market. BEA has integrated its Web services-development tool and support for Web services standards into its main product suite.[2]

---

1. Vendors' products are evolving rapidly. Please check individual company Web sites for the most current information.

BEA has released the newest version of *WebLogic Platform 7.0*, which consists of the *WebLogic Server 7.0*, *WebLogic Integration 7.0*, *WebLogic Portal 7.0* and *WebLogic Workshop*. WebLogic Server 7.0 incorporates support for SOAP message handling and a full UDDI implementation. WebLogic Integration includes application integration, business-process management and business-to-business integration.[3] WebLogic Portal 7.0 offers portal, personalization and e-commerce components.

Workshop is a Web services-development tool that provides an integrated development environment that minimizes the amount of coding required to create and deploy Web services. The developer can focus on a Web services' capabilities, and Workshop handles the core XML, SOAP and WSDL programming. Workshop also offers debugging and testing tools. Web services built with WebLogic Workshop currently can be deployed on numerous Java-based servers.[4]

Workshop generates J2EE *Enterprise JavaBean (EJB)* files, a technology that creates reusable *server-side* (i.e., located on servers) *business logic* (i.e., programming code that processes data according to the application's business rules). The EJBs then are deployed as Web services on the WebLogic Server, which handles the Web service interaction components such as SOAP-message processing, and provides security and management functions. Figure 8.1 shows WebLogic Server's *administration console*, which administrators use to access security and server configuration features, and obtain information about deployed Web services.

BEA makes many evaluation versions of its products available for download at **commerce.bea.com/downloads/weblogic_server.jsp**. Full versions of the products also are available at this site.

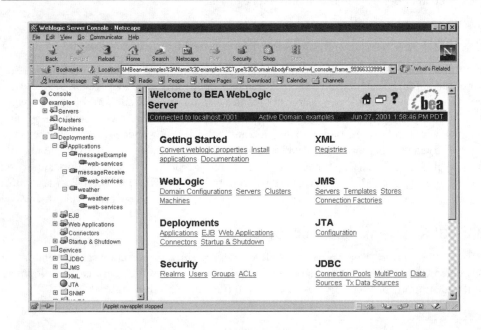

Fig. 8.1   WebLogic Server main administration console. (Courtesy of BEA.)

8.2.2 Hewlett-Packard, e-Speak and the HP Web Services Platform

Hewlett-Packard (**www.hp.com**, HP), a company best known for its hardware products, has entered the Web services market by marketing a series of new software applications. In March 2002, Hewlett-Packard launched the HP *Netaction* software suite, which allows developers to create and deploy Web services.[5]

HP is credited with releasing the first product that enabled services over the Internet, called *e-Speak*. Rather than upgrade e-Speak to support emerging standards (e.g., SOAP, WSDL) as companies began developing Web services as we know them, HP offered e-Speak as an open-source product. HP calls its new platform, *HP Web Services Platform 2.0*, which fully supports Web services standards, the next generation of e-Speak.

The HP Web Services Platform 2.0, a part of the Netaction suite, allows developers to create, deploy, integrate, register and discover Web services. The platform was created using the Java 2 Enterprise Edition; however, the platform is designed to integrate with both Java and .NET architectures. The Web Services Platform contains a SOAP server and developer tools such as the *Service Composer* and the *Registry Composer*.[6] The Service Composer generates WSDL files and is available as part of the Web Services Platform package and as a separate download.[7] The Registry Composer enables developers to deploy and publish Web services to UDDI-compliant registries.[8] We discuss UDDI registries in detail in Chapter 7, UDDI, Discovery and Web Services Registries.

HP also offers the *Web Services Registry* so that developers can install private UDDI registries on networks. The registry package includes the HP Registry Composer software and the *HP Web Services Registry Management Tool*, which enables a developer to publish to a registry. HP is one of four companies that maintains public UDDI registry implementations, referred to collectively as the *UDDI Business Registry (UBR)*. The UBR is a public UDDI registry through which companies can discover third-party services and promote their own services.

The *Web Services Transactions* software is another component of the Netaction suite. Web Services Transactions incorporates capabilities of an emerging Web services standard—Business Transaction Protocol (BTP)—to enable complex transactions of long duration.[9] We discuss BTP in detail in Chapter 5, XML and Derivative Technologies.

HP offers downloads of the Web Services Platform, Web Services Registry, Web Services Transactions and others at **www.hpmiddleware.com/downloads**.

8.2.3 IBM Web Services: WebSphere, DB2, Lotus and Tivoli

IBM's *dynamic e-business* vision promotes using the Internet to manage business-to-business interactions that support evolving business strategies and processes (**www.ibm.com**).[10] To further this vision, IBM incorporated Web services technologies into all its *middleware* applications (i.e., the layer of integration software between an enterprise's network and applications), including WebSphere, DB2, Lotus and Tivoli.[11] In this section, we examine IBM's middleware products and their support for Web services standards, as well as an IBM site, alphaWorks, that focuses on emerging technologies. IBM also has created a technology for designing and deploying Web services, called the *Web Services Toolkit*, which is available at alphaWorks. We discuss the Web Services Toolkit in detail in Chapter 6, Understanding SOAP and WSDL.

The *WebSphere Application Server* is IBM's main deployment platform for Web-based applications. In mid-2001, IBM incorporated support for XML, SOAP, WSDL and UDDI into the WebSphere Application Server, enabling developers to deploy Web services on that platform.[12] In November 2001, IBM released a set of tools that further support Web services development on WebSphere:

- *WebSphere Studio Application Developer* allows developers to build, test and deploy J2EE applications, including Web services.

- *WebSphere Studio Site Developer* contains a Web services development environment, including a private UDDI repository, to create, manage and maintain interactive applications.[13]

At the time of this writing, IBM was beta-testing a third tool for WebSphere Web services development:

- *Enterprise Developer for Multiplatforms* is a development environment that offers integration of Web services in complex e-business systems.[14]

IBM's enterprise database, DB2, also has integrated Web services technologies. The *DB2 XML Extender* translates XML objects to standard *Structured Query Language (SQL)* data, and vice-versa. SQL (pronounced as its individual letters or as "sequel") is a language used to query and manipulate databases. By translating XML objects to a database-specific language, DB2 XML Extender allows Web services to query databases efficiently. The DB2 XML Extender is not limited to IBM's DB2 database; it is capable of manipulating all types of databases.[15]

Lotus Notes and *Domino* also provide support for Web services standards such as XML, SOAP and UDDI.[16] Lotus Notes is a task-management application that provides e-mail, calendar and scheduling capabilities.[17] Lotus Domino is a Web-server software that provides such functionality as e-mail, calendar management and document collaboration.[18]

IBM's *Tivoli* network-management software incorporates Web services technology via the *Web Services Manager*—an application that monitors the performance of Web services transactions—and the *SecureWay Policy Director*—an application that provides security for Web services transactions.[19] IBM offers evaluation software for many applications. Downloads for IBM's evaluation software are available at **www-1.ibm.com/ support/all_download_drivers.html**.

IBM maintains the alphaWorks (**www.alphaworks.ibm.com**) Web site to provide numerous resources to developers working in emerging technologies, including Web services and XML (Fig. 8.2). The site includes access free, open-source software that is in early development, including business-to-business programming tools and programming utilities and a demonstration area that shows all the technical details of real, working Web services, including programming code. alphaWorks also provides information on Web services architectures and links to licensable technologies and development resources. This site has been the basis for many of IBM's commercial tools.

8.2.4 Microsoft and the .NET Platform

Microsoft introduced the term "Web services" during the June 2000 launch of its .NET initiative.[20] At this early stage, Microsoft is one of the dominant companies in the Web services market—some estimates consider the company to be almost a year ahead of others in

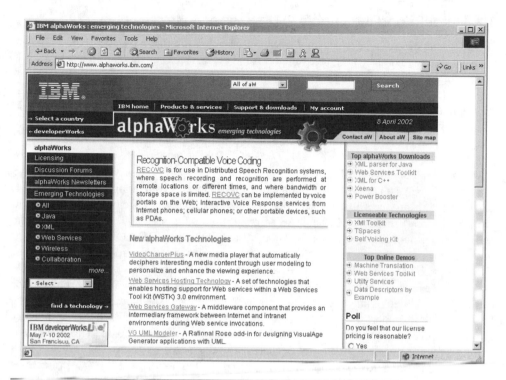

Fig. 8.2   IBM alphaWorks Web site. (Courtesy of IBM alphaWorks, www.ibm.com/alphaworks.)

the development of Web services technologies.[21] We discuss Microsoft's .NET and Web services strategies in detail in Chapter 9, .NET Web Services: A Conceptual Overview.

Microsoft's computing and Web services strategies center around the .NET initiative, which offers a highly integrated and interoperable computing environment that can be implemented using the *Visual Studio .NET* integrated development environment. Visual Studio .NET enables programmers to design Web services in a variety of languages, including C++, C# and Visual Basic® .NET.[22] However, .NET technologies are available only for Windows 2000 and XP. For Windows developers working in older Windows platforms or Windows 2000/XP systems that do not have .NET, Microsoft created the Microsoft SOAP Toolkit. We discuss the Microsoft SOAP Toolkit in Chapter 6, Understanding SOAP and WSDL.

In March 2001, Microsoft introduced .NET My Services, a set of Web services targeted at individual consumers and organizations. My Services offers authentication, alerts and storage of personal information (e.g., profile, calendar, and electronic wallet) to individual customers and businesses.[23] Microsoft designed My Services to be compatible with its own, proprietary centralized registries. Therefore, organizations intending to use My Services must store information in Microsoft's databases. Many organizations were uncomfortable allowing Microsoft to manage confidential customer information. As a result, Microsoft modified its strategy. Instead of maintaining My Services data in central registries, Microsoft is packaging the Web services technology with other software such as Windows XP. This enables companies to maintain their own secure data repositories.[24]

8.2.5 Oracle and the Oracle 9i Developer Suite

Oracle (**www.oracle.com**) is another major organization that has entered the Web services market. Oracle has integrated support for Web services standards into one of its primary products, the *Oracle 9i Developer Suite*.[25]

Oracle 9i Developer Suite incorporates various proprietary technologies, such as *JDeveloper 4*, in the creation of Web services.[26] *Oracle9i JDeveloper 4* helps programmers develop and deploy Web services via such tools as the *Web Services Publishing wizard*, which enables programmers to publish general and technical information about their Web services.[27]

The *Oracle 9i Application Server (Oracle9iAS)* is an integrated software product for developing and deploying e-business portals, applications and Web services.[28] Oracle9iAS provides an open, standards-based architecture that enables organizations to integrate third-party software products to develop Web services applications efficiently. According to Oracle, the latest release of Oracle9iAS offers 250 new features.[29] The product supports Web services standards, including SOAP, XML, WSDL and UDDI; Oracle9iAS also supports *ebXML*, an emerging business-process technology that will incorporate Web services. We discuss ebXML in Chapter 5, XML and Derivative Technologies.

Another feature of Oracle9iAS is *Dynamic Services*—a Web services environment for developing and deploying XML documents as Web services. Dynamic Services supports SOAP and will support the UDDI registry standard when it is formalized. Some industry observers have questioned Oracle's reasons for not incorporating the de facto open standards for Web services technologies in all of its products; the company emphasizes that it supports some standards and plans to adopt others as they are formalized.[30] Applications developed with Dynamic Services are available for delivery through various clients, including Web browsers, mobile devices or local applications. Dynamic Services also provides additional features, including service management and security.[31] Oracle offers various products for download, including evaluation versions, at **otn.oracle.com/software/content.html**.

8.2.6 Sun Microsystems, iPlanet and the Sun ONE Platform

Sun Microsystems' (**www.sun.com**) Web services strategy is based on the *Sun™ Open Net Environment (Sun ONE)*, which consists of three components—a vision, an architecture and a conceptual model for developing standards-based software. Sun also considers support from solutions consultants and collaborative programs to be another essential part of the strategy.[32]

The Sun One vision incorporates a model for software development, in which critical business information and applications are available at any time to any type of device, including cell phones and PDAs. Sun ONE's goal is to help developers create networks of distributed applications or Web services that are highly reliable and promote the reuse of components and services.[33]

The Sun ONE architecture is designed to be scalable to ensure reliable access to services. Scalability is crucial, in that as new technologies and new components are added to systems, more demands are placed on system resources, potentially degrading service.[34]

Three products compose the Sun ONE platform: the *Solaris™ Operating Environment*, the *Infrastructure Software* (formerly *iPlanet* Web applications[2]) and the SunONE *Studio*

---

2. Note: All iPlanet products now are called Sun ONE.

(formerly *Forte*^{TM}—i.e., an integrated development environment that provides tools for developing Java applications). The Infrastructure Software includes the Sun ONE *Directory Server* and the Sun ONE *Portal Server*, which offer user authentication and personalization. Other Infrastructure Software capabilities include scheduling management, billing and communication.[35] Sun ONE also allows programmers to deploy Web services using third-party products. By integrating disparate products, programmers can develop Web services infrastructures that best suit their companies' requirements. Sun ONE incorporates support for open standards, including SOAP, J2EE, UDDI and ebXML, to help ensure high levels of interoperability and system integration.[36] For a list of Sun software downloads, visit **wwws.sun.com/software/download**.

Sun ONE promotes the notion that a company's *data, applications, reports, and transactions (DART)*, which compose the conceptual DART model, can be published as services online. Using the DART model, companies can organize business applications and processes that involve data, applications, reports and transactions so that programmers can map business elements to corresponding services.[37]

Sun considers its consulting, *iForce* and *SunTone* services and solutions to be integral parts of the Sun ONE strategy. Companies employ Sun's *Professional Services* consultants to help develop and deploy business systems.[38] Sun's iForce initiative is a community of software and services developers, called *iForce partners*, that work to design solutions for Sun customers. Sun has established *iForce Ready Centers*, at which customers collaborate with Sun and Sun partners to solve development and deployment issues. Using a non-competitive partnering model that encourages collaboration, iForce produces *iForce Solution Sets* that customers can deploy with relative ease.[39]

SunTone, another Sun program, promotes the development of software and services that help create reliable systems. Sun certifies companies that have achieved a certain level of reliability, scalability and security in various areas, including infrastructure, hardware, software and storage. At the time of this writing, more than 160 organizations have received SunTone certification and more than 1500 companies have applied for certification.[40] Sun also is sponsoring the *Liberty Alliance Project*, a collaborative initiative to store and maintain confidential information, which is crucial to the success of Web services (see the Liberty Alliance Project feature).

Liberty Alliance Project

To facilitate e-commerce, organizations have developed single sign-on services (SSOs) that store users' authentication information and enable automatic sign-on (i.e., users do not have to enter usernames and passwords) at participating Web sites. Often, these services maintain users' personal data, such as social security numbers, and financial information, such as credit-card numbers. Microsoft's single sign-on service, .NET Passport, supports a centralized model, in which Microsoft stores and maintains all customer data that can be accessed by Passport business partners.

Liberty Alliance Project (Cont.)

As an alternative to the .NET Passport model, Sun has formed the Liberty Alliance Project (**www.projectliberty.org**), which seeks to establish standards for maintaining identification information over the Internet.[41] More than 40 major companies are working to develop a federated network-identity system that both individuals and businesses can implement.[42]

The federated approach offers an authentication model in which users (either individuals or businesses) can choose which organization(s) will hold the identity information that enables single sign-on.[43] For example, if an online computer retailer sends a customer to a printer vendor's Web site, the user must first agree to the transfer of identity information, as well as exactly which information is transferred. Liberty Alliance is developing specifications based on open standards that support other identity systems (e.g., .NET Passport) and allow users to access the single sign-on service using many types of devices, such as cell phones and PDAs. In a Liberty Alliance single sign-on system, users will be able to authorize transactions and access private information in a secure system.[44]

Liberty Alliance member corporations agree to support the Sun ONE architecture and Web services open standards.[45] Members also pledge to support the development, deployment and evolution of a single sign-on authentication scheme.[46] Figure 8.3 depicts the Liberty Alliance Web site. We discuss single sign-on technologies in detail in Chapter 12, Web Services Security.

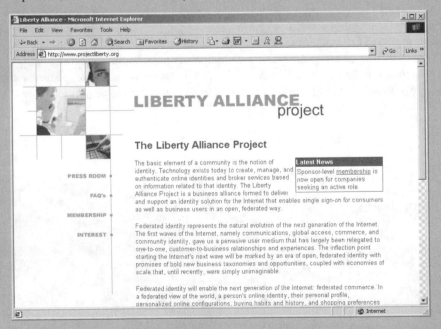

Fig. 8.3   Liberty Alliance Web site. (Courtesy of Liberty Alliance Project.)

8.3 Mid-Sized Vendors and Their Web Services Strategies

As dominant vendors develop their Web services products and market strategies, mid-sized vendors also are creating Web services platforms and/or integrating support for Web services into products. Several mid-sized vendors already have contributed products to an increasingly competitive Web services market. This section discusses three of these vendors: Borland, IONA and SilverStream.

8.3.1 Borland

Borland (**www.borland.com**) designs *rapid application development (RAD)* software for Windows and UNIX operating systems. RAD software tools help developers create applications and Web services quickly. Borland also has released a toolkit for developing Java Web Services and is reportedly developing one for its C++ development environment.[47]

Delphi 6 and *Kylix 2* are Borland's rapid application development environments for Windows and Linux, respectively. These environments support cross-platform interoperability—Delphi 6 applications can communicate with applications developed on Kylix 2 without modification, and vice versa. Both IDEs support the Web services standards SOAP, UDDI and WSDL and have three components that help developers create and deploy Web services: *BizSnap*, *WebSnap* and *DataSnap*. With BizSnap, programmers can incorporate Web services into new or existing programs that interact with consumers or business partners. WebSnap and DataSnap allow developers to create Web-based applications and integrate databases into applications, respectively. Kylix and Delphi provide wizard-directed SOAP-message creation, WSDL importing and other capabilities for building and deploying Web services.[48] Borland makes trial versions of Delphi 6 and Kylix 2 available for download at **www.borland.com/products/downloads/download_kylix.html**.

8.3.2 IONA and the Orbix E2A Platform[3]

Over the past few years, *IONA* has shifted its focus from EAI products that used CORBA to integrate applications to using Web services for application integration.[49] Believing that most future applications will be constructed using Web services, IONA incorporates Web services standards in all its products.[50]

The *Orbix End-to-Anywhere (E2A)* platform, IONA's primary product line, offers a high level of interoperability, enabling virtually any applications on any devices to communicate. The E2A platform consists of two product lines, the Orbix E2A *Application Server Platform* and the Orbix E2A *Web Services Integration Platform* (Fig. 8.4). The Web Services Integration Platform is available in three editions: *XMLBus*, *Collaborate* and *Partner*.[51]

---

3. We discuss IONA's Web services development platform in detail in Chapter 10, Java Web Services: A Conceptual Overview and in the *Deitel Developer Series* book, *Java Web Services for Experienced Programmers*.

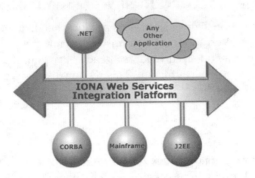

The Application Server Platform is a server platform on which Web services can be deployed by IONA's other products, particularly XMLBus Edition. The XMLBus Edition is IONA's Web services-development platform. This Java-based platform provides a framework for developing, deploying, monitoring and managing Web services. XMLBus also offers wizard-driven development and real-time testing, debugging and monitoring utilities. The XMLBus Edition includes the IONA *Security Service,* which addresses security concerns associated with Web services. Security Service allows developers to use an existing database of user information for authenticating Web services clients.[52] The XMLBus is available in four versions—standalone (typically installed with Tomcat), IONA's J2EE ASP, BEA WebLogic or IBM WebSphere. IONA recently released a version of XMLBus that contains a new feature, called the *Operational Flow Designer*, which provides a visual environment in which developers create Web services from JavaBeans or Enterprise Java Beans.

The Orbix E2A *Business Process Engine* helps programmers focus on the *business logic* (i.e., rules to execute some task performed by a business) that supports Web services, rather than the programming-code details of the Web services. This tool, available in the Collaborate Edition, provides a visual environment in which a programmer coordinates and combines business tasks to create a single process, then exposes that process as a Web service.[53] The Collaborate and Partner editions are platforms that enable organizations to integrate business processes with those of partners. The Collaborate Edition offers a suite of tools and solutions appropriate for larger enterprises; the Partner Edition is ideal for small-to medium-size businesses that do not require the Collaborate Edition's extensive tools.[54] IONA allows users to download evaluation versions of the XMLBus Edition, as well as full versions of other products, at **www.iona.com/downloads**.

8.3.3 SilverStream Software and the eXtend Product Line

In June 2002, the networking software company Novell purchased SilverStream Software, an organization whose products support Web services standards. The purchase allows Novell to use SilverStream's established J2EE-based development, integration and deployment platform to enter the Web services market.[55]

SilverStream's *eXtend* product suite consists of four applications: *eXtend Composer*, *eXtend Director*, *eXtend Workbench* and *eXtend Application Server*. The Composer, Workbench and Director products support dynamic Web-application development capabilities. Each application can be installed as standalone software or as a package and can be integrated into the eXtend Application Server or other servers, including IBM WebSphere, BEA WebLogic and Oracle 9i.

The eXtend Application Server is SilverStream's J2EE-based application server. It serves as a foundation for Composer, Director and Workbench and supports all major Web services standards. The product includes security, server management and administration features. It also incorporates Web services by including SilverStream's *jBroker Web* software.

SilverStream's jBroker product line encompasses a set of middleware application. One application, jBroker Web, enables a developer to build and run Web services using Java. jBroker Web provides support for producing XML from Java objects and vice versa, as well as wizards for generating WSDL and remote interfaces. When using jBroker Web, developers are unaware that they are communicating with a Web service, because jBroker Web treats Web services like any other application. As a result, development occurs rapidly and more efficiently. SilverStream offers jBroker Web for free to accommodate smaller organizations that do not need full J2EE functionality.[56] Evaluation versions of Silver-Stream software are available at **www.silverstream.com/Website/app/ en_US/DownloadsLanding**.

8.4 Start-Up Web Services Platform Vendors

New companies already have had an impact on the Web services market. Unlike established organizations, new companies do not have to alter legacy applications or shift their technological focus—instead, they have tailored their products from the start to support Web services and Web service development. This section overviews Cape Clear, Systinet, The Mind Electric and the products each company offers. We discuss these companys' Web services deployments products in Chapter 10, Java Web Services: A Conceptual Overview. We also demonstrate these Web services-deployment products in the *Deitel Developer Series* book, *Java Web Services for Experienced Programmers*.

8.4.1 Cape Clear Software: CapeConnect and CapeStudio

Cape Clear Software offers a Web services integration platform and a development environment, which allows developers to create and deploy Web services. Cape Clear's *CapeConnect* is an open-standards-based integration platform. Through features such as a *Deployment Wizard* and a *WSDL Generator*, CapeConnect allows developers to convert program components into Web services with little or no code. The platform can be integrated with J2EE and .NET and can incorporate applications written in Java, CORBA, C++, C#, Visual Basic and Perl. The latest version of CapeConnect also allows Microsoft SQL databases to be exposed as Web services.[57]

CapeStudio is a rapid application development (RAD) environment included with CapeConnect (Fig. 8.5). CapeStudio deploys Web services on the CapeConnect platform via two main components: *WSDL Assistant* and *CapeStudio Mapper*. The WSDL Assistant generates proxies (which enable a Web service client to access a Web service) from a

WSDL file; this allows a developer to focus on the application's business logic. CapeStudio Mapper is an XML-to-XML translation utility. Using CapeStudio Mapper, developers can use a graphical environment to link a business component, such as an inventory, to an XML document so that inventory information can be exposed as a Web service.[58]

Cape Clear also hosts and maintains a developer resource forum known as *CapeScience*, at **capescience.capeclear.com** (Fig. 8.6). The site contains Web services news, tutorials and a chat room.[59] CapeStudio and other software utilities are available as free downloads from the CapeScience site, **capescience.capeclear.com/downloads**.

8.4.2 Systinet

Systinet (**www.systinet.com**), formerly Idoox, develops Web services infrastructure products.[60] Systinet's flagship product is the *Web Applications and Services Platform (WASP)*, which allows organizations to develop, test and deploy enterprise Web services. WASP can run as a standalone server or can run on numerous platforms, including Apache Tomcat, BEA WebLogic, IBM WebSphere, Sun ONE and J2EE. The WASP family of products includes the *WASP Server*, *WASP Developer*, *WASP UDDI*, the *WASP Secure Identity* and a technology that is in its early development stage, *WASP TX*.[61]

The WASP Server is available for both Java and C++ and is free for small deployments. WASP Server provides scalability, comprehensive security and a management framework to support complex, enterprise Web service implementations.[62]

The WASP Developer is a plug-in extension for numerous Java integrated development environments (e.g., Sun ONE Studio, Borland JBuilder and Eclipse). This way, developers can create, debug, test and implement Web services in the development environment with which they are most familiar. With this application, developers can turn a Java class into a Web service and deploy the service quickly. The WASP Developer allows programmers to locate Web services via registries, import WSDL files and generate code to communicate with Web services.[63]

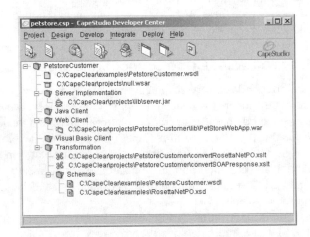

Fig. 8.5   CapeStudio Developer Center. (Courtesy of Cape Clear Software, Inc.)

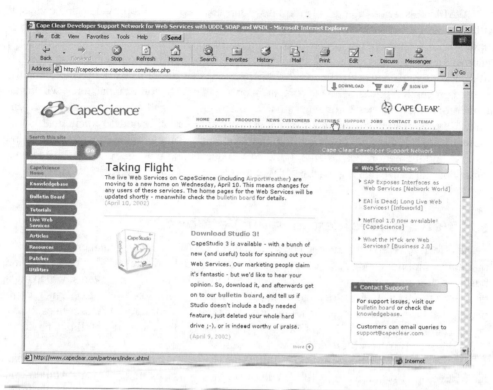

Fig. 8.6   CapeScience Web services developer resource home page. (Courtesy of Cape Clear Software, Inc.)

WASP UDDI is an implementation of the UDDI Version 2 specification that enables developers to create private UDDI registries. WASP UDDI offers powerful query services and security features such as authentication and authorization of clients.[64]

WASP Secure Identity is a platform-independent authentication service that provides a single sign-on option for Web services. When a user logs into the service, WASP Secure Identity, the service generates a *security token* with which a user can access other Web services. Secure Identity uses Security Assertions Markup Language (SAML), an emerging standard for exchanging security information, to format the token. We discuss single sign-on and SAML in detail in Chapter 12, Web Services Security.

Systinet also has released a Technology Preview, called WASP TX, which is a loosely coupled transaction-management service, based on the Business Transaction Protocol (BTP). Systinet offers its products free for download at **www.systinet.com/download.html**.

8.4.3 The Mind Electric

The Mind Electric (TME™) is a company that offers the *GLUE* and *GAIA* platforms. GLUE is a widely used, small, Java-based platform designed for creating and deploying Web services. GLUE uses *Electric XML*, which is TME's Java toolkit for parsing XML documents. TME considers GLUE to be appropriate for most early Web services implementation, but the company offers GAIA to support more mature Web services systems.

GAIA is a service-oriented platform that connects Web services providers and clients. It offers service discovery, *load balancing* (a technology that distributes requests among multiple servers to prevent one server from being overloaded) and *failover* (if one server fails, another server receives requests with no interruption in service) to Web services on any platform. It uses *grid computing* (i.e., a type of networking that performs work by employing the unused processing power of all the computers on a network) to connect machines, which can range from enterprise-level computers to PDAs. The grid design links computers in a decentralized fashion, so that if any node on the network crashes, other nodes remain unaffected. Decentralized designs are common in high-traffic, high-volume environments such as the Internet and the national electricity grid. GAIA connects and manages services hosted on a variety of platforms, making it a type of Web services operating system.[65]

8.5 Web Services Management Vendors

To be effective, Web services must be well managed. Web services management software maintains, monitors and secures Web services, as well as facilitates service brokering and business-process management. These features are crucial to enterprise systems, which must guarantee the security, integrity and reliability of transactions. According to Gartner, companies that do not use management platforms will fail to incorporate Web services in any significant manner.[66] We discuss QoS and Web services brokering in detail in Chapter 3, Web Services Business Models.

Several vendors, including AmberPoint, interKeel, Talking Blocks and WestGlobal, have developed solutions to facilitate enterprise Web services management. AmberPoint (`www.amberpoint.com`), a recently formed company, has created the AmberPoint *Management Foundation* product. The company is releasing a basic management application and plans to add products to increase the program's functionality. The base application can integrate with both Java and .NET architectures, monitor a system on which Web services are deployed and perform problem resolution by correcting or alerting the user to problems. The application offers tools that enable systems administrators to track the content of business Web services transactions by type, performance and use. Additionally, AmberPoint offers an access-control system that allows developers to monitor and control service requests according to the content offered by the services (i.e., the confidentiality level of the content).[67] Future AmberPoint products will enable companies to define and manage quality-of-service agreements and detect, route and correct systems errors. The products also will detect errors that occur in Web service business content and can facilitate business collaborations.[68]

interKeel (`www.interkeel.com`) offers several brokering and management Web services products packaged in the *interKeel Business Composer (iBC)* suite. The first component, *iBC Services Broker*, forms a layer between Web service requests and published Web services. When applications running on J2EE servers make service requests, the Services Broker maps the requests to available services. The *iBC Console* component provides business-management views of available services. From this component, a manager can monitor and manage a company's Web services. The *iBC Repository* is a central, private store of information pertaining to all the services that an enterprise supports.[69]

Talking Blocks (`www.talkingblocks.com`) is a Web services management vendor that offers the Talking Blocks *Management Suite*, composed of a *Services Network*,

Mediation, *Interop* and *Control* tools. The Services Network provides integration, control and *change management*—i.e., network versioning, upgrading and adapting—for enterprise Web services. The Services Network allows a company to define Web services, differentiate the levels of service and change the services via a *Contracts and Service Registry*. Mediation performs load balancing and failover to prevent interrupted services. Using Mediation, service requests can be routed to differentiate service levels based on the request or the service requestor. Talking Blocks Interop allows organizations to integrate legacy applications or protocols into a Web services network without re-coding. Talking Blocks Control provides centralized administration of a Web services network. Using Control, an organization can monitor activity, receive alerts and perform diagnostic tests on a network.[70]

WestGlobal (`www.westglobal.com`) offers the *mScape*™ Web services management application. Using mScape, a developer can monitor many aspects of Web services, including Service Level Agreements, metering and load balancing. Security mechanisms are based on the business context—mScape places stronger security on the more vital information that is exposed via a Web service. mScape provides real-time graphical views of the Web services in the system and of the business processes that underlie the Web services functions.[71]

8.6 Web Services Workflow Vendors

Workflow is the sequence of operations used to accomplish a process or transaction. In a simple Web services interaction (one in which a single client invokes a single Web service), it is relatively easily to define the necessary workflow. However, it is more difficult to coordinate and manage scenarios in which multiple Web services are combined to complete a complex process. Realizing the need to organize Web services interactions, many organizations are developing technologies that define and coordinate Web services workflow.[72] One example is the Web Services Workflow Language (WSFL), which we discuss in Chapter 5, XML and Derivative Technologies. This section introduces several vendors—including Avinon, Collaxa, Eltegra and Versata—that offer Web services workflow products.[4]

Avinon (`www.avinon.com`) offers the *NetScenario* business-services-management suite, which coordinates a business's Web services. The *NetScenario Platform* includes the *NetScenario Studio* and the *NetScenario Business Server*. The NetScenario Studio allows a developer to model processes and to describe the workflow and business logic that the processes contain. The Business Server works with application servers so that a developer can implement a services-driven system that provides security, personalization and process integration. Avinon also offers pre-configured services so that companies offer dynamic, Web-based services immediately. These pre-packaged services are available in the Avinon ServiceCenter solution.[73]

Collaxa (`www.collaxa.com`) approaches Web services management as a two-part process. First, a Web service is published, then it is *orchestrated*. According to Collaxa, orchestration involves integrating Web services to create collaborative business processes that perform transactions.[74] Orchestrating Web services involves coordination (including

---

4. Microsoft's BizTalk also is a workflow tool. We discuss BizTalk in Chapter 9, .NET Web Services: A Conceptual Overview.

asynchronous communications supported by the Business Transaction Protocol), management (including administration, change management and controlling versions) and activity monitoring (including business reporting or Web service auditing). Collaxa offers the *Web Service Orchestration Server,* which allows developers to integrate Web services into enterprise systems to perform complex transactions and processes. The server supports Web services standards, as well as the Business Transaction Protocol (BTP) and ebXML technologies.[75]

EXADEL (`www.exadel.com`) offers EXADEL™, a suite of products for creating business services. The EXADEL *Service Container*, *Web Flow Engine* and *Process Orchestrator* all use *X-Studio*, a graphical modeling environment for packaging Web Services, then building Web and/or Web services-based applications. X-Studio provides a graphical interface in which developers can "drag-and-drop" components, thereby replacing coding with visual representations of business logic. The Service Container provides mechanisms to package legacy-application components into services or to engineer new services. The Process Orchestrator provides business-process-management capabilities to orchestrate services into process-centric applications. The Web Flow Engine orchestrates services into process-centric Web applications, enabling developers to manage complex flow logic.[76] A trial version is available for download at the EXADEL Web site.

Savvion™ (`www.savvion.com`) uses a Java-based platform to automate business processes among employees, customers and business partners. Savvion's primary business-process-management platform, *BusinessManager*™, allows developers to convert business processes to Web applications to automate internal or external business processes. Savvion has built support for Web services into its BusinessManager. Using Web services technologies, developers can publish processes as services and add Web services to existing business-process applications.[77]

Versata's (`www.versata.com`) primary product, the *Logic Server*, focuses on organizational business logic. In response to the growing support for Web services, Versata has developed the *Web Services and XML Add-On* for the Logic Server so that developers using Logic Server can orchestrate and consume Web services. By using this new product in the Logic Server, developers can encapsulate business processes as Web services and publish the services as components in a system.[78]

8.7 Enterprise Application Integration (EAI) Vendors

In Chapter 4, Web Services and Enterprise Computing, we introduced enterprise application integration (EAI) and how organizations can use Web services to integrate applications. Web services pose certain potential challenges to Enterprise Application Integration (EAI) vendors, in that Web services are less expensive and easier to implement for certain situations than are most EAI applications. Dale Skeen, CTO of EAI vendor Vitria, believes Web services will eventually replace EAI: "I think traditional EAI, which was concerned with messaging middleware and connectivity, is dead. Web services will provide the universal way to connect."[79] Many EAI vendors have responded to the advent of Web services by incorporating standards support into their software solutions.[80] This section overviews the Web services support offered by EAI vendors SeeBeyond, Tibco, Vitria and webMethods.

8.7.1 SeeBeyond

SeeBeyond (**www.seebeyond.com**) constructs enterprise portals that make company information available to employees and business partners. To integrate Web services into portal systems, SeeBeyond developed a SOAP wizard, which helps create Web services connections and provides the means to expose any business process as a Web service. This wizard is a part of SeeBeyond's *e*Way Intelligent Adaptor for SOAP*. e*Way Intelligent Adaptors provide added functionality for SeeBeyond's primary portal product, the *e*Integration Suite*, which contains four components. The first, *e*Gate Integrator*, is a scalable tool that connects computers to share files. The second product is the *e*Exchange Partner Manager*. Using e*Exchange, a company can set up and manage business transactions with partners and outside companies. The *e*Insight Business Process Manager* manages processes and enables real-time business transactions. The final e*Integration Suite product, *e*Index Global Identifier*, helps companies manage customer information by creating links and cross-references to information.[81]

8.7.2 Tibco

Tibco is incorporating Web Services Flow Language (WSFL) and Business Process Modeling Language (BPML) technologies to enhance its support for Web services. Tibco has developed *BusinessWorks™* and *Business Process Management (BPM) 2.0* software to integrate Web services technologies in Tibco's main EAI products, *ActivePortal™* and *ActiveExchange™*.[82] With BusinessWorks, developers create Web services from existing applications without additional coding. This functionality enables programmers to aggregate services and information provided by other Web services, thereby creating compound Web services. BusinessWorks also offers security mechanisms for Web services as well as component monitoring and management. BPM 2.0 provides a graphical user interface that enables companies to coordinate Web services workflow among organizations.[83]

8.7.3 Vitria

Vitria Technology (**www.vitria.com**) has played an important role in developing EAI concepts, standards and technologies. Vitria's products focus on standards that enable companies to purchase and sell products and update inventory databases. Vitria incorporated support for Web services in its enterprise integration software, *BusinessWare*. Several technology layers comprise Vitria's BusinessWare. The first layer, a *Business Process* layer, allows a developer to view business processes that reside in the system. An *EAI* layer enables a developer to manage system integration. The next layer is a *B2B* layer, which manages external business processes with partners and supports technologies such as RosettaNet and BizTalk. Finally, a *Real-time Analysis* layer gathers and processes business data so that managers can make strategic decisions based on processed information.[84] This software allows a developer to define, compose, wrap, call and register any BusinessWare process as a Web service. Using BusinessWare, a developer can create Web services encompassing multiple stages, such as a mortgage application—BusinessWare allows Web services to store data, then process it with other data when another step finishes.[85]

8.7.4 webMethods

The webMethods company was formed in 1996 to enable businesses to update legacy applications and integrate business systems. webMethods has incorporated support for Web services standards in its *Integration Platform*. This product allows companies to create infrastructure for Web services and applications by enabling developers to establish SOAP servers or clients and expose any integration platform as a Web service. UDDI is supported, and registry entries can be created via a Web browser. Web services developed with the platform can be monitored and managed using webMethods' GUI-based utilities. By employing these utilities, developers can enable or disable services and manage user access control.[86] The platform also offers security features.[87]

8.8 Small and Niche Vendors

As Web services gain acceptance, vendors will respond to new business requirements with niche products. One example is a company that has developed a Web services platform that can be embedded in ISV products (see the Clear Methods: Steam and the Water Language feature). Another example is WebCollage, which produces software that facilitates online business partnerships using Web services.

Clear Methods: Steam and the Water™ Language

Clear Methods (`www.clearmethods.com`) is a company that provides products to enable independent software vendors (ISVs) to embed Web services and XML technologies in their software applications. Clear Methods' primary technology, *Steam*, is based on the Water language (`www.waterlang.org`), a new, open, object-oriented Web services programming language. The Water language represents data, logic and presentation using *ConciseXML*, which offers a compact syntax that is compatible with XML 1.0.

Steam consists of two components. The first, the *Steam Engine*, is a secure Web service and XML execution engine. The second, the *Steam IDE*, is an integrated development environment that provides an editor, debugger and test system for XML documents and programs. Both technologies can be used as standalone tools or embedded in other software applications.

Steam enables ISVs to integrate new XML vocabularies and standards into their products. Steam provides multiple Web service interfaces that support SOAP, WSDL and UDDI. For ISVs that want to store application data in an XML format, Water provides a concise and flexible XML-based representation that can support complex non-hierarchical data structures, as well as general-purpose business logic. For ISVs that sell workflow or business-modeling tools with visual-programming environments, Steam offers an XML-based object model to represent complex application data.

Steam products support a flexible deployment model and can run on the client or the server. The Water language and the Steam IDE are available for download at `www.waterlang.org`. [*Note*: Various employees at Deitel & Associates, Inc., hold small equity positions in Clear Methods.]

The flagship product of WebCollage (**www.webcollage.com**), WebCollage *Syndicator*, is a platform for businesses to package and deliver Web applications as Web services. Syndicator consists of the *Syndicator Server*, the *Provider Center* and the *Partner Center* Web-based management tools.[88]

The Provider Center is a collection of tools to manage Web services. It consists of the *Packaging Center*, *Partner Manager* and *Administration Center*. The Packaging Center uses WSDL to describe Web services so that clients can locate the specific services. The *Partner Manager* allows business managers to maintain and add to lists of partners that access a company's Web services. The Administration Center is a utility that provides real-time administration of the Syndicator server. The Partner Center provides an *extranet* (i.e., a private network for sharing business information) from which business partners can select Web services.[89]

WebCollage also offers business consulting and technical services. In addition, Web-Collage consultants help companies determine which applications should be shared with partners and how to measure the effectiveness of such partnerships. Once a business solution has been determined, a WebCollage technical team can implement the solution using WebCollage Syndicator and its various utilities.[90]

In this chapter, we have discussed numerous vendors and their products that facilitate the creation and/or deployment of Web services. In the next chapter, .NET Web Services: A Conceptual Overview, we introduce Microsoft's integrated development environment, Visual Studio .NET, and its capabilities for creating and consuming Web services. The chapter overviews the Global XML Web Services Architecture (GXA), a set of specifications that build on core Web services standards. The chapter also examines how Web services are consumed from wireless-device applications and explores specific .NET Web services.

8.9 Summary

As Web services standards develop, organizations are realizing the importance of implementing Web services as soon as possible. Companies worldwide are formulating strategies to adopt Web services technologies in their earliest stages. Gartner forecasts that 75 percent of corporations with annual earnings exceeding $100 million dollars will have incorporated Web services by mid-2002.

Although Web services standards are still in their early stages, many vendors have created Web services platforms, which consist of programming tools with which developers construct and deploy Web services and server software. Web services platforms "hide" many of the programmatic details and enable programmers to create and deploy Web services easily.

How does an IT manager decide on a Web services solution provider? First, a manager must match Web services products to the company's requirements. Second, the manager must determine the level of vendor support offered to clients. For example, some companies might feel more comfortable trusting a smaller vendor that offers more personalized service and support. Other organizations might prefer the support and product variety provided by a large, established vendor like IBM or Sun. The major corporations that are offering Web services products and support include BEA, Hewlett-Packard, IBM, Microsoft, Oracle and Sun Microsystems.

Enterprise-software vendors participate in the Web services industry in several ways. Major organizations often join Web services standards consortia to be involved in the early development of the technologies. Large companies also incorporate support for Web services standards into new versions of already-established products. This way, clients purchasing the new versions have the option to develop and publish Web services if they choose. Typically, larger vendors also offer development toolkits that enable clients to create and deploy Web services. These strategies can result in enterprise-software vendors supplying and supporting clients' Web services.

As dominant vendors develop their Web services products and market strategies, midsized vendors also are creating Web services platforms and/or integrating support for Web services into products. Several mid-sized vendors—including Borland, IONA and SilverStream—already have contributed products to an increasingly competitive Web services market.

New companies already have had an impact on the Web services market. Unlike established organizations, new companies do not have to alter legacy applications or shift their technological focus—instead, they have tailored their products from the start to support Web services and Web service development. Start-up companies that offer Web services platforms include Cape Clear, Systinet and The Mind Electric.

To be effective, Web services must be well managed. Web services management software maintains, monitors and secures Web services, as well as facilitates service brokering and business-process management. These features are crucial to enterprise systems, which must guarantee the security, integrity and reliability of transactions. According to Gartner, companies that do not use management platforms will fail to incorporate Web services in any significant manner. Companies that offer Web services management software include AmberPoint, interKeel, Talking Blocks and West Global.

Workflow is the sequence of operations used to accomplish a process or transaction. In a simple Web services interaction (one in which a single client invokes a single Web service), it is relatively easily to define the necessary workflow. However, it is more difficult to coordinate and manage scenarios in which multiple Web services are combined to complete a complex process. Realizing the need to organize Web services interactions, many organizations are developing technologies that define and coordinate Web services workflow. One example is the Web Services Workflow Language (WSFL). Companies that are developing workflow tools include Avinon, Collaxa, Savvion and Versata.

As Web services gain acceptance, vendors will respond to new business requirements with niche products. One example is WebCollage, which is a platform for businesses to package and deliver Web applications as Web services.

8.10 Internet and Web Resources

www.webservices.org
The Web Services Community Portal contains the latest news regarding Web services and Web services vendors. There is also a collection of articles and papers relating to Web services technologies.

www.esj.com/webservices
Web Services Report provides up-to-date news about Web services vendors and technologies.

www.soaprpc.com
SoapRPC is a resource site for SOAP, .NET, Sun ONE, HP Netaction and other technologies relating to advances in Web services technology.

www.microsoft.com/net

Microsoft's .NET site provides information on the .NET initiative. It provides resources from product information to news, events and downloads.

www.microsoft.com/myservices

Microsoft's My Services site provides information about My Services technologies. Users can sign up, and businesses can find out how to get licensed for My Services support.

www.sun.com/sunone

Sun Microsystems' Sun ONE initiative site explains the Open Net Environment and provides news about the products and its users.

www.projectliberty.org

The site for Sun's Liberty Alliance project provides information about the group and its goals.

java.sun.com/j2ee

The Java 2 Platform, Enterprise Edition site offers a set of resources and documentation. A download section offers various development kits and toolkit add-ons.

www-3.ibm.com/e-business

IBM's e-Business initiative page links to information about e-Business products and solutions.

www-1.ibm.com/services

This site provides news and information about IBM's Global Services Consulting services.

www-124.ibm.com/developerworks/oss

IBM's developerWork's Web site hosts open-source projects in which IBM is participating, including several XML- and Web services-related projects.

www.alphaworks.ibm.com

This IBM site is dedicated to emerging technologies. It features Web services development platforms such as the Web Services Toolkit and other Web services applications available for download.

www.hp.com/products1/softwareproducts/software/netaction

This site highlights Hewlett-Packard's Netaction software suite. It contains information about the Netaction initiative and the products that compose the suite.

www.hpmiddleware.com/products/hp_web_services

Hewlett-Packard's Web services site contains information about Web services and allows developers to download the HP Web Services Platform.

otn.oracle.com/tech/webservices

Oracle's Web services site details Oracle's products that integrate Web services.

www.bea.com

BEA Systems offers information about its services and the products that compose the company's computing solutions, including applications for developing Web services.

www.iona.com

This site contains news about IONA products and solutions, links to download various IONA products and a Web services developer resource.

www.silverstream.com

The SilverStream site includes information about its products and services; resources for developers, business and investors; and a customer support section.

www.capeclear.com

The Cape Clear site describes the CapeConnect and CapeStudio products and provides news, information and product updates.

www.seebeyond.com

SeeBeyond's site lists product information, company news, Web seminars, events and case studies.

www.capescience.com
The CapeScience Developer Support Network is hosted and maintained by Cape Clear Software. This resource for Web services developers includes bulletin boards, tutorials and software downloads.

www.tibco.com
This site details Tibco's products and services, including company information, articles and Web services strategies.

www.vitria.com
Vitria's site provides information on the company's goals, its products and how the company incorporates Web services into products.

www.webmethods.com
This site contains information about the software and services provided by webMethods and its corporate partners.

www.borland.com
This site offers demonstrations of Borland's Kylix 2, Delphi 6 and other products that incorporate Web services.

www.eltegra.com
The Eltegra site details the company's Web services strategy, Exadel suite and Web services strategy.

www.consilient.net
This Web site offers news and information about the company's business partners, products and services.

www.themindelectric.com
The Mind Electric's site offers information about their infrastructure software, GLUE and GAIA platforms, and offers versions of GLUE and GAIA for download.

www.webcollage.com
The WebCollage site provides an overview about the company and its products.

www.clearmethods.com
This site explains the company's Web services platform and offers licensing and contact information.

WORKS CITED

1.   W. Wong, "Why Web Services Make Business Sense," 8 November 2001 <**news.com.com/ 2009-1017-275442.html?legacy=cnet**>.

2.   <**www.bea.com/about/index.shtml**>.

3.   "BEA WebLogic Integration Introduction," <**www.bea.com/products/weblogic/ integration/index.shtml**>.

4.   J. O'Donnell, "Weblogic Workshop Beta Review," 27 March 2002 <**www.theserverside.com/reviews/thread.jsp?thread_id=12690**>.

5.   W. Wong, S. Shankland, "Hardware Powerhouse HP Shows its Software Side," <**news.com.com/2100-1001-252910.html**>.

6.   <**www.hp.com/products1/softwareproducts/ middleware_businessprocess/overview.html**>.

7.   A. Gonsalves, "IBM, HP To Unveil Web Services Tools At JavaONE," <**www.informationweek.com/story/IWK20020322S0022**>.

8.   "HP Registry Composer Product Specification," <**www.hpmiddleware.com/ downloads/PDF/RegistryComposer_specsheet.pdf**>.

9. "HP Netaction Product Suite," <**www.hp.com/products1/softwareproducts/software/netaction/netaction_brochure.pdf**>.

10. "Web Services by IBM," <**www-3.ibm.com/software/solutions/webservices/overview.html**>.

11. "The XML Cover Pages: IBM Global Services and IBM WebSphere Platform to Support IBM's Web Services Infrastructure," 22 May 2001 <**xml.coverpages.org/ni2001-05-22-b.html**>.

12. D. Davis, "IBM Takes an End-to-End Approach to Web Services," IBM Analyst Report February 2002: 2.

13. C. Sadtler and A. Jacob. "An Introduction to IBM WebSphere Studio Application Developer," <**www.redbooks.ibm.com/redpapers/pdfs/redp0414.pdf**>.

14. "Enterprise Developer for Multiplatforms," <**www-3.ibm.com/software/ad/studio.edm**>.

15. "The XML Cover Pages: IBM Global Services and IBM WebSphere Platform to Support IBM's Web Services Infrastructure," 22 May 2001 <**xml.coverpages.org/ni2001-05-22-b.html**>.

16. T. Kontzer and A. Gonsalves. "Lotus Embraces Web Services, But Will Customers?," 4 February 2002 <**www.informationweek.com/story/IWK20020201S0029**>.

17. "Lotus Notes/Domino 6 FAQ," <**www-103.lotus.com/ldd/nfr6welcome.nsf/9ef083dbcc1d1c5c8525695b0050c564/7475e7329c25f71085256b60004dcdb9?OpenDocument**>.

18. "The XML Cover Pages: IBM Global Services and IBM WebSphere Platform to Support IBM's Web Services Infrastructure," 22 May 2001 <**xml.coverpages.org/ni2001-05-22-b.html**>.

19. K. Ohlson, "Big Blue to Trumpet Web Services Scheme," *Network World* 14 May 2001: 1, 68.

20. J. Brock, "Leaders of the Web Services Pack," *InfoWorld* 17 November 2001: 46.

21. W. Wong. "Why Web Services Make Business Sense," <**news.com.com/2009-1017-275442.html?legacy=cnet**>.

22. "Visual Studio .NET Enables Developers to Rapidly Build and Deploy XML Web Services and Applications," 8 February 2002 <**www.microsoft.com/presspass/features/2002/feb02/02-08vsnet.asp**>.

23. ".NET My Services Overview," 8 October 2001 <**www.microsoft.com/myservices/services/overview.asp**>.

24. T. Olavsrud, "Microsoft Puts .NET My Services on Hold," 11 April 2002 <**www.internetnews.com/dev-news/article/0,,10_1007961,00.html**>.

25. M. Migliore. "For Oracle, Web Services Is Old Hat," <**www.esj.com/webservices/columns/article.asp?EditorialsID=9**>.

26. "Oracle 9i Developer Suite," <**zdnetbusiness.cnet.com/enterprise/0-6119586-701-4932333.html**>.

27. M. Biggs, "Oracle9i JDeveloper 4 Spells Services," <**www.javaworld.com/javaworld/jw-01-2002/jw-0125-iw-oracle_p.html**>.

28. "Oracle9i Application Server," <**technet.oracle.com/products/ias/content.html**>.

29. M. Migliore, "Oracle Warms Up to Web Services at OpenWorld," 6 December 2001 `<www.esj.com/webservices/news/article.asp?EditorialsID=81>`

30. S. Hildreth, "Web Services: Market Roundup," `<e-serv.ebizq.net/wbs/hildreth_2.html>`.

31. Oracle Dynamic Services FAQ `<technet.oracle.com/products/dynamic_services/htdocs/general_faq/general_faq.html>`.

32. "Sun™ Open Net Environment (SunONE)," `<wwws.sun.com/software/sunone>`.

33. "Sun ONE Overview: Vision," `<wwws.sun.com/software/sunone/overview/vision>`.

34. "The Sun™ Open Net Environment (SunONE) Architecture," `<wwws.sun.com/software/sunone/overview/architecture/index.html>`.

35. "The Sun™ Open Net Environment (Sun ONE) Architecture," `<wwws.sun.com/software/sunone/docs/arch/chapter2.pdf>`.

36. R. Adhikari, "Sun Extends Web Services Strategy," *Application Development Trends* December 2001: 12.

37. "Sun ONE Overview: DART Model," `<wwws.sun.com/software/sunone/overview/dart/index.html>`.

38. "Consulting," `<www.sun.com/service/sunps>`.

39. "iForce Initiative," `<www.sun.com/aboutsun/media/presskits/iforce>`.

40. "SunTone Press Resources," `<www.sun.com/aboutsun/media/presskits/suntone>`.

41. `<www.projectliberty.org>`.

42. M. Berger, "Liberty Alliance Bolsters Ranks," *InfoWorld* 10 December 2001: 20.

43. A. Shikiar, "Network Identity and the Liberty Alliance Project," `<www.opengroup.org/security/shikiar.pdf>`.

44. S. Morrison, "Sun Unveils Alliance on Web ID System," *Financial Times* 27 September 2001: 18.

45. R. Adhikari, "Sun Extends Web Services Strategy," *Application Development Trends* December 2001: 12.

46. `<www.projectliberty.org>`.

47. B. Swart, "Delphi 6 and Kylix 2 Web Services," *Web Services Journal* February 2002: 50–51.

48. J. Borck, "Taking the Open Road to Web Services," *InfoWorld* 3 December 2001: 48.

49. T. Sullivan and S. Costello, "Vendors Graft Wares onto Web Services," *InfoWorld* 5 November 2001: 24.

50. C. M. Purpi, "Iona Reinvents Its Strategy…Again," *Software Development Times* 15 November 2001: 4.

51. `<www.iona.com/products>`.

52. R. Karpinski, "Iona Advances Web Services Platform, Adds Security: JavaOne," 25 March 2002 `<www.internetweek.com/story/INW20020325S0009>`.

53. J. R. Borck, "Catch the Services Bus," 10 January 2002 `<www.infoworld.com/articles/tc/xml/02/01/14/020114tciona.xml>`.

54. `<www.iona.com/products/webserv.htm>`.

55. D. Connor, "Novell Buys Into Web Services," *NetworkWorld* 17 June 2002: 12.

56. D. Rubinstein, "SilverStream Completes Middleware Picture," 1 January 2002 `<www.sdtimes.com/news/045/story4.htm>`.

57. E. Scannel, "Cape Clear Looks to Meld EAI, Web Services," 7 March 2002 `<ww1.infoworld.com/cgi-bin/fixup.pl?story=http://www.infoworld.com/articles/hn/xml/02/03/07/020307hncapeclear.xml&dctag=middleware>`.

58. R. Irani, "CapeConnect Three From Cape Clear Software," 31 October 2001 `<www.webservicesarchitect.com/content/articles/irani06print.asp>`.

59. "About CapeScience," `<www.capescience.com/about.html>`.

60. P. Resende, "Systinet Surfaces to Sell its Web Services Software," *Mass High Tech* 25–31 March 2002: 3.

61. "WASP Products Overview," `<www.systinet.com/products/overview.html>`.

62. "WASP Products Overview," `<www.systinet.com/products/overview.html>`.

63. "WASP Products Overview," `<www.systinet.com/products/overview.html>`.

64. J. Ackerman, "Systinet's WASP UDDI Standard 3.1," 8 March 2002 `<dcb.sun.com/practices/profiles/systinet_wasp.jsp>`.

65. `<www.themindelectric.com/gaia/features.html>`.

66. "Talking Blocks Management Suite," `<www.talkingblocks.com/tb_product_brief.pdf>`.

67. `<www.amberpoint.com>`.

68. R. Kapinski, "AmberPoint Debut Web Services Management Platform," 10 June 2002 `<www.internetwk.com/story/INW20020610S0001>`.

69. "interKeel At-a-Glance," `<www.interkeel.com/downloads/ik-factsheet.pdf>`.

70. "Talking Blocks Management Suite," `<www.talkingblocks.com/tb_product_brief.pdf>`.

71. `<www.westglobal.com>`.

72. M. Hudson, "Going with the Flow," *Intelligent Enterprise* 18 September 2001: 52–53.

73. "Business Service Management: Toward the Service-Driven Enterprise," *Avinon White Paper* March 2002: 5.

74. "Collaxa Web Services Orchestration Server," `<www.collaxa.com/product.jsp?from =homepage>`.

75. D. Taft, "Orchestrating Web Services," 3 June 2002 `<www.eweek.com/print_article/0,3668,a%253D22557,00.asp>`.

76. `<www.eltregra.com>`.

77. "BusinessManager," `<www.savvion.com/products/enterprise.htm>`.

78. "Versata Logic Server: Web Services & XML Add-On," `<www.versata.com/products/inSuite/webservicesandxml.add-on.html>`.

79. M. Vizard and S. Gillmor, "Vitria's CTO Explains the Impact of Web Services on Application Integration," *InfoWorld* 15 January 2002 `<www.infoworld.com/articles/hn/xml/02/01/15/020115hnvitria.xml>`.

80. H. Harreld, "EAI Seeks to Remold," *InfoWorld* 1 April 2002: 33.

81. R. Karpinski, "SeeBeyond Boosts Web-Services Support In Integration Platform," Insurance & Technology 28 February 2002 `<www.insurancetech.com/story/techWire/INW20020228S0009>`.

82. "Tibco Ties Business Processes, Web Services," 20 May 2002 `<www.webservices.org/index.php/article/articleprint/401/-1/3>`.

83. "Tibco Ties Business Processes, Web Services," 20 May 2002 `<www.webservices.org/index.php/article/articleprint/401/-1/3>`.

84. "BusinessWare: The Leading E-business Platform," `<www.vitria.com/library/brochures/vitria_businessware_brochure.pdf>`.

85. H. Harreld, "Vitria Marries Web Services, BPM," InfoWorld 19 May 2001 `<www.infoworld.com/cgi-bin/fixup.pl?story=http://www.infoworld.com/articles/hn/xml/02/05/19/020519hnvitria.xml&dctag=webservices>`.

86. "Implementing Enterprise Web Services With The Webmethods Integration Platform," *webMethods White Paper* March 2002: 4–5.

87. `<www.webmethods.com/content/1,1107,EnterpriseWebServices,FF.html>`.

88. `<www.webcollage.com>`.

89. "Modules,"`<www.webcollage.com/html/products/management_modules.shtml>`.

90. `<www.webcollage.com>`.

.NET Web Services:
A Conceptual Overview

Objectives

- To introduce the .NET Framework and Visual Studio® .NET.
- To explain the basics of a .NET Web service.
- To examine the Global XML Web Services Architecture (GXA) and its specifications.
- To overview Microsoft's tools that allow developers to create .NET applications (including Web services) for wireless devices.
- To discuss Web services' relationship to Microsoft BizTalk® and .NET Enterprise Servers.

A client is to me a mere unit, a factor in a problem.
Sir Arthur Conan Doyle

...if the simplest things of nature have a message that you understand, rejoice, for your soul is alive.
Eleonora Duse

9.1 Introduction[1]

In June 2000, Microsoft announced its .NET initiative, a broad new vision for incorporating the Internet and the Web in development, delivery and use of software. Web services are a key component of the .NET strategy, and Microsoft provides extensive tools for developing and interacting with Web services. This chapter introduces Microsoft's integrated development environment, Visual Studio .NET, and its capabilities for creating and consuming Web services. We then overview the *Global XML Web Services Architecture (GXA)*, a set of specifications that build on core Web services standards to provide additional discovery, security and routing capabilities. The chapter also examines how Web services are consumed from wireless-device applications and explores specific .NET Web services. We conclude by discussing Microsoft BizTalk, .NET Enterprise servers and their support for Web services. Appendix B, Implementing Web Services in Visual Basic .NET, provides complete, working examples of .NET Web services and .NET Web service clients.

---

1. This chapter focuses on creating and consuming Web services using Visual Studio .NET, a development tool that handles many low-level programming details. There are other tools and techniques that developers can use to create .NET Web services and Web service clients. Many such tools and techniques are beyond the scope of this book, and we do not discuss them here.

9.2 .NET Overview

Before explaining .NET's support for Web services, we must provide a general overview of the .NET platform. A key aspect of the .NET strategy is its independence from a specific programming language. Rather than forcing developers to use a single language, Microsoft enables developers to create .NET applications in any .NET-compatible language. This means that programmers can contribute to the same application, writing code in the .NET languages (such as Visual Basic® .NET, Visual C++ .NET and C#) in which they are most proficient.

Learning to program using a .NET-compatible language is relatively simple, especially for experienced programmers. Both Visual Basic .NET and Visual C++ .NET resemble their earlier versions, whereas the new language C# (pronounced "C sharp") incorporates aspects of C++ and Java. Using the tools and capabilities provided by Visual Studio .NET, both experienced programmers and novices can develop sophisticated .NET applications. (We discuss Visual Studio .NET in Section 9.2.2.)

The .NET strategy also promotes software reuse. Microsoft's .NET Framework, which we discuss in Section 9.2.1, includes tools for *porting*, or adapting, existing software components (such as those written in Visual Basic 6 or Visual C++ 6) to .NET. This minimizes the tedious and counterproductive task of recreating software. Developers can write new components in .NET-compatible languages, then assemble applications by combining existing and new components.

Web services, which are central to the .NET initiative, extend the concept of software reuse to the Internet by allowing developers to reuse software components that resides on another machine or platform. Employing Web services as reusable building blocks, programmers can concentrate on their specialties without having to implement every component of an application. For example, a company developing an e-commerce application can subscribe to Web services that process payments and authenticate users—this enables programmers to focus on other, more unique aspects of the e-commerce application.

9.2.1 .NET Framework

The Microsoft *.NET Framework* is at the heart of the .NET strategy. This framework manages and executes applications and Web services, provides a class library (called the *Framework Class Library*, or *FCL*), enforces security and supplies many other programming capabilities. The FCL contains reusable components that programmers can incorporate into their applications—this saves programmers from having to create new software entirely from the ground up. Details of the .NET Framework can be found in the *Common Language Specification* (*CLS*), a specification that defines the common features of .NET languages and contains information about the storage of data types, objects and so on. The CLS has been submitted for standardization to the European Computer Manufacturers Association (ECMA). Standardizing the CLS is similar to publishing the .NET Framework's blueprints—once the CLS is standardized, anyone can build the framework by following the specification. This will simplify the process of porting the .NET Framework to other platforms. The .NET Framework currently exists only for the Microsoft Windows® platform, but organizations are developing versions of the framework for other platforms, such as Linux and the FreeBSD operating system.

Another central part of the .NET framework is the *Common Language Runtime (CLR)*, which executes programs written in any .NET-compatible programming language. .NET programs are compiled in two steps. First, a program is compiled into the *Microsoft Intermediate Language (MSIL)*, which defines instructions for the CLR. Code translated into MSIL from multiple programming languages and sources can be woven together by the CLR. MSIL then is compiled into machine code for a specific platform. Because most platforms use different machine languages, compiling first to a common format such as MSIL increases portability between platforms and interoperability between languages. MSIL allows various platforms to support .NET and, at the same time, preserve separate methods of handling memory management, security and other details.

Microsoft also offers a version of the .NET Framework called the *.NET Compact Framework*. This version enables developers to create applications for limited-resource devices, such as mobile phones and PDAs. Applications built using the Compact Framework can run on any device that has the Compact Framework installed. Users download applications onto a device through a wireless Internet connection or a connection from a PC. Once downloaded to the device, many applications do not require an Internet connection. We discuss the .NET Compact Framework and other wireless technologies in Section 9.5.

9.2.2 Visual Studio® .NET

Visual Studio .NET is Microsoft's *integrated development environment* (*IDE*)—software used to create, document, run and debug programs conveniently. IDEs facilitate *rapid application development* (*RAD*) by enabling developers to produce working programs relatively quickly. Visual Studio .NET allows developers to create programs in a variety of .NET programming languages and also offers editing tools for manipulating several types of files. These and other features make Visual Studio .NET a powerful tool for creating business-critical and mission-critical applications.[2]

The Visual Studio .NET IDE provides a sophisticated environment for *visual programming*, a technique by which prepackaged components can be "dragged and dropped" into an application. Visual Studio .NET's tools facilitate code reuse by making it easy to build applications from preexisting code. Programmers can use predefined controls to set up connections to databases, organize and add files in an application and much more. Through visual programming, developers can incorporate predefined features in programs without having to know the details of those features. Visual programming also enables developers to use wizards to modify elements of their applications.

Figure 9.1 displays a simple application opened in Visual Studio .NET. This type of project is known as a *Windows application*, because it displays a graphical user interface (GUI) and, therefore, contains at least one window. Windows applications execute within the Windows operating system.

The large, gray box (called a *form)* represents a Windows application. Programmers customize forms by adding *controls*. Collectively, the form and controls comprise the program's graphical user interface (GUI), or the visual components through which a user interacts with a program.

The top of the IDE window (the *title bar* in Fig. 9.1) displays information about the application, such as the name of the application and the application's programming language. The name of each open document is listed on a tab. In this example, the documents are the **Start Page** (a page that provides helpful links for the user) and **Form1.vb** (the application). To view a document, click its tab.

2. Programs created in Visual Studio .NET often are referred to as applications, projects or solutions.

Toolbar   Tabs   Title bar   Menu   **Solution Explorer**

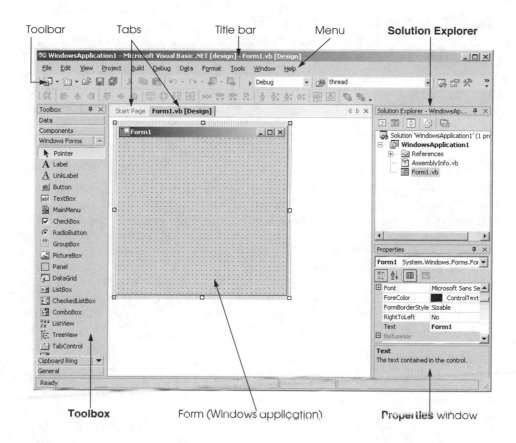

Toolbox   Form (Windows application)   Properties window

Fig. 9.1   Visual Studio .NET environment after a new application has been created.

The top of the IDE contains several menus (**File**, **Edit**, **View**, etc.) that enable developers to perform basic tasks. For example, new projects can be created by selecting the **File** menu, then option **New**, and finally option **Projects....** This opens the **New Project** dialog, where developers specify the type of project they would like to create, as well as the name and location of that project.

The *toolbar* contains icons that represent commands. Rather than navigating through menus to locate certain commonly used commands, the programmer can access these commands from the toolbar. Some icons allow programmers to execute multiple commands. Click the *down arrow* beside an icon to display related commands.

Visual Studio .NET provides windows for exploring files and customizing controls. In Fig. 9.1, we display essential windows for developing .NET applications. The ***Solution Explorer*** window lists all the files in the solution. The ***Toolbox*** contains reusable software components (or controls) that developers can use to customize applications. Using visual programming, programmers can "drag and drop" controls onto a form, instead of writing code themselves. Each control has its own set of properties. These properties specify information about a control, such as its size, color and position. The ***Properties*** window allows programmers to manipulate form or control properties.

9.2.3 ASP (Active Server Pages) .NET

Microsoft's *Active Server Pages (ASP) .NET*, another integral part of the .NET initiative, is a technology for creating dynamic Web content marked up as HTML. Like Windows applications, Web pages built with ASP .NET are designed using Visual Studio .NET. ASP .NET developers can create multi-tier, database-intensive applications quickly by employing .NET's object-oriented languages and the FCL's *Web controls*. Web controls are similar to the controls in Windows applications, but are designed specifically for Web pages. ASP .NET is a sophisticated technology—it includes optimizations for performance, testing and security.

The simplest way to create a Web service in Visual Studio .NET is by creating an *ASP .NET Web service*, or a Web service that is built using ASP .NET technology. Using ASP .NET to build a Web service provides several benefits. First, ASP .NET itself is built upon the .NET Framework, which allows the Web service to employ features of the .NET Framework, such as memory management, interoperability and software reuse. The Web service also benefits from the ASP .NET optimizations mentioned earlier.

When a developer creates Web services using ASP .NET and Visual Studio .NET, many programming details are hidden. For example, developers do not need to create WSDL documents for their Web services, because ASP .NET generates these descriptions. Visual Studio .NET also creates a testing and documentation Web page, which provides information about the Web service and its methods.

9.3 .NET Web Services Basics

In .NET, a Web service is an application stored on one machine that can be accessed by another machine over a network. In its simplest form, a Web service created in .NET is a *class*, or a logical grouping of methods that simplifies program organization. Methods are defined within a class to perform tasks and return information when their tasks are complete. .NET Web service classes contain certain methods (called *Web service methods*) that are specified as part of the Web service. These methods can be invoked remotely using either document-style or RPC-based messaging, which we introduced in Chapter 6, Understanding SOAP and WSDL.

To create a Web service in Visual Studio .NET, a developer first creates a project of type **ASP .NET Web Service**. Visual Studio .NET then generates a file to contain the Web service code (which implements the Web service), an *ASMX file* (which provides documentation for the Web service) and a DISCO file (which potential clients use to discover the Web service) (Fig. 9.2). We discuss these files in more detail shortly. [*Note*: When a developer creates an application in Visual Studio .NET, the IDE typically generates several files. We have chosen to show only those files that are specific to Web services applications.]

When a developer creates an **ASP .NET Web Service** application, Visual Studio .NET provides a code file to contain the Web service class and any other code that is part of the Web service implementation.[3] The Web service class defines all methods that the Web service exposes to remote applications. Any methods (or additional classes) that the developer wants to incorporate in the Web service are added to this class. Developers must tag as a *Web method* each method that they want to expose. We explain how to tag methods in Appendix B, Implementing Web Services in Visual Basic .NET.

---

3. By default, Visual Studio .NET creates only one code file for the Web service implementation. More complex Web services can contain many code files.

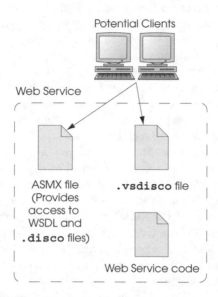

Fig. 9.2 Web service components.

Once the developer adds the necessary programming logic to the Web service code file and successfully compiles the application, then a client application can consume the Web service. However, clients must be able to find the Web service and learn about its capabilities. Discovery of Web services (DISCO) is a Microsoft-specific technology used to locate Web services in a particular directory on a server. There are three types of discovery files: **.disco** files, **.vsdisco** files and **.map** files (**.map** files are discussed later in this section). As we illustrate in Fig. 9.2, **.vsdisco** files are placed in the Web service application, whereas **.disco** files are accessed via the ASMX page. All three DISCO files contain XML that can help clients locate Web service files. A **.disco** file contains markup that specifies references to a Web service's WSDL file and other DISCO documents. A **.vsdisco** file, on the other hand, returns markup (which also contains references to the Web service's WSDL file and DISCO documents) when requested. If a potential client requests a **.vsdisco** file, the .NET Framework analyzes the directory in which the **.vsdisco** file is located, as well as that directory's subdirectories. The .NET Framework then generates markup (using the same syntax as that of a **.disco** file) that contains references to all Web services in that directory and the directory's subdirectories. For security reasons, developers can specify in the **.vsdisco** file that certain directories should not be searched when the markup is generated.[1] Normally, the **.vsdisco** file contains only markup specifying which directories should not be searched. It is important to note that developers usually do not view **.vsdisco** markup. Although a developer can open a **.vsdisco** file in a text editor and examine its markup, **.vsdisco** files are intended to be requested (i.e., viewed in a browser). Every time this occurs, new DISCO markup is generated and displayed.

The reader might be wondering why a developer would want to use one type of DISCO file over another. Developers benefit from **.vsdisco** files, because the files contain a small amount of data and provide up-to-date information on the Web service files provided by a server. However, **.vsdisco** files generate more overhead than **.disco** files do, because a search must be performed every time a **.vsdisco** file is accessed. Thus, some developers find it more convenient to keep **.disco** files up-to-date manually. Many systems use both files. As we discuss later in this section, Web services created using ASP .NET contain the functionality to generate a **.disco** file when it is requested. This **.disco** file contains references to files in the current Web service only.[4] Thus, a developer typically places a **.vsdisco** file at the root of a server; When accessed, this file locates the **.disco** files for Web services on the system and uses these **.disco** files' markup to return information about the entire system.

Once a client locates a Web service, the client must access details regarding the Web service's functionality and how to access that functionality. Although WSDL documents supply this information, WSDL can be difficult to understand. Visual Studio .NET generates an ASMX file when a Web service is constructed to offer a more easily understood description of the Web service. The ASMX file (which is in the form of an ASP .NET Web page) can be viewed in a Web browser and contains descriptions of Web service methods and ways to test these methods. To view more technical information about the Web service, developers can access the WSDL file (which also is generated by ASP .NET). We will demonstrate how to do this shortly.

The ASMX file in Fig. 9.3 displays information about the **HugeInteger** Web service. This Web service, which we use as an example, is designed to perform calculations with integers that contain a maximum of 100 digits (most programming languages cannot easily perform calculations using integers this large). The Web service provides client applications with methods that take two "huge integers" and determine which one is larger or smaller, whether the two numbers are equal, their sum and their difference.

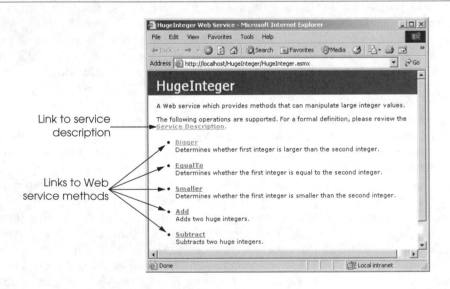

Fig. 9.3 ASMX file rendered in a Web browser.

4. Although in this instance **.disco** files contain references to files in only one Web service, both **.disco** files can contain references to files in several Web services.

The top of the page provides a link to the Web service's ***Service Description*** (Fig. 9.4). The service description is a WSDL file that defines available Web services methods and ways in which clients can interact with those methods. Rather than creating an actual WSDL file, ASP .NET generates WSDL information dynamically. If a client requests the Web service's WSDL file (either by appending **?WSDL** to the ASMX file's URL or by clicking the **Service Description** link), ASP .NET generates the WSDL description, which is then returned to the client and displayed in the Web browser. Because the WSDL file is generated when it is requested, clients can be sure that the WSDL contains the most current information.[2]

As mentioned earlier, the **.disco** file for the Web service is accessed via the ASMX page. Like WSDL data, the **.disco** information for an ASP .NET Web service is not a physical file.[5] The .NET Framework generates this file when a client requests it (by appending **?DISCO** to the ASMX's URL). Readers might be wondering why someone would access a **.disco** file this way—if potential clients know the URL of the Web service's ASMX file, then they have discovered the Web service already. However, **.disco** files also may be accessed when a client requests a **.vsdisco** file. For instance, recall that accessing a **.vsdisco** file causes the .NET Framework to search for Web services. When this occurs, the .NET Framework actually searches for ASMX files, **.disco** files and **.vsdisco** files.[3] This way, the information in a **.disco** file may be returned to a potential client that does *not* know the URL of any ASMX files on this machine.

Fig. 9.4   Service description for a Web service.

5. It is common for XML documents to be created dynamically and manipulated programmatically, but never saved to disk.

Below the **Service Description** link, the ASMX page shown in Fig. 9.3 lists the methods that the Web service offers. Clicking any method name requests a test page that describes the method (Fig. 9.5). After explaining the method's arguments, the test page allows users to test the method by entering the proper parameters and clicking **Invoke**. (We discuss the process of testing a Web service method shortly.) Below the **Invoke** button, the page displays sample request-and-response messages using SOAP, HTTP GET and HTTP POST. These protocols are the three options for sending and receiving messages in Web services. The protocol that transmits request and response messages also is known as the Web service's *wire format*, because it defines how information is sent "along the wire." SOAP is the more commonly used wire format, because both HTTP GET and HTTP POST are tied to HTTP, whereas SOAP can be sent along other transport protocols.

Figure 9.5 depicts the test page for the **HugeInteger** method **Bigger**. From this page, users can test the method by entering **Value**s in the **first:** and **second:** fields, then clicking **Invoke**. The method executes, and a new Web browser window opens to display an XML document that contains the result (Fig. 9.6).

Now that we have discussed the different files that compromise a .NET Web service, let us examine a .NET Web service client (Fig. 9.7). A .NET client can be any type of .NET application, such as a Windows program (which displays a GUI) or a Web application (which displays Web content). Developers can consume Web services from their applications by the process of *adding a Web reference*. This process adds files to the client application that enable the client to access the Web service. To add a Web reference in Visual Studio .NET, the developer right-clicks the project name in the **Solution Explorer** and selects option **Add Web Reference…**. In the resulting dialog, the developer specifies the Web service to consume. Visual Studio .NET then adds an appropriate Web reference to the client application.

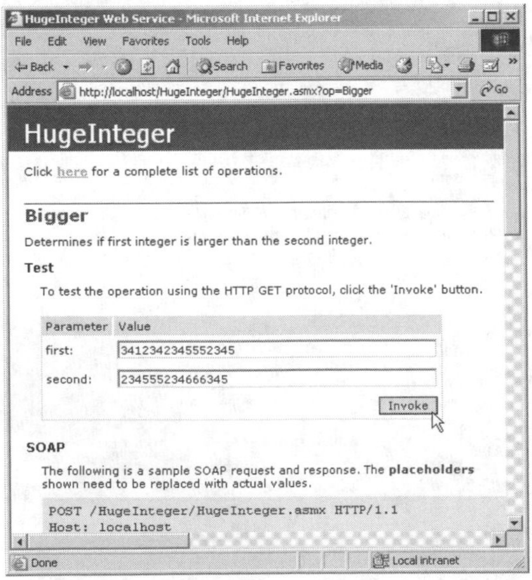

Fig. 9.5   Invoking a Web service method from a Web browser.

Fig. 9.6   Results of invoking a Web service method from a Web browser.

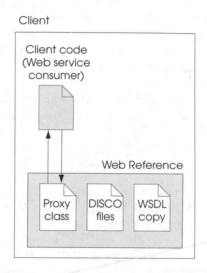

Fig. 9.7   .NET Web service client after Web reference has been added.

The Web reference added to the client application consists of a folder (named **Web References**) containing a copy of the WSDL file, DISCO files and a proxy class (we discuss proxy classes shortly). The **Web References** folder includes two DISCO files— a **.disco** file and a **.map** file. The **.disco** file contains references to the locations of the Web service's ASMX and WSDL files. The **.map** file contains references to Web service files, such as WSDL and DISCO documents. These references can be used to update a Web reference if necessary.[4]

When developers specify the Web service they want to consume, Visual Studio .NET accesses the Web service's WSDL file and makes a copy of it, which will be stored as a file in the **Web References** folder.[6] The information in the WSDL file is used to create the *proxy class*, which handles all the "plumbing" required for Web service method calls. Whenever the client application calls a Web service method, the application actually calls

---

6. A copy of the WSDL file provides the client application with local access to the Web service's description. To ensure that the WSDL file is current, Visual Studio .NET provides an **Update Web Reference** option, which performs the process of updating the files in the **Web References** folder.

a corresponding method in the proxy class. This method takes the name of the Web service method that is being called and its arguments, then formats them so that they can be sent as a request in a SOAP message. The Web service receives this request and executes the method call, sending back the result as another SOAP message. When the client application receives the SOAP message containing the response, the proxy class decodes it and formats the results so that the client application can access them. The information is then returned to the client. The proxy class contains methods that can make either synchronous or asynchronous calls to Web services.[5] Figure 9.8 depicts interactions among the client code, proxy and Web service.

Just as .NET clients contain proxy classes to handle SOAP requests/responses, .NET Web services include their own proxy-like functionality. However, this functionality is provided by the .NET Framework, rather than being contained in a physical file (as is the proxy for the client).

It is important to note that the .NET environment hides from the programmer most of the details we have just discussed. Many aspects of Web service creation and consumption—such as generating WSDL, ASMX files, proxy classes and DISCO files—are handled by Visual Studio .NET and ASP .NET. Although developers are relieved of the tedious process of creating these files, developers can modify the files if necessary.

9.4 Global XML Web Services Architecture (GXA)

As we discussed in previous chapters, Web services technologies are designed to be simple and open, containing only the necessary features to transmit data between applications across a network. However, as organizations begin to use Web services in enterprise systems, core standards such as SOAP, WSDL and UDDI do not provide sufficient support for Web services. For example, how can Web services transmissions be secured? How are SOAP messages routed through multiple nodes? How does one company locate another company's Web services? How are partner relationships and Web services interactions managed electronically?

To address such problems, Microsoft has created the *Global XML Web Services Architecture* (*GXA*), a series of specifications that extend SOAP and provide additional capabilities to Web services developers. Microsoft designed the specifications to supply the higher-level functionality that businesses require to implement complex Web services. GXA provides a general-purpose architecture, meaning that the specifications can be used in various Web service scenarios, regardless of complexity. The specifications are modular—therefore, they can be used separately or together to extend the functionality of GXA as needed. Microsoft plans to submit the GXA specifications for standardization, which will establish GXA as an open architecture.[6]

GXA specifications include *WS-Security*, *WS-Inspection*, *WS-Routing* and *WS-Referral*. WS-Inspection is a specification that helps programmers locate Web services' WSDL files and UDDI descriptions. WS-Routing allows developers to define routing information for a SOAP message. Developers can use WS-Routing to indicate in a SOAP envelope the path that a SOAP message should take.[7] WS-Referral enables developers to modify routing information dynamically (i.e., a SOAP message's path may be changed as the SOAP message moves from one node to another).[8] WS-Security provides security for Web services transmissions.

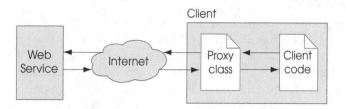

Fig. 9.8   Interaction between Web service and Web service client.

Figure 9.9 summarizes GXA's specifications, and Fig. 9.10 illustrates the relationships among the specifications. Notice that each specification enhances SOAP and that each specification is its own unit. The following sections discuss each specification in detail.

Specification	Description
WS-Inspection	Specification that facilitates the discovery of WSDL files and UDDI descriptions.
WS-Routing	Specification that allows developers to define routing information for a SOAP message statically.
WS-Referral	Specification that allows developers to define routing information for a SOAP message dynamically.
WS-Security	Specification that enables developers to secure Web services transmissions.

Fig. 9.9   Current GXA specifications.

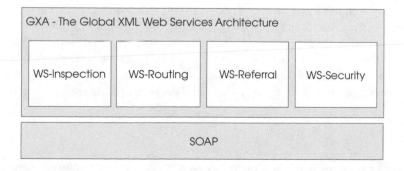

Fig. 9.10   SOAP provides the base for GXA specifications.

9.4.1 WS-Inspection[7]

WS-Inspection is a GXA specification created by Microsoft and IBM that addresses Web services discovery. WS-Inspection defines a syntax for creating *WS-Inspection documents*, which provide references to Web services available on a particular server. WS-Inspection's syntax is XML-based, so WS-Inspection documents contain references that are easy to understand, maintain and format into useful links.

As we discussed in Chapter 7, UDDI, Discovery and Web Services Registries, UDDI allows developers to discover Web services by searching registries for services with specific capabilities. Why, then, would an organization want to use WS-Inspection? Whereas UDDI enables developers to discover Web services on the basis of functionality, WS-Inspection enables developers to discover Web services on the basis of location (i.e., Web services at a specific server). For example, some companies maintain relationships with partners that involve using each other's Web services. In these situations, a company might have access to a partner's server and might want to determine what Web services are available at that server. WS-Inspection is ideal for this purpose.

WS-Inspection information is stored in a document with a **.wsil** extension, known as a *WS-Inspection file* or a *WS-Inspection document*. WS-Inspection markup uses a **service** element to describe a Web service. The **service** element contains additional elements that provide further information about the Web service—including the **name** element, which identifies the service within the WSIL document; the **abstract** element, which provides a text description of the service; and a **description** element, which supplies references to service-description documents (usually WSDL files). In addition to the **service** element, a WSIL document can contain **link** elements, which supply links to other WSIL documents.

The WS-Inspection specification also includes *bindings*—i.e., extensions to WS-Inspection—that provide additional information to a **description** or a **link** element. Current bindings include the *WSDL binding* and the *UDDI binding*. The WSDL binding enables more specific referencing of a WSDL service description. For instance, a WSDL file can contain descriptions for several Web services; the WSDL binding enables the developer to specify one specific service within such a file. The UDDI binding enables the referencing of UDDI entries. Due to WS-Inspection's extensible nature, more bindings can be created as they are needed.

For WS-Inspection files to be useful, they must be easily accessible to developers searching for Web services. One way to make a WS-Inspection file available is to name the file **inspection.wsil** and place it in a standard location—this is usually the root directory of a Web server, which is the topmost folder on the server that contains the organization's Web services. Placing a WSIL file in the root directory is sometimes referred to as *publishing the file*. Another way of providing access to an inspection document is to include a link to the document on a company's Web site. This is sometimes referred to as the *Linked* technique.[9]

---

7. Information in this section is based primarily on K. Ballinger, et al., "Web Services Inspection Language (WS-Inspection) 1.0." **<msdn.microsoft.com/library/en-us/dnglob-spec/html/ws-inspection.asp>**.

9.4.2 WS-Routing[8]

WS-Routing is a specification for defining the path of a SOAP message from sender to final recipient. Using WS-Routing, developers can specify exactly where a SOAP message should go, where it should stop along the way and the order in which the stops should be made. WS-Routing also enables developers to define the paths of SOAP-message responses.

SOAP allows developers to indicate a series of intermediaries through which a SOAP message should pass, but it is difficult to specify the order in which the message reaches these intermediaries. This is because a SOAP message can be transmitted over various transport protocols, and each transport protocol defines its own way of specifying a message path. For example, a SOAP message might travel across HTTP from its sender to an intermediary, then travel across SMTP from the intermediary to the final recipient—it would be complex and difficult to define the SOAP message's path in relation to all possible transport protocols. A developer can specify the message path by "binding" a SOAP message to a particular transport protocol, then using that protocol to define the message's path. However, this means that the SOAP message can travel only over that particular protocol.

WS-Routing provides a solution to this problem by enabling developers to specify a message path, regardless of the transport mechanism. The WS-Routing specification defines a syntax that developers can include in the header of a SOAP message. The syntax's elements can specify the message's ultimate destination (using the **to** element), its point of origin (using the **from** element) and any intermediaries (using the **via** element). WS-Routing also provides the **fwd** and **rev** elements, which specify the forward and reverse message path, respectively, and the **id** and **relatesTo** elements, which enable a message to reference another message. This could be useful when an error message (known as a *fault message*, or *fault*) is being sent in response to another message. The **id** and **relatesTo** elements can be used in the fault message to reference the original message that caused the error. The **fwd** element contains a list of **via** elements, which specify intermediaries; the order of the **via** elements indicates the order in which the intermediaries should be reached.

When the message arrives at an intermediary (or its final destination), the receiver follows an algorithm to process the message. The receiver removes the first **via** element from the **fwd** element and determines if the message has arrived at the proper intermediary. If so, the message is forwarded to the next receiver (specified by the next **via** element). If the removed **via** element does not reference the message's current location, an error message is returned to the original sender. If the removed **via** element was the last **via** element, the message is forwarded to the final destination, which is specified by the **to** element.

If an intermediary receives a message with no **via** elements (or no **fwd** element), the intermediary analyzes the **to** element to determine whether the current location is the final destination. If it is, the message has reached its final destination. If not, a fault is generated.

The reverse message path is generated as the message travels from the sender to the receiver (provided that the **rev** element exists in the SOAP header). For example, when an intermediary removes the first **via** element from the **fwd** element, a corresponding **via**

---

8. Information in this section is based primarily on H. Nielsen and S. Thatte, "Web Services Routing Protocol (WS-Routing)," October 2001 `<msdn.microsoft.com/library/en-us/dn-globspec/html/ws-routing.asp>`.

element is added to the **rev** element. Thus, the WS-Routing information for the return path is created as the message moves from intermediary to intermediary.

Figure 9.11 illustrates the actions of a SOAP message that contains WS-Routing information. [*Note*: The WS-Routing information in this figure is not displayed in its actual XML-based format.] The SOAP message begins at location **A**. Notice that **A** is specified in the **from** element, and **E**, the destination of this message, is specified in the **to** element. The path is specified in element **fwd**, which, in this case, indicates that the message should stop at intermediaries **B**, **C** and **D**, in that order. Notice that, as the message travels from one intermediary to the next, the current location is removed from the **fwd** element and added to the **rev** element. Keep in the mind that the SOAP header is, in fact, being modified as it moves from one intermediary to another.

9.4.3 WS-Referral[9]

The previous section discussed WS-Routing, which enables developers to specify the path of a SOAP message. However, it is not necessary to define a SOAP message's entire path before the message leaves its sender. When an intermediary receives a message that does not have a specified next intermediary, that intermediary uses its own built-in routing information (referred to as *routing entries*), along with the ultimate destination indicated in the SOAP message, to determine the next intermediary. The message then is forwarded to the appropriate intermediary.

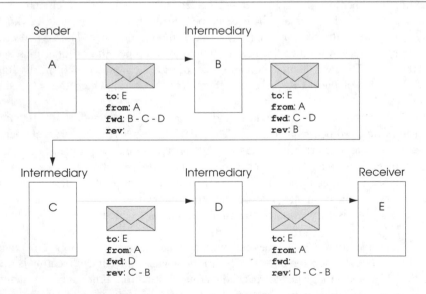

Fig. 9.11   SOAP message with WS-Routing information.

9. Information in this section is based primarily on H. Nielsen, et al., "Web Services Referral Protocol (WS-Referral)," October 2001 <**msdn.microsoft.com/library/en-us/dnglob-spec/html/ws-referral.asp**>. Note that this document is in draft form and is therefore likely to change in the future.

It is sometimes essential for a developer to modify an intermediary's routing entries. For instance, the developer might want to remove an unnecessary intermediary from the message path or inform other intermediaries of a new intermediary that can be used. WS-Referral is a specification for modifying routing entries and, thus, the paths of SOAP messages. WS-Referral can be used to modify only the routing entries of intermediaries known as SOAP routers. A SOAP router is a SOAP node that relays SOAP messages.[10] SOAP routers have the ability to process WS-Referral statements, which are discussed momentarily. WS-Referral can provide different SOAP routers with information about each other, which enables a SOAP message path to be changed dynamically.

The *WS-Referral Statement* is a statement used to modify routing entries. A WS-Referral statement contains a **for** element, which specifies the SOAP routers to which the statement should be applied. If a SOAP router receives a WS-Referral statement for which it is listed in the **for** element, the statement then is applied to that SOAP router. After the **for** element, an **if** element appears, which contains the conditions under which the statement should be applied. If the **if** element conditions are met, the message is sent to the next SOAP router, which is specified in a **go** element. WS-Referral statements are normally used to add or remove SOAP routers from a path.

WS-Referral statements can be delivered to a SOAP router in one of two ways. The first method, called a *WS-Referral Registration Message Exchange*, involves placing the WS-Referral statement in the body of a SOAP message, then sending the message to a SOAP router. In this scenario, the SOAP message is known as a *WS-Referral registration*. The SOAP router either can accept or reject the statement. The second method, known as *WS-Referral Header*, involves sending the WS-Referral statement in the header of a SOAP message.

In some situations, developers want to know what WS-Referral statements have been delivered to a SOAP router. For this purpose, WS-Referral provides the *WS-Referral Query Message Exchange*. Using WS-Referral Query Message Exchange, a query is sent (via a SOAP message) to a SOAP router. This query, which is stored in the body of the SOAP message, can be used to determine what WS-Referral statements are located at the SOAP router. The SOAP router returns a response message containing results of the query.

9.4.4 WS-Security[10]

WS-Security provides SOAP extensions that enable a developer to build secure Web services. Web services developers have numerous security options, but most do not address Web services-specific security issues. Low-level security options, such as firewall-based rules, Secure Sockets Layer (SSL) and Virtual Private Networks (VPN), do not provide ways of authenticating messages and are ill equipped to secure large numbers of SOAP messages sent to multiple intermediaries over different transport protocols.[11] ASP .NET can provide authentication, but this authentication can be used only with HTTP; Web service messages transmitted over different protocols would require an alternate form of authentication.[11]

---

10. Information in this section is based primarily on B. Atkinson, et al., "Web Services Security (WS-Security)," April 2002 **<msdn.microsoft.com/library/en-us/dnglobspec/ html/ws-security.asp>**.

11. Many of the security-related terms in this section are defined in Chapter 11, Computer and Internet Security, and Chapter 12, Web Services Security.

Developers also can employ high-level options to ensure Web services security. One option is to leverage the capabilities of the .NET Framework. The FCL provides classes that enable developers to modify SOAP messages as they are sent back and forth between the Web service and the client. The developer can use this functionality to encrypt and decrypt information in the SOAP message at various stages of the message transmission.

Although these solutions provide security and are relatively simple, none are designed for the particular security needs of Web services. Microsoft, IBM and Verisign have developed various specifications to address Web services security. WS-Security (Web Services Security Language) is a SOAP-based specification that enables developers to enhance the security of SOAP messages. The specification enables developers to authenticate Web service users and ensure that messages remain private (*message confidentiality*) and unmodified (*message integrity*).

WS-Security defines ways of authenticating users by attaching security tokens to SOAP messages. WS-Security is extensible; therefore it supports multiple security-token formats. The specification is designed to be compatible with commonly used security models, such as SSL, PKI and Kerberos. WS-Security also can be used in conjunction with XML Signature and XML Encryption, which are W3C security technologies used to specify digital signatures and encrypt data, respectively.[12]

The creators of WS-Security stress that the specification does not define a "complete security solution." WS-Security was created as a foundation on which programmers can build other Web services specifications. Some of these specifications already are under development, including *WS-Policy*, *WS-Trust* and *WS-Privacy*:

- WS-Policy will enable developers to specify the limitations and capabilities of senders and receivers.

- WS-Trust will define how different organizations can set up and maintain trust relationships.

- WS-Privacy will allow organizations to specify privacy policies.

The next set of specifications will include *WS-Secure Conversation*, *WS-Federation* and *WS-Authorization*:

- WS-Secure Conversation will define how to manage message exchanges, including authenticating Web services and Web service clients.

- WS-Federation will enable the management of trust relationships across different B2B and authorization systems.

- WS-Authorization will allow developers to manage the access privileges of Web services.[13]

These new specifications will facilitate secure Web services transactions between companies.

Microsoft also has announced that it is creating a set of technologies, called *Trust-Bridge*, to provide federated security across trust domains. This new software, built upon WS-Security, will allow business partners to access information on each other's systems as easily as if they were accessing information on their own systems. Web services technology and WS-Security will provide authentication, enabling authorized users to access remote systems without constantly re-entering usernames and passwords.[14] Figure 9.12 illustrates the different specifications and software being built on top of WS-Security. Notice that TrustBridge has been shaded differently than the specifications; this is because TrustBridge will encompass a set of technologies, rather than a specification.

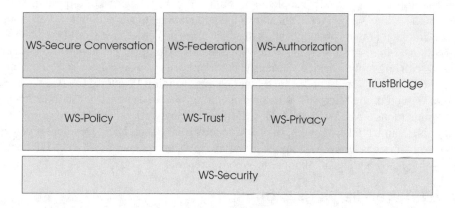

Fig. 9.12 WS-Security as a base for new specifications and software.

9.5 Mobile Internet Toolkit and .NET Compact Framework

As cell phones, personal digital assistants (PDAs) and other hand-held devices become more common, the demand for wireless applications is growing rapidly. In response, Microsoft and other software vendors have created tools for developing wireless Web content and wireless applications. Using Microsoft's tools, programmers can create applications for mobile devices using languages such as C#, Visual Basic .NET and Java. As wireless application-development tools improve, programming for wireless devices is becoming increasingly similar to programming for non-mobile devices. This means that .NET programs can consume Web services from wireless-device applications using techniques similar to those we describe throughout this chapter.

Microsoft already provides several tools that facilitate programming for mobile devices. .NET developers can use Microsoft's *Mobile Internet Toolkit* (*MIT*)[12] to build wireless Web content that runs on a variety of mobile devices. When a wireless client requests an MIT application, the request is sent to the server; the necessary business logic is performed, and a response is returned to the client. An application built using the MIT can determine the type of device that is running the application, then send the appropriate markup to the client. Running MIT applications normally requires frequent interaction with a Web server.

Developers also can create .NET applications for mobile devices using the *.NET Compact Framework* (*CF*) and *Smart Device Extensions* (SDE).[13] The .NET Compact Framework is a subset of the .NET Framework designed to run on various mobile devices. The Smart Device Extensions are extensions to Visual Studio .NET that enable developers to create applications for devices running the .NET Compact Framework.[15] Unlike applica-

---

12. The Mobile Internet Toolkit (now available as Beta software) can be downloaded from **msdn.microsoft.com/downloads/default.asp?url=/downloads/sample.asp?url=/msdn-files/027/001/817/msdncompositedoc.xml**.

13. The Compact Framework (now available as Beta software) and SDE can be downloaded by following the directions at **msdn.microsoft.com/vstudio/device/sdebeta.asp**. The SDE also ships with Visual Studio .NET.

tions developed using the MIT, applications built using the CF and SDE require little or no interaction with a Web server. This allows the applications to run without a Web connection (a Compact Framework application that consumes a Web service would require a Web connection). Microsoft is working to develop the .NET Compact Framework so that it can be used with any mobile device. Currently, the framework is available only for Pocket PC, Stinger (Microsoft's smart phone) and other devices running Windows CE (Compact Edition), a version of the Microsoft Windows operating system designed for mobile devices.

Applications created with the MIT or Compact Framework are developed using Visual Studio .NET and .NET languages, such as C# and Visual Basic .NET. Developers can consume Web services from these applications in the same manner as from .NET applications—that is, by adding an appropriate Web reference.

9.6 .NET Web Services Examples

In the previous sections, we discussed how developers can create and consume Web services in .NET. Microsoft is using the tools and capabilities we describe to develop a variety of Web services marketed to businesses and consumers. We examined one of these Web services, Microsoft .NET Passport, in Chapter 3, Web Services Business Models. This section explores several other Microsoft .NET Web services, including the Microsoft MapPoint .NET and the services that comprise Microsoft .NET My Services.

9.6.1 .NET My Services

Microsoft's *.NET My Services* is a set of service-to-consumer (S2C) Web services that store users' personal information—such as username and password pairs, appointment schedules, travel information and credit-card data. For example, *.NET Profile* maintains a user's nicknames, photographs and important dates; *.NET Contacts* provides an electronic address book; *.NET Inbox* aggregates e-mail and voice-mail messages in a central location; and *.NET Wallet* stores financial data and records.[16] Microsoft plans to integrate .NET My Services into nearly every product and service that the company controls, including the Windows operating system, applications such as *Microsoft Office*, portals such as MSN (**www.msn.com**) and Microsoft bCentral (**www.bcentral.com**), Microsoft wireless operating systems and the *Xbox* video-game console.[17] This means that .NET My Services users will be able to access information and related services from almost anywhere by using a computer, cell phone or other networked device. Furthermore, because information will be synchronized between all access points, users can change their information once, then see the updated data reflected in any application that connects to the services.

Microsoft originally planned to operate .NET My Services itself, maintaining all user data in central databases. Partner companies, such as travel and financial organizations, would participate by offering services through the .NET My Services infrastructure—for example, an online travel agent might send an updated travel itinerary directly to a customer's .NET My Services calendar. However, partners voiced concerns about security and privacy, and some partners indicated that they would prefer to manage data and services internally. In response, Microsoft is not releasing .NET My Services in 2002; the company might redesign the service infrastructure and market the services to corporations in 2003.[18] According to Charles Fitzgerald, a Microsoft general manager for platform strategy, "We are not ruling out operating these services....But the model in which we are sole operator is something that we are refining."[19]

However, Microsoft is continuing direct operation of two core .NET My Services components.[20] One available service is Microsoft *.NET Passport*, a single sign-on and authentication system that we discuss in Chapter 3, Web Services Business Models. The other service is Microsoft *.NET Alerts*, a notification system (Fig. 9.13). Individuals who sign up to use .NET Alerts (**www.microsoft.com/myservices/alerts/default.asp**) specify information or events for which they want to receive notices. Users can ask to be sent sports scores, reminded of friends' birthdays or informed when a certain stock or eBay auction item reaches a particular price. The alerts can be directed to any e-mail address, an MSN or Windows Messenger account or a Web-enabled cell phone or PDA.[21]

9.6.2 MapPoint .NET

To create certain application features, developers must incorporate geographic information, such as maps, directions and spatial analysis. For example, imagine that a programmer is building a Web site for a fast-food chain—the programmer might want the site to provide driving directions between an address input by a user and the nearest franchise. Similarly, a CRM application might need to include mapping data so that marketers can analyze the geographic distribution of a company's customers. Microsoft offers a traditional software product, called *Microsoft MapPoint*, that supplies geographic data that programmers can include in applications. However, MapPoint contains an enormous amount of information—which takes up significant space in memory—and the software must be updated frequently to reflect geographic changes. Organizations that employ traditional MapPoint software often require specialized staffs and servers to maintain the necessary data.

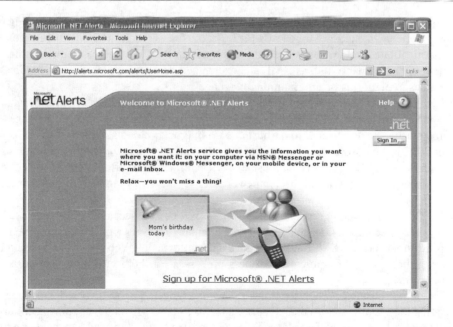

Fig. 9.13   Microsoft .NET Alerts home page. (Courtesy of Microsoft Corporation.)

Microsoft has turned its MapPoint software into a Web service, which simplifies the process of including geographic data in applications. The MapPoint Web service, called *Microsoft MapPoint .NET*, provides an API whose methods enable developers to find a location's latitude and longitude coordinates, search for points of interest within a specified radius, access and manipulate maps and retrieve driving directions between two locations. The most significant advantage of MapPoint .NET is that Microsoft maintains all MapPoint .NET data on centralized servers. The MapPoint .NET staff keeps this information current, so organizations do not have to update MapPoint software or employ specialized staffs to maintain the data. MapPoint .NET also provides the *Customer Service Extranet Application*, which allows clients to upload their own geographic data and manage their accounts online. Many companies—including Expedia and CarPoint—have recognized the benefits of MapPoint .NET and are incorporating it into corporate applications and Web sites.[22]

Microsoft provides the *MapPoint .NET Basic Services SDK* free for download at **msdn.microsoft.com/library/default.asp?url=/library/en-us/ dnmapnet/html/mapintronet.asp**. This limited software-development kit includes a portion of the API, geographic data and two environments in which programmers develop and test their applications. Developers also can use the full MapPoint .NET Web service on either a per-user or per-transaction basis, but this requires the developer to subscribe to MapPoint. For purchasing information, visit **www.microsoft.com/mappoint/net/buy**.

9.7 Microsoft BizTalk®, XLANG and .NET Web Services

To transfer data effectively, businesses need tools that enable communication among disparate systems. One tool is Microsoft's *BizTalk* ("business talk"), an XML-based technology that facilitates and manages business transactions. BizTalk creates an environment in which data can be marked up as XML and exchanged between applications, regardless of differences in platforms or programming languages.

BizTalk encompasses three parts: The BizTalk Server, the BizTalk Framework and the BizTalk Schema Library. The *BizTalk Server* (*BTS*) parses and translates all messages (or documents) that are sent to and from a business via Internet protocols, such as HTTP. BizTalk Server 2002 is Microsoft's BizTalk server. The *BizTalk Framework* is a Schema for structuring messages exchanged between businesses. The Framework offers a specific set of core tags. Businesses can download the Framework to use in their organizations and can create new Schemas.

BizTalk also is used to define business processes. For instance, a developer can use BizTalk to specify certain actions to occur when a company receives a customer's payment. As discussed in Chapter 5, XML and Derivative Technologies in Web Services, defining and enforcing these types of automated business processes can help businesses cut costs and reduce errors.

To define business processes, BizTalk uses *XLANG*, an XML-based language for describing the specific actions that comprise a business process and the circumstances under which those actions should take place. XLANG also can be used to track the state of a business process. Microsoft's BizTalk Server contains the *BizTalk Orchestration Designer*, a tool that uses XLANG to define business processes. An XLANG document that defines a set of business processes is called an *XLANG Schedule*. The BizTalk Orchestration Designer is a visual development tool that makes creating business processes more intuitive; a developer can visually create an *XLANG Schedule Drawing*, which can be compiled and run as an XLANG Schedule.[23]

Certain business processes may need to be executed at different locations. BizTalk allows Web services to be consumed from business-process applications, which means that an action in a business process can be implemented via a call to a Web service. For example, imagine a business process that, under various circumstances, applies a discount to a product (by changing the product's price in an inventory database). If a Web service exists that can apply the discount, the business process's developer can save time and effort by simply calling that Web service.

BizTalk also allows developers to expose business processes as Web services. For instance, if a developer would like to execute a business process as a part of an application, the developer can invoke that business process from outside the BizTalk Server. To access a business process in this way, the business process must be exposed as a Web service, which can be done using Visual Studio .NET. The developer creates the Web service, then invokes the XLANG schedule from the Web service (the FCL provides methods to perform this task). Consuming the Web service from Visual Studio .NET can be performed using the same steps used to consume any other Web service.[24]

To facilitate a more streamlined integration of Web services and BizTalk, Microsoft has created the *BizTalk Server 2002 Web Services Toolkit for Microsoft .NET*. This toolkit simplifies interactions between BizTalk and Web services and allows developers to create BizTalk documents using Visual Studio .NET. This toolkit also provides developers with samples and design guidelines.[25] Figure 9.14 summarizes the BizTalk terminology introduced in this section.

BizTalk Term	Description
Framework	A specification that defines a format for BizTalk messages.
Schema Library	A repository of BizTalk Framework XML Schemas.
Server	An application that helps businesses process message documents. For more information, visit **www.microsoft.com/biztalkserver**.
JumpStart Kit	A set of tools for developing BizTalk applications.
XLANG	An XML-based language used to describe the specific actions that comprise a business process and the circumstances under which those actions should take place.
BizTalk Orchestration Designer	A tool that uses XLANG to define business processes. The tool is included in Microsoft's BizTalk Server application.
XLANG Schedule	An XLANG document that defines a set of business processes.
XLANG Schedule Drawing	A document created (and viewed visually) in the BizTalk Orchestration Designer. This document can be compiled and run as an XLANG schedule.

Fig. 9.14 BizTalk terminology.

9.8 Web Services and .NET Enterprise Servers

As we discussed earlier in this chapter, Microsoft's .NET strategy provides many tools to facilitate application development. The .NET initiative also includes the *.NET Enterprise Servers*, which are server applications designed to Web-enable businesses quickly and efficiently. These servers offer extensive support for tasks such as orchestrating business processes (using BizTalk Server 2002), building e-commerce sites (using *Commerce Server 2002*) and managing databases (using *SQL Server 2000*).

Microsoft supplies toolkits for some .NET Enterprise Servers—these toolkits are designed to integrate Visual Studio .NET and Web services with the solutions provided by the .NET Enterprise Servers. Two of the most prevalent toolkits are the *SQL Server 2000 Web Services Toolkit for Microsoft .NET* and the BizTalk Server 2002 Web Services Toolkit for Microsoft .NET (discussed briefly in Section 9.7). These toolkits work with SQL Server and BizTalk Server, respectively, and are available as free downloads. The SQL Server 2000 Web Services Toolkit for Microsoft .NET enables developers to create Web services from existing stored procedures, which are methods used to access and manipulate data in a database.[26]

Another toolkit designed to work with the .NET Enterprise Servers is the *Exchange 2000 XML Web Services Toolkit. Microsoft Exchange 2000* is a server application that provides messaging and collaboration support for employees and business partners (i.e., support for communication between employees and business partners). As with Microsoft's toolkit for SQL Server, Microsoft's toolkit for Exchange enables users to expose messaging and collaborative solutions as Web services. Developers then can use the services in their applications.[27]

Additional .NET Enterprise Servers include *Microsoft Application Center,* which facilitates the deployment and management of Web applications; *Microsoft Mobile Information Server*, which provides support for mobile Web content; and *Microsoft Internet Security and Acceleration Server*, which enforces security and improves performance across networks. Microsoft is extending many of its .NET Enterprise Servers to support Web services interactions.

This chapter examined Web services in the context of Microsoft's .NET initiative. Microsoft has been instrumental in creating Web services standards, including SOAP, WSDL, UDDI and the GXA specifications. The company also provides extensive tools to facilitate Web services development, deployment and consumption. However, Microsoft is only one of many software vendors that is developing Web services standards, tools and applications. In the next chapter, Java Web Services: A Conceptual Overview, we present Web services technologies designed to run on Java platforms. The chapter focuses on the Java Web Services Development Pack (JWSDP), Sun Microsystems's newest toolkit for creating, deploying and consuming Web services. We also discuss several Web service development platforms that enable developers to create Web services from Java classes, such as WASP, Axis, CapeConnect and GLUE.

9.9 Summary

Microsoft's .NET initiative is a broad vision for incorporating the Internet and the Web in development, delivery and use of software. The .NET strategy promotes software reuse. Web services, which are central to the .NET initiative, extend the concept of software reuse to the Internet by allowing developers to reuse software components that resides on another machine or platform.

When a developer creates a .NET Web service, Visual Studio .NET generates a file to contain the Web service code (which defines the Web service), an ASMX file (which provides documentation for the Web service) and a DISCO file (which potential clients use to discover the Web service). Discovery of Web services (DISCO) is a Microsoft-specific technology used to locate Web services in a particular directory on a server. An ASMX file is constructed to offer a more easily understood description of the Web service. To view more technical information about the Web service, developers can access the WSDL file.

Developers can consume Web services from their applications by adding a Web reference. The Web reference added to a client application consists of a folder containing a copy of the WSDL file, DISCO files and a proxy class. The Web reference also contains a copy of the Web service's WSDL file. When developers specify the Web service they want to consume, Visual Studio .NET accesses the Web service's WSDL file and makes a copy of it. The information in the WSDL file is used to create the proxy class, which handles all the "plumbing" required for Web service method calls.

Microsoft's Global XML Web Services Architecture (GXA) is a set of specifications that provides higher-level functionality necessary to implement complex Web services. WS-Inspection defines a syntax for creating WS-Inspection documents, which provide references to Web services available on a particular server. WS-Routing is a specification for defining a SOAP message's path from sender to final recipient. WS-Referral can be used to modify routing entries and, thus, the paths of SOAP messages. WS-Security enables developers to enhance Web services security by authenticating users and ensuring that messages remain private (message confidentiality) and unmodified (message integrity).

Microsoft provides several tools that facilitate programming for mobile devices. .NET developers can use Microsoft's Mobile Internet Toolkit (MIT) or the .NET Compact Framework to build mobile applications. Applications created with the MIT or Compact Framework are developed using Visual Studio .NET and .NET languages. Developers can consume Web services from these applications in the same manner as from other .NET applications—by adding an appropriate Web reference.

Microsoft is using the tools and capabilities we describe to develop Web services marketed to businesses and consumers. Microsoft's .NET My Services is a set of Web services that store users' personal information—such as username and password pairs, appointment schedules, travel information and credit-card data. Available services include .NET Passport, a single sign-on and authentication system, and .NET Alerts, a notification system. Microsoft MapPoint .NET provides an API that enables developers to find a location's latitude and longitude coordinates, search for points of interest within a specified radius, access and manipulate maps and retrieve driving directions between two locations. One significant advantage of MapPoint .NET is that Microsoft maintains all MapPoint .NET data on centralized servers.

BizTalk can be used to define business processes. XLANG is used to describe the specific actions that comprise a business process and the circumstances under which those actions should take place. An action in a business process can be implemented via a call to a Web service. BizTalk also allows developers to expose business processes as Web services. Microsoft has created the BizTalk Server 2002 Web Services Toolkit for Microsoft .NET, which simplifies interactions between BizTalk and Web services.

The .NET initiative also includes the .NET Enterprise Servers, which are server applications designed to Web-enable businesses quickly and efficiently. Microsoft supplies toolkits for some .NET Enterprise Servers—these toolkits are designed to integrate Visual Studio .NET and Web services with the solutions provided by the .NET Enterprise Servers.

9.10 Internet and Web Resources

UDDI and DISCO

www.develop.com/conferences/conferencedotnet/materials/W4.pdf
This document introduces discovery technologies, specifically UDDI and DISCO, and how they can be used to locate Web services.

msdn.microsoft.com/library/default.asp?url=/library/en-us/cpguide/html/cpconwebservicediscovery.asp
Microsoft Developers Network published this article, which provides background DISCO information for .NET developers.

msdn.microsoft.com/msdnmag/issues/02/02/xml/xml0202.asp
This article begins with background information on Web services in .NET, then covers UDDI and DISCO in detail. The article also includes example code.

msdn.microsoft.com/library/default.asp?url=/library/en-us/cpguide/html/cpconenablingdiscoveryforwebservice.asp
This site, part of the *.NET Framework Developer's Guide*, provides background DISCO information, as well as links to related documentation.

GXA

msdn.microsoft.com/library/en-us/dngxa/html/gloxmlws500.asp
This article introduces the Global XML Web Services Architecture.

Security

msdn.microsoft.com/vstudio/techinfo/articles/XMLwebservices/security.asp
Security options for protecting Web services transmissions are examined in this *Microsoft Developers Network* article.

msdn.microsoft.com/library/en-us/dnglobspec/html/ws-security.asp
This site provides the WS-Security specification.

.NET Examples and Case Studies

www.microsoft.com/myservices/services/default.asp
This site offers information regarding .NET My Services, including links to technical articles, FAQs and more.

www.microsoft.com/myservices/alerts
At this site, Microsoft introduces the features of .NET Alerts and provides links to related technical articles and FAQs.

www.mp2kmag.com
MP2K, a Web-based magazine, discusses many aspects of MapPoint technology.

www.microsoft.com/net/use/casestudies.asp
This site contains links to Web services case studies that discuss .NET Web services implementations by Expedia, Dollar Rent A Car and other organizations.

.NET Compact Framework and the Mobile Internet Toolkit

msdn.microsoft.com/vstudio/device/mitdefault.asp
Microsoft's Mobile Internet Toolkit (MIT) is the topic of this site, which includes an overview, links to Hotfixes, articles and a list of tested devices.

www.asp.net
This site provides sample code, tutorials and articles related to the Mobile Internet Toolkit (MIT).

msdn.microsoft.com/vstudio/device/compactfx.asp
This white paper provides a general overview of the .NET Compact Framework, including links to downloads and a FAQ page.

BizTalk and XLANG

www.gotdotnet.com/team/xml_wsspecs/xlang-c/default.html
This site contains the XLANG specification.

msdn.microsoft.com/library/en-us/dnbiz2k2/html/bts_wp_net.asp
This article provides information on BizTalk, Web services, and how to use .NET with Microsoft BizTalk Server.

.NET Enterprise Servers

www.microsoft.com/servers
This site links to information regarding the .NET Enterprise Servers.

WORKS CITED

1. A. Skonnard, "Publishing and Discovering Web Services with DISCO and UDDI," *MSDN Library* February 2002 **<msdn.microsoft.com/msdnmag/issues/02/02/xml/xml0202.asp>**.

2. R. Tabor, *Microsoft® .NET XML Web Services* (Indianapolis, IN: Sams Publishing 2002) 48.

3. "Deploying XML Web Services in Managed Code," *MSDN Library* **<msdn.microsoft.com/library/default.asp?url=/library/en-us/vbcon/html/vbtskDeployingWebServices.asp>**.

4. R. Basiura, et al., *Professional ASP .NET Web Services* (Birmingham UK: Wrox Press 2001) 250–251.

5. R. Tabor, *Microsoft® .NET XML Web Services* (Indianapolis IN: Sams Publishing 2002) 302.

6. "An Introduction to GXA: Global XML Web Services Architecture," *MSDN Library* February 2002 **<msdn.microsoft.com/library/en-us/dngxa/html/gloxmlws500.asp>**.

7. "Web Services Specifications," *MSDN Library* **<msdn.microsoft.com/library/default.asp?url=/library/en-us/dnglobspec/html/wsspecsover.asp>**.

8. H. Nielsen, et al., "Web Services Referral Protocol (WS-Referral)," October 2001 **<msdn.microsoft.com/library/en-us/dnglobspec/html/ws-referral.asp>**.

9. S. Short, *Building XML Web Services for the Microsoft .NET Platform* (Redmond WA: Microsoft Press 2002).

10. "Web Services Referral Specification Index Page," **<msdn.microsoft.com/library/default.asp?url=/library/en-us/dnglobspec/html/wsreferspecindex.asp>**.

11. "XML Web Services Security," *Visual Studio .NET Technical Resources* **<msdn.microsoft.com/vstudio/techinfo/articles/XMLwebservices/security.asp>**.

12. "Web Services Specifications," *MSDN Library* <**msdn.microsoft.com/library/default.asp?url=/library/en-us/dnglobspec/html/wsspecsover.asp**>.

13. "Security in a Web Services World: A Proposed Architecture and Roadmap," April 2002 <**msdn.microsoft.com/library/en-us/dnwssecur/html/securitywhitepaper.asp**>.

14. "Microsoft's Federated Security and Identity Roadmap," June 2002 <**msdn.microsoft.com/library/en-us/dnwebsrv/html/wsfederate.asp**>.

15. "About .NET Compact Framework and Smart Device Extensions," <**www.gotdotnet.com/team/netcf**>.

16. ".NET My Services Frequently Asked Questions," <**www.microsoft.com/myservices/services/faq.asp**>.

17. "Microsoft outlines their business model for .NET My Services," 23 September 2001 <**www.webservices.org/article.php?sid=281**>.

18. J. Markoff, "Microsoft Has Shelved Its Internet Persona Service," *The New York Times* 11 April 2002 <**www.nytimes.com/2002/04/11/technology/11NET.html**>.

19. D. Clark and R. Buckman, "Microsoft Modifies Web Plan, Lets Firms Manage Services," *The Wall Street Journal* 12 April 2002: A16.

20. C. Adam, ".NET My Services Road Map — Report from the PDC 2001," 23 October 2001 <**www.webservices.org/index.php/article/articleprint/88/-1/10/**>.

21. T. Olavsrud, "Microsoft Launches .NET Alerts Preview," 8 October 2001 <**www.internetnews.com/asp-news/print/0,,3411_898911,00.html**>.

22. S. Lombardi, "Introducing Microsoft MapPoint .NET," April 2002 <**msdn.microsoft.com/library/en-us/dnmapnet/html/mapintronet.asp**>.

23. "BizTalk Orchestration Designer Environment," *MSDN Library* <**msdn.microsoft.com/library/default.asp?url=/library/en-us/bts_2002/htm/lat_sched_concept_oehj.asp**>.

24. U. Roxburgh, "Orchestrating XML Web Services and Using the Microsoft .NET Framework with Microsoft BizTalk Server," February 2002 <**msdn.microsoft.com/library/en-us/dnbiz2k2/html/bts_wp_net.asp**>.

25. "Microsoft Extends XML Web Services Support in .NET Enterprise Servers Through Visual Studio .NET," February 2002 <**www.microsoft.com/presspass/press/2002/feb02/02-13ServerVSpr.asp**>.

26. "Microsoft Extends XML Web Services Support in .NET Enterprise Servers Through Visual Studio .NET," February 2002 <**www.microsoft.com/presspass/press/2002/feb02/02-13ServerVSpr.asp**>.

27. "TechEd 2002: Microsoft Extends XML Web Services Support Into Every Facet of the .NET Enterprise Server Family," April 2002 <**www.microsoft.com/presspass/press/2002/apr02/04-10serverdayonepr.asp**>.

RECOMMENDED READING

Gailey, J. H. "Introducing .NET My Services," *MSDN Library* September 2001 <**msdn.microsoft.com/library/default.asp?url=/library/en-us/dndotnet/html/myservintro.asp**>.

Kulchenko, P. "Web Services Acronyms, Demystified," *XML.com* January 2002 <**www.xml.com/pub/a/2002/01/09/soap.html**>.

Roxburgh, U. "Orchestrating XML Web Services and Using the Microsoft .NET Framework with Microsoft BizTalk Server," February 2002 **<msdn.microsoft.com/library/ en-us/dnbiz2k2/html/bts_wp_net.asp>**.

Short, S. *Building XML Web Services for the Microsoft .NET Platform* (Redmond WA: Microsoft Press 2002).

Tabor, R. *Microsoft® .NET XML Web Services* (Indianapolis, IN: Sams Publishing) 2002.

Thilmany, C. and T. McKinney, "BizTalk: Implement Design Patterns for Business Rules with Orchestration Designer," *MSDN Magazine* **<msdn.microsoft.com/msdnmag/ issues/01/10/BizTalk/print.asp>**.

"XML Web Services Technology Map," *MSDN Library* **<msdn.microsoft.com/library/ default.asp?url=/library/en-us/dndotnet/html/ Techmap_websvcs.asp>**.

10

Java Web Services: A Conceptual Overview

Objectives

- To become familiar with Java technologies for building Web services.
- To understand how Java technologies implement Web services standards.
- To explore software platforms for delivering Java Web services.
- To learn about accessing Web services from clients with limited resources, such as handheld devices and cell phones.

...And many a message from the skies, ...
Robert Burns

Attachment is the great fabricator of illusions; reality can be attained only by someone who is detached.
Simon Wei

I will not answer until I am addressed correctly.
Mary Hamilton

It is the mark of a good action that it appears inevitable in retrospect.
Robert Louis Stevenson

Outline

10.1 Introduction

Since its initial release in June 1995, Java has become one of the most popular programming platforms for building many types of applications. Originally promoted as a language for building interactive Web pages and animations, Java has evolved into a complete platform that provides a rich set of *Application Program Interfaces* (*APIs*) for building embedded applications, desktop applications, dynamic Web components, distributed systems and enterprise-class applications.

A primary feature of the Java platform is its portability. Java-based applications can execute on any operating system and hardware platform that supports Java. This portability, along with Java's support for XML and standard networking technologies, makes

Java ideal for building Internet applications of all kinds, including those based on Web services.

We begin this chapter by introducing several popular Web services platforms used to expose Web services via Java classes. We then introduce the *Java Web Services Developer Pack* (*JWSDP*), Version 1.0, which Sun Microsystems released in June 2002. This developer pack includes the primary APIs and reference implementations for building Java-based Web services and clients. Perhaps the most important part of the JWSDP is the *Java XML Pack*, which includes the following items:

- Java API for XML Messaging (JAXM), v1.1,

- Java API for XML Processing (JAXP), v1.2

- Java API for XML Registries (JAXR), v1.0_01

- Java API for XML-based RPC (JAX-RPC), v1.0

- SOAP with Attachments API for Java (SAAJ), v1.1

In this chapter, we discuss these APIs and technologies that enable Java developers to build standards-based, interoperable Web services and Web services clients. In Appendix C, Implementing Web Services in Java, we demonstrate portions of these APIs with Live-Code™ examples. To conclude this chapter, we introduce *Java 2 Micro Edition* (*J2ME*) and discuss how a *J2ME client* can invoke a Web service.

10.2 SOAP-Based Web Services Platforms

XML messaging is the foundation by which Web services clients and servers communicate. Popular protocols such as XML-RPC (discussed in Section 10.4) and SOAP (discussed in Chapter 6, Understanding SOAP and WSDL) are only two XML messaging schemes that clients can use to communicate. A typical Web service transaction is comprised of two entities—the client and the service. A client invokes a remote Web service by creating an XML message—either a SOAP message or XML-RPC invocation. The client sends the XML message via HTTP, Simple Mail Transport Protocol (SMTP) or another network protocol. The transmitted XML message contains the necessary information for the Web services platform to deserialize the request—i.e., map the XML data types defined in the message to an implementation-specific form that the targeted Web service can use. The transformed request is then delegated to the appropriate handling service. Figure 10.1 depicts a typical interaction between a client and a Java Web service.

Standards developed for Web services focus primarily on communication protocols and Web service description. No standardized approaches exist for implementing Java Web services. In a multiplatform environment, this means that various platforms differ in their requirements on how a Java Web services platform and its hosted Web services should communicate. Similarly, each Java Web services platform has its own preferred way of handling deployment, custom serialization and deserialization, performance optimization and other issues. Developing Java Web services, in some cases, involves adapting a service implementation to the specific requirements of the Java Web services-hosting platform.

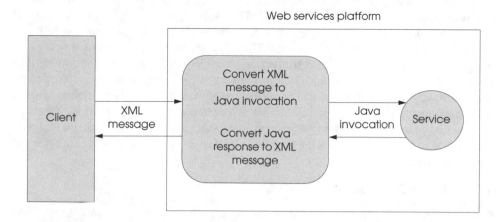

Fig. 10.1 Web service typical invocation process.

Fortunately, certain Java-based Web services platforms now enable developers to pre-serve the implementation of Java classes that are deployed as Web services. Such platforms enable Java classes that will be deployed as Web services to be unaware of the XML mes-sages that clients use to invoke their published functionality. These Java Web services plat-forms handle service creation, method invocation and the response process on behalf of the Java classes. While these aspects of Java Web services platforms are not standardized, most Java-based Web services platforms discussed in this section facilitate Java Web services development by providing these capabilities. Examples of these Web services platforms are Apache's Axis, Cape Clear's CapeConnect, IONA's XMLBus 5.0, The Mind Electric's GLUE and Systinet's Web Applications and Services Platform (WASP). We discuss Axis in Chapter 6, Understanding SOAP and WSDL; the other platforms are covered briefly in Chapter 8, Web Services Platforms, Vendors and Strategies.

10.2.1 Axis

Apache's *Axis* is a restructured successor to the popular Apache SOAP 2.2. Designed to of-fer greater flexibility than its predecessor, Axis provides developers with a substantial set of customization options. Axis is developed using servlet technology,[1] so Axis enables de-velopers to create a Web services-ready platform by installing the Axis distribution on any servlet-capable application Web server.

Architecture
The Axis engine encompasses a network of message-processing elements. A typical inter-action with an Axis Web service starts at the *Transport Listener*. The Axis Transport Lis-tener receives all incoming XML messages. Axis converts each XML message into a **MessageContext** object that represents the XML message. The **MessageContext** object is the internal representation that Axis uses to process incoming and outgoing mes-

---

1. A servlet is a Java technology that extends the functionality of a server. A servlet adheres to the request-response message model—a servlet receives a request from a client, performs some func-tion upon receiving that request, then returns a response to the client.

sages. Each **MessageContext** object is sent to a chain of *message handlers* that process the **MessageContext** object sequentially. The **MessageContext** object then is sent to the targeted service's *provider*, which is responsible for mapping the method calls and parameters to its corresponding Java class. This sequence of events also occurs when a reply is sent back to the client. The corresponding provider obtains the results from the Java class, packages the results into a **MessageContext** object and sends the object to a response chain of message handlers. The **MessageContext** object is processed sequentially and sent to the Transport Listener, which constructs a SOAP message from the information contained in the **MessageContext** object and sends the message to the receiving client. Figure 10.2 shows the flow of an XML message to an Axis Web service and back to the client.

10.2.2 CapeConnect 3.1

Cape Clear's CapeConnect 3.1 enables developers to deploy Java services, EJBs and COR-BA systems in Web services environments. CapeConnect is a stand-alone environment that enables developers to unify legacy systems and Web services protocols without writing code.

The CapeConnect 3.1 package includes a set of graphical deployment tools, a UDDI registry and extensive documentation that provides developers with what they need to create Web services out of existing systems.

Architecture

The CapeConnect system is composed of three major components—the *CapeConnect Gateway*, the *CapeConnect XML Engine* and the *Enterprise Adaptors* (Fig. 10.3). The CapeConnect Gateway is a servlet that acts as the common entry-point for all client requests. All SOAP requests from clients outside the network's firewall are first sent to the CapeConnect Gateway. The CapeConnect Gateway servlet forwards all client requests to the CapeConnect XML Engine servlet. Clients that reside within a firewall may send XML requests directly to the XML Engine servlet.

The CapeConnect XML Engine servlet uses an Enterprise Adaptor to convert the XML request to a Java or CORBA call and invoke the corresponding Java or CORBA service. The Java or CORBA service's response is sent back to the client through the same chain that handled the incoming request.

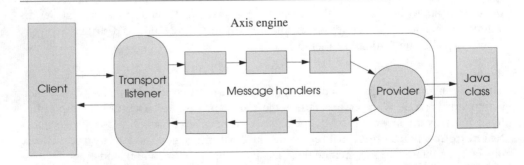

Fig. 10.2 Axis platform architecture.

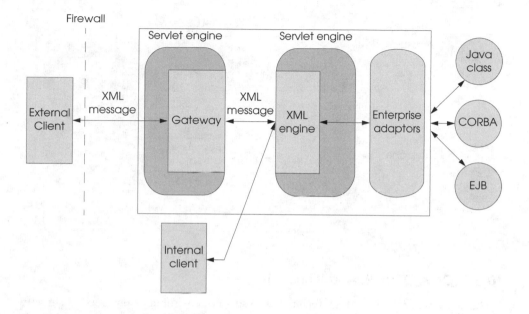

Fig. 10.3 CapeConnect platform architecture.

10.2.3 GLUE Standard 2.1

The Mind Electric's GLUE is an implementation of a full-featured Web services environment. To reduce Web service complexity, GLUE provides a straightforward API designed to simplify the Web services development process. Developers also can use GLUE to create Web services clients. The standard release provides a Web server, servlet engine and XML parser.

Architecture

The GLUE Web services platform is composed of several elements. The first is the transport layer, which receives XML messages and converts them to corresponding Java objects. GLUE provides several default XML-to-Java mappings. Developers also can create mappings for custom objects. The transport layer sends each Java object that corresponds to an incoming XML message to the handling **IService** *implementation*. **IService** implementations act as wrapper objects that delegate all incoming XML messages to the appropriate Java class. Responses are sent back to the **IService**, which in turn sends the response to the transport layer. The transport layer creates and sends an XML response message that contains the invocation results on the **IService** wrapper class. GLUE enables developers to provide their own **IService** implementations. In the event that a developer deploys a service that does not implement interface **IService**, a default implementation **ObjectService** wraps the submitted service. Figure 10.4 illustrates the GLUE architecture.

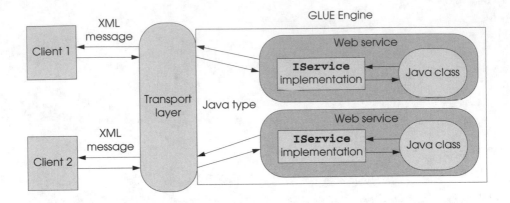

Fig. 10.4   GLUE engine architecture.

10.2.4 IONA Orbix E2A XMLBus 5.1

XMLBus 5.1 standalone is a fully featured Web services environment designed to simplify the Web service creation and deployment process. The XMLBus 5.1 standalone release is comprised of a Web services deployment platform and a set of tools that enable developers to test, deploy and manage Web services. The XMLBus 5.1 standalone package includes a Web services container, a Web service builder tool, a Web services management tool, a multipurpose Web services client console, SOAP message analyzing tool and a UDDI browser.

Architecture
The main component of the XMLBus standalone release is the XMLBus Web services container. The XMLBus Web services container receives XML messages, converts the XML messages to Java representations and invokes the corresponding Java services. The XML-Bus Web services container stores Web services in *XAR files*, which contain all information related to a given Web service—Java classes, property files (i.e., text files that contain information that is likely to be changed, in such a way that changing this information does not require re-compilation), WSDL documents and XML conversion information.

Figure 10.1 illustrates an interaction between a client and a Web service deployed in an XMLBus container. A client sends an XML request to the XMLBus Web services container. The XMLBus Web services container finds the XAR file that corresponds to the XML request. The XAR archive contains information regarding how to convert an XML message into a Java type. Based on the information contained in the XAR file, the XMLBus Web services container invokes the Java service. The Java service returns the results of the method invocation. The XMLBus Web services container converts this information into an XML response and sends it back to the client.

10.2.5 WASP Lite

Web Applications and Services Platform (WASP) Lite is Systinet's entry-level Web services platform. WASP Lite provides developers with tools for implementing, testing, debugging and managing Web services. WASP Lite is targeted to the small-business environment.

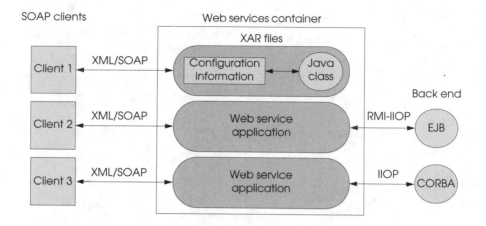

Fig. 10.5 XMLBus architecture.

Architecture

WASP's Web services engine (Fig. 10.6) is composed of four levels—the XML message handling layer, the XML message protocol support layer, a message-adaptation layer and the Java-class layer. Each layer handles an aspect of the messaging process by which XML message requests are delegated to corresponding Java services.

Each XML message that a client sends to a given Java Web service is first handled by the transport layer. Once the transport layer receives the XML message, the XML message is sent to a system-level interceptor layer. The system-level interceptor layer handles system-level policies that are applicable to each XML message (e.g., authentication). The system-level interceptor sends the processed XML message to the dispatcher layer, which in turn determines which Java service is responsible for handling the XML request.

When the dispatcher determines the Java Web service that corresponds to the XML message request, the dispatcher sends the XML message to the set of message interceptors associated with the Java Web service. These service-level message interceptors are particular to each Java Web service.

The service-level interceptors send the XML message to the XML message protocol support layer. The XML message protocol support layer identifies the XML-messaging protocol of the XML message request—XML-RPC, SOAP or application-specific protocols. The XML message protocol support layer is responsible for creating a generic XML message that contains header and body parts.

The XML protocol support layer then sends the XML message to the message adaptation layer, which converts the processed XML message request into an implementation-specific form that the Java service can use. The Java class transmits its invocation results to the client through the chain of layers that initially processed the request.

10.3 Java API for XML Registries (JAXR)

In Chapter 7, UDDI, Discovery and Web Services Registries, we introduced the concepts of discovery and discussed various Web services registry implementations. Registries enable businesses to post information about themselves, such as contact information, avail-

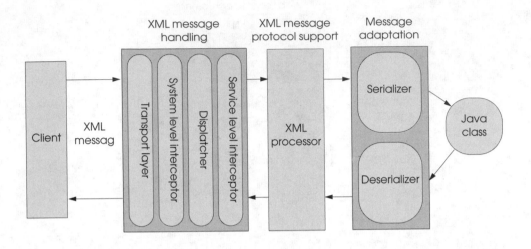

Fig. 10.6 WASP engine architecture.

able services, business classification and information on how to invoke services. Figure 10.7 demonstrates the process of establishing a business relationship through a registry. A business posts an entry in a registry (Step 1). The entry contains information about the business and the services that the business provides. Clients obtain this information from the registry (Step 2). Clients analyze this information and determine what services the clients want to employ (Step 3). The client uses the contact information to contact the business and negotiate access rights to the desired services (Step 4). Once the client and business agree on a payment method, access times and other factors, the client invokes the Web service provided by the business (Step 5).

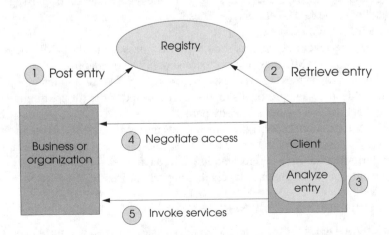

Fig. 10.7 Web services posting, discovery and invocation.

10.3.1 Java API for XML Registries (JAXR) Architecture

Java API for XML Registries (JAXR) defines a standard architecture that enables clients to use *JAXR providers* to access different types of registries, such as those that conform to the UDDI and ebXML specifications. A JAXR provider is an implementation of the JAXR API that 1) maps JAXR objects to protocol-specific entries in the target XML registry, and 2) provides implementations of generic JAXR interfaces. JAXR providers also might choose to expose specific functionality of an XML registry through provider-specific interfaces.

JAXR provides developers with an abstraction of concepts common to all XML registries. JAXR providers are responsible for mapping these general concepts to more specific entities within a target XML registry. This enables clients to use JAXR interfaces to interact with different XML registries. JAXR providers also may choose to expose specific functionality of an XML registry through provider-specific interfaces. Figure 10.8 shows the pluggable JAXR architecture.

10.3.2 Capabilities and Capability Profiles

The JAXR model enables developers to use different types of XML registries. Each type of registry supports a set of operations that are common to all registries, but also supports registry-specific operations. The JAXR model aggregates *capabilities* of various XML registries, so developers are not limited to the set of operations that are common to all XML registries.

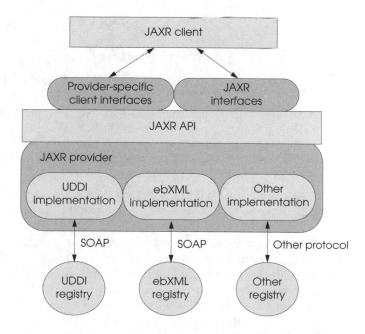

Fig. 10.8 JAXR architecture.

A capability is a measure by which JAXR classifies an operation an XML registry supports. Capabilities help clients determine what methods within the JAXR interfaces to use when interacting with an XML registry. JAXR defines support for numerous XML registries, such as UDDI and ebXML, so not all registries support the same set of operations defined by the JAXR API. Clients must consult the provider's JAXR API documentation to understand what set of JAXR interface methods to use. Alternately, a provider can supply specific interfaces that define the operations clients can use.

The current JAXR specification defines support for two XML registry types, or *profiles*—UDDI registries and ebXML registries. The set of capabilities supported by a given profile is known as a *capability profile*. The capability profile of UDDI registries is a subset of the capability profile of ebXML registries. JAXR providers that support the capability profile for ebXML registries also support the capability profile for UDDI registries (Fig. 10.9). This means that an application that is written to interact with a UDDI registry also can communicate with an ebXML registry. Developers need only to modify the JAXR provider, rather than the implementation of the JAXR client. This correspondence does not apply to applications written for ebXML registries that are transported to UDDI registries.

JAXR classifies an XML registry's capability set by levels. JAXR classifies UDDI registries as level **0** and ebXML registries as level **1**. JAXR providers distinguish the capability support for their provider-specific interfaces by specifying this information in the API documentation. For example, JAXR API documentation specifies that the methods for interfaces **BusinessLifeCycleManager** and **BusinessQueryManager** are level **0**. This means that JAXR providers that support UDDI registries must implement the methods defined in interfaces **BusinessLifeCycleManager** and **BusinessQueryManager**. JAXR providers that support ebXML registries also must support these methods.

10.4 JAX-RPC-Based Java Web Services

The *Java API for XML-based Remote Procedure Calls* (*JAX-RPC*) enables Java programmers to create and access XML-based Web services over a network. RPC originally was developed in the 1980s for enabling a procedural program (e.g., a program written in C or another procedural programming language) to call a function that resides on another computer as conveniently as if that function were part of the same program running on the same computer. A goal of RPC is to allow programmers to concentrate on the required tasks of an application—whether function calls are local or remote is transparent to the programmer. RPC hides the details that enable the application to communicate over a network, as well as performing all the networking and *marshaling of data* (i.e., packaging of function arguments and return values for transmission over a network).

Web services evolved from the need to integrate applications written in many different languages with many different data formats. Whereas RPC requires the use of a single programming language and communications protocol, Web services technology enables integration among many different languages and protocols. By relying on XML—the de facto standard for marking up data—and HTTP—the de facto standard protocol for communication over the Web—SOAP provides such integration. JAX-RPC enables Java programmers to take advantage of these distributed-computing advances by providing a clean, simple API for creating and interacting with XML-based Web services.

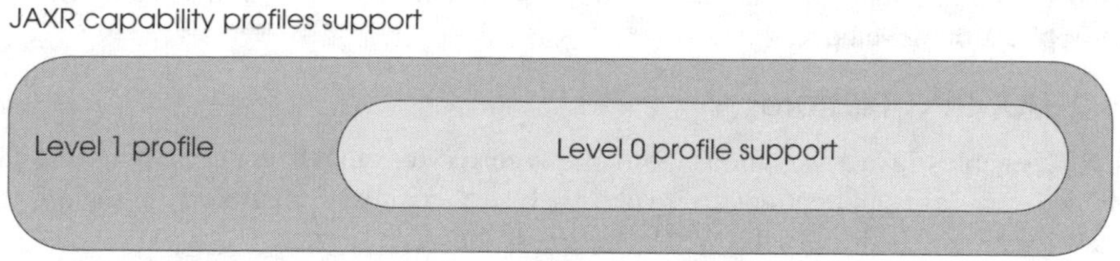

JAXR capability profiles support

Fig. 10.9 JAXR currently supports two capability profiles.

Web services involve technologies like SOAP and WSDL, from which JAX-RPC inherits its *interoperability*—JAX-RPC is programming-language independent and data-format independent. For example, a JAX-RPC Web service does not need to know the data formats that clients send, because client requests are sent as SOAP messages that conform to the SOAP specification. Similarly, a JAX-RPC client does not need to know the Web services's underlying programming language to access the Web service, because the service's WSDL document specifies how to interact with the service.

10.4.1 JAX-RPC Overview

JAX-RPC provides a generic mechanism that enables developers to create and access Web services using XML-based remote procedure calls. While such Web services can communicate over any transport protocol, the current release of JAX-RPC (Version 1.0) uses SOAP as the application protocol and HTTP as the transport protocol. Future versions likely will support other transport protocols as they become available.

When Web service providers publish their Web services to XML registries (e.g., UDDI or ebXML registries), providers may supply service interfaces or WSDL definitions for these services. The JAX-RPC specification defines a mapping of Java data types (e.g., **int**, **String** and *JavaBeans*)[2] to WSDL definitions. When a client locates a service in an XML registry, the client retrieves the WSDL definition to get the service-interface definition. To access the service using Java, the client must transform the WSDL definitions to Java types. The **xrpcc** tool, included in the JWSDP, generates Java classes from the WSDL definitions.

Figure 10.10 shows the JAX-RPC architecture. The service side contains a *JAX-RPC service runtime environment* and a *service endpoint*. The service runtime environment is a software application that manages incoming client connections, and processes incoming and outgoing XML messages (e.g., SOAP messages) on behalf of the Web service. The service runtime environment translates incoming XML messages to simple Java method invocations, which hides the details of XML messaging from the Web-service developer. The service endpoint is the Java class that implements the functionality of the Web service. The client side contains a JAX-RPC client runtime environment and a client application. The client runtime environment processes incoming and outgoing XML messages (e.g., SOAP

---

2. JavaBeans are Java classes that adhere to a specific design pattern—for each attribute that a Java-Bean contains, the JavaBean must provide accessor methods (i.e., a *set* and a *get* method) whose names are the attribute name prefixed by "set" and "get," respectively. For example, a JavaBean that contains attribute **color** must provide public methods **setColor** and **getColor**.

messages) for the client application, which hides the details of XML messaging from the client-application developer.

10.4.2 JAX-RPC Features

JAX-RPC enables Java applications to invoke Web services that execute on non-Java platforms and non-Java applications to invoke Web services that execute on Java platforms. The service client needs only the WSDL to access the Web service.

JAX-RPC hides the details of SOAP from the developer, because the JAX-RPC service/client runtime environment performs the mapping between remote method calls and SOAP messages. The JAX-RPC runtime system also provides APIs for accessing Web services via static *stub*s (local objects that represent the remote services) or dynamic proxies (objects that are generated during runtime), or invoking the Web services dynamically through the *Dynamic Invocation Interface (DII)*.

The JAX-RPC reference implementation provides the **deploytool** to deploy a JAX-RPC service onto Tomcat. The JAX-RPC reference implementation also provides the **xrpcc** tool to generate ties (server-side objects that represent the services), stubs and other service and client-side artifacts (such as a WSDL document). The **deploytool** is a GUI utility that creates a file that, when deployed on Tomcat, exposes the JAX-RPC Web services. The **deploytool** also generates the deploy descriptor (**web.xml**) and a service WSDL document. If we supply **xrpcc** with a remote-interface definition, it generates stubs, ties, a WSDL document and a configuration file used during deployment. If we supply **xrpcc** with a WSDL document, it generates stubs, ties, a server-configuration file and the remote-interface definition. Most developers use an existing WSDL document to access a Web service. For example, to access Web services via static stubs, clients use **xrpcc** to generate the service's stub from the service's WSDL document, then invoke the Web service through the stub.

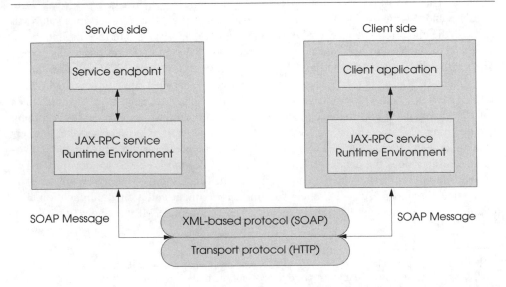

Fig. 10.10 JAX-RPC architecture.

DII enables Web service clients to make method calls on Web services without knowing the service's stub information. DII clients can build method calls dynamically based on the WSDL document of the service. To invoke the RPC using DII, Web service clients must know the following information in advance:

1. Web service endpoint (i.e., location, such as a URL),
2. interface name of the Web service,
3. name of the method call,
4. a list of the parameters,
5. return type of the method call,
6. service target namespace, which defines the namespaces used in the WSDL document,
7. type namespace to register the *serializers/deserializers* (which provide the mapping between Java objects and their XML presentations),
8. SOAP action, which indicates the intent of the SOAP request (an empty-string value indicates that the HTTP request contains the SOAP request's intent),
9. encoding style, which defines the serialization rules used to deserialize the SOAP message.

The Web service's WSDL document provides all this information. Writing clients with DII is more complicated than writing clients with static stubs. However, DII clients are much more flexible, because DII clients can specify the remote procedure calls' properties (such as Web service name, remote method input parameters, remote method return type) at run-time.

Using static stubs requires the programmer to generate the stubs using **xrpcc**. Using DII requires the programmer to do more coding. Using dynamic proxy (a class that is generated at run time) requires neither the stubs nor extra coding. To use the dynamic proxy, the clients must have access to the WSDL document and be able to extract service-based information from the WSDL document.

10.5 Introduction to Java API for XML Messaging (JAXM)

In this section, we introduce the *Java API for XML Messaging* (*JAXM*), which enables applications to communicate using XML-based messaging protocols, such as SOAP. We begin with an overview of other Java messaging technologies—Java Messaging Service (JMS) and JavaMail—and discuss how JAXM differs from them. We then discuss how *JAXM applications* can use the *SOAP with Attachments API for Java* (*SAAJ*) to create and manipulate SOAP messages. We also describe how these use JAXM to send and receive XML-based messages to and from Web services. We then introduce the role of a *message provider*, which allows JAXM applications to send and receive messages asynchronously. We diagram architectures of the two types of JAXM applications: one that uses a message provider and one that does not. We then discuss the advantages and disadvantages for each type of JAXM application.

10.5.1 Java Messaging APIs

The Java platform provides three different types of messaging APIs: the Java Messaging Service (JMS), JavaMail and JAXM. These technologies share the common goal of enabling components to send and receives messages. However, the technologies differ in that each provides support for a distinct messaging infrastructure. Developers use JMS to build applications for *Message-Oriented-Middleware (MOM)*[3] infrastructures, JavaMail to build e-mail applications and JAXM to build applications that produce and consume Web services (or to build any application that supports XML-based messaging). Of course, these messaging infrastructures are not mutually exclusive—for example, it is common for JAXM applications to use JavaMail to send e-mail notifications to users.

JMS enables components to transfer messages via the *point-to-point* and *publish/subscribe messaging models*. In the point-to-point model, the sending component sends a message to a *message queue*, which "forwards" that message to the target component. This model requires that only one target component can consume messages from a message queue. By contrast, the publish/subscribe model allows zero or more *subscribers* to consume messages that other components *publish*. The publish/subscribe model uses the notion of *topics* (analogous to message groups). Publishers send messages to a topic on a server. Clients with active subscriptions to the topic then receive those messages.

JavaMail enables components to send messages via e-mail. JavaMail provides APIs for creating and sending mail, determining the mailing protocols through which to send the mail, and storing and retrieving mail from servers. A message in JavaMail contains a header and a body. The header contains information such as a **From** address, the **To**, **CC** and **BCC** addresses, and the date on which the mail was sent. The message body contains the actual message content. JavaMail supports several Internet-mail protocols, such as IMAP, SMTP and POP3.

JAXM enables components to transfer XML-formatted messages (e.g., SOAP messages) and is often useful when building business-to-business (B2B) applications. JAXM supports both *synchronous* and *asynchronous messaging*. In synchronous messaging, a JAXM application sends a message request to a Web service and waits for a message response. From the perspective of the JAXM application that sends the request, synchronous messaging appears to be identical to JAX-RPC's remote method calls. However, unlike JAX-RPC, JAXM supports asynchronous messaging, in which a JAXM application that sends a request does not wait for a response from the Web service. The asynchronous approach is ideal in situations where the response from a Web service invocation depends on a "human factor." For example, a JAXM application might invoke a Web service to place an order for a product; however, before the receiving application can notify the sending application that the order has been shipped, workers physically must transport the merchandise from a warehouse to a delivery vehicle. This process could take an indeterminate amount of time, so it is not feasible for the sending application to wait for a response.

10.5.2 JAXM and SAAJ

The Java API for XML Messaging (JAXM) and the SOAP with Attachments API for Java (SAAJ) enable a *JAXM application* to send and receive SOAP messages to and from Web services. In addition, developers can use JAXM and SAAJ to create and expose Web services. Essentially, JAXM contains only one package, called **javax.xml.messaging**, which provides classes and interfaces for creating special types of servlets (called **JAXM-Servlet**s) that can send and receive SOAP messages. SAAJ also contains only one pack-

---

3. An application that serves as a messaging system, typically used for enterprise applications.

age, called **javax.xml.soap**, which provides classes and interfaces for creating and manipulating SOAP messages. Specifically, these messages must conform to the SOAP 1.1 specification and the SOAP with Attachments W3C Note. The Java Web Service Developer Pack Early-Access releases integrated SAAJ with JAXM—that is, JAXM contained both packages **javax.xml.messaging** and **javax.xml.soap**. The JWSDP current release (Version 1.0) "extracted" SAAJ from JAXM, enabling other applications (e.g., JAX-RPC applications) to produce and consume SOAP messages without depending on the JAXM specification. For additional information regarding SOAP 1.1 and SOAP with Attachments, see Chapter 6, Understanding SOAP and WSDL.

10.5.3 Standalone JAXM Clients and JAXM Web Services

A *standalone JAXM client* invokes Web services synchronously (i.e., the client must wait for a response from the service). In this respect, a standalone JAXM client acts similarly to a JAX-RPC client. A standalone JAXM client does not use a message provider (which the next section describes in greater detail) to forward requests to, or listen for requests from, a Web service. In Section 10.5.4, we show how a message provider enables a JAXM client to provide Web services, in addition to consuming them. A standalone JAXM client generally is not suited for providing Web services; thus, JAXM clients are used most commonly for invoking Web services.

Figure 10.11 models the flow of execution for a standalone JAXM application. The execution begins when the standalone JAXM client creates a SOAP request (Step 1) to send to a **JAXMServlet** (Step 2), which is a type of servlet that receives only SOAP requests in the form of HTTP **post** requests. After sending the SOAP request, the standalone client *blocks*, or halts its program execution, until it receives a SOAP response from the **JAXM-Servlet**. Upon receiving a SOAP request, the **JAXMServlet** typically uses the information in the request (Step 3) to invoke some method of an object that provides the Web service functionality (Step 4). Usually, the **JAXMServlet** first extracts any parameters from the SOAP request and passes them as arguments to this method. The method returns a result to the **JAXMServlet** (Step 5), which encapsulates the result in a SOAP response (Step 6) and returns the response to the client (Step 7). When the client receives the response, the client resumes program execution (Step 8).

It is important to note that JAXM clients do not necessarily have to transfer SOAP messages only to JAXM-based Web services, nor are JAXM-based Web services required to transfer SOAP messages only to JAXM clients. Both components are completely transparent to each other, which promotes interoperability. For example, a standalone JAXM client can send a SOAP message to a Web service deployed via JAX-RPC, just as easily as that client can send a SOAP message to a Web service deployed via JAXM. As another example, a JAXM-based Web service can receive a SOAP message that a JAX-RPC client created.

10.5.4 JAXM Application with Message Provider

In the previous section, we introduced the standalone JAXM application, which uses synchronous communication. We explained that, using this type of communication, the client blocks, or halts, activity after sending a SOAP request. The client resumes activity only upon receiving a SOAP response from the Web service. Since the client halts activity, the client is unable to offer Web services in conjunction with invoking another one, which is a central character-

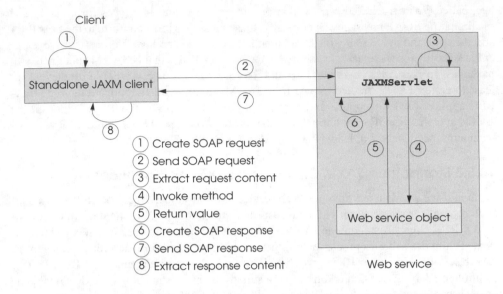

Client

1 Create SOAP request
2 Send SOAP request
3 Extract request content
4 Invoke method
5 Return value
6 Create SOAP response
7 Send SOAP response
8 Extract response content

Fig. 10.11 Flowchart for a JAXM standalone client invoking a Web service via a **JAXMServlet**.

istic of many Web-service-based B2B applications. To circumvent this problem, JAXM applications can use a message provider. which handles sending and receiving messages, thus enabling a JAXM application to perform other functions after sending a SOAP request. Essentially, a message provider acts as a listener for messages. When the provider receives a message, the provider forwards the message to various endpoints. As we will see, using a provider enables a JAXM application to send and receive messages asynchronously. Rather than sending a SOAP request directly to the Web service, the JAXM application sends the SOAP request to the message provider, which in turn sends the request to the Web service. Upon receiving a SOAP request from the JAXM application, the message provider informs the JAXM application that it will, at some point, send the request to the Web service. Eventually, the Web service sends a SOAP response back to the message provider, which forwards the response to a separate component (e.g., a **JAXMServlet**) in the JAXM application. The JAXM servlet component processes the SOAP response accordingly. This form of communication is known as asynchronous messaging.

Figure 10.12 depicts a B2B scenario in which a JAXM application places a book order from another JAXM application. One JAXM application belongs to a company that purchases books, and the other JAXM application belongs to a company that sells books. Each JAXM application uses a message provider to send and receive SOAP messages. The execution begins when a book buyer selects the ISBN of a book and quantity to order from an HTML page. Clicking the **Submit** button sends the ISBN and quantity as part of a **get** request to a servlet called **PlaceOrderServlet** (Step 1). **PlaceOrderServlet** uses the JAXM API to encapsulate the ISBN and quantity values in a SOAP request, then sends the request to the message provider **Provider1** (Step 2). This message provider sends the request over the network to another message provider **Provider2** (Step 3), which belongs to the company that sells books. **Provider2** forwards the request to the

BookOrder Web service (Step 4), which is comprised of **JAXMServlet Book-OrderServlet** and the **BookOrder** Web service object. **BookOrderServlet** uses the **BookOrder** object to place the order (Step 5), and the **BookOrder** object then returns some confirmation of whether the order has been placed (Step 6). **Book-OrderServlet** stores this confirmation in a SOAP response, then sends the response back to **Provider2** (Step 7). **Provider2** returns this response to **Provider1**, which belongs to the company that made the original request (Step 8). **Provider1** forwards the response to the **Confirmation** Web service, which is comprised of **JAXMServlet ConfirmationServlet** and the **Confirmation** Web service object (Steps 9–10). We provide the Java-based implementation for this architecture in Appendix C, Implementing Web Services in Java.

10.6 Introduction to Java 2 Micro Edition

Wireless devices enable users to access Web services at any time and from virtually any location. This is convenient for services such as checking stock quotes or discovering a list of activities in the area. In this section, we introduce *Java 2 Micro Edition* (*J2ME*™), which is Sun Microsystems' Java platform for developing applications for various consumer devices, such as set-top boxes, Web terminals, embedded systems, mobile phones and pagers. We briefly discuss the J2ME API, then describe how a J2ME client can access Web services.

Sun introduced J2ME to provide suitable functionality for consumer devices. The other Java platforms—Java 2 Standard Edition (J2SE™) and Java 2 Enterprise Edition (J2EE™)—do not provide such functionality. J2SE provides an API for building desktop applications, and J2EE provides an API for building scalable enterprise business solutions. However, prior to the release of J2ME, Sun did not provide a standard platform for building applications that operate on devices with limited resources (e.g., limited memory, means of input, display, power, bandwidth, etc.). Realizing the need to provide a platform that enabled developers to create applications for this market, Sun developed J2ME.

A common misconception is that developers use J2ME to create applications only for wireless devices. In fact, J2ME enables developers to write applications for other consumer devices, such as Web terminals and paging devices. Our treatment of J2ME involves building applications for wireless devices—specifically mobile phones.

10.6.1 CLDC and MIDP

The J2ME platform defines two central technologies that enable developers to build J2ME applications, as well as guarantee that these applications will run on any J2ME-compatible device. The first technology is a *configuration*, which includes 1) a *Java Virtual Machine (JVM)*[4] that enables J2ME programs to execute on a J2ME device and 2) a set of APIs enabling developers to create applications that run on devices with limited resources. The second technology is a *profile*, which provides a set of APIs that enable developers to create applications that run on specific devices (e.g., mobile phones), which in turn use configurations. In this section, we discuss the *Connected Limited Device Configuration* (*CLDC*) and the *Mobile Information Device Profile* (*MIDP*), which collectively offer developers a

---

4. The Java Virtual Machine (JVM) is an environment that executes Java applications.

set of APIs to write J2ME applications called *MIDlet*s and deploy them across several types of mobile devices.

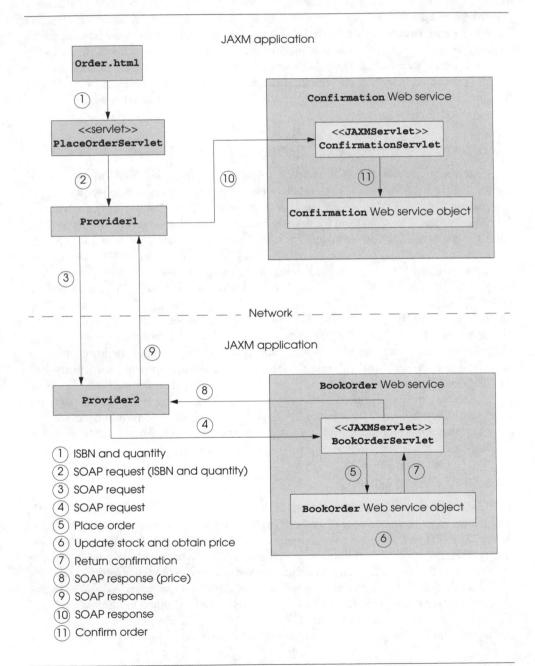

Fig. 10.12 Flowchart for a JAXM client that uses a message provider to order books from another JAXM application.

Connected Limited Device Configuration (CLDC)

The *Connected Limited Device Configuration (CLDC)* is a set of APIs that allows developers to create applications for devices that have limited resources. The J2ME CLDC contains both a virtual machine and a set of classes with which developers can create and execute programs on resource-limited devices. The *KVM*—the virtual machine offered by the CLDC—runs J2ME applications (as the JVM runs J2SE applications). The "K" in KVM represents the word "kilo," because J2ME applications are small enough to be measured in kilobytes, rather than in megabytes, as most other software applications are.

One challenge of J2ME programming is that the API does not contain certain data types and classes that developers often "take for granted" in other Java platforms. For example, J2ME does not include floating-point operations. Also, J2ME does not provide specific "convenience" methods, such as a class that parses a string into smaller substrings (a process known as *tokenizing*). As wireless-device technology advances, it is possible that future versions of J2ME will support such features.

Mobile Information Device Profile

The *Mobile Information Device Profile (MIDP)* is a set of APIs that allows developers to handle mobile-device-specific issues, such as creating user interfaces, permitting local storage and defining the lifecycles of MIDP client applications (MIDlets). Devices that run applications using the MIDP are called *MIDP devices*. Such devices include cell phones and pagers.

MIDP contains several packages for constructing MIDlet user interfaces, networking between MIDlets and other systems, permitting local storage, and defining the *MIDlet lifecycle*—i.e., the execution sequence of a MIDlet. To conform to the MIDP specification, a MIDP device requires a monochrome display of at least 96 pixels x 54 pixels, a two-way wireless network, some input device (such as a one-handed keypad or touch screen), at least 128 kilobytes for CLDC/MIDP classes and at least 32 kilobytes for the KVM. A MIDlet runs on any device that meets these requirements.

10.6.2 MIDlets

A *MIDlet* is a Mobile Information Device application that runs on a MIDP device. MIDlet developers store one or more MIDlets in a single file called a *MIDlet suite*. Developers place the MIDlet suite on a server. The MIDP device then downloads the MIDlet suite using a program called the *Application Management Software (AMS)*, which is located on the MIDP device. The AMS is responsible for downloading the MIDlet suite from the server, opening the MIDlet suite, then launching the user-specified MIDlet on the MIDP device. After launching the MIDlet, the AMS is responsible for the MIDlet's *lifecycle*, which comprises three states during MIDlet execution. The first state is the *active state*, which allows the MIDlet to display content and accept user input. The MIDlet then waits for user input or another notification from the AMS. The AMS can place a MIDlet in the *paused state*, in which the MIDlet may not process user input. The final state is the *destroyed state*, in which the AMS terminates the MIDlet's execution and clears the device's memory for another application.

Figure 10.13 shows an example of a MIDlet called **WelcomeMIDlet**. When the user presses the **Launch** button, the AMS launches **WelcomeMIDlet**, which in turn displays **"Welcome to J2ME!"** on the device's main screen. Sun provides the *Java 2 Micro Edition Wireless Toolkit* to develop and deploy MIDlets. The current version of the toolkit (Release 1.0.3) is available for download at the following URL:

`java.sun.com/products/j2mewtoolkit/download.html`

This toolkit contains several emulators for MIDP applications. Throughout this section, we show sample J2ME application outputs using the Sun MIDP-device emulator, which is shown in Fig. 10.13.

10.7 Using J2ME to Access Web Services

At the time of this writing, Sun Microsystems has not provided a standard Web service API that is compatible with J2ME. In addition, because of J2ME's limited configuration and profile, a J2ME client cannot use the relatively large Web service APIs that Sun already provides, such as the APIs included in the JWSDP. Due to this limitation, a J2ME client may invoke a Web service in one of two ways. The first way is for a J2ME client to use a separate component that is capable of handling SOAP messages. This component, which is known as a *proxy*, acts on behalf of the J2ME client. The J2ME client sends to the component any information necessary to invoke a Web service. The component then encapsulates this information in a SOAP request and sends the request to the Web service. After receiving the SOAP response from the Web service, the component extracts the result from the SOAP response, then returns the result to the J2ME client. The second way is for a J2ME client to use a proprietary (non-standard) API to handle SOAP messages. Using this approach, the J2ME client can create, send and receive SOAP messages, thus negating the need to use a proxy. One such API is called kSOAP, provided by Enhydra (**www.enhydra.org**).

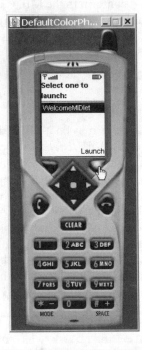
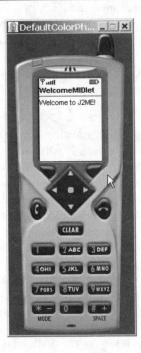

Fig. 10.13 `WelcomeMIDlet` displays a welcome message on a MIDP device. Reproduced with permission by Sun Microsystems, Inc.© Copyright 2002, Sun Microsystems, Inc. All Rights Reserved.

10.7.1 Accessing Web Services via a Separate Component

Figure 10.14 shows the sequence of a J2ME client invoking a Web service via a proxy, such as a servlet. Step 1 of Fig. 10.14 shows the J2ME client making a *get* request to a servlet, which is located on the server from which the MIDlet application was originally download-ed. The *get* request should contain all information (i.e., parameters) necessary to invoke the Web service. Upon receiving the request, the servlet can use a Web service API, such as JAXM, to create a SOAP request. The servlet uses the parameters from the *get* request to populate the SOAP request. Note that the servlet must create the SOAP request, because the J2ME client lacks this functionality. The servlet then sends the SOAP request to the Web service (Step 2), which ultimately returns a SOAP response back to the servlet (Step 3). Since a J2ME client cannot parse a SOAP message, the servlet must extract the result from the SOAP response and send the result to the J2ME client (Step 4).

   Figure 10.15 shows the output of a MIDlet that uses a servlet to invoke a Web service that returns a list of Deitel books. The left-most image shows the user selecting the Web service that the MIDlet should invoke (which, in the example, is the Book Titles Web service). The center image shows the user specifying that the MIDlet should send the SOAP message via a servlet. Usually, a MIDlet would not display this screen—the MIDlet develop-er determines how the MIDlet invokes a Web service, and this process is transparent to the application's user. The right-most image shows the final result of the Web service invo-cation on the J2ME client.

10.7.2 Accessing Web Services via Proprietary Software

In the previous example, we examined how a J2ME client can use a separate component to act as a proxy for accessing a Web service. Now, we describe how to use proprietary soft-ware—namely, Enhydra's kSOAP—to build a J2ME client that is capable of handling SOAP messages. Using this approach enables the client to send the request directly to a Web service, thus eliminating the overhead created by the proxy.

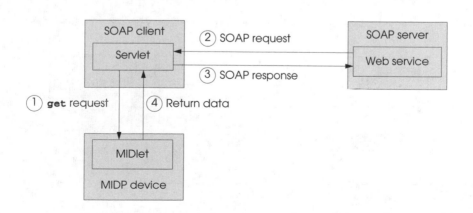

Fig. 10.14 Flowchart for a J2ME client invoking a Web service via a servlet.

Fig. 10.15 MIDlet invoking a Web service that obtains a list of book titles via a servlet proxy. Reproduced with permission by Sun Microsystems, Inc.© Copyright 2002. Sun Microsystems, Inc. All Rights Reserved.

Enhydra's kSOAP API enables a J2ME client to create, send and receive SOAP messages. Enhydra also provides the kXML API, which the kSOAP API uses to create the XML-based messages. Specifically, kSOAP handles SOAP messaging, and kXML handles XML-document generation and parsing. Enhydra's kSOAP v.0.99 and kXML v.1.2.1 packages are contained in **ksoap.zip** and **kxml.zip**, respectively.[5] Figure 10.16 shows the sequence of a J2ME client invoking a Web service via kSOAP. Note that this approach is much simpler than using a component proxy. The MIDlet uses kSOAP to send a SOAP request to the Web service (Step 1), which then returns a SOAP response to the MIDlet (Step 2).

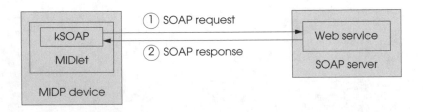

Fig. 10.16 Flowchart for a J2ME client invoking a Web service via Enhydra's kSOAP.

5. These are available for download at **ksoap.enhydra.org/software/downloads/index.html** and **kxml.enhydra.org/software/downloads/index.html**.

Figure 10.17 shows the output of a MIDlet that uses kSOAP to invoke a Web service that returns a list of Deitel books. Note that the image that shows the Web service invocation's result is identical to the image in Fig. 10.15.

10.8 Summary

Java has evolved into a complete platform that provides a rich set of Application Program Interfaces (APIs) for building embedded applications, desktop applications, dynamic Web components, distributed systems and enterprise-class applications. A primary feature of the Java platform is its portability, which makes Java ideal for building Internet applications of all kinds, including those based on Web services.

In June 2002, Sun Microsystems release the Java Web Services Developer Pack (JWSDP), Version 1.0, which includes the primary APIs and reference implementations for building Java-based Web services and clients. The JWSDP contains the Java XML Pack, which includes the Java API for XML Messaging (JAXM), v1.1, the Java API for XML Processing (JAXP), v1.2, the Java API for XML Registries (JAXR), v1.0_01, the Java API for XML-based RPC (JAX-RPC), v1.0, and the SOAP with Attachments API for Java (SAAJ), v1.1.

Java classes can be deployed as Web services via a Java Web service platform. Each platform has its own preferred way of handling issues such as deployment, custom serialization and deserialization and performance optimization. Examples of Web services platforms are Apache's Axis, Cape Clear's CapeConnect, IONA's XMLBus 5.0, The Mind Electric's GLUE and Systinet's Web Applications and Services Platform (WASP).

Fig. 10.17 MIDlet invoking a Web service that obtains a list of book titles via Enhydra's kSOAP. Reproduced with permission by Sun Microsystems, Inc.© Copyright 2002. Sun Microsystems, Inc. All Rights Reserved.

The Java API for XML Registries (JAXR) defines a standard architecture that enables clients to use JAXR providers to access different types of registries, such as those that conform to the UDDI and ebXML specifications. A JAXR provider maps JAXR objects to protocol-specific entries in the target XML registry and provides implementations of generic JAXR interfaces.

JAX-RPC enables developers to build applications that expose and access Web services using XML-based remote procedure calls. When Web service providers publish their Web services to XML registries, providers may supply service interfaces or WSDL definitions for these services. JAX-RPC defines a mapping of Java data types to WSDL definitions. When a client locates a service in an XML registry, the client retrieves the WSDL definition to get the service-interface definition. To access the service using Java, the client must transform the WSDL definitions to Java types.

The service side contains a JAX-RPC service runtime environment and a service endpoint. The service runtime environment translates incoming XML messages to Java method invocations. The service endpoint is the Java class that implements the Web service functionality. The client side contains a JAX-RPC client runtime environment and a client application. The client runtime environment processes incoming and outgoing XML messages for the client application.

The Java API for XML Messaging (JAXM) enables applications to communicate using XML-based messaging protocols, such as SOAP. JAXM applications can use the SOAP with Attachments API for Java (SAAJ) to create and manipulate SOAP messages. JAXM applications send and receive XML-based messages to and from Web services. JAXM applications often use message providers, which allow the applications to send and receive messages asynchronously.

Sun Microsystems provides the Java 2 Micro Edition (J2ME™) for developing applications for various consumer devices, such as mobile phones and pagers. A J2ME client may use a separate component, such as a servlet, to act as a proxy for accessing a Web service. A J2ME client also can use proprietary software, such as Enhydra's kSOAP, for sending and receiving SOAP messages. The latter approach enables the client to send the request directly to a Web service, thus eliminating the overhead created by the proxy.

10.9 Internet and Web Resources

java.sun.com/webservices
Sun's Web services site contains tutorials on Java Web services and offers downloads of the JWSDP.

javaboutique.internet.com/tutorials/Axis
This site explains how to create a Web service using Axis.

javaworld.com/javaworld/javaone01/j1-01-apis.html
This article overview Sun's Web services APIs.

www-106.ibm.com/developerworks/webservices
IBM's Web Services Zone is a comprehensive resource for Java Web services developers. The site includes tutorials, articles, discussion forums and programming tools available for download.

11

Computer and Internet Security

Objectives

- To understand the basic concepts of security.
- To understand public-key/private-key cryptography.
- To learn about popular security protocols, such as SSL.
- To understand digital signatures, digital certificates and certificate authorities.
- To become aware of various threats to secure computer systems, such as viruses and denial-of-service attacks.
- To learn about Virtual Private Networks and IPSec.

Three may keep a secret, if two of them are dead.
Benjamin Franklin

Attack—Repeat—Attack.
William Frederick Halsey, Jr.

Private information is practically the source of every large modern fortune.
Oscar Wilde

There must be security for all—or not one is safe.
The Day the Earth Stood Still, screenplay by Edmund H. North

No government can be long secure without formidable opposition.
Benjamin Disraeli

Outline

11.1 Introduction

As e-businesses and Web services gain widespread adoption, individuals and organizations are transmitting highly confidential information over the Internet. Consumers are submitting credit-card numbers to e-commerce sites, and businesses are exposing proprietary data on the Web. At the same time, organizations are experiencing increasing numbers of security breaches. Both individuals and companies are vulnerable to data theft and hacker attacks that can compromise data, corrupt files and crash systems. For these reasons, security is crucial to the success of e-business and Web services. In a memo to all Microsoft employees, Bill Gates stated that the company's highest priority is trustworthy computing—i.e., ensuring that Microsoft applications are reliable, available and secure. Gates's security emphasis has been echoed across the computing industry as organizations work to improve Internet and network security.[1]

There are five fundamental requirements for a successful, secure transaction: *privacy, integrity, authentication, authorization* and *non-repudiation. The privacy issue is*: How do you ensure that the information you transmit over the Internet has not been captured or passed to a third party without your knowledge? *The integrity issue is*: How do you ensure that the information you send or receive has not been compromised or altered? *The authentication issue is*: How do the sender and receiver of a message verify their identities to each other? *The authorization issue is*: How do you manage access to protected resources on the basis of user credentials? *The non-repudiation issue is*: How do you legally prove that a message was sent or received? Network security must also address the issue of *availability*. How do we ensure that the network, and the computer systems to which it connects, will operate continuously?

In this chapter, we explore the fundamentals of Internet security, including secure electronic transactions and secure networks. We discuss how to achieve e-commerce and network security using current technologies—including cryptography, Public Key Infrastructure (PKI), digital signatures, Secure Sockets Layer (SSL) and Virtual Private Networks (VPNs). We also examine authentication and authorization solutions, firewalls and intrusion detection systems. The next chapter, Web Services Security, overviews the standards and protocols used to secure Web services. XML Signature and XML Encryption provide authentication, integrity and privacy for Web services transmissions. The Security Assertions Markup Language (SAML) and Extensible Access Control Markup Language (XACML) address authentication and authorization in Web services applications. A new standard created by Microsoft, IBM and VeriSign, WS-Security, encrypts information and ensures the privacy of Web services transmissions. All these technologies are based on the security concepts described in this chapter.

11.2 Ancient Ciphers to Modern Cryptosystems

The channels through which data passes are inherently unsecure; therefore, any private information transmitted through these channels must somehow be protected. To protect information, data can be encrypted. *Cryptography* transforms data using a *cipher*, or *cryptosystem*—a mathematical algorithm for encrypting messages. A *key*—a string of digits that acts as a password—is input to the cipher. The cipher uses the key to make data incomprehensible to all but the sender and intended receivers. Unencrypted data is called *plaintext*; encrypted data is called *ciphertext*. The algorithm encrypts the data, and the key acts as a variable—using different keys results in different ciphertext. Only the intended receivers should have the corresponding key to decrypt the ciphertext into plaintext.

First used by the ancient Egyptians, cryptographic ciphers have been used throughout history to conceal and protect valuable information. Ancient cryptographers encrypted messages by hand, usually with a method based on the alphabetic letters of the message. The two main types of ciphers were *substitution ciphers* and *transposition ciphers*. In a substitution cipher, every occurrence of a given letter is replaced by a different letter; for example, if every "a" were replaced by a "b," every "b" by a "c," etc., the word "security" would encrypt to "tfdvsjuz." The first prominent substitution cipher was credited to Julius Caesar, and is referred to today as the *Caesar Cipher*. Using the Caesar Cipher, every instance of a letter is encrypted by replacing by the letter in the alphabet three places to the right. For example, using the Caesar Cipher, the word "security" would encrypt to "vhfxulwb."

In a transposition cipher, the ordering of the letters is shifted; for example, if every other letter, starting with "s," in the word "security" creates the first word in the cipher-text and the remaining letters create the second word in the ciphertext, the word "security" would encrypt to "scrt euiy." Complicated ciphers combine substitution and transposition ciphers. For example, using the substitution cipher in combination with the transposition cipher, the word "security" would encrypt to "tdsu fvjz." The problem with many historical ciphers is that their security relied on the sender and receiver to remember the encryption algorithm and keep it secret. Such algorithms are called *restricted algorithms*. Restricted algorithms are not feasible to implement among a large group of people. Imagine if the security of U.S. government communications relied on every U.S. government employee to keep a secret; the encryption algorithm could easily be compromised.

Modern cryptosystems are digital. Their algorithms are based on the individual *bits* or *blocks* (a group of bits) of a message, rather than letters of the alphabet. A computer stores data as a *binary string*, which is a sequence of ones and zeros. Each digit in the sequence is called a bit. Encryption and decryption keys are binary strings with a given *key length*. For example, 128-bit encryption systems have a key length of 128 bits. Longer keys have stronger encryption; it takes more time and computing power to break the encryption.

Until January 2000, the U.S. government placed restrictions on the strength of crypto-systems that could be exported from the United States by limiting the key length of the encryption algorithms. Today, the regulations on exporting cryptography products are less stringent. Any cryptography product may be exported as long as the end user is not a foreign government or from a country with embargo restrictions.[2]

11.3 Secret-Key Cryptography

In the past, organizations wishing to maintain a secure computing environment used *symmetric cryptography*, also known as *secret-key cryptography*. Secret-key cryptography uses the same secret key to encrypt and decrypt a message (Fig. 11.1). In this case, the sender encrypts a message using the secret key, then sends the encrypted message to the intended recipient, who decrypts the message using the same secret key. A fundamental problem with secret-key cryptography is that before two people can communicate securely, they must find a secure way to exchange the secret key. One approach is to have the key delivered by a courier, such as a mail service or FedEx. While this approach may be feasible when two individuals communicate, it is not efficient for securing communication in a large network, nor can it be considered completely secure. The privacy and the integrity of the message would be compromised if the key is intercepted as it is passed between the sender and the receiver. Also, since both parties in the transaction use the same key to encrypt and decrypt a message, one cannot authenticate which party created a message. Finally, to keep communications private with each receiver, a sender needs a different secret key for each receiver. As a result, organizations would have huge numbers of secret keys to maintain for each user.

An alternative approach to the key-exchange problem is to have a central authority, called a *key distribution center* (*KDC*). The key distribution center shares a (different) secret key with every user in the network. In this system, the key distribution center generates a *session key* to be used for a transaction (Fig. 11.2). Next, the key distribution center distributes the session key to the sender and receiver, encrypted with the secret key they each share with the key distribution center. For example, suppose a merchant and a customer want to conduct a secure transaction. The merchant and the customer each have unique secret keys that they share with the key distribution center. The key distribution center generates a session key for the merchant and customer to use in the transaction. The key distribution center then sends the session key for the transaction to the merchant, encrypted using the secret key the merchant already shares with the center. The key distribution center sends the same session key for the transaction to the customer, encrypted using the secret key the customer already shares with the key distribution center. Once the merchant and the customer have the session key for the transaction, they can communicate with each other, encrypting their messages using the shared session key.

Using a key distribution center reduces the number of courier deliveries (again, by means such as mail or FedEx) of secret keys to each user in the network. In addition, users can have a new secret key for each communication with other users in the network, which greatly increases the overall security of the network. However, if the security of the key distribution center is compromised, then the security of the entire network is compromised.

One of the most commonly used symmetric encryption algorithms is the *Data Encryption Standard* (*DES*). Horst Feistel of IBM created the *Lucifer* algorithm, which was chosen as the DES by the United States government and the National Security Agency (NSA) in the 1970s.[3] DES has a key length of 56 bits and encrypts data in 64-bit blocks. This type of encryption is known as a *block cipher*. A block cipher is an encryption method that creates groups of bits from an original message, then applies an encryption algorithm to the block as a whole, rather than as individual bits. This method reduces the amount of computer processing power and time required, while maintaining a fair level of security. For many years, DES was the encryption standard set by the U.S. government and the *American National Standards Institute* (*ANSI*). However, due to advances in technology and computing speed, DES is no longer considered secure. In the late 1990s, specialized *DES cracker machines* were built that recovered DES keys after just several hours.[4] As a result, the old standard of symmetric encryption has been replaced by *Triple DES*, or *3DES*, a variant of DES that is essentially three DES systems in a row, each with its own secret key. Though 3DES is more secure, the three passes through the DES algorithm result in slower performance. The United States government recently selected a new, more secure standard for symmetric encryption to replace DES. The new standard is called the *Advanced Encryption Standard* (*AES*). The *National Institute of Standards and Technology* (*NIST*)—which sets the cryptographic standards for the U.S. government—chose *Rijndael* as the encryption method for AES. Rijndael is a block cipher developed by Dr. Joan Daemen and Dr. Vincent Rijmen of Belgium. Rijndael can be used with key sizes and block sizes of 128, 192 or 256 bits. Rijndael was chosen over four other finalists as the AES because of its high security, performance, efficiency, flexibility and low memory requirement for computing systems.[5] For more information about AES, visit `csrc.nist.gov/encryption/aes`.

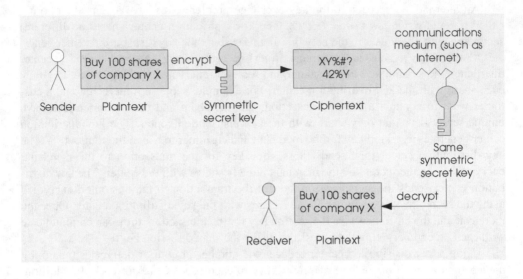

Fig. 11.1   Encrypting and decrypting a message using a secret key.

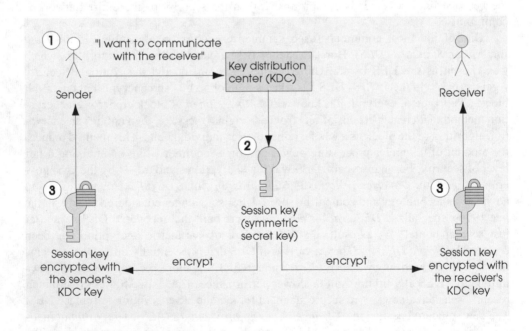

Fig. 11.2   Distributing a session key with a key distribution center.

11.4 Public-Key Cryptography

In 1976, Whitfield Diffie and Martin Hellman, researchers at Stanford University, developed *public-key cryptography* to solve the problem of exchanging keys securely. Public-key cryptography is asymmetric. It uses two inversely related keys: a *public key* and a *private key*. The private key is kept secret by its owner, whereas the public key is freely distributed. If the public key is used to encrypt a message, only the corresponding private key can decrypt it (Fig. 11.3). Each party in a transaction has both a public key and a private key. To transmit a message securely, the sender uses the receiver's public key to encrypt the message. The receiver then decrypts the message using his or her unique private key. Assuming that the private key has been kept secret, the message cannot be read by anyone other than the intended receiver. Thus the system ensures the privacy of the message. The defining property of a secure public-key algorithm is that it is "computationally infeasible" to deduce the private key from the public key. Although the two keys are mathematically related, deriving one from the other would take enormous amounts of computing power and time, enough to discourage attempts to deduce the private key. An outside party cannot participate in communication without the correct keys. The security of the entire process is based on the secrecy of the private keys. Therefore, if a third party obtains the private key used in decryption, the security of the whole system is compromised. If a system's integrity is compromised, the user can simply change the key, instead of changing the entire encryption or decryption algorithm.

Either the public key or the private key can be used to encrypt or decrypt a message. For example, if a customer uses a merchant's public key to encrypt a message, only the merchant can decrypt the message, using the merchant's private key. Thus, the merchant's identity can be authenticated, since only the merchant knows the private key. However, the merchant has no way of validating the customer's identity, since the encryption key the customer used is publicly available.

If the decryption key is the sender's public key and the encryption key is the sender's private key, the sender of the message can be authenticated. For example, suppose a customer sends a merchant a message encrypted using the customer's private key. The mer-

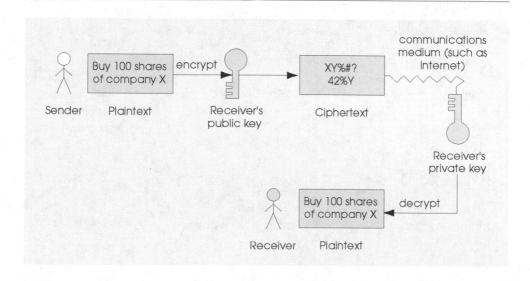

Fig. 11.3   Encrypting and decrypting a message using public-key cryptography.

chant decrypts the message using the customer's public key. Since the customer encrypted the message using his or her private key, the merchant can be confident of the customer's identity. This process authenticates the sender, but does not ensure confidentiality, as anyone could decrypt the message with the sender's public key. This systems works as long as the merchant can be sure that the public key with which the merchant decrypted the message belongs to the customer, and not a third party posing as the customer. The problem of proving ownership of a public key is discussed in Section 11.9, Public-key Infrastructure, Certificates and Certificate Authorities.

These two methods of public-key encryption can actually be used together to authenticate both participants in a communication (Fig. 11.4). Suppose a merchant wants to send a message securely to a customer so that only the customer can read it, and suppose also that the merchant wants to provide proof to the customer that the merchant (not an unknown third party) actually sent the message. First, the merchant encrypts the message using the customer's public key. This step guarantees that only the customer can read the message. Then the merchant encrypts the result using the merchant's private key, which proves the identity of the merchant. The customer decrypts the message in reverse order. First, the customer uses the merchant's public key. Since only the merchant could have encrypted the message with the inversely related private key, this step authenticates the merchant. Then the customer uses the customer's private key to decrypt the next level of encryption. This step ensures that the content of the message was kept private in the transmission, since only the customer has the key to decrypt the message. Although this system provides extremely secure transactions, the setup cost and time required prevent widespread use.

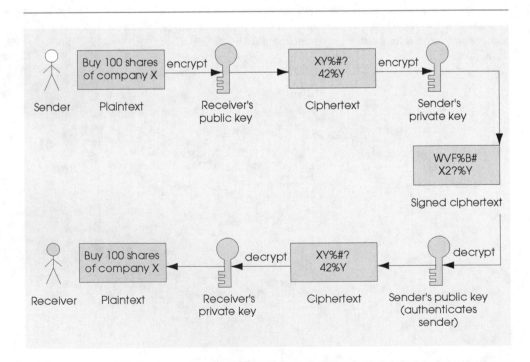

Fig. 11.4   Authentication with a public-key algorithm.

The most commonly used public-key algorithm is *RSA*, an encryption system developed in 1977 by MIT professors Ron Rivest, Adi Shamir and Leonard Adleman.[6] Today, most Fortune 1000 companies and leading e-commerce businesses use their encryption and authentication technologies. With the emergence of the Internet and the World Wide Web, their security work has become even more significant and plays a crucial role in e-commerce transactions. Their encryption products are built into hundreds of millions of copies of the most popular Internet applications, including Web browsers, commerce servers and e-mail systems. Most secure e-commerce transactions and communications on the Internet use RSA products. For more information about RSA, cryptography and security, visit **www.rsasecurity.com**.

Pretty Good Privacy (*PGP*) is a public-key encryption system used for the encryption of e-mail messages and files. PGP was designed in 1991 by Phillip Zimmermann.[7] PGP can also be used to provide digital signatures (see Section 11.8, Digital Signatures) that confirm the author of an e-mail or public posting.

PGP is based on a "web of trust;" each client in a network can vouch for another client's identity to prove ownership of a public key. The "web of trust" is used to authenticate each client. If users know the identity of a public key holder, through personal contact or another secure method, they validate the key by signing it with their own key. The web grows as more users validate the keys of others. To learn more about PGP and to download a free copy of the software, go to the MIT Distribution Center for PGP at **web.mit.edu/network/pgp.html**.

11.5 Cryptanalysis

Even if keys are kept secret, it may be possible to compromise the security of a system. Trying to decrypt ciphertext without knowledge of the decryption key is known as *cryptanalysis*. Cryptologists are constantly researching commercial encryption systems to ensure that the systems are not vulnerable to a *cryptanalytic attack*. The most common form of cryptanalytic attacks are those in which the encryption algorithm is analyzed to find relations between bits of the encryption key and bits of the ciphertext. Often, these relations are only statistical in nature and incorporate an analyzer's outside knowledge about the plaintext. The goal of such an attack is to determine the key from the ciphertext.

Weak statistical trends between ciphertext and keys can be exploited to gain knowledge about the key if enough ciphertext is known. Proper key management and key expiration dates on keys help prevent cryptanalytic attacks. When a key is used for long periods of time, more ciphertext is generated that can be beneficial to an attacker trying to derive a key. If a key is unknowingly recovered by an attacker, it can be used to decrypt every message for the life of that key. Using public-key cryptography to exchange secret keys securely allows a new secret key to encrypt every message.

11.6 Key Agreement Protocols

A drawback of public-key algorithms is that they are not efficient for sending large amounts of data. They require significant computer power, which slows communication. Public-key algorithms should not be thought of as replacements for secret-key algorithms. Instead, public-key algorithms are used most often to exchange secret keys securely. The process by which two parties can exchange keys over an unsecure medium is called a *key agreement protocol*. A *protocol* sets the rules for communication—e.g., which encryption algorithm(s) to use.

The most common key agreement protocol is a *digital envelope* (Fig. 11.5). With a digital envelope, the message is encrypted using a secret key (Step 1), and the secret key is encrypted using public-key encryption (Step 2). The sender attaches the encrypted secret key to the encrypted message and sends the receiver the entire package. The sender could also digitally sign the package before sending it to prove the sender's identity to the receiver (Section 11.8, Digital Signatures). To decrypt the package, the receiver first decrypts the secret key using the receiver's private key. Then, the receiver uses the secret key to decrypt the actual message. Since only the receiver can decrypt the encrypted secret key, the sender can be sure that only the intended receiver is reading the message.

11.7 Key Management

Maintaining the secrecy of private keys is crucial for keeping cryptographic systems secure. Most compromises in security result from poor *key management* (e.g., the mishandling of private keys, resulting in key theft) rather than attacks that attempt to guess the keys.[8]

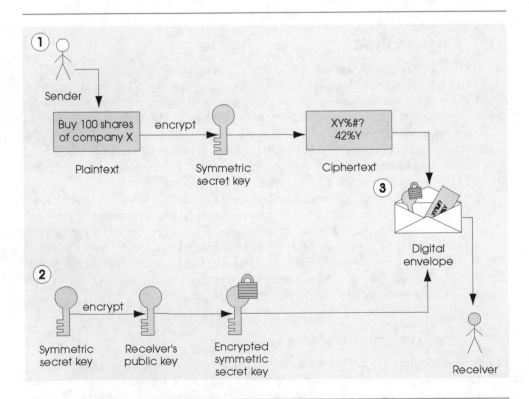

Fig. 11.5 Creating a digital envelope.

A main component of key management is *key generation*—the process by which keys are created. A malicious third party could try to decrypt a message by using every possible decryption key, a process known as *brute-force cracking*. Key-generation algorithms are sometimes unintentionally constructed to choose from only a small subset of possible keys. If the subset is too small, then the encrypted data is more susceptible to brute-force attacks. Therefore, it is important to have a key-generation program that can generate a large number of keys as randomly as possible. Keys are made more secure by choosing a key length so large that it is computationally infeasible for a malicious third party to try all combinations.

11.8 Digital Signatures

Digital signatures, the electronic equivalents of written signatures, were developed to be used in public-key cryptography to solve the problems of authentication and integrity (see Microsoft Authenticode feature). A digital signature authenticates the sender's identity, and, like a written signature, it is difficult to forge.

To create a digital signature, a sender first takes the original plaintext message and runs it through a *hash function*, which is a mathematical calculation that gives the message a *hash value*. A hash value identifies a message uniquely. If a malicious party changed the message, the hash value would also change, thus enabling the recipient to detect that the message was altered. The *Secure Hash Algorithm* (*SHA-1*) is the current standard for hashing functions. Using SHA-1, the phrase "Buy 100 shares of company X" would produce the hash value *D8 A9 B6 9F 72 65 0B D5 6D 0C 47 00 95 0D FD 31 96 0A FD B5*. An example of SHA-1 is available at **home.istar.ca/~neutron/messagedigest**. At this site, users can input text or files into a program to generate the hash value. The hash value is also known as a *message digest*. The chance that two different messages will have the same message digest is statistically insignificant. *Collision* occurs when multiple messages have the same hash value. It is computationally infeasible to compute a message from its hash value or to find two messages with the same hash value.

Next, the sender uses the sender's private key to encrypt the message digest. This step creates a digital signature and validates the sender's identity, since only the owner of that private key could encrypt the message. A message that includes the digital signature, hash function and the encrypted message is sent to the receiver. The receiver uses the sender's public key to decipher the original digital signature (this establishes the message's authenticity—i.e., it came from the sender) and reveal the message digest. The receiver then uses his or her own private key to decipher the original message. Finally, the receiver applies the hash function to the original message. If the hash value of the original message matches the message digest included in the signature, there is *message integrity*; the message has not been altered in transmission.

There is a fundamental difference between digital signatures and handwritten signatures. A handwritten signature is independent of the document being signed. Thus, if someone can forge a handwritten signature, they can use that signature to forge multiple documents. A digital signature is created using the contents of the document. Therefore, your digital signature is different for each document you sign.

Digital signatures do not provide proof that a message has been sent. Consider the following situation: A contractor sends a company a digitally signed contract, which the contractor later would like to revoke. The contractor could do so by releasing the private key and then claiming that the digitally signed contract came from an intruder who stole the contractor's private key. *Timestamping*, which binds a time and date to a digital document, can help solve the problem of non-repudiation. For example, suppose the company and the contractor are negotiating a contract. The company requires the contractor to sign the contract digitally and then have the document digitally timestamped by a third party called a *timestamping agency*. The contractor sends the digitally-signed contract to the timestamping agency. The privacy of the message is maintained since the timestamping agency sees only the encrypted, digitally-signed message (as opposed to the original plaintext message). The timestamping agency affixes the time and date of receipt to the encrypted, signed message and digitally signs the whole package with the timestamping agency's private key. The timestamp cannot be altered by anyone except the timestamping agency; since no one else possesses the timestamping agency's private key. Unless the contractor reports the private key to have been compromised before the document was timestamped, the contractor cannot legally prove that the document was signed by an unauthorized third party. The sender could also require the receiver to sign the message digitally and timestamp it as proof of receipt. To learn more about timestamping, visit **AuthentiDate.com** (**www.authentidate.com**).

The U.S. government's digital-authentication standard is called the *Digital Signature Algorithm* (*DSA*). The U.S. government recently passed digital-signature legislation that makes digital signatures as legally binding as handwritten signatures. This legislation is expected to increase e-business dramatically. For the latest news about U.S. government legislation in information security, visit **www.itaa.org/infosec**. For more information about the bills, visit the following government sites:

> **thomas.loc.gov/cgi-bin/bdquery/z?d106:hr.01714:**
> **thomas.loc.gov/cgi-bin/bdquery/z?d106:s.00761:**

The W3C and the Internet Engineering Task Force created the XML Signature specification as a standard for encrypting XML documents. For more information on, and examples of, XML signatures, see Chapter 12, Web Services Security.

11.9 Public-Key Infrastructure, Certificates and Certificate Authorities

One problem with public-key cryptography is that anyone with a set of keys could potentially assume another party's identity. For example, a customer wants to place an order with an online merchant. How does the customer know that the Web site indeed belongs to that merchant and not to a third party that posted a site and is *masquerading* as a merchant to steal credit-card information? *Public Key Infrastructure* (*PKI*) provides a solution to these problems. PKI integrates public-key cryptography with *digital certificates* and *certificate authorities* to authenticate parties in a transaction. The XML Key Management Specification (XKMS) defines a set of protocols for implementing PKI in Web services. We discuss XKMS and provide an example XKMS-generated document in Chapter 12, Web Services Security.

A digital certificate is a digital document used to identify a user and issued by a *certificate authority* (*CA*). A digital certificate includes the name of the subject (the company or individual being certified), the subject's public key, a serial number, an expiration date, the signature of the trusted certificate authority and any other relevant information (Fig. 11.6). A CA is a financial institution or other trusted third party, such as *VeriSign*. Once issued, the digital certificates are publicly available and are held by the certificate authority in *certificate repositories*.

The CA signs the certificate by encrypting either the subject's public key or a hash value of the public key using the CA's own private key. The CA has to verify every subject's public key. Thus, users must trust the public key of a CA. Usually, each CA is part of a *certificate authority hierarchy*. This hierarchy is similar to a chain of trust in which each link relies on another link to provide authentication information. A certificate authority hierarchy is a chain of certificate authorities, starting with the *root certificate authority*, which is the Internet Policy Registration Authority (IPRA). The IPRA signs certificates using the *root key*. The root key signs certificates only for *policy creation authorities*, which are organizations that set policies for obtaining digital certificates. In turn, policy creation authorities sign digital certificates for CAs. CAs then sign digital certificates for individuals and organizations. The CA takes responsibility for authentication, so it must check information carefully before issuing a digital certificate. In one case, human error caused VeriSign to issue two digital certificates to an imposter posing as a Microsoft employee.[9] Such an error is significant; the inappropriately issued certificates can cause users to download malicious code *unknowingly* onto their machines (see Authentication: Microsoft Authenticode feature).

Fig. 11.6   Portion of a VeriSign digital certificate. (Courtesy of VeriSign, Inc.)

Authentication: Microsoft Authenticode

How do you know that the software you ordered online is safe and has not been altered? How can you be sure that you are not downloading a computer virus that could wipe out your computer? Do you trust the source of the software? With the emergence of e-commerce, software companies are offering their products online, so that customers can download software directly onto their computers. Security technology is used to ensure that the downloaded software is trustworthy and has not been altered. *Microsoft Authenticode*, combined with VeriSign digital certificates (or *digital IDs*), authenticates the publisher of the software and detects whether the software has been altered. Authenticode is a security feature built into Microsoft Internet Explorer.

To use Microsoft Authenticode technology, each software publisher must obtain a digital certificate specifically designed for the purpose of publishing software; such certificates may be obtained through certificate authorities, such as VeriSign (Section 11.9). To obtain a certificate, a software publisher must provide its public key and identification information and sign an agreement that it will not distribute harmful software. This requirement gives customers legal recourse if any downloaded software from certified publishers causes harm.

Microsoft Authenticode uses digital-signature technology to sign software (Section 11.8). The signed software and the publisher's digital certificate provide proof that the software is safe and has not been altered.

When a customer attempts to download a file, a dialog box appears on the screen displaying the digital certificate and the name of the certificate authority. Links to the publisher and the certificate authority are provided so that customers can learn more about each party before they agree to download the software. If Microsoft Authenticode determines that the software has been compromised, the transaction is terminated.

To learn more about Microsoft Authenticode, visit the following sites:

```
msdn.microsoft.com/workshop/security/authcode/signing.asp
msdn.microsoft.com/workshop/security/authcode/authenti-
code.asp
```

VeriSign, Inc., is a leading certificate authority. For more information about VeriSign, visit **www.verisign.com**. For a listing of other digital-certificate vendors, please see Section 11.16.

Periodically changing key pairs is necessary in maintaining a secure system, as a private key may be compromised without a user's knowledge. The longer a key pair is used, the more vulnerable the keys are to attack and cryptanalysis. As a result, digital certificates are created with an expiration date, to force users to switch key pairs. If a private key is compromised before its expiration date, the digital certificate can be canceled, and the user can get a new key pair and digital certificate. Canceled and revoked certificates are placed on a *certificate revocation list* (*CRL*). CRLs are stored with the certificate authority that issued the certificates. It is essential for users to report immediately if they suspect that their private keys have been compromised, as the issue of non-repudiation makes certificate owners responsible for anything appearing with their digital signatures. In states with laws on digital signatures, certificates legally bind certificate owners to any transactions involving their certificates.

CRLs are similar to old paper lists of revoked credit-card numbers that were used at the points of sale in stores.[10] This makes for a great inconvenience when checking the validity of a certificate. An alternative to CRLs is the *Online Certificate Status Protocol* (*OCSP*), which validates certificates in real-time. OCSP technology is currently under development. For an overview of OCSP, read "X.509 Internet Public Key Infrastructure Online Certificate Status Protocol—OCSP" located at **ftp.isi.edu/in-notes/ rfc2560.txt**.

Many people still consider e-commerce unsecure. However, transactions using PKI and digital certificates can be more secure than exchanging private information over phone lines, through the mail or even than paying by credit card in person. After all, when you go to a restaurant and the waiter takes your credit card in back to process your bill, how do you know the waiter did not write down your credit-card information? In contrast, the key algorithms used in most secure online transactions are nearly impossible to compromise. By some estimates, the key algorithms used in public-key cryptography are so secure that even millions of today's computers working in parallel could not break the codes in a century. However, as computing power increases, key algorithms considered strong today could be broken in the future.

Digital-certificate capabilities are built into many e-mail packages. For example, in Microsoft Outlook, you can go to the **Tools** menu and select **Options** and the **Security** tab. At the bottom of the dialog box, you will see the option to obtain a digital ID. Selecting the option will take you to a Microsoft Web site with links to several worldwide certificate authorities. Once you have a digital certificate, you can sign your e-mail messages digitally.

To obtain a digital certificate for your personal e-mail messages, visit **www.veri sign.com** or **www.thawte.com**. VeriSign offers a free 60-day trial, or you can purchase the service for a yearly fee. Thawte offers free digital certificates for personal e-mail. Web server certificates may also be purchased through VeriSign and Thawte; however, they are more expensive than e-mail certificates.

11.9.1 Smart Cards

One of the fastest growing applications of PKI is the *smart card*. A smart card generally looks like a credit card and can serve many different functions, from authentication to data storage. The most popular smart cards are *memory cards* and *microprocessor cards*. Memory cards are similar to floppy disks. Microprocessor cards are similar to small computers, with operating systems, security and storage. Smart cards also have different *interfaces* with which they interact with reading devices. One type of interface is a *contact interface*, in which smart cards are inserted into a reading device and physical contact between the device and the card is necessary. The alternative to this method is a *contactless interface*, in which data is transferred to a reader via an embedded wireless device in the card, without the card and the device having to make physical contact.[11]

Smart cards store private keys, digital certificates and other information necessary for implementing PKI. They may also store credit card numbers, personal contact information, etc. Each smart card is used in combination with a *personal identification number* (*PIN*). This application provides two levels of security by requiring the user to both possess a smart card and know the corresponding PIN to access the information stored on the card.

As an added measure of security, some microprocessor cards will delete or corrupt stored data if malicious attempts at tampering with the card occur. Smart card PKI allows users to access information from multiple devices using the same smart card.

11.10 Security Protocols

Everyone using the Web for e-business and e-commerce needs to be concerned about the security of their personal information. In this section, we discuss network security protocols, such as *Internet Protocol Security (IPSec),* and transport layer security protocols such as *Secure Sockets Layer (SSL).* Network security protocols protect communications between networks; transport layer security protocols are used to establish secure connections for data to pass through.

11.10.1 Secure Sockets Layer (SSL)

Currently, most e-businesses use SSL for secure online transactions, although SSL is not designed specifically for securing transactions. Rather, SSL secures World Wide Web connections. The Secure Sockets Layer (SSL) protocol, developed by Netscape Communications, is a non-proprietary protocol commonly used to secure communication between two computers on the Internet and the Web.[12] SSL is built into many Web browsers, including Netscape Communicator and Microsoft Internet Explorer, as well as numerous other software products. It operates between the Internet's TCP/IP communications protocol and the application software.[13]

In a standard correspondence over the Internet, a sender's message is passed to a *socket,* which receives and transmits information from a network. The socket then interprets the message through *Transmission Control Protocol/Internet Protocol (TCP/IP).* TCP/IP is the standard set of protocols used for connecting computers and networks to a network of networks, known as the Internet. Most Internet transmissions are sent as sets of individual message pieces, called *packets.* At the sending side, the packets of one message are numbered sequentially, and error-control information is attached to each packet. IP is primarily responsible for routing packets to avoid traffic jams, so each packet might travel a different route over the Internet. The destination of a packet is determined by the *IP address*—an assigned number used to identify a computer on a network, similar to the address of a house in a neighborhood. At the receiving end, the TCP makes sure that all of the packets have arrived, puts them in sequential order and determines if the packets have arrived without alteration. If the packets have been accidentally altered or any data has been lost, TCP requests retransmission. However, TCP is not sophisticated enough to determine if packets have been maliciously altered during transmission, as malicious packets can be disguised as valid ones. When all of the data successfully reaches TCP/IP, the message is passed to the socket at the receiver end. The socket translates the message back into a form that can be read by the receiver's application.[14] In a transaction using SSL, the sockets are secured using public-key cryptography.

SSL implements public-key cryptography using the RSA algorithm and digital certificates to authenticate the server in a transaction and to protect private information as it passes over the Internet. SSL transactions do not require client authentication; many servers consider a valid credit-card number to be sufficient for authentication in secure purchases. To begin, a client sends a message to a server. The server responds and sends its digital certificate to the client for authentication. Using public-key cryptography to communicate securely, the client and server negotiate *session keys* to continue the transaction. Session keys are secret keys that are used for the duration of that transaction. Once the keys are established, the communication proceeds between the client and the server by using the session keys and digital certificates. Encrypted data is passed through TCP/IP, just as regular packets travel over the Internet. However, before sending a message with TCP/IP, the SSL protocol breaks the information into blocks, compresses it and encrypts it. Conversely, after the data reaches the receiver through TCP/IP, the SSL protocol decrypts the packets, then decompresses and assembles the data. These extra processes provide an extra layer of security between TCP/IP and applications. SSL is primarily used to secure *point-to-point connections*—transmissions of data from one computer to another.[15] SSL allows for authentication of the server, the client, both or neither. However, in most e-business SSL sessions, only the server is authenticated. The Transport Layer Security (TLS) protocol, designed by the Internet Engineering Task Force, is similar to SSL. For more information on TLS, visit **www.ietf.org/rfc/rfc2246.txt**.

Although SSL protects information as it is passed over the Internet, it does not protect private information, such as credit-card numbers, once the information is stored on the merchant's server. When a merchant receives credit-card information with an order, the information is often decrypted and stored on the merchant's server until the order is placed. If the server is not secure and the data is not encrypted, an unauthorized party can access the information. Hardware devices, such as *peripheral component interconnect (PCI) cards* designed for use in SSL transactions, can be installed on Web servers to process SSL transactions, thus reducing processing time and leaving the server free to perform other tasks.[16] Visit **www.sonicwall.com/products/trans.asp** for more information on these devices. For more information about the SSL protocol, check out the Netscape SSL tutorial at **developer.netscape.com/tech/security/ssl/protocol.html** and the Netscape Security Center site at **www.netscape.com/security/index.html**.

11.10.2 IPSec and Virtual Private Networks (VPN)

Networks allow organizations to link multiple computers together. *Local area networks (LANs)* connect computers that are physically close, generally in the same building. *Wide area networks (WANs)* are used to connect computers in multiple locations using private telephone lines or radio waves. Organizations are now taking advantage of the existing infrastructure of the Internet—the publicly-available wires—to create *Virtual Private Networks (VPNs)*. VPNs connect multiple networks, wireless users and other remote users. VPNs use the Internet infrastructure that is already in place, therefore they are more economical than private networks such as WANs.[17] Encryption allows VPNs to provide the same services as private networks do—over a public network.

A VPN is created by establishing a secure *tunnel* through which data passes between multiple networks over the Internet. *IPSec (Internet Protocol Security)* is one of the technologies used to secure the tunnel through which the data passes, ensuring data privacy and integrity, as well authenticating users.[18] IPSec, developed by the *Internet Engineering Task Force (IETF)*, uses public-key and symmetric-key cryptography to ensure data integrity, authentication and confidentiality. The technology takes advantage of the standard that is already in place, in which information travels between two networks over the Internet via the *Internet Protocol (IP)*. Information sent using IP, however, can easily be intercepted.

Unauthorized users can access the network by using a number of well-known techniques, such as *IP spoofing*—a method in which an attacker simulates the IP of an authorized user or host to get access to resources that would otherwise be off-limits. The SSL protocol enables secure, point-to-point connections between two applications; IPSec enables the secure connection of an entire network. The Diffie-Hellman and RSA algorithms are commonly used in the IPSec protocol for key exchange, and DES or 3DES are used for secret-key encryption (depending on system and encryption needs). An IP packet is encrypted, then sent inside a regular IP packet that creates the tunnel. The receiver discards the outer IP packet, then decrypts the inner IP packet.[19] VPN security relies on three concepts—authentication of the user, encryption of the data sent over the network and controlled access to corporate information.[20] To address these three security concepts, IPSec is composed of three pieces. The *Authentication Header* (*AH*) attaches additional information to each packet, which verifies the identity of the sender and proves that data was not modified in transit. The *Encapsulating Security Payload* (*ESP*) encrypts the data using symmetric key ciphers to protect the data from eavesdroppers while the IP packet is being sent from one computer to another. The *Internet Key Exchange* (*IKE*) is the key-exchange protocol used in IPSec to determine security restrictions and to authenticate the encryption keys.

VPNs are becoming increasingly popular in businesses. However, VPN security is difficult to manage. To establish a VPN, all of the users on the network must have similar software or hardware. Although it is convenient for a business partner to connect to another company's network via VPN, access to specific applications and files should be limited to certain authorized users versus all users on a VPN.[21] Firewalls, intrusion detection software and authorization tools can be used to secure valuable data (see section 11.13). For more information about IPSec, visit the IETF's *IPSec Working Group* Web site (**www.ietf.org/html.charters/ipsec-charter.html**).

11.11 Authentication and Authorization

As we discussed throughout the chapter, authentication and authorization are two of the fundamental requirements for e-business and Web services security. In this section, we will discuss technologies used to authenticate users in a network, such as *Kerberos*, *biometrics* and *single sign-on*.

11.11.1 Kerberos

Firewalls do not protect users from internal security threats to their local area network. Internal attacks are common and can be extremely damaging. For example, disgruntled employees with network access can wreak havoc on an organization's network or steal valuable proprietary information. It is estimated that 70 percent to 90 percent of attacks on corporate networks are internal.[22] *Kerberos* is a freely available, open-source protocol developed at MIT. It employs secret-key cryptography to authenticate users in a network and to maintain the integrity and privacy of network communications.

Authentication in Kerberos is handled by a main Kerberos system and a secondary *Ticket Granting Service* (*TGS*). This system is similar to the key distribution centers described in Section 11.3, Secret-key Cryptography. The main Kerberos system authenticates a client's identity to the TGS; the TGS authenticates client's rights to access specific network services.

Each client in the network shares a secret key with the Kerberos system. This secret key may be used by multiple TGSs in the Kerberos system. The client starts by entering a login name and password into the Kerberos authentication server. The authentication server maintains a database of all clients in the network. The authentication server returns a *Ticket-Granting Ticket* (*TGT*) encrypted with the client's secret key that it shares with the authentication server. Since the secret key is known only by the authentication server and the client, only the client can decrypt the TGT, thus authenticating the client's identity. Next, the client sends the decrypted TGT to the Ticket Granting Service to request a *service ticket*. The service ticket authorizes the client's access to specific network services. Service tickets have a set expiration time. Tickets may be renewed by the TGS.

11.11.2 Biometrics

An innovation in security is likely to be *biometrics*. Biometrics uses unique personal information, such as fingerprints, eyeball iris scans or face scans, to identify a user. This system eliminates the need for passwords, which are much easier to steal. Have you ever written down your passwords on a piece of paper and put the paper in your desk drawer or wallet? These days, people have passwords and PIN codes for everything—Web sites, networks, e-mail, ATM cards and even for their cars. Managing all of those codes can become a burden. Recently, the cost of biometrics devices has dropped significantly. Keyboard-mounted fingerprint-scanning, face-scanning and eye-scanning devices are being used in place of passwords to log into systems, check e-mail or access secure information over a network. Each user's iris scan, face scan or fingerprint is stored in a secure database. Each time a user logs in, his or her scan is compared with the database. If a match is made, the login is successful. Two companies that specialize in biometrics devices are Iridian Technologies (**iriscan.com**) and Keytronic (**www.keytronic.com**). For additional resources, see Section 11.16.

Currently, passwords are the predominant means of authentication; however, focus is beginning to shift to smart cards and biometrics. Microsoft recently announced that it will include the *Biometric Application Programming Interface* (*BAPI*) in future versions of Windows, which will make it possible for companies to integrate biometrics into their systems.[23] *Two-factor authentication* uses two means to authenticate the user, such as biometrics or a smart card used in combination with a password. Though this system could potentially be compromised, using two methods of authentication is more secure than just using passwords alone.

Keyware Inc. has already implemented a wireless biometrics system that stores user voiceprints on a central server. Keyware also created *layered biometric verification* (*LBV*), which uses multiple physical measurements—face, finger and voice prints—simultaneously. The LBV feature enables a wireless biometrics system to combine biometrics with other authentication methods, such as PIN and PKI.[24]

Identix Inc. also provides biometrics authentication technology for wireless transactions. The Identix fingerprint scanning device is embedded in handheld devices. The Identix service offers *transaction management* and *content protection* services. Transaction management services prove that transactions took place, and content protection services control access to electronic documents, including limiting a user's ability to download or copy documents.[25]

One of the major concerns with biometrics is the issue of privacy. Implementing fingerprint scanners means that organizations will be keeping databases with each employee's fingerprint. Do people want to provide their employers with such personal information? What if that data is compromised? To date, most organizations that have implemented biometrics systems have received little, if any, resistance from employees.

11.11.3 Single Sign-On

To access multiple applications or Web services on different servers, users must provide a separate password for authentication on each. Remembering multiple passwords is cumbersome. People tend to write their passwords down, creating security threats.

Single sign-on systems allow users to login once with a single password. Users can access multiple applications. It is important to secure single sign-on passwords, because if the password becomes available to hackers, all applications can be accessed and attacked.

There are three types of single sign-on services: *workstation logon scripts*, *authentication server scripts* and *tokens*. Workstation logon scripts are the simplest form of single sign-on. Users login at their workstations, then choose applications from a menu. The workstation logon script sends the user's password to the application servers, and the user is authenticated for future access to those applications. Workstation logon scripts do not provide a sufficient amount of security since user passwords are stored on the PC in plaintext. Anyone who can access the workstation can take the user's password. Authentication server scripts authenticate users with a central server. The central server controls connections between the user and the applications the user wishes to access. Authentication server scripts are more secure than workstation logon scripts, because passwords are kept on the server, which is more secure than the individual PC.

The most advanced single sign-on systems use token-based authentication. Once a user is authenticated, a non-reusable token is issued, enabling the user to access specific applications. The logon for creating the token is secured with encryption or with a single password, which is the only password that the user needs. A key problem with token authentication is that all applications must be built to accept tokens, rather than traditional logon passwords.[26] Currently, the three leaders in the development of single sign-on technology are the Liberty Alliance Project (**www.projectliberty.org**), Microsoft and AOL Time Warner.[27] The Liberty Alliance Project is a consortium of technology and security organizations working to create an open single sign-on solution. Microsoft's Passport and AOL Time Warner's Magic Carpet are also viable solutions, though they are proprietary. To protect the privacy of information submitted to single sign-on and other applications, the *Platform for Privacy Preferences* (*P3P*) gives users control over the personal information that sites collect (see the feature, P3P: Placing Privacy Control in the Hands of Users).

11.12 Security Attacks

Recent cyberattacks on e-businesses have made the front pages of newspapers worldwide. *Denial-of-service attacks* (*DoS*), *viruses* and *worms* have cost companies billions of dollars. In this section, we will discuss the different types of attacks and the solutions you can implement to protect your information.

P3P: Placing Privacy Control in the Hands of Users

The Platform for Privacy Preferences (P3P) (`www.w3.org/P3P`) allows users to define their own privacy preferences for browsing and shopping online. Sites specify privacy policies in XML policy files that indicate what personal information the sites collect about users and what they do with this information. Many people prefer to keep personal information—such as names, credit-card numbers and mailing addresses—private. Most sites provide written privacy policies, but these can be lengthy and full of confusing legal terms. With P3P, users set privacy preferences on their browsers. When a user reaches a site with a P3P policy, the user's computer determines what information to disclose to the site on the basis of the defined preferences. P3P saves time and helps ensure that user privacy is protected.

Microsoft is encouraging the adoption of P3P for consumer privacy protection—the company includes P3P in Internet Explorer 6.0 and Microsoft Passport technology. In Internet Explorer, users can choose between several predefined levels of security (from accepting all cookies to blocking all cookies, with intermediate settings that restrict cookies from certain kinds of sites). A user can also specify certain sites for which the privacy preferences can be overridden. When the user reaches a P3P-enabled site, the computer compares the site's privacy policies to the user's personal privacy settings. If the site provides an acceptable amount of privacy, Internet Explorer lets the user continue to browse the site without interruption and allows the site to store personal information in cookies. If the user reaches a site with a privacy policy that violates the privacy preferences, the Internet Explorer window alerts the user and allows the user to choose what personal information to disclose to the site. Any cookies that violate the user's privacy preferences are rejected. IBM's P3P Policy Editor, a visual tool for generating P3P-compliant policy files in XML, is available for download at `www.alphaworks.ibm.com/tech/p3peditor`.

11.12.1 Denial-of-Service (DoS) Attacks

A denial-of-service attack occurs when a system is forced to behave improperly. In many DoS attacks, unauthorized traffic takes up a network's resources, restricting access for legitimate users. Typically, the attack is performed by flooding servers with data packets. Denial-of-service attacks usually require the power of a network of computers working simultaneously, although some skillful attacks can be achieved with a single machine. Denial-of-service attacks can cause networked computers to crash or disconnect, disrupting service on a Web site or even shutting down critical systems such as telecommunications or flight-control centers

Another type of denial-of-service attack targets the *routing tables* of a network. Routing tables are the road map of a network, providing directions for data to get from one computer to another. This type of attack is accomplished by modifying the routing tables, thus disabling network activity. For example, the routing tables can be changed to send all data to one address in the network.

In a *distributed denial-of-service attack*, the packet flooding does not come from a single source, but from many separate computers. Actually, such an attack is rarely the concerted work of many individuals. Instead, it is the work of a single individual who has installed viruses on various computers, gaining illegitimate use of the computers to carry out the attack. Distributed denial-of-service attacks can be difficult to stop, since it is not clear which requests on a network are from legitimate users and which are part of the attack. In addition, it is particularly difficult to catch the culprit of such attacks, because the attacks are not carried out directly from the attacker's computer.

Who is responsible for viruses and denial-of-service attacks? Most often the responsible parties are referred to as *hackers* or *crackers*. Hackers and crackers are usually skilled programmers. According to some, hackers break into systems just for the thrill of it, without causing any harm to the compromised systems (except, perhaps, humbling and humiliating their owners). Either way, hackers break the law by accessing or damaging private information and computers. Crackers have malicious intent and are usually interested in breaking into a system to shut down services or steal data. In February 2000, distributed denial-of-service attacks shut down a number of high-traffic Web sites, including Yahoo!, eBay, CNN Interactive and Amazon. In this case, a cracker used a network of computers to flood the Web sites with traffic that overwhelmed the sites' computers. Although denial-of-service attacks merely shut off access to a Web site and do not affect the victim's data, they can be extremely costly. For example, when eBay's Web site went down for a 24-hour period on August 6, 1999, its stock value declined dramatically.[28]

11.12.2 Viruses and Worms

Viruses are pieces of code—often sent as attachments or hidden in audio clips, video clips and games—that attach to, or overwrite other programs to replicate themselves. Viruses can corrupt files or even wipe out a hard drive. Before the Internet was invented, viruses spread through files and programs (such as video games) transferred to computers by removable disks. Today, viruses are spread over a network simply by sharing "infected" files embedded in e-mail attachments, documents or programs. A worm is similar to a virus, except that it can spread and infect files on its own over a network; worms do not need to be attached to another program to spread. Once a virus or worm is released, it can spread rapidly, often infecting millions of computers worldwide within minutes or hours.

There are many classes of computer viruses. A *transient virus* attaches itself to a specific computer program. The virus is activated when the program is run and deactivated when the program is terminated. A more powerful type of virus is a *resident virus*, which, once loaded into the memory of a computer, operates for the duration of the computer's use. Another type of virus is the *logic bomb*, which triggers when a given condition is met, such as a *time bomb* that is activated when the clock on the computer matches a certain time or date.

A *Trojan horse* is a malicious program that hides within a friendly program or simulates the identity of a legitimate program or feature, while actually causing damage to the computer or network in the background. The Trojan horse gets its name from the story of the Trojan War in Greek history. In this story, Greek warriors hid inside a wooden horse, which the Trojans took within the walls of the city of Troy. When night fell and the Trojans were asleep, the Greek warriors came out of the horse and opened the gates to the city, letting the Greek army enter the gates and destroy the city of Troy. Trojan horse programs can be particularly difficult to detect, since they appear to be legitimate and useful applications.

Also commonly associated with Trojan horses are *backdoor programs*, which are usually resident viruses that give the sender complete, undetected access to the victim's computer resources. These types of viruses are especially threatening to the victim, as they can be set up to log every keystroke (capturing all passwords, credit card numbers, etc.) No matter how secure the connection between a PC supplying private information and the server receiving the information, if a backdoor program is running on a computer, the data is intercepted before any encryption is implemented.

Two of the most famous viruses to date are *Melissa*, which struck in March 1999, and the *ILOVEYOU virus* that hit in May 2000. Both viruses cost organizations and individuals billions of dollars. The Melissa virus spread in Microsoft Word documents sent via e-mail. When the document was opened, the virus was triggered. Melissa accessed the Microsoft Outlook address book on that computer and automatically sent the infected Word attachment by e-mail to the first 50 people in the address book. Each time another person opened the attachment, the virus would send out another 50 messages. Once in a system, the virus infected any subsequently saved files.

The ILOVEYOU virus was sent as an attachment to an e-mail posing as a love letter. The message in the e-mail said "Kindly check the attached love letter coming from me." Once opened, the virus accessed the Microsoft Outlook address book and sent out messages to the addresses listed, helping to spread the virus rapidly worldwide. The virus corrupted all types of files, including system files. Networks at companies and government organizations worldwide were shut down for days trying to remedy the problem and contain the virus. This virus accentuated the importance of scanning file attachments for security threats before opening them.

Why do these viruses spread so quickly? One reason is that many people are too willing to open executable files from unknown sources. Have you ever opened an audio clip or video clip from a friend? Have you ever forwarded that clip to other friends? Do you know who created the clip and if any viruses are embedded in it? Did you open the ILOVE YOU file to see what the love letter said?

Most antivirus software is reactive, going after viruses once they are discovered, rather than protecting against unknown viruses. New antivirus software, such as Finjan Software's SurfinGuard® (**www.finjan.com**), looks for executable files attached to e-mail and runs the executables in a secure area to test if they attempt to access and harm files. For more information about antivirus software, see the **McAfee.com**: Antivirus Utilities feature.

11.12.3 Software Exploitation, Web Defacing and Cybercrime

Another problem plaguing e-businesses is *software exploitation* by hackers. In addition to updating virus and firewall programs constantly, every program on a networked machine should be checked for vulnerabilities. However, with millions of software products available and vulnerabilities discovered daily, this becomes an enormous task. One common vulnerability exploitation method is a *buffer overflow*, in which a program is overwhelmed by an input of more data than it has allocated space for. Buffer overflow attacks can cause systems to crash or, more dangerously, allow arbitrary code to be run on a machine. *BugTraq* was created in 1993 to list vulnerabilities, how to exploit them and how to repair them. For more information about BugTraq, visit **www.security-focus.com**.

`McAfee.com`: Antivirus Utilities

`McAfee.com` provides a variety of antivirus utilities (and other utilities) for users whose computers are not continuously connected to a network, for users whose computers are continuously connected to a network (such as the Internet) and for users connected to a network via wireless devices, such as personal digital assistants.

For computers that are not continuously connected to a network, McAfee provides its antivirus software *VirusScan®*. This software is configurable to scan files for viruses on demand or to scan continuously in the background as the user does his or her work.

For computers that are network and Internet accessible, McAfee provides its online `McAfee.com` Clinic. Users with a subscription to McAfee Clinic can use the online virus software from any computer they happen to be using. As with VirusScan software on stand-alone computers, users can scan their files on demand. A major benefit of the Clinic is its *ActiveShield* software. Once installed, ActiveShield can be configured to scan every file that is used on the computer or just the program files. It can also be configured to check automatically for virus definition updates and notify the user when such updates become available. The user simply clicks on the supplied hyperlink in an update notification to connect to the Clinic site and clicks on another hyperlink to download the update. Thus, users can keep their computers protected with the most up-to-date virus definitions at all times, an important factor in protection from viruses.

McAfee.com *VirusScan Wireless* provides virus protection for Palm™ handhelds, Pocket PC and other handheld devices. VirusScan Wireless is installed on the user's PC. Each time the user syncs the handheld device, the software scans for viruses. If a virus is detected, the sync is terminated until the user deletes the virus. For more information about McAfee, visit `www.mcafee.com`. Also, check out Norton security products from Symantec, at `www.symantec.com`. Symantec is a leading security software vendor. Its product Norton™ Internet Security 2002 provides protection against hackers, viruses and threats to privacy for both small businesses and individuals.

Web defacing is another popular form of attack, wherein the crackers illegally enter an organization's Web site and change the contents. CNN Interactive has issued a special report titled "Insurgency on the Internet," with news stories about hackers and their online attacks. Included is a gallery of defaced sites. One notable case of Web defacing occurred in 1996, when Swedish crackers changed the Central Intelligence Agency Web site to read "Central Stupidity Agency." The vandals put obscenities, political messages, notes to system administrators and links to adult-content sites on the page. Many other popular and large Web sites have been defaced. Defacing Web sites has become overwhelmingly popular amongst crackers today, causing archives of attacked sites (with records of more than 15,000 vandalized sites) to close because of the volume in which sites were being vandalized daily.[29]

Cybercrime can have significant financial implications on an organization.[30] Companies need to protect their data, intellectual property, customer information, etc. Implementing a *security policy* is key to protecting an organization's data and network. When developing a security plan, organizations must assess their vulnerabilities and the possible threats to security. What information do they need to protect? Who are the possible attackers and what is their intent—data theft or damaging the network? How will the organization respond to incidents?[31] For more information about security and security plans, visit **www.cerias.com** and **www.sans.org** (see the SANS Institute: Security Research and Education feature). Visit **www.baselinesoft.com** to check out books and CD-ROMs on security policies. Baseline Software's book, *Information Policies Made Easy: Version 7* includes over 1000 security policies. This book is used by numerous Fortune 200 companies.

The rise in cybercrimes has prompted the U. S. government to take action. Under the National Information Infrastructure Protection Act of 1996, denial-of-service attacks and distribution of viruses are federal crimes punishable by fines and jail time. For more information about the U. S. government's efforts against cybercrime or to read about recently prosecuted cases, visit the U.S. Department of Justice Web site, at **www.usdoj.gov/criminal/cybercrime/compcrime.html**. Also check out **www.cybercrime.gov**, a site maintained by the Criminal Division of the U. S. Department of Justice.

The *CERT® (Computer Emergency Response Team) Coordination Center* at Carnegie Mellon University's Software Engineering Institute responds to reports of viruses and denial-of-service attacks and provides information on network security, including how to determine if a system has been compromised. The site provides detailed incident reports of viruses and denial-of-service attacks, including descriptions of the incidents, their impact and solutions. The site also includes reports of vulnerabilities in popular operating systems and software packages. The *CERT Security Improvement Modules* are excellent tutorials on network security. These modules describe the issues and technologies used to solve network security problems. For more information, visit the CERT Web site, at **www.cert.org**.

To learn more about how you can protect yourself or your network from hacker attacks, visit AntiOnline™, at **www.antionline.com**. This site has security-related news and information, a tutorial titled "Fight-back! Against Hackers," information about hackers and an archive of hacked sites. You can find additional information about denial-of-service attacks and how to protect your site at **www.denialinfo.com**.

11.13 Network Security

The goal of network security is to allow authorized users access to information and services, while preventing unauthorized users from gaining access to, and possibly corrupting, the network. There is a trade-off between network security and network performance: Increased security often decreases the efficiency of the network.

In this section, we will discuss the various aspects of network security. We will discuss firewalls, which keep unauthorized users out of the network, and authorization servers, which allow users to access specific applications based on a set of pre-defined criteria. We will then look at intrusion detection systems that actively monitor a network for intrusions and attacks. Finally, biometric authentication will be discussed. In Chapter 12, Web Services Security, we will examine how Web services affect network security.

11.13.1 Firewalls

A basic tool in network security is the *firewall*. The purpose of a firewall is to protect a *local area network* (*LAN*) from intruders outside the network. For example, most companies have internal networks that allow employees to share files and access company information. Each LAN can be connected to the Internet through a gateway, which usually includes a firewall. For years, one of the biggest threats to security came from employees inside the firewall. Now that businesses rely heavily on access to the Internet, an increasing number of security threats are originating outside the firewall—from the hundreds of millions of people connected to the company network by the Internet.[32] A firewall acts as a safety barrier for data flowing into and out of the LAN. Firewalls can prohibit all data flow not expressly allowed, or can allow all data flow that is not expressly prohibited. The choice between these two models is up to the network security administrator and should be based on the need for security versus the need for functionality.

There are two main types of firewalls: *packet-filtering firewalls* and *application-level gateways*. A packet-filtering firewall examines all data sent from outside the LAN and automatically rejects any data packets that have local network addresses. For example, if a hacker from outside the network obtains the address of a computer inside the network and tries to sneak a harmful data packet through the firewall, the packet-filtering firewall will reject the data packet, since it has an internal address, but originated from outside the network. A problem with packet-filtering firewalls is that they consider only the source of data packets; they do not examine the actual data. As a result, malicious viruses can be installed on an authorized user's computer, giving the hacker access to the network without the authorized user's knowledge. The goal of an application-level gateway is to screen the actual data. If the message is deemed safe, then the message is sent through to the intended receiver.

Using a firewall is probably the most effective and easiest way to add security to a small network.[33] Often, small companies or home users who are connected to the Internet through permanent connections, such as DSL lines, do not employ strong security measures. As a result, their computers are prime targets for crackers to use in denial-of-service attacks or to steal information. It is important for all computers connected to the Internet to have some degree of security for their systems. Numerous firewall software products are available. Several products are listed in the Web resources in Section 11.16.

Air gap technology is a network security solution that complements the firewall. It secures private data from external traffic accessing the internal network. The *air gap* separates the internal network from the external network, and the organization decides which information will be made available to external users. *Whale Communications* created the *e-Gap System*, which is composed of two computer servers and a *memory bank*. The memory bank does not run an operating system, therefore hackers cannot take advantage of common operating system weaknesses to access network information.

Air gap technology does not allow outside users to view the network's structure, preventing hackers from searching the layout for weak spots or specific data. The e-Gap *Web Shuttle* feature allows safe external access by restricting the system's *back office*, which is where an organization's most sensitive information and IT-based business processes are controlled. Users who want to access a network hide behind the air gap, where the authentication server is located. Authorized users gain access through a single sign-on capability, allowing them to use one log-in password to access authorized areas of the network.

The e-Gap *Secure File Shuttle* feature moves files in and out of the network. Each file is inspected behind the air gap. If the file is deemed safe, it is carried by the File Shuttle into the network.[34]

Air gap technology is used by e-commerce organizations to allow their clients and partners to access information automatically, thus reducing the cost of inventory management. Military, aerospace and government industries, which store highly sensitive information, use air gap technology.

11.13.2 Intrusion Detection Systems

What happens if a hacker gets inside your firewall? How do you know if an intruder has penetrated the firewall? Also, how do you know if unauthorized employees are accessing restricted applications? *Intrusion detection systems* monitor networks and application *log files*—files containing information on files, including who accessed them and when—so if an intruder makes it into the network or an unauthorized application, the system detects the intrusion, halts the session and sets off an alarm to notify the system administrator.[35]

Host-based intrusion detection systems monitor system and application log files. They can be used to scan for Trojan horses, for example. *Network-based intrusion detection* software monitors traffic on a network for any unusual patterns that might indicate DoS attacks or attempted entry into a network by an unauthorized user. Companies can then check their log files to determine if indeed there was an intrusion and if so, they can attempt to track the offender. Check out the intrusion detection products from Cisco (**www.cisco.com/warp/public/cc/pd/sqsw/sqidsz**), Hewlett-Packard (**www.hp.com/security/home.html**) and Symantec (**www.symantec.com**).

The *OCTAVE*[SM] (*Operationally Critical Threat, Asset and Vulnerability Evaluation*) *method*, under development at the Software Engineering Institute at Carnegie Mellon University, is a process for evaluating security threats of a system. There are three phases in OCTAVE: building threat profiles, identifying vulnerabilities, and developing security solutions and plans. In the first stage, the organization identifies its important information and assets, then evaluates the levels of security required to protect them. In the second phase, the system is examined for weaknesses that could compromise the valuable data. The third phase is to develop a security strategy as advised by an analysis team of three to five security experts assigned by OCTAVE. This approach is one of the firsts of its kind, in which the owners of computer systems not only get to have professionals analyze their systems, but also participate in prioritizing the protection of crucial information.[36]

SANS Institute: Security Research and Education

The *System Administration, Networking and Security Institute* (*SANS*), founded in 1989, is a security research and education organization with over 96,000 members (**www.sans.org**). SANS sells security training, certification programs and publications. The organization also offers several free, publicly-available services such as security alerts and news.

SANS Institute: Security Research and Education (Cont.)

Each year, SANS publishes the *Roadmap to Security Tools and Services Poster*—a resource that includes information about key security technologies, lists of security vendors that specialize in each technology and URLs with additional security information. The poster also includes directions on how to order approximately 20 white papers. To order a copy of the poster and to request copies of the technical white papers, go to **www.sans.org/tools.php**.

The SANS Information Security Reading Room is an excellent resource for security information. The site has hundreds of articles and case studies organized by security topic. Topics include authentication, attacking attackers, intrusion detection, securing code, standards and many more. For more information, visit **www.sans.org/infosecFAQ/index.htm**.

SANS offers three free newsletters. *SANS NewsBites* is a free weekly e-mail newsletter that lists key security news articles with a short summary of each article and a link to the complete resource. Go to **www.sans.org/newlook/digests/newsbites.htm** to view the latest newsletter, to view past newsletters or to subscribe. *Security Alert Consensus* (*SAC*) is a weekly summary of new security alerts and countermeasures. Subscribers can opt to receive information on specific operating systems based on their particular needs. The *SANS Windows Security Digest* lists Windows NT security updates, threats and bugs. To subscribe to any of the SANS e-mail newsletters, go to **www.sans.org/sansnews**.

The SANS *Global Incident Analysis Center* (*GIAC*) records current attacks and analyzes each attack. Network and systems administrators can use this information to help them defend their networks and systems against attacks. Reports are made readily available to the public at **www.giac.org** and **www.incidents.org**.

11.14 Steganography

Steganography is the practice of hiding information within other information. The term literally means "covered writing." Like cryptography, steganography has been used since ancient times. Steganography allows you to take a piece of information, such as a message or image, and hide it within another image, message or even an audio clip. Steganography takes advantage of insignificant space in digital files, in images or on removable disks.[37] Consider a simple example: If you have a message that you want to send secretly, you can hide the information within another message, so that no one but the intended receiver can read it. For example, if you want to tell your stockbroker to buy a stock and your message must be transmitted over an unsecure channel, you could send the message "BURIED UNDER YARD." If you have agreed in advance that your message is hidden in the first letters of each word, the stock broker picks these letters off and sees "BUY."

An increasingly popular application of steganography is *digital watermarks* for intellectual property protection. An example of a conventional watermark is shown in Fig. 11.7. A digital watermark can be either visible or invisible. It is usually a company logo, copyright notification or other mark or message that indicates the owner of the document. The owner of a document could show the hidden watermark in a court of law, for example, to prove that the watermarked item was stolen.

Digital watermarking could have a substantial impact on e-commerce. Consider the music industry. Music publishers are concerned that MP3 technology is allowing people to distribute illegal copies of songs and albums. As a result, many publishers are hesitant to put content online, as digital content is easy to copy. Also, since CD-ROMs are digital, people are able to upload their music and share it over the Web. Using digital watermarks, music publishers can make indistinguishable changes to a part of a song at a frequency that is not audible to humans, to show that the song was, in fact, copied. Microsoft Research is developing a watermarking system for digital audio, which would be included with default Windows media players. In this digital watermarking system, data such as licensing information is embedded into a song; the media player will not play files with invalid information.

Blue Spike's Giovanni™ digital watermarking software uses cryptographic keys to generate and embed steganographic digital watermarks into digital music and images (Fig. 11.8). The watermarks can be used as proof of ownership to help digital publishers protect their copyrighted material. The watermarks are undetectable by anyone who is not privy to the embedding scheme, and thus the watermarks cannot be identified and removed. The watermarks are placed randomly.

Digital watermarking capabilities are built into some image-editing software applications, such as Adobe PhotoShop 7.0 (`www.adobe.com`). Digimarc (`www.digimark.com`) is an example of a company that offers digital watermarking solutions.

In the last few chapters, we discussed the technologies involved in building and running an Web services, and how to secure online transactions and communications. In Chapter 12, Web Services Security, we will discuss the technologies, protocols and standards used to secure Web services.

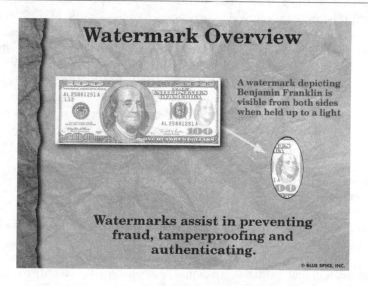

Fig. 11.7   Example of a conventional watermark. (Courtesy of Blue Spike, Inc.)

Fig. 11.8   An example of steganography: Blue Spike's Giovanni digital
watermarking process. (Courtesy of Blue Spike, Inc.)

11.15 Summary

The field of security places emphasis on privacy, integrity, authentication, authorization and non-repudiation. Cryptography transforms data by using a cipher, or cryptosystem—a mathematical procedure for encrypting messages. A key—a string of digits that acts as a password—is input to the cipher. The algorithm uses the key to make data incomprehensible to all but the sender and intended receiver. Secret-key cryptography uses the same secret key to encrypt and decrypt a message. One of the most commonly used symmetric encryption algorithms is DES. The new standard is called AES. Rijndael was chosen as the AES candidate. Public-key cryptography was designed to solve the problem of exchanging keys securely. Public-key cryptography is asymmetric and uses two inversely related keys: a public key and a private key. The most common key agreement protocol is a digital envelope. With a digital envelope, the message is encrypted using a secret key, and the secret key is encrypted using public-key encryption.

Digital signatures, the electronic equivalent of written signatures, were developed to be used in public-key cryptography to solve the problems of authentication and integrity. A digital signature authenticates the sender's identity, and, like a written signature, is difficult to forge. Timestamping, which binds a time and date to a digital document, can help solve the problem of non-repudiation. Public Key Infrastructure (PKI) integrates public-key cryptography with digital certificates and certificate authorities to authenticate parties in a transaction. A digital certificate is a digital document used to identify a user public key that is issued by a certificate authority. Trying to decrypt ciphertext without knowledge of the decryption key is known as cryptanalysis.

SSL is primarily used to secure point-to-point connections—transmissions of data from one computer to another. Virtual Private Networks (VPNs) use the Internet infrastructure that is already in place. VPNs provide the same services as private networks but use a different technique for connecting devices. IPSec uses public-key and symmetric key cryptography to ensure user authentication, data integrity and confidentiality. IPSec enables the secure connection of an entire VPN.

A denial-of-service attack occurs when a network's resources are taken up by an unauthorized individual, leaving the network unavailable for legitimate users. Viruses are computer programs that attach to, or overwrite other programs to replicate themselves. Viruses can corrupt files or even wipe out a hard drive. Software exploitation by hackers can cause systems to crash or, more dangerously, allow arbitrary code to be run on a machine.

The goal of network security is to allow authorized users access to information and services, while preventing unauthorized users from gaining access to, and possibly corrupting, the network. A basic tool in network security is the firewall. The purpose of a firewall is to protect a local area network (LAN) from intruders outside the network. Air Gap technology secures a business' data from external traffic accessing the internal network. Kerberos authenticates users in a network and maintains the integrity and privacy of network communications. Intrusion-detection systems monitor networks and alert administrators to unauthorized access of applications.

Biometrics uses unique personal information, such as fingerprints, eyeball iris scans or face scans, to identify a user and eliminate the need for passwords. Steganography is the practice of hiding information within other information. Digital watermarking could have a substantial impact on e-commerce. Using digital watermarks, music publishers can make indistinguishable changes to a part of a song at a frequency that is not audible to humans, to show that the song was, in fact, copied.

11.16 Internet and Web Resources

Security Resource Sites

www.securitysearch.com
This is a comprehensive resource for computer security, with thousands of links to products, security companies, tools and more. The site also offers a free weekly newsletter with information about vulnerabilities.

www.esecurityonline.com
This site is a great resource for information on online security. The site has links to news, tools, events, training and other valuable security information and resources.

theory.lcs.mit.edu/~rivest/crypto-security.html
The *Ronald L. Rivest: Cryptography and Security* site has an extensive list of links to security resources, including newsgroups, government agencies, FAQs, tutorials and more.

www.w3.org/Security/Overview.html
The *W3C Security Resources* site has FAQs, information about W3C security and e-commerce initiatives and links to other security related Web sites.

web.mit.edu/network/ietf/sa
The Internet Engineering Task Force (IETF), which is an organization concerned with the architecture of the Internet, has working groups dedicated to Internet Security. Visit the *IETF Security Area* to learn about the working groups, join the mailing list or read the latest drafts of the IETF's work.

dir.yahoo.com/Computers_and_Internet/Security_and_Encryption
The *Yahoo Security and Encryption* page is a great resource for security and encryption Web sites.

www.counterpane.com/hotlist.html
The Counterpane Internet Security, Inc., site includes links to downloads, source code, FAQs, tutorials, alert groups, news and more.

www.rsasecurity.com/rsalabs/faq
This site is an excellent set of FAQs about cryptography from RSA Laboratories, one of the leading makers of public key cryptosystems.

www.nsi.org/compsec.html
Visit the National Security Institute's *Security Resource Net* for the latest security alerts, government standards, and legislation, as well as security FAQs links and other helpful resources.

www.itaa.org/infosec
The Information Technology Association of America (ITAA) *InfoSec* site has information about the latest U.S. government legislation related to information security.

staff.washington.edu/dittrich/misc/ddos
The *Distributed Denial of Service Attacks* site has links to news articles, tools, advisory organizations and even a section on security humor.

www.infoworld.com/cgi-bin/displayNew.pl?/security/links/
security_corner.htm
The Security Watch site on **Infoword.com** has loads of links to security resources.

www.antionline.com
AntiOnline has security-related news and information, a tutorial titled "Fight-back! Against Hackers," information about hackers and an archive of hacked sites.

www.microsoft.com/security/default.asp
The Microsoft security site has links to downloads, security bulletins and tutorials.

www.grc.com
This site offers a service to test the security of your computer's Internet connection.

www.sans.org
Sans Institute presents information on security updates, along with new research and discoveries.

www.ntbugtraq.com
This site provides a list and description of various Windows NT Security Exploits/Bugs encountered by Windows NT users. One can download updated service applications.

www.securitystats.com
This computer security site provides statistics on viruses, web defacements and security spending.

Magazines, Newsletters and News sites

www.networkcomputing.com/consensus
The *Security Alert Consensus* is a free weekly newsletter with information about security threats, holes, solutions and more.

www.atstake.com/security_news
Visit this site for daily security news.

www.infosecuritymag.com
Information Security Magazine has the latest Web security news and vendor information.

www.ieee-security.org/cipher.html
Cipher is an electronic newsletter on security and privacy from the Institute of Electrical and Electronics Engineers (IEEE). You can view current and past issues online.

securityportal.com
The *Security Portal* has news and information about security, cryptography and the latest viruses.

www.scmagazine.com
SC Magazine has news, product reviews and a conference schedule for security events.

www.cnn.com/TECH/specials/hackers
Insurgency on the Internet from CNN Interactive has news on hacking, plus a gallery of hacked sites.

Government Sites for Computer Security

www.cit.nih.gov/security.html
This site has links to security organizations, resources and tutorials on PKI, SSL and other protocols.

cs-www.ncsl.nist.gov
The *Computer Security Resource Clearing House* is a resource for network administrators and others concerned with security. This site has links to incident-reporting centers, information about security standards, events, publications and other resources.

www.cdt.org/crypto
Visit the Center for Democracy and Technology for U. S. cryptography legislation and policy news.

www.epm.ornl.gov/~dunigan/security.html
This site has links organized by subject and include resources on digital signatures, PKI, smart cards, viruses, commercial providers, intrusion detection and several other topics.

www.alw.nih.gov/Security
The *Computer Security Information* page is an excellent resource, providing links to news, news-groups, organizations, software, FAQs and an extensive number of Web links.

www.fedcirc.gov
The Federal Computer Incident Response Capability deals with the security of government and civil-ian agencies. This site has information about incident statistics, advisories, tools, patches and more.

axion.physics.ubc.ca/pgp.html
This site has a list of freely available cryptosystems, discussions of each system and links to FAQs and tutorials.

www.ifccfbi.gov
The Internet Fraud Complaint Center, founded by the Justice Department and the FBI, fields reports of Internet fraud.

www.disa.mil/infosec/iaweb/default.html
The Defense Information Systems Agency's *Information Assurance* page includes links to sites on vulnerability warnings, virus information and incident-reporting instructions, and other helpful links.

www.nswc.navy.mil/ISSEC/
The objective of this site is to provide information on protecting your computer systems from security hazards. Contains a page on hoax versus real viruses.

cs-www.ncsl.nist.gov/
The Computer Security Resource Center provides services for vendors and end users. The site in-cludes information on security testing, management, technology, education and applications.

Advanced Encryption Standard (AES)

csrc.nist.gov/encryption/aes
The official site for the AES includes press releases and a discussion forum.

www.esat.kuleuven.ac.be/~rijmen/rijndael/
Visit this site for information about the Rijndael algorithm.

home.ecn.ab.ca/~jsavard/crypto/co040801.htm
This AES site includes an explanation of the algorithm with helpful diagrams and examples.

Internet Security Vendors

www.rsasecurity.com
RSA is one of the leaders in electronic security. Visit its site for more information about its current products and tools, which are used by companies worldwide.

www.checkpoint.com
Check Point™ Software Technologies is a leading provider of Internet security products and services.

www.opsec.com
The Open Platform for Security (OPSEC) has over 200 partners that develop security products and solutions using the OPSEC to allow for interoperability and increased security over a network.

www.baltimore.com
Baltimore Security is an e-commerce security solutions provider. Their UniCERT digital certificate product is used in PKI applications.

www.ncipher.com
nCipher is a vendor of hardware and software products, including an SSL accelerator that increases the speed of secure Web server transactions and a secure key management system.

www.antivirus.com
ScanMail® is an e-mail virus detection program for Microsoft Exchange.

www.zixmail.com
Zixmail™ is a secure e-mail product that allows you to encrypt and digitally sign your messages

web.mit.edu/network/pgp.html
Visit this site to download *Pretty Good Privacy*® freeware. PGP allows you to send messages and files securely.

www.certicom.com
Certicom provides security solutions for the wireless Internet.

www.raytheon.com
Raytheon Corporation's *SilentRunner* monitors network activity to find internal threats.

SSL

developer.netscape.com/tech/security/ssl/protocol.html
This Netscape page has a brief description of SSL, plus links to an SSL tutorial and FAQs.

www.netscape.com/security/index.html
The Netscape Security Center is an extensive resource for Internet and Web security. You will find news, tutorials, products and services on this site.

psych.psy.uq.oz.au/~ftp/Crypto
This FAQs page has an extensive list of questions and answers about SSL technology.

Public-key Cryptography

www.entrust.com
Entrust produces effective security software products using Public Key Infrastructure (PKI).

www.cse.dnd.ca
The Communication Security Establishment has a short tutorial on Public Key Infrastructure (PKI) that defines PKI, public-key cryptography and digital signatures.

www.magnet.state.ma.us/itd/legal/pki.htm
The Commonwealth of Massachusetts Information Technology page has loads of links to sites related to PKI that contain information about standards, vendors, trade groups and government organizations.

www.ftech.net/~monark/crypto/index.htm
The Beginner's Guide to Cryptography is an online tutorial and includes links to other sites on privacy and cryptography.

www.faqs.org/faqs/cryptography-faq
The *Cryptography FAQ* has an extensive list of questions and answers.

www.pkiforum.org
The PKI Forum promotes the use of PKI.

www.counterpane.com/pki-risks.html
Visit the Counterpane Internet Security, Inc.'s site to read the article "Ten Risks of PKI: What You're Not Being Told About Public Key Infrastructure."

Digital Signatures

www.ietf.org/html.charters/xmldsig-charter.html
The *XML Digital Signatures* site was created by a group working to develop digital signatures using XML. You can view the group's goals and drafts of their work.

www.elock.com
E-Lock Technologies is a vendor of digital-signature products used in Public Key Infrastructure. This site has an FAQs list covering cryptography, keys, certificates and signatures.

www.digsigtrust.com
The Digital Signature Trust Co. is a vendor of Digital Signature and Public Key Infrastructure products. It has a tutorial titled "Digital Signatures and Public Key Infrastructure (PKI) 101."

Digital Certificates

www.verisign.com
VeriSign creates digital IDs for individuals, small businesses and large corporations. Check out its Web site for product information, news and downloads.

www.thawte.com
Thawte Digital Certificate Services offers SSL, developer and personal certificates.

www.belsign.be
Belsign issues digital certificates in Europe. It is the European authority for digital certificates.

www.certco.com
Certco issues digital certificates to financial institutions.

www.openca.org
Set up your own CA using open-source software from The OpenCA Project.

Firewalls

www.interhack.net/pubs/fwfaq
This site provides an extensive list of FAQs on firewalls.

www.spirit.com/cgi-bin/report.pl
Visit this site to compare firewall software from a variety of vendors.

www.zeuros.co.uk/generic/resource/firewall
Zeuros is a complete resource for information about firewalls. You will find FAQs, books, articles, training and magazines on this site.

www.thegild.com/firewall
The *Firewall Product Overview* site has an extensive list of products, with links to each vendor's site.

www.watchguard.com
WatchGuard® Technologies provides security solutions for medium to large organizations.

Kerberos

www.nrl.navy.mil/CCS/people/kenh/kerberos-faq.html
This site is an extensive list of FAQs on Kerberos from the Naval Research Laboratory.

web.mit.edu/kerberos/www
Kerberos: The Network Authentication Protocol is a list of FAQs provided by MIT.

www.contrib.andrew.cmu.edu/~shadow/kerberos.html
The Kerberos Reference Page has links to several informational sites, technical sites and other helpful resources.

www.pdc.kth.se/kth-krb
Visit this site to download various Kerberos white papers and documentation.

Biometrics

www.iosoftware.com/products/integration/fiu500/index.htm
This site describes a security device that scans a user's fingerprint to verify identity.

www.identix.com
Identix specializes in fingerprinting systems for law enforcement, access control and network security. Using its fingerprint scanners, you can log on to your system, encrypt and decrypt files and lock applications.

www.keytronic.com
Key Tronic manufactures keyboards with fingerprint recognition systems.

IPSec and VPNs

www.checkpoint.com
Check Point™ offers combined firewall and VPN solutions. Visit their resource library for links to numerous white papers, industry groups, mailing lists and other security and VPN resources.

www.ietf.org/html.charters/ipsec-charter.html
The IPSec Working Group of the Internet Engineering Task Force (IETF) is a resource for technical information related to the IPSec protocol.

www.icsalabs.com/html/communities/ipsec/certification/certified_products/index.shtml
Visit this site for a list of certified IPSec products, plus links to an IPSec glossary and other related resources.

www.vpnc.org
The Virtual Private Network Consortium, which has VPN standards, white papers, definitions and archives. VPNC also offers compatibility testing with current VPN standards.

Steganography and Digital Watermarking

www.bluespike.com
Blue Spike's *Giovanni* watermarks help publishers of digital content protect their copyrighted material and track their content that is distributed electronically.

www.outguess.org
Outguess is a freely available steganographic tool.

`www.cl.cam.ac.uk/~fapp2/steganography/index.html`
The Information Hiding Homepage has technical information, news and links related to digital watermarking and steganography.

`www.demcom.com`
DemCom's *Steganos Security Suite* software allows you to encrypt and hide files within audio, video, text or HTML files.

Newsgroups

`news:comp.security.firewalls`

`news:comp.security.unix`

`news:comp.security.misc`

`news:comp.protocols.kerberos`

WORKS CITED

1.   B. Gates, "Bill Gates: Trustworthy Computing," 17 January 2002 `<www.wired.com/news/business/0,1367,49826,00.html>`.

2.   "RSA Laboratories' Frequently Asked Questions About Today's Cryptography, Version 4.1," 2000 `<www.rsasecurity.com/rsalabs/faq>`.

3.   `<www-math.cudenver.edu/~wcherowi/courses/m5410/m5410des.html>`.

4.   M. Dworkin, "Advanced Encryption Standard (AES) Fact Sheet," 5 March 2001.

5.   `<www.esat.kuleuven.ac.be/~rijmen/rijndael>`.

6.   `<www.rsasecurity.com/rsalabs/rsa_algorithm>`.

7.   `<www.pgpi.org/doc/overview>`.

8.   `<www.rsasecurity.com/rsalabs/faq>`.

9.   G. Hulme, "VeriSign Gave Microsoft Certificates to Imposter," *Information Week* 3 March 2001.

10.   C. Ellison and B. Schneier, "Ten Risks of PKI: What You're not Being Told about Public Key Infrastructure," *Computer Security Journal* 2000.

11.   "What's So Smart About Smart Cards?" *Smart Card Forum*.

12.   S. Abbot, "The Debate for Secure E-Commerce," *Performance Computing* February 1999: 37–42.

13.   T. Wilson, "E-Biz Bucks Lost Under the SSL Train," *Internet Week* 24 May 1999: 1, 3.

14.   H. Gilbert, "Introduction to TCP/IP," 2 February 1995 `<www.yale.edu/pclt/COMM/TCPIP.HTM>`.

15.   RSA Laboratories, "Security Protocols Overview," 1999 `<www.rsasecurity.com/standards/protocols>`.

16.   M. Bull, "Ensuring End-to-End Security with SSL," *Network World* 15 May 2000: 63.

17.   `<www.cisco.com/warp/public/44/solutions/network/vpn.shtml>`.

18.   S. Burnett and S. Paine, *RSA Security's Official Guide to Cryptography* (Berkeley: Osborne/McGraw-Hill, 2001) 210.

19.   D. Naik, *Internet Standards and Protocols* Microsoft Press 1998: 79–80.

20.   M. Grayson, "End the PDA Security Dilemma," *Communication News* February 2001: 38–40.

21. T. Wilson, "VPNs Don't Fly Outside Firewalls," *Internet Week* 28 May 2001.

22. S. Gaudin, "The Enemy Within," *Network World* 8 May 2000: 122–126.

23. D. Deckmyn, "Companies Push New Approaches to Authentication," *Computerworld* 15 May 2000: 6.

24. "Centralized Authentication," **<www.keyware.com>**.

25. J. Vijayan, "Biometrics Meet Wireless Internet," *Computerworld* 17 July 2000: 14.

26. F. Trickey, "Secure Single Sign-On: Fantasy or Reality," *CSI* **<www.gocsi.com>**.

27. L. Musthaler, "The Holy Grail of Single Sign-On," *Network World* 28 January 2002: 47.

28. "Securing B2B," *Global Technology Business* July 2000: 50–51.

29. T. Bridis, "U.S. Archive of Hacker Attacks To Close Because It Is Too Busy," *The Wall Street Journal* 24 May 2001: B10.

30. R. Marshland, "Hidden Cost of Technology," *Financial Times* 2 June 2000: 5.

31. F. Avolio, "Best Practices in Network Security," *Network Computing* 20 March 2000: 60–72.

32. R. Marshland, 5.

33. T. Spangler, "Home Is Where the Hack Is," *Inter@ctive Week* 10 April 2000: 28–34.

34. "Air Gap Technology," *Whale Communications* **<www.whale-com.com>**.

35. O. Azim and P. Kolwalkar, "Network Intrusion Monitoring," *Advisor.com/Security* March/April 2001: 16–19.

36. "OCTAVE Information Security Risk Evaluation," 30 January 2001 **<www.cert.org/ octave/methodintro.html>**.

37. S. Katzenbeisser and F. Petitcolas, *Information Hiding: Techniques for Steganography and Digital Watermarking* (Norwood: Artech House, Inc., 2000) 1–2.

12

Web Services Security

Objectives

- To explain how traditional security methods can protect Web services transmissions.
- To discuss Web services security standards, including Security Assertion Markup Language (SAML) and XML Signature.
- To introduce XML Key Management Specification (XKMS) and XML Encryption.
- To explore emerging Web services standards, including WS-Security.
- To discuss how Web services affect network security.

Outline

12.1 Introduction

According to a Hurwitz Group study, security is the biggest obstacle to enterprise Web services adoption.[1] Web services move transactions beyond firewalls and enable outside entities to invoke applications, potentially giving outsiders access to sensitive information. As a result, Web services present new security challenges. Although existing security standards protect data as it travels over the Internet, Web services require additional measures to secure data.[2]

In Chapter 11, Computer and Internet Security, we provided a general introduction to computer and network security. This chapter builds on the foundation established in the previous chapter by focusing on Web services-specific security issues. We explore developing standards for Web services security, including Security Assertion Markup Language (SAML), XML Key Management Specification (XKMS), XML Signature and XML Encryption. We also describes how Web services affect network security and security policies.

Effective Web services security allows clients to access appropriate services while keeping sensitive information confidential. To access a secured Web service, users must provide some form of authentication, such as a login name combined with a password or digital certificate. Smart cards and biometrics provide stronger authentication. However, even when users are authenticated, login names, passwords and transmissions can be compromised if communications are not encrypted. Web services require end-to-end security for transactions that span multiple computers.

Interoperability is fundamental to Web services security, because transmissions often occur across multiple platforms and must be secured at all times. Software vendors are realizing the need for interoperable security and are cooperating to develop appropriate security standards. For example, the Web services security panel at *InfoWorld*'s *Next-Generation Web Services Conference* included representatives from Borland (**www.borland.com**), McAfee (**www.mcafee.com**) and SmartPipes (**www.smartpipes.com**). Software vendors and consortia—including the Liberty Alliance (**www.projectliberty.org**), Oblix (**www.oblix.com**) and Netegrity (**www.netegrity.com**)—are developing solutions to strengthen user authentication and to promote interoperability among Web services platforms.

Well-defined and well-documented security policies, as well as proper implementation, administration and maintenance, are crucial to any security infrastructure.[3] Thus far, organizations have been responsible for creating their own security policies, resulting in disparate security policies across organizations. The emergence of Web services is forcing industry to develop security-policy standards so that organizations can communicate effectively without compromising their security policies.[4]

Web services introduce more security and privacy concerns than previous technologies did. Standards used to implement Web services—such as XML, WSDL, UDDI and SOAP—do not directly address authorization issues such as access control and user-privilege rights.[5] The fundamental security requirements discussed in the previous chapter— privacy, integrity, authentication, authorization and non-repudiation—are essential in Web services transactions. To address Web services-specific security issues, software vendors and vendor consortia are developing new security standards. For example, SAML addresses Permissions Management Infrastructure (PMI)-related security concerns. XKMS establishes a specification for registering and distributing encryption keys for Public Key Infrastructure (PKI). XML Encryption protects data during transmissions. *XML Signature* adds authentication to files through various signature algorithms. The strong security provided by these technologies is crucial as Web services are implemented in business-critical and mission-critical systems.

12.2 Basic Security for Transmissions over HTTP

This section discusses the basic authentication and security features described in the HTTP specification (**www.w3.org/Protocols**). HTTP enables Web servers to authenticate users before allowing access to resources. A Web server might check a user's credentials (e.g., username and password) against a database before granting or denying access. HTTP security employs secret-key cryptography, message digests and other technologies discussed in the previous chapter. However, the methods outlined in the HTTP specification are weak (for example, HTTP provides no process for encrypting the body of a message). For stronger security, HTTP security should be used with other security technologies, such as SSL and Kerberos.

In *challenge-response authentication* (the method used in HTTP), users must provide specific authentication information to verify their identities. When an unauthenticated user attempts to view a protected resource over an HTTP connection, the server returns a **401 Unauthorized** response. The user must provide the server with a username and a password to access the resource. This username and password are established previously via some other method—such as an e-mail message. If the user's credentials are unacceptable, the server returns a **403 Forbidden** response and denies access to the resource. When used alone, challenge-response authentication (as defined in the HTTP specification) is a relatively weak security solution, because passwords and credentials are transmitted in plain-text. However, encryption and transport-layer security can be used with the protocol to provide stronger security.[6]

Digest authentication, part of the HTTP 1.1 specification, is a protocol in which a user's credentials are submitted to the server as a *checksum* (i.e., a message digest—discussed in Section 11.8, Digital Signatures). A message digest is a unique value derived from the message content. Checksums for digest authentication are generated using a username, password, the requested URI, the HTTP method and a unique value (known as a *nonce value*) generated by the server for each transmission. Digest authentication protects usernames and passwords from eavesdropping attackers, because credentials are not transmitted plain-text. MD5, the default algorithm used to create the checksum, generates a 128-bit message digest on the basis of the given input. Like message digests used in digital signatures, the generated checksums are unique to the input; therefore, no two are the same.[7] Although digest authentication is a step above basic authentication, this design does not encrypt the message content, which means that the content is vulnerable to interception. Also, both the server and the client must support digest authentication for authentication to take place. The HTTP 1.1 specification encourages using digest authentication with other authentication methods, such as public keys and Kerberos.[8]

A server also can restrict access on the basis of an IP address, password or public key. A server can disallow access to all or portions of a site for users with a certain IP address or from a specific *IP subnet* (e.g., a set of similar IP addresses, such as **123.123.45.23** and **123.123.67.89**). However, this method is vulnerable to IP spoofing (see Section 11.10.2, IPSec and Virtual Private Networks) and should be used in combination with other authorization techniques.

Password authentication also raises several concerns. Users often generate passwords using personal information (e.g., birthdays, pets' names, etc.), and crackers can compromise such passwords easily. Also, simple password authentication does not encrypt message content, so data can be compromised if a cracker intercepts transmissions. Public-key cryptography and other security methods should be used with basic HTTP security to ensure transmission security.

12.3 Web Services and Secure Sockets Layer (SSL)

Many of the Web services security technologies discussed in this chapter are still under development or are just being introduced to the market (see the WS-Security: A New Standard Protecting Web Services feature). Therefore, Web services must rely on established security standards until Web services-specific technologies mature.[9]

Secure Sockets Layer (SSL) is considered the next step beyond basic security for Web services (for introductory information on SSL, see Section 11.10.1, Secure Sockets Layer). The SSL protocol secures the channel through which data flows between a client and server and enables authentication of both parties. However, there are several problems with using SSL to secure Web services transmissions. SSL employs user credentials and certificates, which are sometimes too large to transmit efficiently between computers. This affects transaction success and disables the ability to record who initiated each step of a transaction.[10] SSL encryption calculations also use considerable processor power, which can slow down transmissions and significantly impede Web service performance. *SSL accelerators* are hardware devices or software programs that handle complex SSL-encryption calculations. Accelerators free server resources, improve performance and can be less expensive than setting up additional servers to handle SSL transactions.

In a transmission where a user provides a credit-card number to a business over an SSL connection, SSL authenticates both parties and guarantees the integrity of the data. However, in Web services interactions, information commonly passes through a third party before reaching its destination. If a user's information passes through another computer before reaching the final recipient, SSL cannot guarantee that the original data was not tampered with during the transmission, because SSL connects only two computers at a time. SSL protects data transmission, but does not provide end-to-end security.

HTTPS secures communications by sending HTTP requests and responses over an SSL connection. HTTPS connections generally take place over port 443, rather than the standard HTTP port 80. A majority of secure online transactions use HTTPS to provide end-to-end security between a client and server or consumer and vendor.

12.4 XML Signature and XML Encryption

XML-based applications raise significant security concerns, in part because XML documents are encoded in plain-text, rather than in a binary form. For example, externally referenced DTDs and stylesheets can be modified to omit, mangle or otherwise alter information. Even worse, these documents can be altered to leave large security holes, enabling anyone to access information. Digital signatures (discussed in Section 11.8, Digital Signatures) solve this problem by verifying document integrity.

WS-Security: A New Standard Protecting Web Services

In an attempt to improve Web services security, Microsoft, IBM and VeriSign have collaborated to create a new Web services security standard. The new specification, *WS-Security*, encrypts information and ensures the confidentiality of Web services transmissions.

WS-Security is the first of six Web services security specifications to be created by IBM and Microsoft. The specification is designed to secure SOAP-message transmissions.[11] Like many Web services security specifications, WS-Security is flexible and provides various security methods—including Kerberos, PKI and SSL. The specification also outlines how to use WS-Security with XML Signature and XML Encryption. According to Microsoft's director of Web services marketing, the proposed security standard will be compatible with any online authentication system, including Microsoft Passport and the Liberty Alliance Project's forthcoming single sign-on system.[12] We discuss Passport in Chapter 3, Web Services Business Models; the Liberty Alliance Project is covered in Chapter 8, Web Services Platforms, Vendors and Strategies.

Six additional security specifications will be added to WS-Security in 2002–2003: WS-Policy, WS-Trust, WS-Privacy, WS-Secure Conversation, WS-Federation and WS-Authorization.[13] *WS-Policy* will define how to express a security policy's capabilities and limitations. XACML, a developing standard for representing security policies in XML, should comply with the WS-Policy standard.

WS-Trust will describe a model for establishing direct or third-party trust relationships. Trust relationships are necessary for issuing certificates used in XML Signature, Public Key Infrastructure (PKI) and the XML Key Management Specification (XKMS).

WS-Security: A New Standard Protecting Web Services (Cont.)

WS-Privacy will define how Web services express and carry out privacy practices. The Platform for Privacy Preferences (P3P) project is a W3C initiative designed to protect user privacy. Microsoft requires sites that use its Passport service to comply with P3P, and P3P will likely influence the WS-Privacy standard.

WS-Secure Conversation will describe how to manage message exchanges—including authenticating participants and establishing and deriving session keys (we discuss session keys in Chapter 11, Computer and Internet Security). *WS-Federation* will define how to manage trust relationships used in SAML, single sign-on and other B2B and authentication systems. Finally, *WS-Authorization* will define the management of authorization data and security policies.[14] To access the WS-Security specification, visit `www-106.ibm.com/developerworks/webservices/library/ws-secure`. Specifications for other WS-Security standards will be available online once the specifications are completed.

XML Trust Center—a vendor-neutral Web services security group sponsored by Verisign—created the Trust Services Integration Kit for building secure Web services using the WS-Security standard. To obtain additional information or to download this toolkit, visit `www.xmltrustcenter.org`.

The W3C's *XML Signature* specification defines an XML-based standard for representing digital signatures. XML Signature was developed by the *XML Signature Working Group*, the first formal joint project between the W3C and the Internet Engineering Task Force (IETF). The specification provides authentication, message integrity and nonrepudiation.[15] The algorithms used in the specification include the *Digital Signature Standard* (*DSS*) public-key algorithm and the *Secure Hash* (*SHA-1*) authentication algorithm (see Chapter 11, Computer and Internet Security). Developers can extend XML Signature to support their own algorithms and security models. An XML signature can sign any type of file, not just XML documents. The signed data can reside either inside or outside the XML document that contains the signature. The data object is cryptographically signed and used in generating a message digest. A *Uniform Resource Identifier* (*URI*) links the signature to the signed data object. XML Signature serves as the foundation for XKMS, SAML and other XML technologies that rely on authentication via digital signatures.[16]

As we explained in Chapter 11, Computer and Internet Security, different inputs to a hashing function produce different outputs. Hash functions verify data integrity, because it is impossible to determine the content of a message from the hash value. However, it is possible for two XML documents to contain the same data, yet differ in the way they are structured.[17] Such structure changes might break the signature between signer and verifier, even if the signed data has not changed. To prevent such problems, XML Signature puts data in *canonical form* before it is signed. If two documents have the same canonical form, they are logically equivalent. Small differences between documents—such as comments and spaces that have no impact on the meaning of an XML document—create different hash values. For this reason, XML Signature computes the hash value using the canonical form of an XML document. The *Canonical XML Specification* provides an algorithm that generates the canonical form of a document by transforming the document into a context as it would be interpreted by an application—this means that logically equivalent documents will produce the same message digest, regardless of structure.

Due to the complexity of online transactions, documents might require signatures from multiple parties. For example, when a customer purchases a book online using a credit card, an XML document containing the customer's name, address, credit-card information and order information is generated and submitted to the book seller and credit-card company (Fig. 12.1). Element **Personal** (lines 7–23) contains information, such as the credit-card number (line 18) and expiration date (line 20) in element **CreditCard** (lines 17–21) and the address information in element **Address** (lines 10–15), that must be protected as it is transmitted over the Internet.

A customer uses a signature to authenticate identity, then submits the information to the seller. The seller checks the integrity of the customer's signature and signs the document before submitting it to the credit-card company. The credit-card company receives signatures that verify the authenticity of the customer and the seller. XML Signature protects buyers against unauthorized purchases with their credit cards, increases the likelihood that retailers receive payments and prevents unauthorized businesses from using credit-card companies' services.

XML Signature provides three types of signatures. An *enveloping signature* contains the signed data as part of the signature. An *enveloped signature* resides within the data to be signed. A *detached signature* is stored separately from the signed data, but contains a reference to the signed data. If the encrypted data is not part of an XML document, a new XML document is created with **EncryptedData** as the root element. The markup in Fig. 12.2 is an example of a detached signature on the **Personal** element in the XML document **Fig12_1.xml** (Fig. 12.1).

```
1   <?xml version="1.0" encoding="UTF-8"?>
2   <!-- Fig. 12.1: Fig12_1.xml                          -->
3   <!-- XML that marks up an online bookstore purchase -->
4
5   <Purchase xmlns="http://examplebookstore.com/purchase">
6      <OrderNumber>99778866</OrderNumber>
7      <Personal>
8         <Name>Joe Smith</Name>
9
10        <Address>
11           <Street>123 Example Street</Street>
12           <City>Maynard</City>
13           <State>MA</State>
14           <Zip>01754</Zip>
15        </Address>
16
17        <CreditCard>
18           <Number>1234123412341234</Number>
19
20           <Expiration>12/04</Expiration>
21        </CreditCard>
```

Fig. 12.1   XML that marks up an online bookstore purchase. (Part 1 of 2.)

```
22
23        </Personal>
24
25        <ItemNumber quantity="1">000459</ItemNumber>
26    </Purchase>
```

Fig. 12.1   XML that marks up an online bookstore purchase. (Part 2 of 2.)

```
1    <?xml version="1.0" encoding="UTF-8"?>
2    <!-- Fig. 12.2: Fig12_2.xml                                -->
3    <!-- Detached XML Signature referencing an external element -->
4
5    <Signature Id="Purchase99778866"
6        xmlns="http://www.w3.org/TR/xmldsig-core">
7
8        <SignedInfo>
9
10           <CanonicalizationMethod Algorithm=
11               "http://www.w3.org/TR/2001/REC-xml-c14n-20010315"/>
12
13           <SignatureMethod Algorithm=
14             "http://www.w3.org/TR/2002/REC-xmldsig-core-20020212#sha1"/>
15
16           <Reference URI=
17               "http://www.example.com/purchase/Fig12_1.xml#Personal">
18
19              <Transforms>
20                 <Transform Algorithm=
21                     "http://www.w3.org/TR/2001/REC-xml-c14n- 20010315"/>
22              </Transforms>
23
24              <DigestMethod Algorithm=
25               "http://www.w3.org/TR/2002/REC-xmldsig-core-20020212#sha1"/>
26
27              <DigestValue>
28              UI12389UUJFA09812JIA9123M10298REIU3JAIDHAWUYE982HA
29              </DigestValue>
30
31           </Reference>
32        </SignedInfo>
33
34        <SignatureValue>
35        FH5K17Z0IHTFR3N08Y1K5U239UFDKDN617ISDJAOWUEHAJR1UR
36        </SignatureValue>
37
38        <KeyInfo>
39           <KeyValue>
40              <X509Data>
41
```

Fig. 12.2   Detached XML Signature referencing an element in an external XML
document. (Part 1 of 2.)

```
42              <X509SubjectName>
43                  CN=Joe Smith, STREET=123 Example Street,
44                  L=Maynard, ST=MA, C=US
45              </X509SubjectName>
46
47              <X509Certificate>
48                  MIICWDCCAgICAQAwDQYJKoZIhvcNAQEEBQAwgbYxCzAJBgNVBAY
49                  TAlpBMRUwEwYDVQQIEwxXZXN0ZXJuIENhcGUxEjAQBgNVBAcTCUN
50                  hcGUgVG93bjEdMBsGA1UEChMUVGhhd3RlIENvbnN1bHRpbmcgY2M
51                  xHzAdBgNVBAsTFkNlcnRpZmljYXRpb24gU2VydmljZXMxFzAVBgN
52                  NVBa87421hjas2e8AYuidhuiaw471298IUAYISUYhu289yasiuy2
53                  JOiwejqwiojWEHuihqwjasndui12897ruhfjAOIQIEOU29081ifU
54                  7IUdhasun2IYEueh12e1iuYWAEAOOOidehqwunJSDNiuy12874js
55                  HH13i87ue1jhjaIUHAuhdnjweoAIJo2iJIAjhXHZBMoKkadsh813
56                  0YAuh893ieHAUhaodiuAIIA9uew8ACLetiX9usdjhds8wyeh1iu8
57                  9821yuAUSHiuhaapAMJXNBZZoiasdzkj02194yw8dyauh1o731i2
58                  D9324DIoetiksadj2q39oi14oiuOSAIDUOI2oismd6o7slau45==
59              </X509Certificate>
60
61          </X509Data>
62        </KeyValue>
63      </KeyInfo>
64    </Signature>
```

Fig. 12.2   Detached XML Signature referencing an element in an external XML document. (Part 2 of 2.)

The **Signature Id** attribute on line 5 identifies the signature. Element **Signed-Info** (lines 8–32) contains information about the signature, including references to the algorithms used and the location of the signed data in the **Reference URI** attribute (lines 16–17). This signature uses the W3C's Canonical XML Version 1.0 Recommendation and the SHA-1 hashing algorithm. To sign an element in an XML document, the reference Uniform Resource Identifier (URI) contains the location of the document, followed by **#** and the name of the element. In our example, **#Personal** (line 17) references and signs the **Personal** element in the XML document. Lines 27–29 contain element **DigestValue**, which contains the message digest generated by the algorithm specified in the **DigestMethod**'s **Algorithm** attribute (lines 24–25). To verify that an XML digital signature is legitimate, the recipient runs the public version of the hashing algorithm on the received file and compares the result with the value in **DigestValue**. If the two values are not equivalent, then the digest might have been generated by a different file, or someone might have tampered with the data.[18] Element **SignatureValue** (lines 34–36) contains the message digest generated by the signature algorithm specified on lines 13–14 in the **SignatureMethod**'s **Algorithm** attribute. The optional **KeyInfo** element (lines 38–63) provides the key or certificate that the signature algorithm uses—in this case, an X.509 Digital Certificate (lines 48–58). Element **X509SubjectName** on lines 42–45 contains information about the key holder. XML Signature supports DSA Signatures, RSA Signatures and symmetric-key authentication codes (see Chapter 11, Computer and Internet Security).[19]

The signature verifies a sender's identity and the data's integrity, but encryption is necessary to prevent the signed data from being read en route. *XML Encryption* handles the encryption and decryption of XML documents that are secured with XML Signature. XML Encryption can protect any form of data, including an XML element and its contents.[20]

XML Encryption allows different elements of an XML document to be encrypted separately (Fig. 12.3).[21] The data to be encrypted is replaced by element **EncryptedData** in the XML document (lines 8–19). Element **CipherData** (lines 11–17) contains information about the ciphertext that is generated when the file is encrypted. The ciphertext is represented in *base-64 encoding*, which uses 64 characters (**a–z**, **A–Z**, **0–9** and the characters **/** and **+**) to represent binary data.[22] In enveloping and enveloped signatures, **CipherValue** (lines 13–15) stores the ciphertext inside the **CipherData** element. In a detached signature, **CipherReference** contains a URL that references the location of the ciphertext.[23]

Using the example of the online book seller, when a user makes a purchase, the bookstore generates an XML document containing the information submitted by the consumer (Fig. 12.1). To send this document to the seller and ensure that the personal information is protected, certain elements of the document must be encrypted.

The document in Fig. 12.3 contains the encrypted personal fields, leaving only the item and order numbers visible. Any unauthorized users attempting to view this document without the designated decryption key can access only the **ItemNumber** and **OrderNumber** of the purchase.

In other cases, the bookstore might want to encrypt only the customer's credit-card information. For example, imagine that the bookstore forwards customers' personal data to a marketing database, but does not want to disclose credit-card data contained in element **CreditCard** (Fig. 12.1, lines 17–21). In Fig. 12.4, element **CreditCard** is replaced by **EncryptedData** (lines 18–28).

```
1   <?xml version="1.0" encoding="UTF-8"?>
2   <!-- Fig. 12.3: Fig12_3.xml                        -->
3   <!-- XML file with the Personal element encrypted -->
4
5   <Purchase xmlns="http://examplebookstore.com/purchase">
6      <OrderNumber>99778866</OrderNumber>
7
8      <EncryptedData xmlns="http://www.w3.org/TR/xmlenc-core"
9         Type="http://www.w3.org/TR/xmlenc-core#Element">
10
11        <CipherData>
12
13           <CipherValue>
14              H3OI2J2MOII12J4NSAKJH2UIAJWI098128321JI78293M92310CDA9
15           </CipherValue>
16
17        </CipherData>
18
19     </EncryptedData>
20
21     <ItemNumber quantity="1">000459</ItemNumber>
22  </Purchase>
```

Fig. 12.3 XML document with the **Personal** element encrypted.

```
1    <?xml version="1.0" encoding="UTF-8"?>
2    <!-- Fig. 12.4: Fig12_4.xml                              -->
3    <!-- XML document with the CreditCard element encrypted -->
4
5    <Purchase xmlns="http://examplebookstore.com/purchase">
6        <OrderNumber>99778866</OrderNumber>
7
8        <Personal>
9            <Name>Joe Smith</Name>
10
11           <Address>
12               <Street>123 Example Street</Street>
13               <City>Maynard</City>
14               <State>MA</State>
15               <Zip>01754</Zip>
16           </Address>
17
18           <EncryptedData xmlns="http://www.w3.org/TR/xmlenc-core"
19               Type="http://www.w3.org/TR/xmlenc-core#Content">
20               <CipherData>
21
22                   <CipherValue>
23                     92UIO2JFSDIOJL051N6HU872IAODMYJ71253LF819EYIYFGT87231
24                   </CipherValue>
25
26               </CipherData>
27
28           </EncryptedData>
29
30       </Personal>
31
32       <ItemNumber quantity="1">000459</ItemNumber>
33   </Purchase>
```

Fig. 12.4 XML document with the **CreditCard** element encrypted.

IBM's XML Security Suite implements XML Signature and XML Encryption. It is designed specifically for B2B transactions and provides support for digital signatures, encryption, access control, public-key cryptography and hash authentication. The XML Security Suite can be downloaded at **www.alphaworks.ibm.com/aw.nsf/ techs/xmlsecuritysuite**.

12.5 XML Key Management Specification (XKMS)

The *XML Key Management Specification (XKMS)* is a specification for registering and distributing encryption keys for Public Key Infrastructure (PKI) in Web services. XKMS was developed by Microsoft, VeriSign and webMethods, but now is a W3C initiative. Current communications and transactions using PKI are problematic, because no Web services PKI standards exist. Proprietary PKI solutions are often expensive, difficult to implement and not interoperable with other businesses' PKI products. XKMS revolutionizes PKI by establishing a platform-independent set of standards that places portions of the PKI workload on the server side, thus freeing application resources for other processes.[24] XKMS works with proprietary PKI solutions to integrate encryption, digital signatures (including revocation and processing of certificates) and authentication. XKMS simplifies the steps necessary to implement PKI (particularly key management), providing an easy and user-friendly method for secure transactions.

XKMS was designed for use with XML Signature and XML Encryption, but also will be compatible with future security technologies. XML Signature and XML Encryption provide a high level of security for XML documents, but do not address *trust management* (the handling of public and private keys), which is essential to successful PKI. XKMS provides the necessary trust management.[25] XKMS is easy to implement, which makes it an ideal solution for mobile PKI (i.e., PKI over wireless networks).

XKMS is comprised of two specifications: the *XML Key Information Service Specification (X-KISS)* and the *XML Key Registration Service Specification (X-KRSS)*. X-KISS is the set of protocols that processes key information (located in an XML signature's **Key-Info** element) associated with XML encrypted data, digital signatures and other aspects of public-key cryptography. X-KISS locates public keys and binds user information to the keys. The XML Signature specification defines **KeyInfo** as an optional element, so it might not contain enough information to ensure trust. The application that receives a signed file can use X-KISS to forward the **KeyInfo** data to an applicable *trust service*—a trusted party that validates signatures and generates and manages key pairs—for parsing and processing. This process delegates certificate processing to a trust-service server and frees the application from complex logic processing.

X-KRSS is the set of certificate-management protocols that addresses the life of a digital certificate—from registration to revocation and recovery. During registration of a certificate, the user registering the key pair submits the public key to a trusted registration server through a digitally signed request. The registration request also can contain name and attribute information. The user shows proof of ownership of the private key by signing the registration request with the private key and providing the server with the public key for decryption.

Figure 12.5 shows a register request sent to an X-KRSS server. Element **Register** (lines 5–113) of an X-KRSS request contains all of the information relevant to the certificate and owner. Element **Status** (line 7) specifies the current stage of the certificate (i.e., registration, recovery and revocation). When registering a digital certificate, character data in **Status** is **Valid**. Element **KeyID** (line 9) contains a name or location that uniquely identifies the key. In this example, **mailto:joesmith@example.com** specifies that the key is bound to the user **joesmith** at **example.com**. As in XML Signature, element **KeyInfo** (lines 11–38) contains information about the key. Element **PassPhrase** (lines 40–42) contains a generated digest of the user's password. If a user's private key is compromised, the user can revoke the key by submitting the password to the server—which generates a hash value based on the submitted password and compares it to the original digested password. Element **AuthInfo** (lines 46–106) contains elements that authenticate the registration request. Digital signatures show proof of key possession (in **ProofOf-Possession**, lines 48–74) and authenticate the keybinding request (in **KeyBinding-Auth**, lines 76–104). The request specifies how the server should respond; in this case, the server returns a key name (line 109) and X.509 digital certificate (line 110).

If a user decides that the previously issued assertions about a certificate are no longer valid or that the private key has been compromised, the certificate can be revoked. If **Status** contains the character data **Invalid**, the server revokes the information it previously held about the certificate. Users also can request that the server recover the assertions about any previously registered certificates. In this case, **Status** contains **Indeterminate**, and the registration server replies to the request with a confirmation response in XML. The server response states whether the registration is accepted (**Accepted**), rejected (**NotFound**) or pending (**Pending**).[26] Once a certificate is registered successfully, it is usable by X-KISS and other trust services.

```
1   <?xml version="1.0" encoding="UTF-8"?>
2   <!-- Fig. 12.5: Fig12_5.xml                        -->
3   <!-- X-KRSS Registration Request for a key pair -->
4
5   <Register>
6      <Prototype Id="keybinding">
7         <Status>Valid</Status>
8
9         <KeyID>mailto:joesmith@example.com</KeyID>
10
11        <KeyInfo>
12           <KeyName>mailto:joesmith@example.com</KeyName>
13
14        <KeyValue>
15           <X509Data>
16
17              <X509SubjectName>
18                 CN=Joe Smith, STREET=123 Example Street,
19                 L=Maynard, ST=MA, C=US
20              </X509SubjectName>
21
22              <X509Certificate>
23                 CWDCCAgICAQAwDQYJKoZIhvcNAQEEBQAwgbYxCzAJBgNVBAY
24                 BMRUwEwYDVQQIEwxXZXN0ZXJuIENhcGUxEjAQBgNVBAcTCUN
25                 hgVG93bjEdMBsGA1UEChMUVGhhd3RlIENvbnN1bHRpbmcgY2M
26                 xHzgNVBAsTFkNlcnRpZmljYXRpb24gU2VydmljZXMxFzAVBgN
27                 NVBa87421hjas2e8AYuidhuiaw471298IUAYISUYhu289yasA
28                 JOiwejqwiojWEHuihqwjasndui12897ruhfjQIEOU29081ifU
29                 7IUdhasun2IYEueh12e1iuYWOOOidehqwunJSDNiuy12874js
30                 HH13i87ue1jhjaIUHAuhdnjweoAIJo2iJIAHZBMoKkadsh813
31                 0YAuh893ieHAUhaodiuAIuew8ACLetiX9usdjhds8wyeh1iu8
32                 9821yuAUSHiuhaapAMJXNBZZoiasdzkj02194yyauh1o731i2
33                 D9324DIoetiksadj2q39oi14oiuOSAIDUoismd6o7slau45==
34              </X509Certificate>
35
36           </X509Data>
37        </KeyValue>
38        </KeyInfo>
39
40        <PassPhrase>
41           Wio923482hUSHuda389OHIA04u3jMNBZhduiWIUYTIUWYoiH3748i=
42        </PassPhrase>
43
44     </Prototype>
45
```

Fig. 12.5 X-KRSS registration request for a key pair. (Part 1 of 3.)

```
46          <AuthInfo>
47             <AuthUserInfo>
48                <ProofOfPossession>
49                   <Signature xmlns="http://www.w3.org/TR/xmldsig-core">
50                      <SignedInfo>
51                         <CanonicalizationMethod Algorithm=
52                         "http://www.w3.org/TR/2001/REC-xml-c14n-20010315" />
53
54                         <SignatureMethod Algorithm=
55                  "http://www.w3.org/TR/2002/REC-xmldsig-core-20020212#sha1" />
56
57                         <Reference URI="#keybinding">
58                            <DigestMethod Algorithm=
59                  "http://www.w3.org/TR/2002/REC-xmldsig-core-20020212#sha1" />
60
61                            <DigestValue>
62                               8JiSOH32zISULqWerualYR1298Lsaeu24WHE79=
63                            </DigestValue>
64
65                         </Reference>
66
67                      </SignedInfo>
68
69                      <SignatureValue>
70                         P98395u04HUSIJS586HDWHa8y98OPHEu3oUIUSu324eh
71                      </SignatureValue>
72
73                   </Signature>
74                </ProofOfPossession>
75
76                <KeyBindingAuth>
77                   <Signature xmlns="http://www.w3.org/TR/xmldsig-core">
78
79                      <SignedInfo>
80                         <CanonicalizationMethod Algorithm=
81                         "http://www.w3.org/TR/2001/REC-xml-c14n-20010315" />
82
83                         <SignatureMethod Algorithm=
84                  "http://www.w3.org/TR/2002/REC-xmldsig-core-20020212#sha1" />
85
86                         <Reference URI="#keybinding">
87                            <DigestMethod Algorithm=
88                  "http://www.w3.org/TR/2002/REC-xmldsig-core-20020212#sha1" />
89
90                            <DigestValue>
91                               fHdnkj394jnKJXOSDJ451RUGP932A94IHFDIohr
92                               984IHiuZXBNMBDLiIOWEIUyfhas8943uihSdho=
93                            </DigestValue>
94
95                         </Reference>
96                      </SignedInfo>
97
```

Fig. 12.5 X-KRSS registration request for a key pair. (Part 2 of 3.)

```
98                    <SignatureValue>
99                        Bo39udIOSijeAZj1MXioisd9u23rKLJSDPASe3fU1232u
100                       Sk0291jfhjZSIO82uiouderiyq90UAES95yyhru398d=
101                   </SignatureValue>
102
103               </Signature>
104           </KeyBindingAuth>
105       </AuthUserInfo>
106   </AuthInfo>
107
108   <Respond>
109       <string>KeyName</string>
110       <string>X509Cert</string>
111   </Respond>
112
113 </Register>
```

Fig. 12.5 X-KRSS registration request for a key pair. (Part 3 of 3.)

Many companies have already realized the benefits of XKMS and are including the framework in upcoming products. For example, Microsoft is incorporating XKMS in its .NET platform. Vordel (**www.vordel.com**), a company specializing in Web services security, supports XKMS in TalkXML—a standards-based suite for securing data transmissions through digital certificates and PKI. Baltimore Technologies developed the *XML Key Management Specification Bulk Operation (X-BULK)*, an extension to XKMS that enables bulk issuance of digital certificates for smart cards and wireless cards.[27]

12.6 Security Assertion Markup Language (SAML)

The *Security Assertion Markup Language (SAML)* is an emerging standard for transferring authentication, authorization and permissions information over the Internet. The *OASIS Security Services Technical Committee (SSTC)* is developing SAML as a standard XML specification for B2B and B2C communications. SAML is a form of *Permissions Management Infrastructure (PMI)*, a system that uses a set of policies to handle access control and authorization for computing systems.[28] Traditionally, PMI implementation has relied on complex proprietary software, which made PMI prohibitively complex and expensive for many businesses. SAML has revolutionized PMI by establishing an open standard that is accessible to more companies. Security assertions in SAML are files containing authentication credentials and other information used to authorize users.[29]

The SAML protocol was developed by combining two competing XML security standards: Securant Technologies' *AuthXML* and Netegrity's *Security Services Markup Language (S2ML)*.[30] Because SAML is designed for use in interoperable applications, businesses can exchange information securely among groups of trusted partners without demanding any security-configuration modifications.[31] SAML is vendor-neutral and is compatible with many XML communication protocols, including BizTalk® (discussed in Chapter 9, .NET Web Services: A Conceptual Overview), SOAP and ebXML.[32]

SAML also provides a method for single sign-on authentication and authorization (discussed in Chapter 11, Computer and Internet Security).[33]

Single sign-on allows users to enter authentication information once to be authenticated across multiple domains. This technology saves time and relieves users from having to remember multiple usernames and passwords. Before SAML, most single sign-on products (including Microsoft Passport) were proprietary.[34] By contrast, interoperability among SAML-based applications can provide single sign-on across disparate sites and platforms. Netegrity developed the *JSAML Toolkit* for implementing SAML-based applications in Java. For more information on this product, visit **www.netegrity.com/products**.

When a user logs into a SAML-enabled application, permission information is stored in *assertions* (Fig. 12.6).[35] A SAML assertion contains information regarding when, how and for which resources a permission was granted. An assertion has fields for an assertion ID, the subject's name, the subject's security domain and the conditions for which an assertion is valid. An assertion also contains the time that it was issued, the issuer and any other necessary information.[36] Since assertions contain the results of successful authentication, they are only as secure as the authentication process.[37] A weak authentication method can compromise the SAML security.

The subject of an assertion can be a user or a program running on behalf of a user. When the assertion containing the subject's information is generated, the authentication authority creates a *SAML token* (a unique identifier containing authentication and authorization data) that allows access to applications that accept the token (such as trusted business partners' applications or other applications within the same company). When a user reaches a site that requires authentication, the token is submitted to a SAML-equipped authority application. This application is the *Policy Enforcement Point* (*PEP*) and is responsible for requesting and enforcing authorization decisions. The PEP sends a request for an authorization decision (Step 1) to a *Policy Decision Point* (*PDP*) that is responsible for making decisions on the basis of existing security policies. The policies that the PDP uses to make decisions (Step 2) are stored in a *Policy Information Point* (*PIP*). SAML accepts several policy formats, including policies created using the Extensible Access Control Markup Language (discussed in Section 12.9). After using relevant security policies to make an authorization decision, the PDP returns an *authorization decision assertion* (Step 3). If the assertion shows an acceptable level of authorization, an attribute assertion is attached to the user's SAML token, and the user can access the protected resources (Step 4).[38] If the assertion does not provide an acceptable level of authentication, the client is redirected to log in again (Step 5) before accessing the protected content (Step 6).

For example, clients looking to remodel their kitchens and find supplies online could visit **BobsAppliances.com**, a site that supports SAML and single sign-on (Fig. 12.6). The clients would log in at this site with the necessary credentials to make an online purchase. If **BobsAppliances.com** had established a trust relationship with **JoesFlooring.com**, Joe's site would be under the same security domain and accept the token from Bob's site. When users buy flooring tiles through Bob's site, they are redirected to Joe's online store. The PEP at **JoesFlooring.com** sends an authorization request and authentication assertions to the PDP. If the credentials in the assertions are accepted by the policies in the PIP, the PDP returns an assertion that allows the user to shop at Joe's site. The user would simply log in at Bob's site and, from that point, could shop at any of the sites that accept the token as acceptable authentication.

SAML also can be used for B2B communication between Bob's Appliances and Joe's Flooring. For example, **JoesFlooring.com** might want to keep its inventory up-to-

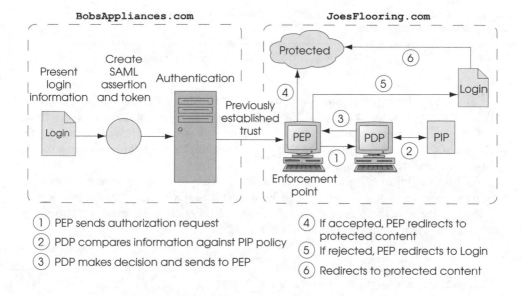

Fig. 12.6 Single sign-on example using SAML.

date with products that complement the appliances from Bob's site. To facilitate this B2B relationship, Joe would need to access Bob's database. Bob and Joe would determine an appropriate level of authentication—such as a secret password that they agree on beforehand or a certificate from a trusted third party—that would authorize access to the sales database. Assuming that the two companies agree on a secret password, the authentication assertion would resemble Fig. 12.7.

```xml
1   <?xml version="1.0" encoding="UTF-8"?>
2   <!-- Fig. 12.7: Fig12_7.xml           -->
3   <!-- Authentication assertion sample -->
4
5   <saml:Assertion MajorVersion="1" MinorVersion="0"
6      AssertionID="123456" Issuer="BobsAppliances.com"
7      IssueInstant="2002-05-05T10:28:00">
8
9      <saml:Conditions
10        NotBefore="2002-05-05T10:28:00"
11        NotAfter="2002-05-05T11:28:00"/>
12
13     <saml:AuthenticationStatement
14        AuthenticationMethod="password"
15        AuthenticationInstant="2002-05-05T10:28:00">
16        <saml:Subject>
17           <saml:NameIdentifier
18              SecurityDomain="BobsAppliances.com"
19              Name="Joe" />
20        </saml:Subject>
```

Fig. 12.7 Authentication assertion sample. (Part 1 of 2.)

```
21
22        </saml:AuthenticationStatement>
23     </saml:Assertion>
```

Fig. 12.7 Authentication assertion sample. (Part 2 of 2.)

This particular assertion states that the user, **Joe** (line 19), was authenticated by a password (line 14) at **10:28:00** on May 5, 2002 (line 15). Element **Conditions** (lines 9–11) states the conditions under which the assertion is valid. This assertion is valid for only one hour after the time of issuance. When Joe reaches the PEP, this assertion provides a history of how **Joe** was authenticated.[39]

In this example, another assertion (called an *attribute assertion*) provides information about the user's attributes. For instance, if the subject **Joe** is a business partner specializing in flooring, the attribute **Partner** (lines 21–29) would contain the content **Flooring**, as it does in the attribute assertion shown in Fig. 12.8.

```
1    <?xml version="1.0" encoding="UTF-8"?>
2    <!-- Fig. 12.8: Fig12_8.xml       -->
3    <!-- Attribute assertion sample -->
4
5    <saml:Assertion MajorVersion="1" MinorVersion="0"
6       AssertionID="654321" Issuer="BobsAppliances.com"
7       IssueInstant="2002-05-05T10:28:00">
8
9       <saml:Conditions
10         NotBefore="2002-05-05T10:28:00"
11         NotAfter="2002-05-05T11:28:00" />
12
13      <saml:AttributeStatement>
14
15         <saml:Subject>
16            <saml:NameIdentifier
17                SecurityDomain="BobsAppliances.com"
18                Name="Joe" />
19         </saml:Subject>
20
21         <saml:Attribute>
22            <saml:AttributeDesignator
23                AttributeName="Partner"
24                AttributeNamespace="http://BobsAppliances.com" />
25
26               <saml:AttributeValue>
27                Flooring
28               </saml:AttributeValue>
29         </saml:Attribute>
30
31      </saml:AttributeStatement>
32   </saml:Assertion>
```

Fig. 12.8 Attribute assertion sample.

After the PDP decides whether to grant permission, it returns an authorization-decision assertion. This assertion states that the user **Joe** is permitted to **read** the sales data for Bob's Appliances (Fig. 12.9).

SAML represents a significant advancement in security for B2B and B2C e-commerce transactions. Baltimore Technologies' (**www.baltimoretechnologies.com**) *SelectAccess 5.0* is the first application to incorporate SAML support.[40] For the latest updates and information on SAML's progress, visit **www.oasis-open.org/committees/ security**.

12.7 Extensible Access Control Markup Language (XACML)

As we discussed in the previous chapter, it is important for companies to establish clear security policies. Organizations must communicate their security policies to various parties— including vendors, customers and clients—and the advent of Web services has increased this need. *Extensible Access Control Markup Language (XACML)*, developed by OASIS (**www.oasis-open.org**), is a markup language that allows organizations to communicate their policies for accessing online information. XACML defines which clients can access information, what information is available to clients, when clients can access the information and how clients can gain access to the information.[41]

XACML is built on the foundations of IBM's *XML Access Control Language* (*XACL*) and the University of Madrid's XML-AC. The OASIS technical committee overseeing the development of this new technology includes members from Baltimore Technologies, IBM, Hewlett-Packard (**www.hp.com**) and Sun Microsystems (**www.sun.com**).[42] XACML security policies can regulate information access using factors such as a client's identity, the client's method of authentication and the port through which the client is communicating.[43] For example, a policy might specify that a document can be read only by senior management authorized by a password and communicating over a secure connection.[44]

```
1   <?xml version="1.0" encoding="UTF-8"?>
2   <!-- Fig. 12.9: Fig12_9.xml                        -->
3   <!-- Authorization decision assertion sample -->
4
5   <saml:Assertion
6       MajorVersion="1" MinorVersion="0"
7       AssertionID="321456" Issuer="BobsAppliances.com"
8       IssueInstant="2002-05-05T10:28:00">
9
10          <saml:Conditions
11              NotBefore="2002-05-05T10:28:00"
12              NotAfter="2002-05-05T11:28:00" />
13
14      <saml:AuthorizationDecisionStatement
15          Decision="Permit"
16          Resource="http://BobsAppliances.com/private/sales_data.xml">
17
18          <saml:Actions Namespace=
19   "http://www.oasis-open.org/committees/security/docs/draft-sstc-
core-25/rwedc">
```

Fig. 12.9 Authorization decision assertion sample. (Part 1 of 2.)

```
20              <saml:Action>Read</saml:Action>
21          </saml:Actions>
22
23          <saml:Subject>
24              <saml:NameIdentifier
25                  SecurityDomain="BobsAppliances.com"
26                  Name="Joe" />
27          </saml:Subject>
28
29      </saml:AuthorizationDecisionStatement>
30  </saml:Assertion>
```

Fig. 12.9   Authorization decision assertion sample. (Part 2 of 2.)

XACML also can enforce *Digital Rights Management* (*DRM*) for content delivered over the Internet. DRM is the set of protocols designed to protect media against piracy and unauthorized access online. As DRM technologies develop, organizations such as the Secure Digital Music Initiative (**www.sdmi.org**) and the Electronic Book Exchange Working Group (**www.ebxwg.org**) oversee DRM developments and establish new technical standards. The permission policies established in XACML can support DRM by declaring that a user has certain access privileges. For instance, an electronic-book distributor can use XACML to allow anyone to view the first chapter of a certain book, but allow only registered users to read the entire work. Registered users that pay an extra fee can print the file.

Working with SAML, XACML policies can provide the basis for authoritative decision-making at a Policy Decision Point. The PEP sends an authorization decision query to the PDP, which consults established security policies. The request must contain the target resource to access and the operation to perform (read, write, etc.) The assertion may also contain optional authentication credentials. Files requiring different levels of security will have different authentication standards. The PDP will return access decisions on the basis of the security policies in place. Building on our example from Section 12.6, imagine that **BobsAppliances.com** wants to allow customers to look at their own purchase histories, but prevent customers from writing to this file or accessing other customers' files. The XACML policy in Fig. 12.10 describes the conditions necessary to view a customer's purchase history stored in **BobsAppliances.com**'s database.

Root element **rule** is comprised of elements that specify the resource protected by the rule, the actions that a user can perform on the resource and the conditions necessary for each action. Attribute **effect** (line 5) contains either the value **"permit"**—which permits the actions outlined in the rule—or **"deny"**—which prohibits the actions outlined in the rule. A description of the policy is placed within the **description** element in lines 8–10. Element **target** (lines 15–41) defines the **resources** (lines 26–35), **subjects** (lines 17–24) and **actions** (lines 37–39).[45]

```
1   <?xml version="1.0" encoding="UTF-8"?>
2   <!-- Fig. 12.10: Fig12_10.xml                                    -->
```

Fig. 12.10 XACML policy that allows customers to view their purchase history.
         (Part 1 of 3.)

```
 3    <!-- XACML policy that restricts access to purchase histories -->
 4
 5    <rule effect="permit"
 6        ruleID="http://www.BobsAppliances.com/customers/policy1"
 7        xmlns="http://www.oasis-open.org/committees/xacml/docs/draft-
      xacml-schema-policy-12.xsd"
 8        xmlns:saml="http://www.oasis-open.org/committees/security/docs/
      draft-sstc-schema-assertion-28.xsd"
 9        xmlns:xsi="http://www.w3.org/2001/XMLSchema-instance"
10        xsi:schemaLocation="http://www.oasis-open.org/committees/xacml/
      docs/draft-xacml-schema-policy-12.xsd">
11        <description>
12         Allow customers to access and read their purchase history at
      BobsAppliances.com
13        </description>
14
15        <target>
16
17            <subjects>
18
19                <saml:Attribute AttributeName="RFC822Name"
20                 AttributeNameSpace="http://www.BobsAppliances.com">
21                    <saml:AttributeValue>*</saml:AttributeValue>
22                </saml:Attribute>
23
24            </subjects>
25
26            <resources>
27
28                <saml:Attribute AttributeName="documentURI"
29                 AttributeNamespace="http://www.BobsAppliances.com">
30                    <saml:AttributeValue>
31                     http://www.BobsAppliances.com/customers/record.*
32                    </saml:AttributeValue>
33                </saml:Attribute>
34
35            </resources>
36
37            <actions>
38                <saml:Action>read</saml:Action>
39            </actions>
40
41        </target>
42
43        <condition>
44
45            <equal>
46                <saml:AttribueDesignator AttributeName="requestor"
47                    AttributeNamespace=
48         "http://www.oasis-open.org/committees/xacml/docs/identifiers/" />
49                <saml:AttributeDesignator
50                    AttributeName="customerID"
```

Fig. 12.10 XACML policy that allows customers to view their purchase history.
(Part 2 of 3.)

```
51                AttributeNamespace=
52              "http://www.BobsAppliances.com/customers/record/custID/" />
53          </equal>
54
55      </condition>
56  </rule>
```

Fig. 12.10 XACML policy that allows customers to view their purchase history.
(Part 3 of 3.)

The PDP compares the **resource**s, **subject**s and **action**s in an authorization decision request to those in the XACML policy's rules before making an authorization decision.[46] In this example, the protected resource (located at **www.BobsAppliances.com/customers/record.***) is the customer's purchase history. Element **actions** (lines 37–39) specifies that an authorized viewer can **read** the resources. The **subject** (lines 17–24) is the customer that is requesting the purchase history. The conditions under which the actions are granted to the customer are contained in element **condition** (lines 43–55). Element **equal** (lines 45–53) contains attributes that must be equal for the conditions to be true—in this case, **requestor** and **customerID** must be equal. The **condition** element also can use **and**, **or** and **not** to create more complex conditional expressions. Like SAML and many other Web service security standards, XACML is changing rapidly; to view the latest specification, visit **www.oasis-open.org/committees/xacml/#documents**.

Figure 12.11 overviews the security standards we cover in this chapter. We list each technology, then summarize its purpose and strengths.

Technology	Fundamentals Addressed	Strengths
Basic HTTP	Authentication	Challenge-response authentication—credentials required for access to protected resources.
Digest Authentication	Authentication, Authorization, Privacy	Authorization credentials are protected through generated checksums, rather than plaintext transmission of passwords and usernames.
SSL (HTTPS)	Authentication, Privacy, Integrity	Authenticates both parties in a transaction. Encrypts data for end-to-end security between a client and server.
XML Signature	Authentication, Integrity	Verifies document integrity and sender identity. Multiple parties can sign a document or parts of a document.

Fig. 12.11 Web services security solutions. (Part 1 of 2.)

Technology	Fundamentals Addressed	Strengths
XML Encryption	Integrity, Privacy	Uses public-key or secret-key cryptography to protect data during transmission. Multiple parties can encrypt a document or parts of a document.
XKMS	Authentication, Privacy, Integrity	Provides XML-based PKI for Web services. Manages key and certificate information. Controls key registration, recovery and revocation.
SAML	Authentication, Authorization Non-Repudiation, Integrity	Designed for interoperable authentication and authorization solutions, including single sign-on. Records when and how a user was authenticated.
XACML	Authorization	XML-based language for creating security policies that can be used with SAML.

Fig. 12.11 Web services security solutions. (Part 2 of 2.)

12.8 Authentication and Authorization for Web Services

As we discussed in Chapter 11, Computer and Internet Security, authentication and authorization are necessary in any security model. Basic authentication and authorization techniques—such as those we discussed in Section 12.2—are not sufficient to secure Web services transactions. The latest Web services products use a combination of security mechanisms, including Kerberos and single sign-on. Microsoft's Passport, Sun's Liberty Alliance and AOL Time Warner's *Screen Name Service* are authentication and authorization systems designed for use with Web services. Web service providers that want to reach the largest number of users should provide authentication and authorization via various popular sign-on services.

Microsoft Passport authenticates and authorizes users for .NET Web services restricted to privileged users. Passport provides single sign-on using Kerberos authentication.[47] In addition to authorizing users for .NET services, Passport has been adopted by many e-businesses, including eBay, Monster and McAfee. Almost 200 million users worldwide are registered for the Passport service, which is required to access several Windows XP applications and Microsoft Hotmail. Microsoft plans to integrate new authentication methods—including digital certificates, biometrics and smart cards—with Passport.[48] All participating Passport sites must adhere to the P3P privacy standard and must provide privacy policies indicating what information they gather from users and how they use the information. To establish a Passport account or to set up a Passport-compliant Web site, visit **www.passport.com**.

The Liberty Alliance (**www.projectliberty.org**) was formed in October 2001 by Sun Microsystems. This organization's goal is to establish non-proprietary single sign-on standards for e-business. Liberty Alliance participants include AOL Time Warner, General Motors, American Express, Mastercard International and RSA Security. The proposed standards seek to secure businesses' and users' confidential information and to establish universal single sign-on methods. Liberty Alliance's specifications are designed to support *decentralized authentication* and interoperability. In decentralized authentication, users are not required to contact a central server to receive authentication, as is necessary in Kerberos and PKI. This increases flexibility and provides an ideal authentication system for wireless communications, in which users might not have access to a central server. The Liberty Alliance will offer an alternative to Microsoft's Passport service.[49] The interfaces designed by the Liberty Alliance could be used with .NET, enabling Passport to operate with other single sign-on systems.

AOL Time Warner developed Screen Name Service (SNS) for Web services authentication and authorization using single sign-on. In January 2002, AOL informally launched SNS, based on the company's *Magic Carpet* single sign-on technology. Screen Name Service combines accounts from AOL's America Online, Compuserve 2000, AOL Instant Messenger, Netscape and NetBusiness into a unified system. Users not registered with any of the previous programs can visit **my.screenname.aol.com** for free registration. SNS was designed to compete with Microsoft .NET's Passport system. Approximately 175 million users are registered for SNS, making it one of the most popular single sign-on products. AOL Time Warner is a member of the Liberty Alliance, but it is unclear whether SNS will be compatible with the Liberty Alliance's proposed specification. Negotiations between Microsoft and AOL to enable Passport and Magic Carpet interoperability failed, because AOL felt that Microsoft operating systems should provide equal support for Magic Carpet and Passport.[50] Businesses that currently support SNS include FedEx, CNN, Time, People and **NBA.com**.

Several emerging standards also provide authentication and authorization for Web services. The XML Key Management Specification (XKMS) manages key pairs used in PKI for encryption and user authentication. SAML transmits authentication, authorization and permissions information via assertions. XACML establishes an interoperable standard for creating security policies and permissions management used in Web services authorization.

12.9 Web Services and Network Security

In Chapter 11, Computer and Internet Security, we discussed aspects of network security, including firewalls and intrusion-detection systems. Web services (and features like single sign-on) create additional network-security concerns. Networks typically authenticate users before allowing access to protected resources. However, Web services often are designed to use single sign-on, which allows access to applications on the basis of another source's authentication credentials. Web services carry transactions beyond corporate firewalls, which places internal resources at a greater risk of attack.

The biggest concern regarding Web services security is the immaturity of underlying standards.[51] As with any new technology, certain vulnerabilities are not discovered until attacks occur in a real-world setting. Most organizations that operate Web services over internal networks are restricting external access to the services until emerging Web services security standards are incorporated in security software. Developers that do offer external access to Web services must take extra steps to protect their applications and networks.[52] A combination of traditional and Web services–specific security methods can be used to protect networks while Web services security standards mature. Encrypting data and using secure channels, such as SSL, protects data integrity and prevents data interception.[53] Firewalls between Web services and internal resources prevent Web service users from accessing protected information. If a computer within a firewall is exploited, an attacker can use that machine to access protected systems on the network. In addition to internal firewalls, a separate firewall should protect Web services from unauthorized visitors and filter traffic from a denial-of-service attacks.

Web services create new security challenges, but also can protect computers on a network. Products under development by Network Associates and Symantec use Web services to search networks for signs of viruses and apply updates to infected computers.[54] As Web services security solutions develop, developers will be forced to decide between traditional security and new Web services-specific security methods. Although we certain technologies are immature, that does not make them insecure. Web services security is an ongoing process, not a one-time solution. Administrators using Web services need to stay apprised of all security developments and update their systems regularly.

Well, that's it for now. We sincerely hope that you have enjoyed reading *Web Services A Technical Introduction*. We encourage developers to investigate the programming appendices that follow, which introduce the fundamentals of XML markup and provide working examples of Visual Basic .NET and Java Web services. Please note that Web services technologies and standards are evolving rapidly. To obtain the most current information on a particular topic, readers should visit the Web resources that we cite throughout the book. Additional Web resources are provided in Appendix D, Best Web Services Web Sites. To learn about the latest developments in Web services and other leading-edge software technologies, readers can register for the new *Deitel*™ *Buzz Online* e-mail newsletter at **www.deitel.com/newsletter/subscribe.html**.

12.10 Summary

Web services move transactions beyond firewalls and enable outside entities to invoke applications, potentially giving outsiders access to sensitive information. As a result, Web services present new security challenges. Although existing security standards protect data as it travels over the Internet, Web services require additional measures to secure data.

In HTTP challenge-response authentication, users must provide specific authentication information to verify their identities. When used alone, challenge-response authentication provides only weak security, because passwords and credentials are transmitted in plain-text. Digest authentication is a protocol in which a user's credentials are submitted to the server as a checksum. Digest authentication protects usernames and passwords from eavesdropping attackers, but does not encrypt the message content, which means that the content is vulnerable to interception. Secure Sockets Layer (SSL) secures the channel through which data flows between a client and server and enables authentication of both parties.

XML-based applications raise significant security concerns, in part because XML documents are encoded in plain-text, rather than in a binary form. Digital signatures solve this problem by verifying document integrity. The W3C's XML Signature specification defines an XML-based standard for representing digital signatures. A signature verifies a sender's identity and the data's integrity, but encryption is necessary to prevent the signed data from being read en route. XML Encryption handles the encryption and decryption of XML documents that are secured with XML Signature.

The XML Key Management Specification (XKMS) is a specification for registering and distributing encryption keys for Public Key Infrastructure (PKI) in Web services. XKMS improves PKI by establishing a platform-independent set of standards and by simplifying the steps necessary to implement PKI.

The Security Assertion Markup Language (SAML) is an emerging standard for transferring authentication, authorization and permissions information over the Internet. SAML is a form of Permissions Management Infrastructure (PMI), a system that uses a set of policies to handle access control and authorization. SAML has revolutionized PMI by establishing an open standard that is accessible to more companies.

Extensible Access Control Markup Language (XACML) is a markup language that allows organizations to communicate their policies for accessing online information. XACML security policies can regulate information access using factors such as a client's identity, the client's method of authentication and the port through which the client is communicating. XACML also can enforce Digital Rights Management (DRM) for content delivered over the Internet.

The biggest concern regarding Web services security is the immaturity of underlying standards. As with any new technology, certain vulnerabilities are not discovered until attacks occur in a real-world setting. Developers that offer external access to Web services must take extra steps to protect their applications and networks. As Web services security solutions develop, organizations must decide between traditional security and new Web services-specific security methods. Web services security is an ongoing process, not a one-time solution. Administrators using Web services need to stay apprised of all security developments and update their systems regularly.

12.11 Internet and Web Resources

General Web Services Security

dcb.sun.com/practices/devnotebook/webserv_security.jsp
This article, titled "Building Security into Web Services," provides an overview of Web services security.

msdn.microsoft.com/vstudio/techinfo/articles/XMLwebservices/security.asp
This Visual Studio .NET site provides an introduction to Web services security in .NET. It discusses Web services, how to restrict access to a Web service, ASP.NET security features and more.

www.infoworld.com/articles/tc/xml/02/01/14/020114tcsecure.xml
This article, titled "The Road to Secure Web Services," discusses the current state of Web services security and solutions that are under development.

msdn.microsoft.com/library/default.asp?url=/library/en-us/dnglob-spec/html/wssecurspecindex.asp
The MSDN *WS-Security Specification Index Page* overviews the WS-Security specification. This site also includes links to the specification, Schema and a security road-map tutorial.

XML Signature

www.ietf.org/html.charters/xmldsig-charter.html
The IETF's *XML Digital Signatures* site discusses the goals of the XML Digital Signature Working Group and includes the latest version of the standards document.

www.w3.org/Signature
The W3C's XML Signature Working Group site includes standards drafts, sample code, tools, SDKs and tutorials.

www.w3.org/TR/xmldsig-requirements
The *XML-Signature Requirements* site lists the design principles for the specification.

www.xml.com/pub/a/2001/08/08/xmldsig.html
This article, titled "An Introduction to XML Digital Signatures," overviews XML Signature technology, including how to create and verify XML digital signatures. Markup examples are also provided.

www-106.ibm.com/developerworks/xml/library/s-xmlsec.html/index.html
This tutorial on XML Encryption and XML Signature technologies includes several markup examples and links to other helpful online tutorials.

www.w3.org/Signature/2001/04/05-xmldsig-interop.html
This site presents the requirements for XML Signature interoperability.

www.xmltrustcenter.org/xmlsig/index.htm
The XML Trust Center includes FAQs, links and resources related to XML signatures and other XML security technologies.

www.webservicesarchitect.com/content/articles/hankison03.asp
This brief tutorial discusses digital signatures and Web services that use XKMS and the XML Digital Signature Specification.

XML Key Management Specification (XKMS)

www.w3.org/TR/xkms
This W3C site provides the specification for XKMS.

www.xmltrustcenter.org/xkms/index.htm
This XKMS resource site includes links to XKMS FAQs, articles and other resources.

www.w3.org/2001/XKMS
The W3C XML Key Management Working Group site contains the specifications, XKMS toolkits from multiple vendors (for Java and .NET) and links to other resources.

www.verisign.com/developer/xml/xkms.html
This site includes an article on integrating XML Signature and XML Encryption with XKMS, as well as links to whitepapers and other free guides.

Security Assertion Markup Language (SAML)

www.oasis-open.org/committees/security
This site contains links to SAML documents, mailing lists and other resources.

www.fawcette.com/xmlmag/2002_02/magazine/columns/collaboration/edejesus
This article discusses how SAML distributes authorization and authentication information.

xml.coverpages.org/saml.html
This site includes information about SAML and links to numerous SAML articles.

XML Encryption

www.w3.org/Encryption/2001
This site includes information about the XML Encryption specification, technical documentation and links to XML Encryption tools and articles.

`www.w3.org/TR/xmlenc-core`
This document explains the process of encrypting data with XML Encryption.

`www.w3.org/Encryption/2001/Overview.html`
The W3C XML Encryption Working Group site contains a mission statement, code, meeting schedules and background information regarding XML Encryption.

`www.xmlhack.com/read.php?item=1431`
This site contains links to information on various XML Encryption topics.

WORKS CITED

1. J. Fontana, "Microsoft Touts Tighter Web Services Security," *Network World* 10 June 2002:1–8.

2. E. Schwartz, "Secure Web Services a Moving Target," *InfoWorld* 17 January 2002 `<www.infoworld.com/articles/hn/xml/02/01/17/020117hntarget.xml>`.

3. M. Andress, "The Road to Secure Web Services," *InfoWorld* 10 January 2002 `<www.infoworld.com/articles/tc/xml/02/01/14/020114tcsecure.xml>`.

4. R. Yasin, "XML Standard to Keep Web Services Secure," *Internet Week* 30 July 2001 `<www.internetweek.com/infrastructure01/infra073001-1.htm>`.

5. R. Yasin, "XML Standard to Keep Web Services Secure," *InternetWeek* 30 July 2001: 21.

6. G. Samtani and D. Sadhwani, "Security and the .NET Framework," *Web Services Journal* February 2002: 34–37.

7. R. Rivest, "The MD5 Message-Digest Algorithm," April 1992 `<theory.lcs.mit.edu/~revisit/Rivest-MD5.txt>`.

8. "HTTP Authentication: Basic and Digest Access Authentication," `<www.ietf.org/rfc/rfc2617.txt>`.

9. S. Vaughan-Nichols, "The Woes of Web Services," 11 February 2001 `<www.byte.com/documents/s=6974/byt1013212280038/0211_vaughan-nichols.html>`.

10. M. Andress, "The Road to Secure Web Services," *InfoWorld* 10 January 2002 `<www.infoworld.com/articles/tc/xml/02/01/14/020114tcsecure.xml>`.

11. "Web Services Security, Version 1.0.," 5 April 2002 `<msdn.microsoft.com/library/en-us/dnglobspec/html/ws-security.asp>`.

12. W. Wong, "Tech Giants Partner on Security Standard," 11 April 2002 `<news.zdnet.co.uk/story/0,,t281-s2108174,00.html>`.

13. J. Fontana, "Whirlwind of Web Services Work on Tap," *Network World* 20 May 2002: 12.

14. M. Milgliore, "IBM, Microsoft and Verisign Release SOAP Security Spec," 11 April 2002 `<www.esj.com/news/article.asp?EditorialsID=174>`.

15. "XML-Signature Syntax and Processing," March 2001 `<community.roxen.com/developers/idocs/rfc/rfc3075.html>`.

16. "XML Signature," `<www.xmltrustcenter.org/xmlsig/index.htm>`.

17. M. Mactaggart, "Enabling XML Security: An Introduction to XML Encryption and XML Signature," September 2001 `<www-106.ibm.com/developerworks/xml/library/s-xmlsec.html>`.

18. E. Simon, P. Madsen and C. Adams, "An Introduction to XML Digital Signatures," 8 August 2001 `<www.xml.com/lpt/a/2001/08/08/xmldsig.html>`.

19. P. Festa, "W3C Backs XML-Based Digital Signature," 14 February 2002 `<zdnet.com.com/2102-1106-838335.html>`.

20. M. Mactaggart, "Enabling XML Security: An Introduction to XML Encryption and XML Signature," September 2001 `<www-106.ibm.com/developerworks/xml/library/s-xmlsec.html>`.

21. M. Andress, "The Road to Secure Web Services," *InfoWorld* 10 January 2002 `<www.infoworld.com/articles/tc/xml/02/01/14/020114tcsecure.xml>`

22. D. Singh, "XML and Binary Data," `<www.topxml.com/xml/articles/binary>`.

23. B. Shaffner, "Protect Sensitive Data with the XML Protocol," *TechRepublic* 11 February 2002 `<www.techrepublic.com/article_guest.jhtml?id=r00820020211sch01.htm>`.

24. C. Boulton, "VeriSign Bows New XML Specs, Services," 29 November 2000 `<www.internetnews.com/dev-news/article.php/10_522211>`.

25. R. Bragg, "Locking Down Web Services," *Enterprise Systems* November 2001: 22–25.

26. "XML Key Management: XML Trust Services," `<www.verisign.com/resources/wp/xml/keyManagement.pdf>`.

27. "W3C Publishes New XKMS 2.0 and X-BULK Working Drafts," 20 March 2002 `<www.webservices.org/index.php/article/articleview/208>`.

28. G. Yost, "PMI: The Tough Sell," *Technical Support* June 2000 `<www.naspa.com/PDF/2000/0600%20TS%20PDFs/T0006014.pdf>`.

29. M. Glaser, "SAML Looks to Allay XML Security Concerns," 8 February 2002 `<dcb.sun.com/practices/webservices/overviews/overview_saml.jsp>`.

30. E. DeJesus, "SAML Brings Security to XML," *XML Magazine* February 2002: 35–37.

31. R. Cover, "The XML Cover Pages: Security Services Markup Language (S2ML)," 21 February 2001 `<xml.coverpages.org/s2ml.html>`.

32. A. Patrizio, "SAML Advances Single Sign-On Prospects," *XML Magazine* March 2002: 10–11.

33. D. Taft, "Services Security Tightens," *eWeek* 29 April 2002: 18.

34. A. Patrizio, "SAML Advances Single Sign-On Prospects," `<www.fawcette.com/xmlmag/2002_03/magazine/departments/marketscan/saml/default.asp>`.

35. "Assertions and Protocol for the OASIS Security Assertion Markup Language," `<www.oasis-open.org/committees/security/docs/draft-sstc-core-27.pdf>`.

36. M. Chanliau, "Security Assertions Markup Language (SAML)," `<www.simc-inc.org/archive0002/February02/Speakers/SAML-SIMC-short>`.

37. J. Byous, "Single Sign-On Simplicity With SAML: An Overview of Single Sign-On Capabilities Based on the Security Assertions Markup Language (SAML) Specification," `<java.sun.com/features/2002/05/single-signon.html>`.

38. J. Byous, "Single Sign-On Simplicity With SAML: An Overview of Single Sign-On Capabilities Based on the Security Assertions Markup Language (SAML) Specification," `<java.sun.com/features/2002/05/single-signon.html>`.

39. M. Glaser, "SAML Looks to Allay XML Security Concerns," 8 February 2002 `<dcb.sun.com/practices/webservices/overviews/overview_saml.jsp>`.

40. J. Fontana, "Baltimore Tech First to Add SAML," *Network World* 29 March 2002: 14.

41. "OASIS eXtensible Access Control Markup Language (XACML)," 9 May 2002 `<www.oasis-open.org/committees/xacml/repository/draft-xacml-schema-policy-13.pdf>`.

42. "XACML - Extensible Access Control Markup Language," 24 April 2001 `<xml.coverpages.org/XACML-PR20010424.html>`.

43. E. DeJesus, "Secure Your Web Services Applications," *.NET Magazine* June 2002:22–26.

44. P. Madsen and C. Adams, "Privacy and XML, Part 2," 1 May 2002 `<www.xml.com/pub/a/2002/05/01/privacy.html>`.

45. "OASIS eXtensible Access Control Markup Language (XACML)," 9 May 2002 `<www.oasis-open.org/committees/xacml/repository/draft-xacml-schema-policy-13.pdf>`.

46. P. Madsen and C. Adams, "Privacy and XML, Part 2," 1 May 2002 `<www.xml.com/pub/a/2002/05/01/privacy.html>`.

47. M. Andress, "The Road to Secure Web Services," *InfoWorld* 10 January 2002 `<www.infoworld.com/articles/tc/xml/02/01/14/020114tcsecure.xml>`.

48. ".NET Passport Overview, "`<www.microsoft.com/myservices/passport/overview.asp>`.

49. M. La Monica, "Web Services Leave a Wake of Security Worries," *InfoWorld* 18 February 2002: 18.

50. "Microsoft Accuses AOL of Net Plot," 4 April 2002 `<msn.com.com/2100-1104-876289.html>`.

51. S. Burns, "Web Services Security—An Overview," 20 November 2001 `<rr.sans.org/managed/web_services.php>`.

52. W. Rash, "Web Services Nightmare," *Software Development Times* 1 November 2001: 31.

53. T. Dyck, "Here Be Dragons: Web Services Risks," *eWeek* 25 March 2002: 42.

54. M. Denton, "Making Web Services Work," *Electronic Commerce World* May 2002: 30–33.

RECOMMENDED READING

Actaggat, A. "Enabling XML Security," September 2001 `<www-106.ibm.com/developerworks/xml/library/s-xmlsec/html>`.

Connolly, P. J. "Getting Serious About Web Services," *InfoWorld* 14 September 2001 `<www.infoworld.com/articles/tc/xml/01/09/17/010917tcsecurity.xml>`.

DeJesus, E. X. "Security Implications of Web Services," 6 June 2001 `<www.webservicesarchitect.com/content/articles/deJesus01.asp>`.

Desmond, P. "Securant, Netegrity Offer Competing Security Standard Proposals," December 2000/January 2001 `<www.softwaremag.com/archive/2000dec/SecurityStandards.html>`.

Dillaway, B. "Implementing XML Key Management Services Using ASP.NET," January 2002 `<msdn.microsoft.com/library/en-us/Dnaspp/html/Im.plementingxkms.asp>`.

Finlay, D. "XML Security Spec Solves PKI Interface Dilemma," *Software Development Times* 1 January 2001 `<www.sdtimes.com/news/021/story1.htm>`.

Fonseca, B. "Authenticating Web Services," *InfoWorld* 3 December 2001 `<www.infoworld.com/articles/fe/xml/01/12/03/011203feauthent.xml>`.

Fonseca, B. "Secure XML Standard Defined for E-Commerce," *InfoWorld* 15 November 2000 `<www.infoworld.com/articles/hn/xml/00/11/15/001115hnnetegrity.xml?p=br&s=4>`.

Lindstrom, P. "Special Report: The Language of XML Security," *Network Magazine* 5 June 2001 <www.networkmagazine.com/article/NMG20010518S0010/3>.

Loeb, L. "XML Signatures: Behind the Curtain," December 2001 <www-106.ibm.com/developerworks/library/s-digsig>.

Messmer, E. "Software Vendors Planning XML-Based Security Spec," *Network World* 15 November 2000 <www.nwfusion.com/news/2000/1115xmlspec.html>.

Messmer, E. "Vendors Jostling Over XML Security Specs," 20 November 2000 <www.nwfusion.com/news/2000/1120xml.html>.

Microsoft. "XML Web Services Security," <msdn.microsoft.com/vstudio/technical/articles/security.asp>.

"Secure XML Standard Defined for E-Commerce," 15 November 2000 <www.itworld.com/AppDev/1503/IW001115hnnetegrity>.

Sundsted, T. "Taking Web Service Security Beyond SSL," 15 October 2001 <dcb.sun.com/practices/devnotebook/beyond_ssl.jsp>.

Vijayan, J. "Web Services, Internet Collaboration Pose Security Challenges for 2002," *Network World* 3 January 2002 <www.nwfusion.com/news/2002/0103sec.html>.

A

Introduction to XML Markup

Objectives

- To create custom markup using XML.
- To understand the concept of an XML parser.
- To use elements and attributes to mark up data.
- To understand the difference between markup text and character data.
- To use **CDATA** sections and processing instructions.
- To understand the concept of an XML namespace.

The chief merit of language is clearness, and we know that nothing detracts so much from this as do unfamiliar terms.
Galen

Every country has its own language, yet the subjects of which the untutored soul speaks are the same everywhere.
Tertullian

The historian, essentially, wants more documents than he can really use; the dramatist only wants more liberties than he can really take.
Henry James

Outline

A.1 Introduction

In Chapter 5, we introduced the Extensible Markup Language (XML) as an essential technology for Web services. In other chapters, we introduced various XML-derived markup languages, such as SOAP and WSDL.

In this appendix, we discuss how to create XML documents by marking up data with programmer-defined tags. We output[1] the XML documents' contents using a Java[2] application we created, named **ParserTest**. This application is included in the Appendix A examples[3] directory at **www.deitel.com**.

A.2 Introduction to XML Markup

In this section, we begin marking up data using XML. Consider a simple XML document (**first.xml**) that marks up a message (Fig. A.1). We output the entire XML document to the command line.

```
1   <?xml version = "1.0" encoding = "UTF-8"?>
2
3   <!-- Fig. A.1 : first.xml                -->
4   <!-- Simple introduction to XML markup -->
5
6   <myMessage id = "643070">
7      <message>Welcome to XML!</message>
8   </myMessage>
```

Fig. A.1   Simple XML document containing a message. (Part 1 of 2.)

---

1. We output to the command-line. We do not include the copyright comment in the output.
2. To run the examples, readers must be familiar with Java programming.
3. Before running the examples in this appendix, execute the batch file (**wsatil_xml.bat**) provided with the book's examples.

```
C:\>java -classpath %CLASSPATH% com.deitel.wsati1.xml.ParserTest
AppendixA/FigA_1/first.xml
<?xml version="1.0" encoding="UTF-8"?>
<!-- Fig. A.1 : first.xml                        -->
<!-- Simple introduction to XML markup -->
<myMessage id="643070">
   <message>Welcome to XML!</message>
</myMessage>
```

Fig. A.1   Simple XML document containing a message. (Part 2 of 2.)

The document begins with the optional *XML declaration* (line 1), which identifies the document as an XML document. The **version** *information parameter* specifies the version of XML used in the document. Currently, there is only one version of XML, 1.0.

The optional **encoding** declaration specifies the method used to represent characters electronically. **UTF-8** is a character encoding typically used for Latin-alphabet characters (e.g., English) that can be stored in one byte. When present, this declaration allows authors to specify a character encoding explicitly. When omitted, either UTF-8 or *UTF-16* (a format for encoding and storing characters in two bytes) is the default. We discuss character encoding in Section A.4.

Portability Tip A.1

*The **encoding** declaration allows XML documents to be authored in a wide variety of human languages.*

Portability Tip A.2

Although the XML declaration is optional, it should be included to identify the version of XML used in the document. Otherwise, in the future, a document without an XML declaration might be assumed to conform to the latest version of XML. Errors or other serious problems may result.

Common Programming Error A.1

Placing anything, including whitespace (i.e., spaces, tabs, carriage returns and line feeds), before an XML declaration is an error.

Good Programming Practice A.1

By convention, XML documents use the file extension **.xml***.*

Lines 3–4 are comments, which begin with **<!--** and end with **-->**. Comments can be placed almost anywhere in an XML document and can span multiple lines. For example, we could have written lines 3–4 as

```
<!-- Fig. A.1 : first.xml
     Simple introduction to XML markup -->
```

Common Programming Error A.2

Placing **--** *between* **<!--** *and* **-->** *is an error.*

In XML, data are marked up using *tags*, which are names enclosed in *angle brackets* (**< >**). Tags are used in pairs to delimit the beginning and end of markup. A tag that begins markup is called a *start tag* and a tag that terminates markup is called an *end tag*. Examples of start tags are **<myMessage>** and **<message>** (lines 6–7). End tags differ from start tags in that they contain a *forward slash* (**/**) character. Examples of end tags are **</message>** and **</myMessage>** in lines 7–8.

Individual units of markup (i.e., everything from a start tag to an end tag, inclusive) are called *elements*, which are the most fundamental building blocks of an XML document. XML documents contain exactly one element—called a *root element* (e.g., **myMessage** in lines 6–8)—that contains all other elements in the document. Elements are embedded or nested within each other to form hierarchies—with the root element at the top of the hierarchy. Nesting allows document authors to create explicit relationships between data. XML documents can contain any number of elements.

Common Programming Error A.3

Improperly nesting XML tags is an error. For example, **<x><y>hello</x></y>** *is an error; here the nested* **<y>** *tag must end before the* **</x>** *tag.*

Good Programming Practice A.2

When creating an XML document, add whitespace to emphasize the document's hierarchical structure. This makes documents more readable to humans.

Common Programming Error A.4

Providing more than one root element in an XML document is an error.

Elements, such as the root element, that contain other elements are called *parent elements*. Elements nested within a parent element are called *children*. Parent elements can have any number of children, but an individual child element can have only one parent. As we will see momentarily, it is possible for an element to be both a parent element and a child element. Element **message** is an example of a child element and element **myMessage** is an example of a parent element.

Common Programming Error A.5

XML is case sensitive. Using the wrong mixture of case is an error. For example, pairing the start tag **<message>** *with the end tag* **</Message>** *is an error.*

In addition to being placed between tags, data can be placed in *attributes,* which are name-value pairs in start tags. Elements can have any number of attributes. In Fig. A.1, attribute **id** is assigned the value **"643070"**. XML element and attribute names can be of any length and may contain letters, digits, underscores, hyphens and periods; they must begin with a letter or an underscore.

Good Programming Practice A.3

XML elements and attribute names should be meaningful. For example, use **<address>** *instead of* **<adr>**.

Common Programming Error A.6

Using spaces in an XML element name or attribute name is an error.

Common Programming Error A.7

Not placing an attribute's value in either single or double quotes is an error.

A.3 Parsers and Well-Formed XML Documents

A software program called an *XML parser*[4] (or an *XML processor*) is required to process an XML document. XML parsers read the XML document, check its syntax, report any errors and allow programmatic access to the document's contents. An XML document is considered *well formed* if it is syntactically correct (i.e., errors are not reported by the parser when the document is processed). Figure A.1 is an example of a well-formed XML document.

If an XML document is not well formed, the parser reports errors. For example, if the end tag (line 8) in Fig. A.1 is omitted, the error message shown in Fig. A.2 is generated by the parser.

Parsers can support the *Document Object Model (DOM)* and/or the *Simple API for XML (SAX)* for accessing a document's content programmatically, using languages such as Java™, Python and C. A DOM-based parser builds a tree structure in memory that contains the XML document's data. A SAX-based parser processes the document and generates *events* (i.e., notifications to the application) when tags, text, comments, etc., are encountered. These events return data from the XML document. Software programs can "listen" for the events to obtain data from the XML document.

```
1   <?xml version = "1.0" encoding = "UTF-8"?>
2
3   <!-- Fig. A.2 : error.xml              -->
4   <!-- XML document missing an end tag -->
5
6   <myMessage id = "643070">
7       <message>Welcome to XML!</message>
```

```
C:\>java -classpath %CLASSPATH% com.deitel.wsati1.xml.ParserTest
AppendixA/FigA_2/error.xml
[Fatal Error] error.xml:24:4: XML document structures must start and
end within
the same entity.
Exception in thread "main" org.xml.sax.SAXParseException: XML docu-
ment structures must start and end within the same entity.
        at org.apache.xerces.parsers.DOMParser.parse(
DOMParser.java:235)
        at org.apache.xerces.jaxp.DocumentBuilderImpl.parse(
DocumentBuilderImpl.java:201)
        at javax.xml.parsers.DocumentBuilder.parse(Unknown Source)
        at com.deitel.jws1.xml.ParserTest.main(ParserTest.java:43)
```

Fig. A.2   XML document missing an end tag.

4. In this appendix, we use the reference implementation for the Java API for XML Processing 1.2 (JAXP), which is part of Early Adoption 2.

The examples we present use DOM-based parsing.[5] We do not discuss SAX-based parsing in this book.

A.4 Characters

In this section, we discuss the collection of characters—called a *character set*—permitted in an XML document. XML documents may contain carriage returns, line feeds and *Unicode*® characters. Unicode is a character set created by the *Unicode Consortium* (**www.unicode.org**). The Unicode Consortium encodes the vast majority of the world's commercially viable languages.

A.4.1 Characters vs. Markup

Once a parser determines that all characters in a document are legal, it must differentiate between markup text and character data. Markup text is enclosed in angle brackets (**<** and **>**). Character data (sometimes called *element content*) is the *text* delimited by the start tag and end tag. Child elements are considered markup—not character data. Lines 1, 3–4 and 6–8 in Fig. A.1 contain markup text. In line 7, the tags **<message>** and **</message>** are the markup text and the text **Welcome to XML!** is character data.

A.4.2 Whitespace, Entity References and Built-In Entities

Spaces, tabs, line feeds and carriage returns are characters commonly called *whitespace characters*. An XML parser is required to pass all character data in a document, including whitespace characters, to the application (e.g., a Java application) consuming the XML document's data.

Figure A.3 demonstrates that whitespace characters are passed by the parser to the application consuming the XML document's data. In this case, we simply print the data returned by the parser.

```
1   <?xml version = "1.0" encoding = "UTF-8"?>
2
3   <!-- Fig. A.3 : whitespace.xml            -->
4   <!-- Demonstrating whitespace, entities -->
5   <!-- and empty elements                   -->
6
7   <information>
8
9      <!-- empty element whose attribute value -->
10     <!-- contains significant whitespace      -->
11     <company name = "Deitel    &amp; Associates, Inc." />
12
13     <!-- start tag contains insignificant whitespace -->
14     <city      >   Sudbury      </city>
15
```

Fig. A.3   Whitespace characters in an XML document. (Part 1 of 2.)

5. Some DOM-based parsers may internally use SAX-based parsing to create the initial tree structure.

```
16
17      <state>Massachusetts</state>
18   </information>
```

```
C:\>java -classpath %CLASSPATH% com.deitel.wsati1.xml.ParserTest
AppendixA/FigA_3/whitespace.xml
<?xml version="1.0" encoding="UTF-8"?>
<!-- Fig. A.3 : whitespace.xml              -->
<!-- Demonstrating whitespace, entities -->
<!-- and empty elements                  -->
<information>

   <!-- empty element whose attribute value -->
   <!-- contains significant whitespace      -->
   <company name="Deitel    &amp; Associates, Inc."/>

   <!-- start tag contains insignificant whitespace -->
   <city>    Sudbury      </city>


   <state>Massachusetts</state>
</information>
```

Fig. A.3   Whitespace characters in an XML document. (Part 2 of 2.)

A parser can inform an application as to whether individual whitespace characters are *significant* (i.e., need to be preserved) or *insignificant* (i.e., need not be preserved). The output window illustrates that the majority of whitespace characters in the document are considered significant. Lines 2 and 6 were considered insignificant by the application as well as the extra space characters in the start tag of line 14. Lines 8, 12 and 15–16 were considered significant because they are part of the character data.

The element in line 11 is called an *empty element,* because it does not contain character data between its start and end tags. The forward slash character closes the tag. Alternatively, this empty element can be written as

```
<company name = "Deitel    &amp; Associates, Inc."></company>
```

Both forms are equivalent.

Almost any character can be used in an XML document, but the characters *ampersand* (&) and *left angle bracket* (<) are reserved in XML and may not be used in character data or in attribute values. To use these symbols in character data or in attribute values, *entity references* must be used. Entity references are special names that begin with an ampersand (&) and end with a *semicolon* (;). XML provides entity references (or *built-in entities*) for the ampersand (&), left-angle bracket (<), right angle bracket (>), apostrophe (') and quotation mark (") characters. XML parsers replace these entity references with their corresponding characters.

 Common Programming Error A.8

Using the left-angle bracket (<) in character data or in attribute values is an error.

Common Programming Error A.9

Using the ampersand (&)—other than in an entity reference—in character data or in attribute values is an error.

A.5 CDATA Sections and Processing Instructions

In this section, we introduce **CDATA** *sections*, which can contain text, reserved characters (e.g., **<**) and whitespace characters and *processing instructions*, which allow document authors to embed application-specific data within an XML document.

Character data in a **CDATA** section are not processed by the XML parser. A common use of a **CDATA** section is for delimiting programming code (e.g., Java, JavaScript and C++), which often include characters such as **&** and **<**. Character data in a **CDATA** section are passed to the application consuming the XML document's data. Figure A.4 presents an XML document that compares text in a **CDATA** section with character data.

Common Programming Error A.10

Placing one or more spaces inside the string **<![CDATA[** *or the string* **]]>** *is an error.*

The first **sample** element (lines 8–12) contains C++ code as character data. Each occurrence of **<**, **>** and **&** is replaced by an entity reference. Lines 15–20 use a **CDATA** section to indicate a block of text that the parser should not treat as character data or markup. **CDATA** sections begin with **<![CDATA[** and terminate with **]]>**. Notice that the **<** and **&** characters (lines 18–19) do not need to be replaced by entity references.

```
 1   <?xml version = "1 0" encoding = "UTF-8"?>
 2
 3   <!-- Fig. A.4 : cdata.xml              -->
 4   <!-- CDATA section containing C++ code -->
 5
 6   <book title = "Russ Tick&apos;s C++ Programming" edition = "8">
 7
 8      <sample>
 9          // sample code
10          if ( this-&gt;getX() &lt; 5 &amp;&amp; value[ 0 ] != 3 )
11             cerr &lt;&lt; this-&gt;displayError();
12      </sample>
13
14      <sample>
15        <![CDATA[
16
17          // sample code
18          if ( this->getX() < 5 && value[ 0 ] != 3 )
19             cerr << this->displayError();
20        ]]>
21      </sample>
22
23      Russ Tick&apos;s C++ programming
24
```

Fig. A.4   Using a **CDATA** section. (Part 1 of 2.)

```
25        <?button cpp = "sample.cpp" ansi = "yes"?>
26    </book>
```

```
C:\>java -classpath %CLASSPATH% com.deitel.wsati1.xml.ParserTest
AppendixA/FigA_4/cdata.xml
<?xml version="1.0" encoding="UTF-8"?>
<!-- Fig. A.4 : cdata.xml                    -->
<!-- CDATA section containing C++ code -->
<book edition="8" title="Russ Tick's C++ Programming">

    <sample>
        // Sample code
        if ( this-&gt;getX() &lt; 5 &amp;&amp; value[ 0 ] != 3 )
            cerr &lt;&lt; this-&gt;displayError();
    </sample>

    <sample>
      <![CDATA[

        // Sample code
        if ( this->getX() < 5 && value[ 0 ] != 3 )
            cerr << this->displayError();
      ]]>
    </sample>

    Russ Tick's C++ programming

    <?button cpp = "sample.cpp" ansi = "yes"?>
</book>
```

Fig. A.4   Using a **CDATA** section. (Part 2 of 2.)

Because a **CDATA** section is not parsed, it can contain almost any text, including characters normally reserved for XML syntax, such as **<** and **&**. However, **CDATA** sections cannot contain the string **]]>**, because this is used to terminate a **CDATA** section. For example,

```
<![CDATA[
    The following characters cause an error: ]]>
]]>
```

is an error.

Line 25 is an example of a processing instruction (or *PI*). Processing instructions have no effect on a document if the application processing the document does not use them. The information contained in a PI is passed to the application that is consuming the XML document's data.

Processing instructions are delimited by **<?** and **?>** and consist of a *PI target* and a *PI value*. Almost any name may be used for a PI target, except the reserved word **xml** (in any mixture of case). In the current example, the PI target is named **button** and the PI value is **cpp = "sample.cpp" ansi = "yes"**. This PI might be used by an application to create a button that, when clicked, displays the entire code listing for a file named

sample.cpp. The **ansi = "yes"** portion of the PI value might be used to indicate that the C++ code is standard C++ compliant.

Software Engineering Observation A.1

Processing instructions provide a means for programmers to insert application-specific information into an XML document without affecting the document's portability.

A.6 XML Namespaces

Object-oriented programming languages, such as Java and standard C++, provide class libraries that group their identifiers (i.e., classes, methods, etc.) into packages and namespaces. These packages and namespaces prevent *naming collisions* between programmer-defined identifiers, third-party identifiers and class library identifiers. For example, a class named **Transaction** might represent a monetary transaction between two large companies; however, a bank might use class **Transaction** to represent a monetary transaction with a Federal Reserve Bank. A naming collision would occur if these two classes were used in the same Java application without their fully qualified package names.

Like Java and standard C++, XML supports *namespaces*[6], which provide a means of uniquely identifying XML elements. Because document authors create their own markup languages or *vocabularies*, namespaces are needed to logically group a vocabulary's elements.

Elements are qualified with *namespace prefixes*, which identify the namespaces to which elements belong. For example,

> **<deitel:book>Java Web Services</deitel:book>**

qualifies element **book** with the namespace prefix **deitel**. This indicates that element **book** is part of namespace **deitel**.

Common Programming Error A.11

*Creating a namespace prefix named **xml** in any mixture of case is an error.*

The markup in Fig. A.5 demonstrates the use of namespaces. This XML document contains two **file** elements that are differentiated using namespaces.

```
1   <?xml version = "1.0" encoding = "UTF-8"?>
2
3   <!-- Fig. A.5: namespace.xml   -->
4   <!-- Demonstrating namespaces -->
5
6   <text:directory xmlns:text = "urn:deitel:textInfo"
7      xmlns:image = "urn:deitel:imageInfo">
8
9      <text:file filename = "book.xml">
10        <text:description>A book list</text:description>
11     </text:file>
12
```

Fig. A.5   XML namespaces demonstration. (Part 1 of 2.)

6. Namespaces in XML is a W3C Recommendation (**www.w3.org/TR/REC-xml-names**).

```
13        <image:file filename = "funny.jpg">
14            <image:description>A funny picture</image:description>
15            <image:size width = "200" height = "100" />
16        </image:file>
17
18    </text:directory>
```

```
C:\>java -classpath %CLASSPATH% com.deitel.wsati1.xml.ParserTest
AppendixA/FigA_5/namespace.xml
<?xml version="1.0" encoding="UTF-8"?>
<!-- Fig. A.5: namespace.xml   -->
<!-- Demonstrating namespaces -->
<text:directory xmlns:image="urn:deitel:imageInfo"
xmlns:text="urn:deitel:textInfo">

   <text:file filename="book.xml">
      <text:description>A book list</text:description>
   </text:file>

   <image:file filename="funny.jpg">
      <image:description>A funny picture</image:description>
      <image:size height="100" width="200"/>
   </image:file>

</text:directory>
```

Fig. A.5   XML namespaces demonstration. (Part 2 of 2.)

Lines 6–7 use attribute **xmlns** to declare two namespace prefixes: **text** and **image**. Each namespace prefix is bound (or mapped) to a series of characters called a *uniform resource identifier (URI)* that uniquely identifies the namespace. Document authors create their own namespace prefixes and URIs.

To ensure that namespaces are unique, document authors must provide unique URIs. Here, we use the text **urn:deitel:textInfo** and **urn:deitel:imageInfo** as URIs. A common practice is to use *Universal Resource Locators (URLs)* for URIs, because the domain names (such as, **www.deitel.com**) used in URLs are guaranteed to be unique. For example, lines 6–7 could have been written as

```
<text:directory xmlns:text =
   "http://www.deitel.com/xmlns-text"
   xmlns:image = "http://www.deitel.com/xmlns-image">
```

These URLs relate to the Deitel & Associates, Inc., domain name. The parser never visits these URLs—they simply represent a series of characters used to differentiate names. The URLs need not refer to actual Web pages or be formed properly.

Lines 9–11 qualify elements **file** and **description** with namespace prefix **text**. Lines 13–16 qualify elements **file**, **description** and **size** with namespace prefix **image**. Notice that namespace prefixes are applied to end tags as well.

To eliminate the need to qualify every element of a particular vocabulary with a namespace prefix, document authors can specify a *default namespace* (i.e., a namespace that does not have a namespace prefix bound to it). Figure A.6 demonstrates the creation and use of default namespaces.

Line 6 declares a default namespace using attribute **xmlns** with a URI as its value. Once this default namespace is declared, child elements belonging to the namespace are not qualified by namespace prefixes. Element **file** (line 9–11) is in the namespace corresponding to the URI **urn:deitel:textInfo**. Compare this to Fig. A.5, where we qualified **file** and **description** with **text** (lines 9–11).

The default namespace applies to the **directory** element and all its child elements that are not qualified with namespace prefixes. However, namespace prefixes can be used to qualify other elements as belonging to different namespaces. For example, the **file** element in line 13 is qualified with **image** to indicate that it is in the namespace corresponding to the URI **urn:deitel:imageInfo**, rather than the default namespace.

```
1   <?xml version = "1.0" encoding = "UTF-8"?>
2
3   <!-- Fig. A.6: defaultnamespace.xml -->
4   <!-- Using a default namespace         -->
5
6   <directory xmlns = "urn:deitel:textInfo"
7      xmlns:image = "urn:deitel:imageInfo">
8
9      <file filename = "book.xml">
10        <description>A book list</description>
11     </file>
12
13     <image:file filename = "funny.jpg">
14        <image:description>A funny picture</image:description>
15        <image:size width = "200" height = "100" />
16     </image:file>
17
18   </directory>
```

```
C:\>java -classpath %CLASSPATH% com.deitel.wsati1.xml.ParserTest
AppendixA/FigA_6/defaultnamespace.xml
<?xml version="1.0" encoding="UTF-8"?>
<!-- Fig. A.6: defaultnamespace.xml -->
<!-- Using a default namespaces      -->
<directory xmlns="urn:deitel:textInfo" xmlns:image="urn:deitel:image-
Info">

   <file filename="book.xml">
      <description>A book list</description>
   </file>

   <image:file filename="funny.jpg">
      <image:description>A funny picture</image:description>
      <image:size height="100" width="200"/>
   </image:file>

</directory>
```

Fig. A.6   Default namespace demonstration.

Software Engineering Observation A.2

*Attribute names need not be qualified with namespace prefixes, because they always are as-
sociated with elements. Attribute names that are not qualified with a namespace prefix do not
belong to any namespace (i.e., a default namespace or the element's namespace).*

A.7 XML Schema[7]

XML documents can reference optional documents that specify how the XML documents
should be structured (i.e., what elements are permitted, what attributes an element can have,
etc.). These optional documents are called *Schemas*. When a Schema document is provided, some parsers (called *validating parsers)* can read the Schema and check the XML document's structure against it. If the XML document conforms to the Schema, then the XML
document is *valid*. Parsers that cannot check for document conformity against the Schema
are called *non-validating parsers*. If an XML parser (validating or non-validating) is able
to process an XML document (that does not have a Schema), the XML document is considered well formed (i.e., it is syntactically correct). By definition, a valid XML document
is also a well-formed XML document. If a document is not well formed, parsing halts, and
the parser issues an error.

In this section, we present a simple Schema example. Figure A.7 shows an XML
instance that conforms to the XML Schema (**simple.xsd**) shown in Fig. A.8. By convention, XML Schema documents use the file extension **.xsd**.

```
1  <?xml version = "1.0" encoding = "UTF-8"?>
2  <!-- Fig. A.7 : simple.xml -->
3  <!-- Simple XML document   -->
4
5  <deitel:note xmlns:deitel = "http://www.deitel.com/wsatiA">
6     Welcome to XML Schema!
7  </deitel:note>
```

Fig. A.7   Simple XML document.

```
1  <?xml version = "1.0" encoding = "UTF-8"?>
2
3  <!-- Fig. A.8 : simple.xsd      -->
4  <!-- Simple XML Schema document -->
5
6  <xsd:schema xmlns:xsd = "http://www.w3.org/2001/XMLSchema"
7     targetNamespace = "http://www.deitel.com/wsatiA">
8
9     <!-- declare element note -->
10    <xsd:element name = "note" type = "xsd:string" />
11
12 </xsd:schema>
```

Fig. A.8   Simple XML Schema document. (Part 1 of 2.)

---

7. For simplicity, we use XSV (XML Schema Validator) to validate XML documents against XML
    Schema. XSV is available for download free of charge from **www.w3.org/XML/Schema**.

```
C:\>xsv simple.xml simple.xsd
<?xml version='1.0'?>
<xsv docElt='{http://www.deitel.com/wstiA}note'
instanceAssessed='true' instanceErrors='0' rootType='string'
schemaDocs='simple.xsd' schemaErrors='0' target='file:/C:/sim-
ple.xml' validation='strict' version='XSV 1.203.2.45/1.106.2.22 of
2002/01/11 16:40:28' xmlns='http://www.w3.org/2000/05/xsv'>
<schemaDocAttempt URI='file:/E:/simple.xsd' outcome='success'
source='command line'/>
</xsv>
```

Fig. A.8   Simple XML Schema document. (Part 2 of 2.)

XML Schema use the namespace URI ***http://www.w3.org/2001/ XMLSchema*** and often use *namespace prefix* ***xsd*** (line 6 in Fig. A.8). Root element ***schema*** contains elements that define the XML document's structure. Line 7 specifies the ***targetNamespace***, which is the namespace for elements that this schema declares. In this case, only one element is declared—***note*** in line 10.

Common Programming Error A.12

Attempting to specify more than one target namespace in a Schema document is an error.

Good Programming Practice A.4

*By convention, Schema authors use either **xsd** or **xs** as the namespace prefix for the URI* ***"http://www.w3.org/2001/XMLSchema".***

In XML Schema, element ***element*** (line 10) defines an element. Attributes ***name*** and ***type*** specify the ***element***'s name and data type, respectively. In this case, the name of the element is ***note*** and its data type is ***string***. Type ***string*** represents a series of Unicode® characters. Because this type corresponds to character data, less-than characters and ampersand characters must be replaced with their corresponding entity references (i.e., ***<*** and ***&***).

Elements that contain only character data (i.e., do not contain attributes and/or child elements) have *simple types*. The XML Schema Recommendation defines many built-in simple data types, some of which are listed in Fig. A.9.[8]

XSV outputs the validation results as XML markup. Notice that ***instanceErrors*** is **0**, indicating that ***simple.xml*** is a valid document (i.e., it conforms to ***simple.xsd***).

Figure A.10 presents a well-formed XML document that does not conform to the XML Schema of Fig. A.8. This invalid document contains two elements (***message*** and ***unexpected***) that are not defined in the XML Schema. Notice that ***instanceErrors*** is non-zero (i.e., **1**), indicating that ***simple.xml*** is invalid (i.e., it does not conform to ***simple.xsd***).

---

8. For a complete list of simple data types visit **www.w3.org/TR/xmlschema-2**.

Data Type	Description
boolean	A logical yes/no or true/false value. Valid values are *true*, *false*, *0* (false) and *1* (true).
date	A Gregorian calendar date in the format *yyyy–mm–dd*.
double	IEEE 754 64-bit double-precision floating-point number.
int	A whole number in the range 2147483648 to –2147483647.
string	A series of Unicode characters. Less-than symbols and ampersands characters must be replaced with their corresponding entity references.
time	Time in the 24-hour format *hh:mm:ss.sss*.

Fig. A.9   Some simple data types.

```
1   <?xml version = "1.0" encoding = "UTF-8"?>
2   <!-- Fig. A.10 : simple_invalid.xml -->
3   <!-- Simple XML document           -->
4
5   <deitel:note xmlns:deitel = "http://www.deitel.com/wsatiA">
6
7       <!-- element not defined in the Schema -->
8       <message>Welcome to XML Schema!</message>
9
10      <!-- element not defined in the Schema -->
11      <unexpected>
12         This document does not conform to the schema
13      </unexpected>
14   </deitel:note>
```

```
C:\>xsv simple_invalid.xml simple.xsd
<?xml version='1.0'?>
<xsv docElt='{http://www.deitel.com/wsatiA}note'
instanceAssessed='true' instanceErrors='1' rootType='string'
schemaDocs='simple.xsd' schemaErrors='0'
target='file:/C:/simple_invalid.xml' validation='strict'
version='XSV 1.203.2.45/1.106.2.22 of 2002/01/11 16:40:28'
xmlns='http://www.w3.org/2000/05/xsv'>
<schemaDocAttempt URI='file:/E:/simple.xsd' outcome='success'
source='command line'/>
<invalid char='39' code='cvc-complex-type.1.2.2' line='3'
resource='file:/E:/simple_invalid.xml'>element {http://www.dei-
tel.com/wsatiA}note with simple type not allowed element children
</invalid>
</xsv>
```

Fig. A.10   XML instance that does not conform to the XML Schema in Fig. 18.2.

In this appendix, we introduced XML. In Appendix B, we introduce Web services development using Visual Basic .NET.

A.8 Summary

XML is a technology for creating vocabularies to describe data of virtually any type in a structured manner. To process an XML document, a software program called an XML parser is required. The XML parser reads the XML document, checks its syntax, reports any errors and allows access to the document's data. An XML document is considered well formed if it is syntactically correct (i.e., the parser did not report any errors due to missing tags, overlapping tags, etc.). Every XML document must be well formed. XML documents may contain carriage return, line feed and Unicode characters.

All XML start tags must have a corresponding end tag and all start- and end tags must be properly nested. Elements define a structure. An element may contain content (i.e., child elements and/or character data). An element may have zero, one or more attributes associated with it that describe the element.

CDATA sections allow the document author to include data that is not intended to be parsed; and may contain text, reserved characters (e.g., **<**) and whitespace characters. Processing instructions allow document authors to embed application-specific data within an XML document.

Because document authors can create their own vocabularies, naming collisions (e.g., conflicts that arise when document authors use the same names for elements) can occur. Namespaces provide a means for document authors to prevent naming collisions.

XML documents can reference optional documents that specify how the XML documents should be structured. These optional documents are called Schemas.

A.9 Internet and Web Resources

www.w3.org/XML
Worldwide Web Consortium Extensible Markup Language home page. Contains links to related XML technologies, recommended books, a time-line for publications, developer discussions, translations, software, etc.

www.w3.org/Addressing
Worldwide Web Consortium addressing home page. Contains information on URIs and links to other resources.

www.xml.com
This is one of the most popular XML sites on the Web. It has resources and links relating to all aspects of XML, including articles, news, seminar information, tools and Frequently Asked Questions (FAQs).

www.xml.org
"The XML Industry Portal" is another popular XML site that includes links to many different XML resources, such as news, FAQs and descriptions of XML-derived markup languages.

www.coverpages.org
Oasis XML Cover Pages home page is a comprehensive XML reference. The site includes links to news, articles, software and events.

html.about.com/compute/html/cs/xmlandjava/index.htm
This site contains articles about XML and Java and is updated regularly.

www.w3schools.com/xml
Contains a tutorial that introduces the reader to XML. The tutorial contains many examples.

java.sun.com/xml/jaxp
Home page of the Sun's JAXP and parser technology.

xml.apache.org
Home page of the Apache Software Foundation. This site contains news, links to Apache projects, Foundation information and downloads.

www.w3.org/XML/Schema#dev
W3C XML Schema home page, which provides links to tools, resources, specifications and development information.

Implementing Web Services in Visual Basic .NET

Objectives

- To create Web services using Visual Studio .NET.
- To create clients that use Web services.
- To use Web services with Windows and Web applications.
- To understand session tracking in Web services.
- To pass programmer-defined data types to Web services.

Protocol is everything.
Francoise Giuliani

They also serve who only stand and wait.
John Milton

Outline

B.1 Introduction

In Chapter 9, .NET Web Services: A Conceptual Overview, we introduced Web services in the context of .NET. We discussed creating .NET Web services and .NET Web service clients, as well as the different pieces that comprise both types of applications. In this appendix, we further explore Web services and the .NET platform by providing examples of .NET Web services and Web service clients. We include the code for each Web service, then provide a sample client application that might use the Web service. Our first example is designed to demonstrate how Web services work in Visual Studio. We then examine more sophisticated Web services that use session tracking and complex data types. We show complete working examples in using our LIVE-CODE™ approach; understanding these examples requires familiarity with Visual Basic .NET, Visual Studio .NET and ASP .NET. If you are unfamiliar with Visual Basic .NET programming, you may want to consider our texts *Visual Basic .NET How To Program* and *Visual Basic .NET For Experienced Programmers*.

B.2 Publishing and Consuming Web Services

This section presents several examples of publishing and consuming a Web service. An application that consumes a Web service actually consists of two main parts: a *proxy* class representing the Web service and a client application that accesses the Web service via an instance of the proxy class. A proxy class transfers the argument to a Web service method from the client application and transfers the result from the Web service method to the client application. Visual Studio .NET generates the proxy class—we demonstrate how this is done momentarily.

Figure B.1 presents the code file for the **HugeInteger** Web service (Fig. B.1). This code file normally is referred to as the *code-behind file*, which is a code file that corresponds to an *ASP .NET page*. In a ASP .NET Web application, the code-behind file provides the functionality for its corresponding ASP .NET page. In an ASP .NET Web service, the code-behind file contains the functionality for the Web service. Documentation for the Web service is provided by the corresponding ASP .NET page.

```
1    ' Fig. B.1: HugeInteger.asmx.vb
2    ' HugeInteger WebService.
```

Fig. B.1   **HugeInteger** Web service. (Part 1 of 6.)

```
3
4    Imports System
5    Imports System.Collections
6    Imports System.ComponentModel
7    Imports System.Data
8    Imports System.Diagnostics
9    Imports System.Web
10   Imports System.Web.Services ' contains Web service classes
11
12   ' performs operation on large integers
13
14   <WebService(Namespace:="http://www.deitel.com",
15      Description := "A Web service that provides methods" _
16      & " for manipulating large integer values." ) > _
17   Public Class HugeInteger
18      Inherits System.Web.Services.WebService
19
20      Private Const MAXIMUM As Integer = 100
21      Public number() As Integer
22
23      ' default constructor
24      Public Sub New()
25
26         ' CODEGEN: This call is required by the ASP.NET Web
27         ' Services Designer
28         InitializeComponent()
29
30         number = New Integer(MAXIMUM) {}
31      End Sub ' New
32
33      ' Visual Studio .NET generated code
34
35      ' property that accepts an integer parameter
36      Public Property Digits(ByVal index As Integer) As Integer
37         Get
38            Return number(index)
39         End Get
40
41         Set(ByVal Value As Integer)
42            If Value >= 0 Then
43               number(index) = Value
44            Else
45               number(index) = 0
46            End If
47         End Set
48
49      End Property ' Property
50
51      ' returns String representation of HugeInteger
52      Public Overrides Function ToString() As String
53         Dim returnString As String = ""
54
55         Dim digit As Integer
```

Fig. B.1   `HugeInteger` Web service. (Part 2 of 6.)

```vb
56
57          For Each digit In number
58              returnString = digit & returnString
59          Next
60
61          Return returnString
62      End Function
63
64      ' creates HugeInteger based on argument
65      Public Shared Function FromString(ByVal value As String) _
66          As HugeInteger
67
68          Dim parsedInteger As New HugeInteger()
69          Dim i As Integer
70
71          For i = 0 To value.Length - 1
72              parsedInteger.Digits(i) = Int32.Parse( _
73                  value.Chars(value.Length - i - 1).ToString())
74          Next
75
76          Return parsedInteger
77      End Function
78
79      ' WebMethod that performs addition of integers
80      ' represented by String arguments
81      <WebMethod( Description := "Adds two huge integers." )> _
82      Public Function Add(ByVal first As String, _
83          ByVal second As String) As String
84
85          Dim carry As Integer = 0
86          Dim i As Integer
87
88          Dim operand1 As HugeInteger = _
89              HugeInteger.FromString(first)
90
91          Dim operand2 As HugeInteger = _
92              HugeInteger.FromString(second)
93
94          ' store result of addition
95          Dim result As New HugeInteger()
96
97          ' perform addition algorithm for each digit
98          For i = 0 To MAXIMUM
99
100             ' add two digits in same column
101             ' result is their sum, plus carry from
102             ' previous operation modulo 10
103             result.Digits(i) = _
104                 (operand1.Digits(i) + operand2.Digits(i)) _
105                     Mod 10 + carry
106
```

Fig. B.1   **HugeInteger** Web service. (Part 3 of 6.)

```vb
107             ' set carry to remainder of dividing
108             ' sums of two digits by 10
109             carry = (operand1.Digits(i) + operand2.Digits(i)) \ 10
110         Next
111
112         Return result.ToString()
113     End Function ' Add
114
115     ' WebMethod that performs subtraction of integers
116     ' represented by String arguments
117     <WebMethod( Description := "Subtracts two huge integers." )> _
118     Public Function Subtract(ByVal first As String, _
119         ByVal second As String) As String
120
121         Dim i As Integer
122         Dim operand1 As HugeInteger = _
123             HugeInteger.FromString(first)
124
125         Dim operand2 As HugeInteger = _
126             HugeInteger.FromString(second)
127
128         Dim result As New HugeInteger()
129
130         ' subtract top digit from bottom digit
131         For i = 0 To MAXIMUM
132
133             ' if top digit is smaller than bottom
134             ' digit then borrow
135             If operand1.Digits(i) < operand2.Digits(i) Then
136                 Borrow(operand1, i)
137             End If
138
139             ' subtract bottom from top
140             result.Digits(i) = operand1.Digits(i) - _
141                 operand2.Digits(i)
142         Next
143
144         Return result.ToString()
145     End Function ' Subtract
146
147     ' borrows 1 from next digit
148     Private Sub Borrow(ByVal hugeInteger As HugeInteger, _
149         ByVal place As Integer)
150
151         ' if no place to borrow from, signal problem
152         If place >= MAXIMUM - 1 Then
153             Throw New ArgumentException()
154
155         ' otherwise if next digit is zero,
156         ' borrow from digit to left
157         ElseIf hugeInteger.Digits(place + 1) = 0 Then
158             Borrow(hugeInteger, place + 1)
159         End If
```

Fig. B.1   **HugeInteger** Web service. (Part 4 of 6.)

```
160
161        ' add 10 to current place because we borrowed
162        ' and subtract one from previous digit
163        ' this is digit borrowed from
164        hugeInteger.Digits(place) += 10
165        hugeInteger.Digits(place + 1) -= 1
166   End Sub ' Borrow
167
168   ' WebMethod returns true if first integer is
169   ' bigger than second
170   <WebMethod( Description := "Determines if first integer is " & _
171      "larger than the second integer." )> _
172   Public Function Bigger(ByVal first As String, _
173      ByVal second As String) As Boolean
174
175      Dim zeroes As Char() = {"0"}
176
177      Try
178         ' if elimination of all zeroes from result
179         ' of subtraction is an empty String,
180         ' numbers are equal, so return False,
181         ' otherwise return True
182         If Subtract(first, second).Trim(zeroes) = "" Then
183            Return False
184         Else
185            Return True
186         End If
187
188         ' if ArgumentException occurs, first number
189         ' was smaller, so return False
190      Catch exception As ArgumentException
191         Return False
192      End Try
193   End Function ' Bigger
194
195   ' WebMethod returns True if first integer is
196   ' smaller than second
197   <WebMethod( Description := "Determines if the first integer " & _
198      "is smaller than the second integer.")> _
199   Public Function Smaller(ByVal first As String, _
200      ByVal second As String) As Boolean
201
202      ' if second is bigger than first, then first is
203      ' smaller than second
204      Return Bigger(second, first)
205   End Function
206
207   ' WebMethod that returns true if two integers are equal
208   <WebMethod( Description := "Determines if the first integer " & _
209      "is equal to the second integer" )> _
210   Public Function EqualTo(ByVal first As String, _
211      ByVal second As String) As Boolean
212
```

Fig. B.1   **HugeInteger** Web service. (Part 5 of 6.)

```
213          ' if either first is bigger than second, or first is
214          ' smaller than second, they are not equal
215          If (Bigger(first, second) OrElse _
216              Smaller(first, second)) Then
217              Return False
218          Else
219              Return True
220          End If
221      End Function ' EqualTo
222  End Class ' HugeInteger
```

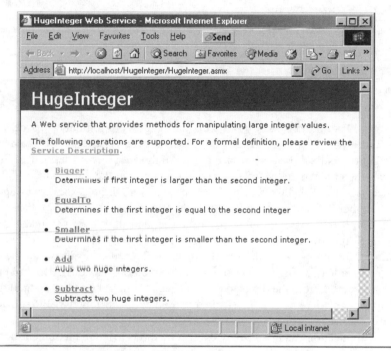

Fig. B.1   HugeInteger Web service. (Part 6 of 6.)

This Web service is designed to perform calculations with integers that contain a maximum of 100 digits. **Long** variables cannot store integers of this size without overflowing. Visual Basic .NET's object-oriented capabilities allow programmers to extend the language's capabilities to handle situations like these. The Web service provides clients with methods that take two "huge integers." The methods determine which number is the largest, whether the two numbers are equal, and the sum and the difference of the two numbers. Any programmer can access this Web service, use the methods and thus avoid writing, testing and debugging over 200 lines of code. We hide portions of the Visual Studio .NET generated code in the code listing. We do this for brevity and presentation purposes.

Line 14 assigns the namespace **http://www.deitel.com** to the **Namespace** property of the **WebService** attribute. In lines 15–16, we use property **Description** to provide a brief description of this Web service. This description appears in the Web service's ASMX file. In line 18, notice that the class derives from **System.Web.Services.WebService**—by default, Visual Studio .NET defines our Web service so that it inherits from class **WebService**. Although a Web service class is not required to derive from **WebService**, this class provides members that are useful in determining information about the client and the Web service itself. For instance, class **WebService** contains a **Session** object, which we will use later to store a user's information between Web service method calls. Several methods in class **HugeInteger** are tagged with the **WebMethod** attributes, which allow methods to be called remotely. Methods not tagged in this manner cannot be called remotely. Like the **WebService** attribute, this attribute contains a **Description** property that provides information about the method in the Web service's ASMX page. Figure B.1 shows the ASMX page.

Good Programming Practice B.1

Specify descriptions for all Web services and Web service methods so that clients can obtain additional information about the Web service and its methods.

Common Programming Error B.1

*Methods tagged with the **WebMethod** attribute cannot be declared **Shared**—for a client to access a Web service method, an instance of that Web service must exist.*

Lines 36–49 define **Property Digits** that enables programmers to access any digit in a **HugeInteger**. Lines 82 and 118 define **WebMethod**s **Add** and **Subtract**, which perform addition and subtraction, respectively. Method **Borrow** (defined in lines 148–166) handles the case where the left operand is smaller than the digit in the right operand. For instance, when 19 is subtracted from 32, we usually go digit by digit, starting from the right. The number 2 is smaller than 9, so we add 10 to 2 (resulting in 12). When 9 is subtracted, the result is 3. We then subtract 1 from the next digit over (3), making it 2. The corresponding digit in the right operand is now the "1" in 19. The subtraction of 1 from 2 is 1, making the corresponding digit in the result 1. The final result, when the resulting digits are put together, is 13. Method **Borrow** is the method that adds 10 to the appropriate digits and subtracts **1** from the digits to the left. Because this is a utility method that is not intended to be called remotely, it is not qualified with attribute **WebMethod** and is declared **Private**.

A client application can invoke only the five methods listed in the screen shot (i.e., the methods qualified with the **WebMethod** attribute).

Let us demonstrate how to create this Web service.[1] To begin, we must create a project of type **ASP.NET Web Service**.[2] Like Web Forms, Web services are stored in the Web server's **wwwroot** directory on the server (e.g., **localhost**). By default, Visual Studio .NET places the solution file (**.sln**) in the **Visual Studio Projects** folder.

Notice that, when the project is created, the code-behind file (**Service1.asmx.vb**) is displayed by default in design view (Fig. B.2). If this file is not open, it can be opened by double-clicking **Service1.asmx**. When creating Web services in Visual Studio .NET, programmers work almost exclusively in the code-behind file. In fact, if a programmer were to open the ASMX file, it would contain only the lines

---

1. Visit the **Downloads/Resources** link at **www.deitel.com** to download the code examples for this book, and visit the FAQs link for step-by-step configuration instructions for the Web Services examples.
2. To create a Web service using Visual Studio .NET, Internet Information Services (IIS) must be running.

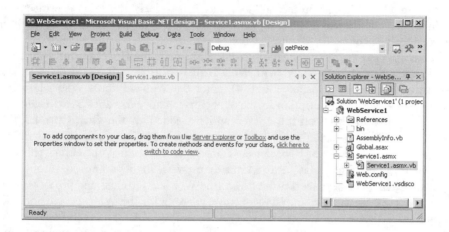

Fig. B.2   Design view of a Web service.

```
<%@ WebService Language="vb" Codebehind="Service1.asmx.vb"
    Class="WebService1.Service1" %>
```

indicating the programming language in which the code-behind file is written, the name of the code-behind file and the class that defines our Web service. [*Note*: By default, the code-behind file is not listed in the **Solution Explorer**. To list the file in the **Solution Explorer**, click the show all files icon.]

It may seem strange that there is a design view for a Web service, when a Web service does not have a graphical user interface. However, more sophisticated Web services contain methods that manipulate more than just strings or numbers. For example, a Web service method could manipulate a database. Instead of typing all the code necessary to create a database connection, we simply drop the proper ADO .NET components into the design view and manipulate them as we would in a Windows or Web application. We present an example that manipulates a database in Section B.4.

Now that we have defined our Web service, we demonstrate how to use it. First, a client application must be created. In this example, we create a Windows application client. Once this application has been created, the client must add a proxy class that accesses the Web service. A proxy class (or proxy) is a class created from the Web service's WSDL file that enables the client to call Web service methods over the Internet. The proxy class handles all the "plumbing" required for method calls to Web service methods. Whenever a call is made in the client application to a Web service method, the application actually calls a corresponding method in the proxy class. This method takes the method name and arguments and then formats them so that they can be sent as a request in a SOAP envelope. The Web service receives this request and executes the method call, sending back the result in another SOAP envelope. When the client application receives the SOAP envelope containing the response, the proxy class parses it and formats the results so that they are understandable to the client. This information then is returned to the client. It is important to note that the proxy class essentially is hidden from the client. The purpose of the proxy class is to make it seem to clients as if they are calling the Web service methods locally—the client should have no need to view or manipulate the proxy class.

We begin by creating a project and then adding a *Web reference* to the project. When we add a Web reference to a client application, the proxy class is created. The client then creates an instance of the proxy class, which is used to call Web service methods.

To create a proxy in Visual Studio .NET, right-click the **References** folder in the **Solution Explorer**, and select **Add Web Reference** (Fig. B.3). In the **Add Web Reference** dialog that appears (Fig. B.4), enter the Web service's Web address, and press *Enter*. When the description of the Web service appears, click **Add Reference** (Fig. B.4). A **Web References** folder will be added to the **Solution Explorer** (Fig. B.5), with a node named after the domain where the Web service is located. In this case, the name is **localhost**, because we are using the local Web server. This means that, when we reference class **HugeInteger**, we will be doing so through class **HugeInteger** in namespace **localhost** (the Web service class and proxy class have the same name). Visual Studio .NET generates a proxy for the Web service and adds it as a reference (Fig. B.5).

The steps that we described previously work well if the programmer knows the appropriate Web service reference. However, what if the programmer is trying to locate a new Web service? There are two technologies that can facilitate this process: *Universal Description, Discovery and Integration (UDDI)* and *Discovery files (DISCO)*.[3] UDDI is a project for developing a set of specifications that define how Web services should be discovered, so that programmers searching for Web services can find them. Microsoft began an ongoing project to facilitate the locating of Web services that conform to certain specifications, allowing programmers to find different Web services through search engines. UDDI organizes and describes Web services, then places this information in a central location. UDDI is covered in detail in Chapter 7, UDDI, Discovery and Web Services Registries. The reader can learn more about this project and view a demonstration by visiting **www.uddi.org** and **uddi.microsoft.com/default.aspx**. Both of these sites contain search tools that make finding Web services fast and easy.

A DISCO file catalogs any Web services that are available in the current directory. There are three types of discovery files: *dynamic discovery* files (**.vsdisco** extension), *static discovery* files (**.disco** extension) and *map files* (**.map** extension). All three DISCO files contain XML that can help clients locate Web service files. **.disco** files contain markup that specifies the locations of a Web service's WSDL file and other DISCO documents. However, developers more commonly use **.vsdisco** files, which are generated dynamically when clients request discovery information. When a potential client requests a **.vsdisco** file, ASP .NET analyzes the directory in which the **.vsdisco** file is located, as well as that directory's subdirectories. ASP .NET then generates a **.disco** file that contains references to all Web services in that directory (and that directory's subdirectories). For security reasons, developers can specify in the **.vsdisco** file that certain directories should not be searched when the **.disco** file is generated.[4]

---

3. DISCO is being replaced with WS-Inspection. WS-Inspection is a SOAP-based specification that defines a syntax for creating WS-Inspection documents, which provide references to Web services available on a particular server.

4. A. Skonnard, "Publishing and Discovering Web Services with DISCO and UDDI," *MSDN Library* February 2002 **<msdn.microsoft.com/msdnmag/issues/02/02/xml/xml0202.asp>**.

Fig. B.3 Adding a Web reference to a project.

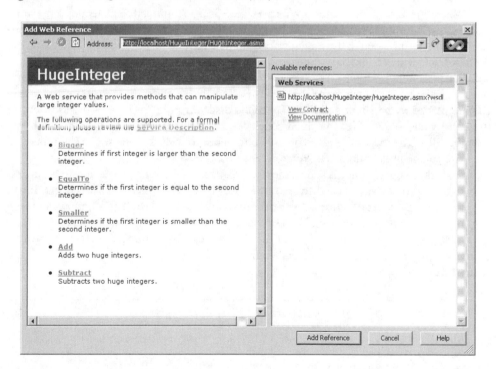

Fig. B.4 Web reference selection and description.

Good Programming Practice B.2

When creating a program that consumes Web services, add the Web reference first. This enables Visual Studio .NET to recognize an instance of the Web service class, allowing Intellisense to help developers use the Web service.

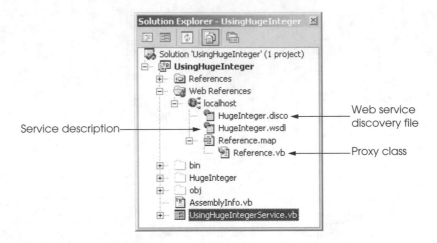

Fig. B.5   Solution Explorer after adding a Web reference to a project.

When a programmer creates a Web service, Visual Studio .NET generates a dynamic discovery file for that Web service. Although a static discovery file is not created as a physical file, the information that would be stored in that file can be accessed by appending the ASMX URL with **?DISCO**.

When a client is adding a Web reference, one of the discovery files is then used to point out the Web service. Once the Web reference is created, a static discovery file and a map file are placed in the client's project. The static discovery file hard-codes the location for the ASMX and WSDL files (by "hard code," we mean that the location is entered directly into the file). The **.map** file also contains references to Web service files. The links in a map file can be used to update a Web reference if necessary.

Once the Web reference is added, the client can access the Web service through a proxy. Because the proxy class (named **HugeInteger**) is located in namespace **localhost**, we must use **localhost.HugeInteger** to reference this class. The Windows Form in Fig. B.6 uses the **HugeInteger** Web service to perform computations with positive integers that are up to 100 digits long. Line 42 creates remoteInteger, of type **localhost.HugeInteger**. This object can now be used to call methods of the **HugeInteger** Web service.

```
1   ' Fig. B.6: UsingHugeIntegerService.vb
2   ' Using the HugeInteger Web Service.
3
4   Imports System
5   Imports System.Drawing
6   Imports System.Collections
7   Imports System.ComponentModel
8   Imports System.Windows.Forms
9   Imports System.Web.Services.Protocols
10
```

Fig. B.6   Using the **HugeInteger** Web service. (Part 1 of 6.)

```vb
11     ' allows user to perform operations on large integers
12     Public Class FrmUsingHugeInteger
13        Inherits Windows.Forms.Form
14
15        ' declare reference to Web service
16        Private remoteInteger As localhost.HugeInteger
17
18        ' HugeInteger operation buttons
19        Friend WithEvents cmdAdd As Button
20        Friend WithEvents cmdEqual As Button
21        Friend WithEvents cmdSmaller As Button
22        Friend WithEvents cmdLarger As Button
23        Friend WithEvents cmdSubtract As Button
24
25        ' input text boxes
26        Friend WithEvents txtSecond As TextBox
27        Friend WithEvents txtFirst As TextBox
28
29        ' labels
30        Friend WithEvents lblPrompt As Label
31        Friend WithEvents lblResult As Label
32
33        Private zeroes() As Char = {"0"}
34
35        ' default constructor
36        Public Sub New()
37           MyBase.New()
38
39           InitializeComponent()
40
41           ' instantiate HugeInteger object
42           remoteInteger = New localhost.HugeInteger()
43        End Sub
44
45        ' Visual Studio .NET generated code
46
47        Public Shared Sub Main()
48           Application.Run(New FrmUsingHugeInteger())
49        End Sub ' Main
50
51        ' determines if two numbers input are equal
52        Private Sub cmdEqual_Click(ByVal sender As System.Object, _
53           ByVal e As System.EventArgs) Handles cmdEqual.Click
54
55           ' ensure HugeIntegers do not exceed 100 digits
56           If SizeCheck(txtFirst, txtSecond) Then
57              Return
58           End If
59
60           ' call Web service method to determine if integers are equal
61           If remoteInteger.EqualTo( _
62              txtFirst.Text, txtSecond.Text) Then
63
```

Fig. B.6   Using the **HugeInteger** Web service. (Part 2 of 6.)

```
64              lblResult.Text = _
65                  txtFirst.Text.TrimStart(zeroes) & _
66                  " is equal to " & _
67                  txtSecond.Text.TrimStart(zeroes)
68          Else
69              lblResult.Text = _
70                  txtFirst.Text.TrimStart(zeroes) & _
71                  " is NOT equal to " & _
72                  txtSecond.Text.TrimStart(zeroes)
73          End If
74
75      End Sub ' cmdEqual_Click
76
77      ' checks if first integer input
78      ' by user is smaller than second
79      Private Sub cmdSmaller_Click(ByVal sender As System.Object, _
80          ByVal e As System.EventArgs) Handles cmdSmaller.Click
81
82          ' make sure HugeIntegers do not exceed 100 digits
83          If SizeCheck(txtFirst, txtSecond) Then
84              Return
85          End If
86
87          ' call Web service method to determine if first
88          ' integer is smaller than second
89          If remoteInteger.Smaller( _
90              txtFirst.Text, txtSecond.Text) Then
91
92              lblResult.Text = _
93                  txtFirst.Text.TrimStart(zeroes) & _
94                  " is smaller than " & _
95                  txtSecond.Text.TrimStart(zeroes)
96          Else
97              lblResult.Text = _
98                  txtFirst.Text.TrimStart(zeroes) & _
99                  " is NOT smaller than " & _
100                 txtSecond.Text.TrimStart(zeroes)
101         End If
102
103     End Sub ' cmdSmaller_Click
104
105     ' checks if first integer input
106     ' by user is bigger than second
107     Private Sub cmdLarger_Click(ByVal sender As System.Object, _
108         ByVal e As System.EventArgs) Handles cmdLarger.Click
109
110         ' ensure HugeIntegers do not exceed 100 digits
111         If SizeCheck(txtFirst, txtSecond) Then
112             Return
113         End If
114
```

Fig. B.6   Using the **HugeInteger** Web service. (Part 3 of 6.)

```
115          ' call Web service method to determine if first
116          ' integer is larger than second
117          If remoteInteger.Bigger(txtFirst.Text, _
118             txtSecond.Text) Then
119
120             lblResult.Text = _
121                txtFirst.Text.TrimStart(zeroes) & _
122                " is larger than " & _
123                txtSecond.Text.TrimStart(zeroes)
124          Else
125             lblResult.Text = _
126                txtFirst.Text.TrimStart(zeroes) & _
127                " is NOT larger than " & _
128                txtSecond.Text.TrimStart(zeroes)
129          End If
130
131       End Sub ' cmdLarger_Click
132
133       ' subtract second integer from first
134       Private Sub cmdSubtract_Click(ByVal sender As System.Object, _
135          ByVal e As System.EventArgs) Handles cmdSubtract.Click
136
137          ' ensure HugeIntegers do not exceed 100 digits
138          If SizeCheck(txtFirst, txtSecond) Then
139             Return
140          End If
141
142          ' perform subtraction
143          Try
144             Dim result As String = remoteInteger.Subtract( _
145                txtFirst.Text, txtSecond.Text).TrimStart(zeroes)
146
147             If result = "" Then
148                lblResult.Text = "0"
149             Else
150                lblResult.Text = result
151             End If
152
153          ' if WebMethod throws exception, then first
154          ' argument was smaller than second
155          Catch exception As SoapException
156             MessageBox.Show( _
157                "First argument was smaller than the second")
158          End Try
159
160       End Sub ' cmdSubtract_Click
161
162       ' adds two integers input by user
163       Private Sub cmdAdd_Click(ByVal sender As System.Object, _
164          ByVal e As System.EventArgs) Handles cmdAdd.Click
165
```

Fig. B.6 Using the **HugeInteger** Web service. (Part 4 of 6.)

```
166            ' ensure HugeInteger does not exceed 100 digits
167            ' and ensure both are not 100 digits long
168            ' which would result in overflow
169
170            If txtFirst.Text.Length > 100 OrElse _
171               txtSecond.Text.Length > 100 OrElse _
172               (txtFirst.Text.Length = 100 AndAlso _
173               txtSecond.Text.Length = 100) Then
174
175               MessageBox.Show("HugeIntegers must not be more " _
176                  & "than 100 digits" & vbCrLf & "Both integers " _
177                  & "cannot be of length 100: this causes an overflow", _
178                  "Error", MessageBoxButtons.OK, _
179                  MessageBoxIcon.Information)
180               Return
181            End If
182
183            ' perform addition
184            lblResult.Text = _
185               remoteInteger.Add(txtFirst.Text, _
186               txtSecond.Text).TrimStart(zeroes)
187
188         End Sub ' cmdAdd_Click
189
190         ' determines if size of integers is too big
191         Private Function SizeCheck(ByVal first As TextBox, _
192            ByVal second As TextBox) As Boolean
193
194            If first.Text.Length > 100 OrElse _
195               second.Text.Length > 100 Then
196
197               MessageBox.Show("HugeIntegers must be less than 100" _
198                  & " digits", "Error", MessageBoxButtons.OK, _
199                  MessageBoxIcon.Information)
200
201               Return True
202            End If
203
204            Return False
205         End Function ' SizeCheck
206      End Class ' FrmUsingHugeInteger
```

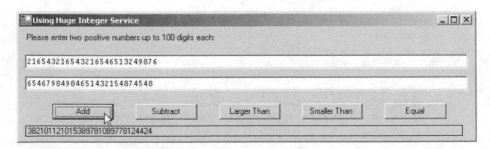

Fig. B.6   Using the **HugeInteger** Web service. (Part 5 of 6.)

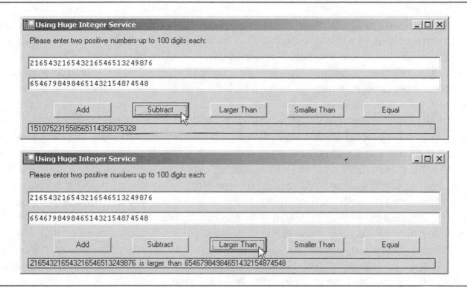

Fig. B.6   Using the **HugeInteger** Web service. (Part 6 of 6.)

The user inputs two integers, each up to 100 digits long. Clicking any button invokes that method's event handler, which performs a remote method call to perform the appropriate calculation. For instance, clicking the **Equal** button causes method **cmdEqual_Click** (lines 52–72) to execute. This method calls another method, **SizeCheck**, on line 56. Method **SizeCheck** is defined on lines 191–205 and ensures that the numbers entered are not too large. If the numbers entered by the user are not too large, the method continues with a call to Web service method **EqualTo** on line 61. The parameters passed to this method include the values entered by the user. If the integers are equal, the user is informed of this fact on lines 64–67. If the integers are not equal, a resulting message is displayed on lines 69–72. The other buttons have similar event handlers. The result of each calculation is displayed, and all leading zeroes are eliminated by **String** method **TrimStart**. Note that **FrmUsingHugeInteger** does not have the capability to perform operations with 100-digit numbers. Instead, it creates **String** representations of these numbers and passes them as arguments to Web service methods that handle such tasks for the programmer.

B.3 Session Tracking in Web Services

Originally, critics accused the Internet and e-businesses of failing to provide the kind of customized service typically experienced in bricks-and-mortar stores. To address this problem, e-businesses began to establish mechanisms by which they could personalize users' browsing experiences, tailoring content to individual users while enabling them to bypass irrelevant information. Businesses achieve this level of service by tracking each customer's movement through the Internet and combining the collected data with information provided by the consumer, including billing information, personal preferences, interests and hobbies.

To provide personalized services to consumers, e-businesses must be able to recognize clients when they request information from a site. The request/response system on which the Web operates is facilitated by HTTP. Unfortunately, HTTP is a stateless protocol—it does not support persistent connections that would enable Web servers to maintain state information regarding particular clients. This means that Web servers have no capacity to determine whether a request comes from a particular client or whether the same or different clients generate a series of requests. To circumvent this problem, sites such as **MSN.com** and **CNN.com** provide mechanisms by which they identify individual clients. A session represents a unique client on the Internet. If the client leaves a site and returns later, the client will still be recognized as the same user. To help the server distinguish among clients, each client must identify itself to the server. The tracking of individual clients, known as *session tracking*, can be achieved in a number of ways. One popular technique involves the use of cookies; another employs .NET's **HttpSessionState** object. Additional session-tracking techniques include the use of input form elements of type **"hidden"** and URL rewriting. Using **"hidden"** form elements, a Web Form can write session-tracking data into a **form** in the Web page that it returns to the client in response to a prior request. When the user submits the form in the new Web page, all the form data, including the **"hidden"** fields, are sent to the form handler on the Web server. When a Web site employs URL rewriting, the Web Form embeds session-tracking information directly in the URLs of hyperlinks that the user clicks to send subsequent requests to the Web server.

In this section, we incorporate session tracking into a Web service. Sometimes, it makes sense for a client application to call several methods from the same Web service. Some methods might be called multiple times. It would be beneficial for such a Web service to maintain state information for the client. Using session tracking is beneficial, because information that is stored as part of the session is not passed back and forth between the Web service and the client. This not only improves the client application's performance, but also simplifies program development.

Storing session information also can provide for a more intuitive Web service. In the following example, we create a Web service designed to assist with the computations involved in playing a game of Blackjack (Fig. B.7). We will then use this Web service to create a dealer that can be used to manipulate our deck of cards. The cards are stored in a **HttpSessionState** object, so that each client has their own deck of cards. Our example uses casino Blackjack rules:

> *Two cards each are dealt to the dealer and the player. The player's cards are dealt face up. Only one of the dealer's cards is dealt face up. If the dealer's card that is face up is either an Ace, 10 or face card, the dealer then checks the card that is face down. If the dealer has a BlackJack, the game is over and all hands are assessed. If not, the player can begin taking additional cards one at a time. These cards are dealt face up, and the player decides when to stop taking cards. If the sum of the player's cards exceeds 21, the game is over, and the player loses. When the player is satisfied with the current set of cards, the player "stays" (i.e., stops taking cards) and the dealer's hidden card is revealed. If the dealer's total is less than 17, the dealer must take another card; otherwise, the dealer must stay. The dealer must continue to take cards until the sum of the dealer's cards is greater than or equal to 17. If the dealer exceeds 21, the player wins. Otherwise, the hand with the higher point total wins. If both sets of cards have the same point total, the game is a push (i.e., a tie) and no one wins.*

The Web service provides methods for dealing cards and for counting the value of the hand. Each card is represented by a **String** in the form "**face suit**," where **face** is a digit representing the card's face, and **suit** is a digit representing the card's suit. After the

Web service is created, we create a Windows application that invokes these methods to implement a game of Blackjack.

Lines 21–23 define method **DealCard** as a **WebMethod**, with property **EnableSession** set to **True**. This property must be set to **True** for session information to be maintained. The Web service can now use an **HttpSessionState** object (called **Session**) to maintain the deck of cards for each client application that wishes to consume this Web service (line 28). We can use **Session** to store objects for a specific client between method calls.

As we discuss shortly, method **DealCard** removes a card from the deck and returns it to the client. Without using a session variable, the deck of cards would need to be passed back and forth with each method call. Not only does the use of session state make the method easy to call (it requires no arguments), but reduces the number of interactions between the client and server.

```vb
1    ' Fig. B.7: BlackjackService.asmx.vb
2    ' Blackjack Web Service which deals and counts card values.
3
4    Imports System
5    Imports System.Collections
6    Imports System.ComponentModel
7    Imports System.Data
8    Imports System.Diagnostics
9    Imports System.Web
10   Imports System.Web.Services
11
12   <WebService(Namespace:="http://www.deitel.com", Description := _
13      "A Web service that provides methods to manipulate a deck " _
14      & "of cards" )> _
15   Public Class BlackjackService
16      Inherits System.Web.Services.WebService
17
18      ' Visual Studio .NET generated code
19
20      ' deals card that has not yet been dealt
21      <WebMethod(EnableSession:=True, Description := "Deal a new " _
22         & "card from the deck." )> _
23      Public Function DealCard() As String
24
25         Dim card As String = "2 2"
26
27         ' get client's deck
28         Dim deck As ArrayList = CType(Session("deck"), ArrayList)
29
30         card = Convert.ToString(deck(0))
31         deck.RemoveAt(0)
32         Return card
33
34      End Function ' DealCard
35
```

Fig. B.7   Blackjack Web service. (Part 1 of 3.)

```
36       <WebMethod(EnableSession:=True, Description := "Create and " _
37          & "shuffle a deck of cards." )> _
38        Public Sub Shuffle()
39
40          Dim temporary As Object
41          Dim randomObject As New Random()
42          Dim newIndex As Integer
43          Dim i, j As Integer
44          Dim deck As New ArrayList()
45
46          ' generate all possible card combinations
47          For i = 1 To 13
48             For j = 0 To 3
49                deck.Add(i & " " & j)
50             Next
51          Next
52
53          ' randomly swap each card with another card
54          For i = 0 To deck.Count - 1
55             newIndex = randomObject.Next(deck.Count - 1)
56             temporary = deck(i)
57             deck(i) = deck(newIndex)
58             deck(newIndex) = temporary
59          Next
60
61          ' add this deck to user's session state
62          Session.Add("deck", deck)
63       End Sub ' Shuffle
64
65       ' computes hand's value
66       <WebMethod( Description := "Compute a numerical value" _
67          & " for the current hand." )> _
68       Public Function CountCards(ByVal dealt As String) As Integer
69
70          ' split String containing all cards
71          Dim tab As Char() = {vbTab}
72          Dim cards As String() = dealt.Split(tab)
73          Dim drawn As String
74          Dim total As Integer = 0
75          Dim face, numAces As Integer
76          numAces = 0
77
78          For Each drawn In cards
79
80             ' get face of card
81             face = Int32.Parse( _
82                drawn.Substring(0, drawn.IndexOf(" ")))
83
84             Select Case face
85                Case 1 ' if ace, increment numAces
86                   numAces += 1
87                Case 11 To 13 ' if jack, queen or king, add 10
88                   total += 10
```

Fig. B.7   Blackjack Web service. (Part 2 of 3.)

```
89                  Case Else ' otherwise, add value of face
90                     total += face
91              End Select
92          Next
93
94          ' if there are any aces, calculate optimum total
95          If numAces > 0 Then
96
97              ' if it is possible to count one Ace as 11, and rest
98              ' 1 each, do so; otherwise, count all Aces as 1 each
99              If (total + 11 + numAces - 1 <= 21) Then
100                 total += 11 + numAces - 1
101             Else
102                 total += numAces
103             End If
104         End If
105
106         Return total
107     End Function ' CountCards
108
109 End Class ' BlackjackService
```

Fig. B.7   Blackjack Web service. (Part 3 of 3.)

Right now, we simply have methods that use session variables. The Web service, however, still cannot determine which session variables belong to which user. This is an important point—if the Web service cannot uniquely identify a user, it has failed to perform session tracking properly. If two clients successfully call the **DealCard** method, the same deck would be manipulated. To uniquely identify various users, the Web service creates a cookie for each user. A client application that wishes to use this Web service will need to store this cookie in a **CookieContainer** object. We discuss this in detail shortly, when we discuss the client application that uses the Blackjack Web service.

Method **DealCard** (lines 23–34) obtains the current user's deck as an **ArrayList**. This data is accessed from the current application's **Session** object on line 28. An **ArrayList** is like a dynamic array (i.e., its size can change at runtime). Method **Add** places an **Object** in the **ArrayList**. Method **DealCard** then removes the top card from the deck (line 31) and returns the card's value as a **String** (line 32).

Method **Shuffle** (lines 38–63) creates an **ArrayList** that represents the card deck, shuffles the cards in the **ArrayList** and stores the **ArrayList** in the client's **Session** object. Lines 47–51 include **For** loops to generate each card (i.e., **String**s in the form "**face suit**"). Lines 54–59 shuffle the deck by swapping each card with another random card in the deck. Line 62 adds the **ArrayList** to the **Session** object to persist the deck between method calls.

Method **CountCards** (lines 68–107) counts the values of the cards in a hand by trying to calculate the highest score possible without exceeding 21. Precautions need to be taken when calculating the value of the cards, because an ace can be counted as either 1 or 11, and all face cards count as 10.

The **String dealt** is tokenized into its individual cards by calling **String** method **Split** and passing it an array containing the tab character, which separates the different cards in a dealt hand. Recall that the numeric and face value of the card is separated by a space. To separate each card (i.e., set of numeric and face values), we must use a different character (in this case, a tab). The **For Each** loop (line 78) counts the value of each card. Lines 81–82 retrieve the first integer—the face—and use that value as input to the **Select Case** statement in line 84. If the card is a **1** (an ace), the program increments variable **aceCount**. Because an ace can have two values, additional logic is required to process aces. If the card is a **13**, **12** or **11** (King, Queen or Jack), the program adds **10** to the total. If the card is anything else, the program increases the total by that value.

In lines 95–104, the aces are counted after all the other cards. If several aces are included in a hand, only one can be counted as 11 (e.g., if two were counted as 11 hand value would exceed 21, which is a losing hand). We then determine whether counting one ace as 11 and the remainder as 1will result in a total that does not exceed 21. If this is possible, line 100 updates the total accordingly. Otherwise, line 102 adjusts the total, counting each ace as 1 point.

Now, we use the Blackjack Web service in a Windows application called **Game** (Fig. B.8). This program uses an instance of **BlackjackService** to represent the dealer, calling its **DealCard** and **CountCards** methods. The Web service keeps track of the player's and the dealer's cards (i.e., all the cards that have been dealt).

The player and dealer each have eleven **PictureBox**es—the maximum number of cards that can be dealt without exceeding 21. These **PictureBox**es are placed in an **ArrayList**, which can be easily indexed to access or modify the card image displayed by each **PictureBox**.

Previously, we mentioned that the client must accept any cookies created by the Web service to identify users. Line 43 in the constructor creates a new **CookieContainer** object for the **CookieContainer** property of **dealer**. Class **CookieContainer** (defined in namespace **System.Net**) is a storage location for **HttpCookie** objects. Creating the **CookieContainer** allows the Web service to maintain a session state for this client. This **CookieContainer** contains a **Cookie** with a unique identifier that the server can use to recognize the client when the client makes future requests.[5]

```
 1    ' Fig. B.8: Blackjack.vb
 2    ' Blackjack game that uses the Blackjack Web service.
 3
 4    Imports System
 5    Imports System.Drawing
 6    Imports System.Collections
 7    Imports System.ComponentModel
 8    Imports System.Windows.Forms
 9    Imports System.Data
10    Imports System.Net ' contains CookieContainer
11
12    ' game that uses Blackjack Web Service
13    Public Class FrmBlackJack
14       Inherits System.Windows.Forms.Form
```

Fig. B.8   Blackjack game that uses the **Blackjack** Web service. (Part 1 of 9.)

5. For simplicity, we have created both our clients and Web services using .NET. The reader should be aware, however, that clients created on other platforms have their own techniques for consuming stateful Web services (i.e., Web services that use session tracking). For information on creating such clients in a different platform, see the Web services documentation for that specific platform.

```
15
16      Private dealer As localhost.BlackjackService
17      Private dealersCards, playersCards As String
18      Private cardBoxes As ArrayList
19      Private playerCard, dealerCard As Integer
20      Friend WithEvents pbStatus As System.Windows.Forms.PictureBox
21
22      Friend WithEvents cmdStay As System.Windows.Forms.Button
23      Friend WithEvents cmdHit As System.Windows.Forms.Button
24      Friend WithEvents cmdDeal As System.Windows.Forms.Button
25
26      Friend WithEvents lblDealer As System.Windows.Forms.Label
27      Friend WithEvents lblPlayer As System.Windows.Forms.Label
28
29      Public Enum GameStatus
30         PUSH
31         LOSE
32         WIN
33         BLACKJACK
34      End Enum
35
36      Public Sub New()
37
38         InitializeComponent()
39
40         dealer = New localhost.BlackjackService()
41
42         ' allow session state
43         dealer.CookieContainer = New CookieContainer()
44
45         cardBoxes = New ArrayList()
46
47         ' put PictureBoxes into ArrayList
48         cardBoxes.Add(pictureBox1)
49         cardBoxes.Add(pictureBox2)
50         cardBoxes.Add(pictureBox3)
51         cardBoxes.Add(pictureBox4)
52         cardBoxes.Add(pictureBox5)
53         cardBoxes.Add(pictureBox6)
54         cardBoxes.Add(pictureBox7)
55         cardBoxes.Add(pictureBox8)
56         cardBoxes.Add(pictureBox9)
57         cardBoxes.Add(pictureBox10)
58         cardBoxes.Add(pictureBox11)
59         cardBoxes.Add(pictureBox12)
60         cardBoxes.Add(pictureBox13)
61         cardBoxes.Add(pictureBox14)
62         cardBoxes.Add(pictureBox15)
63         cardBoxes.Add(pictureBox16)
64         cardBoxes.Add(pictureBox17)
65         cardBoxes.Add(pictureBox18)
66         cardBoxes.Add(pictureBox19)
67         cardBoxes.Add(pictureBox20)
```

Fig. B.8   Blackjack game that uses the **Blackjack** Web service. (Part 2 of 9.)

```vbnet
68          cardBoxes.Add(pictureBox21)
69          cardBoxes.Add(pictureBox22)
70    End Sub ' New
71
72    ' Visual Studio .NET generated code
73
74    ' deals cards to dealer while dealer's total is
75    ' less than 17, then computes value of each hand
76    ' and determines winner
77    Private Sub cmdStay_Click(ByVal sender As System.Object, _
78          ByVal e As System.EventArgs) Handles cmdStay.Click
79          cmdStay.Enabled = False
80          cmdHit.Enabled = False
81          cmdDeal.Enabled = True
82          DealerPlay()
83    End Sub ' cmdStay_Click
84
85    ' process dealer's turn
86    Private Sub DealerPlay()
87
88       ' while value of dealer's hand is below 17,
89       ' dealer must take cards
90       While dealer.CountCards(dealersCards) < 17
91          dealersCards &= vbTab & dealer.DealCard()
92          DisplayCard(dealerCard, "")
93          dealerCard += 1
94          MessageBox.Show("Dealer takes a card")
95       End While
96
97       Dim dealersTotal As Integer = _
98          dealer.CountCards(dealersCards)
99       Dim playersTotal As Integer = _
100         dealer.CountCards(playersCards)
101
102      ' if dealer busted, player wins
103      If dealersTotal > 21 Then
104         GameOver(GameStatus.WIN)
105         Return
106      End If
107
108      ' if dealer and player have not exceeded 21,
109      ' higher score wins; equal scores are a push
110      If dealersTotal > playersTotal Then
111         GameOver(GameStatus.LOSE)
112      ElseIf playersTotal > dealersTotal Then
113         GameOver(GameStatus.WIN)
114      Else
115         GameOver(GameStatus.PUSH)
116      End If
117
118   End Sub ' DealerPlay
119
```

Fig. B.8   Blackjack game that uses the **Blackjack** Web service. (Part 3 of 9.)

```vbnet
120         ' deal another card to player
121         Private Sub cmdHit_Click(ByVal sender As System.Object, _
122            ByVal e As System.EventArgs) Handles cmdHit.Click
123
124            ' get player another card
125            Dim card As String = dealer.DealCard()
126
127            playersCards &= vbTab & card
128            DisplayCard(playerCard, card)
129            playerCard += 1
130
131            Dim total As Integer = _
132               dealer.CountCards(playersCards)
133
134            ' if player exceeds 21, house wins
135            If total > 21 Then
136               GameOver(GameStatus.LOSE)
137            End If
138
139            ' if player has 21, they cannot take more cards
140            ' dealer plays
141            If total = 21 Then
142               cmdHit.Enabled = False
143               DealerPlay()
144            End If
145
146         End Sub ' cmdHit_Click
147
148         ' deal two cards each to dealer and player
149         Private Sub cmdDeal_Click(ByVal sender As System.Object, _
150            ByVal e As System.EventArgs) Handles cmdDeal.Click
151
152            Dim card As String
153            Dim cardImage As PictureBox
154
155            ' clear card images
156            For Each cardImage In cardBoxes
157               cardImage.Image = Nothing
158            Next
159
160            pbStatus.Image = Nothing
161
162            dealer.Shuffle()
163
164            ' deal two cards to player
165            playersCards = dealer.DealCard()
166            DisplayCard(0, playersCards)
167            card = dealer.DealCard()
168            DisplayCard(1, card)
169            playersCards &= vbTab & card
170
```

Fig. B.8   Blackjack game that uses the **Blackjack** Web service. (Part 4 of 9.)

```
171          ' deal two cards to dealer, only display face
172          ' of first card
173          dealersCards = dealer.DealCard()
174          DisplayCard(11, dealersCards)
175          card = dealer.DealCard()
176          DisplayCard(12, "")
177          dealersCards &= vbTab & card
178
179          cmdStay.Enabled = True
180          cmdHit.Enabled = True
181          cmdDeal.Enabled = False
182
183          Dim dealersTotal As Integer = _
184             dealer.CountCards(dealersCards)
185
186          Dim playersTotal As Integer = _
187             dealer.CountCards(playersCards)
188
189          ' if hands equal 21, it is a push
190          If dealersTotal = playersTotal AndAlso _
191             dealersTotal = 21 Then
192             GameOver(GameStatus.PUSH)
193
194          ' if dealer has 21, dealer wins
195          ElseIf dealersTotal = 21 Then
196             GameOver(GameStatus.LOSE)
197
198          ' if player has 21, player has blackjack
199          ElseIf playersTotal = 21 Then
200             GameOver(GameStatus.BLACKJACK)
201          End If
202
203          playerCard = 2
204          dealerCard = 13
205       End Sub ' cmdDeal_Click
206
207    ' displays card represented by card value in
208    ' PictureBox with number card
209    Public Sub DisplayCard(ByVal card As Integer, _
210       ByVal cardValue As String)
211
212          ' retrieve appropriate PictureBox from ArrayList
213          Dim displayBox As PictureBox = _
214             CType(cardBoxes(card), PictureBox)
215
216          ' if String representing card is empty,
217          ' set displayBox to display back of card
218          If cardValue = "" Then
219             displayBox.Image = _
220                Image.FromFile("blackjack_images\\cardback.png")
221             Return
222          End If
223
```

Fig. B.8   Blackjack game that uses the **Blackjack** Web service. (Part 5 of 9.)

```
224            ' retrieve face value of card from cardValue
225            Dim faceNumber As Integer = Int32.Parse( _
226               cardValue.Substring(0, cardValue.IndexOf(" ")))
227
228            Dim face As String = faceNumber.ToString()
229
230            ' retrieve card's suit from cardValue
231            Dim suit As String = cardValue.Substring( _
232               cardValue.IndexOf(" ") + 1)
233
234            Dim suitLetter As Char
235
236            ' determine suit
237            Select Case (Convert.ToInt32(suit))
238               Case 0 ' suit is clubs
239                  suitLetter = "c"
240               Case 1 ' suit is diamonds
241                  suitLetter = "d"
242               Case 2 ' suit is hearts
243                  suitLetter = "h"
244               Case Else ' suit is spades
245                  suitLetter = "s"
246            End Select
247
248            ' set displayBox to display appropriate image
249            displayBox.Image = Image.FromFile( _
250               "blackjack_images\\" & face & suitLetter & ".png")
251
252         End Sub ' DisplayCard
253
254      ' displays all player cards and shows
255      ' appropriate game status message
256      Public Sub GameOver(ByVal winner As GameStatus)
257
258         Dim tab As Char() = {vbTab}
259         Dim cards As String() = dealersCards.Split(tab)
260         Dim i As Integer
261
262         For i = 0 To cards.Length - 1
263            DisplayCard(i + 11, cards(i))
264         Next
265
266         ' push
267         If winner = GameStatus.PUSH Then
268            pbStatus.Image = _
269               Image.FromFile("blackjack_images\\tie.png")
270
271         ' player loses
272         ElseIf winner = GameStatus.LOSE Then
273            pbStatus.Image = _
274               Image.FromFile("blackjack_images\\lose.png")
275
```

Fig. B.8   Blackjack game that uses the **Blackjack** Web service. (Part 6 of 9.)

```
276          ' player has blackjack
277          ElseIf winner = GameStatus.BLACKJACK Then
278             pbStatus.Image = _
279                Image.FromFile("blackjack_images\\blackjack.png")
280
281          ' player wins
282          Else
283             pbStatus.Image = _
284                Image.FromFile("blackjack_images\\win.png")
285          End If
286
287          cmdStay.Enabled = False
288          cmdHit.Enabled = False
289          cmdDeal.Enabled = True
290
291       End Sub ' GameOver
292
293    End Class ' FrmBlackjack
```

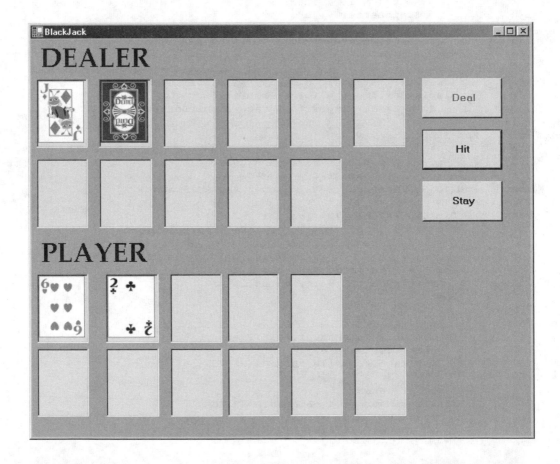

Fig. B.8   Blackjack game that uses the **Blackjack** Web service. (Part 7 of 9.)

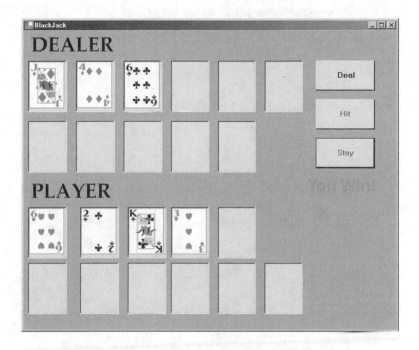

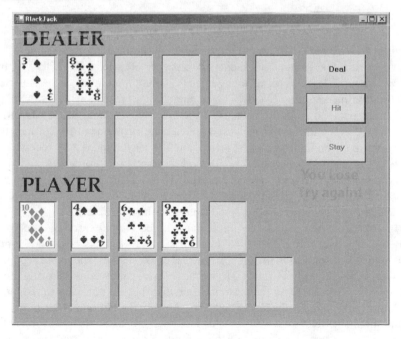

Fig. B.8   Blackjack game that uses the **Blackjack** Web service. (Part 8 of 9.)

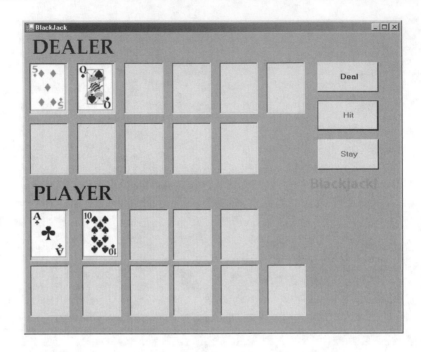

Fig. B.8   Blackjack game that uses the **Blackjack** Web service. (Part 9 of 9.)

Method **GameOver** (line 256–291) displays all the dealer's cards (one of which is face-down during the game) and shows the appropriate message in the status **PictureBox**. Method **GameOver** receives as an argument a member of the **GameStatus** enumeration (defined in lines 29–34). The enumeration represents whether the player tied, lost or won the game; its four members are **PUSH**, **LOSE**, **WIN** and **BLACKJACK**.

When the player clicks the **Deal** button (event handler on lines 149–205), all the **PictureBox**es are cleared, the deck is shuffled, and the player and dealer receive two cards each. If both obtain scores of 21, method **GameOver** is called and is passed **GameStatus.PUSH**. If only the player has 21 after the first two cards are dealt, **GameOver** is called and is passed **GameStatus.BLACKJACK**. If only the dealer has 21, method **GameOver** is called and is passed **GameStatus.LOSE**.

If **GameOver** is not called, the player can take additional cards by clicking the **Hit** button (event handler on line 121–146). Each time a player clicks **Hit**, the player is dealt one card, which is displayed in the GUI. If the player exceeds 21, the game is over, and the player loses. If the player has exactly 21, the player is not allowed to take any more cards.

Players can click the **Stay** button to indicate that they do not want to risk being dealt another card. In the handler for this event (lines 77–83), the **Hit** and **Stay** buttons are disabled, and method **DealerPlay** is called. This method (lines 86–118) forces the dealer to keep taking cards until the dealer's hand is worth 17 or more. If the dealer exceeds 21, the player wins; otherwise, the values of the hands are compared, and **GameOver** is called with the appropriate argument.

Method **DisplayCard** (lines 209–252) retrieves the appropriate card image. It takes as arguments an integer representing the index of the **PictureBox** in the **ArrayList** that must have its image set and a **String** representing the card. An empty **String** indicates that we wish to display the back of a card; otherwise, the program extracts the face and suit from the **String** and uses this information to find the correct image. The **Select Case** statement (lines 237–246) converts the number representing the suit into an integer and assigns the appropriate character to **suitLetter** (**c** for clubs, **d** for diamonds, **h** for hearts and **s** for spades). The character **suitLetter** is used to complete the image's file name.

B.4 Using Web Forms and Web Services

In the previous examples, we have accessed Web services from Windows applications. However, we can just as easily use them in Web applications. Because Web-based businesses are becoming more and more prevalent, it often is more practical for programmers to design Web services as part of Web applications. Figure B.9 presents an airline reservation Web service that receives information regarding the type of seat the customer wishes to reserve and makes a reservation if such a seat is available.

The airline reservation Web service has a single **WebMethod**—**Reserve** (line 38–85)—which searches its seat database to locate a seat matching a user's request. If it finds an appropriate seat, **Reserve** updates the database, makes the reservation and returns **True**; otherwise, no reservation is made, and the method returns **False**.

Reserve takes two arguments—a **String** representing the desired seat type (the choices are window, middle and aisle) and a **String** representing the desired class type (the choices are economy and first class). Our database contains four columns: The seat number, the seat type, the class type and a column containing either **0** or **1** to indicate whether the seat is reserved. Lines 50–53 define an SQL query that retrieves the number of available seats matching the requested seat and class type. The statement in lines 54–55 executes the query. If the result of the query is not empty, the application reserves the first seat number that the query returns. The database is updated with an **UPDATE** statement, and **Reserve** returns **True**, indicating that the reservation was successful. If the result of the **SELECT** query is not successful, **Reserve** returns **False**, indicating that no seats available matched the request.

```
1    ' Fig. B.9: Reservation.asmx.vb
2    ' Airline reservation Web Service.
3
4    Imports System
5    Imports System.Data
6    Imports System.Diagnostics
7    Imports System.Web
8    Imports System.Web.Services
9    Imports System.Data.OleDb
10
```

Fig. B.9   Airline reservation Web service. (Part 1 of 3.)

```vbnet
11      ' performs reservation of seat
12      <WebService(Namespace:="http://www.deitel.com/", Description := _
13         "Service that enables a user to reserve a seat on a plane.")> _
14      Public Class Reservation
15         Inherits System.Web.Services.WebService
16
17         Friend WithEvents oleDbDataAdapter1 As _
18            System.Data.OleDb.OleDbDataAdapter
19
20         Friend WithEvents oleDbDeleteCommand1 As _
21            System.Data.OleDb.OleDbCommand
22
23         Friend WithEvents oleDbConnection1 As _
24            System.Data.OleDb.OleDbConnection
25
26         Friend WithEvents oleDbInsertCommand1 As _
27            System.Data.OleDb.OleDbCommand
28
29         Friend WithEvents oleDbSelectCommand1 As _
30            System.Data.OleDb.OleDbCommand
31
32         Friend WithEvents oleDbUpdateCommand1 As _
33            System.Data.OleDb.OleDbCommand
34
35         ' Visual Studio .NET generated code
36
37         ' checks database to determine if matching seat is available
38         <WebMethod(Description := "Method to reserve a seat.")> _
39         Public Function Reserve(ByVal seatType As String, _
40            ByVal classType As String) As Boolean
41
42            ' try database connection
43            Try
44               Dim dataReader As OleDbDataReader
45
46               ' open database connection
47               oleDbConnection1.Open()
48               .
49               ' set and execute SQL query
50               oleDbDataAdapter1.SelectCommand.CommandText = _
51                  "SELECT Number FROM Seats WHERE Type = '" & _
52                  seatType & "' AND Class = '" & classType & _
53                  "' AND Taken = '0'"
54               dataReader = _
55                  oleDbDataAdapter1.SelectCommand.ExecuteReader()
56
57               ' if there were results, seat is available
58               If dataReader.Read() Then
59
60                  Dim seatNumber As String = dataReader.GetString(0)
61                  dataReader.Close()
62
```

Fig. B.9   Airline reservation Web service. (Part 2 of 3.)

```
63                    ' update first available seat to be taken
64                    oleDbDataAdapter1.UpdateCommand.CommandText = _
65                        "Update Seats Set Taken = '1' WHERE Number = '" _
66                        & seatNumber & "'"
67
68                    oleDbDataAdapter1.UpdateCommand.ExecuteNonQuery()
69
70                    Return True
71                End If
72
73                dataReader.Close()
74
75            Catch exception As OleDbException ' if connection problem
76                Return False
77
78            Finally
79                oleDbConnection1.Close()
80            End Try
81
82            ' no seat was reserved
83            Return False
84
85        End Function ' Reserve
86
87    End Class ' Reservation
```

Fig. B.9   Airline reservation Web service. (Part 3 of 3.)

Earlier in this appendix, we displayed a Web service in design view (Fig. B.2), and we explained that design view allows the programmer to add components to a Web service in a visual manner. In our airline reservation Web service (Fig. B.9), we used various data components. Figure B.10 shows these components in design view. Notice that it is easier to drop these components into our Web service using the **Toolbox** rather than typing the equivalent code.

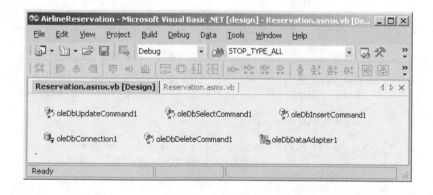

Fig. B.10   Airline Web Service in design view.

Figure B.11 presents the ASPX listing for the Web Form through which users can select seat types. This page allows users to reserve a seat on the basis of its class and location in a row of seats. The page then uses the airline-reservation Web service to carry out users' requests. If the database request is not successful, the user is instructed to modify the request and try again.

```
1   <%-- Fig. B.11: TicketReservation.aspx          --%>
2   <%-- A Web Form that allows users to select the type --%>
3   <%-- of seat they wish to reserve.              --%>
4
5   <%@ Page Language="vb" AutoEventWireup="false"
6      Codebehind="TicketReservation.aspx.vb"
7      Inherits="MakeReservation.TicketReservation"%>
8
9   <!DOCTYPE HTML PUBLIC "-//W3C//DTD HTML 4.0 Transitional//EN">
10  <HTML>
11     <HEAD>
12       <title>Ticket Reservation</title>
13       <meta content="Microsoft Visual Studio.NET 7.0" name=GENERATOR>
14       <meta content="Visual Basic 7.0" name=CODE_LANGUAGE>
15       <meta content=JavaScript name=vs_defaultClientScript>
16       <meta name=vs_targetSchema content=
17          http://schemas.microsoft.com/intellisense/ie5>
18     </HEAD>
19     <body MS_POSITIONING="GridLayout">
20
21       <form id=Form1 method=post runat="server">
22
23         <asp:DropDownList id=seatList style="Z-INDEX: 105;
24            LEFT: 23px; POSITION: absolute; TOP: 43px"
25            runat="server" Width="105px" Height="22px">
26
27            <asp:ListItem Value="Aisle">Aisle</asp:ListItem>
28            <asp:ListItem Value="Middle">Middle</asp:ListItem>
29            <asp:ListItem Value="Window">Window</asp:ListItem>
30
31         </asp:DropDownList>
32
33         <asp:DropDownList id=classList style="Z-INDEX: 102;
34            LEFT: 145px; POSITION: absolute; TOP: 43px"
35            runat="server" Width="98px" Height="22px">
36
37           <asp:ListItem Value="Economy">Economy</asp:ListItem>
38           <asp:ListItem Value="First">First</asp:ListItem>
39
40         </asp:DropDownList>
41
42         <asp:Button id=reserveButton style="Z-INDEX: 103;
43            LEFT: 21px; POSITION: absolute; TOP: 83px"
44            runat="server" Text="Reserve">
45         </asp:Button>
```

Fig. B.11   ASPX file that takes reservation information. (Part 1 of 2.)

```
46
47              <asp:Label id=Label1 style="Z-INDEX: 104;
48                 LEFT: 17px; POSITION: absolute; TOP: 13px"
49                 runat="server">Please select the type of seat and
50                 class you wish to reserve:
51              </asp:Label>
52
53           </form>
54        </body>
55    </HTML>
```

Fig. B.11   ASPX file that takes reservation information. (Part 2 of 2.)

This page defines two **DropDownList** objects and a **Button**. One **DropDown-List** displays all the seat types from which users can select. The second lists choices for the class type. Users click the **Button**, named **reserveButton**, to submit requests after making selections from the **DropDownList**s. The code-behind file (Fig. B.12) attaches an event handler to this button.

```
1    ' Fig. B.12: TicketReservation.aspx.vb
2    ' Making a reservation using a Web Service.
3
4    Imports System
5    Imports System.Collections
6    Imports System.ComponentModel
7    Imports System.Data
8    Imports System.Drawing
9    Imports System.Web
10   Imports System.Web.SessionState
11   Imports System.Web.UI
12   Imports System.Web.UI.WebControls
13   Imports System.Web.UI.HtmlControls
14
15   ' allows visitors to select seat type to reserve, and
16   ' then make the reservation
17   Public Class TicketReservation
18      Inherits System.Web.UI.Page
19
20      Protected WithEvents Label1 As Label
21      Protected WithEvents reserveButton As Button
22      Protected WithEvents classList As DropDownList
23      Protected WithEvents seatList As DropDownList
24      Private Agent As New localhost.Reservation()
25
26      ' Visual Studio .NET generated code
27
28      Private Sub Page_Load(ByVal sender As System.Object, _
29         ByVal e As System.EventArgs) Handles MyBase.Load
30
31         If IsPostBack
32            classList.Visible = False
```

Fig. B.12   Code-behind file for the reservation page. (Part 1 of 3.)

```
33              seatList.Visible = False
34              reserveButton.Visible = False
35              Label1.Visible = False
36          End If
37      End Sub
38
39      ' calls Web Service to try to reserve specified seat
40      Private Sub reserveButton_Click(ByVal sender As _
41          System.Object, ByVal e As System.EventArgs) _
42          Handles reserveButton.Click
43
44          ' if WebMethod returned true, signal success
45          If Agent.Reserve(seatList.SelectedItem.Text, _
46              classList.SelectedItem.Text.ToString) Then
47
48              Response.Write("Your reservation has been made." _
49                  & "  Thank you.")
50
51              ' WebMethod returned False, so signal failure
52          Else
53              Response.Write("This seat is not available, " & _
54                  "please hit the back button on your browser " & _
55                  "and try again.")
56          End If
57
58      End Sub ' reserveButton_Click
59
60  End Class ' TicketReservation
```

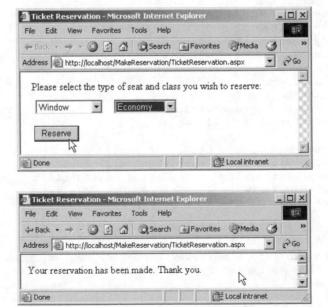

Fig. B.12   Code-behind file for the reservation page. (Part 2 of 3.)

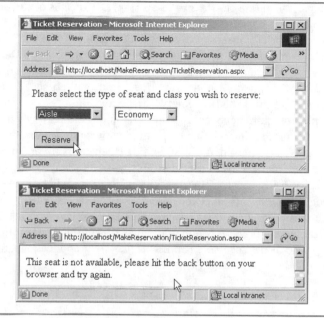

Fig. B.12   Code-behind file for the reservation page. (Part 3 of 3.)

Line 24 creates a **Reservation** object. When the user clicks **Reserve**, the **reserveButton_Click** event handler executes, and the page reloads. The event handler (lines 40–58) calls the Web service's **Reserve** method and passes it the selected seat and class type as arguments. If **Reserve** returns **True**, the application displays a message thanking the user for making a reservation; otherwise, the user is notified that the type of seat requested is not available, and the user is instructed to try again.

B.5 Programmer-Defined Types in Web Services

It is possible to create more sophisticated Web services by using programmer-defined types. These types can be passed to and returned from Web service methods. Web service clients also can use programmer-defined types, because the proxy class created for the client contains these type definitions. There are, however, some subtleties to keep in mind when using programmer-defined types in Web services; we point these out as we encounter them in the next example.

The example in this section presents a math tutoring program. The Web service generates random equations of type **Equation**. The client inputs information about the kind of mathematical example that the user wants (addition, subtraction or multiplication) and the skill level of the user (1 creates equations using one-digit numbers; 2, two-digit numbers; and 3, three-digit numbers); it then generates an equation consisting of random numbers that have the proper number of digits. The client receives the **Equation** and uses a Windows Form to display the math questions to the user.

Data types passed to and from Web services must be supported by SOAP. Programmer-defined types that are sent to or from a Web service are serialized, so that they can be passed in XML format. This process is called *XML serialization*.

In this example, we define class **Equation** (Fig. B.13). This class is included in the Web service project and contains variables, properties and methods. Before explaining class **Equation**, we briefly discuss the process of returning objects from Web service methods. Any object returned by a Web service method must have a default constructor. Although all objects can be instantiated by a default **Public** constructor (even if this constructor is not defined explicitly), a class returned from a Web service explicitly must define a constructor, even if its body is empty.

A few additional requirements apply to programmer-defined types in Web services. Any variables of the programmer-defined type that we wish to access at runtime must be declared **Public**. We also must define **Get** and **Set** accessors for any properties that we wish to access at runtime. The Web service needs to have a way both to retrieve and to manipulate such properties, because objects of the custom type will be converted into XML (when the objects are serialized) then converted back to objects (when they are deserialized). During serialization, the property value must be read (through the **Get** accessor); during deserialization, the property value of the new object must be set (through the **Set** accessor). If only one of the accessors is present, the client application cannot access the property.

```vb
1   ' Fig. B.13: Equation.vb
2   ' Class Equation that contains information about an equation.
3
4   Imports System
5
6   Public Class Equation
7
8      Private mLeft, mRight, mResult As Integer
9      Private mOperation As String
10
11     ' required default constructor
12     Public Sub New()
13        Me.New(0, 0, "+")
14     End Sub ' New
15
16     ' constructor for class Equation
17     Public Sub New(ByVal leftValue As Integer, _
18        ByVal rightValue As Integer, _
19        ByVal operationType As String)
20
21        mLeft = leftValue
22        mRight = rightValue
23        mOperation = operationType
24
25        Select Case operationType
26
27           Case "+" ' addition operator
28              mResult = mLeft + mRight
29           Case "-" ' subtraction operator
30              mResult = mLeft - mRight
```

Fig. B.13   Class that stores equation information. (Part 1 of 3.)

```
31              Case "*" ' multiplication operator
32                  mResult = mLeft * mRight
33          End Select
34      End Sub ' New
35
36      Public Overrides Function ToString() As String
37
38          Return Left.ToString() & " " & mOperation & " " & _
39              mRight.ToString() & " = " & mResult.ToString()
40      End Function ' ToString
41
42      ' readonly property returning String representing
43      ' left-hand side
44      Public Property LeftHandSide() As String
45          Get
46              Return mLeft.ToString() & " " & mOperation & " " & _
47                  mRight.ToString()
48          End Get
49
50          Set(ByVal Value As String)
51          End Set
52      End Property
53
54      ' readonly property returning String representing
55      ' right-hand side
56      Public Property RightHandSide() As String
57          Get
58              Return mResult.ToString()
59          End Get
60
61          Set(ByVal Value As String)
62          End Set
63      End Property
64
65      ' left operand get and set property
66      Public Property Left() As Integer
67          Get
68              Return mLeft
69          End Get
70
71          Set(ByVal value As Integer)
72              mLeft = value
73          End Set
74      End Property
75
76      ' right operand get and set property
77      Public Property Right() As Integer
78          Get
79              Return mRight
80          End Get
81
```

Fig. B.13   Class that stores equation information. (Part 2 of 3.)

```
82              Set(ByVal Value As Integer)
83                 mRight = Value
84              End Set
85          End Property
86
87          ' get and set property of result of applying
88          ' operation to left and right operands
89          Public Property Result() As Integer
90              Get
91                 Return mResult
92              End Get
93
94              Set(ByVal Value As Integer)
95                 mResult = Value
96              End Set
97          End Property
98
99          ' get and set property for operation
100         Public Property Operation() As String
101             Get
102                Return mOperation
103             End Get
104
105             Set(ByVal Value As String)
106                Operation = Value
107             End Set
108         End Property
109     End Class 'Equation
```

Fig. B.13   Class that stores equation information. (Part 3 of 3.)

Common Programming Error B.2

*Failure to define explicitly a **Public** constructor for a type being used in a Web service results in a runtime error.*

Common Programming Error B.3

*Defining only the **Get** or **Set** accessor of a property for a programmer-defined type being used in a Web service results in a property that is inaccessible to the client.*

Common Programming Error B.4

*Clients of a Web service can access only that service's **Public** members. To allow access to **Private** data, programmers should provide **Public** properties.*

Now, let us discuss class **Equation** (Fig. B.13). Lines 17–34 define a constructor that takes three arguments—two **Integers** representing the left and right operands and a **String** that represents the algebraic operation to carry out. The constructor sets the **mLeft, mRight** and **mOperation** variables, then calculates the appropriate result. The default constructor (lines 12–14) calls the other constructor and passes some default values. We do not use the default constructor, but it must be defined in the program.

Class **Equation** defines properties **LeftHandSide**, **RightHandSide**, **Left**, **Right**, **Operation** and **Result**. The program does not need to modify the values of these properties, but an implementation for the **Set** accessor must be provided.

LeftHandSide returns a **String** representing everything to the left of the "=" sign, and **RightHandSide** returns a **String** representing everything to the right of the "=" sign. **Left** returns the **Integer** to the left of the operator (known as the left operand), and **Right** returns the **Integer** to the right of the operator (known as the right operand). **Result** returns the answer to the equation, and **Operation** returns the operator. The program does not need the **RightHandSide** property, but we have chosen to include it in case other clients choose to use it. Figure B.14 presents the **Generator** Web service that creates random, customized **Equation**s.

```vb
1   ' Fig. B.14: Generator.asmx.vb
2   ' Web Service to generate random equations based on the
3   ' operation and difficulty level.
4
5   Imports System
6   Imports System.Collections
7   Imports System.ComponentModel
8   Imports System.Data
9   Imports System.Diagnostics
10  Imports System.Web
11  Imports System.Web.Services
12
13  <WebService(Namespace:="http://www.deitel.com/", Description:= _
14     "Web service that generates a math equation.")> _
15  Public Class Generator
16     Inherits System.Web.Services.WebService
17
18     ' Visual Studio .NET generated code
19
20     <WebMethod(Description:="Method to generate a " _
21        & "math equation.")> _
22     Public Function GenerateEquation(ByVal operation As String, _
23        ByVal level As Integer) As Equation
24
25        ' find maximum and minimum number to be used
26        Dim maximum As Integer = Convert.ToInt32( _
27           Math.Pow(10, level))
28
29        Dim minimum As Integer = Convert.ToInt32( _
30           Math.Pow(10, level - 1))
31
32        Dim randomObject As New Random()
33
34        ' create equation consisting of two random numbers
35        ' between minimum and maximum parameters
36        Dim equation As New Equation( _
37           randomObject.Next(minimum, maximum), _
38           randomObject.Next(minimum, maximum), operation)
39
40        Return equation
41     End Function ' Generate Equation
42  End Class ' Generator
```

Fig. B.14   Web service that generates random equations.

Web service **Generator** contains only one method, **GenerateEquation**. This method takes as arguments a **String** representing the operation we wish to perform and an **Integer** representing the difficulty level. Figure B.15 demonstrates the result of testing this Web service. Notice that the return value from our Web service method is XML. However, this example differs from previous ones in that the XML specifies the values for all **Public** properties and variables of the object that is being returned. The return object has been serialized into XML. Our proxy class takes this return value and deserializes it into an object that then is passed to the client. [*Note*: It is important to understand that an **Equation** object is *not* being passed back and forth between the Web service and the client. Rather, the information in the object is being sent in the form of XML. This information, once received, can be used by the client. Clients created using .NET will take the information and create a new object. Clients created on other platforms, however, may use the information differently. Readers creating clients on other platforms should check the Web services documentation for the specific platform they are using, to see how their client may process complex data types.]

Lines 26–30 define the lower and upper bounds for the random numbers that the method generates. To set these limits, the program first calls **Shared** method **Pow** of class **Math**—this method raises its first argument to the power of its second argument. **Integer maximum** represents the upper bound for a randomly generated number. The program raises **10** to the power of the specified **level** argument and passes this value as the upper bound. For instance, if **level** is **1**, **maximum** is **10**; if **level** is **2**, **minimum** is **100**; and so on. Variable **minimum**'s value is determined by raising **10** to a power one less than **level**. This calculates the smallest number with **level** digits. If **level** is **2**, **min** is **10**; if **level** is **3**, **minimum** is **100**; and so on.

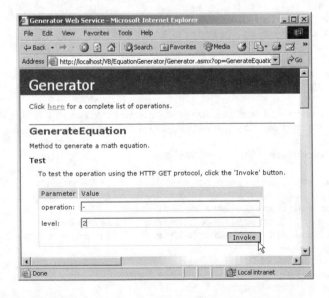

Fig. B.15   Returning an object from a Web service method. (Part 1 of 2.)

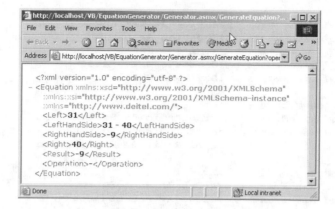

Fig. B.15   Returning an object from a Web service method. (Part 2 of 2.)

Lines 36–38 create a new **Equation** object. The program calls **Random** method **Next**, which returns an **Integer** that is greater than or equal to a specified lower bound, but less than a specified upper bound. This method generates a left operand value that is greater than or equal to **minimum**, but less than **maximum** (i.e., a number with **level** digits). The right operand is another random number with the same characteristics. The operation passed to the **Equation** constructor is the **String operation** that was received by **GenerateEquation**. The new **Equation** object is returned.

Figure B.16 lists the math-tutoring application that uses the **Generator** Web service. The application calls **Generator**'s **GenerateEquation** method to create an **Equation** object. The tutor then displays the left-hand side of the **Equation** and waits for user input. In this example, the program accesses both class **Generator** and class **Equation** from within the **localhost** namespace—both are placed in this namespace when the proxy is generated.

The math-tutor application displays a question and waits for input. The default setting for the difficulty level is **1**, but users change this at any time by selecting a level from among the bottom row of **RadioButton**s. Clicking any of the levels invokes its **Click** event handler (lines 78–94), which sets integer **level** to the level selected by the user. Although the default setting for the question type is **Addition**, the user also can change this at any time by selecting one of the top-row **RadioButton**s. Doing so invokes the radio-button event handlers on lines 97–121, which set **String operation** so that it contains the symbol corresponding to the user's selection.

```
1    ' Fig. B.16: Tutor.vb
2    ' Math Tutor program.
3
4    Public Class FrmTutor
5        Inherits System.Windows.Forms.Form
6
7        Friend WithEvents cmdGenerate As Button
8        Friend WithEvents cmdOk As Button
```

Fig. B.16   Math tutor application. (Part 1 of 4.)

```vbnet
9
10       Friend WithEvents txtAnswer As TextBox
11       Friend WithEvents lblQuestion As Label
12
13       Friend WithEvents pnlOperations As Panel
14       Friend WithEvents pnlLevel As Panel
15
16       ' select math operation
17       Friend WithEvents subtractRadio As RadioButton
18       Friend WithEvents addRadio As RadioButton
19       Friend WithEvents multiplyRadio As RadioButton
20
21       ' select question level radio buttons
22       Friend WithEvents levelOne As RadioButton
23       Friend WithEvents levelTwo As RadioButton
24       Friend WithEvents levelThree As RadioButton
25
26       Private operation As String = "+"
27       Private level As Integer = 1
28       Private equation As localhost.Equation
29       Private generator As New localhost.Generator()
30
31       ' Visual Studio .NET generated code
32
33       ' generates new equation on Click event
34       Private Sub cmdGenerate_Click(ByVal sender As _
35          System.Object, ByVal e As System.EventArgs) _
36          Handles cmdGenerate.Click
37
38          ' generate equation using current operation
39          ' and level
40          equation = generator.GenerateEquation(operation, _
41             level)
42
43          ' display left-hand side of equation
44          lblQuestion.Text = equation.LeftHandSide
45
46          cmdOk.Enabled = True
47          txtAnswer.Enabled = True
48       End Sub ' cmdGenerate_Click
49
50       ' check user's answer
51       Private Sub cmdOk_Click(ByVal sender As _
52          System.Object, ByVal e As System.EventArgs) _
53          Handles cmdOk.Click
54
55          ' determine correct result from Equation object
56          Dim answer As Integer = equation.Result
57
58          If txtAnswer.Text = "" Then
59             Return
60          End If
61
```

Fig. B.16 Math tutor application. (Part 2 of 4.)

```vbnet
62              ' get user's answer
63              Dim myAnswer As Integer = Int32.Parse( _
64                 txtAnswer.Text)
65
66              ' test if user's answer is correct
67              If answer = myAnswer Then
68
69                 lblQuestion.Text = ""
70                 txtAnswer.Text = ""
71                 cmdOk.Enabled = False
72                 MessageBox.Show("Correct! Good job!")
73              Else
74                 MessageBox.Show("Incorrect. Try again.")
75              End If
76           End Sub ' cmdOk_Click
77
78           Private Sub levelOne_Click(ByVal sender As Object, _
79              ByVal e As System.EventArgs) Handles levelOne.Click
80
81              level = 1
82           End Sub ' levelOne_Click
83
84           Private Sub levelTwo_Click(ByVal sender As Object, _
85              ByVal e As System.EventArgs) Handles levelTwo.Click
86
87              level = 2
88           End Sub ' levelTwo_Click
89
90           Private Sub levelThree_Click(ByVal sender As Object, _
91              ByVal e As System.EventArgs) Handles levelThree.Click
92
93              level = 3
94           End Sub ' levelThree_Click
95
96           ' set add operation
97           Private Sub addRadio_Click(ByVal sender As Object, _
98              ByVal e As System.EventArgs) Handles addRadio.Click
99
100             operation = "+"
101             cmdGenerate.Text = "Generate " & addRadio.Text & _
102                " Example"
103          End Sub ' addRadio_Click
104
105          ' set subtract operation
106          Private Sub subtractRadio_Click(ByVal sender As Object, _
107             ByVal e As System.EventArgs) Handles subtractRadio.Click
108
109             operation = "-"
110             cmdGenerate.Text = "Generate " & subtractRadio.Text & _
111                " Example"
112          End Sub ' subtractRadio_Click
113
```

Fig. B.16   Math tutor application. (Part 3 of 4.)

```
114      ' set multiply operation
115      Private Sub multiplyRadio_Click(ByVal sender As Object, _
116         ByVal e As System.EventArgs) Handles multiplyRadio.Click
117
118         operation = "*"
119         cmdGenerate.Text = "Generate " & multiplyRadio.Text & _
120            " Example"
121      End Sub ' multiplyRadio_Click
122   End Class ' FrmTutor
```

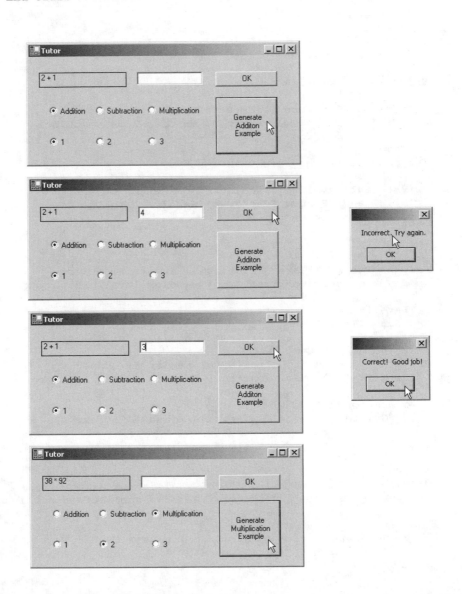

Fig. B.16   Math tutor application. (Part 4 of 4.)

Event handler **cmdGenerate_Click** (lines 34–48) invokes **Generator** method **GenerateEquation**. The left-hand side of the equation is displayed in **lblQuestion** (line 44), and **cmdOk** is enabled (line 46) so that the user can enter an answer. When the user clicks **OK**, **cmdOk_Click** (lines 51–76) determines whether the user provided the correct answer.

This appendix familiarized the reader with the creation of Web services in .NET. In the next appendix, we discuss how to implement Web services in Java.

B.6 Summary

A Web service in .NET has two main parts: an ASMX file and a code-behind file. The ASMX file can be viewed in any Web browser and displays information about the Web service. The code-behind file contains the Web service's implementation.

An application that consumes a Web service consists of two main parts: a proxy class for the Web service and a client application that accesses the Web service via the proxy. A proxy class handles the task of transferring the Web service method call and its arguments into a SOAP message that is sent from the client to the Web service. The proxy likewise handles the transfer of information from the SOAP response to the client. When a client creates a Web reference to a Web service, Visual Studio .NET generates the proxy class, based on the Web service's WSDL file. Whenever a call is made in a client application to a Web service method, a method in the proxy class is called. This method takes the method name and arguments passed by the client and formats them so that they can be sent as a request in a SOAP message.

Class **WebService** provides members that determine information about the user, the application and other topics relevant to the Web service. A Web service is not required to inherit from class **WebService**. A programmer specifies a class as a Web service by tagging it with the **WebService** attribute. A programmer specifies a method as a Web service method by tagging it with a **WebMethod** attribute.

UDDI (Universal Description, Discovery and Integration) is a project for developing a set of specifications that define how Web services should be discovered so that clients searching for Web services can find them. A DISCO (discovery) file specifies the locations of relevant Web service files. There are three types of discovery files: dynamic discovery files (**.vsdisco** extension), static discovery files (**.disco** extension) and map files (**.map** extension). Once a Web reference is created, a static discovery file is placed in the client's project. The static discovery file contains the locations of the ASMX and WSDL files. When dynamic discovery files are accessed, ASP .NET generates a list of Web services stored in the discovery file's directory.

To store session information, the **EnableSession** property of the **WebMethod** attribute must be set to **True**. When storing session information, a Web service must have a way of identifying users between method calls. The approach is implemented using cookies, which are stored in a **CookieContainer**.

Types can be defined by a programmer and used in a Web service. These types can be passed into or returned from Web service methods, because the types are defined in the proxy class created for the client. Custom types that are sent to or from a Web service are serialized as XML. When an object is returned from a Web service, all its **Public** properties and variables are marked up in XML. This information then can be deserialized into an object on the client side.

B.7 Internet and Web Resources

msdn.microsoft.com/webservices
This Microsoft site includes .NET Web service technology specifications and white papers with XML/SOAP articles, columns and links.

msdn.microsoft.com/soap
This Microsoft site includes documentation, headlines and overviews SOAP. ASP .NET examples that use SOAP are available at this site.

www.xmlwebservices.cc
This site offers a wealth of information on Web services, as well as samples and answers to FAQs. This site also provides links to relevant articles and sites, including sites on how to consume .NET Web services from other platforms.

Newsgroups

communities.microsoft.com/newsgroups/default.asp?icp=dotNET
This site brings you to several Microsoft newsgroups, all on .NET-related topics.

Implementing Web Services in Java

Objectives

- To build a JAX-RPC application that enables a client to invoke a Voting Web service.
- To build a JAXM-based B2B application.
- To examine the role of a message provider in a JAXM application to ensure asynchronous messaging.
- To build a Java client capable of invoking Web services.

The great thing about being an architect is you can walk into your dreams.
Harold E. Wagoner

To serve is beautiful, but only if it is done with joy and a whole heart and a free mind.
Pearl S. Buck

We provide the music, and you provide the audience.
Leopold Stokowski

If two laws conflict with each other, the courts must decide on the operation of each.
John Marshal

Outline

C.1 Introduction

In Chapter 10, Java Web Services: A Conceptual Overview, we introduced the *Java API for XML Remote Procedure Call* (*JAX-RPC*) and the *Java API for XML Messaging* (*JAXM*)—technologies that Sun Microsystems provides for building Web services and the clients that invoke those Web services. In that chapter, we examined the theory behind these emerging technologies and discussed scenarios in which developers might use each API. This appendix shows the technologies "at work," as we use the APIs and the Java programming language to develop two example programs. The first example uses JAX-RPC to build a Web service that tallies votes for favorite programming languages. This example demonstrates a synchronous communication architecture, in which a client halts its activity after sending a SOAP request to a Web service. The client resumes activity when it receives a SOAP response from the Web service. Our second example uses JAXM to build a business-to-business (B2B) architecture for purchasing and selling books. This example demonstrates asynchronous communication, in which a client may proceed with its activities immediately after sending a SOAP request to a Web service, without having to "wait" for a SOAP response. As we will see, the client contains a separate component called a *message provider* that handles sending and receiving SOAP messages. We compare and contrast JAX-RPC and JAXM, as well as contrast synchronous and asynchronous communication, throughout these examples.

To conclude this appendix, we build a Java-based client capable of invoking a Web service that provides stock information. We show how a WSDL document participates in informing the client which Web services are available. Although neither the client nor the Web service uses JAX-RPC or JAXM, we include this example to introduce some of the proprietary Java-based APIs for invoking Web services.

We show complete working Java examples in the form of LIVE-CODE™, so understanding these examples requires some familiarity with Java programming. If you are unfamiliar with the Java programming language, please refer to our text *Java How to Program, Fourth Edition*. We deploy both JAX-RPC and JAXM applications via servlets—a Java request-response technology that enables developers to extend the functionality of a server. For more information on implementing Web services in Java, please refer to our book *Java Web Services for Experienced Programmers*.

C.2 Software Installation

To be able to run the examples included in this appendix, you need to download and install the Java Web Services Developer Pack (JWSDP) and the Cloudscape database. The JWSDP includes the *Java XML Pack, Tomcat Java Servlet* and *JavaServer Pages containers*, a registry server and the *Ant build tool*. The Java XML Pack also provides the JAX-RPC and JAXM. As of this writing, the current version of JWSDP is 1.0. The Cloudscape database is included in the *Java 2 Enterprise Edition Software Development Kit (J2EE)* version 1.3.1.

C.2.1 JWSDP Download and Installation

Before installing the JWSDP, make sure that the *Java 2 Standard Edition Software Development Kit (J2SE)* version 1.3.1 or higher has been installed. The JWSDP v1.0 is available for download at

```
java.sun.com/webservices/downloads/webservicespack.html
```

Select a platform and click **Continue** to download the file. To install JWSDP 1.0 on the Windows platform, run **jwsdp-1_0-windows-i586.exe**, which is the download file for Windows. The installation is straightforward. During the installation, you must specify the location of the J2SE installation and the directory where you want to install the JWSDP. After installing the JWSDP, make sure to set the **%JWSDP_HOME%** environment variable to the directory in which JWSDP is installed and include **%JWSDP_HOME%\bin** in the path.

C.2.2 Setting Up the Apache Tomcat Server

Tomcat is a fully functional implementation of the Java Server Pages (JSP) and servlet standards. It includes a Web server, so it can be used as a standalone test container for JSPs and servlets. Tomcat also can be specified as the handler for JSP and servlet requests received by popular Web servers such as the Apache Software Foundation's Apache Web server or Microsoft's Internet Information Server (IIS). Tomcat is integrated into the Java 2 Enterprise Edition reference implementation from Sun Microsystems.

The Java Web Services Developer Pack includes the most recent release of Tomcat (version 4). Installation of the JWSDP will install Tomcat. For Tomcat to work correctly, you must define environment variables **JAVA_HOME**, **CATALINA_HOME** and **TOMCAT_HOME**. **JAVA_HOME** should point to the directory containing your Java installation (ours is **d:\jdk1.3.1**), and both **CATALINA_HOME** and **TOMCAT_HOME** should point to **%JWSDP_HOME%/bin**.

Testing and Debugging Tip C.1

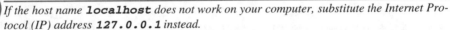

On some platforms you may need to restart your computer for the new environment variables to take effect.

After setting the environment variables, you can start the Tomcat server. Open a command prompt (or shell) and change directories to **TOMCAT_HOME**. In this directory are the files **startup.bat** and **startup.sh**, for starting the Tomcat server on Windows and UNIX (Linux or Solaris), respectively. The Tomcat server executes on Transmission Control Protocol (TCP) port 8080 to prevent conflicts with standard Web servers, which typically execute on TCP port 80. To prove that Tomcat is executing and can respond to requests, open your Web browser and enter the URL

```
http://localhost:8080/
```

This should display the Tomcat documentation home page. The host **localhost** indicates to the Web browser that it should request the home page from the Tomcat server on the local computer.

If the Tomcat documentation home page does not display, try the URL

```
http://127.0.0.1:8080/
```

The host **localhost** translates to the IP address **127.0.0.1**.

Testing and Debugging Tip C.2

*If the host name **localhost** does not work on your computer, substitute the Internet Protocol (IP) address **127.0.0.1** instead.*

Note that the **TOMCAT_HOME** directory also contains the files **shutdown.bat** and **shutdown.sh**, which are used to stop the Tomcat server on Windows and UNIX (Linux or Solaris), respectively.

C.2.3 Deploying a Web Application

JSPs, servlets and their supporting files are deployed as part of *Web applications*. Normally, Web applications are deployed in the **webapps** subdirectory of the **%JWSDP_HOME%** directory. A Web application has a well-known directory structure in which all the files that are part of the application reside. This directory structure can be created by the server administrator in the **webapps** directory, or the entire directory structure can be archived in a *Web application archive file*. Such an archive is known as a *WAR file* and ends with the **.war** file extension. When a WAR file is placed in the **webapps** directory, Tomcat extracts the WAR-file contents into the appropriate **webapps** subdirectory structure. We already have created this directory structure for all the examples in this appendix, which are available from our Web site, **www.deitel.com**. We explain how to deploy each example in this appendix in the sections that discuss each example.

C.2.4 Cloudscape Database Download and Installation

Several examples in this book use the Cloudscape database, which is included in the Java™ 2 Enterprise Edition Software Development Kit (J2EE SDK) v. 1.3.1. This is available for download at

```
java.sun.com/j2ee/sdk_1.3
```

After installing the J2EE SDK, make sure to set the **%J2EE_HOME%** environment variable to the directory in which J2EE is installed. Also, make sure to set include **%J2EE_HOME%/bin** in the path.

Cloudscape represents each database as a directory with the same name as the database. For example, Cloudscape will store a database called **books** in a directory called **books**. The scripts needed to create all databases are available to download from our Web site **www.deitel.com**. Each script has extension **sql**, and the script's name is identical to the name of the database that the script creates—for example, **books.sql** is needed to create the **books** database. Place each script in the **%J2EE_HOME%/cloudscape** directory. We also provide **createDatabase.bat** on our Web site, which is a batch file that creates a database from a script. To create a database, type

```
createDatabase script
```

For example, to create the books database, type

```
createDatabase books.sql
```

Each Web application that accesses a Cloudscape database must have **RmiJDBC.jar** and **cloudclient.jar** in the **lib** directory of the Web-application directory. Figure C.1 shows this relationship. **RmiJDBC.jar** and **cloudclient.jar** are located in the **%J2EE_HOME%/lib/cloudscape** directory.

To start Cloudscape (assuming **%J2EE_HOME%/bin** is included in the path), type in a command shell:

```
cloudscape -start
```

Web application directory and file structure

```
webapps
   WEB-INF
      web.xml
      classes
          Web-application classes (some of which use Cloudscape)
      lib
         RmiJDBC.jar
         cloudclient.jar
```

Fig. C.1   Directory and file structure for a Web application that uses the Cloudscape database.

To stop Cloudscape, type in a command shell:

```
cloudscape -stop
```

Also, make sure to start Cloudscape before starting Tomcat. When Tomcat starts, the Web applications that use Cloudscape will attempt to load the database drivers—if Cloudscape is not operational, Tomcat will report an error.

C.3 JAX-RPC Vote Service

In this section, we present a simple JAX-RPC Web service that tallies votes for the users' favorite programming languages. The Vote service returns an array of JavaBean type object; each JavaBean represents the vote for one programming language. The four major steps in this example include:

1. Defining a service interface that declares methods that clients can invoke on the remote service.

2. Defining the service implementation for the service interface. [*Note*: By convention, the service implementation class has the same name as the interface and ends with **Impl**.]

3. Deploying the service to the Web server. In this example, we use Apache's Tomcat, which is part of the JWSDP.

4. Defining the client application that interacts with the service.

Figure C.2 shows the structure of this example. Before providing the code for the example, we discuss the limited set of JAX-RPC-supported Java types.

C.3.1 JAX-RPC-Supported Java Types

JAX-RPC supports only a subset of Java types, because the data types transmitted by the remote procedure calls must map to SOAP XML data types. When a Web service receives a remote method call from its client, the JAX-RPC runtime service environment first transforms the XML representation of the call arguments to their corresponding Java types. This process is known as *deserialization*. The JAX-RPC runtime service environment then passes the Java representation of the call arguments to the service implementation to process the remote call. After the call is processed, the JAX-RPC runtime service environment transforms the return object to its XML representation. This process is known as *serialization*. The XML representation of the return object is then sent back to the client. The serialization/deserialization process happens both at the client and at the service.

JAX-RPC supports Java primitive types and their corresponding wrapper classes. JAX-RPC supports a subset of standard Java classes as well, including **BigDecimal**, **BigInteger**, **Calendar**, **Date** and **String**. The JWSDP 1.0 final release also supports a set of classes that implement the **java.util.Collection** interface. These classes are: **Vector**, **ArrayList**, **LinkedList**, **Stack**, **HashMap**, **HashTable**, **HashSet**, **Properties**, **TreeMap** and **TreeSet**.

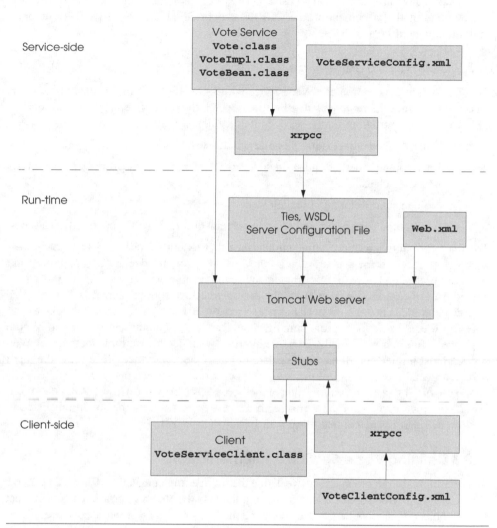

Fig. C.2 Vote example structure.

In addition to the aforementioned supported types, JAX-RPC supports objects of Java classes that satisfy the following conditions:

1. The class does not implement *java.rmi.Remote*.

2. The class has a *public* default constructor.

3. The class's public fields are JAX-RPC-supported Java types.

4. Java classes may follow the JavaBean's *set* and *get* method-design patterns. Bean properties must be JAX-RPC-supported Java types. In addition, each bean property must have a *setter* and *getter* methods.

Finally, Java arrays also can be used in JAX-RPC as long as the member type of the array is one of the aforementioned JAX-RPC-supported Java types. JAX-RPC supports multidimensional Java arrays as well.

C.3.2 Defining **Vote** Service Interface

The first step in the creation of a Web service with JAX-RPC is to define the remote interface that describes the *remote methods* through which the client interacts with the service. There are some restrictions on the service interface definition:

1. The interface must extend **java.rmi.Remote**.

2. Each public method must include **java.rmi.RemoteException** in its **throws** clause.

3. No constant declarations are allowed.

4. All method parameters and return types must be JAX-RPC-supported Java types.

To create a remote interface, define an interface that extends interface **java.rmi.Remote**. Interface **Remote** is a *tagging interface*—it does not declare any methods, and therefore places no burden on the implementing class. Interface **Vote** (Fig. C.3)—which extends interface **Remote** (line 9)—is the remote interface for our second JAX-RPC Web service example. Lines 12–13 declare method **addVote**, which clients can invoke to add votes for the users' favorite programming languages. Note that although the **Vote** remote interface defines only one method, remote interfaces can declare multiple methods. A Web service must implement all methods declared in its remote interface. Recall that the input parameters and return values of the methods declared in a service interface must be JAX-RPC-supported types. The return value of method **addVote** is an array of **VoteBean** objects. When we implement the **VoteBean** class, we must follow the conditions listed in Section C.3.1 to ensure compatibility with JAX-RPC.

C.3.3 Defining **Vote** Service Implementation

After defining the remote interface, we define the service implementation. Class **VoteImpl** (Fig. C.4) is the Web service endpoint that implements the **Vote** interface. Clients interact with an object of class **VoteImpl** by invoking method **addVote** of interface **Vote**. Method **addVote** enables the client to add a vote to the database and obtain a tally of votes.

```
1   // Vote.java
2   // VoteService interface declares a method for adding votes and
3   // returning vote information.
4   package com.deitel.jws.jaxrpc.voteservice;
5
6   // Java core packages
7   import java.rmi.*;
8
9   public interface Vote extends Remote {
10
```

Fig. C.3   **Vote** interface defines the service interface for the Vote Web service. (Part 1 of 2.)

```
11          // obtain vote information from server
12          public VoteBean[] addVote( String languageName )
13             throws RemoteException;
14       }
```

Fig. C.3   Vote interface defines the service interface for the Vote Web service.
(Part 2 of 2.)

```
 1       // VoteImpl.java
 2       // VoteImpl implements the Vote remote interface to provide
 3       // a VoteService remote object.
 4       package com.deitel.jws.jaxrpc.voteservice;
 5
 6       // Java core packages
 7       import java.rmi.*;
 8       import java.sql.*;
 9       import java.util.*;
10
11       // Java extension packages
12       import javax.servlet.*;
13
14       // Java XML packages
15       import javax.xml.rpc.server.*;
16       import javax.xml.rpc.JAXRPCException;
17
18       public class VoteImpl implements ServiceLifecycle, Vote {
19
20          private Connection connection;
21          private PreparedStatement sqlUpdate, sqlSelect;
22
23          // setup database connection and prepare SQL statement
24          public void init( Object context )
25             throws JAXRPCException
26          {
27             // attempt database connection and
28             // create PreparedStatements
29             try {
30
31                // cast context to ServletEndpointContext
32                ServletEndpointContext endpointContext =
33                   ( ServletEndpointContext ) context;
34
35                // get ServletContext
36                ServletContext servletContext =
37                   endpointContext.getServletContext();
38
39                // get database driver from servlet context
40                String dbDriver =
41                   servletContext.getInitParameter( "dbDriver" );
42
```

Fig. C.4   VoteImpl defines the service implementation for the Vote Web service.
(Part 1 of 3.)

```
43          // get database name from servlet context
44          String voteDB =
45             servletContext.getInitParameter( "voteDB" );
46
47          Class.forName( dbDriver ); // load database driver
48
49          // connect to database
50          connection = DriverManager.getConnection( voteDB );
51
52          // PreparedStatement to add one to vote total for a
53          // specific language
54          sqlUpdate =
55             connection.prepareStatement(
56                "UPDATE surveyresults SET vote = vote + 1 " +
57                "WHERE name = ?" );
58
59          // PreparedStatement to obtain surveyresults table's data
60          sqlSelect =
61             connection.prepareStatement( "SELECT name, vote " +
62                "FROM surveyresults ORDER BY vote DESC" );
63
64       } // end try
65
66       // for any exception throw a JAXRPCException to
67       // indicate that the servlet is not currently available
68       catch ( Exception exception ) {
69          exception.printStackTrace();
70
71          throw new JAXRPCException( exception.getMessage() );
72       }
73
74    } // end method init
75
76    // implementation for interface Vote method addVote
77    public VoteBean[] addVote( String name ) throws RemoteException
78    {
79       // obtain votes count from database then update database
80       try {
81
82          // set parameter in sqlUpdate
83          sqlUpdate.setString( 1, name );
84
85          // execute sqlUpdate statement
86          sqlUpdate.executeUpdate();
87
88          // execute sqlSelect statement
89          ResultSet results = sqlSelect.executeQuery();
90
91          List voteInformation = new ArrayList();
92
```

Fig. C.4   **VoteImpl** defines the service implementation for the Vote Web service.
(Part 2 of 3.)

```
93          // iterate ResultSet and prepare return string
94          while ( results.next() ) {
95
96              // store results to VoteBean List
97              VoteBean vote = new VoteBean(
98                  results.getString( 1 ), results.getInt( 2 ) );
99              voteInformation.add( vote );
100         }
101
102         // create array of VoteBeans
103         VoteBean[] voteBeans =
104             new VoteBean[ voteInformation.size() ];
105
106         // get array from voteInformation List
107         voteInformation.toArray( voteBeans );
108
109         return voteBeans;
110
111     } // end try
112
113     // handle database exceptions by returning error to client
114     catch ( Exception exception ) {
115
116         //throw the exception back to the client
117         throw new RemoteException( exception.getMessage() );
118     }
119
120 } // end method addVote
121
122 // close SQL statements and database when servlet terminates
123 public void destroy()
124 {
125     // attempt to close statements and database connection
126     try {
127         sqlUpdate.close();
128         sqlSelect.close();
129         connection.close();
130     }
131
132     // handle database exception
133     catch ( Exception exception ) {
134         exception.printStackTrace();
135     }
136
137 } // end method destroy
138
139 } // end class VoteImpl
```

Fig. C.4   **VoteImpl** defines the service implementation for the Vote Web service.
(Part 3 of 3.)

Class **VoteImpl** implements remote interface **Vote** and interface **ServiceLife-cycle** (line 18). Interface **ServiceLifecycle** allows service endpoint classes to setup access to external resources, such as databases. We use a Cloudscape database in this example to store the total number of votes for each programming language in the database. Not all Web services are required to implement interface **ServiceLifecycle**. However, implementing interface **ServicelLifecycle** provides a convenient way to define lifecycle methods for the service that corresponds to the servlet's lifecycle (e.g., database connection).

Lines 24–74 implement method **init** of interface **ServiceLifecycle** to setup access to a Cloudscape database, which stores the total number of votes for each programming language in the database. The JAX-RPC runtime system invokes method **init** when the service endpoint class is instantiated. Lines 32–33 cast the parameter (**context**) of method **init** to **ServletEndpointContext**. Lines 36–37 invoke method **getServletContext** of class **ServletEndpointContext** to get the servlet context. Lines 40–45 get the database driver and name that is specified in **web.xml**. Line 47 loads the class definition for the database driver. Line 50 declares and initializes a **Connection** (package **java.sql**). The program initializes **connection** with the result of a call to **static** method **getConnection** of class **DriverManager**, which attempts to connect to the database specified by its URL argument. Lines 54–62 invoke **Connection** method **prepareStatement** to create SQL **PreparedStatement**s for updating the number of votes for the client's selected programming language and getting the vote count for each programming language.

Lines 77–120 implement method **addVote** of interface **Vote**. Line 83 sets the parameter of **sqlUpdate** to the programming language that was selected by the user. After setting the parameter for the **PreparedStatement**, the program calls method **executeUpdate** of interface **PreparedStatement** to execute the **UPDATE** operation. Line 89 calls method **executeQuery** of interface **PreparedStatement** to execute the **SELECT** operation. **ResultSet results** stores the query results. Lines 91–107 process the **ResultSet** and store the results in an array of **VoteBean**s. Line 109 returns the **VoteBean**s to the client.

Lines 123–137 implement method **destroy** of interface **ServiceLifecycle**. Lines 127–129 close statements and the database connection to release the database resources.

Class **VoteBean** (Fig. C.5) stores data that represents the vote count for each programming language. Line 17 provides the **public** no-argument constructor. Lines 27–36 provide *get* methods for each piece of information. Lines 39–48 provide *set* methods for each piece of information. These *get* and *set* methods follow JavaBeans design patterns.

```
1   // VoteBean.java
2   // VoteBean maintains vote information for one programming language.
3   package com.deitel.jws.jaxrpc.voteservice;
4
5   // Java core packages
6   import java.io.*;
7
8   // Java extension packages
9   import javax.swing.*;
10
```

Fig. C.5   VoteBean stores the vote count for one programming language. (Part 1 of 2.).

```
11   public class VoteBean implements Serializable {
12
13       private String languageName; // name of language
14       private int count; // vote count
15
16       // public no-argument constructor
17       public VoteBean() {}
18
19       // VoteBean constructor
20       public VoteBean( String voteLanguage, int voteCount )
21       {
22           languageName = voteLanguage;
23           count = voteCount;
24       }
25
26       // get language name
27       public String getLanguageName()
28       {
29           return languageName;
30       }
31
32       // get vote count
33       public int getCount()
34       {
35           return count;
36       }
37
38       // set language name
39       public void setLanguageName( String voteLanguage )
40       {
41           languageName = voteLanguage;
42       }
43
44       // set vote count
45       public void setCount( int voteCount )
46       {
47           count = voteCount;
48       }
49
50   } // end class VoteBean
```

Fig. C.5   **VoteBean** stores the vote count for one programming language.
(Part 2 of 2.).

C.3.4 Service Deployment

In this section, we discuss how to generate the service-side artifacts (e.g., ties, WSDL documents) using **xrpcc** and how to deploy the service on Tomcat. To generate a WSDL document, **xrpcc** reads an XML configuration file that lists remote interfaces. **VoteServiceConfig.xml** (Fig. C.6) is the configuration for our **Vote** service example. **VoteServiceConfig.xml** follows the standard syntax provided by JWSDP to create the configuration file. The **xrpcc** tool uses the **VoteServiceConfig.xml** to generate the WSDL file and other service-side classes for the **Vote** service. The root element **configuration** contains one **service** element that corresponds to remote service. The **name** attribute of element **service** (line 5) indicates the service name. The **targetNamespace** attribute specifies the target namespace for the generated WSDL document (line 6). The **typeNamespace** attribute (line 7) specifies the target namespace within the **types** section of the WSDL document. The **packageName** attribute specifies the fully qualified package name of the generated stubs, ties and other classes (line 8). The value of attribute **packageName** does not need to match the package name of any of the remote interfaces. Element **interface** (lines 10–13) defines the fully qualified name of the service interface via its attribute **name**, and the fully qualified name of the service implementation via its attribute **servantName**. Element **interface** defines a service port in the WSDL file.

Using **xrpcc** requires that we include the location of the service-interface definition and implementation in the classpath. Compile the source code and place the classes in directory **voteserviceoutput**. It is necessary to create directory **voteserviceoutput** before compiling the source code. Execute the following **xrpcc** command

```
xrpcc -classpath voteserviceoutput -d voteserviceoutput
      -server -keep VoteServiceConfig.xml
```

to create service-side classes and the WSDL document. Option **classpath** specifies where **xrpcc** can find the service interface and implementation classes. Option **d** specifies the directory in which to place the generated files. Option **server** specifies that only server-side files should be generated.

The **xrpcc** tool also generates server configuration file **VoteService_Config.properties**, which is used by the JAX-RPC runtime environment. We may modify **VoteService_Config.properties** (in directory **voteserviceoutput**) to make the service WSDL document available from the service endpoint. Open **VoteService_Config.properties** with your a text editor and append the following line:

```
wsdl.location=/WEB-INF/VoteService.wsdl
```

```
1   <?xml version="1.0" encoding="UTF-8"?>
2   <configuration
3     xmlns = "http://java.sun.com/xml/ns/jax-rpc/ri/config">
4
5     <service name = "VoteService"
6        targetNamespace = "http://www.deitel.com/VoteService.wsdl"
7        typeNamespace = "http://www.deitel.com/VoteService/type"
8        packageName = "com.deitel.jws.jaxrpc.voteservice">
9
10       <interface
11          name = "com.deitel.jws.jaxrpc.voteservice.Vote"
12          servantName =
13             "com.deitel.jws.jaxrpc.voteservice.VoteImpl"/>
14    </service>
15  </configuration>
```

Fig. C.6   **VoteServiceConfig.xml** is the configuration file for generating the Vote Web service artifacts using **xrpcc**.

to the end of the file. By doing so, the service WSDL document is accessible at

```
http://localhost:8080/jaxrpc-voteapp/vote/endpoint?WSDL
```

Suppose the service is deployed into **/jaxrpc-voteapp** Web context.

To deploy the Vote Web service to Tomcat, we need to:

1. Write a deployment descriptor.

2. Create a Web context, which, for this example, is **jaxrpc-voteapp**.

3. Copy required classes to directory **jaxrpc-voteapp\WEB-INFO\classes** and required libraries to directory **jaxrpc-voteapp\WEB-INFO\lib**.

Web.xml (Fig. C.7) is the deployment descriptor for the **Vote** service. Two **context-param** elements (lines 14–19 and 21–26) specify the database name and database driver. The URL **jdbc:cloudscape:rmi:languagesurvey** specifies the *protocol* for communication (**jdbc**), the *subprotocol* for communication (**cloudscape:rmi**) and the name of the database (**languagesurvey**). Element **servlet** (lines 28–44) describes the **JAXRPCServlet** servlet that is distributed with the JWSDP 1.0 final release. Servlet **JAXRPCServlet** is a JAX-RPC implementation for dispatching the request to the Web service implementation. In our case, the **JAXRPCServlet** dispatches the client request to the **VoteImpl** class. When the **JAXRPCServlet** receives an HTTP request that contains a SOAP message, the servlet retrieves the data that the SOAP message contains, then dispatches the method call to the service-implementation class via the tie. Element **servlet-class** (lines 34–36) specifies the compiled servlet's fully qualified class name—**com.sun.xml.rpc.server.http.JAXRPCServlet**. The **JAXRPCServlet** obtains information about the server-configuration file, which is passed to the servlet as an initialization parameter. Element **init-param** (lines 37–42) specifies the name and value of the initialization parameter needed by the **JAXRPCServlet**. Element **param-name** (line 38) indicates the name of the initialization parameter, which is **configuration.file**. Element **param-value** (lines 39–41) specifies the value of the initialization parameter, **/WEB-INF/VoteService_Config.properties** (generated by **xrpcc**), which is the location of the server-configuration file. Element **servlet-mapping** (lines 47–50) specifies **servlet-name** and **url-pattern** elements. The URL pattern enables the server to determine which requests should be sent to the **JAXRPCServlet**.

```
1   <?xml version="1.0" encoding="UTF-8"?>
2
3   <!DOCTYPE web-app
4       PUBLIC "-//Sun Microsystems, Inc.//DTD Web Application 2.3//EN"
5       "http://java.sun.com/j2ee/dtds/web-app_2_3.dtd">
6
7   <web-app>
8       <display-name>
9           Java Web service JAX-RPC Vote service Example
10      </display-name>
11
```

Fig. C.7   **web.xml** for deploying the Vote service. (Part 1 of 2.)

```
12       <description>Vote service Application</description>
13
14       <context-param>
15           <param-name>voteDB</param-name>
16           <param-value>
17               jdbc:cloudscape:rmi:languagesurvey
18           </param-value>
19       </context-param>
20
21       <context-param>
22           <param-name>dbDriver</param-name>
23           <param-value>
24               COM.cloudscape.core.RmiJdbcDriver
25           </param-value>
26       </context-param>
27
28       <servlet>
29           <servlet-name>JAXRPCEndpoint</servlet-name>
30           <display-name>JAXRPCEndpoint</display-name>
31           <description>
32               Endpoint for Vote Service
33           </description>
34           <servlet-class>
35               com.sun.xml.rpc.server.http.JAXRPCServlet
36           </servlet-class>
37           <init-param>
38               <param-name>configuration.file</param-name>
39               <param-value>
40                   /WEB-INF/VoteService_Config.properties
41               </param-value>
42           </init-param>
43           <load-on-startup>0</load-on-startup>
44       </servlet>
45
46       <!-- Servlet mappings -->
47       <servlet-mapping>
48           <servlet-name>JAXRPCEndpoint</servlet-name>
49           <url-pattern>/endpoint/*</url-pattern>
50       </servlet-mapping>
51
52       <session-config>
53           <session-timeout>60</session-timeout>
54       </session-config>
55   </web-app>
```

Fig. C.7 `web.xml` for deploying the Vote service. (Part 2 of 2.)

Figure C.8 shows the resulting **jaxrpc-voteapp** Web-application deployment
directory structure. We assume that J2EE is already installed. Because the Vote Web service implementation uses a Cloudscape database, we need to include both **cloud-
client.jar** and **RmiJdbc.jar** in directory **jaxrpc-voteapp\WEB-INF\lib**.
These JAR files are available from directory **%J2EE_HOME%\lib\cloudscape**,
where **J2EE_HOME** is the J2EE installation directory. Directory **jaxrpc-
voteapp\WEB-INF\classes** contains all classes in directory **voteservice-**

output, including **Vote.class**, **VoteImpl.class**, **VoteBean.class** and other classes generated by **xrpcc**.

We can verify whether the Vote Web service is deployed successfully. To verify the deployment, start Tomcat and point your browser to

http://localhost:8080/jaxrpc-voteapp/endpoint

Figure C.9 shows the result of this action.

C.3.5 Client Invocation

Next, we demonstrate how to write a Java client of the Vote Web service using JAX-RPC. Class **VoteServiceClient** (Fig. C.10) is the client application that invokes remote method **addVote** to add votes and obtain voting information. The **vote** package name (line 16) is specified in the configuration file passed to **xrpcc**.

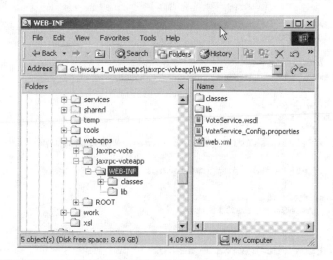

Fig. C.8   Vote Web service Web application directory and file structure.

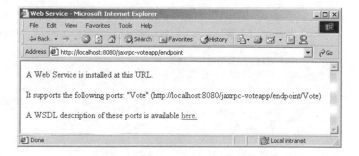

Fig. C.9   Result of verification of the service's deployment.

In the **VoteServiceClient** constructor (lines 23–56), lines 26–50 create a **JButton voteButton** to invoke the Vote service. Lines 52–54 add the **voteButton** to the content pane. When users click **voteButton**, they must select their favorite programming language, which invokes method **showVotes** to get the vote result.

Method **showVotes** gets the service stub (lines 59–95) and casts the service stub to service interface (line 69). Line 72 invokes method **addVote** of the service interface to get an array of **VoteBean**s that contains vote information for each programming language. Lines 74–86 extract the vote information from the array and display the information in a **JOptionPane** message dialog.

```
1    // VoteServiceClient.java
2    // VoteServiceClient display the survey window.
3    package com.deitel.jws.jaxrpc.voteclient;
4
5    // Java core packages
6    import java.awt.*;
7    import java.awt.event.*;
8
9    // Java extension packages
10   import javax.swing.*;
11
12   // Java XML packages
13   import javax.xml.rpc.*;
14
15   // client packages
16   import vote.*;
17
18   public class VoteServiceClient extends JFrame
19   {
20      private static String endpoint;
21
22      // VoteServiceClient constructor
23      public VoteServiceClient()
24      {
25         // create JButton for getting Vote service
26         JButton voteButton = new JButton( "Get Vote Service" );
27         voteButton.addActionListener(
28
29            new ActionListener() {
30
31               // action for the voteButton
32               public void actionPerformed( ActionEvent event )
33               {
34                  String[] languages =
35                     { "C", "C++", "Java", "VB", "Python" };
36
37                  String selectedLanguage = ( String )
38                     JOptionPane.showInputDialog(
39                     VoteServiceClient.this,
40                     "Select Language", "Language Selection",
41                     JOptionPane.QUESTION_MESSAGE,
42                     null, languages, "" );
```

Fig. C.10 VoteServiceClient is the client for the Vote Web service. (Part 1 of 3.)

```
43
44                      showVotes( selectedLanguage );
45
46              } // end method actionPerformed
47
48          } // end ActionListener
49
50      ); // end call to addActionListener
51
52      JPanel buttonPanel = new JPanel();
53      buttonPanel.add( voteButton );
54      getContentPane().add( buttonPanel, BorderLayout.CENTER );
55
56  } // end VoteServiceClient constructor
57
58  // connect to Vote Web service and get vote information
59  public void showVotes( String languageName )
60  {
61      // connect to Web service and get vote information
62      try {
63
64          // get Web service stub
65          Stub stub = ( Stub )
66              ( new VoteService_Impl().getVotePort() );
67
68          // cast stub to service interface
69          Vote vote = ( Vote ) stub;
70
71          // get vote information from Web service
72          VoteBean[] voteBeans = vote.addVote( languageName );
73
74          StringBuffer results = new StringBuffer();
75          results.append( "Vote result: \n" );
76
77          // get vote information from voteBeans
78          for ( int i = 0; i < voteBeans.length ; i++) {
79              results.append( "    "
80                  + voteBeans[ i ].getLanguageName() + ":" );
81              results.append( voteBeans[ i ].getCount() );
82              results.append( "\n" );
83          }
84
85          // display Vote information
86          JOptionPane.showMessageDialog( this, results );
87
88      } // end try
89
90      // handle exceptions communicating with remote object
91      catch ( Exception exception ) {
92          exception.printStackTrace();
93      }
94
95  } // end method showVotes
```

Fig. C.10 **VoteServiceClient** is the client for the Vote Web service. (Part 2 of 3.)

```
96
97      // execute VoteServiceClient
98      public static void main( String args[] )
99      {
100         // configure and display application window
101         VoteServiceClient client = new VoteServiceClient();
102
103         client.setDefaultCloseOperation( EXIT_ON_CLOSE );
104         client.pack();
105         client.setSize( 250, 65 );
106         client.setVisible( true );
107
108      } // end main
109
110   } // end class VoteServiceClient
```

Fig. C.10 `VoteServiceClient` is the client for the Vote Web service. (Part 3 of 3.)

Figure C.11 is the configuration file that **xrpcc** uses to generate the client-side classes. Element **wsdl** (lines 4–7) specifies the location of the WSDL file and the fully qualified package name of the client-side classes. The package name might differ from the package name of **VoteServiceClient**.

The command

> `xrpcc -d voteclientoutput -client VoteClientConfig.xml`

generates the client-side classes for the Vote service in directory **voteclientoutput**. **VoteClientConfig.xml** (Fig. C.11) is the configuration file passed to **xrpcc**.

Figure C.12 shows all the JAR files that are required to compile and execute client-side applications. Directories **%JWSDP_HOME%\common\lib** and **%JWSDP_HOME%\common\endorsed** contain these JAR files, where **%JWSDP_HOME%** is the installation directory of JWSDP.

To run the client application, type:

> `java -classpath voteclientoutput;%CLASSPATH%`
> `    com.deitel.jws.jaxrpc.voteclient.VoteServiceClient`

The **%CLASSPATH%** variable contains all the JAR files listed in Fig. C.12. Fig. C.13 shows the output of the client application.

```
1    <?xml version="1.0" encoding="UTF-8"?>
2    <configuration
3       xmlns = "http://java.sun.com/xml/ns/jax-rpc/ri/config">
4       <wsdl location =
5          "http://localhost:8080/jaxrpc-voteapp/endpoint?WSDL"
6          packageName = "vote">
7       </wsdl>
8    </configuration>
```

Fig. C.11 `VoteClientConfig.xml` that `xrpcc` uses to generate client-side classes from WSDL document.

JAR files required for compilation	JAR files required for execution
`jaxrpc-api.jar`	`jaxrpc-api.jar`
`jaxrpc-ri.jar`	`jaxrpc-ri.jar`
	`saaj-api.jar`
	`saaj-ri.jar`
	`mail.jar`
	`activation.jar`

Fig. C.12 JAR files required to compile and execute client-side applications.

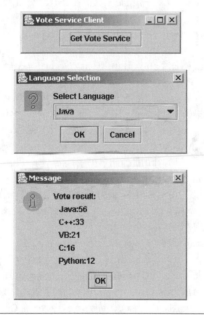

Fig. C.13 Output of the Vote service client.

C.4 JAXM BookBuyer and BookSeller Applications

In Section C.3, we used JAX-RPC to expose a Web service and to build a client that invoked that Web service via synchronous communication. The client sends a SOAP request to the Web service, then halts activity until it receives a SOAP response. Because the client halts activity, this client is unable to offer Web services in conjunction with invoking another service, which is a central characteristic of many Web service-based B2B applications. To circumvent this problem, JAXM applications may use a *message provider*, which handles the sending and receiving of messages, thus enabling a JAXM application to perform other functions after sending a SOAP request. Rather than enable the JAXM application to send a SOAP request directly to the Web service, we require the JAXM application to send the SOAP request to the message provider, which in turn sends the request directly to the Web service. Upon receiving a SOAP request from the JAXM application, the message provider informs the JAXM application that it will, at some point, send the request to the Web service. Eventually, the Web service sends a SOAP response back to the message provider. The message provider forwards the response to a separate component of the JAXM application, which then processes the SOAP response accordingly. This form of communication is known as *asynchronous messaging*.

C.4.1 JAXM Application Overviews

We now create a B2B application that involves two JAXM applications used for placing book orders. One JAXM application belongs to a company that orders books (which we call **BookBuyer**), and the other JAXM application belongs to a company that sells books (which we call **BookSeller**). Each JAXM application uses a message provider to send and receive SOAP messages. Figure C.14 illustrates the architecture for our program.

Suppose a **BookBuyer** employee wishes to order a book from **BookSeller**. From an HTML page, the employee selects the ISBN of a book and the quantity to order. Clicking the **Submit** button sends the ISBN and quantity as parts of a **get** request to servlet **Book-BuyerServlet** (Step 1). The servlet uses the JAXM API to encapsulate the ISBN and quantity values in a *SOAPMessage* object and sends the **SOAPMessage** to the message provider **BuyerProvider** (Step 2). Class **SOAPMessage** (of package **javax.xml.soap**) is the base class of all JAXM classes to represent SOAP messages transmitted between clients and Web services. Note that both **BookBuyerServlet** and **BuyerProvider** are located on the **BookBuyer** server. The **BuyerProvider** sends the **SOAPMessage** over the network to another message provider **SellerProvider** (Step 3), which is located on the **BookSeller** server. **SellerProvider** forwards the message to **BookOrderServlet** (Step 4)—a *JAXMServlet* subclass that exposes the **BookOrder** Web service. (We discuss later how to use subclasses of class **JAXM-Servlet** to expose Web services.) **BookOrderServlet** uses a **BookOrderImpl** object (Step 5) to obtain the total cost from the database (Steps 6–7). **BookOrder-Servlet** stores this value in a **SOAPMessage**, then sends the **SOAPMessage** to **SellerProvider** (Step 8). This provider returns this **SOAPMessage** to **BuyerProvider** (Step 9), which forwards the **SOAPMessage** to a **ConfirmationServlet** (Step 10)—a **JAXMServlet** that confirms the book order. **ConfirmationServlet** updates the database that contains the company's book stock and inserts an order into the database that contains the company's orders (Step 11). A **BookBuyer** employee, at any time, can use **ViewOrderServlet** to view the orders (Steps 12–13) made in the transactions between the JAXM applications.

C.4.2 Message Provider Setup

Before we examine the code for our JAXM applications, we must initialize the message providers that each application uses. The JAXM Reference implementation contains a **Provider Administration** tool that allows developers to initialize the message providers. Accessing this tool requires a user name and password, which **tomcat-us-ers.xml** specifies (located in **%JWSDP_HOME%/conf**). Edit this file to create a username and password, in the manner shown in Fig. C.15. For example, lines 9–10 specify that user name **deitel** has password **admin** and assumes the roles **admin**, **manager** and **provider**.

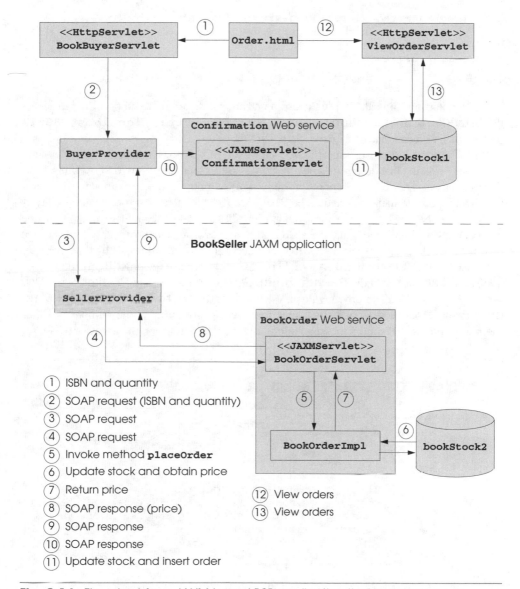

BookBuyer JAXM application

BookSeller JAXM application

1. ISBN and quantity
2. SOAP request (ISBN and quantity)
3. SOAP request
4. SOAP request
5. Invoke method **placeOrder**
6. Update stock and obtain price
7. Return price
8. SOAP response (price)
9. SOAP response
10. SOAP response
11. Update stock and insert order
12. View orders
13. View orders

Fig. C.14 Flowchart for a JAXM-based B2B application that uses a message provider to order books from another JAXM-based B2B application.

```
1    <?xml version='1.0'?>
2
3    <!-- Fig. C.15: Tomcat-users.xml -->
4    <tomcat-users>
5
6      <role rolename="admin"/>
7      <role rolename="manager"/>
8      <role rolename="provider"/>
9      <user username="deitel" password="admin"
10        roles="admin,manager,provider"/>
11
12   </tomcat-users>
```

Fig. C.15 Deployment descriptor for JAXM **Provider Administration** tool.

After starting Tomcat, supply the username and password that you specified to access the **Provider Administration** tool, which is located at **http://localhost:8081/ jaxm-provideradmin/index.jsp**. (Fig. C.16).

JAXM providers must support SOAP. However, SOAP does not specify any message-addressing scheme that determines how providers are to send and receive SOAP messages. For this reason, JAXM providers often use *profiles*, which are specifications for how providers should route their messages. The **Provider Administration** tool enables a developer to specify and customize the available profiles. A JAXM client then sends to the provider a SOAP message that adheres to a particular profile. The provider determines the profile to which the message adheres, then acts according to the values set by the developer in the **Provider Administration** tool. In our example, we use the ebXML profile to send and receive messages. In the **Provider Administration** tool, select **Profiles > ebXML > HTTP** (Fig. C.17). The browser displays **Provider Properties** and **Endpoint Mapping** fields. **Provider Properties** specifies such information as the number of times that the provider will send a message upon failure (called a *retry*), the delay between re-

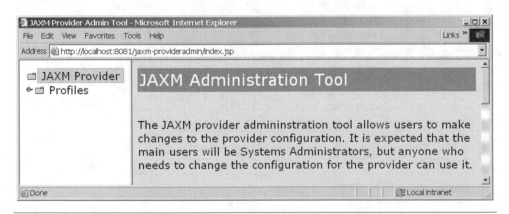

Fig. C.16 JAXM **Provider Administration** tool. (Reproduced with permission by Sun Microsystems, Inc.© Copyright 2002. Sun Microsystems, Inc. All Rights Reserved.)

tries, and the directory in which Tomcat logs information. **Endpoint Mapping** provides a list of URI-to-URL mappings. The URI is merely a string with which a JAXM client identifies the URL of a particular provider.

We create two URI-to-URL mappings: one for the provider that sends the ISBN and quantity values, and one for the provider that returns the price. In **Available Actions**, select **Create New Endpoint Mapping**. Figure C.18 shows the URI-to-URL mapping for **BuyerProvider**—URI **urn:com.deitel.jaxm.buyerProvider** maps to the URL **http://localhost:8081/jaxm-provider/receiver/ebxml**. This URL points to the provider included in the JAXM reference implementation. We now create a second URI-to-URL mapping that corresponds to **SellerProvider**. URI **urn:com.deitel.jaxm.sellerProvider** should map to the URL **http://localhost:8081/jaxm-provider/receiver/ebxml**. For simplicity, note that both the **BookBuyer** and **BookSeller** JAXM applications use the same message provider. In a real-world application, each company would have access to its own provider, which would reside on a separate system, thus enabling each provider to have a unique URL. However, each JAXM application identifies the providers via the URIs, which have different values. Therefore, the JAXM applications are unaware of the providers' true locations. From the perspectives of the JAXM applications, both are using two separate providers. Figure C.19 shows the final endpoint mappings for our JAXM applications.[1]

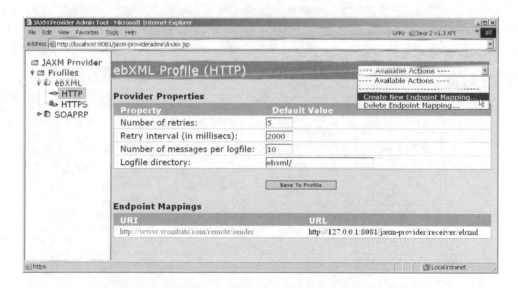

Fig. C.17 JAXM **Provider Administration** tool **ebXML Profile**. (Reproduced with permission by Sun Microsystems, Inc.© Copyright 2002. Sun Microsystems, Inc. All Rights Reserved.)

---

1. Disregard the **http://www.wombats.com/remote/sender** endpoint mapping—this belongs to an application in the JAXM tutorial, and we do not use it in our applications.

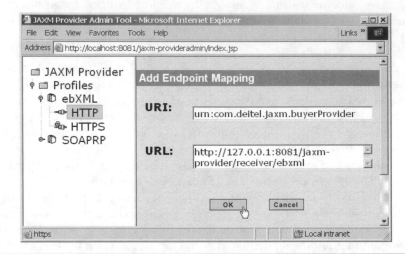

Fig. C.18 Creating an endpoint mapping in the JAXM **Provider Administration** tool. (Reproduced with permission by Sun Microsystems, Inc.© Copyright 2002. Sun Microsystems, Inc. All Rights Reserved.)

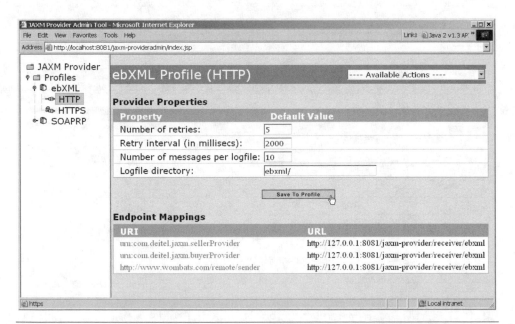

Fig. C.19 Final endpoint mappings in the JAXM **Provider Administration** tool. (Reproduced with permission by Sun Microsystems, Inc.© Copyright 2002. Sun Microsystems, Inc. All Rights Reserved.)

Developers must configure each JAXM application to run in a servlet container, such as Tomcat. In addition to configuring the **web.xml** deployment descriptor, developers also must configure another deployment descriptor, called **client.xml**, for each JAXM application. Figure C.20 is the `client.xml` for the JAXM application that sends the ISBN and quantity values and receives the price. Each `client.xml` document must have element `ClientConfig` (lines 10–29) as its root element. Element `ClientConfig` must contain elements `Endpoint`, `CallbackURL` and `Provider`. Element **Endpoint** (lines 13–15) defines a URI that the JAXM application uses to identify itself. Note that this value must be consistent with the value that the **Provider Administration** tool defines. When a provider receives a message, the provider "forwards" the message to a receiving `JAXMServlet`. `CallbackURL` (lines 19–21) specifies the URL of the **JAXMServlet** that receives these messages. In our example, line 20 specifies that `ConfirmationServlet`, which we discuss later, receives messages sent to this message provider. Element `Provider` (lines 24–27) defines the URI-to-URL mapping of the message provider to identify the location of the provider. Line 26 specifies that the **BookBuyer** JAXM application uses the message provider included in the JAXM reference implementation.

Deployment

Now that we configured the JAXM providers, we explain how to deploy both JAXM applications. Figure C.21 and Fig. C.23 show the files and associated directory structures needed to deploy **Book Buyer** and **Book Seller** via the Java Web Services Developer Pack. **Book Buyer** and **Book Seller** use the `bookStock1` and `bookStock2` databases, respectively. The scripts (`bookStock1.sql` and `bookStock2.sql`) that build these databases are available on our Web site, **www.deitel.com**.

```
1   <?xml version="1.0" encoding="ISO-8859-1"?>
2
3   <!-- Fig. C.20: Client.xml -->
4   <!-- Deployment descriptor for BookBuyer JAXM client -->
5
6   <!DOCTYPE ClientConfig
7       PUBLIC "-//Sun Microsystems, Inc.//DTD JAXM Client//EN"
8       "http://java.sun.com/xml/dtds/jaxm_client_1_0.dtd">
9
10  <ClientConfig>
11
12      <!-- URI of buyerProvider Endpoint -->
13      <Endpoint>
14          urn:com.deitel.jaxm.buyerProvider
15      </Endpoint>
16
17      <!-- URL of JAXMServlet that buyerProvider calls upon -->
18      <!-- receiving SOAPMessages                          -->
19      <CallbackURL>
20          http://127.0.0.1:8080/bookbuyer/confirmOrder
21      </CallbackURL>
22
23      <!-- URL of buyerProvider -->
```

Fig. C.20 Deployment descriptor for the **BookBuyer** JAXM client, which uses **buyerProvider** to send ISBN and quantity values to the **BookOrder** Web service. (Part 1 of 2.)

```
24    <Provider>
25      <URI>http://java.sun.com/xml/jaxm/provider</URI>
26      <URL>http://127.0.0.1:8081/jaxm-provider/sender</URL>
27    </Provider>
28
29  </ClientConfig>
```

Fig. C.20 Deployment descriptor for the **BookBuyer** JAXM client, which uses **buyerProvider** to send ISBN and quantity values to the **BookOrder** Web service. (Part 2 of 2.)

Book Buyer Web application directory and file structure

```
bookbuyer/
   WEB-INF/
      web.xml
      classes/
         client.xml
         com/
            deitel/
               jws1/
                  jaxm/
                     bookbuyer/
                        sender/
                           BookBuyerServlet.class
                           ViewOrderServlet.class
                           bookStock.properties
                           Endpoint.properties
                        receiver/
                           ConfirmationServlet.class
                           bookStock.properties
      lib/
         cloudclient.jar
         RmiJDBC.jar
   XSL/
      viewOrder_XHTML.xsl
```

Fig. C.21 Web application directory and file structure for deploying Book Buyer.

To run this application properly, the classpath must include all proper JAXM and SAAJ (SOAP with Attachments API for Java) files. Figure C.23 lists the JAR files provided by JAXM and SAAJ. Include these files, which are located in **%JWSDP_HOME%/common/lib**, in the classpath when compiling and running all JAXM applications that we show in this appendix. Also include the JAXP classes, which are located in **%JWSDP_HOME%/common/lib** and **%JWSDP_HOME%/common/endorsed**.

Book Seller Web application directory and file structure

```
bookseller/
    order.html
    WEB-INF/
        web.xml
        classes/
            client.xml
            com/
                deitel/
                    jws1/
                        jaxm/
                            bookseller/
                                receiver/
                                    BookOrderServlet.class
                                    Endpoint.properties
                            services/
                                BookOrder.class
                                BookOrderImpl.class
                                bookStock.properties
        lib/
            cloudclient.jar
            RmiJDBC.jar
```

Fig. C.22 Web application directory and file structure for deploying Book Seller.

API	Associated JAR files	Location

JAXM	`jaxm-api.jar`
	`jaxm-runtime.jar`
	`jaxm-provider`
	`jaxm-provideradmin`
		`%JWSDP_HOME%/common/lib`

SAAJ	`saaj-api.jar`
	`saaj-ri.jar`
	`dom4j.jar`
	`activation.jar`
	`mail.jar`
	`commons-logging.jar`
		`%JWSDP_HOME%/common/lib`

JAXP	`jaxp-api.jar`
	`dom.jar`
	`sax.jar`
	`xalan.jar`
	`xercesImpl.jar`
	`xsltc.jar`
		`%JWSDP_HOME%/common/lib`
		`%JWSDP_HOME%/common/endorsed`

Fig. C.23 JAXM, SAAJ and JAXP associated JAR files.

C.4.3 JAXM Applications: Code Walkthrough

In this section, we examine the code for our applications. When the user presses the **Submit** button on the HTML page, the Web browser sends the ISBN and quantity values via a **get** request to **BookBuyerServlet** (Fig. C.24). Class **BookBuyerServlet** is an **HttpServlet** that uses the JAXM API to send these values as a **SOAPMessage** to its message provider. Lines 29–91 define method **init**, which initializes a connection to **BuyerProvider**. A *ProviderConnection* object, which belongs to package **javax.xml.messaging**, represents the connection. Lines 36–37 obtain a default *ProviderConnectionFactory* (i.e., the one that the JAXM reference implementation supplies) by invoking **static** method **newInstance** of class **ProviderConnectionFactory**. Line 38 calls method **createConnection** of the **ProviderConnectionFactory** to create a **ProviderConnection**, which represents a connection to the message provider. Using this connection, **BookBuyerServlet** sends **SOAPMessage**s to **BuyerProvider**, which in turn can send them to another JAXM application (in this case, to **SellerProvider**). Each provider requires the developer to specify endpoints in the form of URIs that determine the URLs of the two message providers (i.e., the sender and the receiver). Lines 41–51 obtain the URIs from **Endpoints.properties** (Fig. C.25). Note that the **from** and **to** values (Fig. C.25, lines 5–6), which **BookBuyerServlet** uses to specify the destination and source providers, match the URI values that we defined via the **Provider Administration** tool. Recall that we also used this tool to customize the ebXML-profile settings. Before **BookBuyerServlet** can create **SOAPMessage**s that use ebXML, **BookBuyerServlet** must determine whether ebXML is available as a profile for **BuyerProvider**. Line 54 calls method **getMetaData** of the **ProviderConnection** to obtain a *ProviderMetaData* object, which contains such information as whether the provider supports ebXML. Line 55 calls method **getSupportedProfiles** of the **ProviderMetaData** object to obtain an array of **String**s, in which each **String** corresponds to a profile that the provider supports. Lines 58–61 determine whether **"ebxml"** is one of these **String**s. If so, then the provider supports ebXML, and lines 65–66 create a *MessageFactory* capable of building **SOAPMessage**s that use ebXML. SAAJ allows the creation of **SOAPMessage** objects via **MessageFactory** method **createMessage**. Invoking method **createMessage** returns a **SOAPMessage** object that contains a header (with content specified by the messaging profile) and an empty body. If not, lines 68–69 throw a **ServletException** to indicate that the provider does not support ebXML.

When the user presses the **Submit** button on the HTML page, the Web browser sends the ISBN and quantity values via a **get** request to **BookBuyerServlet**, which in turn invokes method **doGet** (lines 94–164). Lines 101–102 use the **MessageFactory** to create an *EbXMLMessageImpl*, which represents a SOAP message that uses ebXML. Class **EbXMLMessageImpl** extends class **SOAPMessage** and belongs to package **com.sun.xml.messaging.ebxml**, which does not belong to the JAXM API (although Sun offers these APIs for ebXML in the JWSDP). Note that method **createMessage** of the **MessageFactory** returns a **SOAPMessage** object. However, because lines 65–66 allow the **MessageFactory** to create SOAP messages that use ebXML, line 102 can cast the returned **SOAPMessage** to an **EbXMLMessageImpl**, without resulting in a **ClassCastException**. Line 105 calls method **setSender** of the **EbXMLMessageImpl** to include the URI of the provider that sends the message. Similarly, line 106 calls method **setReceiver** of the **EbXMLMessageImpl** to include the URI of the provider that will receive the message. Both methods require as arguments *Party* objects (of package **com.sun.xml.messaging.ebxml**), which act as wrappers for the URI values. We obtain these URI values from **Endpoint.properties** (Fig. C.25); recall that the URI values must match those values defined in the **Provider Administration** tool. Methods **setSender** and **setReceiver** include the URI values in the ebXML message header. When **BookBuyerServlet** sends this message to **BuyerProvider**, **BuyerProvider** uses the header to determine the location to send the message (which in this case, is **SellerProvider**).

```
1    // Fig. C.24: BookBuyerServlet.java
2    // BookBuyerServlet uses a message provider (BuyerProvider)
3    // to send messages to SellerProvider.
4    package com.deitel.jws1.jaxm.bookbuyer.sender;
5
6    // Java core packages
7    import java.io.*;
8    import java.util.*;
9
10   // Java extension packages
11   import javax.servlet.http.*;
12   import javax.servlet.*;
13   import javax.xml.messaging.*;
14   import javax.xml.soap.*;
15
16   // ebXML packages
17   import com.sun.xml.messaging.ebxml.*;
18
19   public class BookBuyerServlet extends HttpServlet {
20
21      private ProviderConnection buyerProvider;
22      private MessageFactory messageFactory;
23
24      // source and destination endpoints for messages
25      private String from, to;
26      private Properties endPointProperties;
27
28      // setup connection to message provider
29      public void init( ServletConfig servletConfig )
30         throws ServletException
31      {
32         super.init( servletConfig );
33
34         // establish connection to provider
35         try {
36            ProviderConnectionFactory providerFactory =
37               ProviderConnectionFactory.newInstance();
38            buyerProvider = providerFactory.createConnection();
39
```

Fig. C.24 **BookBuyerServlet** encapsulates ISBN and quantity values in a **SOAPMessage** and sends the message to a JAXM message provider. (Part 1 of 4.)

```
40        // obtain URL of properties file
41        java.net.URL endPointURL = getClass().getResource(
42           "Endpoint.properties" );
43
44        // load properties file
45        endPointProperties = new Properties();
46        endPointProperties.load( new FileInputStream(
47           endPointURL.getPath() ) );
48
49        // obtain source and destination endpoints
50        from = endPointProperties.getProperty( "from" );
51        to = endPointProperties.getProperty( "to" );
52
53        // obtain supported profiles for provider
54        ProviderMetaData metaData = buyerProvider.getMetaData();
55        String[] profiles = metaData.getSupportedProfiles();
56
57        // determine whether ebXML profile is supported
58        boolean isProfileSupported = false;
59        for ( int i = 0; i < profiles.length; i++ )
60           if ( profiles[ i ].equals( "ebxml" ) )
61              isProfileSupported = true;
62
63        // use ebXML profile, if supported
64        if ( isProfileSupported )
65           messageFactory =
66              buyerProvider.createMessageFactory( "ebxml" );
67        else
68           throw new ServletException( "Profile ebxml is " +
69              "not supported." );
70     }
71
72     // handle exception in connecting to provider
73     catch ( JAXMException jaxmException ) {
74        throw new ServletException( jaxmException.getMessage() +
75           "\nUnable to connect to message provider." );
76     }
77
78     // handle exception if unable to locate Endpoint.properties
79     catch ( FileNotFoundException fileNotFoundException ) {
80        throw new ServletException(
81           fileNotFoundException.getMessage() +
82           "\nUnable to locate Endpoint.properties." );
83     }
84
85     // handle exception in loading properties file
86     catch ( IOException ioException ) {
87        throw new ServletException( ioException.getMessage() +
88           "\nUnable to load Endpoint.properties." );
89     }
90
```

Fig. C.24 **BookBuyerServlet** encapsulates ISBN and quantity values in a **SOAPMessage** and sends the message to a JAXM message provider. (Part 2 of 4.)

```
91        } // end method init
92
93        // invoked when client makes get request
94        public void doGet( HttpServletRequest request,
95           HttpServletResponse response ) throws ServletException
96        {
97           // create ebXML message for buyerProvider
98           try {
99
100              // create ebXML message
101              EbXMLMessageImpl message =
102                 ( EbXMLMessageImpl ) messageFactory.createMessage();
103
104              // set send and receive provider
105              message.setSender( new Party( from ) );
106              message.setReceiver( new Party( to ) );
107
108              // store ISBN in message attachment
109              AttachmentPart isbnAttachment =
110                 message.createAttachmentPart();
111              isbnAttachment.setContent( request.getParameter(
112                 "ISBN" ), "text/plain" );
113
114              // store quantity in message attachment
115              AttachmentPart quantityAttachment =
116                 message.createAttachmentPart();
117              quantityAttachment.setContent( request.getParameter(
118                 "Quantity" ), "text/plain" );
119
120              // add ISBN and Quantity attachments to message
121              message.addAttachmentPart( isbnAttachment );
122              message.addAttachmentPart( quantityAttachment );
123
124              // send message from buyerProvider to Web service
125              buyerProvider.send( message );
126
127              // display HTML confirmation message to client
128              response.setContentType( "text/html" );
129              PrintWriter out = response.getWriter();
130              String viewOrderURL =
131                 endPointProperties.getProperty( "viewOrderURL" );
132              out.println( "<html>" );
133              out.println( "<body>Order placed." );
134              out.println( "Visit <a href=" + viewOrderURL + ">" );
135              out.println( viewOrderURL + "</a>" );
136              out.println( "to view order status.</body>" );
137              out.println( "</html>" );
138           }
139
```

Fig. C.24 BookBuyerServlet encapsulates ISBN and quantity values in a **SOAPMessage** and sends the message to a JAXM message provider. (Part 3 of 4.)

```
140        // handle exception in using message provider
141        catch ( JAXMException jaxmException ) {
142           throw new ServletException( jaxmException.getMessage() +
143              "\nError in using message provider." );
144        }
145
146        // handle exception in creating SOAP messages
147        catch ( SOAPException soapException ) {
148           throw new ServletException( soapException.getMessage() +
149              "\nUnable to create SOAP message." );
150        }
151
152        // handle exception if servlet not initialized
153        catch ( NullPointerException nullException ) {
154           throw new ServletException( nullException.getMessage() +
155              "\nServlet not initialized properly." );
156        }
157
158        // handle exception in writing HTML to client
159        catch ( IOException ioException ) {
160           throw new ServletException( ioException.getMessage() +
161              "\nServlet not initialized properly." );
162        }
163
164     } // end method doGet
165
166  } // end class BookBuyerServlet
```

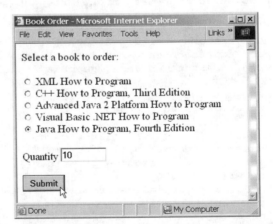

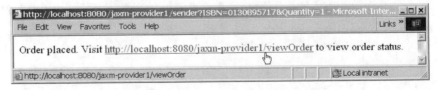

Fig. C.24 BookBuyerServlet encapsulates ISBN and quantity values in a
SOAPMessage and sends the message to a JAXM message provider.
(Part 4 of 4.)

```
1   # Fig. C.25: Endpoint.properties
2   # Properties file for Endpoint mappings.
3
4   # URI values for Endpoint mappings
5   from=urn:com.deitel.jaxm.buyerProvider
6   to=urn:com.deitel.jaxm.sellerProvider
7
8   # URL of servlet to view orders
9   viewOrderURL=http://localhost:8080/bookbuyer/viewOrder
```

Fig. C.25 Properties file that **BookBuyerServlet** uses to determine the URIs for Endpoints.

Before **BookBuyerServlet** sends the ebXML message, **BookBuyerServlet** must populate the message with the ISBN and quantity values. We can do this via *attachments*, which are additional units of information that exist outside the SOAP envelope but are included in the SOAP-message transfer. Using attachments to store values is often more efficient than using XML, because JAXM applications can obtain values from attachments without having to parse entire XML documents to locate values. The JAXM API provides an **AttachmentPart**, which belongs to package **javax.xml.soap**, to represent an attachment. Lines 109–112 create an **AttachmentPart** that stores the ISBN value. Similarly, lines 115–118 create an **AttachmentPart** that stores the quantity value. Lines 121–122 attach the **AttachmentPart**s to the ebXML message.

Line 125 sends the ebXML message to the message provider by invoking method **send** of the **ProviderConnection** and passing the **EbXMLMessageImpl** as an argument. Because **BookBuyerServlet** is using a message provider, it does not have to wait for a response from the receiving provider. Note that this communication is asynchronous. The receiving JAXM application has no obligation to return a message that contains a price. However, our architecture (Fig. C.14) showed that the receiving JAXM application, at some point, will send this message to the original sending JAXM application. This application then updates a database that stores orders and prices. Lines 128–137 create an HTML page that confirms that **BookBuyerServlet** has placed the order, and provides a link to **ViewOrderServlet** (which we will present in Fig. C.31), which allows the user to view the contents of this database. Thus, the only way the user can confirm that the entire transaction occurred is by polling **ViewOrderServlet** repeatedly, and seeing if an additional order has been included in the database. This is one means of confirmation via asynchronous communication—an alternative architecture might send a confirmation notification via e-mail to the client.

When **BookBuyerServlet** sends the ebXML message to **BuyerProvider**, **BuyerProvider** examines the message header to determine where to send the message. Recall that line 106 declared that **BuyerProvider** should send the message to the endpoint that maps to URI **urn:com.deitel.jaxm.sellerProvider**. Using the **Provider Administration** tool, we specified that this URI maps to **http://localhost:8081/ jaxm-provider/receiver/ebxml**, which is the URL for the message provider included in the JAXM reference implementation. When **SellerProvider** receives the message, **SellerProvider** must "forward" that message to a **JAXMServlet**. We specify the **JAXMServlet** that receives the message in the **client.xml** deployment descriptor of Fig. C.26. Each JAXM application requires a unique **client.xml**, so the

client.xml in Fig. C.26 differs from the one in Fig. C.20, which we created for the JAXM application that sends the ISBN and quantity values. Lines 13–15 declare an **Endpoint** element that contains the URI for **SellerProvider**. Note that this value matches the URI value that we established in the **Provider Administration** tool. Lines 19–21 declare a **CallbackURL** element, which contains the URL of the **JAXMServlet** (**BookOrderServlet**) that will receive the SOAP message from **SellerProvider**. Lines 24–27 define the URI-to-URL mapping of the message provider.

According to the deployment descriptor in Fig. C.26, **SellerProvider** sends a SOAP message to **BookOrderServlet** (Fig. C.27) upon receiving a message. Note that line 22 declares **BookOrderServlet** as a **JAXMServlet** subclass. Earlier in the text, we mentioned that we can use subclasses of class *JAXMServlet* to expose Web services. Technically, when we deploy a **JAXMServlet** subclass in a servlet container such as Apache Tomcat, we expose a Web service. To expose the **BookOrder** Web service, we create class **BookOrderServlet** as a subclass of **JAXMServlet** and deploy it in Tomcat. Class **JAXMServlet** belongs to package **javax.xml.messaging** and extends class **javax.servlet.http.HttpServlet**. Method **init** (lines 32–92) overrides method **init** of class **HttpServlet**. Method **init** initializes **BookOrderServlet** by establishing a connection to **SellerProvider** (lines 39–41), obtaining the endpoint URI for **SellerProvider** (lines 44–52) from **Endpoint.properties** (Fig. C.28), and ensuring that **SellerProvider** supports the ebXML profile (lines 55–70).

```
1    <?xml version="1.0" encoding="ISO-8859-1"?>
2
3    <!-- Fig. C.26: Client.xml -->
4    <!-- Deployment descriptor for BookSeller JAXM client -->
5
6    <!DOCTYPE ClientConfig
7        PUBLIC "-//Sun Microsystems, Inc.//DTD JAXM Client//EN"
8        "http://java.sun.com/xml/dtds/jaxm_client_1_0.dtd">
9
10   <ClientConfig>
11
12       <!-- URI of SellerProvider Endpoint -->
13       <Endpoint>
14           urn:com.deitel.jaxm.sellerProvider
15       </Endpoint>
16
17       <!-- URL of JAXMServlet that sellerProvider calls upon -->
18       <!-- receiving SOAPMessages                          -->
19       <CallbackURL>
20           http://127.0.0.1:8080/bookseller/orderBook
21       </CallbackURL>
22
23       <!-- URL of sellerProvider -->
24       <Provider>
25           <URI>http://java.sun.com/xml/jaxm/provider</URI>
```

Fig. C.26 Deployment descriptor for the **BookSeller** JAXM application, which uses **SellerProvider** to receive SOAP messages that contain ISBN and quantity values. (Part 1 of 2.)

```
26          <URL>http://127.0.0.1:8081/jaxm-provider/sender</URL>
27     </Provider>
28
29   </ClientConfig>
```

Fig. C.26 Deployment descriptor for the **BookSeller** JAXM application, which uses **SellerProvider** to receive SOAP messages that contain ISBN and quantity values. (Part 2 of 2.)

```
1   // Fig. C.27: BookOrderServlet.java
2   // Class BookOrderServlet receives an ebXML message that
3   // contains a book's ISBN and the quantity of that book to order.
4   package com.deitel.jws1.jaxm.bookseller.receiver;
5
6   // Java core packages
7   import java.io.*;
8   import java.util.*;
9
10  // Java extension packages
11  import javax.servlet.http.*;
12  import javax.servlet.*;
13  import javax.xml.messaging.*;
14  import javax.xml.soap.*;
15
16  // ebXML packages
17  import com.sun.xml.messaging.ebxml.*;
18
19  // Deitel packages
20  import com.deitel.jws1.services.BookOrderImpl;
21
22  public class BookOrderServlet extends JAXMServlet
23     implements OnewayListener {
24
25     private ProviderConnection sellerProvider;
26     private MessageFactory messageFactory;
27
28     // source and destination endpoints for messages
29     private String from;
30
31     // setup connection to message provider
32     public void init( ServletConfig servletConfig )
33        throws ServletException
34     {
35        super.init( servletConfig );
36
37        // establish connection to provider
38        try {
39           ProviderConnectionFactory providerFactory =
40              ProviderConnectionFactory.newInstance();
41           sellerProvider = providerFactory.createConnection();
42
```

Fig. C.27 **BookOrderServlet** exposes the **BookOrder** Web service. (Part 1 of 4.)

```
43                // obtain URL of properties file
44                java.net.URL endpointURL = getClass().getResource(
45                   "Endpoint.properties" );
46
47                // load properties file
48                Properties endpointProperties = new Properties();
49                endpointProperties.load( new FileInputStream(
50                   endpointURL.getPath() ) );
51
52                from = endpointProperties.getProperty( "from" );
53
54                // obtain supported profiles for provider
55                ProviderMetaData metaData = sellerProvider.getMetaData();
56                String[] profiles = metaData.getSupportedProfiles();
57
58                // determine whether ebXML profile is supported
59                boolean isProfileSupported = false;
60                for ( int i = 0; i < profiles.length; i++ )
61                   if ( profiles[ i ].equals( "ebxml" ) )
62                      isProfileSupported = true;
63
64                // use ebXML profile, if supported
65                if ( isProfileSupported )
66                   messageFactory =
67                      sellerProvider.createMessageFactory( "ebxml" );
68                else
69                   throw new ServletException( "Profile ebxml is " +
70                      "not supported." );
71             }
72
73             // handle exception in connecting to provider
74             catch ( JAXMException jaxmException ) {
75                throw new ServletException( jaxmException.getMessage() +
76                   "\nUnable to connect to message provider." );
77             }
78
79             // handle exception if unable to locate Endpoint.properties
80             catch ( FileNotFoundException fileNotFoundException ) {
81                throw new ServletException(
82                   fileNotFoundException.getMessage() +
83                   "\nUnable to locate Endpoint.properties." );
84             }
85
86             // handle exception in loading properties file
87             catch ( IOException ioException ) {
88                throw new ServletException( ioException.getMessage() +
89                   "\nUnable to load Endpoint.properties." );
90             }
91
92       } // end method init
93
```

Fig. C.27 **BookOrderServlet** exposes the **BookOrder** Web service.
(Part 2 of 4.)

```
94      // invoked when sellerProvider sends message to InfoServlet
95      public void onMessage( SOAPMessage requestMessage )
96      {
97          // call BookOrder service and return result to sender
98          try {
99
100             // create response message from request message
101             EbXMLMessageImpl responseMessage =
102                 new EbXMLMessageImpl( requestMessage );
103
104             // specify that the message should be returned to sender
105             String to = responseMessage.getFrom().toString();
106
107             // specify sender and receiver for message
108             responseMessage.setReceiver( new Party( to ) );
109             responseMessage.setSender( new Party( from ) );
110
111             // obtain ISBN and Quantity attachments from message
112             Iterator attachments = responseMessage.getAttachments();
113             AttachmentPart isbnAttachment =
114                 ( AttachmentPart ) attachments.next();
115             AttachmentPart quantityAttachment =
116                 ( AttachmentPart ) attachments.next();
117
118             // obtain ISBN and Quantity from attachments
119             String isbn = ( String ) isbnAttachment.getContent();
120             Integer quantity = new Integer(
121                 ( String ) quantityAttachment.getContent() );
122
123             // invoke BookOrder Web service to place order
124             BookOrderImpl service = new BookOrderImpl();
125             Double price = new Double(
126                 service.orderBook( isbn, quantity.intValue() ) );
127
128             // store price in message attachment
129             AttachmentPart priceAttachment =
130                 responseMessage.createAttachmentPart();
131             priceAttachment.setContent( price.toString(),
132                 "text/plain" );
133
134             // add price attachments to message
135             responseMessage.addAttachmentPart( priceAttachment );
136
137             // send message back to sending provider
138             sellerProvider.send( responseMessage );
139         }
140
141         // handle exception in invoking BookOrder Web service
142         catch ( SOAPException soapException ) {
143             soapException.printStackTrace();
144         }
145
```

Fig. C.27 BookOrderServlet exposes the **BookOrder** Web service.
(Part 3 of 4.)

```
146            // handle exception in EbXMLMessageImpl creation
147            catch ( IOException ioException ) {
148               ioException.printStackTrace();
149            }
150
151         } // end method onMessage
152
153      } // end class BookOrderServlet
```

Fig. C.27 **BookOrderServlet** exposes the **BookOrder** Web service.
(Part 4 of 4.)

```
1    # Fig. 15.15: Endpoint.properties
2    # Properties file for message-provider Endpoint mapping.
3
4    # URI values for Endpoint mapping to message provider
5    from=urn:com.deitel.jaxm.sellerProvider
```

Fig. C.28 Properties file that **BookOrderServlet** uses to determine the URI
Endpoint for its provider.

A **JAXMServlet** may implement two types of messaging architectures: *request-response* and *one-way*. The request-response messaging architecture requires the **JAXM-Servlet** to send a response to the client that sent the request. The client cannot perform other operations while waiting for a response. We refer to this as synchronous messaging. The one-way messaging architecture does not require the **JAXMServlet** to send a response message. We refer to this as asynchronous messaging. Package **javax.xml.messaging** provides interfaces *ReqRespListener* and *Oneway-Listener* for **JAXMServlet**s to implement request-response and one-way messaging, respectively. Both **ReqRespListener** and **OnewayListener** provide method **onMessage**, which the **JAXMServlet** invokes whenever it receives a SOAP message via an HTTP **post** request. Method **onMessage** receives as an argument a **SOAPMessage** object that represents the incoming SOAP request. However, **ReqRespListener**'s method **onMessage** returns to the client a **SOAPMessage** object that represents the SOAP response, whereas **OnewayListener**'s method **onMessage** returns **void**. Because the return type for **OnewayListener**'s **onMessage** method is **void**, the method implementation cannot return a **SOAPMessage**. The JAXM client delegates the method invocation to a message provider, so the JAXM client is not required to wait for a response. This is efficient for such scenarios in which a confirmation message is dependent on a "human factor." For example, a shipping-order confirmation depends on human workers to transport merchandise from a warehouse to a vehicle.

Class **BookOrderServlet** implements interface **OnewayListener** (line 23) to ensure asynchronous communication. **BookOrderServlet** invokes method **onMessage** (lines 95–151) upon receiving a SOAP message. Using the ebXML profile, method **onMessage** invokes the **BookOrder** Web service to obtain a price, attaches the price to an ebXML message, then returns the message to **BuyerProvider**. Lines 101–102 create an **EbXMLMessageImpl** from the incoming **SOAPMessage**. Line 105 retrieves from the ebXML-message header the URI of the provider that sent the message. Line 108 uses this information to set the **to** field in the ebXML response message's header. Note that this approach relies exclusively on the reliability of the message sender to have included the correct provider URI in the **from** field. However, if a malicious client sent an erroneous value, **SellerProvider** would fail to map the URI to a valid URL and would not send the response message.

Line 112 invokes method **getAttachments** of the **EbXMLMessageImpl** to obtain an **Iterator** that contains all **AttachmentPart**s associated with the incoming message. Using the **Iterator**, lines 113–116 obtain the two **AttachmentPart**s that contain the ISBN and quantity values. Lines 119–121 extract these values from the **AttachmentPart**s by invoking method **getContent** from each **Attachment-Part**. Lines 124–126 invoke method **orderBook** on a **BookOrderImpl** object (Fig. C.29), which handles the logic for the **BookOrder** Web service. Lines 18–56 define the class constructor that establishes a connection to the **bookStock2** database, which holds information on price and quantity for books. Method **orderBook** (lines 59–109) takes as arguments a **String** that represents a book's ISBN and an **int** that specifies the quantity of books to order. Using these arguments and the connection to the **bookStock2** database, method **orderBook** calculates the cumulative price for the requested books. Method **orderBook** returns either a **double** that represents this price, or a **-1** value if the books are unavailable. **BookOrderServlet** (Fig. C.27) then creates an **Attach-mentPart** to store the price and append the **AttachmentPart** to the **EbXMLMes-sageImpl** (lines 129–135). Line 138 sends the ebXML message to **SellerProvider**, which in turn sends the message back to **BuyerProvider**.

```
1   // Fig. C.29: BookOrderImpl.java
2   // Class BookOrderImpl handles the logic for the BookOrder Web
3   // service, which determines the price of a book, based on that
4   // book's ISBN and the quantity of books to order.
5   package com.deitel.jws1.services;
6
7   // Java core packages
8   import java.io.*;
9   import java.util.*;
10  import java.sql.*;
11
12  public class BookOrderImpl
13     implements com.deitel.jws1.services.BookOrder {
14
15     private Connection connection; // connection to database
16
17     // constructor to initialize database connection
18     public BookOrderImpl()
19     {
20        // load JDBC driver and establish connection to database
21        try {
22
23           // obtain URL of properties file
24           java.net.URL propertyURL = getClass().getResource(
25              "bookStock.properties" );
```

Fig. C.29 **BookOrderImpl** handles the logic for the **BookOrder** Web service, which uses ISBN and quantity values to obtain a price from a database. (Part 1 of 3.)

```
26
27          // load properties file
28          Properties databaseProperties = new Properties();
29          databaseProperties.load( new FileInputStream(
30             propertyURL.getPath() ) );
31
32          // load JDBC driver
33          Class.forName( databaseProperties.getProperty(
34             "jdbcDriver" ) );
35
36          // establish database connection
37          connection = DriverManager.getConnection(
38             databaseProperties.getProperty( "databaseURI" ) );
39       }
40
41       // handle exception if database driver does not exist
42       catch ( ClassNotFoundException classNotFoundException ) {
43          classNotFoundException.printStackTrace();
44       }
45
46       // handle exception in making Connection
47       catch ( SQLException sqlException ) {
48          sqlException.printStackTrace();
49       }
50
51       // handle exception in loading properties file
52       catch ( IOException ioException ) {
53          ioException.printStackTrace();
54       }
55
56    } // end constructor
57
58    // obtain price of book based on book's ISBN and quantity
59    public double orderBook( String isbn, int quantity )
60    {
61       // detemine book availability, then determine price
62       try {
63
64          // SQL query to database
65          Statement statement = connection.createStatement(
66             ResultSet.TYPE_SCROLL_INSENSITIVE,
67             ResultSet.CONCUR_READ_ONLY );
68
69          // make query to determine number of available books
70          ResultSet resultSet = statement.executeQuery( "SELECT" +
71             " quantity, price FROM books WHERE isbn = " + isbn );
72
73          int availableBookCount = 0;
74
```

Fig. C.29 **BookOrderImpl** handles the logic for the **BookOrder** Web service, which uses ISBN and quantity values to obtain a price from a database. (Part 2 of 3.)

```
75      // obtain quantity associated with isbn from database
76      if ( resultSet != null ) {
77          resultSet.next();
78          availableBookCount = resultSet.getInt( "quantity" );
79      }
80
81      // determine whether quantity exceeds number of
82      // available books in database
83      if ( availableBookCount < quantity ) {
84          statement.close();
85          return -1;
86      }
87      else {
88
89          // determine price for one book
90          double pricePerBook = resultSet.getDouble( "price" );
91          int newQuantity = availableBookCount - quantity;
92
93          // update database to decrement number of books
94          statement.execute( "UPDATE books " +
95              "SET quantity = " + newQuantity +
96              " WHERE isbn = " + isbn );
97          statement.close();
98
99          return pricePerBook * quantity;
100     }
101 }
102
103 // handle exception in executing Statement
104 catch ( SQLException sqlException ) {
105     sqlException.printStackTrace();
106     return -1;
107 }
108
109 } // end method orderBook
110
111 } // end class BookOrderImpl
```

Fig. C.29 **BookOrderImpl** handles the logic for the **BookOrder** Web service,
which uses ISBN and quantity values to obtain a price from a database.
(Part 3 of 3.)

According to the **client.xml** deployment descriptor of Fig. C.20, **BuyerPro-vider** sends a SOAP message to **ConfirmationServlet** (Fig. C.30) upon receiving that message. Method **init** (lines 23–77) initializes the servlet by establishing a connection to **BuyerProvider** to receive messages (lines 30–32) and opening a connection to database **bookStock1** (lines 35–49).

Class **ConfirmationServlet** implements interface **OnewayListener** (line 17) to ensure asynchronous communication. **BookOrderServlet** invokes method **onMessage** (lines 80–151) upon receiving a SOAP message. Line 86 obtains an **Iterator** that contains the **AttachmentPart**s associated with the incoming message. Lines 87–92 obtain the three **AttachmentPart**s that contain the ISBN, quantity and price values, and lines 95–99 extract these values from the **AttachmentPart**s. If the books were ordered successfully (i.e., the price value does not equal **-1**), lines 123–124 update the quantity of books in the **bookStock1** database. In addition, lines 127–130 insert an order entry in the **bookStock1** database.

```java
1   // Fig. C.30: ConfirmationServlet.java
2   // JAXMServlet that receives messages from BuyerProvider.
3   package com.deitel.jws1.jaxm.bookbuyer.receiver;
4
5   // Java core packages
6   import java.sql.*;
7   import java.io.*;
8   import java.util.*;
9
10  // Java extension packages
11  import javax.xml.messaging.*;
12  import javax.xml.soap.*;
13  import javax.servlet.*;
14  import javax.servlet.http.*;
15
16  public class ConfirmationServlet extends JAXMServlet
17     implements OnewayListener {
18
19     private ProviderConnection buyerProvider;
20     private Connection connection; // connection to database
21
22     // setup connection to message provider
23     public void init( ServletConfig servletConfig )
24        throws ServletException
25     {
26        super.init( servletConfig );
27
28        // establish connection to provider
29        try {
30           ProviderConnectionFactory providerFactory =
31              ProviderConnectionFactory.newInstance();
32           buyerProvider = providerFactory.createConnection();
33
34           // obtain URL of properties file
35           java.net.URL propertyURL = getClass().getResource(
36              "bookStock.properties" );
37
38           // load properties file
39           Properties databaseProperties = new Properties();
40           databaseProperties.load( new FileInputStream(
41              propertyURL.getPath() ) );
42
43           // load JDBC driver
44           Class.forName( databaseProperties.getProperty(
45              "jdbcDriver" ) );
46
```

Fig. C.30 **ConfirmationServlet** receives SOAP messages from **BuyerProvider** and confirms that an order has been placed. (Part 1 of 4.)

```
47        // establish database connection
48        connection = DriverManager.getConnection(
49           databaseProperties.getProperty( "databaseURI" ) );
50     }
51
52     // handle exception in provider connection
53     catch ( JAXMException jaxmException ) {
54        throw new ServletException( jaxmException.getMessage() +
55           "\nUnable to connect to provider." );
56     }
57
58     // handle exception if database driver does not exist
59     catch ( ClassNotFoundException classNotFoundException ) {
60        throw new ServletException(
61           classNotFoundException.getMessage() +
62           "\nUnable to load database driver." );
63     }
64
65     // handle exception in making Connection
66     catch ( SQLException sqlException ) {
67        throw new ServletException( sqlException.getMessage() +
68           "\nUnable to make database connection." );
69     }
70
71     // handle exception in loading properties file
72     catch ( IOException ioException ) {
73        throw new ServletException( ioException.getMessage() +
74           "\nUnable to load bookStock.properties." );
75     }
76
77  } // end method init
78
79  // invoked upon receiving message
80  public void onMessage( SOAPMessage message )
81  {
82     // determine whether order was successful
83     try {
84
85        // obtain ISBN, Quantity and Price attachments
86        Iterator attachments = message.getAttachments();
87        AttachmentPart isbnAttachment =
88           ( AttachmentPart ) attachments.next();
89        AttachmentPart quantityAttachment =
90           ( AttachmentPart ) attachments.next();
91        AttachmentPart priceAttachment =
92           ( AttachmentPart ) attachments.next();
93
94        // obtain ISBN, Quantity and Price from attachments
95        String isbn = ( String ) isbnAttachment.getContent();
96        Integer quantity = new Integer(
97           ( String ) quantityAttachment.getContent() );
```

Fig. C.30 **ConfirmationServlet** receives SOAP messages from **BuyerProvider** and confirms that an order has been placed. (Part 2 of 4.)

```
98              Double price = new Double (
99                 ( String ) priceAttachment.getContent() );
100
101             // ensure book availability
102             if ( price.doubleValue() < 0 ) {
103                 System.err.println( isbn + " is unavailable" );
104                 return;
105             }
106
107             // SQL query to database
108             Statement statement = connection.createStatement(
109                 ResultSet.TYPE_SCROLL_INSENSITIVE,
110                 ResultSet.CONCUR_READ_ONLY );
111
112             // make query to determine number of available books
113             ResultSet resultSet = statement.executeQuery( "SELECT" +
114                 " quantity FROM books WHERE isbn = " + isbn );
115
116             // update BookStock1 databases content
117             if ( resultSet != null ) {
118                 resultSet.next();
119                 int newQuantity = resultSet.getInt( "quantity" ) +
120                     quantity.intValue();
121
122                 // update quantity of books in database
123                 statement.execute( "UPDATE books SET quantity = " +
124                     newQuantity + " WHERE isbn = " + isbn );
125
126                 // place order (ibsn, quantity and price) in database
127                 statement.execute( "INSERT INTO orders " +
128                     "( isbn, quantity, price ) VALUES ( '" + isbn +
129                     "' , '" + quantity + "' , '" + price.toString() +
130                     "' )" );
131             }
132
133         statement.close();
134     }
135
136     // handle exception in accessing database
137     catch ( SQLException sqlException ) {
138         sqlException.printStackTrace();
139     }
140
141     // handle exception in parsing SOAP message
142     catch ( JAXMException jaxmException ) {
143         jaxmException.printStackTrace();
144     }
145
```

Fig. C.30 ConfirmationServlet receives SOAP messages from
BuyerProvider and confirms that an order has been placed.
(Part 3 of 4.)

```
146            // handle exception in obtaining message attachments
147            catch ( SOAPException soapException ) {
148               soapException.printStackTrace();
149            }
150
151         } // end method onMessage
152
153      } // end class ConfirmationServlet
```

Fig. C.30 **ConfirmationServlet** receives SOAP messages from **BuyerProvider** and confirms that an order has been placed. (Part 4 of 4.)

At this point, the transaction between **BuyerProvider** and **SellerProvider** is complete. To view the order status, the **BookBuyer** employee should use the link to the **ViewOrderServlet** on the HTML page that **BookBuyerServlet** generated. **ViewOrderServlet** (Fig. C.31) is an **HttpServlet** that displays the contents of the **bookStock1** database as XHTML. Method **init** (lines 32–79) initializes the servlet by establishing a connection to the **bookStock1** database (41–55) and creating factories for building XML documents and applying XSLT (lines 58–61). **ViewOrderServlet** stores the contents of the database as an XML document, then applies a style sheet to render the output as XHTML.

```
1    // Fig. C.31: ViewOrderServlet.java
2    // ViewOrderServlet enables a user to view the status of orders
3    // created by the JAXM applications.
4    package com.deitel.jws1.jaxm.bookbuyer.sender;
5
6    // Java core packages
7    import java.io.*;
8    import java.util.*;
9    import java.sql.*;
10   import java.text.NumberFormat;
11
12   // Java extension packages
13   import javax.servlet.http.*;
14   import javax.servlet.*;
15   import javax.xml.parsers.*;
16   import javax.xml.transform.*;
17   import javax.xml.transform.dom.*;
18   import javax.xml.transform.stream.*;
19
20   // W3C XML packages
21   import org.w3c.dom.*;
22
23   public class ViewOrderServlet extends HttpServlet {
24
25      private Connection connection; // connection to database
26
```

Fig. C.31 **ViewOrderServlet** displays the orders placed by the **BookBuyer** and **BookSeller** JAXM applications. (Part 1 of 6.)

```java
27      // factories for creating XML and applying XSLT
28      private DocumentBuilderFactory factory;
29      private TransformerFactory transformerFactory;
30
31      // setup database connection for servlet
32      public void init( ServletConfig servletConfig )
33         throws ServletException
34      {
35         super.init( servletConfig );
36
37         // initialize connection to database
38         try {
39
40            // obtain URL of properties file
41            java.net.URL propertyURL = getClass().getResource(
42               "bookStock.properties" );
43
44            // load properties file
45            Properties databaseProperties = new Properties();
46            databaseProperties.load( new FileInputStream(
47               propertyURL.getPath() ) );
48
49            // load JDBC driver
50            Class.forName( databaseProperties.getProperty(
51               "jdbcDriver" ) );
52
53            // establish database connection
54            connection = DriverManager.getConnection(
55               databaseProperties.getProperty( "databaseURI" ) );
56
57            // create factory to build XML Documents
58            factory = DocumentBuilderFactory.newInstance();
59
60            // create factory to apply XSLT
61            transformerFactory = TransformerFactory.newInstance();
62         }
63
64         // handle exception if database driver does not exist
65         catch ( ClassNotFoundException classNotFoundException ) {
66            classNotFoundException.printStackTrace();
67         }
68
69         // handle exception in making Connection
70         catch ( SQLException sqlException ) {
71            sqlException.printStackTrace();
72         }
73
74         // handle exception in loading properties file
75         catch ( IOException ioException ) {
76            ioException.printStackTrace();
77         }
78
```

Fig. C.31 ViewOrderServlet displays the orders placed by the **BookBuyer** and **BookSeller** JAXM applications. (Part 2 of 6.)

```
79        } // end method init
80
81        // invoked upon receiving message
82        public void doGet( HttpServletRequest request,
83           HttpServletResponse response ) throws ServletException
84        {
85           // determine whether order was successful
86           try {
87
88              // SQL query to database
89              Statement statement = connection.createStatement(
90                 ResultSet.TYPE_SCROLL_INSENSITIVE,
91                 ResultSet.CONCUR_READ_ONLY );
92
93              // make query to extract order information
94              ResultSet resultSet = statement.executeQuery( "SELECT" +
95                 " orderID, isbn, quantity, price FROM orders" );
96
97              Document orderXmlDocument = null;
98
99              // view order information
100             if ( resultSet != null )
101                orderXmlDocument = createXML( resultSet );
102
103             if ( orderXmlDocument != null )
104                applyXSLT( "XSL/viewOrder_XHTML.xsl",
105                   orderXmlDocument, response );
106
107             statement.close();
108          }
109
110          // handle exception in accessing database
111          catch ( SQLException sqlException ) {
112             sqlException.printStackTrace();
113          }
114
115          // handle exception in applying XSLT
116          catch ( IOException ioException ) {
117             ioException.printStackTrace();
118          }
119
120       } // end method doGet
121
122       // create XML document from ResultSet
123       private Document createXML( ResultSet resultSet )
124          throws SQLException
125       {
126          // use ResultSet to build XML document
127          try {
128             DocumentBuilder builder = factory.newDocumentBuilder();
129             Document document = builder.newDocument();
130
```

Fig. C.31 **ViewOrderServlet** displays the orders placed by the **BookBuyer** and **BookSeller** JAXM applications. (Part 3 of 6.)

```
131            // create orders root Element
132            Element orders = document.createElement( "orders" );
133            document.appendChild( orders );
134
135            // store ID, isbn, quantity and price in order Element
136            while ( resultSet.next() ) {
137
138               // create order Element for each order
139               Element order = document.createElement( "order" );
140
141               // obtain ID, isbn, quantity and price from resultSet
142               Integer ID =
143                  new Integer( resultSet.getInt( "orderID" ) );
144               String isbn = resultSet.getString( "isbn" );
145               Integer quantity =
146                  new Integer( resultSet.getInt( "quantity" ) );
147               Double price =
148                  new Double( resultSet.getDouble( "price" ) );
149
150               // create Elements for ID, isbn, quantity and price
151               Element orderID =
152                  document.createElement( "orderID" );
153               Element orderIsbn = document.createElement( "isbn" );
154               Element orderQuantity =
155                  document.createElement( "quantity" );
156               Element orderPrice =
157                  document.createElement( "price" );
158
159               // append elements as children to Element order
160               order.appendChild( orderID );
161               order.appendChild( orderIsbn );
162               order.appendChild( orderQuantity );
163               order.appendChild( orderPrice );
164
165               // create NumberFormat to format price to US locale
166               NumberFormat priceFormatter =
167                  NumberFormat.getCurrencyInstance( Locale.US );
168
169               // store ID, isbn, quantity and price information
170               orderID.appendChild(
171                  document.createTextNode( ID.toString() ) );
172               orderIsbn.appendChild(
173                  document.createTextNode( isbn ) );
174               orderQuantity.appendChild(
175                  document.createTextNode( quantity.toString() ) );
176               orderPrice.appendChild( document.createTextNode(
177                  priceFormatter.format( price ) ) );
178
179               // append each order Element to root Element orders
180               orders.appendChild( order );
181            }
182
```

Fig. C.31 **ViewOrderServlet** displays the orders placed by the **BookBuyer** and **BookSeller** JAXM applications. (Part 4 of 6.)

```
183        return document;
184     }
185
186     // handle exception in parsing
187     catch ( ParserConfigurationException parserException ) {
188        parserException.printStackTrace();
189        return null;
190     }
191
192  } // end method createXML
193
194  // apply XSLT style sheet to XML document
195  private void applyXSLT( String xslFile, Document xmlDocument,
196     HttpServletResponse response ) throws IOException
197  {
198     // apply XSLT
199     try {
200
201        // open InputStream for XSL document
202        InputStream xslStream =
203           getServletContext().getResourceAsStream( xslFile );
204
205        // create StreamSource for XSLT document
206        Source xslSource = new StreamSource( xslStream );
207
208        // create DOMSource for source XML document
209        Source xmlSource = new DOMSource( xmlDocument );
210
211        // get PrintWriter for writing data to client
212        PrintWriter output = response.getWriter();
213
214        // create StreamResult for transformation result
215        Result result = new StreamResult( output );
216
217        // create Transformer for XSL transformation
218        Transformer transformer =
219           transformerFactory.newTransformer( xslSource );
220
221        // transform and deliver content to client
222        transformer.transform( xmlSource, result );
223
224     }
225
226     // handle exception transforming content
227     catch ( TransformerException transformerException ) {
228        transformerException.printStackTrace();
229     }
230
231  } // end method applyXSLT
232
233 } // end class ViewOrderServlet
```

Fig. C.31 ViewOrderServlet displays the orders placed by the **BookBuyer** and **BookSeller** JAXM applications. (Part 5 of 6.)

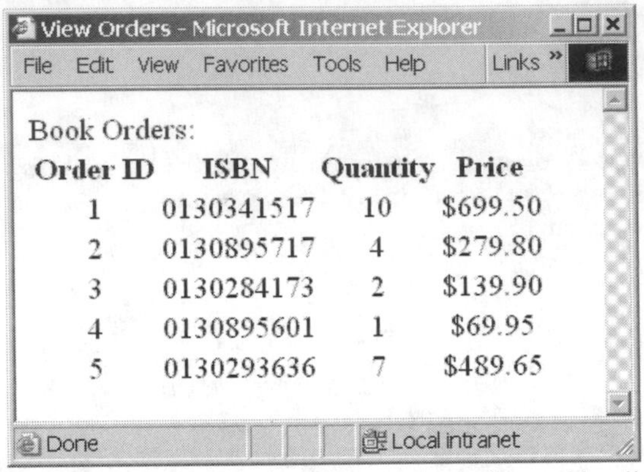

Fig. C.31 **ViewOrderServlet** displays the orders placed by the **BookBuyer** and **BookSeller** JAXM applications. (Part 6 of 6.)

When the user accesses **ViewOrderServlet** via a Web browser, **ViewOrderServlet** invokes method **doGet** (lines 82–120). Lines 94–95 obtain the values for each order ID, ISBN, quantity and price from the database. Line 101 invokes method **createXML** (lines 123–192) to build the XML document from the **ResultSet** that contains these values. Lines 132–133 create root element **orders**. For each order, line 139 creates an element **order**, to which lines 160–163 append elements **orderID**, **isbn**, **quantity** and **price**. Line 180 appends each **order** element to element **orders**, and line 183 returns the XML document to method **doGet**. Lines 104–105 pass this document to method **applyXSLT** (lines 195–231), which applies **viewOrder_XHTML.xsl** (Fig. C.32) to the XML document, then sends the content to the Web browser as XHTML.

```
1   <?xml version="1.0"?>
2
3   <!-- Fig. C.32: viewOrder_XHTML.xsl   -->
4   <!-- XHTML stylesheet                 -->
5
6   <xsl:stylesheet version = "1.0"
7      xmlns:xsl = "http://www.w3.org/1999/XSL/Transform">
8
9      <xsl:output method = "xml" omit-xml-declaration = "no"
10        doctype-system = "DTD/xhtml1-strict.dtd"
11        doctype-public = "-//W3C//DTD XHTML 1.0 Strict//EN"/>
12
13     <!-- specify the root of the XML document -->
14     <!-- that references this stylesheet       -->
15     <xsl:template match = "orders">
16        <html xmlns="http://www.w3.org/1999/xhtml">
17
18           <head>
19              <title>View Orders</title>
20           </head>
```

Fig. C.32 XSL document that **ViewOrderServlet** uses to render **bookStock1** database contents as XHTML. (Part 1 of 2.)

```
21
22            <body>
23                <div class = "header">Book Orders:</div>
24
25                <table class = "orders">
26                    <tr>
27                        <th>Order ID</th>
28                        <th>ISBN</th>
29                        <th>Quantity</th>
30                        <th>Price</th>
31                    </tr>
32
33                    <xsl:apply-templates
34                        select = "order"/>
35
36                </table>
37
38            </body>
39        </html>
40    </xsl:template>
41
42    <xsl:template match = "order">
43        <tr>
44            <td align = "center">
45                <xsl:value-of select = "orderID"/>
46            </td>
47
48            <td align = "center">
49                <xsl:value-of select = "isbn"/>
50            </td>
51
52            <td align = "center">
53                <xsl:value-of select = "quantity"/>
54            </td>
55
56            <td align = "center">
57                <xsl:value-of select = "price"/>
58            </td>
59        </tr>
60    </xsl:template>
61
62 </xsl:stylesheet>
```

Fig. C.32 XSL document that **ViewOrderServlet** uses to render **bookStock1** database contents as XHTML. (Part 2 of 2.)

C.5 Building a Java Client that Invokes a Web Service

In this section, we show how to use the Java programming language to build a client capable of invoking Web services. We build a Java client that uses an online WSDL document to access a Web service that provides stock quotes based on a company symbol.

We construct a client that accesses a Web service from **www.xmethods.com** (Fig. C.33). This site provides access to numerous Web services, ranging from services that perform and return simple mathematical calculations to services that provide credit-card validation. **XMethods** contains a **Service List**, which categorizes each Web service by **Publisher**, **Style**, **Service Name**, **Description** and **Implementation**. The **Publisher** is the Web site of the company that promotes the Web service. The **Style** represents how each SOAP message is encoded (either as a remote-procedure call or as a document). The **Service Name** is a link to the URL of the Web service. The **Description** provides a textual description of the service. The **Implementation** is the name of the Web service environment on which the service has been deployed. The Web service for which we construct a client is the **Delayed Stock Quote** (which, at the time of this writing, is located at the bottom of the page). When given a company stock symbol, this Web service returns a 20-minute delayed stock quote for the company associated with that symbol.

Select the **Delayed Stock Quote** item under the **Service Name** field in the **XMethods** Web site to view information for this Web service (Fig. C.34). This page contains a link to the WSDL document that contains the information needed to access the **Delayed Stock Quote** Web service. Note that the URL of the WSDL document is

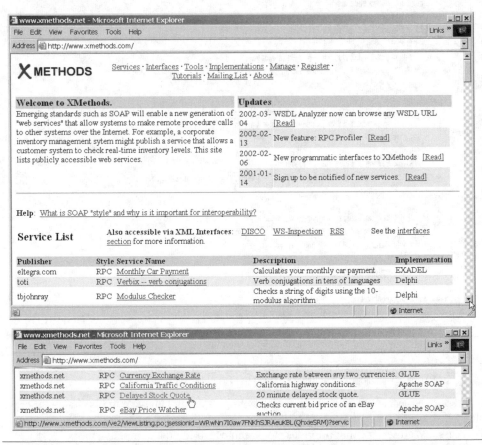

Fig. C.33 `www.xmethods.com` provides access to several Web services. (Courtesy of XMethods, Inc.)

```
http://services.xmethods.net/soap/urn:xmethods-delayed-
quotes.wsdl
```

We use this URL momentarily when we build the client that accesses this service.

If you access this URL via Internet Explorer, the browser displays the WSDL document (Fig. C.35). (Note that using Netscape might require downloading the WSDL document to disk, then viewing it in an appropriate editor.) Lines 12–18 define two messages called **getQuoteResponse1** and **getQuoteRequest1**, which are of Java types **float** and **String**, respectively. Lines 20–26 define a method called **getQuote**, which receives a **getQuoteRequest1** message as a parameter and must return a **getQuoteResponse** message. Logically, the **getQuote** methods receive as a parameter a **String** that represents a company's stock symbol and return a **float** that represents the stock quote for the company associated with that symbol. Lines 28–47 provide the **binding** information (i.e., how that Web service is accessed), by specifying that clients can access the Web service using a remote procedure call in the form of a SOAP message over HTTP. Lines 49–58 provide the **service** element that provides the location (URL) of the Web service.

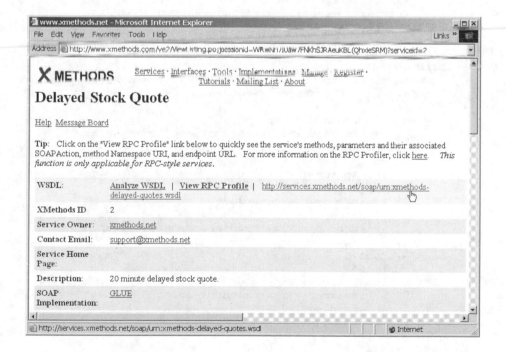

Fig. C.34 Delayed Stock Quote Web service information. (Courtesy of XMethods, Inc.)

```
 1    <?xml version="1.0" encoding="UTF-8"?>
 2    <definitions name="net.xmethods.services.stockquote.StockQuote"
 3        targetNamespace="http://www.themindelectric.com/wsdl/
net.xmethods.services.stockquote.StockQuote/"
 4        xmlns:tns="http://www.themindelectric.com/wsdl/
net.xmethods.services.stockquote.StockQuote/"
 5        xmlns:electric="http://www.themindelectric.com/"
 6        xmlns:soap="http://schemas.xmlsoap.org/wsdl/soap/"
 7        xmlns:xsd="http://www.w3.org/2001/XMLSchema"
 8        xmlns:soapenc="http://schemas.xmlsoap.org/soap/encoding/"
 9        xmlns:wsdl="http://schemas.xmlsoap.org/wsdl/"
10        xmlns="http://schemas.xmlsoap.org/wsdl/">
11
12        <message name="getQuoteResponse1">
13            <part name="Result" type="xsd:float" />
14        </message>
15
16        <message name="getQuoteRequest1">
17            <part name="symbol" type="xsd:string" />
18        </message>
19
20        <portType
21            name="net.xmethods.services.stockquote.StockQuotePortType">
22            <operation name="getQuote" parameterOrder="symbol">
23                <input message="tns:getQuoteRequest1" />
24                <output message="tns:getQuoteResponse1" />
25            </operation>
26        </portType>
27
28        <binding
29            name="net.xmethods.services.stockquote.StockQuoteBinding"
30            type="tns:net.xmethods.services.stockquote.StockQuotePort-
Type">
31            <soap:binding style="rpc"
32                transport="http://schemas.xmlsoap.org/soap/http" />
33            <operation name="getQuote">
34                <soap:operation
35                    soapAction="urn:xmethods-delayed-quotes#getQuote" />
36                <input>
37                    <soap:body use="encoded"
38                        namespace="urn:xmethods-delayed-quotes"
39                        encodingStyle="http://schemas.xmlsoap.org/soap/
encoding/" />
40                </input>
41                <output>
42                    <soap:body use="encoded"
43                        namespace="urn:xmethods-delayed-quotes"
44                        encodingStyle="http://schemas.xmlsoap.org/soap/
encoding/" />
45                </output>
46            </operation>
47        </binding>
48
```

Fig. C.35 WSDL document for the **Delayed Stock Quote** Web service. (Part 1 of 2.)

```
49    <service
50      name="net.xmethods.services.stockquote.StockQuoteService">
51      <documentation>
52        net.xmethods.services.stockquote.StockQuote web service
53      </documentation>
54      <port name="net.xmethods.services.stockquote.StockQuotePort"
55        binding="tns:net.xmethods.services.stockquote.StockQuote-
Binding">
56          <soap:address location="http://66.28.98.121:9090/soap" />
57      </port>
58    </service>
59 </definitions>
```

Fig. C.35 WSDL document for the **Delayed Stock Quote** Web service. (Part 2 of 2.)

We use **Forte for Java, release 3.0** (**Community Edition**), as the Web service-development environment to construct our Web service client. This software is available free for download at

   www.sun.com/forte/ffj/buy.html

The **WASP Developer Advanced 3.0.1—version 3.1.1** module includes a toolkit that enables developers to create and deploy Web services and a WASP server that hosts Web services. This module is free for download through the Forte **Update Center**. After installing Forte, select **Tools > Update Center**. Select and install the **WASP Developer Advanced 3.0.1** module (Fig. C.36).

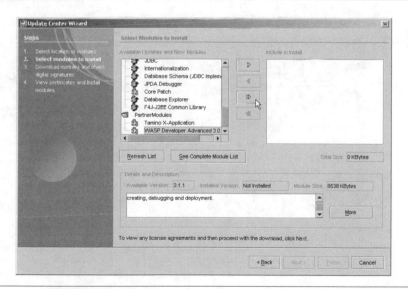

Fig. C.36 **WASP Developer Advanced 3.0.1** module installation via **Forte for Java Update Center.** (Courtesy of Systinet. Reproduced with permission by Sun Microsystems, Inc.© Copyright 2002. Sun Microsystems, Inc. All Rights Reserved.)

When using a module such as the WASP Developer Advanced module for Forte to build a client that accesses Web services, it is often unnecessary to analyze the WSDL in this much detail. To use an existing WSDL document to create a Web service client in Forte, do the following:

1. Select **File > New**. In the **Template Chooser**, select **Web Services > Create Web Service** (Fig. C.37), then press **Next**.

2. Specify the name of the Web Service (e.g., Delayed Stock Quote) in the **Name** field, and specify the package structure (e.g., `com.deitel.jws1.services`) in the **Package** field (Fig. C.38), then press **Next**.

3. Specify **Internet** as the means by which to download the WSDL document (Fig. C.39), then press **Next**.

4. Enter the WSDL-document URL (Fig. C.40), then press **Next**.

5. Select the Web service to invoke (Fig. C.41). (Only the Delayed Stock Quote Web service exists in this example.) Press **Next**.

6. We will create our own implementation class. Click **Next** when prompted to **Select Implementation Class** (Fig. C.42).

7. The module uses the WSDL document to fill Web service properties. Click **Finish** to accept the specified property values (Fig. C.43).

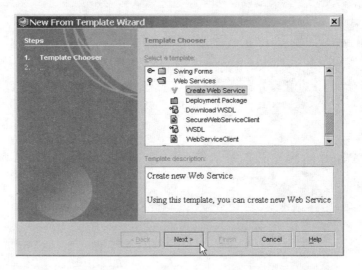

Fig. C.37 Creating a Web service from a remote WSDL document using the **WASP Developer Advanced** module (Step 1). (Courtesy of Systinet. Reproduced with permission by Sun Microsystems, Inc.© Copyright 2002. Sun Microsystems, Inc. All Rights Reserved.)

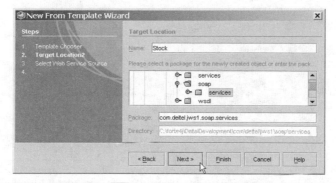

Fig. C.38 Creating a Web service from a remote WSDL document using the **WASP Developer Advanced** module (Step 2). (Courtesy of Systinet. Reproduced with permission by Sun Microsystems, Inc.© Copyright 2002. Sun Microsystems, Inc. All Rights Reserved.)

Fig. C.39 Creating a Web service from a remote WSDL document using the **WASP Developer Advanced** module (Step 3). (Courtesy of Systinet. Reproduced with permission by Sun Microsystems, Inc.© Copyright 2002. Sun Microsystems, Inc. All Rights Reserved.)

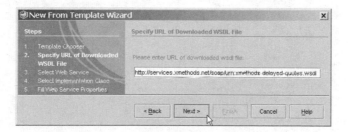

Fig. C.40 Creating a Web service from a remote WSDL document using the **WASP Developer Advanced** module (Step 4). (Courtesy of Systinet. Reproduced with permission by Sun Microsystems, Inc.© Copyright 2002. Sun Microsystems, Inc. All Rights Reserved.)

Fig. C.41   Creating a Web service from a remote WSDL document using the **WASP Developer Advanced** module (Step 5). (Courtesy of Systinet. Reproduced with permission by Sun Microsystems, Inc.© Copyright 2002. Sun Microsystems, Inc. All Rights Reserved.)

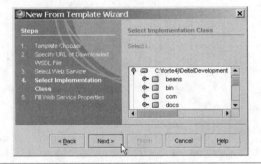

Fig. C.42   Creating a Web service from a remote WSDL document using the **WASP Developer Advanced** module (Step 6). (Courtesy of Systinet. Reproduced with permission by Sun Microsystems, Inc.© Copyright 2002. Sun Microsystems, Inc. All Rights Reserved.)

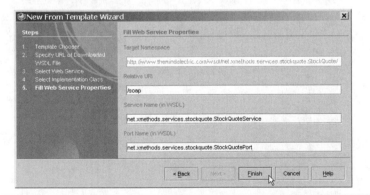

Fig. C.43   Creating a Web service from a remote WSDL document using the **WASP Developer Advanced** module (Step 7). (Courtesy of Systinet. Reproduced with permission by Sun Microsystems, Inc.© Copyright 2002. Sun Microsystems, Inc. All Rights Reserved.)

We now program the interface through which the client interacts with the Delayed Stock Quote Web service. We create interface **Stock** and store it in the **com.deitel.jws1.services** directory (Fig. C.44). Interface **Stock** provides only one method—**getQuote** (line 9)—which clients should use to access the Delayed Stock Quote Web service. This method should receive as an argument a **String** that indicates a company's stock symbol and should return a **float** that represents the company's current stock value (delayed by 20 minutes). Note that we could have created interface **Stock** manually by analyzing the WSDL document in Fig. C.35. lines 22–25 specify that interface **Stock** contains only method (called **getQuote**) which receives a **getQuoteRequest1** (which lines 16–18 define as a **String**) and returns a **getQuoteResponse1** (which lines 12–14 define as a **float**). However, creating interfaces manually by analyzing WSDL documents is a time-consuming and error-prone process, so using a tool that provides automatic interface generation is usually preferable to, and more efficient than, coding interfaces manually.

We now create class **StockClient** (Fig. C.45)—the client that uses a WSDL document to access the Delayed Stock Quote Web service. Lines 14–16 import the WASP APIs that enable the client to communicate with the server that exposes the Delayed Stock Quote service. Line 19 imports interface **Stock**, which **Stock-Client** uses to communicate (via the remote server) with the Delayed Stock Quote Web service.

StockClient has three central GUI elements:

- A **JLabel** (line 44) that displays the value of a company's stock that **Stock-Client** receives from the Delayed Stock Quote service;

- A **JComboBox** (lines 48–53) that enables the user to select from a list of company stock symbols.

- A **JButton** (lines 56–90) that, when clicked, notifies the remote server to invoke method **getQuote** from the Delayed Stock Quote service.

```
1   // Fig. C.44: Stock.java.
2   // Stock is the interface through which clients can invoke the
3   // Delayed Stock Quote Web service.
4   package com.deitel.jws1.services;
5
6   public interface Stock {
7
8       // service to receive stock quote for associated stock symbol
9       float getQuote( String symbol );
10  }
```

Fig. C.44 **Stock** serves as an interface for clients to access the Delayed Stock Quote Web service.

```
1   // Fig. C.45: StockClient.java.
2   // StockClient uses the WASP API for Java and an online WSDL
3   // document to access a Web service that generates stock quotes.
```

Fig. C.45 **StockClient** uses the WASP APIs and an online WSDL document to invoke the Delayed Stock Quote Web service. (Part 1 of 4.)

```
4   package com.deitel.jws1.wsdl.client;
5
6   // Java core packages
7   import java.awt.*;
8   import java.awt.event.*;
9
10  // Java extension packages
11  import javax.swing.*;
12
13  // WASP packages
14  import org.idoox.webservice.client.WebServiceLookup;
15  import org.idoox.webservice.client.WebServiceLookupException;
16  import org.idoox.wasp.Context;
17
18  // Deitel packages
19  import com.deitel.jws1.services.Stock;
20
21  public class StockClient extends JFrame {
22
23     private final static int FRAME_WIDTH = 400;
24     private final static int FRAME_HEIGHT = 100;
25
26     // interface for accessing Delayed Stock Quote Web service
27     private Stock service;
28
29     // URL of Web service
30     private final static String SERVICE_URL =
31        "http://66.28.98.121:9090/soap";
32
33     // WSDL-document URL
34     private final static String WSDL_URL =
35        "http://services.xmethods.net/soap/" +
36        "urn:xmethods-delayed-quotes.wsdl";
37
38     public StockClient( String title )
39     {
40        super( title );
41        getContentPane().setLayout( new GridLayout( 2, 2 ) );
42
43        // JLabel to display stock quote after invoking Web service
44        final JLabel resultsLabel = new JLabel();
45
46        // JComboBox for selecting company from which to receive
47        // associated stock quote
48        final JComboBox symbolComboBox = new JComboBox();
49        symbolComboBox.addItem( "SUNW" );
50        symbolComboBox.addItem( "MSFT" );
51        symbolComboBox.addItem( "INTL" );
52        symbolComboBox.addItem( "IBM" );
53        symbolComboBox.addItem( "CSCO" );
54
```

Fig. C.45 StockClient uses the WASP APIs and an online WSDL document to invoke the Delayed Stock Quote Web service. (Part 2 of 4.)

```
55          // JButton invokes remote Web Service
56          JButton serviceButton = new JButton( "Get Stock Quote" );
57          serviceButton.addActionListener(
58             new ActionListener() {
59
60                // invoked when user presses JButton
61                public void actionPerformed( ActionEvent event )
62                {
63                   // use WASP APIs to access Web service
64                   try {
65
66                      // get object that performs Web-service lookup
67                      WebServiceLookup serviceLookup =
68                         ( WebServiceLookup ) Context.getInstance(
69                            Context.WEBSERVICE_LOOKUP );
70
71                      // lookup Web service from registry
72                      service = ( Stock ) serviceLookup.lookup(
73                         WSDL_URL, Stock.class, SERVICE_URL );
74
75                      // invoke Web service to receive stock quote
76                      float quote = service.getQuote(
77                         ( String ) symbolComboBox.getSelectedItem() );
78
79                      resultsLabel.setText( "Stock Quote: " +
80                         Float.toString( quote ) );
81                   }
82
83                   // handle exception if unable to find Web service
84                   catch ( WebServiceLookupException exception ) {
85                      exception.printStackTrace();
86                   }
87
88                } // end method actionPerformed
89             }
90          );
91
92          // store JLabel, JComboBox and JButton JFrame
93          getContentPane().add( new JLabel( "Select company:" ) );
94          getContentPane().add( symbolComboBox );
95          getContentPane().add( resultsLabel );
96          getContentPane().add( serviceButton );
97
98       } // end constructor
99
100      // return StockClient frame size
101      public Dimension getPreferredSize()
102      {
103         return new Dimension( FRAME_WIDTH, FRAME_HEIGHT );
104      }
105
```

Fig. C.45 StockClient uses the WASP APIs and an online WSDL document to invoke the Delayed Stock Quote Web service. (Part 3 of 4.)

```
106     // instantiate StockClient GUI
107     public static void main( String args[] )
108     {
109        StockClient client =
110           new StockClient( "Stock Quote Service" );
111        client.setDefaultCloseOperation( EXIT_ON_CLOSE );
112        client.pack();
113        client.setVisible( true );
114     }
115
116 }  // end class StockClient
```

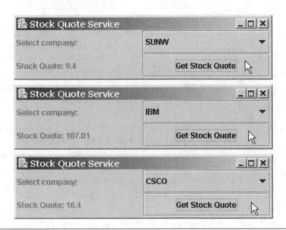

Fig. C.45 `StockClient` uses the WASP APIs and an online WSDL document to invoke the Delayed Stock Quote Web service. (Part 4 of 4.)

When the user clicks the **JButton**, method **actionPerformed** (lines 61–88) uses the WASP APIs to invoke the Web service. The WASP API objects use the WSDL document in Fig. C.35 to invoke the service. Lines 67–73 use a **WebServiceLookup** to obtain a remote reference to the **Stock** object. The lookup operation requires the URLs of the **Stock** object and the WSDL document, which are defined in lines 30–31 and 34–36, respectively. The Delayed Stock Quote service's associated WSDL document contains the Web service URL (Fig. C.35, line 56), and the **Delayed Stock Quote** information page (Fig. C.34) contains the WSDL-document URL.

Lines 76–77 pass the company stock symbol that the user specified from the **JComboBox** to method **getQuote** on the remote **Stock** object. If the Web service invocation was successful, the Web service returns a **float** that represents the value of the stock associated with that company. Lines 79–80 display the result in the **JLabel**.

In this appendix, we constructed two major architectures that used the Java API for XML Remote Procedure Calls (JAX-RPC) and the Java API for XML Messaging (JAXM), respectively. We also demonstrated how to build a Java client that uses a WSDL document to invoke Web services. If you found this material to be informative and wish to further your study in Java-based Web services, we recommend our book Java Web Services. In this book, we provide more examples of systems that use these technologies. In addition, we introduce several of the other technologies in the Java Web Services Development Pack, such as the Java API for XML Parsing (JAXP) and the Java API for XML Registries

(JAXR). We also show how to use some of the most widely employed Web service environments (e.g., Apache's Axis, The Mind Electric's Glue, Systinet's WASP, CapeClear's CapeConnect and Iona's XMLBus) to expose methods in Java classes as Web services.

C.6 Summary

The Java API for XML Remote Procedure Call (JAX-RPC) and the Java API for XML Messaging (JAXM) are technologies that Sun Microsystems provides for building Web services and the clients that invoke those Web services. The Java Web Services Developer Pack (JWSDP) includes the Java XML Pack, Tomcat Java Servlet and JavaServer Pages containers, a registry server and the Ant build tool. The Java XML Pack provides JAX-RPC and JAXM.

To create a JAX-RPC-based Web service and client, we must perform four steps: 1) define a service interface that declares methods that clients can invoke on the remote service; 2) define the service implementation for the service interface; 3) deploy the service to the Web server; 4) define the client application that interacts with the service.

JAX-RPC can be used to expose a Web service and to build a client capable of invoking Web services via synchronous communication. The client sends a SOAP request to the Web service, then halts activity until it receives a SOAP response. Because the client halts activity, this client is unable to offer Web services in conjunction with invoking another service, which is a central characteristic of many Web service-based B2B applications. To circumvent this problem, JAXM applications may use a message provider, which sends and receives messages on the JAXM application's behalf, thus enabling a JAXM application to perform other functions after sending a SOAP request. This form of communication is known as asynchronous messaging.

The Java programming language also can be used to build clients capable of invoking Web services. These clients can be made to download WSDL documents to gather information on specific Web services. The clients then can be made to invoke these services.

C.7 Internet and Web Resources

java.sun.com/webservices
This Sun Microsystems site focuses on Java technology and Web services. It offers tutorials, FAQs and downloads of the Java Web Services Developer Pack.

java.sun.com/xml/jaxrpc
Links to JAX-RPC specifications, downloads and tutorials are available at this site.

archives.java.sun.com/archives/jaxrpc-interest.html
This site provides archived discussions from a JAX-RPC forum.

developer.java.sun.com/developer/technicalArticles/WebServices/ getstartjaxrpc/
This site offers an article that explains how to use JAX-RPC in Web services development.

developer.java.sun.com/developer/community/chat/JavaLive/2002/ jl0402.html
The Java Developer Connection maintains this moderated forum devoted to JAX-RPC.

www.fawcette.com/javapro/2002_05/magazine/features/shorrell/
An article that explains JAX-RPC fundamentals is available at this site.

`forums.java.sun.com/forum.jsp?forum=331`
This site provides a discussion forum on a range of Java Web services topics, including JAXM, JAX-RPC and the Java Web Services Developer Pack.

`www.infoworld.com/articles/fe/xml/02/03/25/020325fejavatca.xml`
A discussion of the technologies that enable Java Web services, including JAXM, is presented in this article.

Best Web Services Web Sites

Objectives

- To learn about key Web services sites.
- To understand the major sections of each Web site.
- To discuss the topics available at each site.

A place for everything and everything in its place
Samuel Smiles

Every tool carries with it the spirit by which it has been created.
Werner Karl Heisenberg

D.1 www.webservices.org

WebServices.org aggregates Web services news and information, including articles about applications, platforms, vendors and event listings. Although certain technical papers and links are available only to members, membership is free—a user must enter a name, password, e-mail address, occupation category, company name, city and country to join.

- **WebServices.org** organizes the information on its site into **Applications**, **Architecture**, **Platforms**, **Vendors**, **Events** and **Feature Papers** sections. Each category is further divided into **Articles**, **Events**, **Papers** and **Members** pages.

- The **Articles** page is the default page for every category—i.e., when the user clicks on a category, such as **Architecture**, the user's browser is directed to the Architecture **Articles** page. The **Events** page displays information about upcoming events related to Web services, such as conferences and specification draft release dates. Only members can view the contents of the **Papers** and **Members** sections. The **Papers** section provides more in-depth, technical treatments of topics than do the articles, and the **Members** page offers the most current articles and information available.

- An **Archive** page lists older articles by category. Every article title links to its full article. A search tool is available on the archive page—results are returned in chronological order to help users locate specific topics.

- The **Forums** page allows users to pose questions, respond to questions and interact with peers. Discussion topics include general questions about Web services, industry-specific Web services questions or technical discussions. Another way for users to interact with the site is via **Polls**. Each poll poses questions about the current state of Web services and measures popular opinion. Only members may vote in the polls, but anyone can view the results.

- The **Links** page refers users to sources outside the site. This section directs users to articles and other sites that cover numerous Web services topics.

- The **Sponsors** section provides links to the Web sites of **WebServices.org** sponsors and offers detailed information on each company's Web services efforts. Several companies sponsor the site, including Red Gate, which offers load-testing for Web services; OpenLink, which develops cross-platform Web services; Blue Titan, a Web services networking company; Cape Clear and IBM. A **Vendors List** page displays an alphabetical list of companies involved in the Web services industry. The page includes product and service information for each and links to company news items that have appeared on the **WebServices.org** site. At the time of this writing, more than 70 vendors are listed.

D.2   www.webservicesarchitect.com

Web Services Architect is an online journal designed to inform professionals about Web services and related technologies. Readers can sign up to receive weekly e-mails that summarize new information on the site. The site aggregates and catalogs technical and business-related articles written by industry experts, as well as providing reader polls. The main sections of the Web site include **Resources**, **Archives**, **Downloads** and a **Reading List**. An **Industry Watch** tracks the latest Web services news, and another section offers links to past articles.

- The home page includes an **Industry Watch** column, which highlights recent Web services articles. Abstracts of recent articles are available on the home page, with links to the full texts. A blue box on the home page highlights *Web Service Architect* announcements, including news, articles, new polls and poll results. Additional articles also can be found on the **Archives** page.

- A **Resources** section contains links to other sites that offer news and information, background on technical aspects of Web services, directories, search engines, links to vendors and white papers.

- Many of the articles on this site are shortened from longer papers. PDF versions of the full articles are available in the **Downloads** section—some downloads must be purchased.

- *Web Services Architect* also provides a **Reading List** page to inform users about technical resources. The reading list includes resources for general topics, as well as particular technologies, including J2EE, .NET, ebXML and SOAP.

D.3 www.w3.org

The World Wide Web Consortium (W3C) is an organization that defines and builds consensus for Internet technologies and standards. The W3C has organized several groups to develop Web services standards, such as the Web Services Architecture Working Group, the XML Protocol Working Group and the Web Services Description Working Group.

- The W3C home page contains a list titled **W3C from A to Z**, which contains links to all the technologies available at the W3C site, including XML and SOAP. To locate more specific topics, a Google Search tool allows users to search only the site or the entire World Wide Web.

- The home page also contains the latest news about the W3C. **Past News** articles can be accessed from a link on the home page. Users can find articles dating back to the founding of the W3C in 1994.

- The **Web Services Activity** page, accessible from the **Web Services** link on the home page, presents the activities of the W3C Web services groups. The page offers information organized under several headings: A **Groups** section includes links to the sites of the individual Web services groups and minutes from group meetings; a **New and Upcoming** section provides information on W3C Web services events, such as recently released drafts; a **Working Drafts in Progress** heading contains a list of proposed standardization drafts; a **Technical Discussion** section allows users to search the W3C's Web Services archive;[1] a **Timeline Publication and Events** section contains chronologically ordered links to publications and events, and a **Bookmarks: Recommended**

---

1. The archive is available at **lists.w3.org/Archives/Public/www-ws**.

Reading page summarizes the W3C Web services standards and links to each technology's specifications.

- By clicking the **Technical Reports** link, a user can view recent W3C publications. Here, users can find links to the current white papers for any W3C technology.

- Links under the **Mission** heading on the home page lead to information about the W3C and its goals. These links outline the W3C's mission and principles, as well as the structure of the organization. Contact and membership information also is available.

D.4   www.oasis-open.org

OASIS is an organization that promotes the use of standards, such as XML and SGML, by developing vertical and horizontal applications based on these standards. EbXML, Universal Business Language (UBL) and Business Transaction Protocol (BTP) are OASIS projects. OASIS initiatives that focus on Web services explicitly include Web Services for Interactive Applications and Web Services for Remote Portals.

- OASIS displays recent press releases and member information on its home page. By clicking a **News** link, users can access all OASIS press releases. There also is a link to **OASIS in the News** from the home page, which provides links to articles that discuss the organization.

- An **Events** page details future Web services conferences. A **Presentations** page chronologically lists conference-presentation outlines that are available for download as PowerPoint slides.

- A **Technical Committees** page describes each OASIS committee's mission and offers a link for more information on individual committees. Individual committee pages overview the mission of the committee, recent announcements, committee members, the committee's progress, articles pertaining to the committee's topic and the minutes to all committee meetings. OASIS provides a **Technical Process** page that details the procedures by which a technical committee is created.

- The **OASIS Network** page provides direct links to other standardization committees such as the one overseeing ebXML. The ebXML home page contains useful information about the initiative, including articles, a FAQ, event listings, resources and white papers.

- OASIS also offers a **Work-in-Progress** list on its home page. This list includes the languages and standards and technologies that OASIS is attempting to develop to enhance XML programming. For example, the UBL Technical committee intends to develop a standard library of XML business documents. A complete list of these works-in-progress can be found by clicking the **More...** link at the bottom of the list.

D.5   www.uddi.org

This site is the home of the UDDI project, a vendor consortium that oversees the development of the UDDI specification and governs implementations of the UDDI Business Registry (UBR). Most of the documents on this site are provided in PDF or Microsoft Word format; some are available in Chinese and Japanese as well as English.

- A **Register** page allows users to upload profiles of their companies to the UBR. Users also can search the UBR using the **Find** tab. Both features allow a user to select either the UDDI Version 1.0 or UDDI Version 2.0 registry implementations.

- The **Specifications** section links to the UDDI Versions 1.0 and 2.0 specifications. On this page, the user can access numerous technical references.

- The **uddi.org** home page lists articles that discuss UDDI. More current articles can be found in the **News** section. All articles can be viewed by clicking the **Archived News Articles...** link on the home page.

- There are two **Forums**—a **General** forum and a **Technical** forum. The forums are hosted by Yahoo Groups, and registered Yahoo users can post to discussions. However, registration is not required to read the discussions.

- A **White Papers** area contains the most recent descriptions of the UDDI standard. The **Technical Notes** and **Best Practices** sections provide a range of technical information, but do not contain actual specifications. The **Solutions** page offers additional technical information for UDDI users. This section details development tools, products, registrars and services.

- The **Events** section lists both past and future events relating to UDDI. Links within the events page direct a reader to event sponsors and Web sites, enabling users to locate additional information about, and sign up for, specific events.

- The **Community** page provides a list and description of businesses that support the UDDI project.

D.6 www.microsoft.com

The Microsoft Developer Network Library is a resource for developers that offers a wide range of Web services information.[2] To access this Web services section, select the **XML Web Services** link from the Microsoft Developers Network Library, **msdn.microsoft.com/library**.

- The Developers Network Library for XML Web Services home page provides several links to introductory information about Web services and .NET technologies that relate to Web services. An **XML Web Services Technology Map** link presents a guide for developers who are new to Web services. The second link, labelled **.NET Technology Map**, provides overviews of technologies r relevant to .NET Web services. The **.NET Six-Week Series Guide** and **Web Services Specifications** are other links that offer introductory information.

- A **Technical Articles** and a **Columns** offer links to general Web services articles that have appeared in *MSDN Magazine*.

- A **Specifications** page includes information on Web services standards—including SOAP, WSDL and UDDI—as well as specifications that comprise the Global XML Web Services Architectures (GXA). Another Microsoft Developer

---

2. Another Web services section is available at **www.microsoft/technet**. Select **Products and Technologies** and choose **Windows Web Services**. The topics on this page relate to security, performance, tutorials, service packs and tools using Microsoft Internet Information Server (IIS).

Network Library section, **Global XML Web Services Architecture**, provides additional resources related to the GXA.

- A **Security Technical Articles** page highlights Web services security concerns. An **Interoperability Resources** includes several articles that explain how developers can ensure the interoperability of their Web services.

- The site offers pages that describe **MapPoint .NET Basic Services** and **.NET Services**. The MapPoint page offers general articles, documentation and technical articles about the MapPoint .NET Web service. The .NET Services page provides articles and documentation for Messenger and .NET Passport.

- An **XML Core** page details the XML standard, XSL and Microsoft's XML implementations.

D.7   www.sun.com

Sun Microsystems offers a large collection of articles that describe Sun's Web services activities. The Web services section of Sun's site is available at **java.sun.com/webservices**.

- The articles on the Web services page are divided into two categories: **Hot Topics** and **News and Articles**. The **Hot Topics** section has links to applications and tutorials for implementing Web services. **News and Articles** includes relevant content about Java, Sun and Web services from a variety of sources.

- Sun also offers a **Downloads** page where developers can access additional resources and technologies. Users can view specifications and download tutorials and developer's packs at this page.

- A **Documentation** page offers links to general information, guides and tutorials, technical articles, API documentation, Release Notes and Frequently Asked Questions on a variety of Web services-related topics, including Java technology and Web services, Java Technology and XML and Java 2 Platform, Enterprise Edition.

- Sun offers a comprehensive Java Web services guide on a **Tutorial** page. The tutorial includes an introduction, technical information about XML, treatments of Web-technology topics, a case study and appendices containing information about development tools.

- A **FAQ** page contains answers to general and technical Web services questions.

- A link to a **White Papers** page offers developers information on a variety of technical issues. Some of the papers are available in Japanese, as well as English.

D.8   www.ibm.com0

IBM's Web Services Zone is a section of DeveloperWorks, IBM's resource for developers. The site provides articles, a discussion forum, columns, tips and a set of the most popular Web Services Zone links, available at **www-106.ibm.com/developerworks/webservices**.

- A **Tools and products** page provides an extensive list of IBM and third-party products and developer applications in a variety of areas, including **Middleware**,

Directory Services, **Application Servers**, **Workflow** and **XML Databases**. For example, the **Directory Services** link takes the user to a preview of IBM's WebSphere UDDI registry, which can be downloaded for evaluation purposes.

- A **Code and components** page offers an extensive list of programming utilities for Web services development. Each component on the page has a brief description and a link to a page that offers more information.

- A Web services **Education** page provides tutorials for several levels of Web services programmers. A **Demonstration** page includes some interactive applications to provide illustrations of Web services in action.

- An **Articles**, **columns & tips** page sorts articles by date, author or title. The **Most Popular Links** page lists the newest and the most frequently accessed articles in the archives, and a **News** link lists Web services articles in reverse chronological order.

- A **FAQs** page provides a set of questions and answers related to IBM's Web Services Toolkit, a Web services development application.

- IBM offers two forums in which developers can discuss technical issues: **The Python Web services developer** and **Web services demos**. The Python forum encourages beginners to participate. The forum directs participants to technical resources to provide fundamental information for each discussion. The Web services demos forum encourages developers to ask questions about demonstration software they have created or they have used.

- The **Events** page includes Webcasts and conferences on a variety of topics, including Web services workshops and Portal conferences.

- IBM's site also contains a section devoted to XML. To locate this page, select **Developers** from the IBM home page, then click the **XML** link. This page offers articles, tools and information about XML standards.

Glossary

A

accessibility   A description of how difficult it is to access a service. A higher accessibility level means that a larger number of users can access the service more easily.

Active Server Pages (ASP) .NET   A technology for creating dynamic Web content marked up as HTML; this technology is part of Microsoft's .NET initiative.

adaptors   Software components that often are part of enterprise-application integration solutions and enable applications to communicate with other applications.

Apache Axis   An open-source toolkit that fully supports SOAP 1.1, supports many features of SOAP 1.2 and offers support for generating WSDL documents. Axis is a re-engineered version of Apache SOAP.

Apache SOAP   An open-source SOAP toolkit that was based on IBM's toolkit, SOAP4J, and supports most features of SOAP 1.1. Apache Axis is the next version of Apache SOAP.

application integration   The process of linking applications so that they can communicate and share data.

Application Management Software (AMS)   A program used to download and open MIDlet suites, and then launch user-specified MIDlets on a MIDP device.

Application Service Providers (ASP)   Software vendors that provide customized business-software applications over the Web. ASPs typically develop a set of commonly used applications, then customize the applications to suit individual clients. Companies typically pay a fee to ASPs to access applications. By using ASPs, companies do not have to develop, maintain or update software.

asset owner   The party that maintains legal control over a Web service and any intellectual property associated with the service; this is often, but not necessarily, the creator of the service.

asynchronous communication   A method of communication that does not require the client to wait for a response from the Web service to continue program execution.

attribute   A name-value pair that provides additional information about an XML element.

authentication   A process through which Web-site visitors or the senders and receivers of messages prove their identities to each other.

authentication capabilities   Security mechanisms that allow a Web service to discern the identity and access rights of a service requestor to prevent nonauthorized users from invoking services.

authorization   The management of access to protected resources based on a user's credentials.

availability   The probability that a service is ready to be used (i.e., available). A higher availability rating means that the service is more likely to be able to process a request at a given time.

B

B2B integration   The process of incorporating aspects of one business's applications, processes or network in other businesses' systems.

base-64 encoding   Encoding that uses 64 characters (**a–z, A–Z, 0–9, /** and **+**) to represent binary data.

biometrics   A security innovation that uses unique personal information, such as fingerprints, eyeball iris scans or face scans, to identify a user.

BizTalk   A technology offered by Microsoft to facilitate and manage business transactions. BizTalk creates an environment in which data can be marked up as XML and exchanged between applications, regardless of differences in platforms or programming languages.

BizTalk Framework   A Schema for structuring BizTalk messages exchanged between businesses.

browse pattern   A feature provided by the UDDI inquiry API that allows service consumers to perform broad searches of UDDI registries to locate businesses, templates, services or **tModel**s.

brute-force cracking   A process in which a malicious third party attempts to decrypt a message by using every possible decryption key.

business-process management   A system for organizing and handling complex computing and e-business tasks, which typically involve interactions between applications.

Business Process Management Initiative (BPMI)   An organization formed to promote the standardization of business processes across applications, platforms and partners. To manage such processes, BPMI developed the Business Process Modeling Language (BPML) and the Business Process Query Language (BPQL).

Business Process Management System (BPMS)   A framework for managing a system of integrated processes, from the strategic planning phase to implementation.

Business Process Modeling Language (BPML)   A meta-language for modeling business processes.

Business Process Query Language (BPQL)   A language designed for deploying business processes.

business tier   The part of a multi-tiered application that controls and processes business rules, including how clients access data, how applications process data and how content is presented to clients. Also called the middle tier or the business-logic tier.

Business Transaction Protocol (BTP)   An XML-based protocol designed to coordinate and manage complex transactions between businesses using Web services or other B2B technologies.

C

canonical form   A form of data used by XML Signature to compute hash values in which logically equivalent documents produce the same hash values, regardless of formatting.

Capability profile   In JAXR, the set of capabilities that a given XML registry type supports.

CapeConnect   A system developed by Cape Clear that enables programmers to deploy Java services, EJBs and CORBA systems in Web service environments by unifying legacy systems and Web service protocols without the need for writing code.

challenge-response authentication   An authentication method used in HTTP security in which users must provide specific authentication information.

change management   The process of versioning, upgrading and adapting systems.

cipher   A mathematical algorithm used to encrypt messages; ciphers also are referred to as cryptosystems.

ciphertext   Encrypted data.

client tier   The part of a a multi-tiered application that provides the user interface through which users communicate with the application. Also called the top tier or presentation tier.

Collaboration-Protocol Agreement (CPA)   In ebXML, a contract formed between trading partners that defines business-transaction guidelines and SLAs.

Collaboration-Protocol Profile (CPP)   In ebXML, an XML document that contains information about a specific organization and the services offered by that organization. A CPP includes information about a service interface and specifies the requirements to exchange documents with a particular trading partner.

Common Language Runtime (CLR)   A central part of the .NET Framework that executes programs written in any .NET-supported language.

Common Language Specification (CLS)   A specification that defines the common features of .NET languages and contains information about the storage of data types, objects and so on.

Component Object Model (COM)   A Microsoft software architecture in which developers use binary program components to build applications that can communicate with other COM-based applications.

Common Object Request Broker Architecture (CORBA)   An industry-standard high-level distributed object framework for building powerful and flexible service-oriented applications.

Connected Limited Device Configuration (CLDC)   A set of APIs that allow developers to create applications for devices that have limited resources— e.g., limited screen size, memory, power, and bandwidth.

corporate portals   Browser-based applications that offer single access points to information or applications aggregated from disparate sources.

cryptanalysis   The process of attempting to decrypt ciphertext without knowledge of the decryption key.

cryptography   A process that uses a cipher to encrypt messages.

custodian   The UDDI Business Registry (UBR) operator node with which a company registers.

Customer Relationship Management (CRM)   A process that encompasses every aspect of interaction between an organization and its customers, including sales, service and support.

D

Data, Applications, Reports and Transactions (DART)   A model that helps programmers develop services on demand. Using DART, companies can organize business applications and processes that involve data, applications, reports and transactions. Programmers apply the DART model and map business elements to corresponding services.

data integration   The most common form of EAI; data integration links databases to applications or other databases.

Data Universal Numbering System (D-U-N-S)   A system by which nine-digit numbers are assigned to businesses as identifiers.

Delphi 6   Borland's rapid-application-development environment for the Windows operating system.

denial-of-service attack   An attack that forces a system to behave improperly, typically performed by flooding servers with data packets.

digital certificate   A digital document used to identify a user; a digital certificate includes the user's name, the user's public key, a serial number, an expiration date, the signature of a trusted certificate authority and any other relevant information.

Digital Rights Management (DRM)   A set of protocols designed to protect media against piracy and unauthorized access online.

digital signatures   Signatures designed for use in public-key cryptography to solve the problems of authentication and integrity.

digital watermark   A visible or invisible mark or message that indicates the owner of a document.

direct discovery   The process of obtaining Web service data from a registry (such as a UDDI or ebXML registry) maintained by the service provider.

discovery   The process of locating Web services, usually through registries.

Distributed Component Object Model (DCOM)   A technology that enables component reusability over a network in Microsoft programming environments.

distributed computing   An arrangement in which an organization's computing is distributed over networks, instead of being performed at a central computer installation.

Document Type Definition (DTD)   A technology that defines an XML document's structure by providing rules to which a document must adhere for that document to be valid. DTDs are used to verify that documents are structured properly and allow machines to validate documents quickly and reliably.

drill-down pattern   A feature provided by the UDDI inquiry API that provides users with programmer-specific information about a particular service, such as integration capabilities and scalability.

Dynamic e-Business   IBM's business strategy that promotes using the Internet to manage B2B interactions that support evolving business strategies and processes.

Dynamic Invocation Interface (DII)   The interface through which the JAX-RPC runtime system invokes a Web service without knowing that service's static information.

E

e-marketplace UDDI   A private UDDI registry that is hosted by an industry and lists businesses that belong to an industry consortium.

electronic business XML (ebXML)   A specification for standardizing XML-based communications among organizations and facilitating electronic business. EbXML uses XML to define, and subsequently automate, business processes.

Electronic Data Interchange (EDI)   A technology that enables businesses to conduct secure, reliable electronic transactions. Every supplier, manufacturer and distributor in a supply chain is linked to the EDI system through a closed network. EDI systems track and document a business's daily accounting and inventory data, including purchase orders, invoices and other transaction information.

element   An individual unit of markup (i.e., everything from a start tag to an end tag). Elements are the most fundamental building blocks of an XML document.

enrollment   A process in which a Web service provider supplies a requestor's identification information to a metering service, which records the requestor's usage information (usually for billing purposes).

Enterprise Application Integration (EAI)   An infrastructure that links multiple applications and databases so that they can share information and business processes. EAI typically uses middleware to connect a company's many applications; interfaces are built to link each separate application to the EAI system. Several types of EAI exist, including data integration, business-process integration and method integration.

Extensible Access Control Markup Language (XACML)   A markup language that allows organizations to communicate their policies for accessing online information. XACML defines which clients can access information, what information clients can access, when clients can access the information and how clients can gain access to the information.

Extensible Markup Language (XML)   A meta-language (i.e., a language used to create other languages) for describing data.

Extensible Stylesheet Language (XSL)   An XML vocabulary used to manipulate data in XML documents for presentation purposes.

extensibility   The ability to change or add features.

F

failover   A technology that, in the event of a server failure, allows another server to receive requests without interruption of the service.

fee-based Web service   A Web service that is accessible only to paying customers.

File Transfer Protocol (FTP)   A protocol used to send files over the Internet.

firewalls   Security barriers that restrict communication between networks.

flat-fee subscription Web service   A Web service payment option in which customers pay for unlimited use of a Web service during a specific period of time. When this time period expires, the customer is notified or billed for continued use.

Framework Class Library (FCL)   A feature of the .NET Framework that contains reusable components that programmers can incorporate into their applications.

free Web service   A payment option that allows customers to access a Web service without charge. The service can be free indefinitely or free for a limited period of time.

G

GAIA   The Mind Electric's service-oriented platform that uses grid computing to connect Web services producers with clients.

Global XML Web Services Architecture (GXA)   A set of specifications that build on core Web services standards to provide additional discovery, security and routing capabilities.

GLUE   A small-footprint implementation designed by Mind Electric that attempts to simplify the process of developing Web services. The standard release provides a Web server, servlet engine and XML parser, and is capable of integrating third-party extensions that enable the use of new transport-layer protocols, registries and WSDL bindings.

graphical user interface (GUI)   The visual components through which a user interacts with a program.

green pages   A component of the UBR's phone-book structure that contains technical information about a company's products, services and Web services.

grid-computing   A type of networking that performs work by employing the unused processing power of all the computers on a network.

H

hash value   A mathematically-calculated value that uniquely identifies a message, thereby enabling a message recipient to detect whether a message has been altered. Hash values also are known as message digests.

horizontal XML vocabulary   An XML vocabulary, such as ebXML, that can be used across industries.

HyperText Markup Language (HTML)   A language for sharing information via hyperlinked text documents.

Hypertext Transfer Protocol (HTTP)   The underlying communications protocol of the World Wide Web. The vast majority of files transferred over the Web use this protocol.

Hypertext Transfer Protocol Secure (HTTPS)   A secure form of HTTP used to transport data on the Web.

I

IBM Web Services Toolkit (WSTK)   A software-development kit that enables programmers to create, invoke and locate Web services. The WSTK includes Web services demonstrations, examples and a runtime environment.

identifier   An alphabetic or numeric value used to uniquely identify companies in the UBR.

independent software vendor (ISV)   A company that specializes in the development and sale of software not directly associated with a specific platform.

indirect discovery   The process of obtaining Web service data through a third-party registry, such as the UDDI Business Registry (UBR).

information tier   The part of a multi-tiered application that is comprised of one or more databases, which together contain the data relevant to the application. Also called the data or bottom tier.

integrated development environment (IDE)   Software used to create, document, run and debug programs conveniently.

integrity   The probability with which a Web service performs its tasks in the exact manner described in the service's WSDL document and/or SLA. A higher integrity rating indicates that the service's functionality resembles more closely the service description in the WSDL document and/or SLA. Integrity also can represent the probability that information sent or received over the Internet has not been compromised or altered.

intermediaries   An intermediate node incorporated into a SOAP transmission model to create a more complex communication architecture.

internal enterprise application integration UDDI   A private UDDI registry that resides behind a company's firewall and is accessible only to select, authorized internal users.

International Organization for Standardization (ISO)   a standards body comprised of representatives from standards organizations in approximately 140 member countries. ISO facilitates international commerce by developing protocols in many diverse areas, from standardized ATM cards to universal systems of measurement. Its work in the information technology arena has included the standardization of SGML, XML's parent language.

Internet Engineering Task Force (IETF)   An international consortium of network and Internet experts who work to further Internet architectures and technologies. The IETF governs the evolution of several standard Internet protocols, such as TCP/IP.

Internet Protocol Security (IPSec)   One of the technologies used to secure the tunnel through which data passes between multiple networks over the Internet, thereby ensuring the privacy and integrity of the data, as well as authenticating users.

interoperability   The ability to communicate and share data across programming languages and platforms.

intrusion detection system   A system that monitors networks and application log files to detect intrusions. If an intruder is detected, the system halts the session and sets off an alarm to notify the system administrator.

inquiry API   An API that enables service consumers to browse UDDI registries for service providers that offer a particular service or type of service.

invocation pattern   A feature provided by the UDDI inquiry API that searches the `bindingTemplate` structure to obtain the current location of a particular Web service.

IONA XMLBus   A Web services environment aimed at simplifying the Web service creation and deployment process. The standalone release includes a Web services container and a set of tools that enable developers to test, deploy and manage Web services.

IP address   An assigned number used to identify a computer on a network.

J

Java 2 Micro Edition (J2ME)   A Sun Microsystems' Java platform that enables programmers to develop applications for various consumer devices, such as set-top boxes, Web terminals, embedded systems, mobile phones and pagers.

Java API for XML Messaging (JAXM)   A Java API that enables applications to send and receive XML-formatted messages (e.g., SOAP messages).

Java API for XML Registries (JAXR)   A Java API that defines a standardized architecture for enabling clients to communicate with XML registries.

Java API for XML-based Remote Procedure Calls (JAX-RPC)   An API that enables Java programmers to create and access XML-based Web services over a network.

Java Messaging Service   A service used to build applications for Message-Oriented-Middleware (MOM) infrastructures.

JavaMail   A Java API used to build e-mail applications.

JAXMServlet   A servlet that receives SOAP requests in the form of HTTP post requests.

JAXR provider   An implementation of the JAXR API that maps JAXR objects to protocol-specific entries in the target XML registry, provides implementations to generic JAXR interfaces and provides clients with additional custom interfaces.

K

Kerberos   A freely-available, open-source protocol that employs secret-key cryptography to authenticate users in a network and to maintain the integrity and privacy of network communications.

key   A string of digits that acts as a password for decrypting ciphertext into plaintext.

key agreement protocol   A process by which two parties can exchange keys over an unsecure medium.

Key Distribution Center (KDC)   A central authority that shares a different secret key with every user on a network.

kSOAP   Proprietary software designed by Enhydra to build J2ME-based applications that handle SOAP messaging.

kXML   Software used by the kSOAP API and by J2ME clients to create and interpret XML-based messages/documents.

Kylix 2   Borland's rapid-application-development environment for the Linux operating system.

L

legacy application   An older application in which companies have invested significant resources; legacy applications often store business data or run critical processes.

Liberty Alliance Project   A business alliance initiated by Sun Microsystems that supports a federated approach to storing and maintaining confidential information. The Liberty Alliance Project aims to develop an open standard for single sign-on authentication that allows organizations to maintain their own data.

load balancing   A technology that distributes requests among multiple servers to prevent one server from being overloaded.

loosely coupled system   A system in which each software component's implementation is independent of those surrounding it.

M

MapPoint .NET   A Web service offered by Microsoft that enables users to find a location's latitude and longitude coordinates, search for points of interest within a specified radius, access and manipulate maps and retrieve driving directions between two locations.

markup language   A way of tagging data to identify the structure and/or describe a document's data.

marshalling   The process of packaging function arguments and return values for transmission over a network.

message handlers   Elements of the Apache Axis engine that sequentially process `MessageContext` objects.

message provider   A component that allows JAXM applications to send and receive messages asynchronously.

message queue   An intermediary enabled by JMS that receives messages from sending components and then forwards these messages to their intended recipients.

messaging framework   A framework in which messages encapsulate information transmitted to and from a Web service.

metering and accounting   The recording of Web service requestors' usage information of fee-based Web services.

Microsoft Intermediate Language (MSIL)   A language that defines instructions for the .NET Common Language Runtime (CLR).

Microsoft .NET Alerts   Part of Microsoft's .NET My Services; .NET Alerts can send notices to users about specified information or events. The notices can be directed to any e-mail address, an MSN or Windows Messenger account or a Web-enabled cell phone or PDA.

Microsoft .NET Passport   Part of Microsoft's .NET My Services; .NET Passport stores users' authentication information and enables automatic sign-on at participating Web sites.

Microsoft SOAP Toolkit   An application that enables developers to deploy Web services on Windows platforms that do not include the .NET framework.

middleware   The integration software between an enterprise's network and applications that links separate applications.

MIDlet   An application that runs on a MIDP device.

MIDlet suite   A single file used to store one or more MIDlets on a server.

Mobile Information Device Profile (MIDP)   A set of APIs that allow developers to handle mobile-device specification issues, such as creating user interfaces, permitting local storage and defining the MIDlet life cycles.

Mobile Internet Toolkit (MIT)   Microsoft's toolkit for developing wireless Web content that can run on a variety of mobile devices.

Multipurpose Internet Mail Extensions (MIME)   A specification that presents a method of encoding various media types to be sent as attachments across the Web.

N

namespace   A capability of XML that provides a means for uniquely identifying XML elements and attributes.

naming collision   A problem that occurs when two different classes with the same name are used in a program without their fully-qualified package names.

***n*-tier architecture**   An architecture in which an application's functionality is divided into separate, logical groupings. The most common *n*-tier architecture is a three-tier architecture, which usually encompasses a data tier, a business tier and a client tier.

.NET Compact Framework   A version of the .NET Framework that enables developers to create applications for devices with limited resources, such as mobile phones and PDAs.

.NET Enterprise Servers   A set of server applications offered by Microsoft and designed to Web-enable businesses.

.NET Framework   A Microsoft framework that manages and executes applications and Web services, provides a class library, enforces security and supplies many other programming capabilities.

.NET My Services   A set of Web services designed by Microsoft to store users' personal information and to provide individualized services accessible from any networked device.

Network Accessible Services Specification Language (NASSL)   A technology designed by IBM to describe Web service information, such as interface and implementation details.

non-repudiation   A process that provides legal proof that a message was sent or received.

O

one-time charge Web service   A Web service payment option allowing customers to make a single payment to access and use a Web service for the duration of that service.

operator node   An organization that hosts an implementation of the UBR; current operator nodes include Microsoft, IBM, Hewlett-Packard and SAP.

operator's council   A committee that governs the UDDI specifications and UDDI-related QoS issues; the council consists of current UBR operator nodes.

Oracle 9i Developer Suite and Application Server   Oracle's platform for developing and deploying Web-based applications.

Orbix E2A Platform   IONA's platform for developing and deploying Web-based applications.

orchestration   The integration of services to create collaborative business processes that perform transactions.

Organization of the Advancement of Structured Information Standards (OASIS)   A standards body comprised of over 400 individual and corporate members working to promote the use of SGML and XML standards. OASIS is involved in numerous Web services initiatives, including ebXML, Web Services for Interactive Applications (WSIA), Web Services for Remote Portals (WSRP) and several XML-based Web services security standards.

P

parameters   Data that procedures require to complete their tasks.

parsing   The use of encoding rules to extract the contents from a message.

partner catalog UDDI   A private UDDI registry that resides behind a company's firewall and is accessible only to authorized users.

Policy Information Point (PIP)   An application that stores security policies used to make authorization decisions.

pay-per-use Web service   A Web service payment option in which customers prepay to use a Web service a specified number of times. When invoked, a mechanism records the interaction; when the prepaid quantity exhausts, the customer is informed that it is time to renew.

performance   A QoS requirement that is comprised of two main factors— throughput and latency. Throughput represents the number of requests that a Web service processes in a given time period; latency represents the length of time that the service takes to respond to each request.

perishable service   A Web service that exists for a fixed period of time. For example, perishable services might provide special-events news coverage—such as information on a specific Olympic games, World Series or presidential campaign.

Permissions Management Infrastructure (PMI)   A system that uses a set of policies to handle access control and authorization for computing systems.

plaintext   Unencrypted data.

point-to-point messaging model   A messaging model in which the sending component sends a message to a message queue, which forwards that message to the target component.

Policy Decision Point (PDP)   An application responsible for making authorization decisions on the basis of existing security policies.

Policy Enforcement Point (PEP)   An application responsible for requesting and enforcing authorization decisions.

Policy Information Point (PIP)   An application responsible for storing authorization decisions.

portal UDDI   A private registry that resides on a company's firewall and contains information about that company's Web services. Although external users can find information in portal UDDI registries, only authorized users can post information.

porting   Adapting existing software to a new programming language.

portlet   An application module that provides specific, real-time information from a portal and presents it to a user.

privacy   The probability that information transmitted over the Internet has not been captured or passed on to a third party without the knowledge or permission of the sender or receiver.

private key   A unique, secret key used to decrypt messages encrypted with a corresponding public key.

private registry   A registry (such as a UDDI or ebXML registry) access to which is limited to certain parties—often partners, affiliates or clients of a particular company.

procedure   A set of instructions that tells an application how to perform a particular task.

procedure call   A command that directs an application to execute a procedure to perform a specific operation. A procedure call contains the name of the operation and the operation's parameters.

proxy   A separate component capable of handling SOAP messages.

proxy class   A class that handles all of the "plumbing" required for Web service method calls.

public cloud   A group of several registries owned and maintained by public operator nodes. The UBR is an example of a public cloud.

public key   A freely-distributed key used to encrypt messages that can be decrypted only by a corresponding private key.

Public Key Infrastructure (PKI)   An infrastructure integrates public-key cryptography with digital certificates and certificate authorities to authenticate parties in a transaction.

public-key cryptography   An asymmetric method of cryptography that uses two inversely related keys to encrypt and decrypt messages.

publish/subscribe messaging model   A messaging model in which one component subscribes to a topic on a server to which another component's messages are published.

publishing API   An access-restricted API that enables companies to post and update information to a UDDI registry.

Q

quality of service (QoS)   A term that refers to the level of service provided by a particular Web service. QoS is comprised of factors that measure how often a service can be used, how well it executes its tasks, how quickly it works and how reliable and secure it is.

R

rapid-application development (RAD) software   Software tools that enable developers to create applications and Web services quickly.

Reasonable and Non-Discriminatory (RAND) agreements   Contracts in which every licensee must pay the same small fee to the licensor. Companies, such as Microsoft and IBM, that hold intellectual-property rights to Web services standards are considering charging RAND fees.

registrar   An organization that assists companies in creating and publishing data, such as business and service descriptions, to be stored in UDDI registries.

reliability   A QoS requirement that describes the ability of a Web service to function correctly and provide consistent service, even in the event of a system or network failure.

remote procedure call (RPC)   A technology by which an application invokes a procedure residing on another computer.

replication   The process of updating records in the UBR so that all instances of those records are identical. Operator nodes perform replication by synchronizing their data at least every twelve hours.

request   A message sent from a client to a Web service asking that the Web service perform a certain operation or provide certain data.

request/response model   A communication architecture in which a client sends a message to a Web server, and the Web server returns information to the client.

response   A message sent from a server to a client containing requested information or the result of a requested operation.

root element   An element that contains all other elements in an XML document.

RosettaNet   A non-profit consortium that is developing an e-business framework to define business processes for the IT, electronics and semiconductor industries.

S

schema   An alternative to a DTD, a schema is an XML document that defines another XML document's structure.

secret-key cryptography   A form of cryptography that uses the same secret key to encrypt and decrypt a message.

Secure Sockets Layer (SSL)   A non-proprietary protocol commonly used to secure communication across the Web.

Security Assertion Markup Language (SAML)   An emerging standard for transferring authentication, authorization and permissions information over the Internet.

service-to-business (S2B)   A business model in which Web services are marketed to and used by businesses.

service-to-consumer (S2C)   A business model in which service providers offer Web services directly to individuals for personal use.

service-to-employee (S2E)   A business model in which Web services are purchased by businesses to improve internal communication and to provide employees with relevant content or applications.

service-level agreement (SLA)   A legal contract in which a service provider outlines the level of service it guarantees for a specific Web service. SLAs cover a specific time period, after which they must be renegotiated.

service-oriented architecture   A model created to illustrate Web service interactions. A typical service-oriented architecture comprises relationships among three entities: a Web service provider, a Web service requester and a Web service broker.

servlet   A Java technology that extends the functionality of a server.

Simple Mail Transfer Protocol (SMTP)   A protocol used to transfer e-mail over the Internet.

Simple Object Access Protocol (SOAP)   An XML-based messaging protocol consisting of a set of standardized XML schemas. SOAP is used to transfer information and instructions between Web services and Web service clients over a network.

single sign-on (SSO) service   A service that stores users' authentication information and enables automatic sign-on at participating Web sites. Microsoft's .NET Passport and Sun Microsystems' Liberty Alliance Project are examples of SSO solutions.

smart card   A card that can perform many different functions, from authentication to data storage. Smart cards store private keys, digital certificates and other information necessary for implementing PKI.

SOAP actor   A SOAP node that processes SOAP messages.

SOAP binding   A process that defines the protocol over which SOAP messages are transported to applications.

SOAP client   Software that creates SOAP messages to interact with Web services.

SOAP Contract Language (SCL)   A technology that employs XML to describe the messages exchanged between applications.

SOAP encoding style   Rules that define the data types of individual data elements within a SOAP message so that receiving systems can process the data correctly.

SOAP message   An XML document that encapsulates information sent to and from a Web service.

SOAP Message Exchange Model   A model that defines how components exchange SOAP messages, as well as the most basic requirements for processing one-way transmissions from a SOAP sender to a SOAP receiver.

SOAP Messages with Attachments document   A technology that enables the attachment of files to SOAP messages. Attachments allow Web services to exchange data that is difficult to represent in XML— such as documents and multimedia files.

SOAP Messaging Object (SMO)   A framework developed by Microsoft that simplifies the creation and processing of XML documents residing in SOAP messages.

SOAP nodes Applications or programming components that understand and process SOAP messages.

SOAP payload The application-specific data contained in a SOAP message; this data is located in the body of the message.

SOAP receiver A SOAP node that receives SOAP messages.

SOAP sender A SOAP node that sends a SOAP message.

SOAP server Software that processes SOAP messages for Web services.

steganography The practice of hiding information within other information.

structured programming A disciplined approach to creating programs that are clear, demonstrably correct and easy to modify.

Structured Query Language (SQL) A programming language used to query and manipulate databases.

stub A local object that represents a remote Web service.

substitution cipher A cipher in which every given letter in a message is replaced by a different letter.

Sun Open Net Environment (Sun ONE) Platform Sun Microsystems' platform for creating and deploying Web-based applications.

supply chain A network of organizations involved in creating a particular product or service.

supply-chain management A process that organizes supply-chain members to better coordinate daily business interactions, such as procurement, transactions, production and distribution.

synchronous communication Communication that suspends the client's execution while the client waits for a response from a Web service.

T

tags Names enclosed in angle brackets and used in pairs to delimit the beginning and end of XML markup.

technology stack A concept that illustrates how technologies build on other technologies.

ties Server-side objects that represent Web services.

tightly coupled system A system in which each software component's implementation is dependent on those surrounding it. If a developer changes a component in a tightly coupled system, the other system components must be altered as well.

timestamping   A process that binds a time and date to an digital document to help solve the problem of non-repudiation.

tokenizing   The process of parsing a string into smaller substrings.

Transmission Control Protocol/Internet Protocol (TCP/IP)   The standard set of protocols used to connect computers and networks to the Internet.

transport layer   An element of the GLUE Web services platform that receives XML messages and converts them to corresponding Java objects.

transport listener   An element of the Apache Axis engine platform that receives all incoming XML messages.

transposition cipher   A cipher in which the order of letters in a message is switched.

TrustBridge   A set of technologies under development by Microsoft that will provide federated security across trust domains.

trusted port   A network port that is not blocked by a firewall.

U

UDDI Business Registry (UBR)   A public UDDI registry in which businesses can publish information about their Web services.

UDDI information model   An information model used in UDDI registries to describe businesses and their Web services. The UDDI information model is comprised of the following components: business information, business service information, binding information, service-specific information and publisher assertion information.

Uniform Resource Identifier (URI)   An identifier that represents the location or address of an object or resource on a network.

Universal Description, Discovery and Integration (UDDI)   A standard that defines an XML-based format in which companies can describe their electronic capabilities and business processes; the standard also provides a method of registering and locating the descriptions on a network, such as the Internet. Part of the information that companies can supply is data regarding available Web services.

Universally Unique Identifier (UUID)   A unique identifier assigned to each `businessEntity` structure by a custodian upon registration.

V

valid document   A document that conforms to a DTD or schema.

validating parser   Software capable of determining whether an XML document conforms to a DTD or schema.

value-added network (VAN)   A closed network that links all members of a production process to an EDI system.

value-added services (VAS)   Services that support Web services transactions and offer consumers additional QoS information about Web services.

vertical language   An XML-based technology that defines specific processes for a single industry or group of industries.

virus   A piece of code that attaches to, or overwrites, other programs to self-replicate and can corrupt files or even wipe out a hard drive. Viruses are often sent as attachments or hidden in audio clips, video clips and games.

visual programming   A technique by which prepackaged components can be "dragged and dropped" into an application.

Visual Studio .NET   Microsoft's IDE, which allows developers to create applications in a variety of .NET programming languages and also offers editing tools for manipulating several types of files.

W

W3C recommendation   A specification presented by a W3C working group that defines a technology. When a W3C technology is moved to recommendation status, this means that the technology is stable for wide deployment in industry.

W3C Working Group   A set of technical experts that work to develop a particular Web technology.

Web Applications and Services Platform (WASP)   A Web services platform developed by Systinet to provide programmers with tools for implementing, testing, debugging and managing Web services.

Web service broker   A networked server or system that maintains a directory or clearinghouse for Web services and acts as a liaison between Web service providers and Web service requesters.

Web service creation   The first stage of the business lifecycle of a Web service. This stage includes design, development, documentation, testing and distribution.

Web Service Deployment Descriptor (WSDD)   A specialized file used to customize the deployment of a Web service.

Web Service Inspection (WS-Inspection)   An XML-based discovery technology developed by IBM and Microsoft that defines how a client application can locate Web services descriptions, such as WSDL documents, that reside on a particular Web server.

Web service interface   A software component that enables other applications to access a Web service over a network.

Web service promotion   A stage in the business lifecycle of a Web service in which service brokers—such as the UDDI registries—enable service requestors to locate the Web service.

Web service provider   A networked server or system that makes a Web service available on the Internet, then publishes the Web service to a service broker.

Web service publication   A stage in the business lifecycle of a Web service in which all necessary pieces of the Web service are made available on the Internet.

Web service requestor   A networked server or system that locates and accesses a Web service by interacting with a service broker to find a Web service that fills a specific computing need.

Web service sale   The final stage of Web services development, which includes accounts management and service auditing.

Web services account manager   A participant in the sale of Web services that collects money from the subscribers to a particular Web service, then distributes the money to the asset owner, hosting company and any other involved parties.

Web services auditor   A party that is responsible for reviewing and evaluating the functionality of Web services.

Web Services Description Language (WSDL)   The XML-based language through which Web services describe themselves to developers and applications over the Internet. WSDL descriptions convey the methods that a Web service provides and how those methods can be accessed.

Web Services Flow Language (WSFL)   An XML-based language created by IBM to incorporate Web services as part of a business's workflow— i.e., the operations required to accomplish a process or transaction.

Web Services for Remote Portals (WSRP)   An initiative started by OASIS to define a standard for allowing Web services to be "plugged into" platforms that aggregate content, such as corporate portals or other Web applications.

Web Services Hosting Technology (WSHT)   A technology that enables Web service providers to implement metering and billing mechanisms easily, without altering the actual code that comprises a Web service. WSHT is part of the IBM Web Services Toolkit 3.0.

Web services toolkit   An application that offers resources to aid developers in the deployment of Web services.

WebLogic Platform   BEA's platform for the creation and deployment of Web-based applications.

WebSphere Application Server   IBM's main deployment platform for Web-based applications.

well-formed document   An XML document that adheres to the XML 1.0 recommendation.

white pages   A component of the UBR's phone-book structure that contains general information about a company, such as its name, address, contact information and identifiers.

workflow   The sequence of operations required to accomplish a process or transaction.

World Wide Consortium (W3C)   An established forum through which qualified individuals and companies can cooperate to develop and standardize technologies for the World Wide Web. The W3C is the largest and most influential standards body that defines Web technologies.

WS-Authorization   A specification under development that will allow developers to manage the access privileges of Web services.

WS-Federation   A specification under development that will enable the management of trust relationships across different B2B and authorization systems.

WS-Policy   A specification under development that will enable developers to specify the limitations and capabilities of senders and receivers.

WS-Privacy   A specification under development that will allow organizations to specify privacy policies.

WS-Referral   A specification that enables developers to modify a SOAP message's routing information dynamically.

WS-Routing   A specification that allows developers to define routing information for a SOAP message.

WS-Security   A Web services security specification designed by Microsoft, IBM and VeriSign to secure the transmission of SOAP messages.

WS-Trust   A specification under development that will define how different organizations can set up and maintain trust relationships.

WSFL flow model   The sequence of steps required by a collection of Web services to accomplish a business process, such as a transaction.

WSFL global model   A model that describes an interaction pattern composition, which specifies how the Web services that comprise a composed Web service relate to each other.

X

XAR files   Files used by the XMLBus Web services container to store all information related to a given Web service, including property files, Java classes, WSDL documents and XML conversion information.

XLANG   An XML-based language used to describe the specific actions that comprise a business process and the circumstances under which those actions should take place.

XML Cover Pages   A collection of online reference materials maintained by OASIS regarding markup language standards.

XML Digital Signature (SOAP-DSIG)   A specification that provides a set of rules for digitally signing SOAP messages, as well as validating message signatures.

XML Encryption   A specification that handles the encryption and decryption of XML documents that are secured with XML Signature.

XML Key Information Service Specification (X-KISS)   The set of protocols used to process key information associated with XML encrypted data, digital signatures and other aspects of public key cryptography.

XML Key Management Specification (XKMS)   A specification for registering and distributing encryption keys for Public Key Infrastructure (PKI) in XML-based Web services.

XML Key Registration Service Specification (X-KRSS)   The set of certificate-management protocols that addresses the life of a digital certificate, from registration to revocation and recovery.

XML parser   A software program that checks an XML document's syntax and enables other software programs to interpret marked-up data.

XML Schema   An XML vocabulary used to describe the structure of XML documents.

XML Signature   A specification that defines an XML-based standard for representing digital signatures.

XML vocabulary   An XML-based markup language developed for a specific industry or purpose.

Y

yellow pages   A component of the UBR's phone-book structure that divides companies into various categories based on the products or services that the companies offer.

Index

X

The DEITEL™ Suite of Products...

Web Services:
A Technical Introduction

© 2003, 400 pp., paper (0-13-046135-0)

Web Services: A Technical Introduction from the DEITEL™
Developer Series familiarizes programmers, technical
managers and project managers with key Web services
concepts, including what Web services are and why
they are revolutionary. The book covers the business
case for Web services—the underlying technologies,
ways in which Web services can provide competitive
advantages and opportunities for Web services-related
lines of business. Readers learn the latest Web-services
standards, including XML, SOAP, WSDL and UDDI;
learn about Web services implementations in .NET
and Java; benefit from an extensive comparison of
Web services products and vendors; and read about
Web services security options. Although this is not a
programming book, the appendices show .NET and
Java code examples to demonstrate the structure
of Web services applications and documents. In
addition, the book includes numerous case studies
describing ways in which organizations are implementing
Web services to increase efficiency, simplify business
processes, create new revenue streams and interact
better with partners and customers.

Java™ Web Services
for Experienced Programmers

© 2003, 700 pp., paper (0-13-046134-2)

Java™ Web Services for Experienced Programmers from the
DEITEL™ Developer Series provides the experienced
Java programmer with 103 LIVE-CODE™ examples and
covers industry standards including XML, SOAP, WSDL
and UDDI. Learn how to build and integrate Web
services using the Java API for XML RPC, the Java
API for XML Messaging, Apache Axis and the Java
Web Services Developer Pack. Develop and deploy
Web services on several major Web services platforms. Register and discover Web services through
public registries and the Java API for XML Registries.
Build Web Services clients for several platforms,
including J2ME. Significant Web Services case studies also are included.

Visual Basic® .NET
for Experienced Programmers

©2003, paper, approximately 1150 pp., (0-13-046131-8)

Visual Basic .NET for Experienced Programmers from the DEITEL™
Developer Series presents experienced programmers with
a concise introduction to programming fundamentals
before delving into more sophisticated topics. Learn how
to create reusable software components with assemblies,
modules and dynamic link libraries. Learn Visual Basic
.NET through LIVE-CODE™ examples of ASP.NET, multithreading, object-oriented programming, XML processing,
mobile application development and Web services.

Visual C++ .NET
for Experienced Programmers:
A Managed Code Approach

© 2003, 1500 pp., paper (0-13-045821-X)

*Visual C++ .NET for Experienced Programmers: A Managed Code
Approach* from the DEITEL™ Developer Series teaches
programmers with C++ programming experience how to
develop Visual C++ applications for Microsoft's new .NET
Framework. The book begins with a condensed introduction
to Visual C++ programming fundamentals, then covers
more sophisticated .NET application-development topics
in detail. Key topics include: creating reusable software
components with assemblies, modules and dynamic link
libraries; using classes from the Framework Class Library
(FCL); building graphical user interfaces (GUIs) with the
FCL; implementing multithreaded applications; building
networked applications; manipulating databases with
ADO .NET and creating XML Web services. In addition,
the book provides several chapters on unmanaged code
in Visual C++ .NET. These chapters demonstrate how to
use "attributed programming" to simplify common tasks
(such as connecting to a database) and improve code
readability; how to integrate managed- and unmanaged-
code software components; and how to use ATL Server
to create Web-based applications and Web services with
unmanaged code. The book features detailed LIVE-CODE™
examples that highlight crucial .NET-programming concepts
and demonstrate Web services at work. A substantial
introduction to XML also is included.

Java™ How to Program Fourth Edition

BOOK / CD-ROM

©2002, 1546 pp., paper
(0-13-034151-7)

The world's best-selling Java text is now even better! The Fourth Edition of *Java How to Program* includes a new focus on object-oriented design with the UML, design patterns, full-color program listings and figures and the most up-to-date Java coverage available.

Readers will discover key topics in Java programming, such as graphical user interface components, exception handling, multithreading, multimedia, files and streams, networking, data structures and more. In addition, a new chapter on design patterns explains frequently recurring architectural patterns—information that can help save designers considerable time when building large systems.

The highly detailed optional case study focuses on object-oriented design with the UML and presents fully implemented working Java code.

Updated throughout, the text includes new and revised discussions on topics such as Swing, graphics and socket- and packet-based networking. Three introductory chapters heavily emphasize problem solving and programming skills. The chapters on RMI, JDBC™, servlets and JavaBeans have been moved to *Advanced Java 2 Platform How to Program*, where they are now covered in much greater depth. (See *Advanced Java 2 Platform How to Program* below.)

Advanced Java™ 2 Platform How to Program

BOOK / CD-ROM

©2002, 1811 pp., paper
(0-13-089560-1)

Expanding on the world's best-selling Java textbook—*Java How to Program*—*Advanced Java 2 Platform How To Program* presents advanced Java topics for developing sophisticated, user-friendly GUIs; significant, scalable enterprise applications; wireless applications and distributed systems. Primarily based on Java 2 Enterprise Edition (J2EE), this textbook integrates technologies such as XML, JavaBeans, security, Java Database Connectivity (JDBC), JavaServer Pages (JSP), servlets, Remote Method Invocation (RMI), Enterprise JavaBeans™ (EJB) and design patterns into a production-quality system that allows developers to benefit from the leverage and platform independence Java 2 Enterprise Edition provides. The book also features the development of a complete, end-to-end e-business solution using advanced Java technologies. Additional topics include Swing, Java 2D and 3D, XML, design patterns, CORBA, Jini™, JavaSpaces™, Jiro™, Java Management Extensions (JMX) and Peer-to-Peer networking with an introduction to JXTA. This textbook also introduces the Java 2 Micro Edition (J2ME™) for building applications for handheld and wireless devices using MIDP and MIDlets. Wireless technologies covered include WAP, WML and i-mode.

C# How to Program

BOOK / CD-ROM

©2002, 1568 pp., paper
(0-13-062221-4)

An exciting new addition to the How to Program series, *C# How to Program* provides a comprehensive introduction to Microsoft's new object-oriented language. C# builds on the skills already mastered by countless C++ and Java programmers, enabling them to create powerful Web applications and components—ranging from XML-based Web services on Microsoft's .NET platform to middle-tier business objects and system-level applications. *C# How to Program* begins with a strong foundation in the introductory and intermediate programming principles students will need in industry. It then explores such essential topics as object-oriented programming and exception handling. Graphical user interfaces are extensively covered, giving readers the tools to build compelling and fully interactive programs. Internet technologies such as XML, ADO .NET and Web services are also covered as well as topics including regular expressions, multithreading, networking, databases, files and data structures.

Also coming soon in the Deitels' .NET Series:

- *Visual C++ .NET How to Program*

Sign up now for the new *Deitel™ Buzz Online* newsletter at:

Visual Basic .NET
How to Program
Second Edition

*©2002, 1400 pp., paper
(0-13-029363-6)*

Teach Visual Basic .NET programming from the ground up! This introduction of Microsoft's .NET Framework marks the beginning of major revisions to all of Microsoft's programming languages. This book provides a comprehensive introduction to the next version of Visual Basic— Visual Basic .NET—featuring extensive updates and increased functionality. *Visual Basic .NET How to Program, Second Edition* covers introductory programming techniques as well as more advanced topics, featuring enhanced treatment of developing Web-based applications. Other topics discussed include an extensive treatment of XML and wireless applications, databases, SQL and ADO .NET, Web forms, Web services and ASP .NET.

Also coming soon in the Deitels' .NET Series:

• *Visual C++ .NET How to Program*

C How to Program
Third Edition

*©2001, 1253 pp., paper
(0-13-089572-5)*

Highly practical in approach, the Third Edition of the world's best-selling C text introduces the fundamentals of structured programming and software engineering and gets up to speed quickly. This comprehensive book not only covers the full C language, but also reviews library functions and introduces object-based and object-oriented programming in C++ and Java. The Third Edition includes a new 346-page introduction to Java 2 and the basics of GUIs, and the 298-page introduction to C++ has been updated to be consistent with the most current ANSI/ISO C++ standards. Plus, icons throughout the book point out valuable programming tips such as Common Programming Errors, Portability Tips and Testing and Debugging Tips.

C++
How to Program
Fourth Edition

*©2003, 1400 pp., paper
(0-13-038474-7)*

The world's best selling C++ book is now even better! Designed for beginning through intermediate courses, this comprehensive, practical introduction to C++ includes hundreds of hands-on exercises, plus roughly 250 complete programs written and documented for easy learning. It also features exceptional insight into good programming practices, maximizing performance, avoiding errors, debugging and testing. The Fourth Edition features a new code-highlighting style that uses an alternate background color to focus the reader on new code elements in a program. The OOD/UML case study is upgraded to the latest UML standard, and includes significant improvements to the exception handling and operator overloading chapters. It features enhanced treatment of strings and arrays as objects using standard C++ classes, string and vector. It also retains every key concept and technique ANSI C++ developers need to master, including control structures, functions, arrays, pointers and strings, classes and data abstraction, operator overloading, inheritance, virtual functions, polymorphism, I/O, templates, exception handling, file processing, data structures and more. *C++ How to Program Fourth Edition* includes a detailed Introduction to Standard Template Library (STL) containers, container adapters, algorithms and iterators.

Getting Started with
Microsoft® Visual C++™
6 with an Introduction
to MFC

©2000, 163 pp., paper (0-13-016147-0)

Internet & World
Wide Web How to
Program,
Second Edition

*©2002, 1428 pp., paper
(0-13-030897-8)*

The revision of this ground-breaking book in the Deitels' *How to Program Series* offers a thorough treatment of

programming concepts that yield visible or audible results in Web pages and Web-based applications. This book discusses effective Web-based design, server- and client-side scripting, multitier Web-based applications development, ActiveX® controls and electronic commerce essentials. This book offers an alternative to traditional programming courses using markup languages (such as XHTML, Dynamic HTML and XML) and scripting languages (such as JavaScript, VBScript, Perl/CGI, Python and PHP) to teach the fundamentals of programming "wrapped in the metaphor of the Web."

Updated material on www.deitel.com and www.prenhall.com/deitel provides additional resources for instructors who want to cover Microsoft® or non-Microsoft technologies. The Web site includes an extensive treatment of Netscape® 6 and alternate versions of the code from the Dynamic HTML chapters that will work with non-Microsoft environments as well.

Wireless Internet & Mobile Business How to Program

©2002, 1292 pp., paper (0-13-062226-5)

While the rapid expansion of wireless technologies, such as cell phones, pagers and personal digital assistants (PDAs), offers many new opportunities for businesses and programmers, it also presents numerous challenges related to issues such as security and standardization. This book offers a thorough treatment of both the management and technical aspects of this growing area, including coverage of current practices and future trends. The first half explores the business issues surrounding wireless technology and mobile business, including an overview of existing and developing communication technologies and the application of business principles to wireless devices. It also discusses location-based services and location-identifying technologies, a topic that is revisited throughout the book. Wireless payment, security, legal and social issues, international communications and more are also discussed. The book then turns to programming for the wireless Internet, exploring topics such as WAP (including 2.0), WML, WMLScript, XML, XHTML™, wireless Java programming (J2ME)™, Web Clipping and more. Other topics covered include career resources, wireless marketing, accessibility, Palm™, PocketPC, Windows CE,

i-mode, Bluetooth, MIDP, MIDlets, ASP, Microsoft .NET Mobile Framework, BREW™, multimedia, Flash™ and VBScript.

Python How to Program

BOOK / CD-ROM

©2002, 1376 pp., paper (0-13-092361-3)

This exciting new book provides a comprehensive introduction to Python— a powerful object-oriented programming language with clear syntax and the ability to bring together various technologies quickly and easily. This book covers introductory-programming techniques and more advanced topics such as graphical user interfaces, databases, wireless Internet programming, networking, security, process management, multithreading, XHTML, CSS, PSP and multimedia. Readers will learn principles that are applicable to both systems development and Web programming. The book features the consistent and applied pedagogy that the *How to Program Series* is known for, including the Deitels' signature LIVE-CODE™ Approach, with thousands of lines of code in hundreds of working programs; hundreds of valuable programming tips identified with icons throughout the text; an extensive set of exercises, projects and case studies; two-color four-way syntax coloring and much more.

e-Business & e-Commerce for Managers

©2001, 794 pp., cloth (0-13-032364-0)

This comprehensive overview of building and managing e-businesses explores topics such as the decision to bring a business online, choosing a business model, accepting payments, marketing strategies and security, as well as many other important issues (such as career resources). The book features Web resources and online demonstrations that supplement the text and direct readers to additional materials. The book also includes an appendix that develops a complete Web-based shopping-cart application using HTML, JavaScript, VBScript, Active Server Pages, ADO, SQL, HTTP, XML and XSL. Plus, company-specific sections provide "real-world" examples of the concepts presented in the book.

Sign up now for the new DEITEL™ Buzz Online newsletter at:

XML How to Program

BOOK / CD-ROM

©2001, 934 pp., paper (0-13-028417-3)

This book is a comprehensive guide to programming in XML. It teaches how to use XML to create customized tags and includes chapters that address standard custom-markup languages for science and technology, multimedia, commerce and many other fields. Concise introductions to Java, JavaServer Pages, VBScript, Active Server Pages and Perl/CGI provide readers with the essentials of these programming languages and server-side technologies to enable them to work effectively with XML. The book also covers cutting-edge topics such as XSL, DOM™ and SAX, plus a real-world e-commerce case study and a complete chapter on Web accessibility that addresses Voice XML. It includes tips such as Common Programming Errors, Software Engineering Observations, Portability Tips and Debugging Hints. Other topics covered include XHTML, CSS, DTD, schema, parsers, XPath, XLink, namespaces, XBase, XInclude, XPointer, XSLT, XSL Formatting Objects, JavaServer Pages, XForms, topic maps, X3D, MathML, OpenMath, CML, BML, CDF, RDF, SVG, Cocoon, WML, XBRL and BizTalk™ and SOAP™ Web resources.

Perl How to Program

BOOK / CD-ROM

©2001, 1057 pp., paper (0-13-028418-1)

This comprehensive guide to Perl programming emphasizes the use of the Common Gateway Interface (CGI) with Perl to create powerful, dynamic multi-tier Web-based client/server applications. The book begins with a clear and careful introduction to programming concepts at a level suitable for beginners, and proceeds through advanced topics such as references and complex data structures. Key Perl topics such as regular expressions and string manipulation are covered in detail. The authors address important and topical issues such as object-oriented programming, the Perl database interface (DBI), graphics and security. Also included is a treatment of XML, a bonus chapter introducing the Python programming language, supplemental material on career resources and a complete chapter on Web accessibility. The text includes tips such as Common Programming Errors, Software Engineering Observations, Portability Tips and Debugging Hints.

e-Business & e-Commerce How to Program

BOOK / CD-ROM

©2001, 1254 pp., paper (0-13-028419-X)

This innovative book explores programming technologies for developing Web-based e-business and e-commerce solutions, and covers e-business and e-commerce models and business issues. Readers learn a full range of options, from "build-your-own" to turnkey solutions. The book examines scores of the top e-businesses (examples include Amazon, eBay, Priceline, Travelocity, etc.), explaining the technical details of building successful e-business and e-commerce sites and their underlying business premises. Learn how to implement the dominant e-commerce models—shopping carts, auctions, name-your-own-price, comparison shopping and bots/ intelligent agents—by using markup languages (HTML, Dynamic HTML and XML), scripting languages (JavaScript, VBScript and Perl), server-side technologies (Active Server Pages and Perl/CGI) and database (SQL and ADO), security and online payment technologies. Updates are regularly posted to www•deitel•com and the book includes a CD-ROM with software tools, source code and live links.

www•deitel•com/newsletter/subscribe•html

Complete Training Courses

Each complete package includes the corresponding *How to Program Series* book and interactive multimedia CD-ROM Cyber Classroom. *Complete Training Courses* are perfect for anyone interested Web and e-commerce programming. They are affordable resources for college students and professionals learning programming for the first time or reinforcing their knowledge.

Each *Complete Training Course* is compatible with Windows 95, Windows 98, Windows NT and Windows 2000 and includes the following features:

Intuitive Browser-Based Interface

You'll love the *Complete Training Courses'* new browser-based interface, designed to be easy and accessible to anyone who's ever used a Web browser. Every *Complete Training Course* features the full text, illustrations and program listings of its corresponding *How to Program* book—all in full color—with full-text searching and hyperlinking.

Further Enhancements to the Deitels' Signature LIVE-CODE™ Approach

Every code sample from the main text can be found in the interactive, multimedia, CD-ROM-based *Cyber Classrooms* included in the *Complete Training Courses*. Syntax coloring of code is included for the *How to Program* books that are published in full color. Even the recent two-color and one-color books use effective multi-way syntax shading. The *Cyber Classroom* products always are in full color.

Audio Annotations

Hours of detailed, expert audio descriptions of thousands of lines of code help reinforce concepts.

Easily Executable Code

With one click of the mouse, you can execute the code or save it to your hard drive to manipulate using the programming environment of your choice. With selected *Complete Training Courses*, you can also load all of the code into a development environment such as Microsoft® Visual C++™, enabling you to modify and execute the programs with ease.

Abundant Self-Assessment Material

Practice exams test your understanding with hundreds of test questions and answers in addition to those found in the main text. Hundreds of self-review questions, all with answers, are drawn from the text; as are hundreds of programming exercises, half with answers.

www·phptr·com/phprinteractive

Sign up now for the new *DEITEL™ Buzz Online* newsletter at:

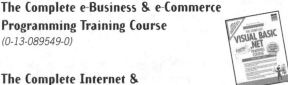

Future Publications

Here are some new titles we are considering for 2002/2003 release:

Computer Science Series: *Operating Systems 3/e, Data Structures in C++, Data Structures in Java, Theory and Principles of Database Systems.*

Database Series: *Oracle, SQL Server, MySQL.*

Internet and Web Programming Series: *Open Source Software Development: Apache, Linux, MySQL and PHP.*

Programming Series: *Flash™.*

.NET Programming Series: *ADO .NET with Visual Basic .NET, ASP .NET with Visual Basic .NET, ADO .NET with C#, ASP .NET with C#.*

Object Technology Series: *OOAD with the UML, Design Patterns, Java™ and XML.*

Advanced Java™ Series: *JDBC, Java 2 Enterprise Edition, Java Media Framework (JMF), Java Security and Java Cryptography (JCE), Java Servlets, Java2D and Java3D, JavaServer Pages™ (JSP), JINI and Java 2 Micro Edition™ (J2ME).*

Deitel™ Buzz Online Newsletter

The Deitel and Associates, Inc. free opt-in newsletter includes:

- Updates and commentary on industry trends and developments
- Resources and links to articles from our published books and upcoming publications.
- Information on the Deitel publishing plans, including future publications and product-release schedules
- Support for instructors
- Resources for students
- Information on Deitel Corporate Training

To sign up for the Deitel™ Buzz Online newsletter, visit `www.deitel.com /newsletter/subscribe.html`.

E-Books

We are committed to providing our content in traditional print formats and in emerging electronic formats, such as e-books, to fulfill our customers' needs. Our R&D teams are currently exploring many leading-edge solutions.

Visit `www.deitel.com` and read the Deitel™ Buzz Online for periodic updates.

Turn the page to find out more about Deitel & Associates!

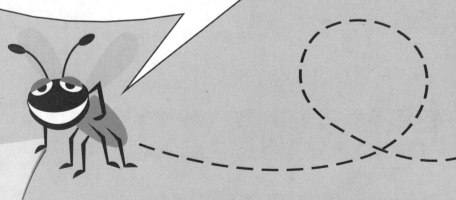